NEW YORK
AND THE UNION

Edited By

STEPHEN L. SCHECHTER and

RICHARD B. BERNSTEIN

New York State Commission
on the
Bicentennial of the United States Constitution
Albany, New York

©New York State Commission on the
Bicentennial of the United States
Constitution, 1990
Albany, New York

Printed in the United States of America

Library of Congress Cataloging in Publication Data

New York and the Union / edited by Stephen L. Schechter and
    Richard B. Bernstein.
        p.   cm.
    Contents: Contributions to the American constitutional experience.
    Includes bibliographical references.
    ISBN 0-945660-05-7
    1. New York (State)—Constitutional history.   2. United States—
Constitutional history.   I. Schechter, Stephen L., 1945-   .
II. Bernstein, Richard B., 1956-   .   III. New York State Commission on the
Bicentennial of the United States Constitution.
KFN5681.N49   1990
342.747′029—dc20   90-5552
[347.470229]   CIP

Contents

RATIFICATION CONFERENCE PAPERS

III. NEW YORK PARTICIPANTS IN THE MAKING OF THE CONSTITUTION, 1787–1789

IV. NEW YORK'S CONTRIBUTIONS TO AMERICAN CONSTITUTIONAL DEVELOPMENT

COLUMBIANS AND CHIEF JUSTICES: JOHN JAY,
CHARLES EVANS HUGHES, HARLAN FISKE STONE

New York State Commission on the Bicentennial of the U.S. Constitution

Hon. Mario M. Cuomo
Governor

Hon. Sol Wachtler
Chief Judge of the
State of New York
Chairman

Hon. Domenick L. Gabrielli
Vice-Chairman

COMMISSIONERS

Hon. Beatrice S. Burstein
Antonia M. Cortese
Edward B. Flink, Esq.
Hon. Kenneth P. LaValle
Hon. Michael McNulty
Dr. Joseph S. Murphy
Hon. Mark Alan Siegel
Hon. Thomas Sobol
Dr. Robert J. Spitzer
Hon. Moses M. Weinstein
Hon. Clifford R. Wharton, Jr.

Stephen L. Schechter
Executive Director

Paul J. Scudiere
Administrative Officer

New York State Education Department
Division of Research and Collections

Foreword

HON. SOL WACHTLER

Chief Judge, New York Court of Appeals
Chairman, New York State Commission
on the Bicentennial
of the United States Constitution

Ever since its creation in 1986, the New York State Commission on the Bicentennial of the United States Constitution has sought not just to celebrate the two hundredth anniversary of the Constitution but also to explain the history we are celebrating.

The Commission has had two important goals: First, we believe that the Constitution is something to understand as well as something to honor. Without understanding the Constitution, its origins and development, and its core principles, we cannot expect to be able to govern ourselves. Second, as New Yorkers we can and should be justly proud of the many contributions that the people of this state have made to the continuing American experiment in self-government. New York State and New York City were the scenes of some of the pivotal events of the process of inventing a nation and a form of government—in February of 1787, the calling of the Federal Convention by the Confederation Congress; in September of 1787, the opening of the ratification campaign; in 1789, the convening of the first Congress, the inauguration of President George Washington, the creation of the machinery of government, and the framing of the Bill of Rights. Even more important, New Yorkers were not passive witnesses to this process. Indeed, they supplied some of the most valuable building blocks of the American constitutional tradition, including the New York Constitution of 1777, *The Federalist*, and some of the most important of the Antifederalist writings.

As an enduring legacy of its work to commemorate the bicentennials of 1787–1789, the New York State Commission on the Bicentennial is sponsoring a series of publications, conforming to high scholarly standards yet accessible to a general audience. *New York and the Union* is the centerpiece of this publication effort. It compiles many of the pamphlets, brochures, and essays published under the auspices of the Commission and distributed, free of charge, to individuals, schools, and other institutions in New York and elsewhere. Taken together, this massive compilation is a proud record of New Yorkers' contributions to the development of American constitutionalism. Just as important, its companion volume, *New York and the Bicentennial*, which assembles publications outlining creative and thoughtful commemorative activities for the bicentennial, demonstrates the scope and enduring value of New York's efforts to make this a substantive as well as a celebratory bicentennial.

In many ways, as New Yorkers and as Americans, we can congratulate ourselves on the accomplishments of our continuing experiments in government. Yet we cannot truly congratulate ourselves unless we know first what it is that should inspire pride. Just as important, we must be aware that this experiment in self-government cannot have any ending; our work as citizens of a constitutional polity is never done. Much remains for us to do—in defining our rights and duties as human beings and as citizens, in ensuring the availability of those rights to all people, and in watching over the instruments and institutions of government that we have adopted to ensure that they continue to perform their constitutional responsibilities. Especially as we witness the struggles of the peoples of Eastern Europe, China, and South Africa for democracy and constitutional government, we hope that *New York and the Union* and *New York and the Bicentennial* will help the people of New York and all others who read them to carry on the task of democratic and constitutional self-government.

Editors' Introduction

The 200th anniversary of the United States Constitution has generated renewed interest in the role of New York and New Yorkers in the ratification of that document—a process of popular consent that legitimized the Constitution and proved the need for completing it with a Bill of Rights. However, that ratification was neither the beginning nor the end of New York's constitutional history. The state's first constitution, adopted in 1777, had been inspired by New York's colonial charters, the development of colonial laws, and the vision of New York's constitution makers. In turn, it exerted a powerful influence on the framing of the federal Constitution a decade later. Its successor state constitutions in 1821, 1846, 1894, and 1938 greatly expanded the powers of government and the protections afforded to our citizens while preserving that basic principle of popular consent.

The Reluctant Pillar: New York and the Adoption of the Federal Constitution (1985; Albany, N.Y.: New York State Bicentennial Commission, 1987) contains essays on the theory, history, people, and places of New York's ratification experience in a basic survey of the period. *New York and the Union* updates that study; in addition, it brings together all of the *New York Notes* and other looseleaf material on New York in the American System published by the New York State Bicentennial Commission. This volume contains more than seventy items organized in four sections, focusing on New York's contributions to the American constitutional experience. The two sections of its companion volume, *New York and the Bicentennial*, recount New York State's contributions to the bicentennial of the Constitution.

New York and the Union

The first section of *New York and the Union* contains various contributions on the origins of constitutionalism in New York, beginning with a general treatment of those origins. Case studies follow on Hiawatha, the Dutch experience, the age of Leisler, John Peter Zenger, the New York experience with church and state, the Albany Congress, the New York Constitution of 1777, and state origins of the national Bill of Rights. This section also includes reprints of *Essays on the Genesis of the Empire State*, published by the New York State Bicentennial Commission in commemoration of the 200th anniversary of the Declaration of Independence.

The second section brings together articles and conference papers on the ratification debate of 1787–88 in New York State. Conference papers were prepared by Jacob E. Cooke, Robert Ernst, Cathy Matson, and John P. Kaminski. The Ratification Conference was co-sponsored with Historic Hudson Valley, organized by Jacob Judd of Lehman College, and held at Federal Hall on May 20–21, 1988, in commemoration of the 200th anniversary of New York State's ratification of the United States Constitution. This section also presents a series of valuable specialized studies by Gaspare J. Saladino cataloguing the newspapers and magazines published in New York, analyzing and explaining the pseudonyms used in the New York "war of words" over the adoption of the Constitution, recounting the means by which the news of the Constitution's ratification in key states was transmitted to the New York ratifying convention meeting in Poughkeepsie, and describing the range and types of celebrations of the adoption of the Constitution in the summer and early fall of 1788. Saladino concludes this section with a comprehensive update of his critical bibliographic guide published in *The Reluctant Pillar*.

The third section presents biographies of New Yorkers who took part in the making and adoption of the Constitution from 1787 to 1789. Included in this section are such well-known figures as Alexander Hamilton and John Jay and such obscure participants as William Duer, Hugh Hughes, and John Lamb. Also included in this section are biographies of New York's two "first ladies"—Cornelia Tappen Clinton and Sarah Livingston Jay—who were married to two of the leading antagonists of the ratification controversy. Governor Clinton receives extensive attention in three papers presented at a conference honoring the memory of the "founding father" of Revolutionary New York; the contributions of John P. Kaminski are particularly noteworthy as previews of his forthcoming biography of Clinton, the first in half a century.

The fourth section profiles New Yorkers who helped shape the development of the Constitution in the nineteenth and twentieth centuries. Susan B. Anthony and Frederick Douglass, James Kent and David Dudley Field, Benjamin Nathan Cardozo and Robert H. Jackson are only some of the cast of characters included in this section, which also includes case studies of such historical topics as New York's participation in the electoral college from 1789 to 1804, the protests launched by the women's suffrage movement during the 1887 centennial of the

Constitution, the contributions of New York's women lawyers to their state and nation, and the surprisingly active and prominent role of President Franklin D. Roosevelt in the commemoration of the sesquicentennial of the New York ratifying convention in 1938.

We acknowledge that there are dozens, if not hundreds, of other New Yorkers who might have been included in this section. We refer the reader to such major reference works as Leonard W. Levy, Kenneth Karst, and Dennis Mahoney, ed., *The Encyclopaedia of the American Constitution*, 4 vols. (New York: Free Press/Macmillan, 1986; update volume in progress) for articles on other notable jurists, amendment advocates, constitutional scholars, and political figures important in American constitutional history.

New York and the Bicentennial

The first section of *New York and the Bicentennial* brings together the guides and other materials designed to support school and community activities dealing with state and national constitutional themes sponsored by the New York State Bicentennial Commission. The contributions to this section will enable educators and community leaders to stage a mock constitutional convention, to produce a play on women and the Constitution, to commemorate the Bill of Rights, to celebrate the Constitution, to organize a "Critical Choices" Town Meeting, to plant a living legacy, to teach about the ratification of the Constitution and the "First Ladies" of New York State, and more. Elsewhere, the Commission has published *Living Together Constitutionally*, a special collection of elementary-school activities organized around themes and concepts of the Pledge of Allegiance.

The reader should be aware that some of the titles in the first section of *New York and the Bicentennial* discuss supplementary materials distributed by the Commission during the bicentennial commemoration, but not available in this volume. For example, the teaching packet for "Creating Your Own Bicentennial Constitution Celebration" included a color slide of Howard Chandler Christy's famous mural, "Scene of the Signing of the Constitution of the United States," painted for the 1937–39 sesquicentennial. It also included a sample program produced by our colleagues at the New York State Imagination Celebration for their tableau recreating the Federal Convention of 1787 at Philadelphia. The four-page pamphlet suggesting educational activities relating to our "First Ladies" teaching packet accompanied biographies of Cornelia Tappen (Mrs. George) Clinton and Sarah Livingston (Mrs. John) Jay, reproduced in Volume I, and a poster of Mrs. Clinton, which is available from the New York State Museum.

The second section of *New York and the Bicentennial* contains the annual and final reports of the New York State Bicentennial Commission established by Chapter 261 of the Laws of 1986. The Commission was in existence for only three years and three months, from the date it became operational on January 5, 1987, to March 31, 1990, when it ceased activities. As stated in its enabling legislation, the Commission's purpose was to promote and coordinate activities commemorating the bicentennial of the United States Constitution and the role of New York State in its adoption. The reports in this section summarize the Commission's activities, publications, and programs for audiences ranging from elementary school to graduate school and beyond. They also include the Commission's grants to worthwhile activities and materials prepared by distinguished co-sponsors to implement the Commission's mandate. In sum, this volume describes the variety of programs and publications developed by and for the Commission to accomplish its mission—its subject is the range of practical implements derived from the biographical and historical materials on the constitutional development of New York State and the American nation found in Volume I of *New York and the Union*.[1]

In three ways, both *New York and the Union* and *New York and the Bicentennial* provide a record of the work of the Commission. First, *New York and the Union* brings together and preserves the looseleaf materials distributed by the Commission which might otherwise be lost due to their ephemeral nature. *New York and the Bicentennial* contains both the guides which were used in conducting the commemorative programs of the Commission and which now can be used to replicate these programs in future years and the Commission's reports chronicling the day-to-day activities of the Commission during its brief history.

Other Commission publications organize contributions on a more thematic basis. *The Reluctant Pillar* contains essays on New York State's ratification of the United States Constitution. *Well Begun: Chronicles of the Early National Period* brings together essays chronicling the establishment of the national government in 1789. *Contexts of the Bill of Rights* contains essays on the origins and adoption of the Bill of Rights. *World of the Founders* presents case studies of community life in late eighteenth-century New York, and *Roots of the Republic: Commentaries on American Founding Documents* provides the reader with texts of colonial, state, and national founding documents from the Mayflower Compact to the United States Bill of Rights with commentary by specialists in constitutional and political history.

By comparison, *New York and the Union* and *New York and the Bicentennial* are more eclectic—yet we hope that readers will find them entertaining and edifying records of the many publications and activities of the New York State Bicentennial Commission prepared to meet the immediate needs of the bicentennial commemoration in New York State. We trust that they will be of use over the years and take this last opportunity to thank some of the many individuals who helped make possible the work of the Commission included in these volumes.

Acknowledgments

New York and the Union and *New York and the Bicentennial* benefit from the contributions of many individuals who have shared their time and expertise. Each author is extended our appreciation for his or her contribution.

A special word of thanks goes to Paul Finkelman who served as editorial consultant for many of the biographical contributions in *New York and the Union.*

We also acknowledge with gratitude the contributions and energy of the many local bicentennial commissions, committees, and other organizations with which this Commission formed so many valuable partnerships in the course of its work.

We also take this opportunity to thank the staff of the Commission, each of whom contributed to this publication. As publications director, Shirley A. Rice was responsible for the editorial production of most of the items in these volumes. Shirley Rice also conceived of the "First Ladies" project, assisted in that effort by Margaret Gordon-Cooke, who also served on the Commission staff. Thomas E. Burke, the Commission's first research director, wrote three of the essays in *New York and the Union* and researched others. Michael J. Phillips, program director, coordinated many of the special events reported in *New York and the Bicentennial.* Stephanie A. Thompson, educational coordinator, organized the educational programs chronicled in that volume, reviewed the educational material presented there, and assisted in preparing the "Critical Choices" material.

Other staff members contributed to the production of these publications and to the many manuscripts and programs which are a part of them. We are grateful to Natalie Irvis and Tracy Sinnott, who han-

dled the secretarial responsibilities of these projects; Margaret Gordon–
Cooke, who managed the financial aspects; Cynthia Shorts, executive
assistant to the director, who helped supervise the administrative work
of the projects; and, collectively, all of the administrative staff who typed
(and retyped) many of the seemingly endless stream of manuscripts
which found their way into these volumes. Finally, a special word of
thanks to Ken Buess and his wife Beth who typeset the manuscripts with
a caring and watchful eye; to Dean John E. Sexton of New York University Law School and his staff (Karen Stember, Eva Menon, April Holder,
and Rhonda Malvey) for their generosity and patience; to Ene Sirvet
of *The Papers of John Jay*, based at Columbia University; and to John
P. Kaminski and Gaspare J. Saladino, co-editors of *The Documentary
History of the Ratification of the United States Constitution*, University of Wisconsin, for their sage advice and good counsel.

Stephen L. Schechter
Richard B. Bernstein

I. Origins of Constitutionalism in New York

"Liberty and Property": New York and the Origins of American Constitutionalism

THE HONORABLE SOL WACHTLER
Chief Judge of the State of New York

and

STEPHEN L. SCHECHTER
New York State Bicentennial Commission

When scholars seek to identify the origins of American constitutionalism, they most frequently look in the direction of the European philosophers—Blackstone, Locke, and Montesquieu. Rarely do they consider the American states and their constitution makers among our constitutional origins.[1]

When research does focus on the states, Massachusetts, Pennsylvania, and Virginia receive the greatest—and often exclusive—attention. While these three states deserve the attention they receive, their constitutional traditions are quite different from that of New York, which also exerted significant influence on the framing of the Constitution.

Massachusetts, Pennsylvania, and Virginia were founded as commonwealths by Whigs who, despite their theological differences, were committed to the idea of a constitution as a covenant binding its members into a community of virtue. By contrast, New York was founded by Dutch merchants and acquired by the English Crown as a commercial republic committed to the idea of a constitution as a framework of rules protecting individual liberty and property in a republican political economy.

The New York tradition of constitutionalism is, at one and the same time, the least romantic and most undervalued of eighteenth-century state constitutional traditions. In this article, we do not seek to claim any premier position for New York State in the origins of American constitutionalism. That would be foolish because it is historically inaccurate. However, we do seek to establish the idea that New York State was a laboratory for the modern commercial republic and its Federalist constitutional traditions.

Colonial Foundations

New York's constitutional order rests on colonial foundations held suspect in the eyes of many of its contemporary observers. When Governor Benjamin Fletcher arrived in 1692, he described New Yorkers as a "divided, contentious impoverished people." Later in the 1690s, John Usher reported: "Am sure if the Roman Catholicks have a place of purgatory. . . . its not soe bad as [this] place is under my Lords Circumstances."[2]

During the eighteenth century, "colonial governors were often warned in their instructions that New Yorkers were 'Unhappily divided' and that 'their Enmity to Each other' was undermining respect for authority."[3] On a visit to New York, John Adams described the politics of this province as "the devil's own incomprehensibles," speculating on another occasion that the peculiarities of New York politics might be due to the very "air or soil of New York."[4]

The ethnic and religious diversity of colonial New York explains much of its distinctiveness and its suspect status in the mind of contemporaries at a time when social diversity and political opposition were perceived as threats to the very meaning of community. The colony's first European settlers were French-speaking Walloons sent to New Netherland by the Amsterdam chamber of the Dutch West India Company. This group was followed by Dutch-speaking settlers from the central provinces and elsewhere in The Netherlands. In 1643, though the total population of New Netherland lagged behind that of New England, William Kieft, the director-general of New Netherland, told Father Isaac Jogues that eighteen languages were spoken in the city of New Amsterdam.

In 1686, Governor Thomas Dongan reported that the city of New York contained not only major groupings of Dutch Calvinists, Anglicans, French Calvinists, Dutch Lutherans, and ordinary Quakers, but also "Singing Quakers, Ranting Quakers; Sabbatarians; Antisabbatarians; Some Anabaptists [;] some Independents; some Jews; in short all sorts of opinions there are some, and the most part, of none at all."

In 1776, one report estimated the number of congregations as follows: "Dutch Reform, 81; Presbyterian, 61; Episcopal, 30; Quaker, 26; Lutheran, 22; Baptist, 16; Congregationalist, 5; Moravian, 3; Associate Presbyterian, 2; Covenanter, 2; Methodist, 1; Jewish, 1."[5]

A second distinguishing feature of colonial New York is the anti-authoritarian attitudes held by many of its ethnic and religious groups. Walloons fought to retain their linguistic identity under Dutch rule. New England Puritans who had settled on Long Island supplied the Whiggish element of provincial politics and were a constant thorn in the side of Dutch and English governors. The Dutch in turn resented English rule. "Then there were French Huguenots and German Palatines whose experience with established authority had been consistently unfortunate; Indians and blacks who encountered discrimination by law, as well as by social custom; tenant farmers with economic grievances against their landlords; and Presbyterians who bridled under Anglican control."[6]

A third distinguishing feature is the religious tolerance that gradually yet inevitably resulted from the necessities of living and working together in a multi-cultural society. The first and most eloquent statement of this tolerance came in 1657 in response to an ordinance issued by Pieter Stuyvesant by which a fine was levied against settlers receiving Quakers in their homes or attending a Quaker meeting. New England settlers in the Long Island town of Flushing responded defiantly by drawing up and signing a document, later known as the Flushing Remonstrance:

> God is a consuming fire, and it is a fearful thing to fall into the handes of the liveing God; wee desire therefore in this case not to judge least wee be judged, neither to condem least wee bee Condemed, but rather let every man stand and fall to his own. . . . our desire is not to offend one of his little ones in whatsoever forme, name or title hee appeares in, whether Presbyterian, Independent, Baptist or Quaker; but shall be glad to see anything of God in any of them.[7]

Equally important, the directors of the Dutch West India Company counselled Stuyvesant against overzealous policies of religious discrimination on the grounds that such acts were bad for business. In a letter of mild rebuke, the directors stated:

> . . . although we heartily desire, that these and other Sectarians remained away from there, yet as they do not, we doubt very much, whether we can proceed against them rigorously without diminishing the population and stopping immigration, which must be

favored at so tender stage of the country's existence. You may therefore shut your eyes, at least not force people's consciences, but allow
every one to have his own belief, as long as he behaves quietly and
legally, gives no offence to his neighbors and does not oppose the
government.[8]

New York is also distinguished by its patterns of foundation and
settlement. New Netherland began as a monopolistic commercial venture established by the Dutch West India Company with the primary
purpose of profiting from the fur trade. From 1624 to 1639, the Company pursued an unsuccessful policy of monopolistic trade, making concessions to Walloon settlers in the Provisional Orders of 1624 and for
the establishment of patroonships in the Freedoms and Exemptions of
1628 and 1629. Finally, in 1639, the Company relinquished its monopoly
and issued Articles and Conditions (joined in 1640 by a revised set of
Freedoms and Exemptions) which established a system of free trade and
free land.

Between 1638 and 1643, the population of New Netherland doubled from under 1,000 to nearly 2,000 inhabitants. Under the new system,
a "master or colonist" received a small patroonship of 200 acres in exchange for the settlement of five family members or servants. Moreover,
trading privileges were expanded to include free trade on virtually all
commodities, including the fur trade, subject only to taxes on certain
imports and exports. Private Amsterdam merchants were now legally
able to trade with New Netherland, and, as one historian notes, "with
their enormous pools of capital and influential connections, they would
succeed where the Company had failed."[9] On the other hand, "once
the Company ceased to be the main employer of labor in the colony,
it found itself burdened with all the responsibilities of government but
little of the privileges and virtually no respect. . . . The only vestige of
the Company monopoly that remained was its right to tax certain imports and exports, but even this right was aimed more at regulation than
revenue."[10]

Under the new system, trade and settlement increased dramatically but not enough to keep pace with population growth in New England and Virginia. By the time of the English conquest in 1664, the
population of New Netherland had not yet reached 9,000 inhabitants,
while the population of New England and Virginia was about 50,000
and 40,000 respectively. By the close of the century, Massachusetts and
Virginia each had close to 60,000 inhabitants, while New York still had
under 20,000.[11]

The relatively slow growth of New York's colonial population was due to two sets of circumstances: First, on the eastern side of the Atlantic, the Amsterdam merchants had to go beyond their countrymen to recruit settlers throughout Europe. This increased the heterogeneity of New York's population but could not keep pace with the mass exodus from England to New England and Virginia; moreover, the resulting social diversity was unattractive to English settlers. Second, on the western side of the Atlantic, Dutch directors-general extended settlement northward 150 miles up the Hudson River to secure the fur trade; however, the result was an insecure frontier subject to Indian attack and hemmed in by the New England empire. No colony was more extensive yet dispersed in its settlement than was New York.

Constitutionalism in Colonial New York

In human terms, the great end of constitutionalism or the rule of law is to satisfy individual and group needs for a sense of certainty about their lives, their liberties, and their property. In republican societies, constitutionalism is based on the freely given consent of the governed; the citizenry or, as is most often the case, their elected representatives, are expected and empowered to make fundamental choices for setting the basic rules by which citizens and their governors are governed. What distinguishes constitutionalism in colonial New York are the inadequacies of provincial security and the lack of popular representation which characterized much of the first 160 years of New York's history.

Among colonial New York's many distinguishing features, it is often forgotten that life in New York was among the least secure of the American colonies. Under Dutch rule, there were frequent clashes with Indians and one war with the English. Under English rule, battles with the Indians continued and Dutch reconquest was attempted. Later in the eighteenth century, New York was deeply involved in the French and Indian Wars, and of course, during the Revolutionary War southern New York was occupied by British forces from 1776 to 1783 while other parts of the state were major battlegrounds.

If one of the distinguishing features of colonial New York was the physical insecurity of life and property due to wartime conditions, another was the political insecurity of liberty and property resulting from changes in authoritarian regimes with no continuing residue of representative government. From 1624 to 1639, New Netherland was governed as the economic monopoly of a joint-stock company. During the period of economic liberalization, from 1640 to 1664, settlers were transformed from company employees to free agents; however, the rights of citizenship remained tightly controlled under an authoritarian regime which allowed for no representation save for minor political concessions granted to certain towns.

Under English rule, New York did not become a royal colony with a permanent representative government until 1691. From 1664 to 1683, New York was governed as a ducal propriety with a thoroughly executive government guaranteed by the king's charter to the Duke of York and maintained by the so-called Duke's Laws of 1664–65. Like the Dutch Provisional Orders, the Duke's Laws served as the colonial constitution setting out an authoritarian form of government and a limited system of privileges. However, as Charles M. Andrews observed: "A ducal domain, such as that of New York, from which revenue was to be extracted, was as foreign to the spirit and trend of the times as was the equally incongruous lordship that the Baltimores were endeavoring to maintain in Maryland during these same eventful years. . . . New York was gradually ceasing to be a propriety except in name. In fact, it was becoming a small, subordinate commonwealth, presenting problems to its governor and other officials that were troublesome to solve because they concerned a community of freemen and not a proprietary estate of land."[12] Still, as late as January 1676, the duke politely rejected the idea of representative government in his domain:

> I have formerly writt to you touching Assemblyes in those countreys and have since observed what severall of your lattest letters hint about that matter. But unless you had offered what qualifications are usual and proper to such Assemblyes, I cannot but suspect they would be of dangerous consequence, nothing being more knowne than the aptness of such bodyes to assume to themselves many priviledges which prove destructive to, or very oft disturbe, the peace of the government wherein they are allowed. Neither do I see any use of them which is not as well provided for, whilst you and your Councell govern according to the laws established . . . But howsoever if you continue of the same opinion, I shall be ready to consider of any proposalls you shall send to that purpose.[13]

Demands for representation, coming mainly from the New England towns on Long Island, increased under English rule, and in 1681 deputies from a number of towns met at Huntington to petition for their "Just Libertys, to present grievances, and to pray for relief."[14] Shortly thereafter, the duke sent Thomas Dongan to New York with instructions that included the following statement: "I have thought fitt that there shall be a General Assembly of all the Freeholders by the persons who they shall choose to represent them in order to consulting with your self while you are selfe and the said Councill what laws are fitt and necessary to be made and established for the good weale and the government of the said Colony and its Dependencyes, and of all the inhabitants thereof."[15]

On September 13, 1683, Governor Dongan issued the necessary writs, and on October 17 New York's first provincial assembly met. No record of its proceedings exists; however, the assembly passed fourteen laws and the "Charter of Libertyes and Priviledges" within three weeks. One of the great mysteries of colonial history is how a small group of representatives, said to be "mainly Dutch," could produce, in so short a time and with so little experience, a charter which neatly set out a representative framework of government and carefully enumerated all of the essential rights of Englishmen accumulated in Magna Carta, the Petition of Right, the Navigation Acts, and other English documents.

Unfortunately for the new experiment, by a twist of history, Charles II died shortly thereafter and was succeeded on February 6, 1685, by his brother, James II, the Duke of York. With his accession to the throne, New York became a royal colony; however, the conjuncture of royal status, chartered rights, and representative government proved short-lived. As king, James had new plans for New York. On May 16, 1686, the Privy Council disallowed New York's charter and in 1688 New York and the Jerseys were consolidated into the Dominion of New England. The Dominion also proved short-lived, collapsing in 1689 following the overthrow of James II in the Glorious Revolution and the accession of William III and Mary II. On May 31, 1689, six weeks after the Boston uprising, part of the militia led by one of its officers, Jacob Leisler, gained control of southern New York. Leisler put together a shaky coalition of provincial government which lasted until the arrival of English troops under the leadership of Colonel Henry Sloughter in March of 1691.

The end of Leislerian government brought a period of long-awaited stability and representative government to New York. On April 9, 1691, with the calling of a representative assembly, "for the first time under the direct authority of the English crown, the period of prerogative and executive government came to an end [and] New York entered the ranks of the regular royal colonies with governor, council, and popular assembly, and a new era in the history of the province began."[16]

Unfortunately, the constitutional status of colonial New York did not improve overnight. One of the first acts of the new anti-Leislerian assembly was to pass a new charter of liberties aimed at quieting rebel forces. Virtually a replica of the 1683 charter, the new charter shared a similar fate and was rejected in England, thereby denying New Yorkers a basic charter of rights for the remainder of their colonial history.

After sixty-seven years, New Yorkers had finally obtained representative government. However, it took another fifty-two years before the governor's council accepted the idea of regularized and hence predictable elections for assembly seats as set out in the Septennial Act of 1743 providing for provincial elections at intervals no greater than seven years. In fact, the Septennial Act closed out and ratified a decade of constitutional reform which included the Zenger trial and the legitimation of the political opposition, assembly control over the provincial budget, the introduction of fiscal responsibility, and the professionalization of the courts and the legal profession.

Constitutionalism, then, came of age in colonial New York nearly 150 years after founding and only 33 years (or one political generation) before independence. The patterns of political and constitutional behavior learned during New York's first century persisted into its second. In the absence of a provincial system of rights and representation, New Yorkers simply learned how to achieve a requisite level of certitude and consent within the arenas of council and community. Without a provincial assembly, interest representation on provincial matters was played out in the governor's council, and this arena nurtured a form of family-based factionalism for which New York soon became famous. At the same time, interest articulation and aggregation, to borrow from the language of political science, began to take root in local communities, aided by a combination of factors including the geographic isolation of upper Hudson communities, the political culture of New England communities on Long Island, and the ethnic and religious diversity of New York City. In the generation before independence, New Yorkers began to learn how to balance the resulting political tendencies toward executive centralization and local noncentralization.

State Constitutional Experience

"The blessings of society," wrote John Adams in 1776, "depend entirely on the constitutions of government." Agreeing with this sentiment, the Second Continental Congress adopted a resolution on May 10, 1776: "That it be recommended to the respective assemblies and conventions of the United Colonies, where no government sufficient to the exigencies of their affairs have been hitherto established, to adopt such government as shall, in the opinion of the representatives of the people, best conduce to the happiness and safety of their constituents in particular and America in general."

Three weeks later, on May 31, George Washington warned of the vastness of the task. "To form a new Government requires infinite care and unbounded attention," Washington stated, "for if the foundation is badly laid, the superstructure must be bad. . . . A matter of such moment cannot be the Work of a day."

Washington's advice notwithstanding, most of the thirteen original states had adopted a constitution within one year of the congressional resolution urging them to do so. New Hampshire and South Carolina adopted constitutions even before the call from Congress (on January 5 and May 26, 1776, respectively). As a corporate colony, Rhode Island converted its colonial charter into a state constitution on May 4 by removing all references to royal authority. On June 29, Virginia adopted a constitution on which it had begun to work even before the congressional resolution of May. Next came New Jersey on July 2, the same day that the Congress declared independence. Most of the remaining states adopted constitutions before the end of 1776. Only two states delayed until 1777, largely owing to the exigencies of war: Georgia on February 5 and New York on April 20.

The foregoing account reminds us that the American Revolution required constitution making as well as war making. During the fifteen-year period from 1776 to 1791, Americans adopted fourteen first state constitutions, seven revised state constitutions, one federal constitution (that is, the Articles of Confederation), one national constitution (that is, the U.S. Constitution of 1787), and its first ten amendments (collectively known as the Bill of Rights).

The principles which these constitutions shared in common are based on the republican theory of popular consent. What distinguishes these constitutions is the type of republican constitutional tradition on which they rest. Two traditions were employed: the older Whig tradition on which most state constitutions were based, and the federalist tradition utilized most clearly in the U.S. Constitution of 1787. As Daniel J. Elazar explains:

> One was based on older *Whig* republican forms brought to American shores by the first British and northwest European colonists and further developed in the intervening four or five generations. The Whig tradition emphasized a communitarian polity and the importance of republican virtue. Individualism was tempered and legislatures as representatives of the community could intervene and regulate behavior in ways which would now be regarded as infringements of individual rights. At the same time, the Whig tradition placed great emphasis on direct, active, continuous,

and well-nigh complete popular control over the legislature and government in general, through such devices as small electoral districts, short tenures of office, many elective offices, sharp separations of power, and procedures approaching constituent instruction of elected representatives.

In facing the task of framing a national constitution, however, a new republican or *federalist* conception of constitutionalism emerged primarily through the work of James Madison. While the federalist idea agreed with the Whig tradition that all powers of government be derived from the people, Madison added the pregnant phrase, "either directly or indirectly." This reflected the federalist effort to cope with the problems of establishing an extended and diverse democratic republic compounded of constituent polities—particularly the problem of majority tyranny. The federalist conception of republican remedies for republican diseases placed greater emphasis on balancing individual and group interests and refining the interests and opinions of the people through such devices as large electoral districts, indirect senatorial elections, longer tenures of office, limited numbers of elective offices and a system of separated but shared powers. The federalist view also saw commerce as a partial way of solving the problem of republican virtue in a large republic.[17]

New York's constitution of 1777 is typically regarded as distinctive because it was the first to provide for a relatively strong chief executive directly elected by the people. However, what distinguishes the New York State Constitution of 1777 is that it was the first state constitution to experiment with the newly emerging federalist tradition of constitutionalism. Several factors help explain how this came about. These factors are war, conservatism, pluralism, and New York's own tradition as a commercial republic.

The exigencies of war were particularly severe in New York State. Because of the threat of British attack, the Fourth Provincial Congress met at White Plains, on July 9, 1776, rather than in New York City, for the purpose of establishing "such a government that they shall deem calculated to secure the rights, liberties and happiness of the good people of this colony; and to continue in force until a future peace with Great Britain shall render the same unnecessary." On August 1, the Provincial Congress, renamed "the Convention of the Representatives of the State of New-York," assigned the task of drafting a constitution to a committee of thirteen—John Jay, Gouverneur Morris, Robert R. Livingston, John Sloss Hobart, William Smith (of Suffolk County), William Duer, John Broome, John Morin Scott, Abraham Yates, Jr., Henry

Wisner, Samuel Townsend, Charles DeWitt of Ulster County, and Robert Yates. James Duane was added later.

British advances forced the Convention northward, first to Fishkill in Dutchess County, and finally to Kingston in Ulster County. Although the constitution-drafting committee was initially ordered to report a draft by August 26, 1776, it did not do so until March 12 of the following year. Beyond the problems caused by the need for constant flight, the committee found it difficult to assemble a quorum because many of the committee members had active military commands, local government responsibilities, or other convention committee assignments.

Wartime conditions were not the only cause for delay. The politics of delay was a tactic of conservatives on this issue, in much the same way as Antifederalists and Federalists alike would use it ten years later on the issue of the ratification of the U.S. Constitution. In a letter to William Duer of June 12, 1777, Robert R. Livingston confided in the use of "well timed delays, indefatigable industry, and a minute attention to every favorable circumstance" in order to prevent the adoption of a radical constitution patterned after that of Pennsylvania, in which the fear of executive power had eliminated the office of governor altogether. John Jay, the principal draftsman of the New York State Constitution, virtually admitted as much when he remarked to his son William that "another turn of the winch would have cracked the cord."

Conservatives or reluctant republicans (many of whom had been Loyalist and would later become Federalist) considered themselves "friends of order" and supporters of energetic government and a strong executive. By contrast, radical republicans (many of whom would later become Antifederalist) considered themselves "friends of liberty" and saw little need for an independent executive in a system in which the legislature represented the people in a mirror-like fashion.

New York State politics was unpredictable because conservative leaders (including city merchants and rural manor lords) believed that they could attract the interest of commercially minded tradesmen in the city and rent-paying tenant farmers in the country. Toward this end, New York conservatives during the Revolutionary period found both a strong executive and an expanded electorate in their interests. This strategy was complicated by the British occupation of New York City, which attracted Loyalists to it and drove radicals out of it. The state constitution of 1777 provided that the current delegates of the five southern counties would serve until elections could be held. These southern delegates belonged to the more radical element.

A third factor of New York State politics is the great diversity of its population. In New York State, the Revolution further divided New

Yorkers in their sentiments, interests, and regions. So sharp were these divisions that the state might have degenerated into civil war had it not been for the British occupation of New York City and the consequent flight of Loyalists to it. Within this context, New York State took so long to adopt a constitution because it had little choice. Practically speaking, it took time for conservatives like John Jay and Gouverneur Morris and radical Whigs like John Morin Scott to learn how to work effectively with one another as members of a drafting committee. Likewise, it took time to reconcile differences over ideology, religion, class, and region.

The provision for a strong yet popularly elected governor represents, in one sense, a necessary wartime compromise between friends of liberty and order. By this compromise, the New York State Assembly became the safeguard of liberty because it was so closely tied to the people. Annual elections were given to farmers with freehold (real property) worth at least 20 pounds, land-renting tenants who paid annual rents of 2 pounds, and tradesmen recognized as "freemen" by the cities of Albany and New York. At the same time, the governor became an acceptable component of energetic government. With a final stroke of innovation, the state constitution established a council of revision in which the governor was forced to share the veto power with state courts, and a council of appointment in which the governor was forced to share the appointment power with state senators.

While their handiwork was clearly a compromise between the forces of liberty and order, the framers of New York State's first constitution also helped to fashion seven building blocks of the modern commercial republic which would receive fuller expression in the U.S. Constitution drafted a decade later.

First, the 1777 constitution provided for a legislature based on proportional representation, representative of all segments of society, yeoman farmers, tenant farmers, city workers, and free blacks.

Second, that document provided for a popularly elected executive with the power to govern energetically. The governor's term of office was three years with no limit on reelection, and the office was vested with "the supreme executive power"; that is, "to take care that the laws are faithfully executed to the best of his ability; and to expedite all such measures as may be resolved upon by the legislature."

Third, the constitution experimented with power-sharing arrangements, involving the judiciary in the review of legislation (subject to a two-thirds override by both houses) and involving the senate in the approval of appointments; both of which found later expression in the U.S. Constitution.

Fourth, the judiciary was given more power than in any other state to date—a share in the review of legislation, a share in impeachments, control of court officers, and a share in judicial selection as members of the council of appointment.[18]

Fifth, although the 1777 constitution contained no separate bill of rights, and underscored the state's reliance on a common-law basis of rights, it did provide a strong guarantee for the free exercise of religion, for trial by jury, for the right to vote, and for due process.

Sixth, the constitution provided for the separation of church and state by barring clergyman from holding public office and rejecting a religious test for holding office.

Seventh, the constitution anticipated population growth in a commercial society by providing for legislative reapportionment based on a septennial census and the naturalization of immmigrants.

In all these respects, the state constitution of 1777 anticipated the national constitution written ten years later.

NOTES

[1] Notable exceptions remain Willi Paul Adams, *The First American Constitutions: Republican Ideology and the Making of State Constitutions in the Revolutionary Era* (published for the Institute of Early American History and Culture, Williamsburg, VA, by the University of North Carolina Press, Chapel Hill, NC, 1980); Donald S. Lutz, *Popular Consent and Popular Control: Whig Political Theory in the Early State Constitutions* (Baton Rouge, LA: Louisiana State University Press, 1980); and Donald S. Lutz, *The Origins of American Constitutionalism* (Baton Rouge, LA: Louisiana State University Press, 1988).

[2] Governor Fletcher to Mr. Blathwayt, NY, September 10, 1692; John Usher's Report on the Northern Colonies, 1698. As quoted in Patricia U. Bonomi, *A Factious People: Politics and Society in Colonial New York* (New York: Columbia University Press, 1971), p. 11.

[3] Bonomi, *A Factious People*, p. 12.

[4] As quoted in Michael Kammen, *Colonial New York: A History* (New York: Charles Scribner's Sons, 1975), p. 341. John Adams to William Tudor, Philadelphia, June 24, 1776; as quoted in Bonomi, p. 17.

[5] Governor Thomas Dongan's Report on the State of the Province, 1686. As quoted in Bonomi, p. 25. Estimates of 1776 quoted in David Maldwyn Ellis, *New York: State and City* (Ithaca, NY: Cornell University Press, 1979), p. 69.

[6] Kammen, *Colonial New York*, p. 342.

⁷As quoted in Oliver A. Rink, *Holland On the Hudson: An Economic and Social History of Dutch New York* (Ithaca, NY: Cornell University Press, 1986), p. 236.

⁸E.B. O'Callaghan and Berthold Fernow, eds., *Documents Relative to the Colonial History of the State of New York*, 14 vols.(1856–1883), XIV, p. 526. On this subject generally, see George L. Smith, *Religion and Trade in Colonial New Netherland: Dutch Origins and American Development* (Ithaca, NY: Cornell University Press, 1973).

⁹Rink, *Holland on the Hudson*, p. 137.

¹⁰Rink, *Holland on the Hudson*, p. 136, 137.

¹¹Kammen, *Colonial New York*, p. 38.

¹²Charles M. Andrews, *The Colonial Period of American History*, 4 vols. (New Haven, CT: Yale University Press, 1937), Vol. III, p. 101.

¹³Andrews, *The Colonial Period of American History*, III, p. 113.

¹⁴*Hempstead Town Records*, September 26, 1681. As quoted in Andrews, *The Colonial Period of American History*, III, p. 113n.

¹⁵Andrews, *The Colonial Period of American History*, III, p. 114.

¹⁶Andrews, *The Colonial Period of American History*, III, p. 137.

¹⁷Daniel J. Elazar, *State Constitutional Design in Federal Systems*, a special issue of *Publius* edited by Daniel J. Elazar and Stephen L. Schechter, vol. 12, no. 1 (Fall 1982), p. 13.

¹⁸Willi Paul Adams, *The First American Constitutions*, p. 268.

Hiawatha: Constitution-maker

DEAN R. SNOW

State University of New York at Albany

The United States Constitution of 1787 is America's oldest surviving constitution, but it was not the first. That distinction may belong to the League of the Iroquois, founded by Hiawatha of Iroquoian legend.

The name "Hiawatha" was made popular by Henry Wadsworth Longfellow in the last century, but at the cost of historical accuracy. Longfellow's Hiawatha has nothing to do with the Hiawatha of Onondaga legend. Longfellow's epic poem is modeled on a Finnish epic, reworked for an Algonquian (not Iroquoian) setting, and supplied with names that he borrowed randomly from a number of sources.

The Hiawatha of Iroquois legend was an Onondaga, one of the tribes of the Five Nations, who joined with an expatriate Huron (usually referred to as the "Peace Maker") to create the League of the Iroquois. The legend of this accomplishment is one of the three great set pieces of Iroquois cosmology. The first is the Creation Myth, which is similar to many others (including that of the Christians) in its beauty and implausibility. The character of Sky Woman, the concept of the earth as the back of a great turtle, the good and evil twins, and the other elements of the creation myth seem not intended to be taken literally, yet tell us much about the Iroquois world view. At the other extreme is the Code of Handsome Lake, the third piece of Iroquois cosmology. Handsome Lake developed the code around the end of the eighteenth century. This was clearly an historical development, and the people involved are well known to us through many documentary sources. Handsome Lake founded a religion based on traditional Iroquois belief and new principles developed to deal with the relatively new personal and social pressures confronting Iroquois people at the time (Fenton, 1978; Tooker, 1978).

The Constitution of the Five Nations lies between the other two pieces of Iroquois cosmology. It has both mythic elements and elements that seem to have the same degree of historical reality as the Code of Handsome Lake. Hiawatha comes through as a real person, who has acquired some mythic attributes over time. Similarly, the Peace Maker seems historically real in the versions of the legend that have come down through oral tradition. Nevertheless, the name of the Peace Maker (Deganawida) is considered sacred by modern Iroquois believers, and they prefer not to hear it spoken. This and other mythic elements characterize the Peace Maker as he appears in the legend describing the origins of the constitution. Consequently, both he and Hiawatha appear to many to have been real people who participated in real events, but the whole is draped in the clothing of Iroquois legend. The result is a story that over the years has lost historic certainty while gaining cultural meaning (Parker, 1968).

Iroquois oral accounts of the founding of the League vary in detail according to local tradition and differences in translation. In some versions, the Peace Maker is the founder, while in others Hiawatha is. In still others, they share the honor equally. Generally, the story involves the departure of Hiawatha from his native Onondaga village, a departure occasioned by the deaths of his seven daughters at the hands of an evil shaman. The grief-stricken Hiawatha wanders eastward picking up magical wampum beads from the bed of a pond after ducks fly away with the pond's water. The Peace Maker has already made his way to Cohoes Falls from Huron country after establishing himself as a person with supernatural powers. He proves his powers to the Mohawk as well, and then is joined by Hiawatha. Together they devise the Condolence Ceremony. The Peace Maker makes fifteen wampum strings from the wampum beads brought by Hiawatha, and defines the fifteen matters of the Requickening Address that they represent. The purpose of the fifteen matters and the ceremony constructed around them is to ''wipe away the tears,'' to ''remove obstructions from the throat,'' to ''wipe the bloodstains from the mat,'' and so on. Clearly, the intent is to end the grieving process and thereby to short-circuit revenge. The Condolence Ceremony became the mechanism for the maintenance of the Great Peace because with it the Iroquois were able to break the cycle of revenge-motivated killing.

According to the legend, Hiawatha and the Peace Maker first convinced the Mohawk to extend the Great Peace between nations. The Oneida agreed next, followed by the Onondaga, Cayuga, and Seneca in turn. The timing of this process is still not certain, but it could have occurred around 1500 A.D., or sometime in the century straddling that date. The glue that held the league together was the Condolence Ceremony, which first reasserted, then disposed of the collective grief of league members when a death occurred. Meetings of the league chiefs began with the ceremony in a ritual clearing of the air.

Although the mutual nonaggression pact created a Great Peace among the five participating Iroquois nations, it did not extend to other nations. It consequently produced a union that would eventually dominate the Northeast. One authority, Daniel Richter, has argued that we should distinguish between the league and the Iroquois Confederacy, a more overtly political institution that was built on league foundations in the course of the seventeenth century. This is a useful distinction because it allows us to distinguish between the league as an entirely Native American institution and the Confederacy, which thrived mainly in the context of Euro-American colonial history.

The Peace Maker and Hiawatha established a code of conduct for the league, having (by one count) 117 specific parts. These draw upon the symbolism of the Great Tree of Peace, the White Roots of Peace, and so on. They also specify the structure of league representatives and the conduct of league affairs. Fifty league chiefs (sachems) are specified. Each office carries a name which a new chief assumes when he is appointed. The Peace Maker had no successor, so his name does not appear in the roll. The name of Hiawatha (Ayonhwathah) appears as the second of nine Mohawk chiefs, but it remains permanently unfilled in his honor. Each nation was assigned a number of league chiefs: the Mohawk, nine; the Oneida, nine; the Onondaga, fourteen; the Cayuga, ten; and the Seneca, eight. Within each nation, these were parcelled out by clan. The Mohawk and Oneida had only three clans (Wolf, Turtle, and Bear) and their sachemships were divided equally between them. However, Onondaga chiefs were divided unequally among eight clans, with one chief (Thadodaho) standing alone as first among equals for the whole league. The Cayuga assigned two or three chiefs from each of four clans. The Seneca made use of four pairs of chiefs drawn from five clans.

All league chiefs were appointed by senior women in dominant family lineages belonging to appropriate clans. Iroquois lineages (clan segments) were and are matrilineal; one's clan identity is determined by that of one's mother. Traditional Iroquois households were matrilocal; the inhabitants of a particular longhouse were closely related women of some particular clan segment, their husbands (necessarily drawn from clan segments belonging to some other clan), and their unmarried children. Select longhouses, each controlled by a senior woman, provided chiefs for so long as they could produce suitable leaders. Village and national affairs were conducted by men appointed in similar ways, but who were not necessarily also league chiefs.

The arrangement seems unfair to modern Americans steeped in Western democratic traditions. Representation from the Five Nations was unequal, and individual appointments were hereditary in a general sense. However, this was a system in which concepts such as "quorum" and "majority rule" had no place. All decisions had to be unanimous, or no action would take place. Debate began with the most junior man present and proceeded to the most senior, with a deliberate development of consensus each step of the way. The confederacy that grew out of the league was disadvantaged in its struggle against French and English colonial powers because it lacked the internal mechanisms to enforce compliance by minority factions when unanimity could not be reached. In this respect, it was flawed in the same way the United States Articles of Confederation were flawed. It worked, but not well enough to compete effectively against nation-states defined in the European tradition.

At the national and village levels, Iroquois clans were divided into two "sides" or "moieties." Among the Mohawk and Oneida, the Turtle and Wolf clans formed one moiety while the Bear clan stood alone as the opposite moiety. The dual division worked differently in detail among the other nations, but everywhere the system allowed for reciprocal cooperation in practical village matters. The moiety system was projected to the league level as well. The Mohawk, Onondaga, and Seneca constituted one side, while the Oneida and Cayuga were the other. When the Tuscarora joined as a sixth nation in the eighteenth century they were incorporated on the Oneida–Cayuga side. At all levels, an important function of a moiety was to perform the Condolence Ceremony for the other moiety.

The operations of the league took on an additional three-part complexity when issues other than condolence arose. In those cases, the Onondaga sat between the Mohawk and Seneca on one side, the Oneida and Cayuga on the other. A further complication that began in the seventeenth century was the designation of influential men as "Pine Tree Chiefs" or "War Chiefs." These tended to be men of considerable ability and charisma who did not happen to come from the clan segments (lineages) that provided league chiefs. The growing power of such men eventually undermined the structure of the league. By the time of the American Revolution, Pine Tree Chiefs had acquired most of the real power and wealth in league communities, and the league chiefs were left with powers that were more symbolic than real.

The Iroquois nations were badly fragmented by colonial wars and the American Revolution. Mohawks now live on six scattered reserves and reservations in Canada and the United States. There are Oneidas in Wisconsin, Ontario, and New York. Some Cayugas live in Oklahoma, and both they and Senecas can be found in several communities in Ontario and New York. The league was recreated at many of these locations in the nineteenth and twentieth centuries. League chief names (and, therefore, offices) are in some cases duplicated in different locations. Other league chief names have been left vacant. Only the Onondaga have remained localized in their traditional homeland. For these reasons and because of their traditional role as Firekeepers for the league, the league structure persists most strongly and coherently at Onondaga.

The importance of the League of the Iroquois for the bicentennial celebration of the U. S. Constitution is that it was the first formal constitution in what is now New York State. Further, it appears to have been a partial model for the Albany Plan of Union, which resulted from the Albany Congress of 1754. Benjamin Franklin drafted the plan for the congress, which included representatives from most of the colonies and the Iroquois nations. The plan called for forty-eight representatives to be chosen unequally by eleven colonies (Georgia and Delaware were not included). The colonial assemblies were to select the members of this "Grand Council." Thus, in terms of basic structure and name, Franklin's proposal bears a striking resemblance to the League of the Iroquois (O'Callaghan 6:853–892).

For further information on the Albany Plan of Union and the importance of the League to it, see Thomas E. Burke, "The Albany Plan of Union," elsewhere in this volume.

FOR FURTHER READING

Fenton, W.A. "Northern Iroquoian Cultural Patterns." In *Handbook of North American Indians*, edited by B.G. Trigger. Vol. 15, 296–321. Washington, D.C.: Smithsonian Institution, 1978.

O'Callaghan, E.B. *Documents Relative to the Colonial History of the State of New York*. 15 vols. Albany: Weed, Parsons, and Company, 1855.

Parker, A.C. "The Constitution of the Five Nations." In *Parker on the Iroquois*, edited by W.A. Fenton. Syracuse: Syracuse University Press, 1968.

Tooker, E. "The League of the Iroquois: Its History, Politics, and Ritual." In *Handbook of North American Indians*, edited by B.G. Trigger. Vol. 15, 418–441. Washington, D.C.: Smithsonian Institution, 1978.

The Dutch–American Connection: The Impact of "The Dutch Example" On American Constitutional Beginnings

JAMES R. TANIS

Bryn Mawr College

From time to time, colonial governors and administrators in North America considered proposals for unification, primarily for defensive purposes. They looked to Europe for inspiration, finding in the Union of Utrecht a model that had served to regularize the confederation known as the United Provinces of the Netherlands.

The Dutch impact on eighteenth-century America has often been told in terms of Knickerbockers and other Hudson Valley provincialisms, but the true heart of the matter lies in the critical political and economic forces by which The Netherlands affected the American scene. Foremost were the traditions of union and liberty, symbolized by the Union of Utrecht, the *de facto* Dutch constitution. Emerging most clearly at the time of the French and Indian War in the 1750s, the Dutch example, as it was often called, continued its positive impact through the period of the Continental Congresses, helping to shape the Articles of Confederation. As the American constitutional debates of 1787 took shape, the Dutch–American comparisons took on new and more critical forms.

On the tenth of September, 1787, the Committee of Style and Arrangement was working in Philadelphia to put the final touches on the newly drafted Constitution. Thomas Jefferson was in Paris attending to the international political and fiscal affairs of the new nation. To

America's representative in The Netherlands, Charles W.F. Dumas, Jefferson wrote: "Happy for us, that when we find our constitutions defective and insufficient to secure the happiness of our people, we can assemble with all the coolness of philosophers and set it to rights, while every other nation on earth must have recourse to arms to amend or to restore their constitutions." Though Jefferson's view proved overly optimistic in the long run, he was well aware of the history of the Dutch constitution—the Union of Utrecht—and he hoped for as much for the newly shaped American constitution.

Much earlier, the Union of Utrecht had been a symbol to many Americans, first of unity, and then of unity and liberty. The Dutch text of the Union had been reprinted in *De Americaanse Almanak* for 1754, the only surviving relic of a series of forty or fifty New York Dutch almanacs. The author of the articles began: "These provinces, that is, the Dutch provinces, consist of a group of commonwealths independent of one another, though united to protect one another against the common enemy." The bloody and unsettling French and Indian War was at hand. The Hudson River Valley was a major passage between the British and the French colonies to the north. Albany, in the middle, was a major center for Indian trade and other Indian affairs.

No American colonists were more pressingly aware of the threat of French and Indian warfare than the Dutch of the upper river valley. The almanac's article describing a defensive union against a common enemy spoke directly to their condition. What was most needed among the disparate colonies was just such a union, one which would respect their prevailing independence and yet provide protection against the common enemy. The timely reminder of the Union of Utrecht must have been welcome to many of the New World Dutch settlers.

The Dutch example, however, was by no means limited to the once-Dutch middle colonies, but was a topic of conversation among their Anglo–American neighbors, as well. In a Boston sermon in 1754, Pastor Jonathan Mayhew observed, "No one that is not an absolute stranger to French ambition, to their policy, to their injustice, to their perfidiousness, can be in any doubt what they aspire at. . . . Their late conduct may well alarm us; especially considering our disunion, or at least want of a sufficient bond of union, amongst ourselves; an inconvenience which, it is to be hoped, we shall not always labour under. And whenever all our scattered rays shall be drawn to a point and proper focus, they can scarce fail to consume and burn up these enemies of our peace, how faintly soever they may strike at present. What *union* can do, we need only look toward those Provinces, which are distinguished by the name of the United, to know."

Though the significance of the Union of Utrecht was as clear, in a general way, to most Dutch–Americans of the mid-eighteenth century as the Declaration of Independence is to most Americans now, the story of Dutch union and of the Dutch struggle for liberty was familiar to any well-read colonist, regardless of national origin. Sir William Temple's *Observations upon the United Provinces of the Netherlands* was a most popular book in the colonies, having passed through numerous editions and translations. (In fact, it may well be the source of the account in *De Americaanse Almanak.*) Though first published in 1673 when Britain and The Netherlands were at war, no book in English detailed the Dutch political scene as adequately. Temple had served as envoy to the United Provinces, and he wrote with understanding and with considerable objectivity. In 1750, when Benjamin Franklin was recommending a course of study for the Philadelphia Academy (now the University of Pennsylvania), Sir William Temple was among the foremost authors cited. Indeed, it appears to have been Temple's work which informed much of Franklin's thinking as he prepared for the Albany Congress of 1754.

That congress was the most significant intercolonial meeting held in the American colonies up to that time. It opened to everyone the question of union, which only later was to eventuate in independence as well as union. The concrete idea of union does not appear to have been widely discussed prior to the congress, but the seeds of union-thinking were widely scattered as a result of the plan which was formulated. No person was as crucial to that elusive-but-hoped-for union as was Benjamin Franklin. In May of 1754, Franklin's famous political cartoon of the "Join or Die" snake spread his ideas throughout the colonies more rapidly than any words could have done. Franklin arrived in Albany in early June with the draft of a plan. "Short Hints," he called it, which he hoped could be developed into a commonly acceptable document of agreement.

The Dutch political example which influenced the discussions at Albany must surely have been reinforced by the setting; most of the city's architecture was more reminiscent of Amsterdam than of Boston or Philadelphia, and a large portion of the population regularly conversed in Dutch. In fact, the English Indian agent, Thomas Pownall, complained that all the Indian negotiations were first conducted in Dutch and then had to be translated into English.

Franklin's "Short Hints" were soon elaborated into a document called "the committee's Short Hints." There are many parallels between this document and the Union of Utrecht. Like the Union of Utrecht, it proposed that "the Several Colonies may each enjoy its own Constitution, Laws, Liberties and Privileges as so many Separate Corporations in one Common Wealth." A Grand Council was proposed to fill the place of the Dutch States General, and a President General to fill that of the king's regent. All of the Albany documents, from Franklin's "Short Hints" to the final Albany Plan, explicitly recognized the royal authority of the British king. Indeed, the original 1579 preface to the Union of Utrecht had stated: ". . . the deputies of the aforesaid provinces . . . have decreed and concluded the following Points and Articles, without thereby in any way desiring to secede from the Holy Roman Empire." A Dutch declaration of independence did, however, follow two years later. The Albany committee's "Short Hints" noted: "Perticular Colonies not to Declare Warr." The Union of Utrecht required "Peace and War not to be made without the consent of all the Provinces." Other technical points of comparison can be made, but far more fundamental than passing analogies was the psychological impact of the Union of Utrecht and its function as a symbol of union among diverse and independent bodies. In fact, though the existence of the Union was well known, the content of the document was little known and even less understood. It is significant that eighteenth-century Americans usually referred to the country as the United Provinces, and only occasionally as The Netherlands. Historically, it is also important to keep in mind the fact that the Union of Utrecht, like the Albany Plan of Union, was not originally conceived as a constitution of fundamental law, but as a means of regularizing a confederation based on pressing historical exigencies.

The Albany Plan was never ratified, in spite of the efforts of Franklin in Pennsylvania and the Livingstons in New York. At that time, young William Livingston led the pro-union struggle and probably stood behind the weekly New York newspaper, the *Instructor*. In the first issue, articles were solicited; but, it noted, "no controversy of any kind shall have admittance." Then, the journal's own editorials proceeded to argue for union. "The only expedient . . . is, that all the Colonies appertaining to the Crown of Great Britain on the Northern Continent of America, be united under a legal, regular, and firm establishment. . . . A coalition, or union of this nature . . . will, in all probability, lay a sure and lasting foundation of dominion, strength, and trade. . . ." Tradition says that the British found the Albany Plan too radical, and the more radical colonists felt that it did not go far enough. Though there is some truth in that observation, reasons both more complex, and at times more mundane, also accounted for its failure to gain acceptance. Its long-term impact, nonetheless, was of great importance to the colonies as their problems shifted from the French government, which had been driven from Canada by the French and Indian War, to the British government, which was increasingly more insensitive to the development of colonial power and identity. The next American congress was the Stamp Act Congress in 1765, called to protest taxation without representation—coincidentally, one of the original causes of the Dutch revolution two centuries earlier.

Though the Albany Plan of Union was never effected, Franklin never lost sight of the Dutch example. Writing in 1768 to alert the English to American restiveness, he noted: "Threescore years did the oppressed United Provinces maintain a war in defence of their liberties against the then powerful kingdom of Spain . . . which was finally obliged to acknowledge their independency in a formal treaty . . . and with a broken strength that has never since been recovered." A decade later, when in France seeking European support for the Revolution, Franklin wrote on behalf of the American commissioners to their agent in The Hague, ". . . in the love of liberty, and bravery in the defence of it, Holland has been our example. We hope circumstances and constitutions, in many respects so similar, may produce mutual benevolence. . . ." The Dutch constitution to which he referred was the Union of Utrecht. The American constitution was the Articles of Confederation, though it would be 1781 before it was signed by Maryland, the last of the states to ratify.

Franklin's constitutional comparison was not news to the Dutch, at least not to all of them. In The Netherlands, an eager young lawyer, Pieter Paulus, was in the midst of writing a three-volume study of the Union of Utrecht in a country then undergoing deep political problems. Paulus had a deep interest in tracing connections between the Utrecht Union and American events. Volume one had been published in 1775 and volume two in 1776. As he was writing the third volume, published in 1777, he received a draft copy of the American Articles of Confederation.

Paulus wrote: "The Union of Utrecht, I must admit, is for the time in which it was constructed, one of the best sets of fundamental laws which human wisdom could frame. . . . I cannot imagine that the wisdom of our forefathers, in the framing of the Utrecht Union, could ever be seen more clearly or impartially than that a powerful posterity of freeborn [American] children are persuaded by it, as they realize that the Mother, who earlier had sought freedom herself . . . designed that each member of society and all civil companies have a natural and inseparable right. Now, I say, the English colonies in North America, after the passage of about two centuries, have vowed to venture all and undergo everything to make themselves totally independent from Great

Britain. . . . As concerns the object of the matter, the reaching of that intention, it has been necessary to come to the same decision, concerning the same fundamental law which our forebears two hundred years ago approved as the most useful. So that some will not consider these remarks hyperbole, I include their *Articles of Confederation and Perpetual Union* in their entirety [in Dutch translation].''

Paulus drew some comparisons between the historical situations in the sixteenth and eighteenth centuries. He admitted that "the American Union, *in some respects*, appears to be argued somewhat neater." He noted certain differences, due to structural forms of government arising from the hereditary "stadtholder," the Dutch chief of state. Indeed, that and other of Paulus' observations were later echoed and elaborated in the American debates in 1787.

It is of interest that one of the conspicuous divergences between Paulus' text and the final American text is in Article XIII, the article which most frequently evoked comparison with the Dutch example when opened to debate by the Continental Congress. The printed text simply reads: "In determining questions, each State shall have one vote." Paulus' text modifies it to read: "Each state shall have one vote in determining all differences in the general congress." The debates in Congress clearly reveal the intention of the Article to allow just one vote on all matters, not only those over which differences arose. The Reverend Dr. John Witherspoon of New Jersey, arguing for one vote for each state regardless of size, several times cited the Dutch model as a positive example validating the procedure. Pennsylvania's Dr. Benjamin Rush, on the other hand, found the Dutch procedure lacking, thus strengthening his case for proportional representation in the vote. "The decay of the liberties of the Dutch republic proceeded from three causes," he wrote, "1. the perfect unanimity requisite on all occasions. 2. their obligation to consult their constituents. 3. their voting by provinces." That Witherspoon's evaluations were overly optimistic in appraising Dutch success and that Rush's historical observations were inaccurate, to say the least, is not really the matter at hand. The fact of importance is the repeated references to the Dutch example.

As one examines the influence of the United Provinces, first in the Albany Congress and later in the Continental Congresses, one is led to a clear affirmation of its symbolic impact on the debates in 1754 and again in 1776. Dutch union and then Dutch liberty became measuring-rods for the colonists. It is the positive effect of the imagined Dutch political paradigm that emerges initially and most importantly. The negative aspects of the then-current Dutch political scene first began to enter the discussion in the congressional debates of 1776. Eleven years later, those negative evaluations gained prominence in the constitutional debates of 1787, most accessibly for modern readers in *The Federalist No. 20*, in which "Publius" (in this case, James Madison) drew extensively on discussions of the Union of Utrecht by Sir William Temple and French *philosophes*. By that time, the symbolic value of the aged and faltering Union of Utrecht was weakened by a more realistic assessment of Dutch political difficulties; indeed, such was the analysis presented by *The Federalist No. 20* in drawing parallels between the defects of the Union of Utrecht and those of the Articles of Confederation.

The Dutch example, as Franklin had called it, had served its practical and polemical purposes. By 1787, American independence had been won and her government established. The Dutch financial support which had undergirded the American Revolution was next called upon to support the young republic. Millions of very tangible Dutch guilders, which made the United States fiscally viable, took the place of the idealized symbol of the United Provinces. Both had been in turn indispensable, first to the thirteen colonies and then to the thirteen states as they struggled to become a new nation.

The Menacing Shadow of Louis XIV and the Rage of Jacob Leisler: The Constitutional Ordeal of Seventeenth-Century New York

JOHN M. MURRIN

Princeton University

Revised version of a lecture co-sponsored by the New York State Commission on the Bicentennial of the United States Constitution and The New Netherland Project, Twelfth Rensselaerswyck Seminar, Albany, New York, September 23, 1989.

The constitutional struggles of seventeenth-century New York may seem remote today. Even from an eighteenth-century perspective they were quite unusual. For Virginia, Massachusetts, and Pennsylvania, we can tell a relatively clean story about the early acceptance of representative institutions and their evolution over time into the era of the American Revolution, the adoption of new state constitutions between 1776 and 1780, and the drafting of the United States Constitution in 1787.

New Yorkers lived through a different history. They had to fight about what others usually took for granted. The ethnic and religious diversity of the population made these struggles quite complex, sometimes as baffling to contemporaries as to later historians who have tried to sort them out. New Yorkers went through a constitutional ordeal in a pluralistic environment. Their experience in the seventeenth century reminds us of other options and other possibilities open to the men and women who settled the mainland colonies. Events did not lead smoothly from the first settlements to 1776 and 1787. This essay explores major aspects of that discontinuity.

I

Jacob Leisler's Rebellion ought to be a simple matter, but it never has been. In June 1689 he assumed the leadership of those New Yorkers who insisted that the colony's government had to repudiate the Roman Catholic Stuart king of England, James II (1685–88), and proclaim its loyalty to James's son-in-law and daughter, the Protestant William, Prince of Orange, and his wife Mary. News of their coronation as King William III (1689–1702) and Queen Mary II (1689–94) would soon reach the province. While in power, Leisler never lost sight of his highest priority—to hold the colony for William and the Protestant cause. Because of William's triumph in England, the story ought to have a happy ending. Surely the new monarch would be able to distinguish his friends from his enemies in New York and would name a governor who would recognize and accept what the Leislerians had done. Instead, William appointed a government dominated by men who had supported James well into the spring of 1689 and had then been displaced by Leisler. In 1691, these angry and vengeful people returned to New York, resumed office, and hanged Leisler for treason.[1]

If we place these events in an intercolonial context, the puzzle only deepens. In April 1689, Boston set the pace for all other colonies when the town overthrew the autocratic government of Sir Edmund Andros and the Dominion of New England. After a few weeks of hesitation, Massachusetts resumed the forms of its charter government, which James II had superseded with the Dominion in 1686. The other New England colonies soon followed this example. In England William and Mary acquiesced in the resumption of charter government by Connecticut and Rhode Island. They also agreed to accept the legitimacy of the previous history of Massachusetts Bay by negotiating a new charter for that province, which went into effect in 1692 and which recognized the validity of such distinctive institutions as the New England town and the land system. Massachusetts retained an elective assembly and won the right to elect its upper house indirectly. The Crown appointed the governor, all judges, and militia officers. The colony also had to grant religious toleration to all Protestants and could no longer restrict the suffrage to full members of the Congregational Church. Although this new regime would be quite different from the Puritan commonwealth of the seventeenth century, it retained many of its traditional privileges. Maryland, the last colony to overturn its government in 1689, also won approval in England for this political upheaval. It became a royal colony in 1692. Its Catholic dynasty, the Calvert family of lords proprietors, lost power until 1716 when the conversion of an heir to Protestantism prompted the Crown to restore the proprietary regime.

In short, New York really stood out. Its rebellion had close parallels elsewhere. Its result was unique. Only in New York did the English state deliberately crush the very people who had struggled to make the Glorious Revolution a success in the colony. New York got its religious and constitutional moorings thoroughly tangled between 1689 and 1691, with very serious consequences for the colony's later history.[2]

II

Because Leisler's Rebellion was a major governmental crisis for New York, we must try to sort out the constitutional ideas or assumptions of the major participants. New York was a highly pluralistic society in 1689. Founded as the Dutch colony of New Netherland, it had been conquered by England in 1664. The constitutional traditions of both countries affected the internal development of the province. So also, to a remarkable degree, did events in France.

For much of the seventeenth century, France was the most tolerant country in Western Europe. Only in France did the law protect the public worship of both Catholics and Protestants (Huguenots). By contrast, England persecuted both Protestant dissenters and Catholics for most of the same period, while the Dutch republic usually left Protestant dissenters alone and "connived" at the private—but not public—worship of peaceable Catholics. Most apologists for the French state believed that only royal absolutism made these arrangements possible, and on varying grounds the French monarchy found many admirers and defenders, both Catholic and Protestant. Charles and James, the two sons of King Charles I of England, came to manhood while in exile in France following their father's execution. They both brought back a softened attitude toward the Catholic Church and a deep respect for absolutism and broad religious toleration. Although no informed Protestant could forget the horrors of St. Bartholomew's Day in August 1572, when furious Catholic mobs had tried to exterminate Protestants in Paris and other French cities, Huguenots and Dutch Protestants generally regarded the French state as a political ally in the seventeenth century, at least until the 1670s. Its intervention against Spain in the Thirty Years' War had been decisive, and in the mid-1660s France had aligned with the Dutch republic against England. Even though the political privileges of Huguenots were restricted in the 1620s, they continued to worship freely and openly well into the 1670s, despite some less visible disabilities and pressures to conform.

These French achievements had a potent impact on Protestants in France and elsewhere. They strongly colored even the political thought of French Huguenots and Dutch Protestants, most of whom were quite eager to placate moderate Catholics in France and reluctant—unlike some radical Protestants in England and Scotland—to justify political resistance by the whole body of the people, as against duly constituted magistrates. While it lasted, French toleration moderated the demands of Huguenot and Dutch political thinkers and prompted the English court after 1660 to implement something similar to the French model, first in New York, later in England. New York may well have been a testing ground for policies too dangerous to attempt at home. And, when French support for the Dutch republic turned suddenly to war and aggression in 1672, and when French toleration died swiftly and brutally in the 1680s, the consequences in The Netherlands, England, and New York would be dramatic and extremely important. Leisler's Rebellion was only one aspect of a broader transatlantic response to the changing policies of Louis XIV (1642–1715).[3]

Both Leislerians and Anti–Leislerians were Anglo–Dutch coalitions. Both had several contemporary models to draw upon, Dutch and English. Within the seven United Provinces of The Netherlands, the central political tension pitted the regent class against the House of Orange. The regents were an oligarchy of merchant families who dominated the public life of Amsterdam and other major cities and usually controlled the governments of the more commercial provinces and the States General of the republic. By the middle of the seventeenth century, they had developed a coherent ideology of "true liberty." It extolled the benefits of decentralized government and broad religious toleration, even of Roman Catholics. It encouraged the maximum exploitation of commercial markets abroad, mostly by eliminating any regulations that hindered the expansion of trade, and it sought to maintain peaceful relations within Europe. Opposed to the regent class, especially in time of war, stood the House of Orange, whose princes had served for generations as the chief military officer of the republic, the *stadholder* of Holland, the wealthiest province in The Netherlands. Or, to give the office its closest equivalent title in the English world, the prince of Orange was the captain-general of Holland and any other province that similarly honored him.

Since the 1560s the princes of Orange had been a rallying point for international Calvinism under siege from hostile Catholic forces, marshalled first by Spain, later (after 1670) by France. Orthodox Calvinists supported the princes of Orange, demanded the suppression of Catholics at home (and sometimes Protestant dissenters as well), and supported an active war effort against the encircling Catholic powers. As late as the 1660s, Dutch Calvinists knew how to justify their ancestors' revolt against Spain, but they still routinely idealized monarchical over republican forms of government, and they had generated no coherent rationale for defending the peculiar mixture of institutions and practices that the United Provinces had become. Regents suspected that, if the Orangists ever got their way completely, they would turn the stadholderate into an authoritarian Protestant monarchy similar to those that had already emerged in the Lutheran states of Germany. For that reason the States General, under intense pressure from Oliver Cromwell in England, excluded William III (then a small boy) from the office of *stadholder* in 1654, and the province of Holland abolished the office itself in 1667.

Twice in the seventeenth century, militant Orangists killed the leader of the regent class as a way of reasserting their power. In 1618–19, just as the Thirty Years' War was getting under way and the famous Synod of Dort was defining orthodoxy for Calvinists everywhere, Prince Maurice of Nassau arrested the Grand Pensionary of Holland, Johan van Oldenbarneveldt, accused him of collusion with Spain, tried him for treason, and executed him. In 1672 an angry Orange mob attacked Jan de Witt and his brother Cornelis in The Hague, killed both, desecrated the bodies, and even cannibalized parts of them. On that occasion, the Orangists suspected the De Witts of sympathy for France at a time when the armies of Louis XIV threatened to overrun the republic, and they did succeed in restoring the office of *stadholder* to youthful William III, who had just come of age. Partly because popular elections had no role in the politics of the Dutch republic, mobs provided a quasi-legitimate way of expressing public discontent, usually on behalf of the House of Orange. Dutch New Yorkers, and probably many of the English as well, understood the significance of these chronic struggles between Orangists and regents. By the mid-1670s, William III had indeed become the Protestant world's most powerful symbol of resistance to Catholicism.[4]

England also provided conflicting constitutional models growing out of the era of civil wars and the interregnum between 1640 and 1660. The resistance of the Long Parliament to Charles I became an open war by 1642 and led to the king's execution in 1649. English Puritans, or strict Calvinists (Presbyterians and Congregationalists), and Protestant radicals (Baptists, Quakers, Seekers, Ranters, Muggletonians, Fifth Monarchy Men, and others) strongly supported Parliament while virtually all defenders of episcopacy backed the Crown and the traditional Church of England. Those who resisted the Crown suspected the royal family of absolutist ambitions, something that even many royalists feared. The Restoration of Charles II in 1660 complicated these alignments in several ways. By then, Charles and his brother James, duke of York (King James II from 1685 to 1688) preferred religious toleration for both Catholics and Protestant dissenters. Most dissenters favored toleration only of all Protestants. The strongly Anglican Parliament tried to suppress both Catholics and dissenters.[5]

These tensions affected New York more acutely than any other colony because in 1664 Charles II made his brother James lord proprietor of the whole area between the Delaware and Connecticut rivers and dispatched a naval force to the Hudson, which compelled the government of New Netherland to surrender to the invading English. James did in New York what the royal family did not dare attempt in England. Influenced by the example of the French state, he created an absolutist government designed to rule through a fixed code of laws without an elective assembly. And, drawing somewhat more loosely upon French experience, he promised toleration to all Christians.[6]

New York's constitutional struggles became violent and extremely complex after 1664 because of the differing expectations and associations that Dutch and English settlers brought to the colony. Within The Netherlands the forces of dynasticism were Orangist and intolerant. In England the Stuart dynasty favored a broader toleration than did virtually anyone else except the Quakers, but even intolerant Anglicans demanded a continuing role for Parliament in the government of the realm. Dutch Calvinists, while committed to the triumph of militant Protestantism, had no experience with representative government in the way that most English settlers understood that term. But English Puritans had learned to place careful limits on the powers of the monarchy. In America they created colonial governments that lodged ultimate power in the legislature, not the governor.

Within New York, even a simple word like "liberty" could thus mean very different things to different groups. To most Englishmen it included some role for an elective assembly. To most Dutchmen it did not. It suggested generous toleration to the duke's men, most merchants, the Catholic minority, and even many of the Yankees who had left orthodox New England to settle on western Long Island (renamed Queens in 1683). To orthodox Calvinists, Dutch and English, it still implied freedom for the true church to impose its will on the community.

For the first decade after the English conquest, the biggest problem faced by the new government was the loyalty of its population. Governor Richard Nicolls arranged an understanding with Governor John Winthrop, Jr., of Connecticut in which New York tacitly abandoned its claim to the Connecticut River as its eastern boundary while asserting control over all of Long Island, the eastern half of which had been under Connecticut's jurisdiction. These Yankees were used to government by an elective assembly and could not be talked out of their convictions. Nicolls also made ambitious plans to settle English colonists on the mainland south and west of Manhattan, only to learn that James had just given the region between the coast and the Delaware River to two courtiers, John Lord Berkeley and Sir George Carteret, who promptly organized their grant as the colony of New Jersey. This arrangement struck all New York governors as particularly troublesome. As a part of New York, the Jersey hinterland would strengthen the whole colony by attracting English newcomers and expanding trade. As a separate province, it would draw English settlers out of New York and magnify greatly the security problems of the duke's colony.[7]

Their anxieties were not misplaced. When England joined France in attacking The Netherlands in 1672, the Dutch responded by sending a major naval expedition into American waters in 1673. After raiding the tobacco fleet in Chesapeake Bay, it turned north and demanded the surrender of poorly defended Fort James. To the jubilation of the Dutch population, the English garrison gave up as easily as the Dutch had in 1664. The invaders restored New Netherland and renamed the city New Orange and its fortifications Fort Willem Hendrik, both after Prince William. They expelled English settlers unwilling to be loyal to the restored Dutch regime and established a stern, Calvinist government. Then, to the consternation of the population, the Dutch States General returned the province to England at the Treaty of Westminster in 1674. For the second time, New Netherland and its capital city became New York, and Fort William was once again Fort James.[8]

James ruled a Dutch population that did not wish to be English and an English population that desired to be freer than he cared to permit. It was not an auspicious formula for success. In no other part of the English Empire would the Glorious Revolution carry a higher and more ambiguous symbolic impact. In 1688–89, James and William, the two men for whom the fort had been twice named and renamed, were contesting for nothing less than the throne of England.

III

Before 1689, most of the important constitutional and legal decisions in New York had been made by men who would become Anti-Leislerians. What precedents had they set? What form of government did they prefer? What anxieties did they arouse?

They were, of course, a diverse coalition. The most important elements of it were the duke's men (people who owed their careers to James), a group of wealthy and interrelated Dutch mercantile families, and a growing number of English merchant newcomers who began to achieve prominence in New York City after 1674. Although they worked together as Anti-Leislerians after 1689, these factions reflected a broad spectrum of ideas about government and constitutionalism, and they clashed frequently with one another before the Glorious Revolution.

The duke's men consisted mostly of soldiers, although they also included some civil officials such as Councillors Mathias and William Nicolls and Collector Matthew Plowman. A fair number of them were Roman Catholics, including Plowman, Lieutenant Governor Anthony Brockholls, and Governor Thomas Dongan (1683–88). They believed they had a mandate to maintain order, secure the duke's (later the king's) revenues, and—somewhat more ambiguously—enforce the English Navigation Acts. So long as James demanded autocratic rule, they were prepared to enforce his will. Yet nearly all of them found this role unappealing and disquieting—perhaps even Sir Edmund Andros, governor of the colony from 1674 to 1680 and of the Dominion of New England from 1686 to 1689. In 1675 he may have tried—without success—to persuade the duke to grant an elective assembly to the colony. Brockholls presided over New York's government from 1681 to 1683 when the court of assizes, which had been designed as the principal bulwark of absolutist rule, demanded and finally got an elective assembly. Dongan implemented this concession, and William Nicolls sat in the first assembly. Even after James revoked this concession by 1686, Dongan kept the assembly alive by successive prorogations until 1687, apparently with the hope that he might yet receive permission to summon a new session. From this perspective the absolutism of James was a policy without a constituency. Even the men who implemented it did not believe in it, and on several occasions they sanctioned efforts to transform it in more conventional directions. Yet James's autocratic principles continued to affect New Yorkers in profound ways.[9]

The crisis of 1689 would force these men to decide to what or whom they were loyal. Their attachment to James was real enough, for they owed him their careers. But as the crisis deepened, they began to realize that they might have to choose between James and the English state. Their natural instinct was to avoid any decision of this kind as long as possible. Both Andros in Boston and Captain Francis Nicholson, his lieutenant governor in New York, first tried to suppress the news that William had landed in England. Boston overthrew Andros before he could reverse himself. Nicholson reacted somewhat differently.

On March 1, Nicholson learned from Philadelphia that William had landed in England, that James had tried to flee to France, and that London had welcomed the prince of Orange. He passed on the news to Andros and tried to suppress it in New York. Neither man yet knew what constitutional decisions were being made in England or that James had actually reached France in a second escape attempt. Who was king? Had perhaps a regency been established to rule in James's name while preserving the succession unaltered? To make a wrong choice on this extremely sensitive issue could ruin a man's career. It seemed far wiser to do nothing irrevocable until the situation became clearer.[10]

After the overthrow of Andros in Boston, Nicholson made his own decision. A loyal servant of James would have prepared for another Anglo–Dutch war (the fourth since 1652). The earliest news of William's invasion stimulated some talk of this kind. Stephanus Van Cortlandt, a member of the council and mayor of New York City, expected war with The Netherlands as of January 1689.[11] As late as April, Robert Livingston, somewhat isolated in the upper Hudson valley, told Albany Sheriff Richard Pretty that "there was a p'sell of Rebels gon out of Holland into England, & the prince of orringe was the hed of them & he might see how [he] got out a gaine, & should come to same end as Mulmoth [i.e., James, duke of Monmouth] did."[12] By late April, a servant of the English state would have expected war with France, not The Netherlands. Spurred to action by a rising of the New England settlers in Suffolk County on eastern Long Island, Nicholson tried to prepare New York for a conflict with France, informed the English secretary of state (rather than someone still in direct contact with James II) what he was doing and why, and created an expanded council of civil and military officers to give him advice and support and to preserve the peace during the crisis.[13]

But, having secured this support at the end of April, Nicholson and three councillors continued to make nearly all important decisions themselves during the critical month of May while the ferment began to spread from Long Island into the city. When Collector Plowman became an issue, they pledged that all revenues paid to him would be used to strengthen the city's defense. Their credibility disintegrated anyway, partly because they never formally proclaimed William and Mary, partly because they could not regard the New England uprising as anything less than rebellion and made open efforts to keep in touch with Andros. To suspicious opponents, these attitudes had to seem pro-French. To Nicholson and his followers, hesitation was mere prudence. They would act to proclaim someone when the English government so ordered and not before. They were not about to repudiate Andros, who in their eyes was still governor of the Dominion of New England, of which New York was but one portion.

With three centuries of hindsight on their predicament, we can understand both their caution and their rage when finally challenged. Nicholson invited the city militia to share with his soldiers the responsibility for guarding Fort James at the southern tip of Manhattan. But when the militia continued to make other demands that seemed to question the loyalty of the garrison, Nicholson made a fatal error. The twenty-eight-year-old commander lost his temper in front of a fifty-two-year-old Dutch militia lieutenant, Hendrik Cuyler, and threatened to burn down the city if the militia did not stop pestering him. Because Nicholson had been part of the English garrison of Tangiers that had burned the city before withdrawing a few years before, this outburst had to seem terrifying. Within days, Nicholson's power collapsed, and the militia took complete charge of the fort. Most of the city refused to believe that anyone appointed by James had really abandoned his cause.[14]

Prominent Dutch mercantile families also formed part of the Anti-Leislerian coalition. They resembled the regent class of The Netherlands in their preference for the broadest possible commercial opportunities and full religious toleration. They did not hesitate to work closely with the Roman Catholics in the duke's service. Probably they were more interested in the liberties of the cities of New York and Albany than in any larger questions about the desirability of representative institutions for the province as a whole. Although they never shed many of their underlying Dutch values, these families—the Philipse, Van Cortlandt, Bayard, Schuyler, and Van Rensselaer clans stood out—were anglicizers, people of Dutch background who were quite prepared to accept the social and political demands of English rule. Because of their behavior during the Dutch reconquest of 1673, they knew that they had to demonstrate their complete loyalty to the English state. They tried to master the conquerors' language and teach it to their children. Their religious commitments were rather flexible. When Anglicans finally organized Trinity Church in the 1690s, Nicholas Bayard, Tunis DeKey, Brandt Schuyler, and Stephanus Van Cortlandt were among those who joined. Such men were willing to serve autocratic regimes under both the Dutch and the English. They also held office from 1683 to 1685 and after 1691 when the colony had a representative assembly. In short, they seemed to take it for granted that they had a right to rule and reacted ferociously when that claim was challenged, especially by lesser Dutchmen.[15]

The least-studied portion of the Anti–Leislerian coalition was a bloc of English newcomers who entered the province in the 1670s and 1680s. Most of them were merchants, although some became lawyers or bookkeepers, and eventually many of them bought land outside the city. Other than Lewis Morris and George Heathcote, few of them have aroused the curiosity of anyone besides genealogists. Yet such men as William Pinhorne, Edward Antill, and John Robinson played important roles in the politics of the era. They believed that New York would never thrive until it guaranteed traditional English liberties to all settlers. Above all, they demanded an assembly and insisted on the principle of no taxation without representation. Without concessions of this kind, they feared, New York might suffer a fatal drain of scarce Englishmen to the freer societies then taking shape in East and West New Jersey and Pennsylvania. In 1676 twenty-five of them threatened to leave the province when New York City imposed a municipal tax upon them.[16] When Andros returned to England in January 1681 after neglecting to renew a revenue act that had expired in November, the merchants led a well-organized tax strike and won the support of the duke's own court of assizes, which sent James a formal petition for an assembly. As of 1681 these reformers still regarded the anglicizing Dutch elite as their principal enemies, families who monopolized too many offices and somehow managed to keep the colony's trade oriented toward Amsterdam instead of England. But by 1683 the duke's men, the anglicizing Dutch elite, and the English merchants were all willing to support the reform program adopted by the province's first elective legislature when it met in October of that year.[17]

IV

The reformers of 1683 had important political allies who would favor the overthrow of Nicholson in 1689, indeed serve as the principal catalyst to that upheaval—the New England population of Long Island and what is now Westchester and The Bronx. These people had been agitating for an assembly since the English conquest of 1664, and their town meetings joined lustily in this call during the turbulent year of 1681.[18]

By then they had more leverage than ever. The duke, who no longer made any effort to deny his conversion to Rome, was in deep political trouble in England where the newly organized Whig party was trying to bar him from succession to the throne. Within the colony prospects began to seem truly alarming between 1680 and 1683. Before leaving the colony, Andros tried to reassert New York's power over East New Jersey by arresting Governor Philip Carteret and trying him in New York for usurping the duke's authority. To the mortification of Andros, the largely English jury of the court of assizes acquitted Carteret in 1680 at about the same time that a Whig attorney general in England upheld important claims of West New Jersey settlers against the duke and his New York governor.[19]

The Quakers knew how to use this opportunity, and their actions transformed the political climate of the Middle Atlantic colonies. In 1674 John Lord Berkeley, one of the New Jersey proprietors, sold his claim to a group of Quakers, who then arranged with Sir George Carteret, the other original proprietor, to divide the province into two distinct colonies, Carteret's East New Jersey and the Quakers' West New Jersey. The families settling West New Jersey next began to implement, by stages, their Concessions and Agreements of 1677, the most radical constitutional system put into practice in any English colony before the American Revolution. This document lodged most political power in a legislature of one hundred delegates, who in turn would choose a weak plural executive of ten men. In the court system, juries were to decide both fact and law while judges merely presided and responded to queries, when anybody bothered to put one to them. The Concessions imposed no military obligations on the settlers, guaranteed full toleration, and offered land on generous terms.[20]

In 1681, William Penn, one of the West Jersey proprietors, intensified the pressure on New York when he obtained his proprietary charter for a colony on the west bank of the Delaware and put an enormous amount of energy into drafting the First Frame of Government for the province. It was less bracing than the West Jersey Concessions, but it still had plenty of potential for enticing Englishmen away from New York. Penn agreed to modifications in early 1683 that became known as the Second Frame of Government, or Charter of Liberties. Meanwhile, Quakers had also gained control of the proprietary claim to East New Jersey, for which they drafted a text, called the Fundamental Constitutions, in 1683. Since the conquest, New York's governors had always worried about the superior liberties of New Englanders as a source of potential discontent within New York. Now the province was surrounded on three sides by much freer societies.[21]

This intercolonial context explains the utter collapse of the duke's absolutist regime almost as soon as Andros left the colony in early 1681. Nobody in authority did anything to punish merchants who refused to pay customs duties. Instead the court of assizes tried and convicted the duke's collector for insisting upon their payment, and then it joined in the popular demand for an assembly. New York thus became swept into the extraordinary ferment of constitutional experimentation that threatened to intoxicate the entire Middle Atlantic region. The immediate result was the summoning of a legislature to draft and implement the province's own Charter of Liberties in 1683.[22]

Governor Dongan issued election writs shortly after his arrival in August 1683. They called for the choice of eighteen representatives, nine to be elected directly, nine indirectly. Oddly, in the predominantly Dutch portions of the province where the settlers had little familiarity with English general elections by the assembled freeholders and freemen, eight representatives were chosen directly by the free holders, four indirectly by committeemen selected in their individual towns, who then met to name representatives. In the heavily English constituencies, five were selected indirectly, only one directly. Quite possibly Dongan was trying to expand English influence within such heavily Dutch communities as New York City and Esopus, where in fact at least three of those elected were English, and to reduce the impact of ordinary New Englanders from Long Island and Westchester. When the assemblymen finally convened in late October, their first item of legislation was New York's Charter of Liberties. The second, James's price for the Charter of Liberties, was a permanent revenue act designed to meet all ordinary costs of government.[23]

This achievement ended absolutism in New York, at least for a heady two-year period, but the Charter of Liberties was a much more cautious document than its counterparts in the Jerseys and Pennsylvania. Unlike the annual elections held in New England (semi-annual in Connecticut), West Jersey, and Pennsylvania, or the staggered triennial elections mandated for East Jersey, the New York Charter of Liberties required only that a *session* of the assembly meet every three years. Although it gave the choice of future assemblymen to the freeholders and freemen of the colony, it said nothing about the frequency of elections. Yet it did include strong guarantees for such civil liberties as trial by jury, equality before the law, and a ban against quartering soldiers in private homes during peacetime. Some provisions, including a clause protecting the dower rights of women, were copied directly from an East Jersey statute of the same year.

The charter became most innovative in defining the religious rights of settlers. All Christians received the freedom to worship with their coreligionists. Subject to approval by two-thirds of the voters, any town on Long Island could levy a tax for the support of the ministry. Religious minorities on Long Island, and all Christian denominations elsewhere in the province, could establish legally enforceable contractual relations between a congregation and its minister. In effect, the government was willing to underwrite the support of any minister whose congregation so desired, a system likely to antagonize only Quakers and Jews, and then only if they lived on Long Island. In full operation it would have anticipated freedom of religion as practiced in modern Canada, rather than the separation of church and state that finally took hold in the United States.[24]

The assembly met again in 1684 and, after new elections occasioned by the death of Charles II, also in 1685. The 1685 choices marked the only true general election in the colony's entire history before the Glorious Revolution—the only occasion, that is, on which freeholders and freemen in all constituencies had an opportunity to vote directly for their representatives. In their three meetings, Dongan's assemblies passed an ambitious legislative program that included a generous present to Dongan and the full imposition of English law even upon the most heavily Dutch portions of the colony. Dongan also granted corporate charters to the cities of New York and Albany in 1686, empowering them to elect their aldermen and common councilmen.[25]

Only after the assembly session of 1685 did the colony learn that James, now king, had approved the permanent revenue act but disallowed the Charter of Liberties. New York's reformers had asked to be as free as their neighbors in other English colonies. As the grand jury at the court of assizes put it in June 1681, New Yorkers wished to be placed "upon Equall Ground with our Fellow Brethren and Subjects of the Realme of England In our Neighbouring Plantacons."[26] James had another idea. He made the province's neighbors as unfree as New Yorkers had been before 1683. The Dominion of New England, which by 1688 included New York and both Jerseys, drew directly upon the absolutist principles in use in New York before the tax strike of 1681 and brought in Andros, a former New York governor, to implement them.

Nevertheless, one huge fact does stand out about the men who agitated for, passed, and implemented the Charter of Liberties. New Englanders aside, virtually none of them would support Jacob Leisler in 1689.

V

The Leislerians were in no sense an organized group in New York before 1689. If we ask what stand future Leislerians had taken during the province's long struggle between absolutism and participatory government, the most interesting finding is that they had not taken part in the contest. They erupted on the scene in May 1689 as angry and frightened supporters of William and the Protestant cause. In trying to prevent subversion by dangerous papist forces, they played the classic Dutch role of an Orange party in New York politics. They soon had their local *stadholder*, too—Captain Jacob Leisler, a wealthy merchant, ship captain, and former army officer from a distinguished Continental European family of renowned ministers, bankers, and lawyers.[27]

Leisler was the highest ranking militia officer willing to assume command of Fort James, which was once again renamed Fort William. Within New York City and western Long Island, those who rallied to Leisler were disproportionately Dutch, the sort of people that the reformers of 1683 had hoped to transform into Englishmen or swamp with English newcomers attracted by the guarantees of the Charter of Liberties. As of June 1689, some of them—but not Leisler—hoped that the Glorious Revolution would lead to a full restoration of Dutch rule in New York.[28] Like his principal opponents, he too chose to be loyal to the English state—they despite the triumph of William of Orange, he because of it.

The English population of New York City overwhelmingly sided against Leisler. Virtually all of the exceptions were men who had chosen to support the restored Dutch regime in 1673–74.[29] The fondness of English merchants for English liberty had not abated. As early as May 1689, several weeks before the militia took over the fort, some of them refused to pay "any Customs and other duties, as illegally established [*sic*]," Nicholson reported to England.[30] At the end of the month, Leisler also refused to pay customs, but his motive was different. He was willing "to pay the Customs to such as should be legally qualified to receive them, which the Papist Plowman was not."[31] He objected to the religion of the collector, not to taxation without consent.

Yet Leisler clearly hoped to unite sincere English Protestants behind his leadership. As he explained in July, his own militia company of one hundred men had been so worked upon by their opponents that by May 31 when they seized the fort their strength had fallen to about forty—a highly cosmopolitan forty. Twenty-five had been born in New York, presumably in the 1660s or earlier and were no doubt mostly Dutch. Eight were born in England, two were French Huguenots, two were Swiss, four were Hollanders, "and I a germane." He then related a most revealing incident:[32]

> here is one merchant borne in old England Joint with us & chosen by one company to represent them, they have stopt his horse & threatened his persone that our burgers will not trust him to their mercy but watches his house with one centry, which is s[ai]d high treason by them [Leisler's opponents], they have scattered them to all parts to incense the people with abominable lees [i.e., lies] making them beleeve that the people are abused by the dutch[,] that i have the fort for the french[,] have listed [i.e., mustered] 25 french[,] that I & my officers are continually drunk & in drunken fitts commits a great dale of insolvency.

This incident requires amplification. Despite Leisler's attempt to unite all Protestants regardless of ethnic background, and despite the explicit effort of one company to use an English merchant as its spokesman, the militia of the city at large would not let the man function in that capacity. The English merchants, who all along had been the city's most consistent advocates of English constitutional liberties, were alienated at the very start of the upheaval, not through any design of Leisler's but through pressures and resentments welling up from below among the Dutch militiamen. Whatever Leisler wished the struggle to be, the English merchants saw it as an ethnic explosion in which they were likely to become the most conspicuous victims. When Leisler challenged a group of them in late June 1689, "threatning before a weeke was to an end to secure them all," his outburst "occasioned severall English merchants & Gentlemen for safety of their lives to depart this Citty."[33] The refusal of some of them to pay customs in the spring of

1689 suggests that they could have been mobilized in a broad coalition designed to resist the Dominion of New England. Ethnic antagonisms made such unity impossible. This perception drove them into alliance with their enemies of the 1670s, James's officeholding clique and the anglicizing Dutch elite.

In expelling the English merchants from their coalition, the Leislerians were also cutting themselves off from the best possible sources available to them for one critical task. Somebody had to present an effective defense of the New York revolution in England. Who else could do it? Leisler never sponsored any but the briefest justifications in the first year of the upheaval. Even though his competence with the English language has been underrated by most historians, he was not fluent enough to become a serious polemicist. Of the other militia captains, Charles Lodwyck was a highly anglicized Dutch merchant who had recently moved to New York from London. He commanded the English language well enough to prepare a paper for the Royal Society in London a few years later, and like Leisler he tried to stamp out expressions of ethnic contempt in his militia company. He also had a real interest in preserving traditional English liberties. In an effort to discredit the arbitrary rule of Nicholson's regime, he provided the revolutionary government in July 1689 with a sworn deposition. He had heard Nicholson claim, he testified, that New Yorkers "could but account ourselves as a conquered people, and therefore we could not so much claim rights and privileges as Englishmen in England but that the prince might lawfully govern us by his own will and appoint what laws he pleases among us." By emphasizing this critical item in the argument for absolutism, Lodwyck indicated that he probably understood English law somewhat better than Leisler. Yet by early 1690 at the latest, he transferred his loyalties to the Anti-Leislerians.[34]

Leisler's most prominent English officeholder was Samuel Edsall, four of whose sons-in-law were important Leislerians. Although Edsall began his career as a hatmaker, he was wealthy by 1689 and owned property in Hackensack, Queens, and New York City. He had also shown strong signs of assimilating into the Dutch community. He acquired burgher rights in New Amsterdam years before the English conquest, and when the English fleet arrived in 1664, it treated him as a Dutchman. He supported the restored Dutch regime in 1673–74. At least two of his four wives were Dutch, and most of his children were raised in the Dutch Reformed Church. No doubt he was thoroughly bilingual by 1689. Yet his political actions before that year made him an extremely awkward spokesman for English constitutional principles. In the public life of East New Jersey, he had consistently supported authoritarian policies and the proprietary governor against the assembly, especially in the dramatic confrontations of 1672 and 1681. The very assembly of 1683 that approved the East Jersey Fundamental Constitutions also demanded Edsall's arrest and trial for "evil and illegal practices" that tended to disturb the public peace. Although the charges were eventually dropped, the assembly clearly regarded him as a menace to the constitutional liberties of the province and hoped to bar him and his associates from office for life. Edsall's prominence on Leisler's council could in no way reassure settlers interested in securing their English liberties.[35]

One other Englishman, Jacob Milborne, might have acted as a Leislerian spokesman in England. After serving as an apprentice in Hartford and Barbados (where he met Lewis and Richard Morris before they moved to New York), he worked from 1668 to 1672 as a bookkeeper to Thomas Delavall, a prominent New Yorker who sat on the provincial council for several years. Milborne became a merchant, and on at least one occasion he represented a client as an attorney before the court of assizes. In 1676, he joined Leisler's fight to guarantee the orthodoxy of the Dutch Reformed Church of Albany against the interference of Andros. Two years later, Andros arrested him for refusing to report to the governor after returning to the colony from a business trip. Milborne pursued Andros to London, sued him for false arrest in 1681, and collected £45. That activity kept him out of the colony during the tax strike that led to the summoning of the 1683 assembly, but Milborne returned to New York about that time and married Samuel Edsall's daughter Johanna before sailing for Rotterdam in 1686. His family had taken radical political stands in England during the civil wars, and his brother William was accused of treason in Bermuda in 1678.

Jacob Milborne probably could have defended the New York revolution in London, and his family contacts may even have been strong enough to get him a hearing. But he was still in Rotterdam on business when the uprising occurred and did not reach New York until August 25, 1689, a few days after Joost Stol sailed for England as the agent of the committee of safety. Leisler did select Milborne as his agent of choice in 1690, once he realized that Stol's mission had failed, but events in Albany seemed so pressing that Leisler decided to keep him in the province, a change that permitted the recently widowed Milborne to marry Leisler's daughter Mary. Instead of explaining New York's revolution to London, he spent much of 1689 and 1690 debating it with the burghers of Albany.[36]

Leisler himself wrote to the king several times in 1689 to explain events in New York. The letters reflect a confident tone that the king would approve what the Leislerians did in the province on his behalf, but in fact William never replied. As the news filtering back from England became more ominous in 1690, Leisler wrote to Bishop Gilbert Burnet and the earl of Shrewsbury to enlist their support, but he received only one reply that we know of, and it was not very helpful. It instructed him to turn over to the incoming governor copies of all papers relating to the proposals carried to England by a second Leislerian agent in 1690. Presumably he would make all appropriate decisions. Although interesting on other grounds, none of these communications tells us anything new about Leisler's constitutional preferences.[37]

What then were the constitutional ideas of the Leislerians? They said little on the subject and were often maddeningly vague, especially in comparison with New Englanders defending their own overthrow of Andros. In an early statement, for example, the Massachusetts revolutionaries denounced the "Illegal and Arbitrary Power" embodied in the Dominion government and asked William and Mary that they not be "left without our share in that Universal Restoration of Charters and English Liberties; Which the whole Nation is at this Day made Happy withall."[38] In a word, they expected the restoration of the Massachusetts Charter of 1629, which had been abrogated by court action in England in 1684. In pursuit of this objective they made strenuous efforts to mobilize public opinion on their behalf on both sides of the Atlantic.[39]

In sharp contrast to the Boston pattern, at no point did the Leislerians request the New York equivalent of the restoration of the Massachusetts charter, which would have meant a return to government under the Charter of Liberties. Instead their enemies began to make these demands, and in 1691 they would try to carry them out.

Yet the Leislerians did issue a few statements about the kind of political future they desired for New York. The militia, in its first pronouncement on May 31 right after taking possession of Fort James, complained of living "thes many years under a wicked arbitrarie Power execissed by our Late popish governr Coll Dongan & severall of his wicked Creatures and Pensionaris" and affirmed their dedication to "our Libertie, propertie and ye Laws." But the statement drew only one negative conclusion—that the militia were "Entirely Opposed to papists and their Religion"—and affirmed one positive commitment—that they would hold the fort until they could deliver it to any Protestant sent by William to take command of it. They made no request for any specific form of constitutional government.[40]

The militia's address to William and Mary a few days later amplified these demands without clarifying them. They complained that they had been governed "in a most arbitrary way [that has] subverted our ancient priviledges making us in effect slaves . . . contrary to the laws of England." They denounced Nicholson as a "pretend protestant" and affirmed "our Religion liberty and property," now about to be gloriously restored under the new monarchs.

What exactly did they mean? An elective assembly was not part of the political heritage of Continental Protestants, who made up most of the militia. In denouncing arbitrary power, such men usually meant something else—governing contrary to established law. Nor was an elective assembly an "ancient priviledge" of New Yorkers, who had enjoyed one for only three years in the colony's entire history of more than sixty years under Dutch and English rule. Were the militia demanding an assembly? I believe they were. But they hardly made their case clear, and most of them were probably thinking in terms of a simple duality that pitted good Protestants against bad Catholics, not in constitutional generalities.[41]

Leisler has left us a few glimpses of his own thoughts on these questions. On June 8, an extemporized committee of safety named him commander of the fort until relieved by William and Mary, and a few days later Leisler wrote to the government of Connecticut. The seizure of the fort, he reported, was in the process of being ratified or upheld by local committees throughout the province. He remarked on the importance of sending "one trusted man . . . to procure in England some privileges." Did he mean a charter? Or less formal concessions? He did not say, but he did add one important explanation (or was it an alternative?): "I wish we may have parte in your Charter, being as I understand in the latitude. If possible I could be informed of the said Charter and priviledges it would be great satisfaction." His own preference, in short, was for a government similar to those of New England. He had no clear idea of exactly what those privileges were, but apparently he had heard about the clause in the Connecticut charter extending its western boundary to the Pacific Ocean. He was willing to explore the possibility of using that provision as a legal basis for merging the two provinces under the Connecticut charter and government.[42]

Later that summer, the Leislerians did send Ensign Joost Stol as their emissary to England. He was a terrible choice. In explaining to the English government what had happened in New York in May and June, he represented himself as the prime mover at every important juncture. Joost Stol organized the militia to take possession of the fort on

May 31. Joost Stol led the militia and citizens in proclaiming William and Mary in mid-June. His statement never even mentions Leisler, who by implication became a mere lackey of the great Joost Stol, who would personally negotiate all outstanding questions with King William. The king did receive him once but did not respond to his petition. Stol never did figure out a way to get appropriate action out of the English government. He was playing politics on a level that he had no chance of mastering.

Yet his petition did suggest political objectives similar to the ones articulated by Leisler in June. Of Stol's seven requests put to the English government, the second asked "that his Majestie might be pleased to grant New Yorke a Charter in the like manner and with same or more priviledges as the citty of Boston, being that the contents of that Charter, dost best agree with the humour and nature of those inhabitants, and with the constitution of the said citty." Here again a note of disquieting ambiguity pervades the petition. Boston had no charter. Massachusetts had had one until 1684; New York City had acquired one in 1686. Was Stol talking about municipal or provincial privileges? Like many contemporaries, he probably used "Boston" as a shorthand expression for Massachusetts or even New England. But in that case to request "the same *or more* priviledges" than the Massachusetts charter of 1629 had conferred upon that colony virtually guaranteed almost instant rejection by the English government, which had been trying to tame the pretensions of Massachusetts since 1660 and would impose a new and more limited charter upon the colony in 1691.[43]

For all of the ambiguity of their statements and for all of the ethnic hostilities that they had to encounter within New York City, let us give the Leislerian spokesmen the benefit of the doubt. They probably hoped to acquire a charter that would confer on New York a set of privileges comparable to those contained in the Massachusetts or Connecticut charters. They were even willing to contemplate annexation to Connecticut, and because Leisler occasionally did exercise jurisdiction over East Jersey, they probably expected a continuing connection with that predominantly English province. Despite the angry resentment that pitted ordinary Dutch militiamen against English New Yorkers, the leaders of the movement always intended to keep the colony as an *English* province and saw New Englanders as their natural allies in this process. The English merchants who had agitated for the Charter of Liberties were another matter.

The unspoken assumption behind these preferences and antagonisms was undoubtedly religious. Leisler believed that fellow Calvinists could get along despite ethnic and social differences. He did not trust English merchants whose constitutional principles were similar to or even more generous than his own if their religious preferences were Anglican rather than strict Calvinist.[44]

Stol's failure coincided with the news that William had appointed a new governor, Colonel Henry Sloughter, who was putting together a council of prominent Anti-Leislerians. Much more urgently this time, the Leislerians dispatched a second emissary to London in 1690, Benjamin Blagge, a ship captain and son-in-law of Edsall. Although this exercise in damage control also failed, Blagge's requests are interesting. He begged the king never to let Nicholas Bayard and his colleagues back into power but instead asked him to approve what the Leisler regime had done in William's name. Finally, Blagge urged that the assembly be empowered to elect the council, an arrangement with no exact equivalent anywhere in New England. It was probably the only expedient Blagge could think of to reverse the appointments already made. The Crown ought to reward its true friends, he explained, "and frustrate the wicked designs of your Ma[jes]tys and their, Enemys on the Place." Like the city militia in June 1689, his goal also seems to have been narrowly political rather than broadly constitutional.[45]

At no point in their two-year struggle did Leislerians offer any theoretical or even legal justification for their constitutional positions. Partly because New York had no printing press, they published very little. Their most significant statement was a two-page pamphlet that appeared in Boston in 1689 and justified the seizure of the fort. Nobody tried to answer Nicholas Bayard's lengthy attack on Leisler's regime that appeared in 1690 in London, where it had tremendous potential for discrediting Leisler in the one place he could be hurt most. The Leislerians also had some exceptionally bad luck. The French captured the vessel containing their first efforts to communicate with the English government, a piece of ill fortune that permitted the Anti-Leislerians to state their case first. For all of these reasons, New York's revolutionary leaders never found a way to explain to the world what they were doing and why they had to do it.[46]

VI

The Leislerians' actions probably conveyed more effective and eloquent messages than any of their formal pronouncements. What they did can tell us much about their constitutional principles.

Leisler was willing to use elections as a legitimating device, but once again he injected a nearly fatal dose of ambiguity into the whole process. With Leisler in *de facto* command in June 1689, the militia ordered county-level elections throughout the province to choose a committee of safety. When it met, it appointed Leisler commander of the fort and began to exercise broad governmental powers over most of the colony. (Some parts, such as Albany, refused to obey.) Leisler also invoked the New York City charter in September and October 1689 to hold new elections and force his opponents, such as Mayor Stephanus Van Cortlandt, to surrender their municipal posts. Elections served Leisler well so long as he had no other source of legitimacy.[47]

This situation changed starting in December 1689 when Leisler accepted a letter from the king addressed to whoever was preserving the peace in New York. Claiming that this document gave him all the powers of a royal lieutenant governor, he dissolved the committee of safety and appointed his own royal council. At that point his government had no elective base at all and with his own people safely in power in New York City, he did not hold elections when they came due under the municipal charter in 1690. In Albany, where the city corporation had resisted him with prolonged success, his eventual triumph meant the overthrow, not just of the officials in power, but of the whole system of government established under the municipal charter of 1686. In November 1689, just before Leisler claimed the prerogatives of a lieutenant governor, his emissary Jacob Milborne had gone to Albany and denounced its charter as "Illegall . . . null & void Since it was graunted by a Popish kings governour & that now ye Power was in the People to choose both new Civill and Military officers as they pleased." Milborne probably was a good deal more radical than Leisler, and his statement contains a formula for a truly popular form of government. But things turned out differently. Once Leisler claimed to be governor, he did use elections in Albany when he reorganized it about a month later, but he also told that touchy community which men he regarded as acceptable choices. There, as in New York City, he was replacing those who had ruled, not introducing a system of annual elections. Instead, elections to Leisler seem to have been a means to an end, not a good in themselves. They were useful so long as they put the right men in office.[48]

As soon as Leisler assumed formal royal powers, he began to encounter ideological resistance based on the rights of Englishmen. As one of their first acts, he and his council proclaimed the laws of 1683 in force throughout the province. At a minimum, this step demonstrated that Leisler accepted the legitimacy of what the assembly of 1683 had done. This action also meant, as Leisler specifically announced, that he had no doubts about the legality of the permanent revenue act and that he had no intention of reviving the disallowed Charter of Liberties, although he was willing to quote it.

A few days after Leisler posted the notice about the revenue act at the customs house, someone tore it down and put in its place a declaration "By the English Freemen of the province of New York." Quoting Magna Carta, it insisted "that no freemen should be any Wise destroyed, but by the Lawfull Judgment of his peers or by the Laws of the Land," and it added passages from a statute of Edward I and the Petition of Right (1628) that affirmed the principle of no taxation without representation. The declaration attacked the revenue act of 1683 as illegal, alleging inaccurately that James had never approved it. The protestors then denounced Leisler's attempt to revive the tax as an assertion of "the unreasonable unlimmited and arbitrary power of the sword against the fundamental rights of the English subjects and contrary to reason Law & Justice" and condemned his government as "the treacherous betrayers of the Rights & priviledges of their Majestyes good Subjects & the Introducers of a miserable brutish Slavery from which his Majesty has Solemnly Given his Royall word to protect and defend us."[49]

Leisler and the council replied quickly. They accused the protestors of a "false construction on the wholesome Lawes of England not regarding An Act of the Freemen represented in Assembly as aforesd Vizt That the Supreame Legislatiue Authority under his Ma[jes]ties &ca shall forever be & reside in a Governr, Councill & the People met in Generall Assembly." Leisler warned that anyone defacing government proclamations would answer at his peril, and a few days later the government arrested two youthful anglicizing Dutchmen, Jacob DeKey, Jr., and Cornelius Depeyster, for the incident at the customs house.[50]

The struggle over English liberties was becoming serious, and Leisler had made an intelligent beginning. When accused of violating Magna Carta and the Petition of Right, he responded by quoting Article One of the Charter of Liberties. The tax was valid because it had been passed by governor, council, and general assembly, as the Charter of Liberties required. By throwing the Charter of Liberties back in the faces of the people who had drafted it, he positioned himself nicely to take the high ground in defense of English liberties, and he forced such opponents as Nicholas Bayard into arguing that the tax was no law because it was passed in exchange for the Charter of Liberties, which James had disallowed. This position could muster great moral force behind it but could not have been sustained as a matter of strict law. The assembly had passed the tax as a separate act, and James had approved it. But the moral argument also demanded some kind of response, and Leisler never gave it.

Thus Leisler, after gaining an initial polemical edge, never followed through with any broader statement of the constitutional principles that his government embodied. He made no attempt to implement the Charter of Liberties for those who regarded it as a binding bargain in exchange for the revenue act, or to revive it for those who conceded the validity of the disallowance. Nor did he suggest any substitute in a region of America that had been awash in daring constitutional schemes since the 1660s. As the constitutional debate continued over the next sixteen months, he permitted his opponents to recapture the Charter of Liberties and the form of government it represented. His opponents kept trying to stigmatize him as an enemy of the Charter of Liberties in particular, and English liberties in general. As Leisler jailed even more of his opponents for extended periods without trial, the accusations began to stick.[51]

Nevertheless Leisler did try to invoke the legitimating power of an English assembly. As expenses mounted in the war against New France, he issued writs for an election in February 1690. His New York City writ was addressed "To the military & civill officers of and ye rest of ye Inhabitants of the city & county of N. Yorrck." The intriguing question is whether "ye rest of ye Inhabitants" mandated a general election by the freeholders and freemen, as established in the Charter of Liberties. It most likely did not, and in any case few communities responded at all, probably because Leisler was drawing ever more narrowly upon a constituency of Continental Protestants, for whom the whole procedure was unusual. Even in Queens, where Leisler did get compliance from the preponderantly New England population, the towns interpreted his writ to require indirect elections similar to those used by Dongan in 1683, not the general elections mandated by the reforming assembly of that year. Each town chose a committee of two men, and those individuals then met separately to select the representatives.[52]

Leisler therefore tried again with new writs in April, and they produced better results in the rest of the province. This time, the writ to heavily Dutch Kings County was addressed only to the ruling cadre, and that small group of men made the choice by themselves, a pattern that was quite familiar to Dutch Protestants. This evidence suggests that Leisler never did invite the freeholders and freemen of the province to participate in a true general election, but then the only one that had ever been held in the entire history of New York had been in 1685.[53]

Beyond fighting the war and rendering his regime secure until he could be relieved by William, Leisler had no legislative agenda. The spring session of the 1690 assembly passed the tax he requested along with a law repealing New York City's monopoly on the bolting of flour. But when the assembly took up the question of the legal rights of Leisler's prisoners under English common law, Leisler prorogued it.[54]

The attempt to collect the tax of April 1690 led to a very serious Anti-Leislerian riot in New York City in June. Of several contemporary accounts, the least partisan indicates that the affair began when a large group of Anti-Leislerians assembled a few blocks from where the Leislerian militia were mustering. After denouncing the tax as arbitrary and illegal, they decided that, with the militia busy elsewhere, they might be able to surprise the fort and free the prisoners. Someone then suggested that they first ask Leisler to free the men, which they did when they happened to meet him coming from the fort. To their immense surprise, he agreed to release the prisoners on bail. Then, as the excited crowd moved closer about him, a bystander (probably his son, Jacob, Jr.) concluded that he was being mobbed and charged the throng with drawn sword. In the melée that followed, someone tried to brain Leisler with a carpenter's adze, a potentially fatal blow, but his followers came to his aid and freed him. Leisler's narrow escape convinced him that the whole incident had been an assassination plot, and he confined another long list of prisoners to the fort. This unhappy resolution probably marked the passing of his last chance to reach some minimal understanding with his opponents about the legal rights of all New Yorkers.[55]

Thereafter Leisler seldom relented from a strategy of confrontation with his opponents. He forced the clergy—particularly Henricus Selyns, his most powerful enemy within the Dutch Reformed ministry —to offer prayers of public thanksgiving for his deliverance. The angry exchange between the two men in church on a Sunday morning shocked the worshippers. Leisler denounced Selyns as "a rascal, which created a great sensation in the house of the Lord." Even in the eyes of many of Leisler's own followers, the politics of rage began to seem both grim and unwise.[56]

This growing estrangement became conspicuous when Leisler summoned a new session of his assembly in September. He issued several writs to fill vacancies, and they show that in Albany and New York City he again expected, not the voters, but the municipal corporations—his people by then—to do the actual choosing. Only in Yankee Queens did his writ also summon the "inhabitants" as well, although I have encountered no evidence to show whether freeholders in fact participated. The Albany writ, so far as I know, marks the only occasion—after the incident at the customs house in December 1689—in which he accorded some legitimacy to the Charter of Liberties. Calling it the "Charter of privilege," he accepted its apportionment of delegates, but not its mode of election.[57]

By the autumn of 1690, Leisler was in fact well advanced in losing the allegiance of the New Englanders on Long Island, and the second session of the assembly with its aftermath largely completed the process. Earlier in the year, when Easthampton had announced its intention to seek reunion with Connecticut, Leisler had dispatched Edsall to that town to dissuade the community. At a formal level Edsall succeeded, but in practice the situation became a stalemate. When Leisler and his council appointed a full slate of militia officers for the province, they included commissions for only one Suffolk town, Huntington, and for only one person in what was already becoming a secessionist town, Easthampton. So far as I am aware, no evidence survives to show that Leisler's government collected taxes in Suffolk (although it did appoint a collector). The county sent delegates to the first session of Leisler's assembly but apparently not the second.[58]

Surviving records tell us little about the assembly session of September–October 1690, but it was probably stormy. Still smarting from being prorogued in April for daring to raise the question of the common-law privileges of Leisler's prisoners, the delegates chose an English speaker, the rather obscure John Spratt, and the assembly resorted to a venerable parliamentary tactic. It demanded a redress of grievances before voting supplies. As its first item of business, it passed on September 18 "A Bill Confirming to the Inhabitants of this Province the Full Privilege and Benefitts of his Majties Laws within this Province." In brief, it demanded trial and due process according to the laws of England for anyone imprisoned for or accused of an offense, and it offered amnesty to all exiles who would return to New York within three weeks of the publication of the law—an effort to win over English merchants who had fled the colony. Nine days later, Leisler finally approved an amended version that made no explicit mention of his prisoners.

The wrangling never paralyzed the proceedings, however, for the assembly passed several other statutes in late September, including an act to explain the April tax. On October 2, the assembly finally voted the new tax that Leisler demanded, and two days later Leisler approved a measure that imposed harsh penalties on anyone refusing to assume office under his government and fines almost as severe on settlers who fled the exposed frontier counties of Albany and Ulster without permission. This series of incidents says a great deal. At a minimum, it tells us that even Leisler's own followers believed that he ought to be much more accommodating on the sensitive question of English liberties.[59]

The tax of October 1690 largely completed the alienation of Yankee Long Island. In Queens, led by longstanding enemies of Leisler's government, over one hundred settlers (perhaps a third of the taxpayers in a county of 500 militia) refused to pay the levy, and by the end of the year they were in various stages of having their property distrained. They called this procedure plunder, and ominous numbers of them took up arms in resistance. Puritan Westchester, however, remained loyal.[60]

Leisler's regime collapsed a few months later. Quite correctly, he refused to surrender the fort to Major Richard Ingoldsby when he arrived with his advance party of redcoats in January 1691 unless Ingoldsby would show him a direct order from the governor, who had been delayed enroute, or a commission from William (rather than James). Ingoldsby disdained to oblige, and the confrontation between them continued for nearly two months as both sides awaited Governor Sloughter's arrival. Leisler occupied the fort and a blockhouse. Ingoldsby took possession of the Town House (seat of the city government) and began to collect several hundred armed militia, mostly from Queens. Still suspecting that Ingoldsby represented James and not William, Leisler issued a proclamation on March 10 ordering his opponents to disperse and an angrier one on March 16. He opened fire the next day, killing two men—a last act of Leislerian rage. Ominously for Leisler, Governor Sloughter then arrived on March 19, and Leisler surrendered the fort to him on the twentieth, only to be arrested, tried, and convicted of treason. Leisler and his English son-in-law, Jacob Milborne, arguing that they were answerable only to the king for their public acts, refused to plead to their indictments. The court condemned them without trial. When Sloughter refused to allow an appeal to England, Leisler and Milborne were hanged on May 16.[61]

VII

What larger significance can we give to this struggle? New York, which had the most diverse population of any mainland English colony, also lived under a Continental European form of government almost continuously until 1689. Whether under the Dutch West India

Company or under James as duke or king, the settlers had to cope with varying forms of absolutism. In constitutional terms, New York thus became the one mainland colony in which royal (though initially proprietary) prerogative became firmly established decades before the province acquired an elective assembly. Virtually everywhere else, the assembly was older than royal government and confronted the first royal governor with an existing set of legislative privileges. In New York, the assembly had to make room for itself against the resistance of a well entrenched and very powerful prerogative.

Nonetheless, Leisler's Rebellion guaranteed that an assembly would become a permanent part of the governing process in New York. From the summoning of Leisler's contentious deputies in 1690 until the present, an assembly has met every year with the single exception of 1707. From the moment of their return in 1691, the Anti-Leislerians took dramatic steps of their own to guarantee the success of this effort. With several interesting amendments, they reenacted the Charter of Liberties of 1683, this time denying toleration to Catholics and requiring annual sessions of the legislature. They also declared all prior legislation void to gain control of a full agenda, and they began passing revenue acts for quite limited terms.[62]

Things did not work out as they planned. William III disallowed the 1691 charter, much as James had revoked the 1683 version. Even more important, the execution of Leisler and Milborne so brutalized the political enviroment that Anti-Leislerians found themselves under constant attack on both sides of the Atlantic. To remain in power, they needed the governor's support, and in the process they became measurably more accommodating on issues of prerogative.[63]

The Leislerian leadership had favored a New-England style charter for the colony as a way of guaranteeing its privileges. Anti-Leislerians had been the main force behind the two Charters of Liberties passed by the assemblies of 1683 and 1691. In securing a legislature that met every year, both sides won. In winning no broader guarantees, they both lost. On this question, their respective positions were much closer together than either realized or could admit. In the face of other disagreements, they found no way to discover how to concur on constitutional questions even when their differences were not large.

Continuing internal divisions and the need to placate the governor also made New York politics far more venal and corrupt after 1691 than was the public life of the colonies in neighboring New England or Pennsylvania. With rival factions bidding for its support, the governorship became the most lucrative office in British North America, a magnet capable of attracting every gentleman of broken fortune who could reach the ear of the duke of Newcastle. Governors also gave away New York real estate in truly enormous grants that undoubtedly retarded the settlement process by comparison with Pennsylvania or even New Jersey. After 1715, smart governors learned that once they had a safe majority in the assembly they could rule nicely for years—provided they did not call a general election. Elections were annual in New England and Pennsylvania, triennial in England from the Glorious Revolution to 1715 and septennial after that. New York had no such protection. Several different governors went from 1716 to 1726 and from 1728 to 1737 without calling new elections. Only in the 1740s did the province get its own Septennial Act. Only in the decade after 1737 did the assembly begin to make significant inroads on the most bloated prerogative in America. Leisler's Rebellion and the struggle it initiated did indeed destroy absolutism in New York, but the upheaval failed to do much to trim royal prerogative. Success in that contest had to wait for another half-century.[64]

VIII

New Yorkers failed to achieve broader constitutional objectives because in the late seventeenth century the politics of rage took precedence over these issues. Behind that rage loomed the threatening visage of Louis XIV, the monarch whose persecution of the Huguenots made it impossible for English Protestants to trust James II, for Dutch Calvinists and New England Puritans in New York to trust Nicholson and his councillors, and for Jacob Leisler to compromise with his opponents on English liberty or avoid bloodshed in his confrontation with Ingoldsby.

This rage also had ideological implications. Continental European Protestant values, religious and political, had to express themselves in unfamiliar English forms. Because the Dutch, English, and French communities all faced internal divisions, the potential for misunderstanding was always enormous. As the political stakes reached a new high in 1689, when everyone agreed that a false step could be fatal, anxiety and dread exploded inexorably into fury.

Both the youthful Nicholson and the middle-aged Leisler (forty-nine in 1689) responded with passion. Nicholson, who believed that he had taken every reasonable precaution to protect the colony from French attack, lost his temper when the militia continued to display its distrust of him and his soldiers. His angry threat to burn the city initiated the process that overturned his government. Leisler, after accepting command of the fort, went through the next year in one towering rage after another. When Philip French arrived in New York City from Boston on June 5, 1689, and objected to being interrogated, a militiaman growled, "Damn you doe not speake one word more or I'l kill you," and led him to Leisler in the fort.[65] Leisler badgered his opponents in person, fiercely and often. "Yo[u']r[e] a Traitour, a Papist, &c," he shouted "in a rage" at Stephanus Van Cortlandt on June 22, "and made the people just ready to knock me in the head," Van Cortlandt complained. A few days later Leisler told Frederick Philipse that "if he should meet [him] again the Divell should take him."[66] Men who had held office for many years became "Roages, Rascalls, and Devills" in an outburst by Leisler on June 25. Nearly everyone who resisted him became a "papist" or a "popish dog." In another confrontation also on June 25, Leisler accosted Nicholas Bayard at the customs house, "cursing and swearing that he would be the death of me," according to Bayard, "sometimes threatening to run mee thorow, to cudgel mee with his kaine, to run mee in the face."[67] Leisler's followers used similar language. They often threatened their opponents with violence—and even death.

On the one occasion when Leisler is known to have remained calm in a dispute with an Anti-Leislerian, the other party found the exchange so singular that he wrote a detailed account of it for Nicholson. In August, Leisler sent a sergeant and two musketeers to summon Captain George McKenzie, one of Nicholson's officers, to the fort. McKenzie refused to admit them to his house. Then, reported McKenzie, "they told me (in a threatening tone), you must go along with us; I said I would not; and bid them show me their warrant, and they held up their musquetts, which I said was not satisfactory to me, upon which they called me the greatest rogue in the whole country and threatened to pull down the house, which words I regarded not." But the next day while McKenzie strolled conspicuously along the Broad Way, Leisler's men arrested him and took him to the fort, where Leisler and two members of his council (Edsall and Peter Delanoy) interrogated him about a letter they had intercepted that he had sent to former Governor Andrew Hamilton of East Jersey, in which McKenzie had advised Hamilton not to trust Leisler's word on any matter of importance. As McKenzie reported,[68]

> Mr. Leisler said he wondered what wrong he had done me that I
> should write so of him to wrong his credit, that if he knew he had
> done me any wrong he would beg pardon for it upon his knees.
> I answered if I did him wrong I would beg his, but I told him I

was provoked first by his calling me a Papist, for so I was told.
He answered it was a very great lye for he had never said so. After
a little pause he put on a more angry look, and said he knew I was
Popishly affected. I answered that is not true. I am as much a protestant as you or any man in the Country. Why, says he, have not
I heard you call Father [John] Smith [the Jesuit who ran a school
in the city] a very good man? Yes replyed I, and so I do still; he
is a very good humoured man, but I never called him so because
he was a Papist, and I was so far from haveing any friendship for
his principlis [sic], that in all the six yeares I had known New York
I never so much as out of curiosity looked into their Chapell.
. . . After a great deal of [such] discourse which what I liked not
I always contradicted, he at last said I might call him what I pleased,
he would pray God to bless me. And then I prayd God might bless
him, in which holy sort of complem[en]t we continued a pretty
while. And at last [he] said he would never do me any prejudice,
and I made answer after the same manner, and so was dismissed
very civilly, which I very much wonder at, for he treated vanden-
burgh (who is one of the troopers) verry far otherwise, forbidding
him to ride in the troop, and that if he should see him ahorseback
he would shoot him down. It would proove tedious to give an account of all that passed betwixt him and I, but the other Committee men and he too spoke with as much smoothness and civility
as I think I have heard, which was pretty strange because new to me.

In a word, the lion had dragged McKenzie to his lair—and did not even
roar. It was a unique occasion, or so McKenzie clearly believed.

Even Leisler's strong supporters often tried to calm him. After the
confrontation between Leisler and Bayard at the customs house, Peter
Delanoy—a member of Leisler's council and a son-in-law of Edsall—
took in Bayard overnight to protect him from the wrath of the crowd
that Leisler had aroused, while the angry men "watched the house and
swore they would kill him."[69] Pierre Daillé, the Huguenot minister of
New York who owed many favors to Leisler, "was accustomed to go
to Commander Leisler, and exhort him to moderation."[70] Writing from
Boston, a Dutch Leislerian reminded his leader, "Sir gustis, with moderation and mersy is becoming all persons in pour [i.e., power]."[71] John
Allyn, the secretary of Connecticut, conveyed the same message much
more angrily in 1690, after Leisler had arrested Major General Fitz-
John Winthrop following the failure of the invasion of Canada. "A
prison is not a catholicon for al State Maladyes, though so much used
by you," he declared, "nor are you incapable of need of, nor aid from
their Majesties subjects in New England, nor could you in any one ac-

tion have more disobliged al New England."[72] Both sessions of Leisler's assembly had been trying to tell him the same thing. When the rebellion finally crashed around Leisler's head in 1691, Gerardus Beekman, until then a member of the council and loyal supporter, deplored the violence that occurred near the fort in March. He blamed these "base and inhuman actions" upon "the Malise of a Colerick man"—Leisler.[73] Of course, Leisler retained the passionate loyalty of thousands of New Yorkers. The public indignation provoked by his execution would otherwise be inexplicable. But even many of his closest associates believed that his fierce temper too often made things worse, not better.

Yet this rage fit a pattern. It had both a biography and a history behind it. Leisler maintained his Calvinist principles throughout his life at a real personal cost. In the 1670s, he and Milborne endured a long and expensive lawsuit in order to challenge the orthodoxy of Nicholas Van Rensselaer, a minister with rather odd theological views who had been thrust upon the Albany congregation by Governor Andros. Similarly, when the Dutch Reformed Church of New York City insisted on naming Selyns (whose theology was Arminian or Cocceian rather than Calvinist) as pastor in the early 1680s, Leisler left the congregation to worship with the French instead. Yet as late as 1684, this Calvinist commitment did not prevent him from maintaining friendly relations with Catholics. Although Dongan had never hidden his Catholicism, Leisler had not always hated and feared him. He accepted his first high office as a militia captain from Dongan in September 1684 and married his daughter Susannah to Michael Vaughton, a Dongan protégé. At this stage in Leisler's career, only his persistent orthodoxy set him apart from other Dutch settlers who were getting ahead by coming to terms with English rulers and institutions. Indeed, four of Leisler's daughters chose Englishmen as their first husbands, or quite possibly Leisler selected his daughters' mates himself.[74]

Then something happened that left Leisler fearfully alarmed. He never explained what it was, but we can guess with reasonable accuracy. Louis XIV revoked the Edict of Nantes in 1685 and culminated a mass persecution of Huguenots that compelled perhaps 160,000 of them to flee from France, the largest forced migration in early modern European history—larger even than the Loyalist migration from the United States during the Revolution or the flight of the emigres from the French Revolution. The expulsion of the Huguenots was the most chilling atrocity in Western Europe during Leisler's lifetime, and its impact soon destroyed both James II and Leisler, the tolerant absolutist and the heir of an earlier generation of Huguenot exiles.

Leisler, the son of a Huguenot clergyman who had escaped Spanish persecution by fleeing to Frankfort, deeply sympathized with the refugees. He paid John Pell £1675.5.0 sterling for land in New Rochelle which he made available to Huguenots as they arrived in New York, and he also worshipped with them in Pierre Daillé's French church. No doubt he knew that James II, whose own record on religious toleration had been excellent until then, was trying ineffectually to suppress the many accounts of Louis's persecution that circulated in England. In the process, James managed only to compromise himself irreparably in Protestant eyes. To Leisler, the news that James had fled to France meant that, if the exiled king somehow triumphed in New York, his victory would mean ruthless Catholic persecution of Protestants.

The stakes were too high for compromise. The maddening thing about the situation, in Leisler's mind, was that too many settlers, particularly those who held office under James, refused to recognize what was happening. Leisler understood the temptations they faced. He had tasted them and found them delectable, but since the repeal of the Edict of Nantes he had put stern Protestant duty ahead of any public career he might have been building. His enemies did not. Only one explanation made sense. They too must be papists, especially that other son of a persecuted émigré clergyman, Nicholas Bayard, who would not admit the urgency of the situation. He was the worst of the pack. Leisler's Orangist followers shared these convictions. They were as frightened and angry as the Orangist crowd in the Hague that killed the De Witt brothers during the French invasion of The Netherlands in 1672.[75]

Leisler was not only enraged, but as he met continued resistance, he was able to sustain his fury for nearly two years. He directed it against Bayard, against Nicholson's other councillors, and against all other recalcitrant officeholders in New York City or elsewhere who would not defer to him as military commander of New York. Only in his gallows speech did he finally concede that wrath, even righteous wrath, is not a subtle political weapon, that he and Milborne had undertaken "great & weighty matters of State affairs requiring at Such an helme more wise & Cunning powerfull Pilotts than either of us ever was." But by forgiving his enemies and dying in an exemplary Christian manner, Leisler only raised the fury of his followers to a new intensity. During the execution, they chanted the seventy-ninth Psalm:[76]

O God, the heathen are come into thine inheritance; thy holy temple have they defiled; they have laid Jerusalem on heaps.

> The dead bodies of thy servants have they given to be meat unto
> the fowls of the heaven, the flesh of thy saints unto the beasts
> of the earth.
> Their blood have they shed like water round about Jerusalem;
> and there was none to bury them.
> Pour out thy wrath upon the heathen that have not known thee,
> and upon the kingdoms that have not called upon thy name.
> For they have devoured Jacob, and laid waste his dwelling place.
> Let the sighing of the prisoner come before thee; according to
> the greatness of thy power preserve thou those that are ap-
> pointed to die;
> And render unto our neighbours sevenfold into their bosom their
> reproach, wherewith they have reproached thee, O Lord.

In May 1691, nobody who mattered was thinking of conciliation.

The rhetoric of rage often obscured important constitutional issues even within the Dutch community. Clashes between Orangist principles and the expectations of New York's proto-regents occurred frequently but seldom found articulate expression. Most of the maneuvering over who would proclaim William and Mary as king and queen
in June 1689, once official word of their accession finally arrived, involved a classic confrontation between an Orangist military leader and
his angry crowd of supporters against the civil officeholders who had
compromised their Protestant identities by cooperating smoothly with
Catholics.[77]

Although Leisler never called himself a *stadholder*, he acted like
one. He clearly believed that in a military emergency civil officeholders
ought to take orders from him as the highest military officer in the colony loyal to William. Whether he ever said, "The Sword must rule and
not the Laws," as Bayard claimed, is irrelevant.[78] He made certain that
official news about the accession of William and Mary reached him
before it got to Mayor Van Cortlandt, and he proclaimed their majesties
at the fort before ordering the mayor to do so later in the day as a civil
officer obliged to obey the province's military commander. Van Cortlandt refused to concede that Leisler had any legal power over him but
tried to make it clear that he approved of William and Mary. Leisler,
of course, did not believe him and accused him of favoring the infant
prince of Wales. Like the regent class in The Netherlands under Oldenbarnevelt and De Witt, Van Cortlandt, Bayard, Philipse, and their associates faced an angry Orangist uprising that certainly threatened their
status. Beyond any doubt, they feared for their lives. So did the English
merchants in New York City, many of whom probably saw in the first

phase of the uprising a repetition from within of the Dutch reconquest of 1673. The English, explained *Domine* Redolphus Varick of Long Island, "had been greatly provoked by their losing the fort a second time."[79]

These encounters ended in a final, terrible irony. For all the violence of their rhetoric, the Leislerians did not kill their enemies. When the Anti-Leislerians returned to power, they purged the Orangist terror from which they had suffered by killing Leisler. The men of moderation and flexibility had none when they most needed it. Instead, they bequeathed a heritage of continuing fury and vengeance to New York politics. Louis XIV never conquered New York, but he quite successfully warped the colony's politics for at least a generation.

Except among the badly outnumbered English merchants of New York City and the increasingly peripheral New Englanders, the battle for English constitutional liberties was always subordinate to the struggle within the Dutch community. Had constitutional systems been the most serious issue of 1689, the quarreling parties could have settled their differences. The confrontation between Orangists and proto-regents prevented the question of English liberties from achieving clear focus. Because the disputants literally could not believe how close together they actually were on basic constitutional questions, New York entered the eighteenth century with a crippled constitution that would take another two generations to repair.

NOTES

[1]For the most recent study of Leisler's Rebellion, see David William Voorhees, " 'In Behalf of the True Protestants Religion': The Glorious Revolution in New York" (Ph.D. dissertation: New York University, 1988).

[2]Important general histories of the Glorious Revolution in America include David S. Lovejoy, *The Glorious Revolution in America* (New York: Harper & Row, Publishers, 1972); and J. M. Sosin, *English America and the Revolution of 1688: Royal Administration and the Structure of Provincial Government* (Lincoln, Neb.: University of Nebraska Press, 1982). For more specific studies, see Richard R. Johnson, *Adjustment to Empire: The New England Colonies, 1675–1715* (New Brunswick, N.J.: Rutgers University Press, 1981); and Lois Green Carr and David William Jordan, *Maryland's Revolution of Government, 1689–1692* (Ithaca, N.Y.: Cornell University Press, 1974).

³See Joseph Lecler, *Toleration and the Reformation* (New York: Association Press, 1960), II, 5-323, 475-506; and Quentin Skinner, *The Foundations of Modern Political Thought* (Cambridge: Cambridge University Press, 1978), II, Chaps. 7-9.

⁴For general studies of The Netherlands, see Simon Schama, *The Embarrassment of Riches: An Interpretation of Dutch Culture in the Golden Age* (New York: Alfred A. Knopf, 1987), esp. Chap. 2; and Pieter Geyl, *The Netherlands in the Seventeenth Century, 2 vols.* (New York: Barnes & Noble Inc., 1961-64). More specialized studies include Jan den Tex, *Oldenbarnevelt*, 2 vols. (Cambridge, Eng.: Cambridge University Press, 1973), esp. II, Chap. 15; Herbert H. Rowen, *John de Witt, Grand Pensionary of Holland, 1625-1672* (Princeton: Princeton University Press, 1978), esp. Chaps. 2, 11, 19, 41; Stephen B. Baxter, *William III and the Defense of European Liberty. 1650-1702* (New York: Harcourt, Brace and World, Inc., 1966); Douglas Nobbs, *Theocracy and Toleration: A Study of the Disputes in Dutch Calvinism from 1600 to 1650* (Cambridge, Eng.: Cambridge University Press, 1938); E. H. Kossmann, "The Development of Dutch Political Theory in the Seventeenth Century," in J. S. Bromley and E. H. Kossman, eds., *Britain and the Netherlands: Papers delivered to the Oxford-Netherlands Historical Conference, 1959* (London: Chatto & Windus, 1960), 91-110; Kossmann, *In Praise of the Dutch Republic: Some Seventeenth-Century Attitudes* (London: Inaugural Lecture, University College, London, May 13, 1963).

⁵For a strong introduction to a vast literature, see J. R. Jones, *Country and Court: England 1658-1714* (Cambridge, Mass.: Harvard University Press, 1978). See also Anne Whiteman, "The Restoration of the Church of England"; Geoffrey F. Nuttall, "The First Nonconformists"; and Roger Thomas, "Comprehension and Indulgence," in Geoffrey F. Nuttall and Owen Chadwick, eds., *From Uniformity to Unity 1662-1962* (London: S.P.C.K., 1962), 19-88, 149-87, and 189-253.

⁶See Michael Kammen, *Colonial New York: A History* (New York: Charles Scribner's Sons, 1975); Oliver A. Rink, *Holland on the Hudson: An Economic and Social History of Dutch New York* (Ithaca, N.Y.: Cornell University Press, 1986); Robert C. Ritchie, *The Duke's Province: A Study of New York Politics and Society, 1664-1691* (Chapel Hill: University of North Carolina Press, 1977); and Joyce D. Goodfriend, " 'Too Great a Mixture of Nations': The Development of New York City Society in the Seventeenth Century" (Ph.D. dissertation: University of California at Los Angeles, 1975).

⁷For a strong intercolonial perspective on these events, see Wesley Frank Craven, *The Colonies in Transition, 1660-1713* (New York: Harper & Row, Publishers, 1968), Chaps. 2-3.

⁸Donald G. Shomette and Ronald D. Haslach, *Raid on America: The Dutch Naval Campaign of 1672-1674* (Columbia: University of South Carolina Press, 1988).

⁹The Andros letter to James is not extant, but see duke of York to Edmund Andros, April 6, 1675, in Edmund Bailey O'Callaghan, ed., *Documents relative to the Colonial History of the State of New York* (Albany: Weed, Parsons and Co., 1856-87), III, 230 (hereafter cited as *NY Col. Docs.*). James commended Andros for not encouraging the settlers in their desire for an assembly. I suspect that Andros raised the question with James in the hope of finding greater flexibility.

¹⁰See the deposition of Zechariah Whitpaine before the Pennsylvania council, February 24, 1688 / 89, in *Minutes of the Provincial Council of Pennsylvania from the Organization to the Termination of the Proprietary Government* (Philadelphia: John Stevens & Co., 1852-53), I, 245-47 (this series is often cited by the binding title, *Colonial Records of Pennsylvania*). Whitpaine left England just after hearing of James's capture during his first attempt to flee. In the late 1640s, Charles I had been held captive for more than a year before his trial and execution by the army and the Rump Parliament. The implications of James's capture had to seem extremely murky to officials in the colonies, such as Nicholson when he received a copy of Whitpaine's deposition on March 1. New-York Historical Society, *Collections* (1868), 241-43. (Hereafter cited as NYHS *Coll.*)

[11]Stephanus Van Cortlandt to Maria Van Rensselaer, January 21, 1688 / 89, in Albert J. F. Van Laer, ed., *Correspondence of Maria Van Rensselaer, 1669-1689* (Albany: University of the State of NewYork, 1935), 188-89.

[12]Richard Pretty to Jacob Milborne, January 15, 1689-90, in Edmund Bailey O'Callaghan, ed., *Documentary History of the State of New York*, octavo edn. (Albany: Weed, Parsons and Co., 1849-51), II, 60. (Hereafter cited as *NY Doc. Hist.*) In 1685 James II had crushed the rising of the duke of Monmouth, a bastard son of Charles II who had considerable support among radical Whigs.

[13]See "Declaration of the Freeholders of Suffolk county, Long Island," May 3, 1689, in O'Callaghan, ed., *NY Col. Docs.* III, 577. They sent a deputation of three men to the city "to demand the Fort to be delivered into the hands of such persons as the country shall chose." For the government's actions from April 26 to May 15, 1689, see NYHS *Coll.* (1868), 244-62, especially the letter "to the principall secretary off State and the Secretary off plantacons" on May 15, pp. 259-62.

[14]For the Leislerian version of this incident, see O'Callaghan, ed., *NY Doc. Hist.* II, 10-13. Nicholson denied that he threatened to burn the city, but he probably did say, "I rather would see the Towne on fire than to be commanded by you." Stephanus Van Cortlandt to Sir Edmund Andros, July 9, 1689, in O'Callaghan, *NY Col. Docs.* III, 593-94. For a study of Nicholson including the Tangiers incident, see Stephen Saunders Webb, "The Strange Career of Francis Nicholson," *William and Mary Quarterly*, 3rd ser., 23 (1966): 513-48.

[15]See Randall H. Balmer, *A Perfect Babel of Confusion: Dutch Religion and English Culture in the Middle Colonies* (New York: Oxford University Press, 1989), esp. Chap. 2.

[16]Herbert L. Osgood, ed., *Minutes of the Common Council of the City of New York, 1675-1776* (New York: Dodd, Mead and Company, 1905), I, 25-26.

[17]Robert C. Ritchie, "London Merchants, the New York Market, and the Recall of Sir Edmund Andros," *New York History*, 57 (1976): 5-30; Peter R. Christoph and Florence A. Christoph, eds., *Records of the Court of Assizes for the Colony of New York, 1665-1682* (Baltimore: Genealogical Publishing Co., Inc., 1983), 271-77. (Hereafter cited as *Recs. Ct. of Assizes.*)

[18]For an interpretation of the period that makes the Long Island towns and their demands the center of the story, see Jerome R. Reich, *Leisler's Rebellion: A Study of Democracy in New York, 1664-1720* (Chicago: University of Chicago Press, 1953), esp. Chaps. 1-2.

[19]William A. Whitehead, ed., *Documents relating to the Colonial History of the State of New Jersey*, 1st ser. (Newark: Daily Journal Establishment; Trenton: The John L. Murphy Publishing Company, 1880-1949), I, 292-319, 323-24 (hereafter cited as *NJ Archives*); Christoph and Christoph, eds., *Recs. Ct. of Assizes*, 260-66. See also John E. Pomfret, *The Province of East New Jersey 1609-1702: The Rebellious Proprietary* (Princeton: Princeton University Press, 1962), Chap. 6. On James's political difficulties in England, see J. R. Jones, *The First Whigs: The Politics of the Exclusion Crisis, 1678-1683* (London: Oxford University Press, 1961).

[20]The only accurate modern text of the West Jersey Concessions is in Mary Maples Dunn, Richard S. Dunn, *et al.*, eds., *The Papers of William Penn* (Philadelphia: University of Pennsylvania Press, 1981-86), I, 387-416. See also John E. Pomfret, *The Province of West New Jersey, 1609-1702: A History of the Origins of an American Colony* (Princeton: Princeton University Press, 1956), esp. Chaps. 6-7; and *The West Jersey Concessions and Agreements of 1676 / 77: A Round Table of Historians*, New Jersey Historical Commission, *Occasional Papers Number 1* (Trenton, 1979).

[21]See Jean R. Soderlund, ed., *William Penn and the Founding of Pennsylvania. 1680-1684: A Documentary History* (Philadelphia: University of Pennsylvania Press, 1983), especially 37-50, 93-140, 265-74; and Aaron Leaming and Jacob Spicer, eds., *The Grants, Concessions, and Original Constitutions of the Province of New Jersey. . .*, 2d edn. (Somerville, N.J.: Honeyman and Company, 1881), 153-66.

[22]See Christoph and Christoph, eds., *Recs. Ct. of Assizes*, 271-77.

[23]Indirect elections prevailed in the three ridings of Long Island and Westchester, among the communities along the Esopus River, and on Martha's Vineyard and its dependencies. Direct elections occurred in New York City, Staten Island, Albany, Schenectady, and Pemaquid. For the writs, see *NY Col. Docs.* XIV, 770-71. For an attempt to reconstruct the membership of the assembly, see John M. Murrin, "English Rights as Ethnic Aggression: The English Conquest, the Charter of Liberties of 1683, and Leisler's Rebellion in New York," in William Pencak and Conrad Edick Wright, eds., *Authority and Resistance in Early New York* (New York: New-York Historical Society, 1988), 56-94. See also Charles Z. Lincoln, ed., *The Colonial Laws of New York from the Year 1664 to the Revolution* (Albany: James B. Lyon, State Printer, 1894-96), I, 111-21.

[24]See John M. Murrin, ed., "The New York Charter of Liberties, 1683 and 1691," in Stephen L. Schechter, ed., *Roots of the Republic* (Madison, Wis.: Madison House, for New York State Commission on the Bicentennial of the United States Constitution, 1990). Although the Charter of Liberties did not officially recognize the religious rights of Jews, they too enjoyed toleration under James.

[25]For all of Dongan's legislation, see Lincoln, ed., *The Colonial Laws of New York* I, 111-77. See also Mrs. Schuyler Van Rensselaer, *History of the City of New York in the Seventeenth Century* (New York: The Macmillan Company, 1909), II, Chap. 23. For the Albany charter, see Joel Munsell, *Annals of Albany* (Albany: J. Munsell, 1850-59), II, 62-87.

[26]Christoph and Christoph, eds., *Recs. Ct. of Assizes*, 275.

[27]David William Voorhees, "European Ancestry of Jacob Leisler," *New York Genealogical and Biographical Record*, 120 (1989): 193-202.

[28]Nicholas Bayard's journal for June 3, 1689, in O'Callaghan, ed., *NY Col. Docs.* III, 639.

[29]For a fuller development of this point, see Murrin, "English Rights as Ethnic Aggression."

[30]Nicholson and the New York Council to the Lords ("Board") of Trade, May 15, 1689, in O'Callaghan, ed., *NY Col. Docs.* III, 575

[31]*Loyalty Vindicated from the Reflections of a Virulent Pamphlet . . .* (1698), in Charles M. Andrews, ed., *Narratives of the Insurrections, 1675-1690* (New York: Charles Scribner's Sons, 1915), 380-81. Although this explanation was made public nine years after the event, I see no reason to doubt it. In one of Leisler's earliest justifications of his actions, he complained that although Plowman "is a rank papist, I cannot get the other Captanes to resolve to turne him out but acts still as before." Leisler to the governor and committee of safety at Boston, June 4, 1689, in O'Callaghan, ed., *NY Doc. Hist.* II, 3-4.

[32]Leisler to William Jones of New Haven, July 10, 1689, in O'Callaghan, ed., *NY Doc. Hist.* II, 9.

[33]Nicholas Bayard's journal, in O'Callaghan, ed., *NY Col. Docs.* III, 601-02.

[34]Lodwyck was admitted to the Dutch Reformed Church in New York City in 1685 by transfer from the Dutch Church in London. After a long career in New York, he died in London about 1724. *New York Genealogical and Biographical Record* 59 (1928), 71; *id.* 40 (1909), 125. On May 31, 1689, his role in the uprising rivalled Leisler's. He was the captain who demanded and received the keys to Fort James from Nicholson. Stephanus Van Cortlandt to Sir Edmund Andros, July 9, 1689, in O'Callaghan, ed., *NY Col Docs.* III, 594. In the next few days he was systematically collecting news as it arrived from abroad and sat with Leisler to sift through this information and interrogate newcomers. *Ibid.*, 586, 587. In July 1689, his militia company agreed to fine any member "who shall rail at any one or make any distinction in Nationality or otherwise." NYHS *Coll.* (1868), 294. For his deposition of July 25, 1689, against Nicholson, see *ibid.*, 295. Yet by early 1690 he was in Boston where on January 25 he joined with the moderate royalists of Massachusetts, many of whom were Anglicans, in petitioning William for a royal govern-

ment. Robert E. Moody and Richard C. Simmons, eds., *The Glorious Revolution in Massachusetts: Selected Documents, 1689-1692* (Boston: Colonial Society of Massachusetts, 1988), 406–07. At least from that point on, his political affiliation remained Anti-Leislerian, prompting Jacob Milborne to question Lodwyck's religious orthodoxy. William Milborne, Jacob's brother and a Baptist minister in Boston, replied that Lodwyck was sound. William Milborne to Jacob Milborne, February 17, 1689/90, in O'Callaghan, ed., *NY Doc. Hist.* II, 72. Lodwyck's contribution to the Royal Society has been published as "New York in 1692," NYHS *Coll.*, 2nd ser., 2 (1849): 241–50.

³⁵See especially the genealogy of Samuel Edsall by Thomas Henry Edsall in *New York Genealogical and Biographical Record* 13 (1882), 191–96. See also NYHS *Coll.* 18 (1885), 23 (his burgher rights in New Amsterdam, 1657); O'Callaghan, ed., *NY Col. Docs.* III: 75 (Edsall required to take an oath of allegiance conquering English in 1664); *Records of the Reformed Dutch Churches of Hackensack and Schraanlenburgh, New Jersey*, I, Pt. 1 (New York: Holland Society of New York, 1891), *passim*; Whitehead, ed., *NJ Archives*, 1st ser., XIII, 53. Edsall's East Jersey career can be traced through Pomfret, *The Province of East New Jersey.* A Connecticut deputation to New York, which commended "Loyall Mr. Samuell Edsall & other good worthy and Loyall gentlemen," obviously had a favorable opinion of him but probably knew little or nothing about his public actions in East New Jersey. Connecticut delegates to Jacob Leisler, June 26, 1689, in O'Callaghan, ed., *NY Doc. Hist.* II, 17.

³⁶The fullest autobiographical statement of Milborne's that has yet come to light is "The Informacon of Jacob Milborne of London Merchant," January 6, 1679/80, Rawlinson Mss A, 175, fol. 83, Bodleian Library, Oxford University. My thanks to Robert C. Ritchie for pointing it out to me and providing me with a copy. See also, Christoph and Christoph, eds., *Recs. Ct. of Assizes*, 127; O'Callaghan, ed., *NY Col. Docs.* III, 300–01; and Voorhees, " 'In Behalf of the True Protestants Religion,' " 450–52. For Leisler's intention to send Milborne to England in 1690, see Leisler to the earl of Shrewsbury, June 23, 1690; and Leisler and the council to same, October 20, 1690, in O'Callaghan, ed., *NY Col. Docs.* III, 733, 751.

³⁷Leisler to William and Mary, August 20, 1689; to the king, January 7, 1689/90; to Bishop Gilbert Burnet, January 7, 1689/90; to the king, March 3, 1689/90; to Burnet, March 3, 1689/90; to the earl of Shrewsbury, June 23, 1690; to the king, October 20, 1690; to Shrewsbury, October 20, 1690, in O'Callaghan, ed., *NY Col. Docs.* III, 614–16, 653–54, 654–57, 700, 700–02, 731–33, 751, 751–54. For the response of the English government, see lords of the council to Governor Henry Sloughter, October 17, 1690, *ibid.*, 750; and the petition of Jacob Leisler and others to Governor Sloughter, n.d. (probably March 1691), in O'Callaghan, ed., *NY Doc. Hist.* II, 360. The English privy councillors almost certainly did not realize that they were authorizing Leisler's execution by conferring full discretionary powers on Sloughter.

³⁸Massachusetts Council of Safety to the King and Queen, May 20, 1689, in Moody and Simmons, eds., *The Glorious Revolution in Massachusetts*, 77–79.

³⁹Besides the material in Mody and Simmons, eds., *The Glorious Revolution in Massachusetts*, see also W. H. Whitmore, ed., *The Andros Tracts*, 3 vols., Publications of the Prince Society, V–VII (Boston, 1868–74). The sheer volume of this material is striking.

⁴⁰O'Callaghan, *NY Doc. Hist.* II, 10–11.

⁴¹Address of the New York militia to William and Mary, June 1689, in O'Callaghan, *NY Col. Docs.* III, 583-84. This document gives no specific date, but it was undoubtedly written shortly after news reached New York from Barbados on June 3 that William and Mary had been proclaimed king and queen in February. See the deposition of John Dischington, June 5, 1689, in *ibid.*, 586.

⁴²Leisler to Major Nathan Gold, June 12, 1689, in O'Callaghan, *NY Doc. Hist.* II, 14–15.

⁴³Representation of Joost Stol, agent for the New York committee of Safety, Nov. 9, 1689, in O'Callaghan, *NY Col. Docs.* III, 629–32, esp. 631 (emphasis added). See also Stol's account of his proceedings, Nov. 16, 1689, *ibid.*, 632–33.

⁴⁴For the fullest explorations of the religious dimensions of Leisler's Rebellion, see Voorhees, " 'In Behalf of the True Protestant Religion' "; and Randall H. Balmer, "Traitors and Papists: The Religious Dimensions of Leisler's Rebellion," *New York History* 70 (1989): 341–72.

⁴⁵Petition of Captain Benjamin Blagge to the king, n.d., in O'Callaghan, *NY Col. Docs.* II, 737.

⁴⁶*An Account of the Proceedings at New York, 1689* (Boston, 1689), Evans No. 39,248. This pamphlet contains the militia's statements of May 31 and June 3, 1689. Nicholas Bayard, *A Modest and Impartial Narrative of Several Grievances and Great Oppressions that the Peaceable and Most Considerable Inhabitants of their Majesties Province of New-York in America Lye Under, by the Extravagant and Arbitrary Proceedings of Jacob Leysler and his Accomplices* (London, 1690), in Andrews, ed., *Narratives of the Insurrections*, 315–54. For Leisler's discovery that his enemies got to England first, see Leisler to Shrewsbury, June 23, 1690, in O'Callaghan, ed., *NY Col. Docs.* III, 731.

⁴⁷Nicholas Bayard mocked the elections of 1689 by insisting that the turnout was very low. Because Leisler was appealing mostly to settlers from Continental European Protestant backgrounds, they would indeed have found the device of popular elections unfamiliar, and yet it still would have served a legitimating function. Bayard, *A Modest Narrative* (1690), in Andrews, ed., *Narratives of the Insurrections*, 328–29. See also Osgood, ed., *Minutes of the Common Council of the City of New York*, I, 207–08.

⁴⁸William III to Francis Nicholson "and in his absence to such as for the time being take care for Preserving the Peace and administering the Lawes in our said Province of New York in America," July 30, 1689, in O'Callaghan, ed., *NY Col. Docs.* III, 606. Leisler's municipal corporation of New York City met several times after its records cease in December 1689, but we do not know how often. For its proceedings, see Osgood, ed., *Minutes of the Common Council of the City of New York*, I, 208–13; David William Voorhees to author, January 23, 1990. For Albany, see Jacob Milborne's speech at a convention at Albany, November 9, 1689; and Jacob Leisler to Captain Joachim Staats, December 28, 1689, in O'Callaghan, ed., *NY Doc. Hist.* II, 113–14, 52–53. See also, Alice P. Kenney, *The Gansevoorts of Albany: Dutch Patricians in the Upper Hudson Valley* (Syracuse: Syracuse University Press, 1969), 16–19.

⁴⁹C.O. 5 / 1081 / 203, British Public Record Office, London. My thanks to David William Voorhees for bringing this text to my attention and for sending me a copy.

⁵⁰Proclamation of December 20, 1689, in O'Callaghan, ed., *NY Doc. Hist.* II, 50–51.

⁵¹See Bayard, *Modest Narrative* (1690), in Andrews, ed., *Narratives of the Insurrections*, 340–44.

⁵²Jamaica town meeting of March 14, 1689/90, in Josephine C. Frost, ed., *Records of the Town of Jamaica, Long Island, New York, 1656–1751* (New York: Long Island Historical Society, 1914), I, 143; Hempstead town meeting of March 17, 1689/90, in Benjamin D. Hicks, ed., *Records of the Town of North and South Hempstead, Long Island, New York* (Jamaica, N.Y.: Long Island Farmer Print., 1896–1904), II, 28. See also, Leisler to Bishop Gilbert Burnet, March 31, 1690, in which he noted that "the people . . . do not convene, according to our writts" for election of the assembly. O'Callaghan, ed., *NY Col. Docs.* III, 702.

⁵³For the New York City writs of February and April, see O'Callaghan, ed., *NY Doc. Hist.* II, 73; for Kings County, see "Flatbush Town Records, Miscellaneous, I: 1652 to 1758," 271–73 (St. Francis College Archives, Brooklyn).

⁵⁴Leisler to Captain John D'Bruyn *et al.*, in O'Callaghan, *NY Doc. Hist.* II, 238. For the legislation of April 1690, only the title survives. The two measures may have been embodied in one comprehensive act, which would have been a very un-English thing to do when one item was a tax and the other was not. See Lincoln, ed., *Colonial Laws of New York* I, 218.

⁵⁵For this version of the riot, see Lawrence H. Leder, ed., " '. . . Like Madmen through the Streets': The New York City Riot of June 1690," *New-York Historical Society Quarterly* 34 (1955): 405–15. For the Leislerian version, see "Depositions respecting the Riot at New-York, &c.," in O'Callaghan, *NY Col. Docs.* III, 740–48.

⁵⁶Leder, ed., " '. . . Like Madmen through the Streets,' " 414.

⁵⁷For the writs, see O'Callaghan, *NY Doc. Hist.* 282–83.

⁵⁸See Samuel Mulford *et al.* to Leisler, Mar. 10, 1689 / 90, in *NY Doc. Hist.* II, 187. For a list of Leisler's civil and military commissions with dates and recipients, see *ibid.*, 347–54. David William Voorhees has found evidence that Suffolk County sent Richard Kedee and Thomas Harris to the April assembly. Voorhees to author, January 23, 1990. Until now all historians have assumed that Suffolk participated in neither session.

⁵⁹The text of the contested bill is in O'Callaghan, *NY Doc. Hist.* II, 355. For the statutes of October 2 and 4, see *ibid.*, 356–57, and Lincoln, ed. *Colonial Laws of New York* I, 219–20. For the others, including the final version of the contested bill, I am indebted to David William Voorhees to author, January 23 and February 23, 1990.

⁶⁰John Clapp to the secretary of state, November 7, 1690, conveying the protests of the freeholders of Hempstead, Jamaica, Flushing and Newtown, in O'Callaghan, ed., *NY Col. Docs.* III, 754–56.

⁶¹See generally O'Callaghan, ed. *NY Col. Docs.* III, 756–69; O'Callaghan, ed. *NY Doc. Hist.* II, 320–46; NYHS *Coll.* (1868), 299–333; and Lawrence H. Leder, ed., "Records of the Trials of Jacob Leisler and his Associates," *New-York Historical Society Quarterly* 36 (1952): 431–57. Those who pleaded not guilty received a jury trial. Leisler and Milborne did not plead and were comdemned without a jury.

⁶²*Journal of the Votes and Proceedings of the General Assembly of the Colony of New York (1692-1765)* (New York: Hugh Gaine, 1764–66), I, 8–9; Lincoln, ed., *Colonial Laws of New York* I, 239–42, 244–48, 248–53. For a fuller discussion of the 1691 Charter of Liberties, see Murrin, ed., "The New York Charter of Liberties, 1683 and 1691."

⁶³For disallowance of the Charter of Liberties of 1691, see Lincoln, ed., *Colonial Laws of New York* I, 244. On New York politics after Leisler, see Thomas J. Archdeacon, *New York City, 1664-1710: Conquest and Change* (Ithaca, N.Y.: Cornell University Press, 1976), Chap. 6; Patricia U. Bonomi, *A Factious People: Politics and Society in Colonial New York* (New York: Columbia University Press, 1971), Chaps. 1–3; Lawrence H. Leder, *Robert Livingston, 1654-1728, and the Politics of Colonial New York* (Chapel Hill: University of North Carolina Press, 1961), Chaps. 5–12; and Eugene R. Sheridan, *Lewis Morris, 1671-1746: A Study in Early American Politics* (Syracuse University Press, 1981), Chaps. 1–3.

⁶⁴Stanley Nider Katz, *Newcastle's New York: Anglo-American Politics, 1732-1753* (Cambridge, Mass: Harvard University Press, 1968), esp. Chap. 2; Beverly McAnear, *The Income of the Colonial Governors of British North America* (New York: Pageant Press, Inc., 1967); and Charles Worthen Spencer, "The Rise of the Assembly, 1691-1760," in Alexander C. Flick, ed., *History of the State of New York* (New York: Columbia University Press, 1933–37), II, 151–99.

⁶⁵Deposition of Philip French, June 7, 1689, in O'Callaghan, ed., *NY Col. Docs.* III, 587.

⁶⁶Stephanus Van Cortlandt to Sir Edmund Andros, July 9, 1689, in O'Callaghan, ed., *NY Col. Docs.* III, 595–96.

⁶⁷Nicholas Bayard's journal, June 25, 1689, in O'Callaghan, ed., *NY Col. Docs.* III, 602, 603.

⁶⁸George McKenzie to Francis Nicholson, August 15, 1689, in O'Callaghan, ed., *NY Col. Docs.* III, 612–14. I have modernized some of the punctuation in this passage.

⁶⁹Stephanus Van Cortlandt to Sir Edmund Andros, July 9, 1689, in O'Callaghan, ed., *NY Col. Docs.* II, 596.

[70]Leislerian members of the Dutch Reformed Church of New York to the Classis of Amsterdam, October 21, 1698, in Hugh Hastings and E. T. Corwin, eds., *Ecclesiastical Records of the State of New York* (Albany: James B. Lyon, State Printer, 1901-16), II, 1256. Hereafter cited as *NY Eccles. Recs.*

[71]Isaac Melyn to Leisler, December 11, 1690, in O'Callaghan, ed., *NY Doc. Hist.* II, 316.

[72]John Allyn to Leisler, September 1, 1690, in O'Callaghan, ed., *NY Doc. Hist.* II, 289.

[73]Petition of Gerrardus Beekman to Governor Henry Sloughter, n.d. (probably April 1691), in O'Callaghan, ed., *NY Doc. Hist.* II, 368-69.

[74]Voorhees, " 'In Behalf of the True Protestants Religion,' " Chap. 5; Edwin R. Purple's genealogy of the Leisler family, *New York Genealogical and Biographical Record* 7 (1876): 145-51; Lawrence H. Leder, "The Unorthodox Domine: Nicholas Van Rensselaer," *New York History* 35 (1954): 166-76; and for the relationship between Vaughton and Dongan, Dongan's report on the state of the Province, *NY Col. Docs.* III, 407-08.

[75]Jon Butler, *The Huguenots in America: A Refugee People in New World Society* (Cambridge, Mass.: Harvard University Press, 1983), esp. Chaps. 1, 2, and 5; J. Thomas Scharf, *History of Westchester County, New York, including Morrisana, Kings Bridge, and West Farms, which Have Been Annexed to New York City* (Philadelphia: L. E. Preston and Co., 1886), I, 27.

[76]O'Callaghan, ed. *NY Doc. Hist.* II, 376-79, esp. 376; Balmer, *A Perfect Babel of Confusion*, 42-43 (italics removed).

[77]The most thoughtful effort to understand Leisler within the context of Anglo-Dutch politics in general and the office of *stadholder* in particular is Donna Merwick, "Being Dutch: An Interpretation of Why Jacob Leisler Died," *New York History* 70 (1989), 373-404.

[78]Bayard, *Modest Narrative* (1690), in Andrews, ed., *Narratives of the Insurrections*, 332.

[79]See the accounts by Van Cortlandt and Bayard of the events of June 22, 1689, in O'Callaghan, ed., *NY Col. Docs.* III, 595-96, 601; Rudolphus Varick to the Classis of Amsterdam, April 9, 1693, in Hastings and Corwin, eds., *NY Eccles. Recs.* II, 1050.

John Peter Zenger, New York, and the Origin of the Bill of Rights

PAUL FINKELMAN

State University of New York at Binghamton

The seditious libel trial, in 1735, of the printer, John Peter Zenger, is particularly important in explaining New Yorkers' sensitivity toward the lack of a bill of rights. For New Yorkers, and others familiar with the case, the Zenger trial was more than just a precedent for freedom of expression. It also illustrated the dangers of a society which did not guarantee due process to all persons accused of crimes.

John Peter Zenger was a German immigrant who learned the art of printing as an apprentice to William Bradford, the colony's official printer, and the publisher of the only newspaper in New York. By the early 1730s, Zenger was an independent printer, publishing handbills, commercial documents, and religious tracts in Dutch. In 1733 he commenced publishing the *New York Weekly Journal*. Two years later, he was tried for seditious libel because of his paper's unrelenting attacks on the colony's officials, especially Governor William Cosby and Chief Justice James DeLancey.

Zenger's road to the courtroom was hardly predictable. Before 1733, he had shown little interest in politics. In that year, a group of New York politicians led by James Alexander, Rip Van Dam, and Lewis Morris, hired Zenger to publish a paper for them. Zenger did the physical printing, but Alexander and Morris provided most of the content.

The paper reprinted the writings of such English essayists as Joseph Addison, Richard Steele, and John Trenchard and Thomas Gordon, the authors of "Cato's Letters." Alexander and Morris supplemented these imported essays with some of their own. The paper stressed the necessity of constitutional restraint on the rulers and the virtues of representative government. The articles also presented a coherent defense of freedom of the press. This defense was significant, because it was the first of its kind in British North America. Finally, Alexander and others indirectly assaulted the Cosby administration through allegory, innuendo, and biting satire. Some essays took the form of historical pieces, which described tyrants taking liberty from the people in classical, medieval, or renaissance states. Others were designed to harm Cosby with humor. Thus, a bogus commercial notice described a "choice parcel of new authorities" that had recently arrived on a ship from "God knows where."

The opposition disliked Cosby for a variety of reasons. Shortly after he arrived in New York, Cosby had sued a leading politician, Rip Van Dam. When Chief Justice Lewis Morris ruled against him, Governor Cosby responded by removing the venerable Morris from his position on the court, and replacing him with the much younger James DeLancey. This action alienated Morris and his many allies. Furthermore, it smacked of an attempt to corrupt justice by punishing jurists for their decisions. This, combined with Cosby's excessive personal venality, made him unpopular with a large number of voters. Campaigning under the slogan "liberty and law," an opposition party defeated Cosby's supporters in a number of elections. Zenger's paper was part of a larger effort by Alexander and Morris to undermine Cosby's authority in New York and to control the colonial legislature. The *Weekly Journal* served this movement well, as the opposition won majorities in the legislature and in the New York City government. The newspaper attacks were successful in part because Cosby was vulnerable. Cosby was greedy and corrupt, even by the rather loose standards of the early eighteenth century. He compounded these faults with political ineptitude and administrative bungling. While not using Cosby's name, Zenger's paper portrayed the governor as a threat to the people's liberty and property. In Zenger's paper, Cosby appeared at best a fool, more likely a knave, and probably a tyrant.

Cosby's conduct in the Zenger affair made his enemies appear to be correct. In January 1734, just two months after the appearance of Zenger's paper, Chief Justice DeLancey, a Cosby appointee, urged a grand jury to indict Zenger for seditious libel. The grand jury, however, refused to act. In October, a second grand jury agreed with the Cosby administration that certain articles in Zenger's paper might be libelous, but the jurors refused to make any determination as to who wrote or published them. Again Zenger was not indicted, and he continued to print the *Weekly Journal*.

In November, the Governor's Council—which consisted of Cosby's hand-picked allies—ordered Zenger arrested on suspicion of publishing a seditious paper. While Zenger sat in jail "denied the use of pen, ink and paper, and the liberty of speech with any persons," the colony's attorney general, Richard Bradley, prepared an indictment against him. After Zenger was finally allowed to speak with his friends, he sought bail. Although his net worth amounted to no more than forty pounds, Zenger's bail was set at an outrageous four hundred pounds by Chief Justice DeLancey.

With the arrest and high bail, the Cosby administration hoped to accomplish two things. First, Cosby and his friends may have thought that the high bail would keep Zenger in jail and thus prevent continued publication of the *Weekly Journal*. Cosby also seemed intent on making an example of Zenger. The high bail would be a warning to anyone who might challenge the government. Zenger's wealthy friends might have bailed him out, but they refrained for three reasons. First, they feared that Cosby would order the arrest of others connected to Zenger and, by demanding high bail in all cases, financially destroy the opposition. Second, Zenger and his friends understood the propaganda value of keeping the relatively poor Zenger in jail because he could not pay an unfair bail. Cosby's enemies saw that keeping Zenger in jail would validate the charge that the governor was a tyrant. Finally, no one expected Zenger to be kept in jail very long. Under English law, Zenger could be held only until the end of the grand jury term, which would be in January. Thus, Zenger's martyrdom would be a relatively short two months. No one in New York expected that the grand jury would actually indict the printer.

The grand jury in fact failed to indict Zenger, but on the last day of the grand jury's term, Attorney General Bradley charged Zenger by an information. An information was usually reserved for a relatively minor crime. Today, for example, a charge of driving above the speed limit would be the equivalent of filing an information against the accused. The use of an information against Zenger smacked of tyranny. Cosby had short-circuited the legal system to guarantee the prosecution of a person who had offended the colony's leaders.

Although charged in January, Zenger was not arraigned until April. During the arraignment, Zenger's lawyers challenged the right of DeLancey to hear the case on the grounds that Morris had been illegally removed as chief justice, and thus DeLancey's appointment also violated the law. Zenger's lawyers argued that judges sat during "good behaviour," rather than at "the pleasure" of the executive, and therefore Cosby had no right to remove Morris simply because he did not like his decision. DeLancey responded by disbarring Zenger's lawyers, and replacing them with a pro-Cosby lawyer. Once again, the Cosby administration appeared to threaten liberty.

Before the trial began, Cosby's henchmen made one final attempt to insure Zenger's conviction. When the sheriff presented the list of potential jurors, he included a number of men who were not legally qualified to serve, including the governor's baker, shoemaker, tailor, candlemaker, and other tradesmen who enjoyed Cosby's patronage. Zenger's court-appointed lawyer, although allied with Cosby, nevertheless protested this fraud, and a jury of freeholders was ultimately chosen.

The case presented two issues for the court to decide. The first concerned who actually published the allegedly seditious newspaper. The second was whether the paper libelled the government. In legal terms, these were known as the "facts" of the case and the "law" of the case. Under precedents dating from the reign of James I, English judges reserved for themselves the right to determine the "law" in seditious libel cases. Thus, the only apparent role for the jury was to determine if Zenger had actually published the *New York Weekly Journal*. Since everyone in New York City knew that Zenger published the paper, the case seemed open and shut.

But, as we know, the case was not open and shut. When the trial finally began on August 4, 1735, Zenger had a new lawyer, Andrew Hamilton of Philadelphia. Hamilton was the best-known attorney in the colonies, and his presence must have surprised and disturbed the inexperienced Chief Justice DeLancey as well as Attorney General Bradley.

Hamilton began by admitting that Zenger had indeed published the newspapers in question, but, Hamilton argued, the supposed allegations against the governor were true, and thus Zenger could not be convicted. The information charged Zenger with publishing "a certain *false, malicious, seditious scandalous* libel." Hamilton asserted that the prosecution had to prove that Zenger's publication was "false." However, to relieve Bradley of that burden, Hamilton offered to prove that what Zenger published was true. Either approach would have put Cosby, and not Zenger, on trial. That is precisely what Hamilton wanted.

Chief Justice DeLancey refused to allow Hamilton to argue "truth as a defense." DeLancey took the traditional English common law position that truth was not a defense to a charge of seditious libel, because even a truthful statement could undermine the government.

Hamilton, however, urged the jury to act as "*honest and lawful men*" who knew what the truth was. Hamilton ignored the judge and appealed directly to the jury, who had lived under Cosby's rule. Hamilton told the jury of cases in English history where power had been usurped. He warned them that the liberty of the people rested in their hands. Hamilton argued that an English jury was always entitled to give a general verdict on both the law and the facts of a case. Chief Justice DeLancey, of course, told the jury to ignore Hamilton and to find Zenger guilty of the "facts of publication."

The jury ignored DeLancey, and acquitted Zenger. This was the first time in Anglo-American legal history that "truth" had been used successfully as a defense in a seditious libel case.

For many years, lawyers and scholars considered Zenger's case a great precedent for freedom of the press. Technically, it was not. Rather, it was the singular victory of one defendant and his brilliant lawyer over an incompetent governor, an inexperienced judge, and an untalented attorney general. The Zenger verdict did not change the law of seditious libel in America or England. The principles of the case—that truth should be a defense and that the jury should decide the entire case— were not adopted in either place until after the American Revolution.

However, in other ways, the case was a clear and valuable precedent. Zenger's narrative was first published in 1736. In 1770, a New Yorker reprinted the narrative during the failed attempt to convict the Revolutionary, Alexander McDougall, of seditious libel. In 1799, during the crisis of the Sedition Act, the Zenger narrative was again reprinted to remind Americans of the need for a free press.

During the ratification struggle of 1787–88, a few Antifederalists reminded Americans of the Zenger case, and what they could learn from it. In New York, "Cincinnatus" asked his readers to consider what would happen under the new Constitution if a "patriotic printer, like Peter Zenger, should incur the resentment of our new rulers, by publishing to the world the transactions which they wish to conceal." Without a guarantee of freedom of the press, "Cincinnatus" believed that a new Zenger would surely be convicted and "The freedom of the press, the sacred palladium of public liberty, would be pulled down." "Cincinnatus" was especially fearful that under Article III of the Constitution, the federal appellate courts might overrule a jury verdict of not guilty. Indeed, "Cincinnatus" was uncertain if under the Constitution a new Zenger would even be entitled to a jury trial. From "Cincinnatus" we learn that the Fifth and Sixth Amendments, as well as the First Amendment, were anticipated by the Zenger case.

Other New Yorkers, such as "Sydney" and "A Son of Liberty," commented on the need to protect a free press. "A Son of Liberty" declared that the failure to protect the press was "intended to give our new masters an opportunity to rivet our fetters the more effectually." Such language could easily have come from Zenger's paper.

New Yorkers were not the only ones who remembered Zenger. In Pennsylvania, "A Democratic Federalist" wrote that "the case of *John Peter Zenger* of New York, ought still to be present in our minds, to convince us how displeasing the liberty of the press is to men in high power." This writer might have had Judge DeLancey in mind when he wrote, "There is no knowing what corrupt and wicked judges may do in process of time, when they are not restrained by express laws."

The Zenger case is not, of course, the sole precedent for the Bill of Rights, or even the First Amendment. It is, however, the earliest American precedent for the notion that a free press was "the sacred palladium of public liberty." For that reason alone, it is important to our understanding of the Constitution and the Bill of Rights.

The Soul and the State: Religious Freedom in New York and the Origin of the First Amendment

PAUL FINKELMAN

State University of New York at Binghamton

On September 12, 1787, five days before the end of the Constitutional Convention, George Mason of Virginia and Elbridge Gerry of Massachusetts sought to remedy the major defect they saw in the proposed Constitution. Gerry moved, and Mason seconded, that a bill of rights be written. Mason noted that "with the aid of the state declarations, a bill might be prepared in a few hours." He might have added that this would be such a simple matter because a number of delegates, including Mason himself, had participated in writing a bill of rights in their own states. They could certainly have written one for the nation. Nevertheless, the Convention defeated this motion with all states voting no.[1]

This rejection of a bill of rights was due to many factors. One of them was the belief that such explicit protections were unnecessary, an argument based on the twin assumptions that the states were the main guarantors of liberty and that the national government under the Constitution lacked power to interfere with the basic rights and liberties of the people.

At the time of the Convention, most Americans looked to their state governments to protect their liberties. As Oliver Ellsworth of Connecticut had explained earlier in the Convention, he turned to the state governments "for the preservation of his rights."[2] Most of the Convention delegates believed that the Constitution was designed to create a stronger national government, not to interfere with the liberties of the people in the existing states. Early in the Convention, Pennsylvania's James Wilson had argued that one purpose of the states was "to preserve the rights of individuals." In opposing the motion by Gerry and Mason, Connecticut's Roger Sherman made much the same point, arguing that "the State Declarations of Rights are not repealed by this Constitution; and being in force are sufficient." He believed that the national legislature might "be safely trusted" not to interfere with the liberties of the people.[3] All the states present agreed with Sherman, and the motion for a bill of rights died.[4] The vote took place in spite of George Mason's proper observation that "The Laws of the U.S. are to be paramount to State Bills of Rights."[5]

The English Background of American Liberty: A Limited Heritage

In 1787, most of the states guaranteed many of the liberties and rights that would ultimately be protected by the Constitution and the Bill of Rights. During the Revolution, only nine states actually wrote a bill of rights, but "the other constitutions contained important provisions of this character."[6] A careful search of the early state constitutions and bills of rights reveals that virtually every clause of the federal Bill of Rights can be found in some earlier state document. Some of the clauses are ubiquitous. Protections of criminal due process, provisions for fair jury trials, and guarantees of habeas corpus are found in most of the early state constitutions. Almost every state protected freedom of the press, while only Pennsylvania and Vermont (the fourteenth state) protected freedom of speech.

Many of the provisions of the early state bills of rights and constitutions derived from an English legal heritage which began to develop in the thirteenth century. This English heritage includes Magna Carta (1215), the evolution of trial procedures under common law, and the Statute of Merton (1236), guaranteeing a right to an attorney in all civil and some criminal matters. As early as 1275, English law limited the power of sheriffs over prisoners, and by 1444 the statutes of the realm recognized the right to bail in most cases. The Petition of Right (1628), the English Bill of Rights (1689), and other statutes adopted during the tumultuous seventeenth century enhanced the rights of Englishmen. A common law right against self-incrimination also began to emerge during the seventeenth century.[7]

Despite these developments during the course of more than five hundred years, by the time of the American Revolution the rights of Englishmen were still quite limited. In England some forms of coerced self-incrimination existed and criminal due process was not fully developed. Anyone criticizing the government in print or with speech could be jailed. Treason remained a vaguely defined crime with barbaric penalties often attached to it. It was relatively easy to charge someone with treason but difficult to defend against such a charge. As the Americans found out during the period immediately preceding the Revolution, the English government claimed the right to conduct the most arbitrary searches, with general rather than specific warrants, to try colonists without juries in distant courts, and to strip the citizens' militias of their arms and ammunition.

Before 1775, the colonists claimed to want their "rights as Englishmen." In fact, by 1775 the colonists had already forged ahead to create rights for themselves that were unavailable to Englishmen. These rights were further augmented by the actual practice of the colonial and post-Revolutionary period. The law of seditious libel illustrates this. The technical law of seditious libel in America remained exactly the same as in England. Under that law, a jury was entitled to find only the facts of a case—whether the defendant actually published the allegedly libelous material. The judge alone decided whether the materials were actually libelous or not. The defendant was not allowed to argue that the offending articles were true and therefore not libelous. Such rules made it difficult for English printers to avoided libel convictions if they offended the government. While these rules technically applied to the American colonies, after the failed prosecution of John Peter Zenger in 1735, the common law of seditious libel was, for all practical purposes, a dead letter.[8] After declaring independence, Americans would specifically protect some of their newly developed rights, such as freedom of the press, in their state constitutions or through state legislation.

However, in one critical area—that of religious freedom and separation of church and state—most of the early states mirrored English practice. In England at the time of the American Revolution, religious toleration was limited; the church and state remained unseparated.[9] Twelve of the fourteen new states (counting Vermont) maintained some sort of religious test for officeholding at their founding.[10] The two exceptions were New York and Virginia.[11]

Equally important, at the founding, New York was the only state to abandon, through a constitutional provision, its previous establishment of an official church. Even Virginia, long remembered for its early strivings for religious freedom, was unable to abandon its establishment of the Anglican Church, which during the Revolution became the Protestant Episcopal Church.

Of all the state constitutions and bills of rights adopted between 1776 and 1784, only New York's came close to establishing complete religious freedom, by providing six of the seven key elements to religious freedom and separation of church and state. The New York Constitution of 1777 contained provisions to: 1) guarantee complete freedom of worship; 2) disestablish a previously established church; 3) absolutely prohibit any future establishment of an official church; 4) promise equal treatment to all religious faiths; 5) remove all religious tests for office holding; and 6) provide protection for the special needs of minority religions, such as exempting Quakers from oaths and military service. The constitution failed in only one aspect of religious freedom, by providing a slight religious test for naturalization, based on abjuring allegiance to all foreign leaders "in all matters, ecclesiastical as well as civil."

Despite this one lapse, only New York, of all the states of the new American Republic, was able to build on its past when it came to defining the relationship between religion and the government. To understand why this was so—and why the New York Constitution of 1777 was such a remarkable exception, pointing the way to a more tolerant future—it is necessary to examine the relationship between religion and the state in seventeenth-century Europe and America.

Religion and the State:
The Seventeenth Century Experience

Virtually all political leaders of the seventeenth century accepted the idea that religious diversity was dangerous to the stability of any government. Most people believed that in any kingdom a ruler and his or her subjects should have the same religion. This was based on the assumption that religious differences could create conflict within the country that might lead to civil war and anarchy. This was certainly true during the brutal wars of the sixteenth century. Thus, the Peace of Augsburg in 1555 ended years of religious wars in the Holy Roman Empire by establishing throughout most of the Empire the concept of *cuius regio, eius religio* (whose the region, his the religion), which allowed local rulers to decide the religion of their subjects. In 1648, European leaders reaffirmed this principle in the Treaty of Westphalia, which ended the Thirty Years' War.

Although England was not a party to either treaty, all English monarchs understood and agreed with the theory behind the treaties.

Indeed, this theory had a special meaning in England, where after the English Reformation the monarch was not merely the head of the nation, but also the head of the Church of England. Thus, to reject the Church of England was, in part, to deny the authority of the monarch. Queen Elizabeth declined to seek "windows into men's souls," and thus tolerated Puritans and other Protestants who wanted to further reform the Church of England; but she was less tolerant of Catholics who, from the official English perspective, took their orders from a foreign ruler, the pope.

By the end of the seventeenth century, England had come to understand the value of limited toleration of religious diversity. Dissenting Protestants, including Puritans, Separatists, Quakers, Presbyterians, and Baptists were tolerated, as long as their allegiance to the Crown remained firm. Under the same conditions, England allowed Jews and Catholics to practice their faith. But limited toleration did not mean religious equality. The Anglican Church remained the established church of the realm, and public office remained closed to anyone who was not a member of that church. Even this limited toleration at the end of the 1690s had not, of course, existed at the beginning of the century.

It is an axiom of American history that some of the earliest English settlers came to the New World in search of religious liberty. However, few colonists had the same notions of religious liberty that Americans accept today. The Separatists and Puritans who left England during most of the seventeenth century were partially or mostly motivated by a desire to be left alone to practice their religion. The Massachusetts Puritans sought religious liberty *for themselves*, but had little patience for those who did not agree with their Puritan theology. Most Americans know that nineteen convicted witches were hanged in Salem in 1692; few learn about the hanging of four Quakers between 1659 and 1661.[12] Statutes in Connecticut allowed similar punishments, but that colony limited its persecution of religious minorities to jail, fines, and banishment. Virginia began with the Anglican Church as *the* church in the colony. Even Maryland, noted as a haven for Roman Catholics, began with the Anglican Church established.[13] The non-English settlements were no different. New Netherland established the Dutch Reformed Church.

The failure to extend religious toleration to non-established faiths in the colonies during the first half of the seventeenth century was both religiously and politically motivated. The Puritans sought to create a godly community—a "City on the Hill"—and thus wanted no dissenters or non-believers amongst them. The colonial settlements, Puritan or Anglican, were precarious. They could not afford to allow religious disputes to distract the colonists. In this sense, the colonies mirrored Europe.

Religious Freedom and Revolutionary Constitution Making: The Importance and Irrelevance of Rhode Island

Over a century before Jefferson and Madison worked through the concept of separation of church and state, Roger Williams in Rhode Island offered a viable system of religious toleration. The theory Williams worked out was based on his belief that any state involvement with religion would corrupt the church. He argued that religious toleration hinged on three points: first, that all members of a society obey the civil officers; second, that no civil officer force anyone to attend religious services nor prevent anyone from attending their peaceful religious services; and third, that no one could disturb someone else's religious services.[14]

By the time of the Revolution, Rhode Island had a variety of Protestant churches, as well as Catholic and Jewish communities. The Rhode Island experience is clearly critical for the development of religious toleration as an intellectual concept.[15] However, for three reasons, the Rhode Island experience did not serve as a particularly useful constitutional precedent for the Revolutionary states or the drafters of the Bill of Rights.

First, by the time of the Revolution the "memory of Roger Williams [had] subsided to such an extent that no library catalogue published in the American colonies listed any of his works. . . . Not until 1773, when the Baptist apologist Isaac Backus rediscovered him, did Williams's thoughts resurface." Most importantly, perhaps, people not living in Rhode Island "showed a complete lack of familiarity with" the history of religious freedom there.[16]

Second, despite the tolerance for minority religions, and the explicit lack of an established church, neither the Rhode Island colony nor the new state was able to divorce itself fully from official religious prejudice. Thus, while all people were free to worship in Rhode Island, at the time of the Revolution only Protestants could vote or hold office.[17] Not until 1842 did Rhode Island give complete political equality to all people, regardless of religion. Jews, who flourished in the colony, did so as second-class citizens.[18] In Rhode Island, toleration did not lead to political equality.

Third, in the 1770s and 1780s, Rhode Island was both constitutionally backward and politically insignificant. The tiny state was geographically and politically isolated from the mainstream of American life. Rhode Island was one of two states (the other was Connecticut) which failed to write a constitution during the Revolutionary period. Thus, the state's long experience with toleration was not formalized or updated in the 1770s. Finally, Rhode Island sent no delegates to the

Constitutional Convention and initially refused to ratify the document. At the Philadelphia Convention, Rhode Island was often cited as an example of bad government. No one, it seems, listened to what happened in Rhode Island, or indeed, cared much about the place.

Religious Freedom and Revolutionary Constitution Making: The Primacy of New York

The history of New York is quite different from that of Rhode Island. Throughout most of its pre-Revolutionary history, New York had an established church—the Dutch Reformed Church until 1664 and the Anglican Church after 1693.[19] Nevertheless, in the era of constitution making, New York moved closer to complete separation of church and state and absolute free exercise of religion than any other new state. The roots of New York's remarkable stand on religious freedom are found in the state's colonial history.

In New York, religious toleration did not develop because of the genius of a single individual, as it had in Roger Williams's Rhode Island. Indeed, it did not even grow out of a philosophy of religious liberty. Rather, religious toleration grew out of the stark realities of colonial life.

Religious Diversity and Tolerance in New Netherland

In the early part of the seventeenth century, The Netherlands became the most tolerant nation in Europe. By the 1620s, Amsterdam's Jews, while officially second-class citizens, "enjoyed virtual freedom of religion in all essential respects." Despite the best efforts of the Dutch Reformed Church, "Roman Catholicism flourished in Amsterdam." By the 1630s "in practice the Roman Catholics had total religious freedom in Amsterdam" although "they could build no churches with towers in the public streets."[20]

This tolerance partially migrated to the New World along with the Dutch flag. From the beginning, officials of the Dutch West India Company realized the virtue of both a religious establishment and religious tolerance. In 1638, the company declared that religion in New Netherland should "be taught and practiced" according to the same "Confession and formalities of union" which were "publicly accepted" in Holland. This meant that the Dutch Reformed Church was the established church of the colony. However, the Dutch West India Company's leaders also declared that this directive should be implemented "without . . . it being inferred from this that any person shall hereby in any wise be constrained or aggrieved in his conscience."[21] This call for toleration was promulgated by company officials in Amsterdam, but, with a few exceptions, the leadership on the scene in New Amsterdam resisted and ignored their superiors in Amsterdam. The history of religion in New Netherland is one of constant conflict between the tolerance of the Heeren XIX,[22] who made up the governing body of the West India Company in Amsterdam, and the intolerance of the local leadership in New Amsterdam, especially under the administration of Peter Stuyvesant.

The Dutch religious and secular leaders in America believed that religious toleration was dangerous to the stability of any government. These Dutch Calvinists "interpreted a harmonious state to mean one in which the magistracy and church worked together to preserve doctrine and therefore civil unity. Conversely, they held that doctrinal diversity must necessarily lead to civil anarchy and disintegration of the state."[23]

These ideas were particularly suited to conditions in the New World. New Netherland was a weak and underdeveloped colony, precariously sandwiched between a French settlement to the north and strong English colonies to the east and south. "Because the colony was intended to be an efficient, disciplined trading center in a strange and unaccommodating wilderness, its leaders thought it essential to enforce existing social controls in a rigorous manner."[24] The rulers of New Netherland naturally established the Dutch Reformed Church.

Initially, the colonial officials were able to sustain religious homogeneity, but this goal could not be maintained. Refugees, including the religiously oppressed, were more likely to move to the New World than prosperous and contented Dutch citizens. The tolerance of The Netherlands also undermined the intolerance of New Netherland. Despite persecution by the local authorities, religious dissenters moved to the colony in the 1640s and 1650s. Their right to remain was usually upheld by the Heeren XIX, who often overruled the colony's governor on these matters. Once they were allowed to live in the colony, they quickly sought other privileges, including citizenship and the right of public religious observance. When denied the latter right, they either appealed to authorities in Holland or practiced in defiance of the law.

Religious minorities reached the colony in the 1640s, but not until the 1650s did their presence lead to political difficulties. In the 1640s the Dutch governor, Willem Kieft, allowed various New England dissidents to settle in the colony, offering them not only religious freedom, but also "the liberty to appoint their own magistrates" subject to the approval of the Dutch leadership. Among those settling in New Netherland was the radical Separatist, Anne Hutchinson, who moved to present-day Westchester County in 1642. These refugees from New England orthodoxy tended to live by themselves in small villages and communities. They did not threaten Dutch hegemony or Dutch Reformed orthodoxy, while at the same time they added much to the colony.[25] Thus, as early as 1640, officials in New Netherland accepted a small number of dissenters because they would help populate the large and mostly empty colony. The fact that these New Englanders were also Calvinists no doubt made the Dutch more tolerant of their presence. While not members of the Dutch Reformed Church, these English settlers were theologically similar and at the same time posed no threat to the colony's established orthodoxy.

The welcome that the English Separatists received did not extend to other non-conformists who sought refuge in New Netherland. In 1653, Peter Stuyvesant, the colony's governor, declared he "would rather relinquish his office than grant permission" to a group of Lutherans who wished to import their own minister from Holland and form their own church.[26] When a handful of Jews arrived a year later, Dominie Johannes Megapolensis, the clerical leader of the Dutch Reformed Church in the colony, sided with Stuyvesant in an attempt to expel them. Megapolensis clearly disliked Jews who, he believed, had "no other God than the unrighteous Mammon, and no other aim than to get possession of christian property." He thought Jews were "godless rascals" and hoped authorities in Holland would order their expulsion. Significantly, he did not make his case on either culturally based or religiously based anti-Semitism. Rather, he defended his position by arguing that if the Jews settled in the community it would be one more step on the road to ethnic and religious chaos. He noted "we have here Papists, Mennonites and Lutherans among the Dutch; also many Puritans or Independents, and many Atheists and various other servants of Baal among the English under this government, who conceal themselves under the name of Christians; it would create a still further confusion, if the obstinate and immovable Jews came to settle here."[27]

Stuyvesant and the Dutch Reformed clerics had mixed success in their attempts to control the growth of other religions. The Dutch West India Company ruled that the Jews were to be allowed "to sail to and trade in New Netherland and to live and remain there." However, neither "Lutheran pastors" nor "any other public worship" except that of the Dutch Reformed Church would be allowed in the colony.[28] Despite laws, fines, and decisions by authorities in the metropolis, religious minorities persisted in seeking the right to worship openly as they chose. The absorption of the Swedish settlement to the south and wars with native

Americans made any suppression of Lutherans unrealistic and impolitic. Ultimately, even the Reformed clergy discovered that "it was not feasible to eliminate the Lutherans because there were too many of them."[29] Meanwhile, Stuyvesant was once more reprimanded for his behavior toward Jews. Authorities in Amsterdam countermanded his refusal to allow them to purchase land and instead instructed the governor that the Jews should be allowed to buy land in a section of the city of "their own choice" so they might "exercise in all quietness their religion within their houses." Jews were furthermore allowed to "quietly and peacefully carry on their business." In the same letter Stuyvesant was admonished to treat the Lutherans "quietly and leniently" and to "let them have free religious exercises in their homes."[30]

In 1657, Stuyvesant refused permission to land to a boatload of Quakers. This was the beginning of the longest and most brutal religious suppression in the colony's history. Over the next six years, a number of Quakers were jailed, expelled, fined, placed at hard labor, and tortured for preaching in the colony. Non-Quakers were also jailed and fined for aiding or harboring Quakers.[31]

This persecution proved futile. Each new persecution seemed to strengthen the Quakers, especially in the English-speaking settlements on Long Island. The persecutions also stimulated some colonists to argue for religious toleration as a duty of Christian love. In the "Flushing Remonstrance" of 1658, thirty-one settlers, including the sheriff, called on Stuyvesant to rescind his orders levying heavy fines on anyone who harbored a known Quaker. The petitioners, who were mostly English, declared that "wee desire therefore in this case not to judge least wee be judged, neither to Condem, least wee bee Condemed, but rather let every man stand and fall on his own." They felt bound by God's law "to doe good unto all men," and thus, by Stuyvesant's decree, they were trapped between the law of God and that of man. Rather than persecute the Quakers, they would allow them freedom, on the theory that "if God justify who can Condem, and if God Condem there is none can justifye."[32] Stuyvesant not only rejected the petition, but arrested the leading petitioners for sedition.

Ultimately, officials in Holland ended the persecutions. The directors of the Dutch West India Company told Stuyvesant that they too wished no Quakers had moved into the colony. But once in the colony, the directors asserted "we doubt very much, whether we can proceed against them rigorously without diminishing the population and stopping immigration, which must be favored at a so tender stage of the country's existence."[33] In other words, the colony could not grow and prosper, and the investors with it, without tolerance. The directors told

the governor to "shut your eyes" to the Quakers, and "not force people's consciences, but allow every one to have his own belief, as long
as he behaves quietly and legally, gives no offence to his neighbors, and
does not oppose the government." The directors pointed out that this
had been the practice in old Amsterdam "and consequently" the city
had "often had a considerable influx of people." New Amsterdam too
"would be benefitted by" this practice.[34]

By the end of the Dutch period, persons of almost any religious
faith were able to live in the colony. Catholics, Jews, and Lutherans,
among others, were allowed to hold their "superstitious" religious services—as the Dutch authorities called them—in private homes. The reason
for this was not the desire to protect religion from government interference that motivated Roger Williams of Rhode Island. This toleration was also not a function of Christian charity, love, or fear of God,
although some in the colony thought it should be, nor was toleration
the result of an Enlightenment philosophy which denied any role for
the government in the saving of souls.

Toleration in New Netherland had almost no theory nor philosophy
behind it. It evolved out of the need to populate a frontier and encourage
trade and commerce. Put simply, the Dutch West India Company put
worldly success above theology. For Peter Stuyvesant "religion was an
important instrument of social control," and the failure to exercise such
control was "an invitation to an anarchy of contesting beliefs."[35]
However, his superiors in Amsterdam understood that too much control of religion might lead to tyranny and would certainly discourage
settlement. Jews, Quakers, Catholics, and others were allowed to settle
and trade in the colony because they could make the colony grow and
prosper. This was the message the Dutch officials conveyed to Stuyvesant whenever he wanted to suppress religious minorities. Stuyvesant
and other overly devout colonial officials were simply told to "shut your
eyes" to persons of other religions, and let everyone in the colony go
about their business. Indeed, business, not religion, was the purpose
of the colony. Toleration stimulated growth and trade. That was reason
enough to allow persons of any faith to practice discreetly their religion
and openly ply their trades.[36]

English Rule and the Continuation of Tolerance

In 1664, an English fleet seized New Amsterdam and, with it, the
entire Dutch empire on the mainland of North America. New Netherland
was renamed New York, after the colony's new proprietor, James, Duke

of York. The English of the 1660s differed little from the rest of Europe in their support for the old concept of *cuius regio, eius religio*—"whose the region, his the religion." Nevertheless, the very fact that England had taken over a Dutch colony meant that a certain amount of religious toleration was necessary because the overwhelming majority of the residents of the colony were not members of the Church of England.

Indeed, the colony that James claimed was probably the most polyglot in the New World. A religious census at the time would have found members of the Dutch Reformed Church, Lutherans from Holland, Germany, and Sweden; French Calvinists; Presbyterians from the British Isles; Puritans, Separatists, Baptists, and Quakers from England, Germany and elsewhere; a variety of other Protestant sects; and small numbers of Jews and Catholics. The only conspicuous absence was anyone who claimed membership in the Church of England.

Most of the residents of this new English colony were members of the Dutch Reformed Church. No official in the "Duke's Colony" ever contemplated expelling them or forcing them to accept the Church of England. This would have been impossible and impractical. Instead, the duke and his deputies adopted an unusually tolerant policy on religious matters. The Articles of Capitulation, which the Dutch were compelled to sign, provided that the "Dutch here shall enjoy the liberty of their consciences in Divine Worship and church discipline."[37] What the duke gave to the Dutch he also had to give to the Protestant dissenters living on Long Island. Initially, all towns in the colony were allowed to establish whatever church they wished. Minority faiths were granted the right to conduct meetings openly. In 1666, Lutherans gained the right, long denied under the Dutch, to build their own churches. In 1674, the duke of York ordered his new governor, Edmund Andros, to "permitt all persons of what Religion soever, quietly to inhabitt wthin ye precincts of yor jurisdiccon, wthout giveing ym any disturbance or disquiet whatsoever, for or by reasons of their differring opinions in matter of Religion."[38] In 1683, the New York Assembly partially codified this tolerance in the colony's Charter of Liberties and Privileges, which declared:

> Noe person or persons which professe ffaith in God by Jesus Christ Shall at any time be any wayes molested punished disquieted or called in Question for any Difference in opinion or Matter of Religious Concernemnt . . . But that all and Every such person or persons may . . . at all times freely have and fully enjoy his or their Judgments or Consciencyes in matters of Religion throughout all the province.[39]

This charter did not separate church and state, but explicitly provided for government support for all Christian churches. John W. Pratt, in his study of religion in New York asserts that the Charter of Liberties "amounted to a full grant of religious freedom to Christians."[40] However, even this understates the reality in New York, because in 1682 the colony's Jews were allowed to have their own house of worship. While not given access to tax monies to support their teachers and clergymen, the Jews nevertheless had complete freedom of public worship, something the Dutch had denied them.[41]

Even without statutes and explicit protections of religion, no one seems to have been turned away from the colony for their religious beliefs. New York was already a commercial entrepôt and something of a melting pot. In 1678, Governor Edmund Andros reported to his superiors in London that he could find "Noe account" of "childrens births or chistenings" because ministers had kept few records. Further complicating his attempts to take a complete census, Andros noted: "There are Religions of all sorts, one Church of England, severall Presbiterians and Independents, Quakers and Anabaptists, of serverall sects, some Jews. . . ." A decade later Andros's successor, Governor Thomas Dongan, reported: "Here bee not many of the Church of England; [a] few Roman Catholicks; abundance of Quakers preachers men and women especially; Singing Quakers, Ranting Quakers; Sabbatarians; Antisabbatarians; Some Anabaptists; some Independents; some Jews; in short of all opinions there are some, and the most part none at all."[42]

In the 1690s, New York altered its virtually unparalleled toleration in four important ways. In the wake of the Glorious Revolution, which overthrew the crypto-Catholic King James II in England and forced Governor Andros to leave the colonies, the New York Assembly adopted a new declaration of the "Rights and Privileges of their Majesties Subjects inhabiting within their Province of New York." The provision on religion declared that all persons could "freely meet" and "worshipp according to their respective perswasions without being hindered or molested." This, in effect, extended full toleration to Jews and any other non-Christians in the colony. However, this clause was immediately modified by a proviso, declaring that it did not apply to "any persons of the Romish Religion."[43] In another change from the early Charter of Liberties, the 1691 document did not provide for the support of ministers of all Christian faiths, "suggesting that the support arrangements in the Duke's Laws and other similar acts were no longer to be recognized."[44] This set the stage for the final change in New York law, an act to establish the Church of England as the colony's official church.

In 1693, the colonial assembly established the Church of England in the four key counties of Queens, Richmond, Westchester, and New York (Manhattan). At the time, the entire colony had only one Anglican clergyman—the chaplain at the fort in New York City. New York was an Anglican colony, but the overwhelming majority of the people were not of that religion. Indeed, it was an English colony, but the majority of the population was not of English descent.

Over the next eighty years, royal officials tried, with varying degrees of effort and success, to expand the power and influence of the Church of England. In the 1690s, Governor Benjamin Fletcher began the process of establishing the Church of England. In addition to securing the 1693 law establishing the Church of England as the colony's official religion, by his own patent he created Trinity Church, making it the established church for New York City. From 1702 until 1708, Edward Hyde, Lord Cornbury, vigilantly strove to make the Church of England the colony's established church in fact as well as in law. His tenure as governor was marked by constant tension over his ruthless and impolitic attempts to impose the Church of England on a non-Anglican population. He attempted to appoint an Anglican clergyman to a vacant Dutch Reformed pulpit in Ulster County, ordered the arrest of Presbyterian clergymen in New York City, and imposed Anglican clergymen on dissenting churches in Queens. "In seven short years this one man had managed to stir up great religious controversy in New York, to fortify dissenting opposition to the Anglican establishment, and to strengthen colonists' attachment to their freedom of conscience and of worship."[45]

Cornbury's departure in 1708 temporarily ended most church-state conflicts in the colony. For most of the next forty years, England focused little attention on the American colonies. "Everyone supposed that the purpose of supporting colonies was to benefit the mother country in accordance with the vague precepts of mercantilist economic theory."[46] During this period, the English discovered what the leaders of the Dutch West India Company had known: religious diversity and tolerance were more likely to lead to economic success than orthodoxy and repression. Sir Robert Walpole's motto, "let sleeping dogs be,"[47] apparently applied to religion in the New York colony. With the exception of outbreaks of anti-Catholic hysteria,[48] New York continued its remarkable tolerance for religious diversity until the late 1750s.

In the 1740s and 1750s, America's first important religious revival, the Great Awakening, and the creation of King's College (later to be renamed Columbia University), revived interfaith hostilities and questions of church and state. In the 1750s, William Livingston (later the first governor of the State of New York) and others attempted to establish King's College as a non-sectarian state-supported institution. While initially somewhat successful, they eventually lost this struggle, and the college became an Anglican institution with financial support from the colonial government. Dissenters in the colony viewed this Anglican triumph as more "evidence of a 'lust for dominion' which would ultimately lead to the suppression of all dissenting sects and a full Anglican church establishment" in New York.[49]

Disestablishment and Religious Freedom in Revolutionary New York

By the beginning of the Revolution, New Yorkers had a mixed heritage of religious liberty to contemplate. Since the 1650s, the colony had had both enormous diversity and toleration. The Dutch Reformed establishment had failed to preserve theological homogeneity in the colony while the establishment of the Church of England had only intensified opinion in favor of tolerance and against orthodoxy. The struggle over King's College in the 1750s underscored the hostility to an Anglican establishment in polyglot New York. Immediately before the Revolution, fear of the imminent appointment of an Anglican bishop for the colonies helped exacerbate tensions between the colonies and Great Britain. However, in the provincial election of 1769, appeals to religious bigotry by the moderate whigs backfired, and helped elect more radical whigs to the colonial legislature.[50] Thus, well before revolutionaries like Jefferson and Paine developed theories of religious liberty based on republican ideology, "New Yorkers had learned in the crucible of day-to-day living in a multifarious society the value of a neutral state which permitted creeds to compete for the spiritual affection of the citizenry."[51]

Given this background, it is not surprising that New York State's first constitution guaranteed religious freedom. Nevertheless, the 1777 constitution is significant for its remarkable degree of religious freedom. More than any other revolutionary state constitution, New York's sought to guarantee full religious freedom. In anticipation of the federal Bill of Rights, the New York constitution recognized the importance of both the free exercise of religion and the separation of church and state.

The 1777 document did not create religious freedom with a few short clauses, as would the federal Constitution and Bill of Rights.[52] Rather, New York's constitution dealt with religion in a variety of elaborate articles. Taken together they created the most tolerant constitutional order in the new nation. On the question of religious freedom, New York took the lead among the new states.

Freedom of Worship

New York's new constitution was not alone in guaranteeing freedom of worship. Most of the states recognized this as necessary in a republican society. This was true even where states maintained established churches. However, many of these early declarations of religious liberty were internally inconsistent in their definition of religious freedom. Maryland, for example, asserted that it was "the duty of every man to worship God in such manner as he thinks most acceptable to him" but in the very next sentence, limited the "protection" of "religious liberty" to "persons, professing the Christian religion." New Hampshire's constitution was similarly confused. The Granite State's bill of rights declared that no one should be "hurt, molested, or restrained in his persons, liberty, or estate for worshipping God, in the manner and season most agreeable to the dictates of his own conscience, or for his religious profession, sentiments or persuasion." However, the next article asserted that "every denomination of christians demeaning themselves quietly, and as good subjects of the state, shall be equally under the protection of the law." Massachusetts had a similar clause, protecting "every denomination of christians. . . ."[53]

New York was not unique in granting freedom of religious practice to all persons.[54] However, the state did set a standard with the detailed explanation it offered for toleration of religious observance. The 1777 constitution declared:

> And whereas we are required, by the benevolent principles of rational liberty, not only to expel civil tyranny, but also to guard against that spiritual oppression and intolerance wherewith the bigotry and ambition of weak and wicked priests and princes have scourged mankind, this convention doth further, in the name and by the authority of the good people of this State, ordain, determine, and declare, that the free exercise and enjoyment of religious profession and worship, without discrimination or preference, shall forever hereafter be allowed, within this State, to all mankind; Provided, that the liberty of conscience, hereby granted, shall not be so construed as to excuse acts of licentiousness, or justify practices inconsistent with the peace or safety of this State.[55]

From the perspective of the twentieth century, it is easy to see that the qualifications at the end of this clause were subject to abuse. One person's religious obligation could easily be seen as "licentious" by the larger community. This is certainly something the followers of Joseph Smith discovered in the 1830s, as they went from New York, to Ohio, to Missouri, to Illinois, and finally to the northern fringes of the Mexican Empire looking for a place where they could follow the dictates of their faith, which included an obligation to practice polygamy. However, from the perspective of the Revolution, this clause was remarkable for three reasons. First, it guaranteed unrestricted freedom to all religions, at a time when many other states were often only willing to promise such freedom to either fellow Protestants or fellow Christians. Second, this freedom was not mere toleration or the sufferance of religious minorities. It was not a gift or an indulgence from the majority to the minority. It was the result of neither *noblesse oblige* nor Christian charity. The clause did not argue for religious toleration as something good Christians should give to others. Rather, the New York constitution expressed the concept of religious liberty as something central to a republican society. The clause condemns religious "bigotry" in an age when many devout persons saw nothing wrong with discrimination against their theological rivals. Finally, the clause acknowledges in frank terms the dangers of religious orthodoxy to a free society and the past manipulation of religion for political purposes by "weak and wicked priests and princes" who "have scourged mankind."[56]

Disestablishment

Given the religious heterogeneity of the new state, it is perhaps not surprising that Revolutionary New York not only disestablished the Anglican Church, but prohibited any future establishment of any church.[57] Surprisingly, no other state adopted a similar clause in the first constitutions adopted in the Revolutionary era. New York had the only state constitution to disestablish unequivocally a previously established church, prohibit any future establishment, and end state support for specific churches. Even Virginia, famous for adopting the nation's first bill of rights, did not disestablish the Anglican Church until 1786, ten years after that state's first constitution.[58] During the Revolution, Virginia, Massachusetts, New Hampshire, and Connecticut failed to disestablish their churches. States which did not have an established church before the Revolution, of course, did not establish them afterwards.

On the question of establishment, the New York constitution might be contrasted with that of South Carolina. The Palmetto State's constitution guaranteed that all "religious societies" which "acknowledge that there is one God and a future state of rewards and punishments'' would be "freely tolerated" in their public worship. However, in the next sentence the constitution also declared that "The Christian Protestant religion shall be deemed, and is hereby constituted and declared to be, the established church of this State."[59] Catholics and Jews were apparently free to live and worship in South Carolina, but they might be denied certain privileges and rights.

The Special Case of Quakers and Pacifists

Quakers and members of other pietistic faiths, including Mennonites and Dunkers, posed three special problems for the framers of eighteenth-century constitutions. The first was rooted in an historical prejudice against members of these groups because of their anti-authoritarian and anti-government beliefs. The second stemmed from the pacifism of adherents to these faiths. The third resulted from their refusal to swear to an oath on grounds that this was blasphemous.

In the seventeenth century, Quakers were notorious for their opposition to most forms of political authority. With little exaggeration, one historian has argued that "As Bolsheviks were feared after the Russian Revolution of the twentieth century, so the very thought of Quakers frightened people of the seventeenth."[60]

The Society of Friends was founded by George Fox in 1652. The religion grew out of Puritanism and is an extreme example of "the relentless movement of the Puritan-Reformed impulse away from the hierarchical, sacramental, and objective Christianity of the Middle Ages toward various radical extremes in which intensely individualistic and spiritual motifs become predominant." Quaker teachings "undermined the establishment by minimizing the liturgical and teaching function of an ordained ministry, abandoning the idea of objective sacraments, and inspiring conduct which was attributed to the promptings of an inner voice. Most ominous of all to the authorities was the phenomenal missionary zeal which flowed from the Quaker conviction of the universality of the Holy Spirit's work."[61] The Friends became known as the "Quakers" because of their shaking or "quaking" while praying and giving sermons.

The reaction of Dutch authorities to their arrival in New Amsterdam illustrates the overwhelming hostility they faced in the early colonies. The description by two Dutch Reformed ministers of the arrival of a shipload of Quakers in New Amsterdam illustrates the consternation they could cause to government officials. In early August 1657, a ship "having no flag" came into the harbor. This ship "fired no salute before the fort, as is usual with ships on their arrival." People in the colony "could not decide whether she was Dutch, French, or English." When a government official boarded the ship, those on board "tendered him no honor or respect." When the ship's master came before the governor of the colony "he rendered him no respect, but stood still with his hat firm on his head, as if a goat." The ship was allowed to remain in the harbor for only a night. The Dutch ministers believed the ship then went to Rhode Island "for that is the receptacle of all sorts of riff-raff people, and is nothing else than the sewer, of New England." Since "all the cranks of New England" had moved there, the Dutch assumed these Quakers would do the same. The ministers regretted that two Quaker women somehow managed to stay behind, and "as soon as the ship had fairly departed, these began to quake and go into a frenzy, and cry out loudly in the middle of the street, that men should repent, for the day of the judgment was at hand." The two women were soon jailed. Other Quakers coming to New Netherland were expelled, jailed, and tortured.[62]

Other colonies were equally intolerant of members of the Society of Friends. Connecticut expelled many Quakers. In 1656, Massachusetts prohibited any ship from bringing Quakers to the colony. Quakers entering the colony were jailed, whipped, fined, and expelled. The Bay Colony eventually hanged four Quakers who returned after being expelled.[63]

New Amsterdam was one of the first places to allow Quaker settlement. However, by 1700 most of the colonies, including Massachusetts, allowed Quaker settlement and religious observance. Meanwhile the Quakers had abandoned their missionary zeal, their "quaking," and their anti-authoritarian behavior. Even though they were no longer disruptive, Quakers were not content unless they could be exempted from church taxes, military service, and swearing oaths. In 1724, the English government intervened on behalf of the Quakers to exempt them from ecclesiastical taxes in Massachusetts.[64] This ruling naturally applied to other colonies.

The questions of military service and oaths were more complicated. Before the Revolution, Quakers were often allowed to affirm their support of the government rather than being forced to swear an oath of allegiance. During the Revolutionary War, this became somewhat more problematic. The Revolution required that citizens accept the new government, and agree to support it. Many Quakers had, in fact, refused to support even the non-military aspects of the Revolution; more than a few openly supported King George III. Yet, whether loyal to the king or the Revolution, they, along with Mennonites, Dunkers, and others, refused to take an oath of allegiance to anyone. Similarly, members of these groups were pacifists and refused to serve in the army. These groups thus raised special problems for the Revolutionary constitution makers.

Pennsylvania, Vermont, New Hampshire, and New York specifically exempted Quakers from both military service and taking oaths. In addition to these states, Massachusetts, Maryland, New Jersey, South Carolina, and Georgia[65] had provisions exempting Quakers from some oaths.[66] These states did not declare that Quakers could not claim conscientious objection from military service. However, they did not guarantee such protection. The text of some of these constitutions indicates that the Revolutionary constitution makers may have specifically rejected the concept of pacifism.

The Maryland constitution, for example, included an elaborate clause exempting "the people called Quakers, those called Dunkers, and those called Menonists" from taking oaths in court cases. Instead they were allowed to "affirm" they would tell the truth.[67] Officeholders, however, were required to swear an oath, which precluded Quakers and others opposed to oaths from taking office. Officeholders were also required to swear they were Christians, thus preventing Jews from holding office.[68] In addition to denying Quakers, other non-jurors, and Jews the right to hold office, the constitution also failed to provide any exemption for the pacifism of these groups. On the contrary, the same Declaration of Rights that recognized their right not to take an oath asserted that the "doctrine of non-resistance" was "absurd, slavish, and Destructive of the good and happiness of mankind."[69] The Maryland legislature did exempt pacifists from serving during the war, and after 1776 there were "few instances where Quakers were refused benefit of laws regarding pacifism."[70] However, Maryland was unwilling to elevate this exception to a basic constitutional right.

The failure of a number of states to exempt Quakers from all oaths and the rejection of military exemptions for Quakers by most states may illustrate the limited notions of religious toleration common in most states. However, these constitutional provisions, and the lack of them, also suggest that hostility to Quakers, present since the colonial period, had not entirely disappeared. In addition, many Quakers were, in fact, Loyalists, and fervent Patriots may have felt it necessary to put all Quakers to the test of swearing their loyalty to the cause, even if such an oath violated their religion.

Even where states attempted to accommodate the Quakers, the results were often mixed. The contrast between Maryland and New York is striking. Both understood the three special needs of Quakers: to be allowed to affirm rather than swear when being called as a witness; to be allowed to affirm rather than swear when taking office or when proving their loyalty; and to be exempt from military service. By accommodating only the first of these, and explicitly rejecting the other two, Maryland seemed to be saying that Quakers were not acceptable as officeholders in the kind of republic Maryland wanted to create. New York took the opposite position, opening its offices to all, while protecting the special needs of some.

Religion and Political Rights

Maryland's use of an oath to discourage or prevent Quaker officeholding was only one of many provisions found in the state constitutions which created political discrimination based on religion. Of the twelve[71] states which wrote constitutions between 1776 and 1784, only two, Virginia and New York, had no explicit religious test for officeholding. The remaining ten states had a variety of clauses which limited the political rights of members of minority religions.

Seven[72] state constitutions—those of New Jersey, North Carolina, Georgia, Vermont, South Carolina, Massachusetts,[73] and New Hampshire—limited officeholding to Protestants.[74] Two constitutions, those of Pennsylvania and Maryland, limited officeholding to Christians. Delaware, in a unique clause, limited officeholding to trinitarians. Thus, of the twelve states adopting constitutions, ten barred Jews from holding office, seven prevented Catholics from holding office, and one, Delaware, prohibited Unitarians, as well as Jews, from holding office. In addition, in Maryland, Georgia, South Carolina, North Carolina, and New Hampshire, Quakers, Mennonites, and members of a variety of other non-juror pietistic religions could not hold office even though they were Protestant Christians.

The two state constitutions which did not contain religious tests for officeholding treated the problem quite differently.[75] Virginia's 1776 constitution did not set out any qualifications for public office. Thus, the document made no provisions for religion in officeholding. The only mention of religion in the document was in Article 16 of the Virginia Declaration of Rights. That article is curious. It asserts that "all men are equally entitled to the free exercise of religion according to the dictates of conscience." This appears to be an unequivocal free exercise clause. However, in the next line, the clause declares "that it is the mutual duty of all to practise Christian forbearance, love, and charity towards each other."[76] It is not clear if this clause was designed to exclude non-Christians from the "free exercise of religion."[77]

Even if Virginia's Article 16 was meant to include all people, of all religions, the Virginia constitution did not go any further in establishing religious freedom. The document did not disestablish the Anglican Church, which remained the established church of the state for another decade. Nor did it prohibit public funding of religion, which continued. It contained no special oath provisions to accommodate Quakers and other nonjurors nor did it exempt pacifists from military service. Finally, while not containing any religious tests for officeholding, it did not ban them, either.

The New York constitution did not explicitly prohibit religious tests for officeholding. The document did, however, make it clear that religion was not a basis for political rights. The constitution also set up a complete separation of church and state, and provided exemptions for nonjurors and pacifists. The tenor of the New York constitution was apparent to all.

With two exceptions, the New York Constitution of 1777 created absolute religious freedom in the state. The first, and perhaps less important, was a clause which prohibited "ministers of the Gospel, or priests of any denominations whatsoever" from holding any civilian or military office in the state. Five other states, Virginia, Delaware, Maryland, North Carolina, and South Carolina, had similar provisions in their constitutions. These provisions were designed to insure a separation of church and state. However misguided they might appear today, these provisions were adopted because people thought they would preserve religious liberty.

Less enlightened was the last provision in the New York constitution, concerning the naturalization of aliens. This clause required that aliens "born in parts beyond the Sea," seeking citizenship in the state "abjure and renounce all allegiance and subjection to all and every foreign king, prince, potentate, and State in all matters, ecclesiastical as well as civil."[78] This clause meant that English-born Anglicans moving to New York would have to reject the authority of the king as the head of their church. During a revolution against the king, such a clause made great sense. However, this does not appear to have been the main thrust of the provision. Rather, the key word in the provision is "potentate," which referred to the pope. Thus, to become a citizen, a foreign-born Catholic would have had to reject allegiance to the pope.

Proposed by John Jay, who was fiercely anti-Catholic, this clause was designed to prevent the naturalization of European-born Catholics. Jay apparently was not fearful that native-born Catholics would be influenced by the pope, or he may have realized that there was no chance of disenfranchising native-born Americans. But, there was a fear of papal influence on Catholics from overseas, and the convention sought to act on these fears. Jay and other draftsmen of the 1777 constitution also thought this oath would reduce the likelihood that "other forms of Old World reaction" would "subvert the new state."[79]

This clause was never enforced, and had no effect on Catholic immigration into New York after 1777. Nevertheless, the clause does indicate that even the most enlightened constitutional draftsmen of Revolutionary America were not capable of fully divorcing themselves from the prejudices and fears of their age.

Conclusions

Stephen Botein has argued that in the founding period "there was near consensus in America for all religions, and against assistance to religious organizations if such assistance discriminated against any Protestant."[80] This statement is only partially true. There was a complete consensus on toleration for mainstream Protestants, with less agreement on the rights of Quakers, Mennonites, Unitarians, as well as Catholics, Jews, and other non-Protestants. In the age of a political revolution, we cannot discount the religiously based political discrimination found in every state constitution but Virginia's and New York's. Nor can we ignore the persistence of established churches, in more than half the new states, including Virginia.

The New York Constitution of 1777 pointed the way for the rest of the nation. When delegates from twelve of the new states met in Philadelphia in 1787, they dealt with religion in only one clause of the new national constitution: they borrowed from New York's constitution by prohibiting any religious test for public office. When the Bill of Rights was later added to the federal Constitution, it incorporated the concept of separation of church and state which had first appeared in New York's Constitution of 1777.

NOTES:

[1] Max Farrand, *Records of the Federal Convention of 1787*, 4 vols. (rev. ed., New Haven: Yale University Press, 1987) 2:587–588; Robert A. Rutland, *Birth of The Bill of Rights* (Chapel Hill: University of North Carolina Press, 1955), 107.

[2] Farrand, *Records*, 1:492.

[3] Farrand, *Records*, 1:354 and 2:588.

⁴Two days later, Sherman again argued against specific protections for liberty on the ground that under a government of limited powers they were unnecessary. He opposed a guarantee of a free press because "The power of Congress does not extend to the Press." Four states were not so sure, but the remaining seven delegations sided with Sherman, and the motion that "the liberty of the Press should be inviolably observed" was defeated. Farrand, *Records*, 2:618. During the ratification struggle, Federalists would make much the same point. In New York, Alexander Hamilton would argue: "Why declare that things shall not be done which there is no power to do? Why, for instance, should it be said that the liberty of the press shall not be restrained, when no power is given by which restrictions may be imposed?" Hamilton, *The Federalist No. 84.*

⁵Farrand, *Records*, 2:588.

⁶William Clarence Webster, "Comparative Study of the State Constitutions of the American Revolution," *Annals of the American Academy of Political and Social Science* 9 (May 1897): 69; Bernard Schwartz, *The Roots of the Bill of Rights*, 5 vols. (New York: Chelsea House, 1980), 2:289. The states with a bill of rights in their constitutions were Virginia, Delaware, Pennsylvania, Maryland, North Carolina, Massachusetts, New Hampshire, and the fourteenth state, Vermont. Connecticut rewrote its colonial charter rather than adopt a new constitution, but in 1776 did adopt a Declaration of Rights. New Jersey, New York, South Carolina, and Georgia did not have a separate bill of rights, but did provide the substance of a bill of rights in their constitutions. Rhode Island retained its colonial charter with some minor modifications, and did *not* adopt a declaration of rights.

⁷Leonard W. Levy, *The Origins of the Fifth Amendment* (New York: Oxford University Press, 1969).

⁸Paul Finkelman, "The Zenger Case: Prototype of a Political Trial," in Michal R. Belknap, *American Political Trials* (Westport: Greenwood Press, 1981), 21–42.

⁹Stephen Botein, "Religious Dimensions of the Early American State," in Richard Beeman, *et al.*, eds., *Beyond Confederation: Origins of the Constitution and American National Identity* (Chapel Hill: University of North Carolina Press, 1987), 318. In 1787, at the time the Convention was meeting in Philadelphia, the English parliament was considering, and rejecting, a bill which would have allowed non-Anglicans to hold public office. In 1791, the same year America adopted the Bill of Rights, Britain imposed a government on the Canadian provinces which established the Anglican church and set aside one-seventh of all land grants for the support of the Anglican clergy. *Ibid.*

¹⁰Rhode Island and Connecticut did not write new constitutions, but continued to maintain religious tests for officeholding.

¹¹Virginia appears to have had no formal religious test for voting or officeholding (with the exception of vestrymen) during the eighteenth century. Although Virginia probably acted in violation of the English law, dissenting Protestants and Catholics both voted and held office there during the seventeenth and eighteenth centuries. An act of 1769 regulating elections contained no religious qualification, and specifically exempted Quakers from having to swear an oath. "An Act for Regulating the election of Burgesses, for declaring their privileges and allowances, and for fixing the rights of electors." Act of November, 1769, *The Statutes at Large; Being a Collection of All the Laws of Virginia* (W.W. Hening, ed., 1821), 8:309–10. During the Revolution, Virginia adopted legislation which made any enfranchised citizen eligible for officeholding. "An Ordinance for regulating the election of delegates . . . ." Act of July, 1775, *Statutes at Large of Virginia* (Hening, ed.), 9:54. The Virginia Declaration of Rights of 1776 is silent on the question of religious tests for officeholding and separation of church and state. Throughout the eighteenth century, Virginia tolerated Protestant dissenters and Catholics, if for no other reason than "the Lords of Trade clearly indicated that religious toleration was a needed accessory to mercantilism." Robert E. and B. Katherine Brown, *Virginia, 1705-1786: Democracy or Aristocracy?* (East Lansing, MI: Michigan State University Press, 1964), 251. However, even on the eve of the Revolution, Virginia authorities prosecuted and jailed dissenting ministers. In 1775 the Virginia legislature failed to pass a bill "exempting his Majesty's Prot-

estant dissenters from the Penalties of certain Laws." Anson Phelps Stokes, *Church and State in the United States*, 2 vols. (New York: Harper Brothers, 1950), 1:370.

[12]Sydney E. Ahlstrom, *A Religious History of the American People* (New Haven: Yale University Press, 1972), 178.

[13]The Maryland charter required that all churches in the colony "be dedicated and consecrated according to the Ecclesiastical Laws of our Kingdom of England." The Charter of Maryland, 1632, Section IV, in Francis N. Thorpe, *The Federal and State Constitutions*, 7 vols. (Washington, D.C.: Government Printing Office, 1909), 3:1678-79.

[14]The best statement of this theory is in Roger Williams to the Town of Providence, January, 1655, reprinted in Edmund Morgan, ed., *Puritan Political Ideas* (Indianapolis: Bobbs-Merrill, 1965), 222-23.

[15]See Edmund Morgan, *Roger Williams: The Church and the State* (New York: W.W. Norton, 1967).

[16]Thomas J. Curry, *The First Freedoms: Church and State in America to the Passage of the First Amendment* (New York: Oxford University Press, 1986), 91.

[17]Curry, *The First Freedoms*, 162-63.

[18]Morton Borden, *Jews, Turks and Infidels* (Chapel Hill: University of North Carolina Press, 1984), 13; Jacob R. Marcus, *The Colonial American Jew, 1492-1776* (Detroit: Wayne State University Press, 1970), 1:314-20, 427-38.

[19]The establishment of the Church of England was, in one expert's words "a strange piece of legislation." John Webb Pratt, *Religion, Politics, and Diversity: The Church-State Theme in New York History* (Ithaca: Cornell University Press, 1967), 40-41. The law did not use the term Church of England, but instead called for public support for "good sufficient Protestant" ministers. Under English law at the time, however, this could only have meant the support of ministers of the Church of England. The law also only applied to the counties of New York, Richmond, Queens, and Westchester. Despite the circumlocution of the statute, courts in the eighteenth century held that the Anglican church was indeed the established church in these counties, and dissenters were forced to pay the salaries of Anglican ministers. *Ibid*, 61-62.

[20]Smith, *Religion and Trade in New Amsterdam*, 98, 103.

[21]This directive is quoted in Henri and Barbara Van Der Zee, *A Sweet and Alien Land: The Story of Dutch New York* (New York: Viking Press, 1978), 91-282.

[22]Literally the "Nineteen Lords Directors."

[23]George L. Smith, *Religion and Trade in New Netherlands* (Ithaca: Cornell University Press, 1973), 64.

[24]John Webb Pratt, *Religion, Politics, and Diversity: The Church-State Theme in New York History* (Ithaca: Cornell University Press, 1967), 6.

[25]Henri and Barbara Van Der Zee, *A Sweet and Alien Land: The Story of Dutch New York* (New York: Viking Press, 1978), 91-92.

[26]Revs. Megapolensis and Drisius to the Classis of Amsterdam, Oct. 6, 1653, in Edward T. Corwin, ed., *Ecclesiastical Records of the State of New York* (Albany: James B. Lyon, 1901), 1:317-18.

[27]Rev. John Megapolensis to the Classis of Amsterdam, Oct. 6, 1653, in *Ecclesiastical Records of New York*, 1:334-36. Although unhappy with their presence in his domain, Megapolensis gave some charity to the Jews, who arrived destitute. Van Der Zee, *A Sweet and Alien Land*, 290-91.

[28]West Indies Company to Peter Stuyvesant, April 26, 1655, *Ecclesiastical Records*, 1:338. Frederick J. Zwierlein, *Religion in New Netherlands* (Rochester: John P. Smith, 1910), 190. This volume is useful for its factual data, although outdated and, at times, quite bigoted in interpretation.

[29]Smith, *Religion and Trade in New Amsterdam*, 213; Zwierlein, *Religion in New Netherlands*, 187-212.

[30]"Directors to Stuyvesant," June 14, 1656, in *Ecclesiastical Records*, 1:352; Pratt, *Religion, Politics, and Diversity*, 15-24; Zwierlein, *Religion in New Netherlands*, 247-65.

³¹In 1657 Dutch authorities in New Netherland tortured the Quaker Robert Hodgson in a variety of ways, including dragging him behind a horse cart, placing him in a vermin-filled dungeon, and severely whipping him and "chaining him to a wheelbarrow in the hot sun until he collapsed." He was later hung by his hands in a prison cell and "whipped until he was near death." After two days in solitary confinement, he was again whipped until near death. Hodgson's ordeal ended when Stuyvesant's own sister convinced him to release Hodgson from prison and expel him from the country. Smith, *Religion and Trade in the New Netherlands*, 223. See also Zwierlein, *Religion in New Netherland*, 213–46.

³²"Remonstrance of the Inhabitants of Flushing, L.I., Against the Law Against Quakers," January 1, 1658, in *Ecclesiastical Records*, 1:412–13.

³³Directors of the Dutch West Indies Company to Stuyvesant, April 16, 1663, in *Ecclesiastical Records*, 1:530.

³⁴*Ibid.*

³⁵Pratt, *Religion, Politics, and Diversity*, 24.

³⁶Pratt argues that the failure to resolve the tension and contradiction between Stuyvesant and the West India Company officials undermined the Dutch colony. *Religion, Politics, and Diversity*, 25. This may be true, although it seems unlikely that a consistent policy of either tolerance or repression would have prevented English seizure of the colony.

³⁷E.B. O'Callaghan and B. Fernow, eds., *Documents Relating to the Colonial History of the State of New York* (Albany: 1853), 2:251.

³⁸Pratt, *Religion, Politics, and Diversity*, 26–35; O'Callaghan and Fernow, *New York Colonial Documents*, 3:218.

³⁹*Colonial Laws of New York*, 1:115.

⁴⁰Pratt, *Religion, Politics, and Diversity*, 34–35.

⁴¹Jacob R. Marcus, *The Colonial American Jew, 1492–1776* (Detroit: Wayne State Press, 1970).

⁴²"Answer of Governor to Enquiries About New York," April 16, 1678 and Governor Dongan's Report on the State of the Province," 1684, in *Ecclesiastical Records*, 1: 709 and 2:879–80; Douglas Greenberg, *Crime in the Colony of New York* (Ithaca: Cornell University Press, 1978), 26; Edwin Scott Gaustad, *Historical Atlas of Religion in America* (New York: Harper and Row, 1962), 2.

⁴³*Colonial Laws of New York*, 1:248. This was followed in 1700 by "An Act against Jesuits and Popish Priests" providing a "perpetual imprisonment" or "death" for such persons found in the colony. *Ibid.*, 1:302.

⁴⁴Pratt, *Religion, Politics, and Diversity*, 39.

⁴⁵Pratt, *Religion, Politics, and Diversity*, 58.

⁴⁶Stanley N. Katz, *Newcastle's New York: Anglo–American Politics, 1732–1753* (Cambridge, Mass.: Harvard University Press, 1968), 10.

⁴⁷Quoted in *ibid.*, 10.

⁴⁸One example of anti-Catholic behavior was the attempt to tie the New York Slave Revolt of 1741 to a Jesuit conspiracy. Daniel Horsmanden, *A Journal of the Proceedings in the Detection of the Conspiracy Formed by Some White People, in Conjunction With Negro and Other Slaves. . . .* (New York: James Parker, 1744); T.J. Davis, *A Rumor of Revolt* (New York: The Free Press, 1985).

⁴⁹Milton Klein, "Church, State, and Education: Testing the Issue in Colonial New York," in Milton M. Klein, *The Politics of Diversity: Essays in the History of Colonial New York* (Port Washington: Kennikat Press, 1974), 99; Pratt, *Religion, Politics, and Diversity*, 60–78.

⁵⁰Patricia Bonomi, *A Factious People: Politics and Society in Colonial New York* (New York: Columbia University Press, 1971), 248–67.

⁵¹Milton Klein, "New York in the American Colonies: A New Look," in Klein, *The Politics of Diversity*, 193.

[52]In addition to the First Amendment, the federal Constitution dealt with religion in two other ways. Wherever the Constitution discussed an oath the document allowed persons to swear or affirm, thus guaranteeing that Quakers could hold office. (Art. II, Sec. 1, Par. 8 and Art. 6, Par. 3). The Constitution also provided that there would be no "religious test" for federal officeholders.

[53]*Maryland Declaration of Rights, 1776*, Article XXXIII; *New Hampshire Bill of Rights, 1783*, Articles V and VI; *Massachusetts Declaration of Rights, 1780*, Art. III. See also *New Jersey Constitution, 1776*, Art. XVIII and XIX; *Delaware Constitution, 1776*, Secs. 2 and 3; *Vermont Declaration of Rights, 1777*, Art. III; *South Carolina Constitution, 1778*, Art. XXXVIII, for similar statements.

[54]See for example, *Virginia Declaration of Rights, 1776*, Art. 16; *Georgia Constitution, 1777*, Art. LVI; *Pennsylvania Declaration of Rights, 1776*, Art. II.

[55]*Ibid.*, Article XXXVIII.

[56]The use of the term "priests" here may have been a slap at Catholicism, but it would have equally applied to the Anglican clergy, which had been a more realistic threat to the New Yorkers. Many Protestants would also have understood the term to apply to the religious leaders of ancient Israel.

[57]*New York Constitution, 1777*, Art. XXXV.

[58]Thomas E. Buckley, *Church and State in Revolutionary Virginia, 1776-1787* (Charlottesville: University of Virginia Press, 1977).

[59]*South Carolina Constitution, 1778*, Article XXXVIII. Five other states limited officeholding to Protestants.

[60]Pratt, *Religion, Politics, and Diversity*, 19.

[61]Sydney E. Ahlstrom, *A Religious History of the American People* 2 vols. (Garden City: Doubleday, 1975), 1:229, 230.

[62]Revs. Johannes Megapolensis and Samuel Drisius to the Classis of Amsterdam, August 14, 1657, *Ecclesiastical Records*, 1:399-400; Zwierlein, *Religion in New Netherlands*, 213-42.

[63]Ahlstrom, *Religious History of the American People*, 1:230-34.

[64]Jacob C. Meyer, *Church and State in Massachusetts, From 1740 to 1833* (Cleveland: Western Reserve University Press, 1930), 13.

[65]Georgia exempted Quaker voters from oaths, but required oaths for all officeholders, thus preventing Quaker officeholders. *Georgia Constitution, 1777*, Art. XIV, XV.

[66]In 1778 Congress passed a test oath for all civilian and military officers of the nation that allowed people to affirm rather than swear, thus allowing Quakers and other nonjurors to serve in the new government. Harold M. Hyman, *To Try Men's Souls: Loyalty Oaths in American History* (Berkeley: University of California Press, 1959), 82-83.

[67]*Maryland Declaration of Rights 1776*, Art. XXXVI. This clause led to some arguments over who actually were Quakers. Thomas O'Brien Hanley, *The American Revolution and Religion: Maryland, 1770-1800* (Washington, D.C.: Catholic University of America Press, 1971), 60. Methodists did not oppose oaths *per se* but did oppose oaths supporting war. Significantly, the document did not exempt Methodists from taking oaths to support the war effort. *Ibid.*, 33, 42-43.

[68]*Maryland Declaration of Rights, 1776*, Art. XXXV. The Maryland framers rejected a provision exempting Quaker and other non-juror office holders from oaths. Hanley, *American Revolution and Religion*, 57-58.

[69]*Maryland Declaration of Rights, 1776*, Art. XXV.

[70]Hanley, *American Revolution and Religion*, 40.

[71]This includes Vermont, but excludes Connecticut, which wrote a brief bill of rights but no constitution and Rhode Island, which wrote neither a bill of rights nor a constitution.

[72]Anson Phelps Stokes, *Church and State in the United States*, 3 vols. (New York: Harper and Row, 1950), the most important study of church and state in America,

inexplicably, and incorrectly, asserts that Maryland limited officeholding to Protestants, but that Georgia, New Jersey, and North Carolina did not.

[73]The *Massachusetts Constitution, 1780,* Chap. VI, Article I, required two oaths of state officials. The first required a belief in "the Christian religion." This would have opened officeholding to Catholics. The second, however, required the person "to renounce and abjure all allegiance, subjection, and obedience to the king, queen, or government of Great Britain . . . and every other foreign prince, person, prelate, state, or potentate . . . civil, ecclesiastical, or spiritual." This oath would have prohibited Roman Catholics (and other orthodox Catholics, had any lived in America at the time) from holding office. It might also have prohibited members of the Church of England from holding office, although not members of the Protestant Episcopal Church, into which the Anglican Church was evolving.

[74]Connecticut limited officeholding to Protestants under its charter, which remained in force.

[75]By statute and under its colonial charter, Rhode Island apparently allowed people of any faith to hold office.

[76]*Virginia Declaration of Rights, 1776,* Art. 16.

[77]Virginia also excluded "all ministers of the gospel, of every denomination" from officeholding. This is discussed below.

[78]*New York Constitution, 1777,* Art. XLII.

[79]Pratt, *Religion, Politics, and Diversity,* 95–97.

[80]Botein, "Religious Dimensions of the Early American State," 319.

The Albany Congress and Constitution Making in Early America

THOMAS E. BURKE

New York State Bicentennial Commission

At Albany, New York, during the summer of 1754, representatives from seven northern colonies turned their inventive political minds to the task of creating a plan of union which would serve to join the colonies of England's North American empire for the purpose of defense against France and her Indian allies without sacrificing the balance of local interests.

In the years after 1690, England fought three wars with her European opponents. In a fourth conflict, the Seven Years' War (1756–63), known in the colonies as the French and Indian War, America was the central theater of war. The immediate cause of the Seven Years' War sprang from a series of clashes between French troops trying to secure the Ohio River valley and soldiers from Virginia, which claimed the territory based on its original seventeenth-century charter. The French built Fort Duquesne at the junction of the Ohio, Allegheny, and Monongahela rivers. A small force under Major George Washington failed to dislodge them.

Anticipating a scale of conflict greater than that of any of the previous wars, delegates of seven colonies met at Albany in 1754 in an effort to coordinate defense plans among themselves and with their Indian allies.

On the morning of June 19, 1754, twenty-three commissioners appeared at the Albany City Hall. In the presence of Lieutenant Governor John DeLancey, they presented the instructions which they had received from their individual colonies. The powers vested in the com-

missioners varied greatly. Those given to the Massachusetts Bay delegation were the most liberal, permitting it not only to make a treaty with
the Indians but to enter "into articles of Union and Confederation."

New York's position, however, was peculiar. Although Lieutenant
Governor DeLancey was present, as were four members of the Council, they did not appear as commissioners and had no special powers
to act in behalf of their colony's government. Nevertheless, the New
York members participated in the activities of the Congress as though
fully qualified to do so. Their immediate concern was an intercolonial
agreement for the installation of military posts in the Indian country,
the expense of which would be shared among the colonies.

Lieutenant Governor DeLancey insisted on organizing the conference and controlling its proceedings as the presiding officer. This high-
handed conduct, however, seems to have been resented by only the
delegation from Massachusetts Bay.

All of the colonies represented at Albany had at least one common objective: the re-establishment of friendly relations between the
Iroquois and the British. At the opening of the Congress, the delegates
were made aware of the danger that the Six Nations (Mohawk, Oneida,
Onondaga, Cayuga, Tuscarora, and Seneca) might be lost to the enemy.
Only a small number of Indians appeared and their behavior indicated
a calculated coldness and air of hostility.

Although DeLancey made it plain that he did not want the other
commissioners to examine the details of New York's past relations with
the Iroquois, the grievances of the Six Nations having to do with the
fur trade and the disposal of their land could not be hidden.

There followed a series of meetings between the commissioners and
the Iroquois. By July 9 these official negotiations had been concluded.
The Iroquois now proclaimed the strength of their loyalty to the English
cause. Most soon left, so loaded down with presents that thirty wagons
were required to transport the gifts to the Indian country.

As early as June 24, however, the question had been raised as to
"whether a Union of all the Colonies is not at present absolutely nec-
essary for their security and defence." The idea was not a new one. Dur-
ing the seventeenth century the New England Confederation had main-
tained itself from 1643 until 1684. In 1686, at the order of King James
II, the governments of Massachusetts, Connecticut, Rhode Island, and
Plymouth Colony were consolidated and in 1688 New York and New
Jersey were added to what became known as the Dominion of New
England. The life of this new colony was brief, however. The Glorious
Revolution in England, which overthrew James II, was followed by po-

litical disturbances within the colonies, such as Leisler's Rebellion in New York in 1689. By 1690, the dominion was dead.

During Queen Anne's War in 1709, the Crown worked out a plan for providing quotas of troops from neighboring colonies for an expedition against Canada which was to depart from Albany. Similarly, in King George's War during the 1740s, there was a "concert" of the New England colonies to provide troops and supplies to attack the French at Cape Breton. Given this past experience of intercolonial co-operation, it is not surprising that when the question of a union was raised at Albany, it was passed by the commissioners "in the affirmative unanimously."

Each delegation was called upon to choose one of its members to serve on a committee to prepare plans of union. The members included Thomas Hutchinson for Massachusetts Bay, Theodore Atkinson for New Hampshire, William Pitkin for Connecticut, Stephen Hopkins for Rhode Island, William Smith for New York, Benjamin Tasker for Maryland, and Benjamin Franklin for Pennsylvania.

As early as 1751, Franklin had produced a rough outline for a colonial union which embodied many of the ideas which would later be found in the 1754 plan. This plan of union was included in a pamphlet on Indian affairs printed by Archibald Kennedy the same year (1751). Kennedy, who had been receiver general and collector of customs for New York since the 1720s, was a faithful servant of the Crown whose interests corresponded with those of Franklin. Kennedy wrote six tracts concerning imperial defense, Indian policy, and the northern colonies between 1750 and 1755.

In his *Pennsylvania Gazette* on May 9, 1754, Franklin had written about the difficulties that the separate colonies faced in dealing with the French. The article was illustrated—the first American political cartoon—by a woodcut of a snake separated into parts, representing the colonies, with the motto beneath it: "Join or Die." In going to Albany, Franklin was already committed to the general idea of establishing a union of the colonies.

Franklin arrived at New York City on June 5 and busied himself with meetings with prominent New Yorkers. He also took time to set down a scheme of union. He called his plan, "Short Hints toward a Scheme for Uniting the Northern Colonies." It included many features of his earlier plan of 1751. One important feature that it discarded was the idea of a voluntary union. Now he favored that the plan be sent to England and established by an act of Parliament. In this manner, the colonies would have the union imposed on them.

The "Short Hints" called for the appointment by the king of a "Governor General" who would be paid by the Crown and who could veto all acts of the Grand Council. The members of the Council were to be chosen by the colonial assemblies with each colony having at least one representative and the larger colonies, several.

Franklin's "Short Hints," however, was not the only plan submitted for consideration by the Congress. Richard Peters of the Pennsylvania delegation also prepared "A Plan for a General Union of the British Colonies of North America." This plan provided for the colonies to be grouped into four divisions: one for New England; another for New York and New Jersey; a third for Virginia, Maryland, and Pennsylvania; a fourth for Georgia, South Carolina, and North Carolina. Each colony would appoint a "Committee of Union" to correspond with the committees of the other twelve colonies. Also, each division would hold an annual meeting of the committees within it which would recommend necessary measures to each of the governments within that division. Each colony was to raise a company of one hundred men, "the Union regiment." There was to be a "Union Fund" raised by the issue of paper money, and a "Fort Fund" to finance the building of forts to protect the frontiers.

Finally, at least one more plan also was formulated, apparently by Thomas Hutchinson of Massachusetts. His plan, like Peters's, adhered more closely to existing colonial arrangements than did Franklin's. Hutchinson suggested grouping the colonies into two unions, a northern and a southern, which would come into existence through an act of Parliament.

Initially, the Congress busied itself with Indian affairs and did not turn to the issue of union until June 28. By that time, the committee on plans of union had concluded to make Franklin's "Short Hints" the basis for the proposed union. The plan was debated for two days. On July 2 the question was put, "whether the Board should proceed to form a plan of Union of the Colonies by Act of Parliamt," and passed in the affirmative.

Although the commissioners had no power to bind their respective colonies, the vote represented the consensus of opinion of the most representative and politically capable and experienced body of colonials from the thirteen colonies to meet prior to the Stamp Act Congress of 1765.

On July 9 the committee on plans submitted its "Representation on the Present State of the Colonies." This was considered paragraph by paragraph. After referring to the need to regulate Indian affairs, certain broad recommendations were presented: that the encroachments of the French be removed; that the Indians be placed under some superintendency; that forts be built within each of the Indian nations; that the sale of Indian lands be regulated; and, finally, that there be a "Union of His Majtys several Governts on the Continent, that so their Councils, Treasure and strength may be employed in due proportion agst their common enemy."

The final draft of the "Plan of Union" seems to have been a fusion of ideas expressed in Franklin's "Short Hints" and the "Plan of a Proposed Union" formulated by Hutchinson. It called for a union of all the continental colonies except for the buffer colonies of Nova Scotia and Georgia. This union would be established by an act of Parliament. The conflict of interests among the colonies suggested to Franklin and some of the other commissioners that this was the only practical means of procuring a lasting plan of union. The "Representation" was forwarded by DeLancey to England to the Board of Trade, together with the other papers relating to the Congress.

Under the "Plan of Union" provision was made for a president general to be appointed and supported by the Crown. There would also be a grand council, the members of which were to be chosen by the respective assemblies with the following allotments: Massachusetts and Virginia, seven representatives each; Pennsylvania, six; Connecticut, five; New York, Maryland, North Carolina, and South Carolina, four each; New Jersey, three; and New Hampshire and Rhode Island, two each. The grand council was to meet at least once a year with the place of meeting, initially, at Philadelphia. To do business, a quorum of twenty-five was needed with one or more members from a majority of the colonies.

The "Plan" directed the president general, with the advice of the grand council, to direct all Indian treaties, to make peace or declare war with the Indians, to provide laws for regulating the Indian trade, and to settle outstanding land claims with the Indians.

To defend the colonies, the president general and the grand council were to raise and support soldiers and to build forts and equip war vessels. For these purposes they were to levy whatever duties, imports, or taxes appeared equal and just. However, it was provided that all acts of the grand council must receive the assent of the president general and were to be sent England for the approval of the privy council, which could disallow such acts within a period of three years.

Finally, a general treasurer and individual treasurers for each government would be appointed by joint action of the president general and the grand council who together could order sums of money in colonial treasuries to be placed in the general treasury. All accounts were to be reported yearly to the assemblies of the colonies.

Historians have seen in this plan certain features that underlay the subsequent establishment of Indian superintendents and the Proclamation Line of 1763 and also the idea of creation of trans–Appalachian colonies and commonwealths as embodied in the Northwest Ordinance of 1787. Historians also have noted that in many respects this plan goes beyond the provincialism of the Articles of Confederation of 1781.

Although Philadelphia, because of its convenient location, was to be the usual meeting place of the grand council, provision was made for its gathering in any colony which might be in need of assistance. Nothing, however, referred to the residence of the president general.

According to a report made by the Massachusetts Bay commissioners to Governor William Shirley of that colony, those attending the Congress were "very near unanimous" on three points: first, that a general union of the colonies was necessary to save them from the French; second, that a scheme for union could only be placed into execution by Parliament; third, that the proportion of the general expense that each colony should bear was to be estimated by the number of members allotted to each on the grand council. Finally, the commissioners agreed that taxation of the colonies should be through measures adopted by the grand council and not by Parliament.

Having completed their work, the commissioners returned home to give an accounting. Except for the Massachusetts delegation, those attending the Congress only had authority to deal with Indian affairs, and had not been specifically delegated by their governments to establish a colonial confederacy. This may explain why most took a passive attitude toward their achievement. Moreover, they did not have long to wait for opposition to their recommendations to develop.

Almost unanimously, the plan of union was ignored or rejected on both sides of the ocean. Colonial governors and assemblies either took no notice of the plan or, like Governor Dinwiddie of Virginia, waited to see how it was received in England. The assemblies in the various colonies refused to transfer their power to a new intercolonial agency.

At the time of the Albany congress, the subject of Indian relations and of colonial defence was being discussed by the statesmen of England. In April 1754, the Board of Trade suggested that the English should build forts all along the disputed frontier, that the colonies should garrison them, and that these forts should serve both for defense against the French and as warehouses for Indian goods and trade.

On June 14, 1754, King George II had ordered the Board of Trade to prepare a plan for the common defense of the colonies. However, in passing on the Albany plan of union to the King, the Board of Trade made no comment except to note, as a serious defect, that not enough provision had been made for the management of Indian affairs. The board recommended that Indian affairs be taken out of the hands of the separate colonies and placed under the domain of commissioners. It specifically suggested that William Johnson of New York, who already carried on extensive trade and diplomatic relations with the Iroquois and other tribes from his estate at today's Johnstown, be given command over the Six Nations. The Board of Trade also was fearful that the proposed intercolonial government would take power away from the Crown. Finally, the outbreak of war with France diverted attention to more immediate issues.

The New York delegation to the Albany Congress consisted of Lieutenant Governor John DeLancey and several members of the governor's council. Although Albany served as the site for the meetings, no members of the local community were involved in preparing, debating, or adopting the plan of union.

Note: The plan of union has been printed in Robert C. Newbold, *The Albany Congress and Plan of Union of 1754* (1955), 184–187.

The Albany Congress and the United States Constitution

The Albany plan survived as the basic idea of federalism during the years after 1754. At the First Continental Congress in 1774, Joseph Gallaway, a conservative Pennsylvanian, proposed a plan of union that was similar to that proposed at Albany except that both Parliament and the intercolonial legislature would be able to legislate for the colonies, each to have a veto on the other. This proposal was narrowly defeated by a vote of six states to five.

At the Second Continental Congress, in June 1775, Benjamin Franklin proposed a plan of confederation also based on the Albany plan. Franklin argued for a scheme of representation proportional to population. Although his plan substituted for the provision granting powers of taxation to the grand council a proposal to allow Congress the right to make requisitions, Congress was to exercise wide power in other areas "necessary to the general welfare." However, this proposal was set aside and not given further consideration.

As finally adopted, the Articles of Confederation preserved that part of the Albany plan which included control of the West by the general government. Franklin tried to introduce the idea of representation in proportion to population, but the Articles continued the voting equality of the states established by the First Continental Congress. In failing to go as far as the Albany Plan of Union in limiting the sovereignty of the states, the Articles fell short of what the commissioners at Albany had proposed more than twenty years earlier. However, a significant achievement representing a principal objective of the Albany Congress—federal control of the western territories—occurred in 1787 with the passage of the Northwest Ordinance in which Congress set up a government for the territories and provided for the admission of new states.

Finally, at Philadelphia in 1787 some of the basic concepts of the Albany Plan of Union were attained at the Constitutional Convention. In 1754, it was proposed that members of the council were to be elected by the colonial legislatures. In a similar manner, in 1781 the Articles of Confederation provided that delegates to the Confederation Congress be named by the state legislatures, and in 1787 the United States Constitution provided that two Senators were to represent each state and that the senators were to be chosen by the state legislatures.

A system of checks and balances was embodied in the Albany Plan of Union as in the federal Constitution. The council was to have the authority to raise, equip, and pay an army and navy, with the consent of the president general. But the president general was to have the power to appoint the officers of the army and navy subject to the council's approval. Similarly, as regards the veto power, even if the president general approved a bill, it still could have been disallowed by the Crown. In this sense, Franklin's plan included the idea of a limit to legislative authority.

The Albany congress produced a document which, although failing to receive acceptance at the time, foreshadowed the adjustment of power, authority, and interest represented in the constitutional compact achieved at Philadelphia over three decades later.

1777: The Political Revolution and New York's First Constitution*

WILLIAM A. POLF

New York State Bicentennial Commission

Fourteen Revolutions

Years before the United States Constitution was written, each of the independent American states adopted constitutions of their own. America's rebellion against British rule destroyed thirteen distinct colonial governments. Each had a direct political link with England; there was no formal political connection between the colonies themselves. As these colonial governments began to collapse under the pressure of the growing rebellion in 1775 and 1776, the revolutionaries recognized that the various congresses and committees which were directing the revolutionary movement within the states would have to be replaced by more permanent governments.

Constitutions were being written and state governments organized even before independence was declared. In January 1776, New Hampshire adopted a preliminary constitution; South Carolina did so in March. (Both states later replaced these hurriedly drafted documents with permanent constitutions.) On May 4, Rhode Island converted its colonial charter into a state constitution by purging all references to royal authority, a method followed by Connecticut in October. Virginia acted in June, and on July 2, the very day the Continental Congress declared independence, New Jersey's constitution became law. Delaware and Pennsylvania adopted constitutions in September, followed by Maryland in November, North Carolina in December, Georgia in February 1777, and New York in April. Vermont proclaimed a constitution in July 1777 even though none of the other states acknowledged the state's independence until the 1780s. (Control of the territory of present-day Vermont was disputed between New York and the Vermont separatists.) In 1780, the temporary government which had been in opera-

*Reprinted, with permission, from *1777: The Political Revolution and New York's First Constitution*, by William A. Polf.

tion in Massachusetts since 1775 was replaced by a permanent constitution.

These first state constitutions made the war for American independence a genuine political revolution. Although the states had united under the Continental Congress to declare their independence, raise an army, and conduct a unified defense against England, the Continental Congress had no political jurisdiction within the states themselves. The creation of state governments gave substance to the declaration of independence: not only were Americans prepared to fight for their independence, but also they were filling the political vacuum caused by the repudiation of British authority. That political vacuum was filled in ways that transformed American political culture. Unique forms of government were established; even though the principles underlying them were ancient, and even though the language had been adopted largely from English law and politics, Americans knew perfectly well that they were undergoing a political revolution unprecedented in scope and originality.

New York's first constitution, like all the others, was an experimental document devised to cope with a political emergency. On July 9, 1776, delegates to a specially elected provincial congress, the fourth since May 1775, convened in White Plains for the purpose of establishing "such a government as they shall deem best calculated to secure the rights, liberties and happiness of the good people of this colony; and to continue in force until a future peace with Great-Britain shall render the same unnecessary." By the time the fourth congress met, peace with Great Britain was unlikely. Seven days earlier, independence had been declared by the Continental Congress. New York's delegates in Philadelphia, lacking specific instructions, refused to vote but instead referred the matter of independence back to the provincial congress. As soon as the meeting at White Plains had begun, the declaration of independence was adopted unanimously. The next day, the provincial congress changed its name to "the Convention of the Representatives of the State of New-York." For nearly a year the convention of representatives and its derivative committee of safety governed the state, while the work of framing a more permanent state government went ahead.

On August 1, the convention assigned the task of drafting a constitution to a committee of thirteen men—John Jay, John Sloss Hobart, William Smith (of Suffolk County), William Duer, Gouverneur Morris, Robert R. Livingston, John Broome, John Morin Scott, Abraham Yates, Jr., Henry Wisner, Samuel Townsend, Charles De Witt, and Robert Yates. James Duane was later added. The committee had to work under the most extreme wartime conditions. Staten Island had already been occupied by the British army when the convention met, forcing it to assemble in White Plains instead of New York City. Planning for the constitution had hardly begun before the convention was forced to flee northward as Long Island and Manhattan fell to the British. Those convention delegates from Suffolk, Queens, Kings, and New York counties who participated in the constitutional deliberations became exiles from their homes; they would not be able to return for more than seven years.

Understandably, the drafting proceeded slowly. Abraham Yates, the chairman, constantly had trouble assembling a quorum of committee members. Several had active military commands which kept them away. Others had local governmental responsibilities or were serving on additional committees. There were also charges that the delay was deliberate. Some committee members were suspected of dragging their feet in the hope of a reconciliation with England, or were believed reluctant to be associated with the drafting of a constitution if New York fell to the British, a real possibility in late 1776 and 1777. A few members insisted that it was a waste of time to debate a constitution while the state's independent existence was still very uncertain.

It was hardly surprising, then, that the drafting process took months, despite the prodding of the convention and complaints from local officials. The committee was initially ordered to report a draft by August 26, but this date passed. Another month went by. Early in October, as criticism began to mount, committee member Henry Wisner informed General George Clinton that "the formation of government goes on very slow indeed; we have done little or nothing about it." Two weeks later, John McKesson, the convention secretary, made an optimistic progress report; the impasse was apparently broken. But once again, the committee was silent. More than five more months passed before James Duane stood in the convention on March 12, 1777, and read the draft the committee had prepared.

The work was still far from over. For another six weeks, the members of the convention subjected the committee draft to an article-by-article scrutiny. Some provisions were scarcely debated; others took days. By the time the convention had finished, many basic changes had been made.

The document that became the state's first constitution reflected the joint efforts of the drafting committee and many of the more than thirty members of the convention who regularly attended during the floor debate. A few people stand out. John Jay—brilliant, detached, reserved—single-handedly reduced the cumbersome, long-winded committee draft into a compact, concisely written document for the convention to consider. During the convention debate, Jay excelled at breaking deadlocks by proposing workable compromises. He often discussed his ideas with Gouverneur Morris. Urbane, sarcastic, cynical, contemptuous of the new popular influences in politics, and utterly self-assured, Morris exerted his influence most strongly during the floor debate, where he displayed superb parliamentary skills to dominate the proceedings. He often got his way, but he could not persuade the members to abolish slavery.

Jay and Morris usually acted in concert with Robert R. Livingston, scion of one of the state's most notable political families. Livingston was frequently bored by the tedious legal argumentation at which Jay excelled, and he wrote Edward Rutledge of South Carolina that he was "sick of power and politics" and would not "give one scene of Shakespeare for 1,000 Harringtons, Lockes, Sidneys and Adams to boot." Yet he helped Jay formulate the compromises that kept the discussion from foundering and, like Morris, was often able to control the floor debate.

Abraham Yates, the former sheriff of Albany County, was selected as chairman of the drafting committee though he lacked the political credentials of Jay, Morris, and Livingston. Yates was the incarnation of the new men of the Revolution, who rose from obscurity to positions of power and who were distrusted and despised by colonial patricians such as Morris. Yates led those convention members who wanted to increase public control over politics.

Others also played important parts: James Duane, a New York City lawyer, and William Duer, an English-born land speculator; Duane and Duer usually supported the actions of Jay, Morris, and Livingston. William Smith of Suffolk County (not to be confused with the loyalist William Smith, Jr.) and Robert Yates, nephew of Abraham Yates, helped to draft the constitution and then to guide it through the convention. Henry Wisner, a farmer and landowner who doubled as a manufacturer of gunpowder, and Thomas Tredwell actively proposed and supported measures designed to increase popular influence in the new state government.

Often at odds, but just as often able to submerge their differences, the convention members finished their work late in the day on April 20, 1777. Thirty-three of the thirty-four members present voted in favor of the constitution; only Peter Livingston dissented. No time was allowed for making a clean copy before the document was rushed to the printer. Convention president Leonard Gansevoort signed his name to the heavily amended last draft, which was covered with erasures and interlineations; words and phrases were crossed out and clauses were written in the margins.

Two days later the constitution was proclaimed.

A Choice of Dishes

"We have a government to form," wrote John Jay early during the drafting of New York's constitution. "God knows what it will resemble. Our politicians, like some guests at a feast, are perplexed and undetermined which dish to prefer." Throughout the states Americans were debating the formation of their new governments. Opinions varied widely on what should be included or what should not, what powers should be granted to whom and how they should be defined or restricted. Although the colonists had obtained an extensive political education during the years of protest against Britain's imperial practices, the debate had focused largely on the erosion of rights and liberties; little attention was paid to planning alternative forms of government if British authority collapsed. When that happened, there was a scramble to fabricate workable structures.

While there was no consensus on just how the governments should be constructed, there were certain basic principles which all the constitution makers accepted. It was universally agreed that, by the act of revolution, the people had become their own political masters; there could be no higher political authority. No one seriously doubted that the new governments would be republican in form. The colonists rejected the royal colonial governments in favor of republicanism, Thomas Jefferson observed in 1777, as easily as "throwing off an old and putting on a new suit of clothes." Americans were also committed to government by law and the protection of basic rights; most agreed on the necessity of distributing power between various branches of government. "It is essential to Liberty," the voters of Boston stated in May 1776, "that the legislative, judicial, and executive Powers of Government be, as nearly as possible, independent of and separate from each other, for where they are united in the same Persons, there will be wanting that natural Check, which is the principal Security against the enacting of arbitrary Laws, and a wanton Exercise of Power in the Execution of them."

Sovereignty of the people, superiority of republicanism, rule of law, protection of rights, separation of powers—few Americans in 1776 would have found fault with any of these basic principles.

But within this framework of principles was a wide range of possible applications. Theory did not necessarily translate smoothly into practice. It was easier to declare that the people were their own political masters than to create mechanisms through which they truly governed themselves. Republicanism was fine in principle, but there were questions about what representation really meant or even who was to be represented. Guaranteeing rights was a laudable objective, but could liberty truly be threatened if the people themselves controlled the government? Nor was it easy to draw distinct lines between various types of political power. Where, for instance, did legislative authority end and executive authority begin? Or where did the process of administering the laws—an executive function—become distinct from interpreting them—a judicial responsibility?

The constitution makers of 1776 and 1777 had to refer to basic principles partly because they lacked exact models to guide them. Republics had existed from time to time since antiquity, but in no case did the conditions completely match those in America. Written constitutions of the kinds Americans were beginning to envision were also rare. The closest thing to a working model was, ironically, the British government. Even though most Americans believed that English politics had become hopelessly corrupt, they also believed that England, with its entrenched traditions expressed in the common law, its commitment to the protection of basic rights and liberties, and its balanced institutions, had the best-constructed government in the world. Americans continually insisted that they were fighting to protect their rights "as Englishmen"; many believed that the American war was being waged to preserve the spirit of English law. Yet even England's form of government could not be followed exactly, particularly since America lacked two of the most conspicuous elements in the English social and political balance—a monarchy and a hereditary nobility.

Ideas flowed into the constitution making process from many sources. Well-educated Americans were familiar with European political and legal literature, both classical and contemporary, English and Continental. Throughout the constitutional discussions are references to the writings of Livy, Cicero, Plato, Plutarch, Thomas Hobbes, Henry St. John (Viscount Bolingbroke), Baron de Montesquieu, Sir Edward Coke, Jean Louis De Lolme, David Hume, Baron de Pufendorf, Jean Jacques Rousseau, the third earl of Shaftesbury, Emmerich de Vattel, and many others. John Adams, who pursued the business of making constitutions with characteristic intensity, absorbed many of the ideas of these and other writers, fashioning them into *Thoughts on Government*, a kind of political manual for Americans. John Jay carried a copy of Adams's book with him as he returned to New York from Philadelphia to participate in the drafting of New York's constitution.

American political thinking was influenced most by the principles of the English Whigs. English Whig thought had taken shape during the English civil wars of the mid-seventeenth century and the politically volatile period of Stuart rule that followed. Through such prominent seventeenth-century theorists as John Milton, James Harrington, Algernon Sidney, and John Locke, Americans were introduced to basic Whig political maxims—the contractual nature of political society, the supremacy of natural rights, the eternal tension between power and liberty, and the ideal of balanced government. In the early eighteenth century, as English politics became more pragmatic and patronage ridden, Whig political rhetoric became more radical in content and strident in tone, particularly as expressed in the essays of Thomas Gordon and John Trenchard.

Trenchard's and Gordon's essays, called *Cato's Letters*, drew a dark, conspiratorial picture of politics. Government, in their view, was very nearly the natural enemy of society. Politicians were invariably corrupt and grasping, intent upon pursuing self-interest at the expense of the public good. Individual liberty was in constant danger from those who ruled. Only a virtuous populace, cautious in granting political authority and ever vigilant against abuses of power, had a chance of establishing and maintaining a free government.

Radical Whiggery reflected the dissatisfaction and suspicion of those excluded from political power. The shrill rhetoric of Trenchard and Gordon and others had little influence in England but appealed to Americans, who were keenly aware of their own isolation from English politics. *Cato's Letters* and similar writings were widely read in the colonies long after they had been forgotten in England. While the earlier Whig writers were a source of basic principles and structural concepts, the radical Whigs provided Americans with an emotional political language capable of giving vent to their own frustrations under British rule.

Not everything in the constitutions was new. Even a political revolution as deep as the one Americans were undergoing could not uproot everything from the political past. Some revolutionaries did not believe it should. Many of those who were forming new governments had substantial experience in the old, and they brought to the constitution drafting process their collective thinking on what should be preserved as well as what should be repudiated. There was substantial political carryover from the old governments, particularly at the local level. Components of the colonial system were often altered only slightly, if at all.

The degree of continuity between the colonial period and statehood varied from state to state, but in every case it was a major factor shaping the new constitutions.

From this combination of principles and experience, general fears and specific aspirations, lofty intentions and pragmatic assumptions, the constitution makers had to find workable formulas for their new governments. Complicating the process further was the fact that Americans did not always agree on what they wanted their revolution to accomplish. Even by July 1776, when independence became the most commonly agreed upon objective, many of those who supported independence believed that it was still possible (and desirable) to reach some sort of reconciliation with England. Others supported independence only reluctantly and would have preferred to defer the business of creating state governments until it was clear whether or not the rebellion would succeed. Nor was there a consensus upon the relationship between independence and the creation of new governments. Some revolutionaries wanted as little change as possible from the colonial system; others saw the war as an opportunity to make drastic reforms in the social and political order. Some Americans were generally unconcerned about the institutional structure of government as long as specific rights were protected; others believed that rights were secure only in properly fabricated governments.

It is understandable, then, that the first constitutions shared certain common features and differed greatly in others. Starting from the political assumptions underlying the revolution throughout the colonies, New York's constitution makers created a state government reflecting their own experience under colonial rule and designed to meet the state's particular needs. Though a hybrid creation, as Jay had anticipated it would be, it proved to be among the most effective of the first state constitutions.

Organizing the Legislature

Americans were convinced that the success of their new governments would depend upon the creation of strong legislatures. Republicanism, for most Americans, meant that the power to make laws resided in elected representatives of the people. Part of the controversy between England and the colonies in the 1760s and early 1770s involved the American claim that Parliament was attempting to usurp the constitutional prerogatives of the colonial assemblies. As the new state governments began to take shape, it was clear that Americans considered their legislatures to be the very embodiment of the revolutionary changes occurring in American society. "It is in their legislatures that the members of a commonwealth are united and combined together into one coherent, living body," a Rhode Island newspaper stated. "This is the soul that gives form, life and unity to the commonwealth."

Most of the state constitutions established bicameral legislatures. In these states, one legislative branch was called the house of delegates, or the house of representatives, or, as in New York, the assembly. This house of the legislature was considered to be closest to the people themselves, most concerned with protecting their welfare, espousing their interests, and guarding their rights. The people expressed their sovereign power most directly through this legislative branch. So it was important, argued John Adams, that each lower house "should be in miniature an exact portrait of the people at large. It should think, feel, reason, and act like them." Although these legislative houses were modeled on the colonial assemblies, each state made important changes designed to make them more representative and more responsive to the public will.

New York's state assembly was basically similar to the lower house in the other states. Assemblymen were to be elected annually, a term of office adopted by every other state except South Carolina. Under the colonial government, assembly terms could last as long as seven years, and the colonial assembly met only when called by the governor. It was not unusual for several years to pass without the assembly's meeting. New York's new constitution, therefore, required that the legislature meet at least once a year. Changes were also made in electoral districts. The colonial government had allowed each county two assemblymen. Additional representatives were granted to the municipal corporation of New York, the township of Schenectady, the borough of Westchester, and the manors of Livingston, Cortlandt, and Rensselaerswyck. These special representatives were eliminated in the state constitution. State assemblymen were to be elected by county, with the size of each county's delegation based on its population. Representation for the two municipal corporations—Albany and New York—was included in their respective counties.

The minimum number of assemblymen was set at seventy, creating a house twice the size of its colonial predecessor. The city and county of Albany had the largest delegation—ten—followed by the city and county of New York with nine. Only two representatives were allowed for the counties of Kings, Richmond, and Gloucester (now in Vermont). All others ranged somewhere in between.

An important innovation was the provision for proportional representation. It was generally agreed that one of the defects of the British government was the failure to reallocate parliamentary seats to reflect shifts in population. Some large metropolitan areas were without representation, while some depopulated areas still had seats in Parliament. The control of these so-called "rotten boroughs" by the Crown or by wealthy members of the aristocracy was regarded by Americans as one of the most conspicuous examples of corruption within the British political system.

New York's constitution provided for a septennial census of "electors and inhabitants" in order to reapportion assembly delegations. Population shifts amounting to one-seventieth of the total number of electors was the basis for increasing or decreasing a county's representation in the assembly. Since the population of the state was expected to grow after the war, the legislature was given the power to create new counties with appropriate assembly delegations until the assembly reached its constitutional maximum of 300 members.

Deciding who should be allowed to vote was a major concern in all the states. Under the colonial system, members of the assemblies were elected by voters possessing a "freehold" (basically, real property) worth £ 40. Most of the state constitution framers accepted the maxim that voting was the privilege of those with a tangible stake in the community. Few Americans advocated universal adult male suffrage, and almost no one believed that women should be allowed to vote. Every state except Vermont imposed at least a nominal property-holding requirement for the franchise, and only in New Jersey was the constitution phrased in a way that did not absolutely exclude women from voting.

New York's constitution committee eliminated the colonial £ 40 stipulation and proposed that all adult male freeholders who had paid taxes should be allowed to vote for assemblymen. This suggestion was substantially revised by the convention. Gouverneur Morris's motion that the franchise be restricted to those with freeholds worth at least £ 20 was adopted by the convention. Also approved was Robert R. Livingston's suggestion to enfranchise land-renting tenants who paid annual rents of £ 2. All "freemen" of the cities of Albany and New York as of October 14, 1775, were also given the vote. (Freemanship was the technical term for those who were legally permitted by a municipal corporation to vote and conduct business within its limits. By the time of the Revolution, it was possible for almost any resident who worked or engaged in trade in Albany or New York to qualify for freeman status.) If they could meet the property requirements, there was no prohibition against free blacks voting, but the constitution specifically restricted the franchise to adult males.

Despite these changes, the legacy of the colonial assemblies was so strong that New Yorkers felt it was a sufficient statement of the powers of the state assembly to declare that "it shall . . . enjoy the same privileges, and proceed in doing business in like manner as the assemblies of the colony of New-York of *right* formerly did. . . ." Conspicuously missing from the constitution was a grant of exclusive power to the assembly to originate money bills, a stipulation that was made in almost every other state that adopted a bicameral legislature. After the Revolution, when the New York senate challenged the assembly's insistence that it alone could initiate legislation on money matters, the assembly cited the precedent of the colonial assemblies.

While the state assemblies were basically patterned upon the colonial assemblies, there was no colonial counterpart for the second branch of the legislature. The closest approximation had been the provincial councils, which, in all the colonies except Massachusetts, Rhode Island, and Connecticut, had been appointed by the Crown on the recommendation of the governors. The colonial councils acted as the upper house of the legislature, often serving as the highest colonial appellate court. But the councils were regarded primarily as buttresses to executive authority, since they served mostly as advisory bodies to the governors. This mixture of legislative, judicial, and executive authority clearly violated the doctrine of the separation of powers, and even those state constitutions that adopted councils modeled on the provincial councils usually stripped them of their legislative roles and made them strictly a part of the executive branch.

Much more innovative than these remodeled councils was the division of legislative authority between two houses with basically similar powers but with different qualifications, different constituencies, and different terms of office. New York, like most other states, called the second house the "senate," a name initially suggested for the Virginia constitution by Thomas Jefferson. The underlying rationale of the state senates was the classical notion that society was a compound of three distinct elements—monarchy, aristocracy, and democracy. In an ideally balanced government, each of these three social components held a share of power, which enabled it to act as a check upon the others. The distribution of power in England between the king, the House of Lords, and the House of Commons was the clearest expression of mixed government; when it was working correctly, Americans believed that there was no better form of government.

Even though America had no monarchy or aristocracy, most of the constitution makers were convinced that a tripartite division of political authority should be instituted in the state constitutions. From their own colonial experience they knew that governors usually tried to extend their power while the people tried to increase their liberty. Going too far in either direction was dangerous. Tyranny lay at one extreme, anarchy at the other. Ideally there should be a mitigating force between the two extremes that would keep them from pulling against each other until the government was torn apart. In theory this was one of the functions of the House of Lords: it kept the king from becoming too despotic, the House of Commons from being too unruly.

John Adams argued forcefully for the creation of state senates. Despite the rhetoric of republican equality that underscored the revolutionary effort, Adams had no doubt that men were not equal in abilities, just as they were rarely equal in estates. Somehow government had to be constructed to insure that men of superior talent had a secure role to play. "To conduct the affairs of a community in a safe and successful way," Adams wrote, "requires all the *wisdom* of the most learned and experienced members of the state, as well as the *vigilance* and particular attention of the peculiar [i.e., exclusive] deputies of the whole people." Adams believed that the "contemplative and well-informed," as he called them, would often lack the popularity necessary to be elected to the assemblies. Some device was necessary to guarantee that such men had a continuing role in government, safe from the tumult of democratic politics, in which they would be able to bring stability and caution to the law-making process. Creating a second legislative branch, chosen by a more restricted electorate and serving longer terms of office, would ideally provide such a forum.

Others saw the senates in less noble terms. Although America lacked the stark class divisions of Europe, many dedicated revolutionaries nevertheless believed that there was an inherent tension between the wealthier and poorer members of American society. Some feared that the war for independence might degenerate into class warfare, with the more numerous poor using the new state governments to plunder the rich. As one Loyalist cynically observed: "A Legislature of Beggars will be Thieves." A second legislative branch chosen by electors of substantial property would provide a minimum of security against the potential danger of the assemblies becoming the exclusive province of the poorer members of society. A kind of artificial aristocracy had to be created, one based not upon inherited titles but upon gradations of wealth.

Many critics of this reasoning pointed out that such a notion was anachronistic in America where, as one writer put it, "none were entitled to any rights but such as were common to all." If the legislatures were to represent all the people equally, what justification could there be for splitting legislative authority? This, in a sense, was like asserting that the people, in whom sovereign power resided, could somehow be their own enemies and that some sort of check could constitutionally be placed upon the exercise of their sovereign will. Despite the seeming paradox in such reasoning, most of the constitution makers in the states agreed with Adams that "a people cannot be long free, nor even happy, whose government is in one assembly."

The members of the committee that drafted New York's constitution apparently never questioned the desirability of dividing legislative authority. A plan calling for a single-house legislature, similar to that in Pennsylvania, circulated early in the drafting process, but received little serious attention. Abraham Yates later recalled a general agreement that there would be elements of "monarchy, aristocracy, and democracy" in the government, a fact strongly suggesting that the drafters decided at the outset to create a legislative upper house.

Once it had been decided to establish a second branch of the legislature, the drafting committee considered several methods to place it at some distance from the pressures of electoral politics. One plan called for the selection of special electors who would choose the senators, an idea later adopted for electing the president of the United States. This proposal was rejected in favor of a high property-holding franchise requirement. At first the committee considered retaining the £ 40 freehold of the colonial era, but this was later raised to £ 100. Senators were to be chosen by an electorate with property five times greater than the assembly electorate. Senators would also serve a much longer term of office than assemblymen, four years as opposed to the one year assembly term. Four senatorial districts consisting of groups of counties were established, and the number of senators to be chosen in each district was stipulated.

The committee's plan for the senate ran into determined opposition on the convention floor. Robert Harper moved to strike the £ 100 franchise requirement, and William Harper proposed a reduction of the term of office from four years to one. Both motions were defeated. A proposal by Henry Wisner to elect the senators, like the assemblymen, by counties also failed to pass. Robert Yates attempted to redraw the senatorial districts in a way that would give New York and Westchester counties an additional senator at the expense of the thinly populated northeast. Like the other efforts to change the committee's plan, Yates's motion was defeated.

A long discussion then followed on reapportionment. Proposals made by Robert and Philip Livingston established the same septennial reapportionment adopted for the assembly, and Gouverneur Morris inserted a clause requiring adjustments in senatorial delegations when changes amounting to one twenty-fourth part of the qualified electorate occurred. Delegates from New York County, apparently afraid that upstate New York might use the reapportionment power to increase their representation at the expense of New York City, objected to this proposal, but all the other counties approved it. With that amendment the senate was complete, essentially as proposed by the drafting committee.

New York's senate was given much the same authority in lawmaking as the assembly. Like the assembly, the senate was the judge of its own members and, when the lieutenant governorship was vacant, had the right to elect its own leader, or "president." The two houses shared the responsibility of appointing delegates to the Continental Congress, and although the assembly had the authority to nominate the state treasurer, both houses had to approve the candidate. Unlike most other states, New York's senate was not specifically denied the right to originate money bills, an omission that caused a conflict between the two houses after the war.

New York had created a legislature broadly similar in structure and powers to those in most other states. Only three states—Pennsylvania, Georgia, and Vermont—departed from the bicameral principle, opting instead for single-house legislatures. Pennsylvania was distinctive for another reason. Since adopting its constitution in September 1776, the state had been in an almost constant state of political turmoil. By April 1777 the situation had become so serious in Pennsylvania that the Continental Congress stepped in to restore order. No state, said New Yorker James Duane, writing from Philadelphia, "ever cried more loudly for a vigilant active and decisive government."

Pennsylvania was an example of what New Yorkers hoped to avoid. Indirectly, the political situation there influenced the creation of New York's executive branch.

Establishing the Executive

Pennsylvania's constitution was among the most innovative of all the first state constitutions. At the center of the government was an all-powerful, single-house legislature. All taxpaying male adults with one year's residence could vote. Adult sons of taxpayers could also vote even if they themselves paid no taxes. There was an elected executive council, modeled on the colonial councils, which shared executive authority with a president elected by the house of representatives and the council. Assemblymen and councillors could serve only four years out of seven. Before becoming law, bills passed by the legislature had to be "printed for the consideration of the people," who could then exercise a sort of veto by ordering their representatives to vote against the bill when it was resubmitted in the next session. The government was to be scrutinized every seven years by a specially elected "council of censors," with the power to probe into every activity and impeach government officials.

Many New Yorkers were critical of Pennsylvania's constitution, particularly the executive clauses. Dividing authority between the president and council, it was felt, hamstrung the executive branch. Too much power had been given to the legislature, critics in New York and elsewhere charged; the executive branch was too weak and too clumsily constructed to provide effective government. Most of the constitution framers in the states agreed that while the legislature should meet only periodically to pass laws, the executive was supposed to keep the administration of the laws in continuous operation. In theory there should be no time during which the executive branch was not functioning. But when James Duane, a member of the committee that drafted New York's constitution, arrived in Philadelphia to attend the Continental Congress, he was appalled to discover that Pennsylvania's executive council had adjourned. "Executive adjourned, say you, how is this possible?" he exclaimed to John Jay. "Sirs, they *have* adjourned. . . . Faith I cannot tell you why—perhaps for Want of Authority to save their Country under their new Constitution, perhaps for Want of Resolution to exercise the power they have. . . . The Civil Governours [have] in effect abdicated for a month. . . ."

William Duer, another New York delegate to the Continental Congress and also a member of the constitution drafting committee in New York, regarded Pennsylvania's difficulties as an extreme example of what was happening in a number of other states. In almost every state where new governments had been established, he wrote from Philadelphia in May 1777, "either from the Contention of Parties, or from a Want of proper Powers being vested in the Executive branches, Disaffection has encreased prodigiously and an Unhappy languor has prevailed in the whole Political System."

But identifying the problem was easier than solving it. Although most Americans recognized that an executive branch was necessary, they were primarily concerned with keeping it from being too strong. Much of the animosity of the pre-Revolutionary years had been directed at the colonial governors, and many of the specific grievances under the colonial governing structure concerned the extent of executive power. Even if Pennsylvania had overreacted, its constitution reflected a dislike and distrust of executive authority shared by most Americans. The states experimented with various methods of establishing workable executive branches, but nearly everywhere the chief executive was almost completely dominated by the legislature and usually had to share authority with an executive council.

New York, however, created one of the strongest executive branches of all the first state constitutions. Several measures adopted in other states to limit executive power were either rejected or ignored in New York. Most states kept the chief executive subservient by giving the legislature the power to elect him; New York's governor was chosen directly by the same electorate qualified to vote for senators. Extremely short terms of office, usually one year, were adopted for the chief executive in most states, and several of them included prohibitions against reelection or limited the number of terms one person could serve. New York established a three-year term with no provision against reelection.

Early in the deliberations of the constitutional committee, the members considered the creation of a "council of state" to "assist the Governor in exercising the Supreme executive Power," as one draft put it. It soon became apparent that similar councils adopted in several other states were hampering executive authority, particularly in Pennsylvania. As late as February 1777 the council of state was still included in committee drafts, but soon after that it disappeared. The subject was not resurrected during the convention debate.

One of the great weaknesses of many other constitutions was the failure to outline clearly the powers of the executive. New York's constitution defined the governor's power unequivocally. He could call the legislature into special session and prorogue it for a maximum of sixty days, a power unprecedented in all the other constitutions. The state militia and navy were firmly under his command. He was obligated to report on the condition of the state at every session of the legislature and to recommend measures for its consideration. All government officials were commissioned by him and reported to him; he was to correspond with the Continental Congress and the other states. Most important, he was "to take care that the laws are faithfully executed." Clearly, New York's governor was expected to govern actively and decisively.

Two powers held by the royal governors had been particularly detested by Americans. The governor's power to veto bills passed by the colonial assemblies had been a continuing source of friction in most colonies. Even more disliked was the governor's control of appointments. Most Americans believed that King George III and his royal predecessors had thoroughly corrupted the English political system through the abuse of patronage, a procedure attempted by the colonial governors in America. Nothing frustrated Americans more, declared the *Pennsylvania*

Packet, than seeing the royal governors "sporting with our persons and estates, by filling the highest seats of justice with bankrupts, bullies, and blockheads."

There was little doubt that the veto and appointment powers would be altered drastically in the new state constitutions. John Adams, who wanted a stronger executive branch than most, did not favor giving "the Governor a Negative" on laws; in only a few states did the chief executive have even a limited role in the veto process. Appointments were also carefully controlled. Several state constitutions gave the appointment power to the legislature; Georgia even went to the extreme of electing most officials who had traditionally been appointed.

Although New York's constitution did not grant the governor exclusive authority to veto laws or make appointments, it did give him a substantial role in both. In fact, at the outset it appeared that the convention was willing to give the veto power to the governor alone. The constitutional committee had made no recommendation on who, if anyone, should be able to reject bills passed by the legislature. On March 13, Joseph Smith of Orange County moved that the governor be added as a third branch of the legislature and, as the convention journal reads, that he "may have a negative upon all laws passed by the Senate and Assembly." This proposal was derived from the ancient English notion that the king had a right to participate actively and directly in the lawmaking process and to reject any objectionable bill.

Smith's proposal caught the convention members off guard. Henry Wisner and James Duane managed to delay the discussion of it until the afternoon. When the convention reconvened, Gouverneur Morris softened Smith's motion by changing it to read that the governor would have no authority to propose or amend laws, only to accept or reject them. Opponents of this weakened version tried to delay the discussion once again, but on the following day, after a long debate, the Smith–Morris measure was adopted.

John Jay and Robert R. Livingston then took the initiative in reversing what the convention had done. Two weeks after the measure had been adopted, they brought it up again. After Jay moved to repeal the Smith–Morris amendment, Livingston then proposed a compromise on the veto power. Bills passed by the legislature would go to a so-called "council of revision," consisting of the governor, the justices of the supreme court, and the chancellor (the highest justice of the equity court system). The governor and any two of the others would have the authority to "revise," or veto, all bills and to return them, along with an explanation, to the legislature. Vetoed bills could be repassed over the veto by a two-thirds vote. Any bill not acted upon by the council within ten days would automatically become law.

Even though a majority of the convention members had supported the Smith–Morris amendment, the Jay and Livingston proposals appealed to them even more. The governor would still have a substantial voice in vetoing bills, but he would have to do so in consultation with the state's highest judicial officials. Jay's proposal was adopted unanimously, and Livingston's passed by a vote of thirty-one to four. Not until Massachusetts finally adopted its constitution in 1780 did any chief executive have more authority in vetoing bills than that of New York.

Much of the debate on the executive clauses concerned appointment power. The drafting committee proposed an arrangement in which the governor would make nominations to the legislature. If four nominees for an office were rejected, then the legislature itself would make the appointment. Since this proposal would have created just the sort of potential for direct clashes between the governor and the legislature that most New Yorkers wanted to avoid, there was little chance that it would survive in the convention debate. Several alternate plans were proposed on the convention floor. Zephaniah Platt of Dutchess County suggested giving the appointment power to the governor and the justices of the supreme court; Gouverneur Morris proposed that all officials usually appointed instead be elected by the senatorial electorate. Neither of these ideas appealed to the convention.

On the following day, John Jay made a compromise proposal. A "council of appointment" would be established, consisting of the governor and four senators, one from each of the senatorial districts, chosen annually by the assembly. No senator would be allowed to serve two years in succession. The governor would make all nominations and preside at meetings of the council but would vote only to break ties. As soon as his plan had been presented, Jay immediately moved to add the assembly speaker to the council.

For the next few days the Jay plan withstood several efforts to either expand or lessen the governor's role in appointments. William Harper was defeated in an effort to have the governor removed from the council; Charles De Witt was unsuccessful in trying to have one assemblyman from each county added. Robert Yates reversed the drafting committee's plan by proposing that the legislature make nominations from which the governor could choose. Thomas Tredwell suggested giving the entire appointment power to the legislature. Both proposals were soundly defeated. Robert R. Livingston and Morris failed in an effort to allow the governor to have a vote on every nomination, and Morris was frustrated in trying to make the council an advisory body only, with no authority to reject nominations. All these proposals were defeated by substantial majorities; most of the convention members clearly preferred the Jay plan.

One substantial change was made in Jay's proposal. On the day before the constitution was adopted, Robert R. Livingston succeeded in having the assembly speaker removed from the council. This prompted several efforts by other members to give the assembly a larger role in appointments. Henry Wisner proposed adding to the council an assemblyman chosen by the assembly itself, and Thomas Tredwell moved to have the council members chosen from the assembly rather than the senate. Neither proposal was adopted. The Jay plan, minus the assembly speaker, was incorporated into the constitution.

With the end of the debate on the appointment power, the executive branch was complete. A substantial majority of the convention members found it satisfactory. Most members apparently shared the concern of Duane and Duer that the other states, especially Pennsylvania, had tipped the governmental balance too far in the direction of the legislature at the expense of the executive. They wanted a governor strong enough to provide stable government and maintain order but not so powerful that his powers might be used dictatorially. Only those who had wanted to make the governor stronger or weaker were unhappy with the results in New York's constitution. Morris groused to his friend Alexander Hamilton that executive authority had been hamstrung by the convention, but in fact New York's executive branch proved to be one of the most workable and effective of any created by the first state constitutions.

The office of governor, like the senate, was a new creation, based on old ideas and traditional models adapted to the unique requirements of American politics. In contrast, the judiciary established by the constitution was much more familiar to New Yorkers than either the executive or legislative branches.

Creating the Courts

Very little is said about the judiciary in the first state constitutions. While the constitution makers paid close attention to designing the legislative and executive branches, they simply adopted with few changes the existing colonial court and legal system. Most of the changes made concerned only the very top of the court structure; the local courts were largely untouched. All the states instituted reforms relating to qualifications for judgeships or terms of office, but in general the details of judicial organization and procedures were left to the legislatures. Each state also adopted the English common law and all applicable parliamentary and colonial statute law that was not in conflict with specific provisions of the constitutions. Since the enforcement of the law was the part of the governmental process that touched the lives of Americans most directly, the continuity in the administration of justice provided an important foundation for an orderly transition from British rule to statehood.

New York's colonial court system was basically similar to those in the other colonies. Each colony had a supreme court with jurisdiction over the inferior civil and law courts. Despite its name, the supreme court could be overruled by the governor and council, and appeals could still go even higher to the king and his privy council. Equity courts in most colonies were separate from law courts, with equity, or "chancery," authority residing in the royal governors. Probate authority in colonial New York was exercised under a unique surrogate system. While the law courts governed probate matters in most colonies, in New York the governor had held probate authority technically since 1686. During the eighteenth century, the control of local surrogate appointments and administration of probate gradually passed to the provincial secretary.

With the severing of the tie to England, some of this structure had to be changed. In New York, equity and probate authority was given to the newly created office of chancellor. County law courts continued under a state supreme court. Over both the chancellor and the supreme court was placed a special appeals court, or "court of errors" as it was called, consisting of the senate, the president of the senate (normally the lieutenant governor), the supreme court justices, and the chancellor. Neither the chancellor nor the supreme court justices could vote on appeals from their respective branches, although they were expected to participate in the deliberations.

This same specially constructed high court was empowered to try impeached public officials. No reform was closer to the heart of the revolutionary generation than the establishment of a method for removing public officials from office. Impeachment of Crown officers by Parliament was an ancient practice in England, but it had never been attempted by the colonial legislatures. While all the state constitutions made provisions for impeachment, they differed widely in stating which officials were liable to impeachment and how the trials were to be conducted. So confused was the impeachment process that James Madison later commented: "The diversified expedients adopted in the Constitutions of the several States prove how much the compilers were embarrassed on this subject."

In New York, as in most states, the impeachment power was given to the assembly. The plan presented to the convention by the constitutional committee had called for a three-fourths vote of the members present to institute an impeachment proceeding, but during the floor debate this was reduced to two-thirds. Impeachment trials were then to be conducted by a special court with the same membership as the court of errors. Impeached officials could still be prosecuted in the regular courts if convicted and removed from office. Early drafts of the constitution had contained lists of those officials who could be impeached. Since this was a politically sensitive matter, the list later disappeared, and the constitution left the question of liability purposely vague. The impeachment process outlined in the New York constitution was very similar to that later adopted in the United States Constitution.

Keeping the judiciary independent of the other branches of government was a fundamental maxim of Whig political theory. This independence was accomplished in most states primarily by prohibiting judges from holding other public offices. New York's top judicial officials were allowed to hold no other office except delegate to the Continental Congress, and the chief judge in the county courts could simultaneously serve only in the state senate. New York's judges were permitted to appoint their own clerks and registers, a device intended to keep these court officers free from the influence of the governor and legislators.

But it was easier to keep the judiciary independent in principle than in practice. Making the senate the highest appellate court was a clear violation of the principle of the separation of powers, as many critics pointed out. Since the chief county judges could, if elected, also serve in the senate, they were potentially in a position to participate in rulings on appeals from their own courts. A similar situation had provoked criticism under the colonial governments. Colonial supreme court justices invariably served also on the governor's council and therefore could participate in ruling on appeals from the supreme court.

Other changes in the court system were intended to insure a degree of public control over judges. In some states judges were appointed by the legislature; in Georgia they were elected. Most states adopted extremely short terms of office, and in all states judges could be impeached. New York's constitution contained relatively fewer restrictions than those of most other states. Judges served during good behavior, or, in the case of the chancellor, the supreme court justices, and the chief county judges, until age sixty. Inferior county judges and justices of the peace had to have their commissions renewed every three years, but there was no mandatory retirement age.

After the revolution the states began to pay more attention to their judicial systems. Americans who had previously concentrated almost entirely on the legislative and executive branches now recognized that the courts did not constitute the coequal branch of government which the principle of separating powers presupposed. During the 1780s, a new role for the courts was conceived. Many Americans began to argue that the courts had an obligation to decide whether laws passed by the legislature violated some higher law or were in conflict with basic constitutional privileges. The right of the courts to decide when a law was, in a sense, legal was an innovative concept resulting directly from the experience of the country under the newly formed state governments. Even though the people expressed their sovereign will through their legislatures, argued a Rhode Island newspaper in 1787, laws were still "liable to examination and scrutiny by the people, that is, by the Supreme Judiciary, their servants for this purpose; and those that militate with the fundamental laws, or impugn the principles of the constitution, are to be judicially set aside as void, and of no effect."

New York, through the Council of Revision, had already gone further than most other states in giving its top judicial officers a role in checking legislation. But even this role was limited, for vetoes could be overridden by the legislature. During the 1780s, some New Yorkers, notably Alexander Hamilton and James Duane, began to argue for full-fledged judicial review. As the judge in a case called *Rutgers v. Waddington*, Duane ruled in 1784 that the courts could decide when the legislature might not foresee the consequences of its actions and inadvertently violate an individual's rights. Although Duane insisted that the courts were doing nothing more than enforcing true legislative intent, his point was clear: even the popularly elected legislatures, the very bodies created to express the public will, were capable of violating that trust and had to be checked.

Judicial review was based on the premise that it was necessary to protect fundamental rights even under a republican form of government. The guarantee of rights had been at the core of the revolutionary impulse, and, in one way or another, influenced the course of constitution making in the states.

Rights and Ballots

Americans justified their rebellion against British rule on the grounds that the British were violating the basic rights of the colonists.

The creation of independent state governments, read the opening clause of New York's constitution, was made necessary by "the many tyrannical and oppressive usurpations of the King and Parliament of Great Britain, on the rights and liberties of the people of the American colonies. . . ." The loss of rights had been at the core of the dispute with England since the beginning. In 1776 and 1777, Americans recognized, as one commentator put it, that the strength of the new governments would depend upon the framers' success in "determining and bounding the power and prerogatives of the rulers [and] ascertaining and securing the rights and liberties of the subjects."

Several states in 1776 and 1777 prefaced their new state constitutions with bills of rights. Pennsylvania characteristically wrote one of the most comprehensive, guaranteeing everything from complete religious liberty to the right of the people to dissolve their government if they saw fit. The committee designated to draft New York's constitution was also ordered to draw up a bill of rights, but the committee members inexplicably ignored this part of their instructions. Later, when the constitution was debated on the convention floor, there was no apparent objection to the absence of the bill of rights. Why the convention members let the matter drop is not known. After waiting nine months for the government to be organized, they probably were anxious to get it into operation and were simply unwilling to become involved in a time-consuming debate over the question of rights.

The absence of a separate bill of rights does not mean that basic rights and liberties were not protected by the constitution. Most of the liberties that Americans were concerned about were encompassed by the common law, which was adopted by all the states. Some specific rights were protected by clauses incorporated directly into the text of New York's constitution; others were covered by implication. A jury trial was assured "in all cases in which it hath heretofore been used in the colony of New York," and New Yorkers were protected against arbitrary or extra-legal proceedings by a clause stating that the legislature shall "at no time hereafter, institute any new court or courts but such as shall proceed according to the course of the common law." New York's constitution, like all the others, incorporated the basic principle that rights granted in the constitution, especially the right to vote, could only be withdrawn by a trial at law or a jury conviction. This provided a safeguard against unlawful arrests or seizures.

One specific liberty which New Yorkers debated at length was freedom of religion. Because New York had one of the most religiously diverse populations in America, it had always been one of the more tolerant colonies toward religious groups. Most New Yorkers were probably predisposed to accept a strong declaration on religious freedom in their new constitution, and when the draft constitution came from the committee, it included such a provision. On the convention floor, John Jay tried to insert a clause that would have barred Catholics from owning property or enjoying civil rights until they had sworn before the state supreme court that their allegiance to the pope did not transcend loyalty to the state. Jay also wanted to make Catholics deny the "damnable doctrine" that the pope could absolve them of sin. When Jay's proposal lost after a long debate, he finally had to content himself with adding to the article on naturalization of foreigners the stipulation that they renounce "all allegiance and subjection to all and every foreign king, prince, potentate and state, ecclesiastical as well as civil."

Just before the adoption of the constitution, the wording of the article on religious liberty was changed to make it even stronger. The clause as it stood stated that "the free Toleration of Religious Profession and Worship shall forever hereafter be allowed. . . ." The convention members agreed unanimously to change it to read: "the free exercise and enjoyment of religious profession and worship without discrimination or preference shall forever hereafter be allowed. . . ." Religious worship was not merely to be "tolerated"; it was to be absolutely free of interference. With these changes New York had adopted one of the strongest constitutional clauses on religious liberty of all the states.

There were also other important religious features in the constitution. Free religious worship was not to be "so construed as to excuse acts of licentiousness or justify practices inconsistent with the peace or safety of this state." Quakers, whose scruples against swearing oaths and bearing arms had always caused problems for colonial authorities, were allowed by the constitution to substitute for the loyalty oath an affirmation of loyalty to the state. They were declared exempt from militia service but were to pay a special tax in lieu of it. Because New Yorkers were also concerned with keeping religion out of politics, another article of the constitution prohibited clergymen from holding any civil or military office. New York was the only state which established no religious test for holding public office. Nor did the constitution make the Protestant religion supreme, a provision included in several other state constitutions.

The constitution makers recognized that workable electoral procedures were an important safeguard of representative government. Voting in the eighteenth century was traditionally done by voice; each voter stood among the assembled voters and openly declared his preferences. Many revolutionaries, convinced that this left voters vulnerable to pressure and intimidation, advocated the adoption of the secret ballot as a corrective, but there was no consensus on the point. Opponents argued that ballots were more susceptible to tampering, particularly since many voters could neither read nor write. Between the time that the ballots were cast and later recorded at a central location, there would be ample opportunities for fraud. Voting by voice, they argued, gave each voter the assurance that his vote was clearly understood by everyone within hearing distance, reducing the possibility that it would be misrecorded.

New Yorkers debated the subject at length during the drafting of the constitution. In November 1776, the drafting committee agreed that the governor and lieutenant governor would be elected by ballot, and this recommendation was subsequently adopted by the convention. A much longer discussion ensued concerning assembly and senate elections. Advocates of the secret ballot, led by Abraham Yates, managed to insert a requirement that the secret ballot be used in elections for the assembly, following it up with five pages of minutely detailed instructions on exactly how the ballots were to be cast, tallied, and recorded. When John Jay revised and edited the committee draft, the five pages of instructions disappeared.

Opponents of the secret ballot marshalled their forces during the floor debate. Led by Gouverneur Morris, they managed to delete the clause requiring the use of the ballot in assembly elections. On April 5, John Jay brought the issue back to life by proposing a compromise: voting during the war would continue to be by voice, but after the war, senators and assemblymen would be elected by ballot. If problems resulted from the use of the secret ballot, the legislature would be empowered to restore voice voting by a two-thirds vote of each house. Despite Morris's objections, the compromise proposal passed thirty-three to four.

Abraham Yates still was not satisfied. He had been absent when the Jay compromise was adopted, and when he returned, he announced that he planned to propose further changes. On the morning of the day that the constitution was finally adopted, Yates moved to remove the clause empowering the legislature to alter the voting procedures. Through skillful parliamentary maneuvering, Morris and Robert R. Livingston managed to keep Yates's proposal from coming to a vote.

The discussion on Yates's proposal was the last substantive issue debated by the convention. After a flurry of last-minute changes, all of which passed unanimously, the constitution was adopted by a vote of thirty-three to one. Peter Livingston voted "nay."

Revolution and Compromise

The forty-two article constitution proclaimed in Kingston on April 22, 1777, was a compromise document. Few of the other state constitutions contained so many provisions specifically designed to split the difference between various political and ideological groupings. Most conspicuous were the councils of appointment and revision, creations which revealed the balance between those who believed that vetoes and appointments were proper executive functions and those who were fearful of erecting an executive branch too much like its colonial predecessor. The jerry-rigged Jay compromise on the secret ballot was an obvious effort to relieve the tension between those New Yorkers who thought that the war should bring basic political changes and those who felt that, even in a revolution, innovations should be adopted cautiously, if at all. Other features for which there had been considerable sentiment early in the drafting process—an article delineating the state's boundaries, a bill of rights, an executive council, a detailed description of the electoral process—fell by the wayside as convention members submerged their differences in order to get the state government into operation.

Because New York's constitution makers were able to compromise during the drafting process, the constitution they produced provided a strong foundation for the new state government. No one, of course, believed that it was perfect, or even that everything would work out as planned. The council of appointment, for instance, was a product of the reaction against the excessive power of the colonial governors. Within a decade, the appointment process was intensely politicized by the emergence of political parties, a development largely unforeseen before the Revolution. There was also considerable uncertainty about the use of the secret ballot in elections for governor. According to William Smith, Jr., there appeared to be a conflict between the constitutional provision for electing the governor by ballot and the law passed by the convention outlining election procedures. Peter Livingston told Smith that the convention members themselves were confused, and Smith reported that in Dutchess County the election inspectors failed to keep a record of the electors and their votes, casting doubt on the legality of the election.

Some convention members were unhappy with all or part of the constitution. Peter Livingston, the only member who voted against adoption, believed it was too democratic; others thought it was not democratic enough. Gouverneur Morris complained that it was "deficient for the Want of Vigor in the executive, unstable from the very Nature of popular elective Governments, and dilatory from the Complexity of the Legislature." Other members criticized it for having too strong a governor and too weak a legislature. John Jay, who contributed more to it than any other member of the convention, was angered by the clause allowing judges to appoint officers of the court. Empowering inferior court judges to license attorneys, he lectured Morris and Livingston, "will fill every County in the State with a Swarm of designing cheating litigious Pettifoggers, who like Leaches and Spiders will fatten on the Spoils of the Poor, the Ignorant, the Feeble and the unwary."

Despite such criticism, the constitution proved to be an effective instrument, particularly in comparison with the first constitutions in most other states. Alexander Hamilton, who later wrote some of the most articulate arguments in favor of the United States Constitution, recognized that the strengths of New York's constitution outweighed the weaknesses. Like Gouverneur Morris, Hamilton was concerned that the executive branch might be too weak and also feared that the senate might degenerate into an exclusive, obstructionist body. But he regarded the core of the constitution as sound. "A representative democracy, where the right of election is well secured and regulated and the exercise of the legislative, executive and judiciary authorities, is vested in select persons chosen *really* and not *nominally* by the people," he wrote Morris, "will in my opinion be most likely to be happy, regular and durable." New York had gone far toward establishing such a government, he continued. "On the whole, though I think there are the defects intimated," he concluded, "I think your Government far the best that we have yet seen, and capable of giving long and substantial happiness to the people."

Hamilton was correct. The constitution of 1777 lasted largely unamended for forty-five years, through a political period nearly as turbulent as the revolutionary era had been. It served the state until a new political generation replaced the one that had created the first state government. Not until 1821 was another constitutional convention called. The resulting constitution guaranteed more individual rights, particularly habeas corpus and freedom of speech, both of which had been protected by statute since 1787. The council of appointment was abolished: the compromise which had been so effective in overcoming obstacles in 1777 proved to be one of the most troublesome features of the first constitution. Some of the nearly 15,000 military and civil offices controlled by the council would now be filled by the legislature; others would be elective; still others were to be filled by the governor acting either alone or with the concurrence of the senate.

The council of revision was also eliminated in 1821. The governor would now have the sole power to veto bills, subject to reversal by the legislature. At the same time, the governor's term of office was reduced from three years to two. (The three-year term was reestablished by amendment in 1874 but once again reduced to two years in 1894.) The secret ballot was made permanent in 1821, and an amendment approved by the voters in 1826 removed the property-holding suffrage requirements for white males. Black males still had to qualify under the 1777 property provisions. Property qualifications for blacks were not removed until 1874, after the fifteenth amendment to the United States Constitution had already made such provisions illegal.

Three more times in the nineteenth century, in 1846, 1867, and 1894, conventions were called to revise the constitution. The new constitution adopted in 1846 contained many new features, including the reduction of the senatorial term from four years to two. Changes in the judicial system were among the most important provisions in the 1846 constitution. The chancery court system and the office of chancellor were abolished and the powers absorbed by the supreme court. A court of appeals consisting partly of the supreme court justices and partly of specially elected appellate judges was substituted for the court of errors created in 1777. In 1867, the court of appeals was restructured: the supreme court justices were removed from it, and provisions were made for a seven-man, elected court.

A clause of the 1846 constitution required that the voters decide every twenty years whether a new constitutional convention should be convened. The first convention held under this provision in 1867 drafted a new constitution, but the voters rejected all except the judicial clauses.

The next constitutional convention, which should have met in 1887, was delayed seven years because of partisan conflict between the governor and the legislature. When it did finally meet in 1894, the constitution was substantially revised. Among the more important changes was the creation of a civil service system. Suffrage for women was debated at length but not adopted.

Three constitutional conventions have met in the twentieth century. The constitution proposed by the convention of 1915 was overwhelmingly defeated. In 1938, a substantially new constitution was approved, but the voters rejected the constitution drafted in 1967. The 1894 constitution was amended sixty-eight times between 1899 and 1937. Adult suffrage without sex discrimination was adopted by amendment in 1917. In 1937, an amendment increased the term for assemblymen from one year to two and the terms for governor and lieutenant governor from two years to four. Between 1939 and 1975, 107 amendments have been adopted.

New York's state constitution, which began as a forty-two article document filling thirty-three printed pages, is now 173 pages long in the legislative manual, not counting the index and the table of contents.

Constitution Making in a Time of Troubles*

PATRICIA U. BONOMI

New York University

The initial period of constitution writing in this country—from 1777 to 1787, when not only state charters but also the Articles of Confederation and the federal Constitution were formulated—was one of the most turbulent decades in the nation's history. The depredations of a long war, economic disruption, and rocketing inflation created conditions of strain and instability that hardly seem conducive to the sober task of constructing new governments. But after reading the papers presented today and reflecting on the interesting points they raise, I would like to suggest that the conditions under which those first constitutions were written may in certain respects have been more favorable than they first appear. Focusing on the document we celebrate today, the New York State Constitution of 1777, a review of the circumstances under which our initial charter was drafted may illustrate the point.

The most compelling circumstance of 1777, one that could never have been far from the thoughts of New York's founding fathers, was the war of independence itself. During the months when the constitution was being drafted, moreover, New York was the very stage upon which the major actions of that war were fought. A thirteen-member drafting committee was appointed by the provisional state legislature from among its own delegates on August 1, 1776. In the same weeks that the committee was to begin its deliberations, everyone's attention was centered on the British fleet, which was standing off New York harbor laden with troops being readied for an invasion. Beginning on August 22, the British forces under General William Howe made their first

*Reprinted from *Essays on the Genesis of the Empire State* (Albany: New York State Bicentennial Commission, 1979), 51–56.

landings at Gravesend Bay, and the contest for Long Island and New York City was under way. Imminent defeat of the hard-pressed American forces which had withdrawn to Brooklyn Heights was narrowly avoided by their evacuation to Manhattan in that celebrated Dunkirk-like operation on the night of August 29–30. By September 12, George Washington had been forced to admit that his position on Lower Manhattan island was itself no longer tenable. As the Continental Army made its hairbreadth escape up the west side of the island, the Convention of the Representatives of the State of New York[1] and its constitutional drafting committee fled also, and by September 15 the British had occupied the city.

It is hardly surprising that no progress was made toward writing a constitution during these harrowing weeks. As Professor Bernard Mason notes, moreover, in addition to serving as a constitution writing body, the convention was performing all the legislative and executive functions of government during this chaotic period. With New York the focal point of the war, the convention was constantly busy requisitioning supplies, raising money, and mustering men for Washington's lines. To make matters worse the area was overrun with Loyalists, especially as the war moved north to Westchester County, and the legislators were forced to devote a large portion of their time to the suppression of Loyalists and the confiscation of their property. John Jay, Robert R. Livingston, and Robert Yates, perhaps the three leading members of the constitutional drafting committee, had also been placed in charge of devising measures to obstruct the Hudson River to the advancing British, efforts that resulted in the laying of the first chain across the river at Fort Montgomery and the construction of a log boom.[2]

All these military and governmental obligations disrupted the drafting committee's efforts to settle down to work, but when the New York convention finally convened at White Plains in late October, it looked as if their labors could begin in earnest. On October 28, however, the Battle of White Plains took place, and once again the legislature had to flee. Pushed from New York City to White Plains, to Fishkill, and eventually to Kingston, all the while keeping but one step ahead of the British Army's rapid advance westward to the Hudson River, the committee members stole whatever time they could from their other duties to discuss the form of government they would propose for their wounded state. John Jay may have foreseen many of these difficulties when in an earlier letter to a friend he had written: "We have a government, you know, to form; and God only knows what it will resemble."[3]

The atmosphere in which these first efforts to frame a constitution took place, then, was one filled with the sounds and perils of war.

A second circumstance that made for a special sense of urgency was the universal wish of the people for a tangible government that would give them an assurance of political legitimacy. New Yorkers, like other Americans of that day, were firmly attached to the idea of a written constitution. They had lived for generations with the shadowy ambiguities of an English constitution whose meaning seemed to change with each new situation. Now they wanted everything to be spelled out and made explicit. They wanted the rules for their new state to be accessible to everyone in a single, written document. For the present, their only government was the Convention of the Representatives of the State of New York, whose combination of both legislative and executive functions was all too reminiscent of the parliamentary system against which they were rebelling. Thus there was a special tone of urgency in the eighteenth-century New Yorkers' insistence that their new state be settled on a legitimate constitutional base. Some Yorkers, like the aristocratic Philip Schuyler, feared that a rudderless ship of state would result in anarchy. "I am very apprehensive," he declared, "that much Evil will arise if a Government is not soon established for this State. The longer it is delayed the more difficult it will be to bring the unprincipled and licentious to a proper Sense of their Duty and we have too many such amongst us."[4] Others feared that an oligarchy would seize power and defeat the very republican principles for which the Revolution was being fought. And everyone was uneasy with the present state of suspension and uncertainty.

These two conditions—the war and the strong public wish for a written frame of government—combined to create a sense of time pressure on the first constitutional drafting committee that would never be duplicated in subsequent constitutional conventions. It may even be that these same qualities of tension and urgency created a sort of optimum environment for the committee's labors. Having the Redcoats at one's back no doubt provided a powerful incentive to focus the mind. The committee members could not quibble over every word and meaning as they might have done under more leisurely circumstances, and the shortage of time thus became the strongest possible inducement to compromise and reconciliation. Moreover, eighteenth-century New Yorkers needed such a prod, for they were just as likely to divide into factions and clashing interests as their descendants have been ever since.[5] But with time a precious resource, private interests had to be set aside and impasses broken so that the committee could forge ahead with its essential work.

It has recently been observed that "few of the other state constitutions contained so many provisions specifically designed to split the difference between various political and ideological groupings" as did New York's.[6] This is not to say that the final document was without faults, however. Certain of its features, especially the Councils of Revision and Appointment, proved unwieldy and later had to be replaced. Nonetheless, the 1777 Constitution served without major revision for over forty years, providing New Yorkers with legitimacy and a working form of government in the crucial early period of transition.

All of New York's major constitutional conventions in succeeding years have been held in times of relative tranquility. The 1821 Convention took place during the so-called "Era of Good Feelings"; the conventions of 1846 and 1894 fell during periods of optimism and expansionism in American life; 1915 and 1938 can be characterized as years of lull before the storm; and 1967 seems almost like another age when we consider the political and cultural upheaval that began the next year. In these more placid years the delegates were freer to engage in political bargaining, to divide into factions, and to indulge their fondness for rhetorical display. No coercions of time or public impatience disciplined their deliberations or forced them to prompt conclusions. And while significant revisions were achieved in these conventions, many reforms became so caught in a tangle of complex maneuvers and turgid language that hopes for implementing them had to be abandoned. All of which gives special weight to Professor Gerald Benjamin's suggestion that means other than formal conventions may offer a more effective avenue to constitutional reform.

Short of another revolution, it is unlikely that we will reproduce the dynamic and often salutary conditions of 1777. Yet it is inevitable and right that our state constitution should change with the times. As Thomas Jefferson once observed about the federal charter: the Constitution "as it is, will, I believe, last my time, and those coming after will know how to repair it to their own minds."[7] Let us hope that present and future New Yorkers will be equal to Jefferson's high expectations.

NOTES:

[1]On July 9, 1776, the Provincial Congress changed its name to the Convention of the Representatives of the State of New York.

[2]The chain was said to have cost some £70,000. Donald F. Clark, comp., *Fort Montgomery and Fort Clinton: Several Contemporary Accounts of the Battle, Monday, 6 October 1777* (Fort Montgomery, New York, 1952), 15.

³John Jay to Edward Rutledge, July 6, 1776, as quoted in William Jay, ed., *The Life of John Jay* (2 vols., New York, 1833), I, 62.

⁴Schuyler to Robert Yates, December 6, 1776, as quoted in Don R. Gerlach, *Philip Schuyler and the American Revolution in New York, 1733–1777* (Lincoln, Nebr., 1964), 297.

⁵See Patricia U. Bonomi, *A Factious People: Politics and Society in Colonial New York* (New York, 1971).

⁶William A. Polf, *1777: The Political Revolution and New York's First Constitution* (Albany, New York State Bicentennial Commission, 1977), 39.

⁷Thomas Jefferson to Thomas Pleasants, Jr., 1821, as quoted in Saul K. Padover, ed., *Thomas Jefferson on Democracy* (New York, 1946), 153.

Constitutional Revision in New York: Retrospect and Prospect *

GERALD BENJAMIN

State University of New York at New Paltz

O n November 8, 1977, New Yorkers will celebrate the bicentennial of the adoption of their first constitution by voting upon whether a constitutional convention should be held to revise the current basic document, adopted in 1895 and last changed in a major way almost a half century ago. Should a convention be mandated, it will be the tenth in the history of the state. Certainly the coincidence in this year of the two hundredth anniversary of the first constitution and a referendum on the current one offers the scholar more than the usual incentive for considering both the past of constitutional revision in New York and the prospects for the future of this process.

Constitutional revision may be achieved in several ways, both formal and informal.[1] Though we are most likely to think of informal revision in connection with executive, legislative, and (especially) judicial action at the national level, it is clear that judicial interpretation or efforts by the political branches may just as effectively alter state constitutions. What else, after all, were the development of moral obligation borrowing and lease-purchase agreements by the Rockefeller administration, or the declaration by the state legislature of a "period of probable usefulness" for certain operating expenditures of local governments? As a practical matter, these techniques, devised to bypass restrictions in the state constitution on state and local fiscal practices, were informal revisions of that document.[2]

In New York, formal revision may occur in either of two ways. One alternative is the passage by two successively elected legislatures of an amendment, which then is offered to the electorate for ratification. The

*Reprinted from *Essays on the Genesis of the Empire State* (Albany: New York State Bicentennial Commission, 1979), 35–50.

second is the holding of a constitutional convention. Such a convention may be called either as a result of a proposition put on the ballot by legislative action or as a result of a provision, added to the state constitution in 1846, that requires the presentation of the following question to the voters every twenty years: "Shall there be a convention to revise the constitution and amend the same?"[3] The 1967 state constitutional convention was called as the result of legislative initiative. This year the question is on the ballot because of the constitutional requirement.

The periodic automatic presentation of the convention question, a practice New York shares with thirteen other states, raises an interesting issue. Generally, analysts are inclined to attribute the emergence of a constitutional convention to "crisis" in a state's political system. Accumulated grievances, intolerable corruption, or other massive malfunctions in state government allow the forces of reform to overcome entrenched interests, this thesis goes, in order to restructure the polity.[4] In New York perhaps the best example of this dynamic is the 1846 convention, which resulted after legislative intransigence blocked action over an extended period of time on a number of pressing issues: judicial reorganization, changes in land law, removal of the property requirement for officeholding, and restriction of the legislative power to incur debt.[5]

The automatic provision, however, allows a convention to be called in the absence of "crisis." Designed to take some of the control of constitutional convention timing out of the hands of a legislature that may itself be a target for change, the result of this provision may be a convention that few knowledgeable observers of state affairs thinks really necessary. This year is a case in point. On the Democratic side, though some preparations for a state constitutional convention have been made by the assembly, Governor Hugh Carey has openly questioned the need for such a meeting.[6] In the major statewide bastion of Republican power, the senate, there have been no preparations at all for a possible affirmative vote on the constitutional convention proposition. The senate leadership has considered the matter, has concluded that from both a partisan and policy perspective there is little to gain from holding a convention, and has decided to remain discreetly silent. Even the good-government groups, usually the leading agitators for constitutional reform, have been relatively inactive. There was one conference in Albany to define issues in March of 1976, but little has happened since.[7] One bellwether group, the state League of Women Voters, will make no recommendation to its members on the constitutional convention proposition this year.

This leadership ennui may be shattered by the actions of the voters in November. In the recent past, the electorate has been full of surprises on constitutional proposition balloting. In 1936, most of the political leaders of the state failed to encourage or actively opposed the holding of a convention. The New York *Times* concurred, urging a "no" vote.[8] Nevertheless, the voters mandated a convention, one that proved to be the most productive of this century. In contrast, in 1956 Governor Averell Harriman, a Democrat, and Republican legislative leaders, determined not to be caught unprepared by the question to be presented in 1957, appointed a constitutional commission to prepare for a convention by doing research on prospective issues. In a close vote, the convention proposition was rejected. (The commission was not, however, a total failure. It provided the initial platform for the successful effort of its chairman, Nelson Rockefeller, to capture the governorship from Harriman, the man who had appointed him.)

Several factors contribute to the unpredictable nature of voting on constitutional convention propositions. In this century, two of four considerations of such propositions were in off election years when voter turnout was traditionally lower. A third consideration, that of 1914, was at a special election held in April and prior to the state's adoption of woman's suffrage. Turnout for this election was about one-fifth of that for the general election for governor held in November of the same year (Table I).

A further point is that even among those voters who turned out, only about half have cast valid ballots on the constitutional convention question. The phenomenon called "ballot fatigue" has taken a massive toll, whether in regular or off election years (Table I). The result is that a self-selected minority, one-half-plus-one of that half of the electorate that votes on the convention question, decides on whether a convention will be held. These voters tend to be an elite—well educated, upper middle class, highly efficacious—and positively oriented toward reform. Nevertheless, in these circumstances, such ephemeral factors as the relative intensity and importance of contests for local office may have a major impact.

In the past, constitutional convention balloting in New York State could be explained in terms of the classic upstate-downstate split. Massive downstate majorities for a convention, linked to a Democratic desire to alter the Republican advantage in state legislative apportionment cemented into the constitution of 1895, were generally opposed by upstate majorities for the status quo. More recently, however, a "New York City v. Rest of the State" explanation has offered us little aid in

TABLE I

Twentieth- Century Constitutional Convention Propositions—New York State

VOTER TURNOUT—NUMBER AND (%)

Total Vote (excluding blanks)

Year	New York City	Outside New York City	Total
1914	103,401 (33.9)	201,890 (66.1)	305,291
1936	1,528,816 (58.7)	1,075,163 (41.3)	2,603,879
1957	1,060,895 (40.7)	1,549,736 (59.3)	2,610,631
1965	1,266,138 (40.2)	1,883,731 (59.8)	3,149,869

Blank Ballots

Year	New York City	Outside New York City	Total
1914	1,604 (31.1)	3,549 (68.9)	5,153 (1.7)*
1936	1,294,375 (43.2)	1,691,839 (56.8)	2,986,214 (52.5)*
1957	1,163,159 (44.6)	1,445,045 (55.4)	2,608,204 (50.0)*
1965	1,386,313 (48.7)	1,562,019 (51.3)	2,948,332 (48.3)*

*Note: The percentages in this column represent that portion of the electorate that actually entered the voting booth in the year indicated but did not vote on the constitutional convention proposition. These percentages should be read separately from other percentages in this table.

understanding constitutional convention proposition balloting (Table II). In the 1965 election (which, similarly to the coming case of 1977, was held in the same year as a New York City mayoral election), though upstate voters provided a slight majority against the convention, their affirmative vote was 54.5 percent of the total for the state (Table III). Indeed, a multivariate analysis of county level voting patterns on the 1965 convention proposition showed supporters of the idea to be affluent, urban, non-homeowning Democrats, but these urban Democrats were located throughout the state, not just in New York City.[9]

TABLE II

TWENTIETH- CENTURY CONSTITUTIONAL CONVENTION PROPOSITIONS—NEW YORK STATE

Vote in New York City—Number & (%)*

	Yes	No	Total
1914	79,305	24,096	103,401
	(76.7)	(23.3)	
1936	1,017,636	511,180	1,528,816
	(66.6)	(33.4)	
1957	651,032	409,863	1,060,895
	(61.4)	(38.6)	
1965	765,723	500,415	1,266,138
	(60.5)	(39.5)	

TWENTIETH-CENTURY CONSTITUTIONAL CONVENTION PROPOSITIONS—NEW YORK STATE

Outside New York City—Number & (%)*

	Yes	No	Total
1914	74,017	127,873	201,890
	(36.7)	(63.3)	
1936	395,968	679,095	1,075,063
	(36.8)	(63.2)	
1957	591,536	958,200	1,549,736
	(38.2)	(62.8)	
1965	915,715	968,016	1,883,731
	(48.6)	(51.4)	

*Blanks and void ballots are not included in totals.

TABLE III

TWENTIETH- CENTURY CONSTITUTIONAL CONVENTION PROPOSITIONS—NEW YORK STATE

AFFIRMATIVE VOTE—NUMBER AND (&)

	New York City	Upstate	Total
1914*	79,305	74,017	153,322
	(51.7)	(48.3)	
1936	1,017,636	395,968	1,413,604
	(72)	(28)	
1957	651,032	591,536	1,242,568
	(52.4)	(47.6)	
1965	765,723	915,715	1,681,438
	(45.5)	(54.5)	

*This was a special election. held on April 7, 1914. Turnout was 21.2 percent of that for the general election for governor in the same year.

A short look at the entrails of long-dead elections surely is not a foolproof way to predict current electoral behavior. What such an analysis does tell us, however, is that despite widespread leadership reluctance, we may indeed once again be surprised by the enigmatic voters of New York this year. If we are, what will the central concerns of a constitutional convention be, and how do these relate to those of conventions held in the past?

Constitutional Values

A few fundamental values have guided constitution making in New York State over the past 200 years. Without doing too much injury to the complexities involved, these may be labeled democracy, liberty, control of government, and effectiveness in government. It may be said further that, in each different historic epoch, a different one of these values has provided the dominant constitutional concern, although not the exclusive one.

Clearly the dominant concern at New York's first constitutional convention was for the degree of democracy that would be allowed in the new polity.[10] In the issues it faced—the basis for representation in the upper and lower houses, the strength of the executive, the nature and extent of property requirements for voting and officeholding, the length of terms of office, direct vs. indirect election of officials—New York was similar to other states.[11] It was the way New York solved these problems that made it more "aristocratic" than its sisters.

From 1777 forward, the question of "How much democracy?" was regularly on the agenda of New York constitutional conventions. The general trend has been toward democratization. Thus in 1821 property qualifications were removed for voting, and in 1846 for officeholding. In 1874 black males were given the unencumbered franchise. Voting for women, debated extensively in 1894, was approved in 1917. This is not to say, of course, that the history of New York has been one of a continual march, onward and upward, toward ever-increased democracy. (Until it was overturned by judicial action in the mid-1960s, the apportionment formula entrenched in the 1895 document, for example, assured a decreasingly democratic state senate.) The point is that democracy has been an enduring central value. In 1967, the consideration of extending the franchise to eighteen-year-olds, though not a major convention issue, was a continuation of this tradition.

A second major focus of constitutional conventions has been upon the assurance of liberty. Though religious freedom and the right to a jury trial were included in the 1777 constitution, it had within it no separate bill of rights. The Bill of Rights Act of the state legislature, passed in 1787, was added to New York's constitution by the 1821 convention. Over time, fundamental liberties have come to be a relatively settled constitutional area, although additions or changes in detail have been made from time to time. In 1938, a bill of rights of labor was added to Article I. In 1967, significant additions were attempted in the state bill of rights, and changes were sought to achieve conformance with the language of the federal constitution. These alterations failed ratification at the polls.

During the middle and late nineteenth century, fears about the excesses of government led to the use of the power of the constitution to constrain action not only in the area of personal liberty, but also in significant substantive areas of public policy. In New York, as in many other states, the use of constitutional amendment to place selected matters beyond the reach of the political branches of government, often in reaction to a crisis of the moment, became a widespread phenomenon. A few examples may be given. In 1846, in reaction to a severe fiscal crisis caused by extensive and inadequately financed state borrowing for public improvements, two amendments were passed. One required a referendum before public debt could be incurred, and another forbade the use of the state's borrowing power for private purposes.[12] In 1894, amendments mandating a merit system in public employment and requiring that the Adirondack forest preserve be kept "forever wild" created additional restrictions on governmental action. Acting upon the notion, common at the time, that state government was a predator that had to be held in check by extraordinary measures, these two nineteenth-century conventions established in New York what has come to be called a "tradition" of legislation through constitutional amendment.[13]

In the twentieth century the focus of reform shifted. The concern was no longer with limiting government, but rather with strengthening it and making it more efficient so that it could meet the compelling social problems of the new century. Several contrasts highlight this point. During the decades just prior to and after the Civil War, in accord with the emphasis on the need to constrain government, having a large number of elected state officials was perceived as a guarantee of democracy and liberty. But by the 1915 convention, reformers, influenced by the newly emergent professional public administration movement, saw these same phenomena as excessive fragmentation, a block to effective governmental action.

Generally, efficiency in government meant strengthening the formal powers of the executive and his control over the state bureaucracy. In 1777, New York's acceptance of a strong executive was a victory for the forces that sought to limit democracy in the new state. In contrast, in 1915 (and into the 1920s when, under the leadership of Governor Alfred E. Smith, the battle was finally won) the desire for a strong executive with control over budget and bureaucracy was justified on the basis of the necessity for making government work better to serve the needs of the people. The target of reform during one period became its goal in another.

Throughout the twentieth century, the central value that constitutional reformers have sought to serve has been government effectiveness. In addition to action on the executive, the importance of this value can be seen in the debates during several constitutional conventions, including the one held in 1967, over such issues as judicial reform and home rule for localities. No issue, however, illustrates the emphasis upon governmental effectiveness more clearly than the drive for constitutional simplification.

The Myths of Constitutional Simplification

No constitution is written on a blank slate. All such documents are attempts at concrete solutions to the pre-eminent political problems of the era in which they are drawn. As time passes, as new problems become the most compelling on the political agenda, new solutions are added to the old. The result is often a document that the incremental processes of history have left expanded and layered, much like the soil in a river delta. No new constitution adopted by New York State has ever been shorter than the one it replaced. The constitution of 1777 was 6,600 words long; our current document contains 45,000 words.

Another point might be reinforced here. Although there may be broad agreement in one era about what constitutes an ideal constitution, agreement is rare from one era to the next. Thus, as one team of scholars has suggested: "Conventions in one era meet to undo the careful reforms of an earlier generation."[14] This is the case in New York, for example, with regard to the constitutional limits on state borrowing power and local taxing authority. Both of these are the results of previous constitutional revision. Both are targeted for change by modern reformers as unnecessary restrictions that hamper governmental effectiveness.[15]

Simplification is an attractive symbol. Who would disagree that the state constitution should be less cluttered, more understandable to New York's citizens? Indeed, demand for simplification is one assumption underlying the idea that most of the constitutional compromises of the past are outmoded and should be swept away. The state constitution, it is argued, should be short like the national document, and concentrate on fundamental principles. And along with this set of propositions goes the view that such ideal documents can only be achieved through comprehensive change in an apolitical environment.

Let us examine these arguments. The first point that may be made is that neither age nor length are, in themselves, negative qualities for constitutions.[16] As Judge Charles Breitel pointed out in 1967, the functions of state government differ from those of the national government, and therefore states may need more detailed documents.[17] Furthermore, the political cultures of some states may require formal revision through amendment rather than informal change through interpretation. As for age, it is interesting that those who denounce New York's 1894 document as a "horse and buggy affair" because of its age accept the federal document as a model, despite its age, on the length criterion![18]

In fact, an examination of the age and length of state constitutions now in force demonstrates that the oldest documents, drawn prior to the Civil War, are about the same length as the modern ones, drawn since World War II. The longest constitutions are the products of the post-Civil War to World War I period. There is no significant statistical correlation between a constitution's modernity and the number of words it contains. The age of New York's Constitution is almost exactly at the mean for the states. Although the document is a long one, there is a tendency among the larger, more socially complex states to have longer documents (Table IV).

TABLE IV

The Constitutions of the Ten Largest States

State	Date of Passage	Length	% of Amendments Passed
California	1879	32,000	59.1
Florida	1969	23,500	*
Illinois	1971	13,200	**
Massachusetts	1780	33,092	92.9
Michigan	1964	20,000	46.7
New Jersey	1948	15,700	70.3
New York	1895	39,000***	73.8
Ohio	1851	31,100	55.2
Pennsylvania	1968	21,500	72.7
Texas	1876	60,000	62.1

*Under the 1969 Florida constitution, popular ratification of constitutional amendments is not required.

**Too few cases for valid comparison.

***Estimates of the length of the New York Constitution vary. The number commonly used inside the state is 45,000 words. This figure is used because it appears in the same source as all other figures used in this table.

Source: Council of State Governments, *Book of the States: 1976–1977* (Lexington, Ky.: The Council, 1976), 163.

But the two greatest myths fostered by the simplification advocates concern the possibility in New York of apolitical reform and comprehensive reform. Careful comparative empirical research has shown that the relative partisanship of a state's constitutional convention is a function of the nature of the delegate selection process and the state's political system. If parties in a state are closely competitive, the selection system is partisan; and if district size is small, constitutional conventions will be partisan.[19] New York's selection system is written into the Constitution. It is based upon partisan election and state senate districts, with a small at-large component.[20] Under these conditions, New York's constitutional conventions will be partisan despite all appeals of good government groups. There is a classic "catch–22" at work. Nonpartisan conventions will require a constitutional amendment to alter the delegate selection process, but such an amendment must be passed by a (partisan) legislature or a (partisan) constitutional convention to reach the voters.

With this reality in mind, the appeals of good government groups in New York for nonpartisanship in constitution making are misdirected.[21] Their efforts should be focused upon altering the delegate selection process. Nevertheless, they persist in seeking to alter the "arena of conflict," in the hope that the comprehensive reforms that they advocate will do better in the convention, a temporary and relatively structured body, than in the structured state legislature.[22] In this hope they are usually disappointed.

Like the hope for apolitical conventions, the aim of comprehensive reform is an all-but-impossible dream in the New York context. The "legislation" in the constitution is there because it protects real interests in the state, interests that will fight hard to retain these protections. Will civil servants risk amendment of their constitutional guarantees, or environmentalists of theirs? Even where these interests may be overcome, the symbolic value of some constitutional provisions that reformers would like to see removed may prevent ratification of changes by the voters. For example, even though constitutional debt and tax limits have been ineffectual, it is difficult to perceive of the voters endorsing their removal just after the state and several of its cities have skirted the brink of fiscal collapse.

Overall constitutional reform failed in New York in 1967, and this state's experience was not unique. Since 1930, there have been twelve comprehensive state constitutional revisions that have succeeded, but twenty-two that have failed.[23] Though superficially an attractive option for total, once-and-for-all cleaning up of the mess, both because of internal dynamics and because of consequent ratification problems, constitutional conventions, especially with ground rules such as those prevailing in New York, promise more than they deliver.

Another problem is apparent. When a convention gathers, its agenda is not limited. Its energies may be captured by an issue of the moment, rather than by the arcane and sometimes complex issues that the advocates of simplification would have it address. In 1967 in New York, the debate over the Blaine Amendment and state aid to parochial schools dominated the constitutional convention and later voter consideration of its work. If a convention is called as a result of this year's balloting, it may well be dominated by another passionate issue, perhaps an amendment seeking to block abortion in the state. How would more technical constitutional issues fare in this environment?

There is a fiction attendant to the comprehensive approach that constitutional amendment through the legislative route is difficult. In fact, research by Albert Sturm has shown that throughout the states this method succeeded about two-thirds of the time, and that, since 1970, it was more effective than attempts at comprehensive change.[24] New York's record is better than average. Between 1894 and 1975, 73.8 percent of constitutional amendments offered to its voters have won approval. Clearly, even when the overall products of constitutional conventions failed in popular referendums, when individual changes were able to gain the approval of two successive sessions of the legislature, they were likely to win acceptance at the polls.

Conclusion

In considering the need for constitutional revision, it is essential to recall the fundamental soundness of the basic principles of the New York document, even when measured by the effectiveness criteria used by modern reformers. One recent piece of research compared seven state constitutions to a model document drafted by the National Municipal League (the reform "ideal") in twenty-nine key categories. Comparisons were made both before and after state constitutional conventions were held. Of the seven documents studied, New York's had the second highest "reform score" at the outset (after Hawaii, admitted to statehood with a new constitution in 1958).[25] The 1967 changes were not adopted, but even without them New York's current constitution is closer to the model on several key criteria than those of most other states. It is important to remember, when considering the need for a constitutional convention in New York, that this is a state in which reform in this century has, in large measure, already successfully redefined the political system.

There are problems with the current New York constitution. There is some unnecessary detail, some material on reapportionment that needs to be altered to bring the document into conformance with federal law and judicial opinions.[26] These are not problems, however, that require a constitutional convention for their resolution. Given the kind of convention New York is likely to have, should one be called, and the problems that body will face, it is a better strategy to seek the necessary constitutional changes through the legislative route. The automatic provision of the state constitution has led this year to a balloting that may call a constitutional convention in the absence of real need in the state, and without the prospect for fundamental change. Sophisticated voters should reject this option this year.

Postscript

Two months after this essay was written, the New York electorate decided by a three-to-two margin not to hold a constitutional convention in 1978. Participation on the convention question was the lowest it has been since 1914. For those who did vote, balloting followed the pattern of the recent past, though upstate rural and suburban hostility was considerably greater than in 1965 or even 1957. In the absence of any burning constitutional issue, New Yorkers decided that the risks (and costs) of a convention were not worth the potential gains. The opportunity offered for automatic periodic reconsideration of the document was rejected, and it was left to the elected political leadership of the state to initiate incremental change in those specific areas in which it could be convincingly demonstrated that it was really needed.

NOTES

[1] Elmer E. Cornwell, Jay S. Goodman, and Wayne R. Swanson, *State Constitutional Conventions* (New York: Praeger, 1975), 7-8.

[2] It is interesting that on the state level the courts have been the most conservative branch with regard to the constitution, especially the debt, taxing, and home rule provisions.

[3] New York State Constitution, Article XIX.

[4] Edward Grant III, "State Constitutional Revision and the Forces That Shape It," *State and Local Government Review* 9 (May 1977): 63-64.

[5] David M. Ellis, *Landlords and Farmers in the Hudson Mohawk Region* (New York: Octagon, 1967), 277-78.

⁶Speaker's Task Force on Constitutional Revision, *Constitutional Revision in New York State* (Albany: processed, 1976); New York State Assembly, Standing Committee on the Judiciary, *Report* (Albany: processed, 1977); *New York Times*, August 8, 1977.

⁷The conference was held March 23, 1977, and was sponsored by the Citizen's Union, the League of Women Voters, Common Cause, and the New York Public Interest Research Group. Proceedings were not published.

⁸Vernon A. O'Rourke and Douglas W. Campbell, *Constitution-Making in a Democracy* (Baltimore: Johns Hopkins University Press, 1943), 63–64

⁹Cornwell, et. al., 41.

¹⁰See Bernard Mason, *The Road to Independence* (Lexington: University of Kentucky Press, 1966), Chapter 7; and William A. Polf. *1777: The Political Revolution and New York's First Constitution* (Albany: New York State Bicentennial Commission, 1977).

¹¹Jackson Turner Main, *The Sovereign States: 1775-1783* (New York: Franklin Watts, 1973), Chapter 5.

¹²Charles Z. Lincoln, *The Constitutional History of New York*, Vol. 2 (Rochester: Lawyer's Cooperative Publishing Company, 1906), 73, 93.

¹³Cornwell, et. al., 20.

¹⁴*Ibid.*, 203.

¹⁵Speaker's Task Force, 8-18.

¹⁶This point is made in Duane Lockard, *Politics of State and Local Government* (New York: Macmillan, 1963), 94.

¹⁷*New York Times*, January 28, 1967.

¹⁸Speaker's Task Force, 4.

¹⁹See Elmer Cornwell, Jay S. Goodman, and Wayne R. Swanson, "State Constitutional Conventions: Delegates, Roll Calls, and Issues," *Midwest Journal of Political Science* 14 (Feb. 1970): 105-130; and Cal Clark and Janet Clark. "The Impact of Party and Electoral Systems on Political Conflict in State Constitutional Conventions," *Western Political Quarterly* 28 (December, 1975): 700-712.

²⁰New York State Constitution, Article XIX, Section 2.

²¹For a statement of the reform view, see League of Women Voters of New York State, *Seeds of Failure: A Political Review of New York State, 1967 Constitutional Convention* (New York: The League, 1973).

²²For a discussion of this concept, see E.E. Schattschneider, *The Semi-Sovereign People* (New York: Holt, Rinehart, and Winston, 1960).

²³Grant, 63.

²⁴Albert L. Sturm, *Thirty Years of State Constitution-Making, 1938-1968* (New York: National Municipal League, 1970), 29-31; and Council of State Governments, *Book of the States, 1976-1977* (Lexington, Ky.: The Council, 1976), 163.

²⁵Cornwell, et. al (1975), 158.

²⁶Assembly Task Force, 28.

John Jay and the New York State Constitution and Courts after Two Hundred Years *

RICHARD B. MORRIS
Late Gouverneur Morris Professor of History, Emeritus,
Columbia University

This two hundredth anniversary of the founding of our state government and of John Jay's contribution thereto requires perhaps a big leap back in time and circumstances. The summer of 1777 presented New York with its darkest prospects. The whole northern front seemed to be verging on collapse. A British force from New York City was readying itself for an advance northward. Fort Ticonderoga had been evacuated, and General John Burgoyne's Redcoats, Hessians, and Indians were pushing ahead relentlessly in their southward drive to Albany. Meantime, British General Sir Henry Clinton was readying his troops for a push northward to join Burgoyne, divide the thirteen states, and smash New York state's refugee government and its Patriot supporters.

By this time in September the tide seemed to be turning. The British were forced to abandon the siege of Fort Stanwix on the Mohawk River, and the Hessians were decimated by General Stark's men fighting outside Bennington, but on the New York State side. Within another week the decisive battle of Saratoga would be in its opening phases—a battle that was to be a turning point of the Revolution, one might say even of world history.

Conscious of their perils, New York's Patriot statesmen moved forward nonetheless with their program to put into effect the state govern-

*Reprinted from *Essays on the Genesis of the Empire State* (Albany: New York State Bicentennial Commission, 1979), 5–11.

ment which their constitution had established—a constitution adopted just a few months before. To guarantee the rule of law, even in wartime, they inaugurated New York State's first judicial system 200 years ago.

It is indeed appropriate that these twin events—the bicentennial of our state government and the two-hundredth anniversary of New York's judicial system, should be commemorated today in this handsome historic residence—for in the years ahead this was to be the home as governor or in retirement of the draftsman of the New York State Constitution and the first chief justice of the state, that remarkable man named John Jay. Indeed, until very recent years, this residence was also the home of his direct descendants. We are surrounded by heirlooms which have been in the continuous possession of the Jay family for more than two centuries, and we are privileged to have members of the family with us today.

We are fortunate, too, that first Westchester County and then the state assumed responsibility for this historic landmark, so well tended and preserved under the direction of Orin Lehman and his staff and our own curator, Lino S. Lipinsky de Orlov.

There are so many other memorable events in the history of the state and nation with which Jay was associated that it would take the better part of a day merely to list them. But to encapsulate: In a little over a year following September 10, 1777, Jay was to become president of the Continental Congress, and then he represented the United States as head of a diplomatic mission to Spain. From Spain he journeyed to Paris in 1782 to join Benjamin Franklin and then to be supported by John Adams in drafting the preliminary and final treaties which ended the war of the American Revolution, giving the United States its independence and a great continental domain, in which negotiations he was the central figure.

When Jay came home he served for a five-year period until 1789 as secretary for foreign affairs under the Confederation, then as *ad interim* secretary of state under President George Washington until Thomas Jefferson returned from Paris to assume the post. In Washington's administration Jay was the first chief justice of the United States, and, while still on the high court, Jay went abroad to negotiate with the British the famous treaty that bears his name.

When Jay returned from England in 1795, he learned that he had been elected governor of New York State to succeed George Clinton, an election he won without so much as having to lift a finger. After two terms as governor, he retired to this country retreat that he had built to his specifications while still governor. For the rest of his life he devoted himself to philanthropic and civic affairs, notably to the freedom of the blacks, a cause that his sons carried on with notable success.

Today, however, I shall only briefly advert to just two aspects of Jay's illustrious career—first in setting up the machinery of state government, and second, in founding the courts.

If any man were to be singled out as the author of the state's first constitution, he is John Jay. He was the chairman of the original committee named in August 1776 to draft a constitution. He and his committee colleagues were all occupied with a variety of war duties that summer and fall—fortifying the Hudson against British naval incursion, rounding up Tories and spies—and so it was not until March that Jay was able to submit the committee's draft to the state convention, which adopted it in modified form on April 20.

Many of the special features of the constitution bore Jay's imprint. Just to name a few:

1) a relatively strong executive elected by the people instead of by the legislature as elsewhere;

2) a council of appointment, on which the governor served to share appointing power;

3) the council of revision, with which the governor shared veto power;

4) the notion of checks and balances;

5) the notion of a tripartite division of powers between the executive, the legislature, and the judiciary;

6) the idea of voting by ballot instead of *viva voce;*

7) the provision for religious freedom—which especially distinguishes this remarkable state constitution.

Jay could not stay for the final debates. On April 17, 1777, he was called away to tend his dying mother at Fishkill, and some changes were introduced by the convention in his absence. Indeed, he was exceedingly unhappy about two of these changes—the first conferred on the judges the power to appoint the clerks of their respective courts. "Patronage and nepotism," Jay charged. The second required attorneys to be separately licensed in *each* court in which they would practice. Jay would have conferred on the supreme court the exclusive power of admitting attorneys. He found the provision, to quote this lawyer, "the most whimsical, crude, and undigested thing I have met with." Why this was devised to spare the supreme court of drudgery, Jay could not understand. Why was it any more drudgery, he asked, than striking a jury or any other business incidental to judicial duties? In short, Jay saw no sense in a provision which required an attorney seeking general license to obtain admission in the supreme court, in three mayor's courts, in *thirteen* inferior courts of common pleas, in *fourteen* sessions courts, "and the Lord knows how often, or in how many courts of oyer and terminer and gaol delivery." Fortunately we have a more common-sense approach to admission to the bar today, and it is basically the one advocated by John Jay.

Jay had a few disappointments. He had hoped to incorporate in the constitution a provision for the abolition of slavery. He wanted New York to act first among the thirteen states in that regard. Gouverneur Morris, his friend and political ally, put up a valiant fight during his absence, but to no avail. Jay was never to lose sight of this goal, and twenty years later, as governor, he affixed his name to an enactment providing for ending slavery in the state. But I shall forgo any further probing of that document, as it will be the subject of the next speaker this afternoon.

And now for the courts. Very little was said about them in the new state constitution. By implication the courts adopted the pre-existent system with few changes. The local courts of colonial days were largely untouched. At the top there were now a supreme court and a chancellor, the latter having jurisdiction over both equity and probate. Over both courts there was placed a special appeals court, or "court of errors," as it was called, consisting of the senate, the supreme court judges, and the chancellor. Neither the chancellor nor the supreme court justices could vote on appeals from their respective branches, although they were expected to participate in the deliberations. This same specially constructed and highly original court was empowered to try impeached officials. In fact, the impeachment process outlined in the New York Constitution bears resemblance to that later adopted in the United States Constitution.

John Jay assumed his official duties as chief justice on September 9, 1777, when he delivered a charge to the grand jury of the supreme court held at Kingston. Something should be said about the circumstances. This was a time when the state senate and assembly were convening, and the system of government established by the new constitution was just being set in motion. According to the note of a contemporary, "the grand inquest was composed of the most respectable characters in the county, and no less than 22 of them attended and were sworn."

This was to be the first of a series of occasions when Jay utilized the custom of charging the grand jury to instruct them in the principles for which the Revolution was being waged, enlighten them about the new constitution, and advise them to do their duty in enforcing the law. Again, as chief justice of the United States some twenty-two years later,

Jay was to seize the opportunity frequently to expound to grand juries the constitutional principles upon which the new nation had been founded, including the supremacy of treaties and the obligation of debtors to pay their debts in conformity with the peace treaty of 1783.

One might have anticipated that Jay, despite some small reservations about a few clauses in the state constitution, which in large part he had written, would seize the occasion to praise the document. And so he did in eloquent language.

"Whoever compares our present with our former Constitution," he declared, "will find abundant reason to rejoice in the exchange, and readily admit that all the calamities incident to this war will be amply compensated by the many blessings flowing from this glorious revolution."

In singling out the more distinctive and commendable aspects of the state constitution, Jay adverted "to those great and equal rights of human nature, which should forever remain inviolate in every society"— including liberty of conscience and the equal protection of the laws (doesn't that have a contemporary ring?) and to the organization of the three branches of the government so "as to promise permanence to the constitution, and give energy and impartiality to the distribution of justice." Security for the citizen, energy in government, impartial justice—what could be loftier goals for government?

Jay's activity on the state bench was limited in time owing to the demands for his services in other wartime activities. As head of the council of safety he was the *de facto* chief executive of the state in the absence of Governor George Clinton, who was at the war front. Jay last sat on the council of revision, the court of appeals one might say, on November 6, 1778, but he did not resign from the court until August 18, 1779, when he accepted appointment by Congress as minister plenipotentiary to Spain. Under the state constitution he was technically permitted to hold his seat on the bench and serve for nine months as president of the Continental Congress.

The September 1777 session of the court was perhaps typical of wartime judicial business. The cases the judges heard involved murder, assault, attempted rape, counterfeiting, and grand larceny, the type of cases which account for most of the business of the court in the following two years. Civil cases were confined to actions of ejectment, lawsuits over real property. But Jay was also required to preside over the courts of oyer and terminer, which were considered separate from the sessions of the Supreme Court proper. Surviving records show that law and order was a major problem, with Jay pronouncing the death sentence against some ten men, sentencing to the gallows men who were found guilty not only of murder and theft, but also of being political enemies of a state under siege from British regulars, Loyalist volunteers, hostile Indians, and lawless ruffians from both camps. In cases like these, it was impossible to draw the line between banditry and treason.

Did Jay feel any compunctions about imposing the death penalty in the case of such crimes? Evidently not, as he was long on record favoring capital punishment on religious and moral grounds.

In sum, at the commencement of our state, 200 years ago, no single man, not even the redoubtable Governor George Clinton, played a more decisive and constructive role in establishing the supremacy of civil power, due process, and constitutional liberties at a time when New York was torn asunder from one end to the other by military conflict and subversion.

There are many other contributions over a long lifetime for which the state and nation should properly pay tribute to John Jay. But the occasion 200 years ago of his inaugurating the judicial system of New York was one of his shining hours. And we assembled here today salute him on this bicentennial commemoration of state government in New York.

New York State's
First Constitution *

BERNARD MASON

Harpur College, State University of New York at Binghamton

When General Washington ordered the reading of the Declaration of Independence to the assembled troops in New York, that *de facto* independent state had not yet caught up with the pace of events. Divided by the growing problems of the collapsing political structure and accompanying symptoms of social strain, the third provincial congress, the revolutionary center of power, had called in May for the election of a provincial congress with authority to draft and put into operation a new form of government for the people. That referendum and election had taken place in June, but the new body had not yet convened.

As mundane as this referendum procedure may seem to us, in the eighteenth century it was revolutionary, and New York was the leader of the vanguard. Pennsylvania, the only other state in 1776 to opt for the employment of this technique, did not act until June. New York's tactic represented a radical deviation because the whole subject of the nature and meaning of written constitutions was the point of convergence of a long and drawn-out debate for much of the revolution. One element within this raging dispute was the question of who had the authority to draft such documents, a question which most of the revolutionary legislatures settled simply by seizing that power for themselves without reference to the electorate. The idea that the voters should choose a special body of delegates to elaborate a frame of government was still a minority concept. The revolutionaries, of course, were drawing in part on Locke's premise of the formulation of a social contract as an expression of the sovereign power of the people. Flowing from the concept of the constitution as the embodiment of a social contract was the

*Reprinted from *Essays on the Genesis of the Empire State* (Albany: New York State Bicentennial Commission, 1979), 13–33.

further notion of the constitution as fundamental law and therefore as superior to statutory law. This distinction between fundamental law and legislative enactment, however, remained to be spelled out. $\mathcal{L}_o$

The fourth provincial congress, or Convention of Representatives of the State of New York, as it quickly renamed itself on July 10, 1776, was not only a wartime legislature but also a constitution writing assemblage. Since the state was to be the center of military campaigning in 1776 and again in 1777, the demands of the war effort and the anxieties deriving therefrom frequently absorbed much of the effort and time of the delegates, not all of whom consistently attended the sessions. The additional burden of devising a republican structure of government often was relegated to a secondary priority but not simply in response to more urgent army needs. Political differences were also partly responsible for reluctance to come to grips with this crucial problem of the distribution of the powers of government. Even though political parties as we know them had not yet evolved, these men brought to the convention political aspirations and animosities to which they gave expression in formal and informal groupings bonded together by diverse interests of kin, property, region, religion, ideology, personal ambition, patronage, and power. In calmer times the fabrication of a stable bloc with which to enact the basic principles of government would have faced formidable obstacles, but the revolutionary wave which swept over the state, thoroughly splintering opinion, practically ruled out the formation of a disciplined coalition. To the more astute delegates it was apparent that only by a series of pragmatic compromises would this body approve a final product with any semblance of unanimity.

One major source of these forebodings lay in the composition of the convention. Of the ninety-eight members, not only had perhaps half come from the middle propertied class, but also the overwhelming majority of these had never held any office prior to the Revolution other than a minor one in the township, district, or county. The remainder of the representatives had their roots among the leading state and county families, the elite.[1] Apprehension among the wealthy stemmed from their fear of the potential militancy of the middle class whom the revolution had stirred to an unexpected pitch. Having lived through two years of turbulence, the elite had good grounds for their perturbation. The revolutionary process had imparted a new consciousness among the middle class and greatly raised its expectations of change and the broadening of the power structure. Naturally, enhancement of the power of the middle class could only occur at the expense of the gentry. However, as the latter quickly perceived, the hobgoblin of a united middle class, striking in wrath against the rich, had little basis in reality because this was a revolution for the acquisition and preservation of property by unfettered competition, as well as for many other things. It was not a revolution to seize and redistribute equally the property of the rich among the population.

Any constitution that emerged from this convention would have to give expression to the revolutionary upheaval, to the reordering of society in accordance with republican values. One of the central issues confronting these people was how to concentrate or diffuse power in order to make manifest the locus of sovereignty in the commonwealth. This general determination of which group or groups were to exercise power would naturally shape the arrangement of the structure of government to be laid down in the constitution, would inevitably subtly sway thinking about checks and balances as well as about the state and local level machinery for the application of that power.

Circulation of conflicting constitutional concepts within the convention induced other anxieties in the minds of those who preferred minimal changes in the status quo. John Jay very perceptively described this state of affairs in a letter to a friend: "We have a government, you know, to form; and God only knows what it will resemble. Our politicians, like some guests at a feast, are perplexed and undetermined which dish to prefer." Jay and other delegates were also aware that the New York newspapers in the spring of 1776 had printed numerous proposals for a future governmental structure, but the influence of these ideas upon the convention is problematical.[2] More relevant for the perplexed in the chamber was a version circulated among them which radically altered the traditional concept of the balance among the three branches of government. Abandoning the British notion of the role of the king as the head of society and government, of an hereditary aristocracy as a check upon the commons, the unknown author chose to assign superior power to an assembly in a bicameral legislature. The lower house would appoint all state officials, including the judiciary, who would hold office during good behavior. Even in military affairs the assembly would have significant input through its nomination of militia officers. Patronage, therefore, lay largely in the hands of the assemblymen. All taxpayers would have the right to vote for and be candidates for both houses, casting secret ballots annually. The executive, a president, chosen by ballot out of the legislature in joint session, would sit for three years but would not possess the veto power. His principal authority would derive from his position as commander-in-chief of the militia and chancellor of the state.

In sharp contrast to the foregoing broadly inclusive plan, another formulation primarily modified the pre-existing colonial establishment to fit an independent republic. Assembly, council, and governor would have essentially the same powers each possessed under British rule, but they would owe their existence to direct or indirect electoral processes. Continued reliance upon the $£$ 40 freehold as a qualification for the suffrage would limit participation in the annual election of assemblymen even though the voters would enjoy a secret ballot. An enhanced prerogative of the assembly was to be the election of the upper house, the council, either from among its own members or outsiders for life terms during good behavior. Furthermore, candidates for the council must own land worth $£$ 10,000. The electorate were not to have any direct voice in the choice of the governor, whom the legislature would select by joint ballot from among the council for a three-year term. Although the governor would appoint all state officers with the advice of the council, he would effectively control patronage. This power in combination with his absolute veto over legislation would make him a force to be reckoned with. The author of this draft must have intended to translate the landed gentry, the traditional leaders of society, into the political rulers, especially since the governor would come from the same class. There were also other concepts floating around the convention which fell politically in between those I have mentioned. Consequently, the men who labored on the committee to elaborate a framework of government did not suffer from a shortage of ideas.

Whatever the mere numbers of middling landholders in the convention may have seemed to presage about the body's performance, their quantity had no discernible effect upon the choice of the committee to report a frame of government. Without direct knowledge of the reasons for the singling out of these thirteen men for this task, it is only possible to suggest the convention's motivations from the characteristics of the group. The geographic distribution had a rough equivalence in that every county except Richmond, Kings, Tryon, and the disputed Vermont area had at least one representative. In regional terms there was also a general balance because the six southern counties had seven members and the eight northern units had six seats. Proportionally to population, however, the northern region was underrepresented. Socially, practically the entire committee stood among the leading state and county families of notables. If some of them were middling landholders, it was only in the sense that they had risen out of that class into the ranks of the affluent. Occupationally, individuals with legal training and experience predominated, comprising eight of the thirteen. Despite this superficial appearance of socio-economic homogeneity, serious political divergencies existed among individuals. If we were to divide the committee into two broad groups, one consisting of those traditionalists who favored the least possible change and the other consisting of those majoritarians who desired as much change as was feasible, the former might have claimed seven men, the latter, six. Although the makeup of the committee suggests that the convention sought to balance conflicting interests and views, it also suggests that the more traditional minded had managed to secure a slight edge.

As one might expect from as closely balanced a group as this one, the drafting committee sparred almost interminably during its infrequent sittings from August 1776 to March 1777 before it concurred upon the final report to the convention. From the extant scraps of its records and other evidence, it would appear not only that clashing opinions impeded progress in completing its task but also that the attendance of members was a sometime affair. Of the thirteen, two never attended, four were often absent, and the remaining seven were present more often than not. This fluctuating attendance affected the contents of the proposed articles because a majority for a particular provision on one occasion became a minority on another when the committee reconsidered it. One suspects from the oblique and cryptic comments of some of the elite that their absorption in other affairs at the expense of committee attendance concealed a deliberate decision to postpone for as long as possible the completion of a draft constitution. Their essential motivation lay in the erroneous assumption that the hammer blows of wartime problems would diminish revolutionary fervor and would reduce, therefore, any general anticipation of enlargement of the power base and of popular participation in political processes.[3]

One fundamental matter which stood unaltered throughout the lengthy process of chopping and changing in the committee, and on the convention floor as well, was the definition of power in the state. Article I stipulated that all authority should derive from the people and their representatives in the legislature, but the ambiguous phraseology could be read to mean that the citizenry and lawmakers were coequal— that by implication the constitution did not bind or restrict the legislature except where explicitly stated. Indeed, the drafts did not mention, let alone spell out, any method for the amendment or revision of the fundamental law. By inference, then, the legislature might amend or revise the constitution by statute, as happened in other states. The idea of a basic law amendable only by special convention as a shield to protect the people against their own representatives had not yet taken hold in New York. Despite this defect, in Article I the constitutional committee had ruled out the monopolization of power by any single group or class in society. Implicit in this position was a decision to check and balance power in its distribution in the governmental structure.

Over these eight months of 1776–77, the drafting committee labored on five drafts, the extant fragments of which exhibit tell-tale signs of shifting sentiment among members. When the committee completed shaping the assembly, for example, it had slightly reduced participation in the balloting by requiring the payment of state or county taxes one year prior to the election, instead of payment within the year preceding it. The restriction may have been aimed at farm wage laborers and seamen who were more itinerant than most groups in the population. The only other revision of note in this section eliminated a provision for the division of each county into equal assembly districts in order to retain the traditional method of at-large elections. Candidates from small election districts would probably be better known among their constituents, and the system would have favored nominees of lesser social status than the competition on a countywide scale. Vacillation over the qualifications for choosing senators illuminated more sharply the divergent views among the committee. An early draft contained language which evinced an intent to set off the senate as a preserve for the landed property interests in society. This passage declared that the freeholders "of right ought to have an ascendancy in the Legislature. . . ." Freeholders were those who had an absolute title to land, or who leased land for one or more lives, or who leased land for more than twenty-one years. Although we have no reliable data on their numbers in 1777, freeholders may have comprised 45 percent of the adult white males. Apparently dissatisified with this assertion of right, the committee struck it out, retaining the qualification that the freehold must have a minimal assessed value of £ 40 per year free of all debts. The last two drafts increased the freehold qualification to £ 100 per year free of all liabilities. The committee had a similar tug-of-war over the governor, both as to his powers and as to who should possess the right to elect him. In both cases the end result reflected the triumph of the more traditionally oriented members, especially since the property qualification for the vote escalated from the £ 40 to £ 100 freehold. Finally, in the matter of county and local officeholders, the committee retreated from its initial stipulation of election by ballot and agreed on appointment by the legislature.

The final version, as clarified, sharpened, and polished by John Jay, fashioned a constitution which did not go as far as that of Pennsylvania in broadening popular participation in the governing structure, but did go further than that of Maryland, and which occupied a kind of left of center position between extremes.[4] The essential features of this middling document revolved around the concept of the people as the sovereign power, but the committee imposed certain rudimentary checks on popular domination of the government through the agency of the senate, governor, and judiciary. Specifically, two classes of electors emerged from this committee report, one of perhaps 75 percent of the adult white males for the assembly, the other of some 30 percent of the adult white males for the senate and governor, but all voting was by secret ballot. As a restriction on officeholding, the draft confined candidacy to freeholders.[5] Mirroring the unhappy experience with royal colonial executive power, the committee sharply curtailed the governor's authority. It stripped him of any legislative role; that is, he had no veto, could not dissolve the houses, and might prorogue them for no more than sixty days in one year. On the other hand, the governor retained a foot in the door as a political power to be reckoned with, first in patronage and second through his annual message to the two houses on the state of the state. In one sphere he had complete control, that of military appointments. Otherwise, he could only nominate officeholders to the legislature who voted them up or down. After each negative vote on an office, the initiative returned to the governor, who might make a maximum of four recommendations, after which the legislature might ignore the executive and make the appointment. The constitution obliged the governor not only to report on conditions in the state but also to recommend action on problems, thus arming him with a potential for embarrassing the legislators or exerting pressure for specific legislation.

Three other sections merit comment for their obvious importance. The committee carefully provided for continuity in the law by accepting English common law and British statutes theretofore applied in New York, as well as all applicable colonial legislation. Furthermore, to forestall endless, complex litigation, the constitutional draftsmen confirmed to the body politic, to corporations, and to private persons the lands, farms, inheritable property, rights, immunities, and franchises granted to them by the kings of Great Britain. Another clause guaranteed the right to trial by jury as then existed in the state. Lastly, the religious provisos were decisively for the separation of church and state and for universal toleration. Having finally discharged its task, the drafting committee handed in its report to the convention on March 12, 1777.

Debate began the next day, extending until April 20 but subject to frequent interruption by other matters. Important though this business of the government's form was, attendance throughout the debate fluctuated from 33 to 45 percent of the convention's membership. Even when the final vote on the entire document occurred on April 20, those present numbered only 33.[6]

Within a couple of weeks of the commencement of its sessions in Kingston, the New York convention had to pause in order to cope with an environmental problem. Perhaps it was symbolic that rebels should gather to conduct their revolutionary government on the second floor of the county jail, which housed a number of Tory captives. Bothered by the noxious odor which emanated from below because the jail was unsanitary, Gouverneur Morris moved successfully to permit the delegates to smoke to preserve their health. Seventeen representatives who voted nay may have regarded the remedy as more damaging to their well-being than the malodorous affliction. John Jay, who opposed his friend's motion, proposed to treat the ailment rather than the symptoms by having the prisoners moved elsewhere, a treatment that probably improved the health of everyone, revolutionary and Tory alike.

The deceptively harmonious treatment of the first article which described the source of governmental authority quickly vanished when the delegates switched their attention to the composition of the legislative branch. The traditionalists had taken umbrage at the elimination of the governor from the legislative process and made a determined effort to reincorporate him in it. The method chosen to accomplish this objective apparently stirred fears among other colleagues because the amendment declared that the legislature would consist of three branches: a governor, who would possess an absolute veto, and two houses. Since some men inferred that the governor would also have authority to originate and amend bills, Gouverneur Morris sought to assuage these apprehensions with a proviso that limited this official solely to approval or dissent. Modified in this fashion, the article won acceptance; but almost three weeks later Jay contrived to eliminate the amendment.

The chief controversies over the assembly circulated around suffrage qualifications, the secret ballot, and the distribution of seats. If the amendments to the electors' qualifications article fell into a pattern, they resembled that of a hesitant swimmer cautiously testing the water's temperature with his toes. Seeking sufficient breadth to assure commitment to the system, yet wishing to confine voting as much as was practicably possible, Robert R. Livingston and Gouverneur Morris introduced the first restriction on the broad franchise, a restriction which necessitated nonfreeholding taxpayers to be renters of farms. Many taxpaying craftsmen and skilled laborers in New York City and farm laborers would find themselves excluded from participation by this device. Although the New York county delegation voted against the Livingston-Morris motion, it did so in splendid isolation. The rural-urban dichotomy was very much alive in the midst of revolution. Phase two of the traditionalist strategy did not unfold until three weeks later when Morris and Thomas Tredwell of Suffolk further qualified the vote in two ways. The one set a minimum assessed value of £20 on the freehold; the other mandated a rent of £ 2 per year for nonfreeholding farmers. Despite John Jay's salvage of the ballot for some of the urban artisans, the overall result of these amendments was to diminish the electorate from perhaps 75 percent to 60 percent of the adult white males. For those who had sought vainly for more inclusive participation of the population, there was consolation in the expansion of the suffrage from its lower prerevolutionary level.

A considerable difference of opinion arose among the traditionalist leaders over the draft's acceptance of the secret ballot. Gouverneur Morris spearheaded the drive to reject this departure from the pre-Revolutionary oral vote, but Robert R. Livingston appears to have opposed him. John Jay, the other key member of the traditionalist leadership, was absent. When the smoke of battle had cleared, Morris had won his point, but the close vote strikingly illustrated the fluidity of political alignments n the convention. Three weeks later John Jay reopened the question with a compromise substitute to inaugurate the secret ballot after the war's end. Although Morris sought to retain the oral vote in the senatorial elections, the convention overwhelmed him. Unfortunately, it is not apparent whether fears of Tory voters in wartime elections initially swung the house in favor of open voting, or whether Jay's credibility and influence persuaded the convention to reverse itself resoundingly.

Desires for maximum authority in the assembly gave direction to the prolonged arguments over county representation. The constitution more than doubled the size of the prewar assembly, awarding county seats roughly in proportion to population. Overall, Albany and Dutchess gained most and Richmond and Kings lost most relative to county population. Aside from county partisanship, enlargement of the lower house to sixty-five members probably also satisfied the aspirations of local notables for a potential place on the stage of the political theatre.

Conflict over the upper house's structure was subdued in comparison with what had occurred in relation to the assembly. Among the thirty-nine members present in convention, a major proposal to broaden the senatorial ballot to all freeholders evinced little sympathy, and Robert Harpur's amendment went down to ignominious defeat without even a recorded vote. In keeping with this demonstration of attitudes, the body then proceeded to shout down by a "great majority" a motion to reduce the length of the senate term from four years to one year. Most of the disharmony over the draft description of the senate sprang from the division of the state into four senate electoral districts and from the number of seats contained therein. The convention unquestionably intended the upper house to be a small, select body of twenty-four persons who would essentially represent the middling and wealthy property holders of the state. From an ideological standpoint, the elite among the revolutionary generation tended to equate wisdom with wealth, and in this sense the New York senate was hopefully expected to be the repository of prudence and intelligent judgment, a check upon the "rash," more popular assembly.

Both houses had specific powers that rendered them independent of the executive and gave them a reserve power against official misconduct. The two houses possessed authority to judge their own members and, unlike the colonial legislature, could neither be adjourned indefinitely nor dissolved by the governor. Moreover, the assembly, as the more popular branch, preserved all the privileges and procedures of the colonial assembly. Both houses shared in the impeachment process, but the senate sat as a court of impeachment with the chancellor and judges of the supreme court.

A mechanism that owed its inception to broad dissonance in the house was the Council of Revision, the body upon which the convention conferred the veto power. Apparently severely fractionated over the problem of the negative on bills, the membership voted tentatively for the absolute veto but persisted in private negotiations to strive for a better *modus vivendi*. Some of the legislators may well have grudgingly swallowed this measure in reaction to the prospect of a veto-proof legislature which would wield such power that it would dominate the state. Unpleasant memories of the colonial experience, however, may have persuaded Jay and others to patch together a more palatable method of checking the houses which combined elements of previously suggested ideas and, therefore, laid a basis for a compromise. Robert R. Livingston resolved the quandary by means of a council of revision to consist of the governor, chancellor, and judges of the supreme court. This group could negative bills by majority vote, but the legislature would have the final voice. As amended on the floor, Livingston's concept provided that the council send a bill back to the originating house, which might override the veto by two-thirds of the entire membership. Having cleared that hurdle, the legislation went to the other house, where two-thirds of those present might override. Although diluted in this fashion, the veto was a device with sufficient punch to give pause to the legislature. Ideologically, the council of revision spoke to the future, albeit cautiously.

Our revolutionary fathers, driven by hard political necessity, did not consistently hew to the line of ideological purity, which in this matter of the veto ought to have applied the principle of the separation of powers. Rather than separating branches, the framers well-nigh merged them in this council. What is essential to our understanding of the link here between ideology and politics is not our familiarity with the notion of separation but instead familiarity with the sources of power. The convention joined the governor, chosen by a limited constituency, with the judges, appointed by the council of appointment. That body consisted of senators who, although selected by the assembly, were originally elected by a more restricted franchise. Second, the chief executive, whose term was three years, labored with judges whose tenure was almost tantamount to life service. Third, the governor could ignore his accountability to the electorate only at the risk of his political reputation, but the judges were accountable to no one. Lack of accountability, as we ought to have learned, promotes authoritarianism. To resist this trend the drafters incorporated the device of the override by both houses, bodies responsible to the voters. The entire structure comprised an intricate web of powers and functions with something for almost everyone.

Patronage—the appointive power—perhaps caused more distraction in the convention than any other single issue. The draft lodged the initiative of nomination to office with the governor with concurrence of both houses, but it quickly became apparent that that provision would not stand. There were several different amendments from the floor, none of which survived. Again, it was the collaboration of Jay, Livingston, and Morris that came up with the winning combination. Essentially, Jay involved the governor and both houses in appointments. Utilizing the idea of the council, he formulated a body which comprised the governor and four senators, one from each senatorial district, but the assembly chose the four senators annually. Within this council of appointment the governor nominated but could only vote to break a tie. Since the thrust on the convention floor was to minimize the assembly's participation in patronage, the crux of the disagreement was how to disperse this power more broadly to evade the more popular branch on the one side and individual aggrandizement in the governor's person on the other. The method chosen allowed indirectly for the interplay of *vox populi* and for the evolution of a patronage system, but it assuaged also some of the fears of the larger propertyholders about the infiltration of government by the nonaffluent.

Adoption of the council of appointment by the convention lends itself to other explanations of course. A complementary inference is the members' conception of the senate as a seat of wisdom wisdom derived from the senators' status as affluent elen ety. Moreover, the underlying mission of the council of was to contrive a supportive, stable bureaucracy whose extend down through the governmental structure into the governor and senators would probably be men of considerable property, their appointees, regardless of factional alignments, would tend to have similar social values, even though they might differ over the means with which to maintain such values. The exclusion of the assembly, therefore, from the sphere of filling offices was potentially a further limitation on popular involvement in government and contrariwise guaranteed larger propertyholders additional means with which to defend their interests in society. Whatever else the affair of the council signified, it sacrificed unequivocally theoretical ideas of the separation of powers to pragmatic necessity.

Perhaps one of the simpler convention tasks involved the delineation of the legal system. There was very little dispute over the retention of the colonial framework for the courts. Three of the major modifications related to judicial tenure, the chancellorship, and a final court of appeals. Reacting to the frustrations of British imperial policy, the Convention of Representatives realized a long, pent-up aspiration when it applied the principle of good behavior rather than the governor's pleasure to the superior bench. The action assured the relative independence of the judges and the integrity of the judicial organization. Anent the second change, the drafters again departed from colonial practice by stripping the governor of his equity and probate jurisdictions and lodging both of these in a chancellor. Lastly, as a substitute for the final appeals jurisdiction of the colonial governor and his council, and of the crown, our founders instituted a court for the trial of impeachments and correction of errors which comprised the judges of the supreme court, the chancellor, and the entire senate. This body possessed authority to try impeached officials and to hear appeals on law from other courts. When cases came to the court of errors which the judges had previously adjudicated, the justices could engage in the deliberations but could not vote on their disposition. Suspicion of lawyers and a desire to inhibit legal obfuscation may have induced the convention to prescribe this mixture of law and politics. Distrust of the power of long-term appointive officials may also have moved the members to check the judges with persons responsible to an electorate. Bench and bar along with the upper house might have drowned in a torrent of litigation had the Convention chosen to revolutionize the body of colonial law, but in their pursuit of stability the drafters opted for minimal mutations.

Accommodation of the legal institutions to the revolutionary order of things necessitated attentiveness to their complexities. New York's laws grew out of the adaptation of English common law, of the application of special British statutes, and of the enactment of provincial statutes. Rather than tinker with each category of law, the framers encompassed them all with several qualifications. Displaying a nice sense of revolutionary chronology, the representatives legalized those portions of the common law that the province had applied and those statutes currently in force, both on April 19, 1775, the day of the battles of Lexington and Concord. They refined this enabling proviso more precisely by nullifying everything in the common law that Yorkers had omitted to adopt, everything in any branch that pertained to an establishment of religion, and everything in all three groups that referred to the sovereignty of the kings of Great Britain. To protect their flanks by legitimating revolutionary actions, the fathers sanctioned the sundry resolutions of the provincial congresses and convention. Basically, the amendments from the floor did not alter the committee report's conception of the state's legal system. Other species of problems also impinged upon or depended upon the structure of the law and received definition in the constitution.

Two of these concerns affected numerous people from the pinnacle of society down to the small landowner and leaseholder. The most serious of these was the validity of land titles which the drafting committee resolved by legalizing all royal grants of lands and leases to individuals and to "bodies corporate and politic" made prior to July 4, 1776. Not content with this sweeping ratification of the status quo, the convention narrowed the scope of the coverage to those individuals and incorporated communities which had received the royal largesse prior to October 14, 1775. A possible inference from this restrictive definition is that the house desired to leave the door open to legislative assault upon the Loyalists, the Anglican church, King's College, and other politically tainted chartered bodies. Implied support for this interpretation derives from the draft which confirmed to corporations and persons not only the soil but also "hereditaments, Rights, Immunities and franchises." None of this terminology remained in the final document.

Although the convention ensured religious pluralism and competition, it verged on restraining complete freedom of worship. John Jay prepared and managed the amendments which would have curtailed liberty of conscience.[7] His first measure amounted to a sweeping denial of toleration both to those who might be defined as sectarian agitators or evangelicals and to Catholics. Authority to determine who was "licentious" or disturbed the peace, or threatened public safety in the pursuit of conscience, would be placed in the hands of the legislature. When the amendment came under very heavy fire, Jay withdrew it rather than witness its demise on the floor, but he renewed the strife with a specifically anti-Catholic proviso which would have blocked the establishment of Catholic churches. Political distinctions in the vote on this section, which was negative, seem to have dissolved; leading moderates, radicals and conservatives were to be found on both sides. Undeterred by his defeat, Jay resumed the fray with a modified version of his first proposal, having stricken out the legislature as inquisitor. Even though Robert R. Livingston moved to substitute a more carefully and precisely worded paragraph, the convention voted him down. Gouverneur Morris salvaged Jay's fundamental concept by the employment of cautious semantics. In effect he offered sanctuary "without discrimination or preference" to all denominations in exchange for sanctions against "acts of licentiousness" and "practices inconsistent with the peace or safety" of the state. Satisfied with this protection of majority interests, the delegates passed overwhelmingly the Morris substitution. Other fundamental human rights did not fare as well in the convention.

New York, like most of the states, did not extend the logic of the Declaration of Independence to the slaves. Gouverneur Morris, however, strove to establish the principle of emancipation in the form of a recommendation for its implementation to the future legislature. The initial test of the main body of the motion without the preamble demonstrated the presence of a favorable majority, but two fears probably undermined its adoption. One was anxiety over arousing among blacks premature expectations which might be dashed. Subsequent frustration might induce the slaves to foment rebellion or to flee to the British forces. Moreover, some revolutionaries who owned slaves might turn against the Revolution and join the British. Much of the discussion of the issue must have occurred off the floor, and its content is unknown. One may surmise, nonetheless, that the drift of sentiment shifted against manumission, because Morris withdrew his motion. Although the conception of freedom for blacks attained the stage of formal debate, the broader context of the universal right to life, liberty, and property never achieved even that status.

The absence of a state bill of rights is not an indication of total indifference among the delegates toward such freedoms. In fact the convention had instructed its constitution drafting committee in August 1776 to frame both a form of government and a bill of rights. Although the committee analyzed the content of proposals for this purpose, it may have persuaded itself that there was no necessity for this special provision, because its report to the convention did not contain one. Furthermore, the prolonged debates on the floor in 1777 afforded ample opportunity to introduce the subject, but no one mentioned it. It has been said that Gilbert Livingston's amendment to bar disfranchisement and the deprivation of constitutional rights was a restatement of article 39 of Magna Charta, but his motion must be understood in the context of the debates. Livingston was substituting his paragraph for one which intended solely to prevent a single legislative house from disqualifying voters or elected candidates, actions that had crippled and humiliated the pre-Revolutionary Livingston faction in the colonial assembly. That the members understood the language as a general guarantee of rights is a moot point. It should also be noted that the last phrase in the substitution opened the door to deprivation of a person's freedoms "by the law of the land and the judgment of his peers." Perhaps the most decisive factor in the determination to omit any statement of general liberties was the loyalist problem. Alarmed, if not frightened, by what the revolutionaries perceived as the great dimensions of this threat, the leaders may have argued that a definition of rights would inhibit the government's flexibility in suppressing counter-revolutionary activities. Indirect corroboration for this explanation may lie in the fate of the prohibitions of ex post facto and attainder laws. The former did not survive the drafting process, and the latter underwent modification on the floor. Jay and Morris revised the clause in order to permit acts of attainder for crimes committed during the war. Not until 1787 were the legislature and executive willing to spell out a bill of rights.

The legislative action on individual rights in 1787 possessed a theoretical magnitude that exceeded the import of the law's particulars. Since the constitution omitted any mention of a process of amendment, it left ambiguous the question of the ultimate sovereignty of the people. The enactment of this fundamental bill of 1787 by ordinary legislative procedures rather than by a special convention or referendum implied the coequal sharing of power by legislators and people. Some decades would elapse before Yorkers comprehended fully the implications of a written constitution as a statement of popular sovereignty.

When the convention had consummated its task of framing a government, it had metamorphosed a leftward leaning draft into a right-of-center constitution with sufficient resilience to accommodate much of the revolutionary impulse. Traditionalist leaders had frustrated the aims of the majoritarians by skillfully interweaving an elaborate network of checks and balances which effectively prevented any single branch from dominating the entire structure. Politically and socially, however, the majoritarians had dealt the hierarchical and deferential order of society a hard blow through their forced penetration of the power structure, a penetration that would make it impossible for the traditionalists ever to turn the clock back to pre-Revolutionary relationships. From this time forward the only open path lay in some form of adaptation to further majoritarian change.

NOTES:

¹See the biographical analysis and description of the constitution in Edward F. Countryman, "Legislative Government in Revolutionary New York" (Ph.D. diss., Cornell University, 1971), Chaps. III, V.

²For these proposals and those discussed below, see Bernard Mason, *The Road to Independence* (Lexington: University of Kentucky Press, 1966), Chap. VII; Gordon S. Wood, *Creation of the American Republic* (New York: W.W. Norton, 1972), Chaps. IV–VI; William H.W. Sabine, ed., *Historical Memoirs of William Smith* (2 vols., Colburn and Tegg, 1956–58), II, 18–21, 26.

³A detailed examination of the committee drafts is in Mason, *Road to Independence*, Chap. VII.

⁴See Elisha P. Douglass, *Rebels and Democrats* (Chicago: Quadrangle Books, 1965), Chaps. IV, XII–XIV; Wood, *Creation of the American Republic*, Chaps. II, VI.

⁵These estimates are based on the data in the 1790 census. See Alfred F. Young, *The Democratic Republicans of New York, 1763–1797* (Chapel Hill: University of North Carolina Press, 1967), Appendix, 585–87.

⁶The several paragraphs below derive from the *Journals of the Provincial Congress, Provincial Convention, Committee of Safety and Council of Safety of the State of New York, 1775–1777* (2 vols., Albany, 1842), I, passim.; and Charles Z. Lincoln, *The Constitutional History of New York* (5 vols., Rochester, 1906), I, passim.

⁷See Richard B. Morris, ed., *John Jay: The Making of a Revolutionary* (New York: Harper and Row, 1975), 392; John W. Pratt, *Religion, Politics and Diversity* (Ithaca: Cornell University Press, 1967), Chaps. IV, V.

"A trust . . . to our children" New York State and the Adoption of the Bill of Rights

Stephen L. Schechter
New York State Bicentennial Commission

On September 25, 1789, the United States Congress, during its first session, approved the Bill of Rights at Federal Hall in New York City, the first federal capital. On October 2, President George Washington transmitted the Bill of Rights in the form of twelve proposed constitutional amendments to the states for ratification. New York State became the seventh state to ratify the Bill of Rights on February 27, 1790; ratification of ten of those amendments originally proposed by Congress was accomplished on December 15, 1791, upon ratification by the eleventh state, Virginia.

Passage of the Bill of Rights was no simple task. One had not been included in the original Constitution of 1787, because the Framers believed it was unnecessary. Their Federalist standardbearers continued to oppose the addition of a bill of rights, even though Antifederalists rallied to correct this shortcoming.

The issue erupted in the ratification debate over the proposed Constitution. In New York State, Federalists led by Alexander Hamilton and others argued for the adoption of the Constitution without a bill of rights, while Antifederalists under the leadership of Governor George Clinton were at the forefront of the battle for a bill of rights, even drafting a proposed version at the New York State ratifying convention in Poughkeepsie.

It was at that ratifying convention that Judge Thomas Tredwell, a Suffolk County delegate, eloquently defended the need for a bill of rights. "No other foundation can any man lay," Judge Tredwell remarked, "which will secure the sacred temple of freedom against the power of the great, the undermining arts of ambition, and the blasts of profane scoffers." Judge Tredwell then set out a theme adopted two hundred years later as the theme of this essay:

> *The liberties of the country are a deposit, a trust, in the hands of individuals . . . which the possessors have no right to dispose of; they belong to our children, and to them we are bound to transmit them. [July 2, 1788]*

New York State's decision to ratify the Constitution, with recommended amendments for a bill of rights, was a major step in the movement toward a national bill of rights which began in the town meetings, print shops, and provincial assemblies of colonial New York. This is the story, stretching back six score years and ten in New York, from the Flushing Remonstrance of 1657 to the New York State ratifying convention of 1788, chronicled in this essay, "A trust . . . to our children." It illustrates the contributions of New Yorkers to the colonial foundation, early state blueprint, and final adoption of the Bill of Rights.

Colonial Foundations

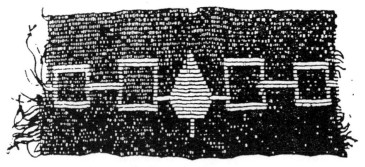

Wampum belt depicting the confederacy of Iroquois nations, ca. 1700.
Courtesy: New York State Museum

Iroquois Belt

Magna Carta may have laid the foundations for an American system of rights, but that system was built out of colonial demands for freedom and their ultimate expression in Revolutionary state constitutions. We must never forget, however, that the Iroquois had established the first patent for constitutional order in the New World when they agreed to the Great Peace.

REMONSTRANCE
Of the Inhabitants of the
Town of Flushing
To Governor Stuyvesant
December 27, 1657

*R*ight Honorable,

You have been pleased to send up unto us a certain prohibition or command that we should not receive or entertain any of those people called Quakers because they are supposed to be by some, seducers of the people. For our part we cannot condemn them in this case, neither can we stretch out our hands against them, to punish, banish or persecute them, for out of Christ God is a consuming fire, and it is a fearful thing to fall into the hands of the living God.

We desire therefore in this case not to judge lest we be judged, neither to condemn lest we be condemned, but rather let every man stand and fall to his own master. We are bound by the Law to do good unto all men, especially to those of the household of faith. And though for the present we seem to be unsensible of the law and the Law giver, yet when death and the Law assault us, if wee have our advocate to seek, who shall plead for us in this case of conscience betwixt God and our own souls; the powers of this world can neither attack us, neither excuse us, for if God justify who can condemn and if God condemn there is none can justify.

And for those jealousies and suspicions which some have of them, that they are destructive unto Magistracy and Ministry, that can not be, for the magistrate hath the sword in his hand and the minister hath the sword in his hand, as witness those two great examples which all magistrates and ministers are to follow, Moses and Christ, whom God raised up maintained and defended against all the enemies both of flesh and spirit; and therefore that which is of God will stand, and that which is of man will come to nothing. And as the Lord hath taught Moses or the civil power to give an outward liberty in the state by the law written in his heart designed for the good of all, and can truly judge who is good, who is civil, who is true and who is false, and can pass definitive sentence of life or death against that man which rises up against the fundamental law of the States General; so he hath made his ministers a savor of life unto life, and a savor of death unto death.

Flushing Remonstrance, 1657.

Flushing Remonstrance (December 27, 1657)

This petition has been called the "First American Declaration of Independence." The English freeholders of Flushing and Jamaica, Long Island, living under Dutch rule, sent this strong protest to Governor Peter Stuyvesant because he had forbidden Quakers living among them to hold religious meetings. This document is a landmark in the fight for freedom of religion in early New York.

Trial of John Peter Zenger (1735)

Born in Germany, John Peter Zenger emigrated to America in 1710, where he began publishing the *Weekly Journal* in 1733. Zenger's newspaper published articles attacking the policies of New York's colonial governor, William Cosby, leading to Zenger's arrest and imprisonment in 1734 on libel charges. Zenger was later acquitted, owing to the brilliant defense of his attorney Andrew Hamilton, who successfully advanced truth as a defense against libel and thereby helped establish freedom of the press in America.

Above: Illustration from Morning Star of Liberty.
Courtesy: New York State Library

Right: Zenger Trial Minute Book, 1735, highlighting the "not guilty" verdict rendered by the jury.
Courtesy: New York State Supreme Court

The New York State Blueprint

POLITICAL ORGANIZATION of NEW YORK STATE
Constitution of 1777

Map of New York State, 1777, showing boundaries of counties and Senate districts. From 1777: The Political Revolution and New York's First Constitution, *by William A. Polf.*

New York State's First Constitution (1777)

New Yorkers had twice (in 1683 and 1691) tried and failed to secure official British approval for a colonial charter setting out individual rights, framing the structure of government, and limiting the powers of government. Meeting at the Senate House in Kingston, amidst the threat of British invasion, New York constitution makers were nearly foiled a third time. Approved on April 20, 1777, by the wartime government of New York, our first constitution became a model for the federal Constitution drafted ten years later.

The state constitution of 1777 provided for the first popularly elected chief executive in America and contained a pathbreaking provision for judicial review. Although the constitution did not contain a separate bill of rights, the constitution contained various individual rights including one of the strongest constitutional provisions of its day, as provided in Article 38 for religious liberty. Owing in no small part to the religious diversity of our state's population, our constitution went beyond the policy of mere toleration to one of non-interference in the "free exercise and enjoyment of religious profession and worship."

Pictured are the principal authors of the constitution of 1777: John Jay, co-author of *The Federalist*, first chief judge of New York State, and first chief justice of the United States Supreme Court; Gouverneur

Morris, who, as a Pennsylvania delegate to the Constitutional Convention, prepared the final text of the United States Constitution, including its eloquent preamble beginning "We the People . . ."; Robert R. Livingston, first chancellor of New York State and a member of the committee chosen by the Second Continental Congress to draft the Declaration of Independence; and Abraham Yates, Jr., an Albany Patriot, avid supporter of Governor George Clinton, and the only one of these constitutional draftsmen who later became an Antifederalist and strongly opposed the adoption of the United States Constitution.

Principal draftsmen of New York's first Constitution

John Jay   *Gouverneur Morris*   *Robert R. Livingston*   *Abraham Yates, Jr.*

New Yorkers Achieve a Bill of Rights

Two hundred years ago, New Yorkers, like other Americans, were still experimenting with their invention of a written constitution. There was no single model, nor was there a single set of rules. Ten years after New York adopted its first state constitution, New Yorkers determined they wanted a bill of rights. Should it be added to their existing constitution? Should their constitution be amended?

On January 26, 1787, four months before the Constitutional Convention met in Philadelphia, the New York State Legislature enacted "An act concerning the rights of citizens of the State."

Little is known about this act, except that it contained a bill of rights and remained a statute or ordinary law until 1821, when many of its important provisions were incorporated within the New York State Constitution. Most of the rights contained in this act concerned the rights of the accused, including "due process of law" and protection from "excessive bail," "excessive fines," and "cruel and unusual punishments." The act also guaranteed the citizen's right of petition, secured freedom of speech in New York State Senate and Assembly proceedings, and prohibited the quartering of soldiers without the homeowners' consent.

New York and the House Erected

New York State Ratifies the Federal Constitution

On September 17, 1787, thirty-nine delegates at the Constitutional Convention in Philadelphia approved and signed the proposed federal Constitution. The Convention then sent the Constitution to the Confederation Congress for further action. Recognizing the controversial nature of that document, the Congress took no action save transmitting the proposed Constitution on to the state legislatures for ratification.

In the ensuing months, New Yorkers hotly debated the strengths and weaknesses of the proposed Constitution. In fact, New York City newspapers flourished during these months and provided a popular forum for the national debate. Antifederalists, led by Governor George Clinton, argued strongly against adopting the new plan, citing the resulting loss of state revenues, excessive congressional powers, and lack of a bill of rights.

Alexander Hamilton

John Jay

Above: The Federalist, *1788. Title page of volume 2.*
Courtesy: New York State Library

Above and right: Alexander Hamilton, author, with John Jay and James Madison, of The Federalist.

James Madison

Federalist leaders included Alexander Hamilton who, as principal author of *The Federalist*, presented the case for the Constitution without a specific bill of rights. Noting that most states had their own bill of rights, that the proposed Constitution already contained various basic rights, and that the Constitution created a Congress of enumerated powers, Hamilton concluded in *The Federalist* No. 84, "the constitution is itself in every rational sense and to every useful purpose, A BILL OF RIGHTS."

In the spring of 1788, voters of New York State elected Antifederalist delegates by a margin of two to one to the New York State ratifying convention. (For this one election, the New York State Legislature removed all voting requirements of race and property; however, women were denied the right to vote.) The convention first met on June 17, 1788, in Poughkeepsie, only to learn a week later that New Hampshire had become the ninth state to ratify the Constitution, thereby bringing that document into effect. So strong was the opposition of Antifederalist delegates to the Constitution, that it took until July 26 for a slim margin of thirty to twenty-seven delegates to approve the Constitution.

Detail from "Delegates at the New York Convention to Ratify the Federal Convention," by Gerald Foster. Alexander Hamilton grasps the hand of Governor George Clinton.
Courtesy: U.S. Postal Service, Poughkeepsie

The final compromise included approval of a list of recommended amendments drawn up by Mayor John Lansing, Jr., of Albany. It is a little-known fact that Lansing's list of recommended amendments included the first American constitutional provision for the phrase "due process of law," probably drawn from the language of New York State's statutory bill of rights of 1787.

New York State was not the first state to draw up a list of recommended amendments for consideration by the first federal Congress. In fact, it was the last state to do so before the Congress drafted a proposed Bill of Rights. As a result, New York's list was the most inclusive. It was also the most forcefully presented, accompanied by a circular letter to all of the states urging them to support a second constitutional convention to secure a bill of rights.

The Bill of Rights Is Added

Congress Drafts the Bill of Rights

When Congress convened in New York City on March 4, it was only forceful acts, such as New York State's circular letter, which convinced a majority of congressmen to consider the need for a bill of rights. The threat of a second convention intensified when Virginia on November 20, 1788, and New York on February 7, 1789, petitioned the not-yet-assembled Congress for another convention. Then, on May 6, Representative John Laurence of New York City presented his state's petition.

On Monday, June 8, 1789, Representative James Madison of Virginia, carrying out his election promise to his constituents, asked the federal House of Representatives to go into a committee of the whole to consider amendments to the Constitution. The House divided, sometimes strongly, over Madison's proposals. The veteran politician George Mason of Virginia maintained that Madison had not gone far enough and was a supporter of "Milk & Water Propositions" that would serve as "A Tub to the Whale," or a diversion for more significant amendments. Representative James Jackson of Georgia dismissed Madison's amendments as "theoretical speculation," "unnecessary" if not "dangerous or improper."

On June 8, the House set the issue aside; and on July 21, Madison "begged the House to endulge him" in further consideration of the matter. The House voted to send Madison's amendments to a select committee which then reported a list of seventeen amendments on July 28. A lengthy debate of those amendments began on August 13.

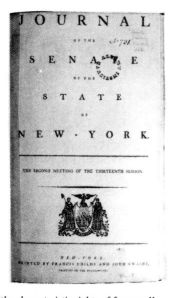

Amos Doolittle after Peter LaCour. "Federal Hall The Seat of Congress." Engraving, 1790. This is the only contemporary depiction of the Inauguration of President George Washington which took place on April 30, 1789. In his inaugural address, Wash-ington endorsed the call for amendments protecting "the characteristic rights of freemen."

Journal of the Proceedings of the State Convention at Poughkeepsie to consider ratifi-cation of the federal Constitution, 1788. Courtesy: New York State Archives

On August 24, 1789, the House achieved the necessary two-thirds majority required by Article V of the Constitution and sent the seventeen proposed amendments to the Senate, which began its considerations on September 2. The Senate consolidated the amendments into a list of twelve, which it approved on September 9, 1789. A conference was called on September 21 to resolve the House–Senate differences. This was accomplished two days later, and on the following day, September 24, the House accepted the committee's report. On September 25, the Senate concurred, and on September 26, copies of the proposed twelve amendments were sent to the states for ratification. (The first two amendments, relating to apportionment of U.S. representatives and compensation of members of Congress, failed to be ratified by the states.)

The States Ratify the Bill of Rights

New Jersey became the first state to ratify the Bill of Rights on November 20, 1789. With little debate, the New York State Legislature ratified the Bill of Rights on February 27, 1790, making New York State the seventh state to do so. Then, after much debate, Virginia brought the Bill of Rights into effect when it became the eleventh state to ratify on December 15, 1791, celebrated today as Bill of Rights Day.

Promise and Reality

Frederick Douglass

Susan B. Anthony
Photo by Gary Gold

Ratification did not extend the promise of the full liberty to all Americans. In 1791, most of the black population in America was subject to the bondage of slavery by both national and state law. It was not until 1821 that slavery was fully abolished in New York State, and, of course, it took a Civil War and a constitutional amendment to abolish slavery throughout the Union.

In 1791, women in New York as well as other states were treated as second-class citizens. They could not vote, hold elective office, obtain a college education, practice most professions, or claim legal control of their children. This condition was recognized by many as unacceptable, and expressed vividly by Mary Wollstonecraft in *A Vindication of the Rights of Woman*, published in London in 1792. However, this was only the beginning of a movement whose members would experience many disappointments before ratification of the Nineteenth Amendment in 1920 recognizing women's right to vote.

In 1791, it was assumed that the opening phrase of the Bill of Rights, "Congress shall make no laws . . . ," was intended to protect individual rights from infringement by Congress, but not by the states. This assumption was confirmed by the U.S. Supreme Court in the case of *Barron* v. *City of Baltimore* in 1833. However, since most American laws have been passed by state legislatures, not Congress, the Bill of Rights reached only a relatively small portion of governmental action until the twentieth century. Beginning in the 1920s, on a case-by-case basis, the U.S. Supreme Court has used the Fourteenth Amendment to apply individual provisions in the Bill of Rights as limits on state law. By the mid 1970s, most of the provisions of the Bill of Rights had been applied to protect individual rights from state action.

New York Ratifies the Bill of Rights: A Chronology

On September 25, 1789, Congress approved twelve amendments to the newly implemented federal Constitution. A week later, on October 2, 1789, President George Washington sent each state an engrossed manuscript listing the proposed amendments. Ratification by three-quarters of the state legislatures was required to adopt any or all of the amendments. By mid-December 1791, eleven states, the required three-quarters, had adopted ten of the amendments—the Bill of Rights. The actual procedure followed in each state varied. In New York, the proposed amendments were considered and approved at the second meeting of the thirteenth session of the state legislature held in New York City from January 13 to April 6, 1790.

The following chronology of New York's ratification is excerpted from the New York State Senate and Assembly journals and the Minutes of the Council of Revision (courtesy of the New York State Library, Division of Manuscripts and Special Collections, Albany, N.Y.), and from Record Group 11 of the National Archives.

January 13, 1790, Wednesday: Governor George Clinton sends a message to the state legislature enclosing the proposed amendments to the federal Constitution.

January 13, 1790, Wednesday: The senate and the assembly, each in its own committee of the whole, considers the governor's message and the papers accompanying it.

January 20, 1790, Wednesday: The senate assigns "Saturday next" for the consideration of the amendments.

January 22, 1790, Friday: The assembly resolves to consider the amendments in a committee of the whole on "Tuesday next."

January 23, 1790, Saturday: The senate, agreeable to the order of the day, considers the amendments in a committee of the whole.

January 26, 1790, Tuesday: The assembly in a committee of the whole chaired by John Watts, Jr. (City and County of New York) considers the proposed amendments. The committee by a vote of 52 to 5 rejects the second amendment: "No law varying the compensation for the services of Senators and Representatives shall take effect, until an election of Representatives shall have intervened." The committee, after agreeing to the other eleven amendments, reports to the assembly, which reads and agrees to the committee report. The assembly appoints Rufus King (City and County of New York), Samuel Jones (Queens County), Jonathan N. Havens (Suffolk County), John Livingston (Columbia County), and Ezekiel Gilbert (Columbia County) as "a committee to report the form of a ratification of the said amendments."

February 4, 1790, Thursday: The senate committee of the whole reports "that a special committee be appointed, to devise and report a mode for the ratification of the amendments, proposed to be made to the Constitution." The senate agrees to the report and appoints James Duane (City and County of New York), Ezra L'Hommedieu (Suffolk County), and Philip Livingston (Westchester County).

February 12, 1790, Friday: Assemblyman Samuel Jones brings in a bill entitled "An act ratifying certain articles in addition to, and amendment of the Constitution of the United States of America, proposed by the Congress"; the assembly reads the bill for the first time and orders a second reading.

February 13, 1790, Saturday: The assembly, for the second time, reads the bill ratifying the proposed amendments and commits it to a committee of the whole.

February 20, 1790, Saturday: In a committee of the whole, Assemblyman John Smith (Suffolk County) moves that the proposed amendments to the Constitution be approved by legislative resolution rather than as an act. His motion is defeated 49 to 2. (John Smith and Jonathan N. Havens voted in the minority.) The committee of the whole agrees to the bill without amendment and reports it to the assembly, which reads the bill, agrees to it, and orders it engrossed. [The rationale for Smith's motion is uncertain. He perhaps believed, from a technical perspective, that the ratification of amendments to the federal Constitution should not take the form of an act but should more properly be done by joint resolution. However, Smith may have believed that a bill ratifying the amendments would be rejected by the Council of Revision, which, at that time, had two Antifederalists and one Federalist in attendance. A joint resolution of the legislature would not have required Council consideration.]

February 22, 1790, Monday: The assembly reads the engrossed bill and passes it. James Gordon (City and County of Albany) and Henry Will (City and County of New York) carry the bill to the senate for its concurrence.

February 22, 1790, Monday: The senate receives the bill ratifying the proposed amendments, reads it, and orders a second reading.

February 23, 1790, Tuesday: The senate reads the bill a second time and refers it to a committee of the whole.

February 24, 1790, Wednesday: Senator James Duane reports that the committee of the whole had gone through the bill without amendment. The senate reads the bill a third time, agrees to it, and orders Lewis Morris (Westchester County) and Peter Schuyler (Montgomery County) to inform the assembly.

February 24, 1790, Wednesday: The assembly receives a message informing that the senate had approved the bill ratifying the proposed amendments to the Constitution. The assembly orders Christopher Tappen (Ulster County) and Zina Hitchcock (Washington and Clinton counties) to deliver the bill to the Council of Revision.

February 25, 1790, Thursday: The Council of Revision (Governor George Clinton, Chief Justice Richard Morris, and Associate Justice Robert Yates in attendance) reads the bill and orders a second reading.

February 27, 1790, Saturday: The Council of Revision reads the bill a second time and resolves, in its standard fashion, "that it does not appear improper to the Council that the said Bill" should become law. The council orders that a copy of its resolution, signed by Governor Clinton, should be delivered to the assembly by Justice Yates.

February 27, 1790, Saturday: The assembly receives the message from the Council of Revision.

March 1, 1790, Monday: The senate receives a message from the assembly stating that the Council of Revision has approved the bill ratifying the proposed amendments.

March 16, 1790, Tuesday: The assembly resolves that, if the senate agrees, Governor Clinton should be "requested to cause an exemplification of the act" ratifying the proposed amendments to the Constitution to be made and to be sent to the president of the United States. Assemblymen Isaac I. Talman (Dutchess County) and John Carpenter (Orange County) deliver this resolution to the senate.

March 19, 1790, Friday: The senate receives the message from the assembly and concurs with the resolution requesting the governor to prepare an exemplification of the act ratifying the proposed amendments which should be sent to the president of the United States. James Clinton (Ulster County) and Peter Schuyler ordered to inform the assembly.

March 27, 1790, Saturday: The exemplification of the act ratifying eleven of the proposed amendments to the Constitution is signed by Governor Clinton and has the Great Seal of the State affixed.

April 2, 1790, Friday: Governor Clinton sends a letter to President George Washington enclosing the exemplification of the act ratifying eleven of the proposed amendments to the Constitution.

April 5, 1790, Monday: President Washington sends Congress New York's exemplification of the act ratifying eleven of the proposed amendments to the Constitution.

This chronology was prepared by John P. Kaminski, co-editor of the *Documentary History of the Ratification of the Constitution and the Bill of Rights, 1787–1791.*

II. New York and the Making of the Constitution, 1787–1788

Key Bicentennial Dates

Congress calls a convention to amend the Articles of Confederation, February 21, 1787

New York legislature elects delegates to the convention at Philadelphia, March 6, 1787

Constitutional Convention achieves its first quorum, May 25, 1787

Constitution signed by delegates, September 17, 1787
[Constitution Day]

First essay of *The Federalist* published, New York City, October 27, 1787

New York legislature calls state ratifying convention, February 1, 1788

New York legislature creates more than 100 towns, March 7, 1788

Popular election of delegates to state ratifying convention, April 29–May 3, 1788

New York State ratifying convention opens June 17, 1788

New Hampshire is ninth state to ratify, thereby satisfying requirements to bring the Constitution into effect, June 21, 1788

Virginia is the tenth state to ratify, June 25, 1788

Federal Procession, New York City, July 23, 1788

New York State convention ratifies Constitution (30 to 27), July 26, 1788

Victory procession, Albany, August 8, 1788

Congress selects New York City as federal capital, September 13, 1788

New York elects its federal representatives, March 3–4, 1789

First federal Congress meets, March 4, 1789

House of Representatives achieves quorum, April 1, 1789

Senate achieves quorum, April 6, 1789

Inauguration of President George Washington, April 30, 1789

New York legislature chooses state's United States Senators,
August 8–16, 1789

Passage of Federal Judiciary Act, September 24, 1789

Bill of Rights proposed by Congress, September 25, 1789

John Jay of New York named first chief justice
of United States, September 26, 1789

New York legislature ratifies Bill of Rights, February 4, 1790

Bill of Rights ratified, December 15, 1791

1787: The Issues

SHIRLEY A. RICE

New York State Bicentennial Commission

In 1787, George Clinton of Ulster County had just begun his fourth term as governor of New York. The state's first chief executive, Clinton was elected to the post in 1777 over Albany's Philip Schuyler, a celebrated military leader and a member of New York's wealthy, aristocratic Dutch community. Clinton's extended control of the governor's office revealed his strength among the farmers of the Hudson Valley countryside. His firmest support sprang from the yeoman and tenant agriculturalists of Orange, Ulster, Albany, Washington, and Montgomery counties.

In New York, the years following the close of the Revolution were marked by depression, plummeting farm prices, the shrinkage of hard currency, and debt. The obligations of the state to public creditors and other related economic hardships were met by the emission of paper money, a move that created a land bank to lend money on real estate collateral. This legislation cemented and increased support for Clinton's policies and helped many distressed farmers to avoid bankruptcy and foreclosure. It also permitted the state to purchase large quantities of federal securities, the interest on which was used to retire outstanding debts incurred during the war.

The cornerstone of New York's financial recovery, however, remained the 5 percent impost, a tariff on imported goods which had been temporarily granted to the Continental Congress to finance military operations. In 1783, Governor Clinton forced a repeal of the grant, diverting the income once more to the state's treasury. At this time, therefore, New York's economy prospered from a tax paid by other states on goods flowing through her ports, a tax which Clinton and his Antifederalists firmly refused to surrender to a national government.

Disputes between New York and her eastern neighbors intensified in the postwar period. Titles to land in New Hampshire and in the re-

New York State, 1788

gion which eventually became Vermont remained clouded until 1790, when a two-state commission finally established the state boundaries. As a result, New York withdrew her claims in return for a cash settlement of $30,000, and Vermont became the fourteenth state in 1791. These events, however, took place only after the framing and adoption of the federal Constitution; in 1787, the Vermont question was a major source of controversy in New York.

The state's policy toward Loyalists and their property holdings also became an important issue in the 1780s. Governor Clinton opposed the return and recovery of Tory elements and urged the passage of severe laws against the supporters of the British monarchy. The New York legislature eventually eliminated many of the restrictions imposed on the Loyalists, but this conservative faction threw its political support toward the Federalists, led by Alexander Hamilton, his father-in-law, Philip Schuyler, and the Livingston family, headed by Chancellor Robert R. Livingston. They believed that the future of the young nation depended on a new and vigorous form of government that put national interests ahead of those of the states.

Interstate economic issues precipitated the call for a convention to propose and discuss remedies. Failure to resolve the problems at a meeting in Annapolis in 1786 led to an urgent demand for representatives from each of the thirteen states to gather in Philadelphia in May of 1787 to attempt the resolution of the difficulties faced by a deteriorating Confederation Congress. The New York legislature selected three men with strong upstate connections: Albany Mayor John J. Lansing, Albany resident and New York State Supreme Court Judge Robert Yates, and New York State Assemblyman and prominent New York City attorney Alexander Hamilton, whose wife, Betsy Schuyler, spent her childhood and youth in an elegant Georgian mansion situated on the southern edge of the city of Albany. All three recognized the need for measures to settle the disputes facing New York and her sister states. The means to achieve those ends, however, separated Hamilton from his fellow delegates. To accomplish their objectives, the Federalists needed to convince thirteen diverse entities to cede some of their cherished prerogatives to an untested national government "in order to form a more perfect union."

No one was more interested in maintaining the sovereignty of the states than Hamilton's staunchest opponent, George Clinton. Opposed to the establishment of a strong central executive, Clinton favored withdrawal if the convention appeared likely to dissolve the Articles of Confederation, under which the states were then associated. When it became obvious that the Federal Convention intended to do just that, Yates and Lansing departed, leaving Hamilton the sole representative from New York. As an unofficial delegate, a circumstance arising from his minority status, Hamilton signed the proposed United States Constitution on September 17, 1787, and began the long and arduous task of persuading New Yorkers to ratify it.

Clintonism and the New Federalism in New York State

STEPHEN L. SCHECHTER
New York State Bicentennial Commission

Judge Thomas Tredwell, a Suffolk County Antifederalist delegate at the New York State ratifying convention of 1788, echoed the sentiments of many of his fellow Antifederalists when he remarked: "In this Constitution, Sir, we have departed widely from the principles and political faith of '76, when the spirit of liberty ran high, and danger put a curb on ambition. Here," Tredwell continued, "we find no security for the rights of individuals, no security for the existence of our state governments; here is no bill of rights, no proper restriction of power; our lives, our property, and our consciences, are left wholly at the mercy of the legislature, and the powers of the judiciary may be extended to any degree short of almighty. Sir, in this Constitution we have not only neglected,—we have done worst,—we have openly violated, our faith,—that is, our *public faith*."[1] (Emphasis added.)

Republicanism was the "public faith" or civil religion about which Tredwell spoke; and popular consent was the central belief on which that faith was founded.

Throughout the Revolutionary Era, New Yorkers, like citizens of other states, debated how best to implement their belief in republicanism. By the end of that era, two well-developed views of government had emerged: Federalism, based on the then novel idea that popular consent could be best realized within a large republic led by a strong national government; and Antifederalism, based on the then conventional idea that popular consent could be maintained only by a national system of states functioning as viable small republics.

Unlike most states, by the late 1780s New York had developed a viable political system with a relatively healthy economy. In fact, under the able leadership of Governor George Clinton, New York had become the very model of an Antifederalist polity with a coherent public philosophy, a successful economic policy, and winning political strategy. In a word, New York worked. It worked because of Clintonism, and that is why its leaders were so reluctant to join the new Union envisioned by Federalist leaders.

The Political Theory of Clintonism

In the late eighteenth century, New York State displayed all the attributes of a rapidly developing country and Clintonism was its integrating force. Clintonism incorporated three basic components: a philosophy of republican society, a policy of postwar economic recovery, and a political strategy for building constituencies and recruiting leaders. These components supplied the building blocks of New York's political society and provided its yeoman citizenry with a sense of political and economic well-being.[2]

The proposed Constitution tested the relative strength of supporters and opponents of Clintonism. At the same time, it provided each side with an opportunity to forge a deeper sense of loyalty among its members. In fact, Alexander Hamilton, a leading opponent of Governor George Clinton and Clintonism, believed that the governor's adamant opposition to the Constitution was a product of his desire "to establish Clintonism on the basis of Antifoederalism."[3]

As a political movement, Clintonism drew much of its support from its founder, George Clinton. Born in 1739 in the Ulster County community of Little Britain, Clinton spent his early years acquiring the credentials, if not the reputation, for leadership. He pursued an early military career in the French and Indian Wars, studied law in New York City under William Smith, obtained a clerkship to the Ulster County Court, and was elected in 1768 to the provincial assembly, where he became a member of the anti-British faction. He was then chosen in 1775 as one of the state's delegates to the Second Continental Congress, appointed a brigadier general by Congress in the spring of 1777 in which capacity he courageously, if unsuccessfully, defended the Hudson Highland. Clinton briefly attended the Fourth Provincial Congress in the Spring of 1777, when he cast only one vote during the considerations of the state's first constitution (a vote against Robert Yates's motion to strengthen the governor's appointment power, a vote which would later haunt Clinton as governor).

In all these capacities, Clinton served with characteristic courage, silence, good judgment, and moderation. In the process, he amassed considerable land holdings; however, much like George Washington, his property and lifestyle retained a republican simplicity.

None of these capacities fully prepared Clinton or his opponents for his electoral victories and administrative successes as the state's first governor. Serving six successive terms, 1777–95, and 1801 to 1804, Governor Clinton is one of the neglected architects of the founding generation. He helped fashion a philosophy, policy, and political strategy of republican government which attracted the support of the state's yeomanry. At the same time, Clinton and Clintonism forever repelled the state's "old guard" and conservative Whig establishment led by figures such as General Philip Schuyler, who lost the race for governor in 1777; Schuyler's son-in-law, Alexander Hamilton, whose dislike for Clinton is legend; and John Jay, the gentleman conservative, who nearly bested Clinton in the gubernatorial race of 1792 and, after Clinton's retirement, won the election of 1795, becoming the state's second governor.

As a political theory, Clintonism had several expositors including John Lansing, Jr., Melancton Smith, Abraham Yates, Jr., "Brutus," "Cato," and, of course, Governor Clinton. Leading the opposition to Clintonism were Alexander Hamilton and John Jay, writing under their own names and under various pseudonyms, including "Publius."

Propositions of Clintonian Theory

1. Clintonism rested on the compact theory of popular consent. An associative, not an individualistic, theory, its basic proposition was best stated by "Brutus": "The origin of society then is to be sought, not in any natural right which one man has to exercise authority over another, but in the united consent of those who associate."[4]

2. Clintonism accepted the idea of popular consent by representation. "In a free republic, although all laws are derived from the consent of the people, yet the people do not declare their consent by themselves in person, but by representatives, chosen by them, who are supposed to know the minds of their constituents, and to be possessed of integrity to declare this mind."[5]

3. Clintonism subscribed to a "mirror" theory of representation, including the ideas that representatives and represented should be of the same class; the dominant class ought to be the middle class; and the ratio of representatives to represented and the number of representatives ought to be sufficiently small and large, respectively, to allow this system to flourish. By contrast, Alexander Hamilton advocated a

"trusteeship" theory of representation, which is based on the ideas that representatives ought to be the most meritorious, that such candidates may well come from the upper class, and that the best security of good representation is "good administration," not the size of the district.[6]

4. Clintonians were not of a single mind regarding the ends of representative government. At one extreme were men like Thomas Tredwell, who remained "friends of liberty," with the view that the first end of government was to secure the safety of the citizenry from government. Others, notably Governor Clinton and Melancton Smith, were of a more pragmatic disposition, subscribing to the view that "liberty first" ought not to prevent reliance on energetic government when necessary. (Governor Clinton sought a stronger federal government in wartime, led state troops against Shays's rebels, and called out the state militia to put down mob attacks.) By contrast, the very hallmark of New York State Federalists was their unapologetic respect for energetic government in peace as well as war, and the belief that strong government is the best protection of, not threat to, liberty.

5. Clintonism was solidly based on the model of a "small republic;" namely, the idea that republican society could survive only in small countries where the attachments to republican principles could be nurtured and sustained. In a large republic, the population is dispersed, territories become ungovernable, extremities rebel, representatives become remote, ambitious men arise, and popular attachments to equality erode.[7]

6. Clintonism reaffirmed its commitment to a strong union of the states, but sharply distinguished between a strong union and a strong national government. The Clintonian or "small republic" view of federalism maintained that a strong union rested on strong states "completed" by a confederation of them. The basic premise was sociological: "The strongest principle of union resides within our domestic walls. The ties of the parent exceed that of any other; as we depart from home, the next general principle of union is amongst citizens of the same state, where acquaintance, habits, and fortunes, nourish affection, and attachment; enlarge the circle still further, and, as citizens of different states, though we acknowledge the same national denomination, we lose the ties of acquaintance, habits, and fortunes, and thus, by degrees, we lessen in our attachments, till, at length, we no more than acknowledge a sameness of species."[8]

7. Clintonism rested on a healthy respect for the yeoman farmer as the model citizen. Nowhere, however, did Clintonism explicitly reject commerce. By contrast, much of Federalist theory, especially as put forward by Alexander Hamilton, rested on the characteristics of social

pluralism, political diversity, and economic development that would result from an extended republic based on commerce.

As political theories, neither Clintonism nor the New Federalism in New York were unique. Their elements were well drawn, articulately advanced, and deeply felt; but they were representative of the prevailing Antifederalist and Federalist theories of the day. What distinguished Clintonism and the opposition to it was the extent to which they had been applied to and reenforced by public policy stances, recruitment vehicles, and electoral strategies.

Politics and Public Policy in the 1780s

In New York State, political principles, interests, and ambition of Clintonians and Anti-Clintonians were tightly braided, and this helps explain their internal strength as well as the intractable differences between them. George Clinton's first gubernatorial election in June 1777 confirmed that his electoral strength lay in the yeomanry outside British-occupied New York City. It was a perfect marriage, not only of convenience, but also of principle and style. Over the next two decades, Governor Clinton and his supporters carefully maintained that marriage, forcing Clinton's opponents to build a somewhat fluid coalition out of the commercial and urban interests of the state, especially in the southern areas where those interests dominated.

The cornerstone of Clintonism was its fiscal and monetary policy.[9] On the issue of property taxation, Clintonians favored, and in 1784 obtained, a special assessment on the southern district. Thereafter, each county contributed a quota, with the southern district paying approximately one-half of that total. In the 1787 legislative session, Alexander Hamilton proposed a reform tax measure designed to replace the county-based quota system with a property-based tax system which most heavily taxed agricultural meadow, pasture, and arable land. Hamilton's efforts failed.

Other economic issues divided Clintonians and Anti-Clintonians. Clintonians supported and Anti-Clintonians opposed the sale of confiscated Loyalist estates, the issuance of paper money, trials for small debts before justices of the peace, increasing legislators' *per diem*, increasing the governor's salary, holding the line on salary and *per diem* increases for judges and state administrative officers, maintaining a low price for vacant land, and maintaining restrictions on foreign trade and on the relief of merchants' prewar debts. Both supported the sale and settlement of unsettled lands, a major source of state revenue.

The impost involved more aspects of the conflict between Clinton-ism and the New Federalism than any other economic policy. Every schoolchild is taught that New York State had an impost, that advocates of a strong federal government led by Alexander Hamilton lobbied state legislatures for years to amend the Articles of Confederation in order to obtain a federal impost, and that the defeat of the proposed federal impost in the New York State legislature on February 15, 1787, precipi-tated the congressional call on February 21 for a convention to meet in Philadelphia for the purpose of drafting amendments to the Articles of Confederation. What was the impost and why was it so popular?

The impost, an *ad valorem* tax on imported goods, was both an economically and politically important source of revenue in New York State. In economic terms, "annual income from the state impost dur-ing the Confederation years ranged between $100,000 and $225,000, and represented one-third to more than one-half of the state's annual in-come."[10] Politically, the tax was ideal from the perspective of Clintoni-ans since it was levied on merchants, many of whom were non-New Yorkers from Connecticut and New Jersey. In this sense, Governor Clin-ton's yeoman constituency could feel doubly relieved since they did not directly feel the impact of the impost on increased consumer prices and could calculate their tax savings from the increased property tax they might otherwise have had to pay.

The political consequences of adopting a federal impost were well understood by both sides. On December 24, 1787, an essay by "A Land-holder" (Oliver Ellsworth) appeared in the *Connecticut Courant*, lam-basting New York State officials for retaining the state impost: "In New-York the opposition is not to this constitution in particular, but the federal impost; it is confined wholly to salary men and their connec-tions, men whose salary is paid by the state impost. This class of citizens are endeavouring to convince the ignorant part of the community that an annual income of fifty thousand pounds, extorted from the citizens of Massachusetts, Connecticut and New-Jersey is a great blessing to the state of New-York." Two weeks later, addressing the Connecticut Con-vention on January 4, 1788, Ellsworth referred to his fellow state citizens as "tributaries" of New York State, and suddenly hiked the annual in-come from the New York State impost to sixty to eighty thousand pounds. In his *Address to the People of the State of New York* of April 17, 1788, Melancton Smith charged "that Connecticut and New-Jersey were very much influenced in their determinations on the question, by local considerations. The duty of impost laid by this state, has been a subject of complaint by those states. . . . To excite in the minds of the people of these states an attachment to the new system, the amount of the revenue arising from our imposts has been magnified to a much larger sum than it produces."

By the time of the state ratifying convention elections of April–May 1788, New York State's political economy and the individual lot of its yeomanry were on relatively solid ground. The price of agricultural goods had remained high throughout the postwar period, Clinton's monetary and fiscal policies were having their intended effects on reducing the state's indebtedness, and Clinton's yeoman constituency could look forward to relatively stable economic conditions of available land, available cash, stable farm prices, and low property taxes.

In New York, then, Herbert J. Storing's thesis of positive Antifederalism can be readily supported.[11] Clintonism was working—as a political philosophy, as a policy of postwar recovery, and as a strategy of political mobilization. As a result, the State of New York had become a viable entity politically as well as economically.

To borrow from psychology, the primary source of opposition by Clintonians to the proposed Constitution was the *gestalt* of Clintonism itself; that is, a configuration of principles, interests, and symbolism so unified as a whole that the reasons for its opposition to the Constitution could not be derived from or attributed to any one of its parts. Clintonians, many of whom were aspiring members of the middle class, could feel good about themselves as citizens—that is, as functioning and consequential members of a viable political system—and it is this sense of political attachment and efficacy that provided the glue which held together the various components of political society in New York.

NOTES

[1] Jonathan Elliot, ed., *Debates in the Several State Conventions on the Adoption of the Federal Constitution . . .*, Second Edition (Philadelphia: J.B.Lippincott Company, 1836), II, 401, 404.

[2] *Cf.*, George Dangerfield, *Chancellor Robert R. Livingston of New York, 1746–1813* (New York: Harcourt, Brace and Company, 1960); and E. Wilder Spaulding, *New York in the Critical Period, 1783–1789* (New York: Columbia University Press, 1932.)

[3] Abraham Bancker to Evert Bancker, Poughkeepsie, June 28, 1788.

[4] "Brutus" II, November 1, 1787.

[5] "Brutus" I, October 18, 1787.

[6] See especially the debate between Melancton Smith and Alexander Hamilton on June 21, 1788, in the New York State ratifying convention.

[7]See especially Robert Yates and John Lansing to Governor George Clinton, "Reasons of Dissent," December 21, 1787; and "Brutus" I, October 18, 1787.

[8]"Cato" III, October 25, 1787.

[9]The discussion of public policy issues draws heavily from the legislative roll-call votes analyzed by Jackson Turner Main in *Political Parties before the Constitution*, published for the Institute of Early American History and Culture (Chapel Hill: University of North Carolina Press, 1973), 120–155.

[10]John P. Kaminski, "New York: The Reluctant Pillar," in *The Reluctant Pillar: New York and the Adoption of the Federal Constitution,* edited by Stephen L. Schechter (1985; Albany, New York: New York State Bicentennial Commission, 1987). 52.

[11]Herbert J. Storing, *What the Anti-Federalists Were For: The Political Thought of the Opponents of the Constitution* (Chicago: University of Chicago Press, 1981).

A Guide to *The Federalist* *

Stephen L. Schechter
New York State Bicentennial Commission

Many things can serve more than one purpose. CERTS, so the jingle goes, is two mints in one; it's a breath mint and a candy mint. So, too, *The Federalist* is three documents in one. It is a campaign document, designed to win popular approval among the voters of New York State for the proposed Constitution; a serious work of political thought, analyzing the nature of free societies; and the authoritative commentary on the Constitution, reflecting the intent of the framers of the Constitution.

The multifaceted character of *The Federalist* is what makes it such a challenge to read with comprehension. To understand *The Federalist*, one must understand its historical context, the rhetoric (i.e., political language) of that time, the political theory of *The Federalist*, the place of that theory in the history of political thought, and how these elements can reinforce one another on the printed page. Based on these criteria, no one can fully understand *The Federalist*, but one can apply these criteria to improve one's understanding of it, and that is the purpose of this guide.

Historical Background

On February 21, 1787, the Congress of the Confederation called for a convention to revise the Articles of Confederation. In the months that followed, all of the states (except for Rhode Island) elected delegates to the convention. That convention, known as the Constitutional Convention, met in the city of Philadelphia from May 25 to September 17. The product of its summertime efforts was a new Constitution, debated in the Congress, September 26–28, and sent without approval to the states.[1]

By the end of 1787, four states had ratified the Constitution, beginning with Delaware, whose license plates now read "First State" to commemorate its early action. By June of 1788, four more states ratified.

Revised version of a paper prepared for the Center for the Study of Federalism, Temple University, with the support of a grant from the National Endowment for the Humanities.

Then, on June 21, New Hampshire became the ninth state to ratify, bringing the Constitution into effect.

New York State was not among those first nine states. In fact, New York did not ratify the Constitution until July 26, 1788, thereby becoming the eleventh to do so. The state legislature delayed the process, first, by waiting until February 1788 to call the convention, and then by scheduling the election for the end of April and the convention for mid-June. But why did the state legislature choose to delay the process? To understand *The Federalist* as a campaign document, one must first understand why New York State waited so long to ratify.

New York was a reluctant state because neither Federalist nor Antifederalist leaders were willing to risk an early decision. As the state's minority party, Federalists wanted late elections in the hope of swaying new voters to their side; they wanted a late convention because they believed they could win over moderate Antifederalist delegates before the convention. And if these two efforts failed, there would be no early defeat in New York to hurt their efforts in other states.

Antifederalists had their own reasons for delay. They were led by George Clinton, the state's first governor, undefeated in every election bid since 1777. Clinton was a smart politician who tried to leave nothing to chance. He realized his forces might have won an early contest, but they also might have lost. He wanted time to assess his statewide strength on this particular issue and to organize the diversity of interests needed to win in a state like New York. He also hoped that, with time, Antifederalists could build an interstate movement for a second constitutional convention. Finally, Clinton did not want New York to be the first big state to reject the Constitution.[2]

How and Why *The Federalist* Was Written

The proposed Constitution was first printed in New York on September 21, 1787, and within a week the debate over its adoption began. A commentary by a Federalist appeared in a New York City newspaper, *The Daily Advertiser*, on September 24. It was answered three days later in the city's only Antifederalist newspaper, *The New-York Journal*, by "Cato" I, the first of seven Antifederalist essays attributed by some to Governor Clinton. Several days later, "Cato" was attacked in a newspaper essay by "Caesar" (once thought to be Alexander Hamilton), and the debate was well underway, nurturing two basic tools of American campaign politics—the print media and the political party.

The Federalist was an important part of the New York debate, with the first essay appearing on October 27, 1787, two days after the unanswered charges of "Cato" III were published.[3] The decision to write the essays was made by Alexander Hamilton and fellow New Yorker John Jay. Though little is known about that decision, it is likely that Hamilton recognized the need for an authoritative series of essays in defense of the proposed Constitution to counter the early onslaught of Antifederalists like "Cato," and that *The Federalist* was intended to serve that purpose.

The essays were written by Alexander Hamilton, John Jay, and James Madison of Virginia under the pseudonym "Publius."[4] A total of eighty-four essays were printed in New York City between October 27, 1787 and May 28, 1788. The essays were first published in New York City newspapers. They were then widely circulated in other newspapers until January 1788 when it was announced that the McLean brothers would print the essays in book form. (The first of the two-volume set was published on March 22, 1788; the second, on May 28.)

The essays were addressed to the "People of the State of New York," and intended to convince New Yorkers of the necessity of ratifying the new Constitution. In particular, the essays were intended to show, in Hamilton's words: "The utility of the UNION to your political prosperity—The insufficiency of the present Confederation to preserve that Union—The necessity of a government at least as equally energetic with the one proposed to the attainment of this object—The conformity of the proposed constitution to the true principles of republican government—Its analogy to your own state constitution—and lastly, The additional security, which its adoption will afford to the preservation of that species of government, to liberty, and to property."[5]

The essays were written on a tight schedule: at first, two were printed each week; later, the schedule was increased to four per week. This did not leave much time for careful study or coordination. As James Madison explained near the end of his life in a private memorandum, the essays "were written most of them in great haste, and without any special allotment [assignment] of the different parts of the subject to the several writers, J.M. [James Madison] being at the time a member of the then Congress [of the Confederation in New York City], and A.H. [Alexander Hamilton] being also a member, and occupied moreover in his profession at the bar [i.e., as a lawyer], which occasionally took him up to Albany."[6]

At the time of their publication, *The Federalist* papers were widely recognized by Federalist and Antifederalist alike as one of the most serious and sophisticated defenses of the Constitution. Federalists generally regarded the essays as the best analysis of the Constitution, though some admitted that they were too "elaborate" and not "well calculated for the common people." (In other words, even friendly readers of the day found them heavy and, at times, difficult reading.)

Today, *The Federalist* is widely regarded as the authoritative statement of the intent of the framers of the Constitution. It is used by lawyers, legal scholars, and judges to interpret the meaning of particular clauses of the Constitution, and by theorists to understand the meaning of the Constitution as a whole. However, its impact on its intended audience—the people of New York—was negligible. A majority of New York voters cast their ballot for Antifederalist convention delegates, and there is no evidence that any of those Antifederalist delegates who later decided to switch their final vote for ratification were influenced by *The Federalist*.

How *The Federalist* Begins

With this background in mind, consider how *The Federalist* begins. Read the following sentence from the first paragraph of the very first essay.

> It has been frequently remarked, that it seems to have been reserved to the people of this country, by their conduct and example, to decide the important question, whether societies of men are really capable or not, of establishing good government from reflection and choice, or whether they are forever destined to depend, for their political constitutions, on accident and force.

Written by Hamilton, this sentence can be read in two ways; namely, as the opening statements of a campaign document and a work of political thought.

As the opening statement of a campaign document, this sentence is a classic gambit—an opening move designed to occupy a favorable position (in this case, the "high ground") with a minimal amount of sacrifices. Consider how the same sentence might read in terms of today's political rhetoric:

> Once again, my fellow Americans, we have an historic opportunity (presented by my friends and me) to show the world that we are a thoughtful people capable of creating good government by careful planning and popular consent, not by being forced to do it or by accidentally blundering into it.

The opening sentence gains added dimension as a campaign statement when its political context is recalled. The overall context was shaped by the desire to buy time, and what better way to do that than to appeal to the "reflective" nature of the voters? The particular context is the newspapers of New York City and what was being printed that week by the opposition.[7]

As an opening statement of political thought, the first sentence of *The Federalist No. 1* suggests that politicians (and Hamilton was one of the best) do not campaign simply to win the votes of the people, they also campaign to govern; in this instance, to inform the public (and by that I mean giving shape and form to the public mind as well as providing it with bits of information) about the better world that will be possible under the new Constitution. This involves the selection and use of words not merely as tactics in an overall strategy but also as concepts in an overall theory.

In this sense, the opening sentence contains two basic ideas that shape America's theory of constitutionalism.[8] Hamilton elegantly phrased those ideas but he did not invent them. In fact, they were so much a part of the eighteenth-century American mind that they were widely used by Federalists and Antifederalists alike.

The two ideas used to introduce *The Federalist* answer the political question: If society is governed by laws, how can laws (and in this instance, the Constitution) be made in a way that the members of society will willingly obey? The answer to this question is, in Hamilton's words, "reflection and choice."

1. **Reflection** is the Enlightenment idea that humankind is a thinking species, capable of improving its lot by thinking before it acts. This idea was shared by both sides in the debate, and it is one of the reasons why the campaign remained a peaceful debate. It was used in *The Federalist No. 1*, but it was also used by Antifederalist "Cato" I: "Deliberate, therefore, on this new national government with coolness; analize[9] it with criticism; and reflect on it with candour. . . . Beware of those who wish to influence your passions, and to make you dupes to their resentments and little interests . . . ." And "Cato" II wrote of the Federalist author "Caesar": "he shuts the door of true deliberation and discussion."

This is not to say that all matters of politics were objects of reason. Reprinted from a Philadelphia statement of August 29, 1787 in the *New Jersey Journal* on September 5, 1787, while the Constitutional Convention was still in session, is an interesting distinction: "The principles of liberty and the principles of government . . . are distinct things: Many understand the former which are matters of feeling, who know nothing of the latter, which are objects of reflection and reason."

2. **Choice** is the republican idea of popular consent. It occurs time and time again throughout *The Federalist* and all other commentaries on the Constitution by Federalists and Antifederalists; it stands for the complex yet simple notion that people will obey laws of their own making (or by representatives of their own choosing) so long as they have confidence in themselves and their representatives. In the heat of debate, some Federalists accused Antifederalists of pandering to the people, while some Antifederalists accused the other side of forgetting the people. However, virtually all were advocates of popular government; and, rhetoric aside, most were advocates of popular government by some form of elected representation.[10]

In sum, then, Federalists and Antifederalists agreed on the need for delay, the worth of cool and reasoned debate, and the goal of government by popular consent. On what did they disagree and how did federalism figure into that debate?

What the Antifederalists Were For:[11]
A Confederacy of Small Republics

Federalists and Antifederalists were both advocates of popular government in its republican form. Where they differed was in the type of republican society they wanted and the type of federal system they thought best suited to secure that society.

Antifederalists were opposed to the proposed Constitution in its original form; like any group bound by opposition, it would have been difficult for them to agree on what they were *for*. It is for this reason that they are remembered as "men of little faith." However, in the late Cecelia Kenyon's phrase, Antifederalists were against the Constitution as proposed because they were for a type of society that they felt would be threatened by the new Constitution; and, as they read what "Publius" had to say, especially in essays such as *The Federalist No. 10*, their fears were undoubtedly confirmed, because "Publius" was quite clear about the different type of society he envisioned.

Much of Antifederalist opinion was united behind the idea that republics had to be small (like ancient Greek city-states, medieval Swiss cantons, or modern American states) to survive. Undoubtedly, part of this opinion was shaped by a desire to preserve the existing status quo. However, another part was an idea which they drew from the French philosopher Montesquieu: the basis of republican government (i.e., popular consent) required a small and intimate setting where citizens

(1) knew one another, (2) shared similar habits and values, and (3) did not have the opportunity to become too unequal in their fortunes, because without these three bonds, people would not trust one another enough to agree on anything (including how to protect themselves against tyranny). Note how "Cato" III relied on these same three bonds in his explanation:

> The strongest principle of union resides within our domestic [i.e., family] walls. The ties of the parent exceed that of any other; as we depart from home, the next general principle of union is amongst citizens of the same state, where acquaintance, habits, and fortunes, nourish affection, and attachment; enlarge the circle still further, &, as citizens of different states, though we acknowledge the same national denomination, we lose the ties of acquaintance, habits, and fortunes, and thus, by degrees, we lessen in our attachments, till, at length, we no more than acknowledge a sameness of species.

"Cato" assumed the existence of a union (see line 1 of the quote) and of national ties (see line 7). What "Cato" could not accept was the idea of a national government. Like other Antifederalists, "Cato" advocated a federal or confederal union of the states. In the eighteenth century, "federal" and "confederal" were used as synonyms. Both terms referred to relations among equals (in this instance, states) entered into voluntarily by compact or covenant. They could be loose relations (as in an alliance or league) or they could be stronger, as in the perpetual union formed by the Articles of Confederation. However, Antifederalists rejected the Federalist argument that federal relations could exist with a national government in the same system.

Today, we might consider Antifederalist attitudes to be "parochial" and "small town"; and we would be right. But does this make "Cato" wrong?

What the Federalists Were For:
An Extended and Compound Republic

Federalists, including "Publius," believed "Cato" was dead wrong. In fact, much of what made the Federalist argument so new to the eighteenth-century mind was (1) the idea that republics should be large and complex, not small and simple; and (2) the constitutional means for accomplishing that task.

In *The Federalist No. 10*, James Madison, as "Publius," set out the reasons step-by-step (i.e., the logic) for a large, compound republic, focusing more on the large-republic element. He resumed this theoretical discussion in *The Federalist No. 51*, focusing on the compound-republic element. In numbers 37 and 39, he considered the constitutional means for securing a large, compound republic. There are other writings where the Federalist experiment is explained,[12] but it is Madison's Tenth, like Beethoven's Fifth, which is most frequently required of the student and, hence, the most widely known. For this reason, let us review Madison's Tenth to discover the reasons for wanting a large, compound republic, and then proceed to numbers 51, 37, and 39 to complete the Madisonian model of republican government.

The Madisonian Model Outlined
A. *The Federalist No. 10* and the Large Republic

1. The greatest danger facing popular government is factionalism, which occurs when a majority or minority unites around a passion or interest adverse to individual rights or the public good. [Why did Madison single out factionalism?][13]

2. Madison rejected the idea of controlling factionalism by removing its causes (see Figure 1).

a. Controlling the people by denying their liberties would be unwise, much like throwing the baby out with the bathwater. (Is factious behavior, as defined by Madison, illegal today? If not, should it be?)[14]

b. Telling people how to think would not work because no one would listen unless they were forced to do so, and that option was rejected (see 2[a] above).

3. Madison accepted the idea of controlling factionalism by controlling its effects.

4. The effects of *minority* factions can be controlled relatively simply by the republican principle of popular consent, by which the majority would defeat the minority faction at the polls. (Did Madison worry too little about minority factions? Was he too tolerant of some of its effects?)

5. The real problem facing popular governments and the "great object" of his essay is how to control the *majority* when it becomes factious.

6. There are two basic ways to control majority factions: control the motives that inspire them and the opportunities for them to organize. These are taken up in (8) and (9) below, respectively, after the essay introduces the distinction between democracies and republics. (Review note 10 in the guide.)

7. Of the two forms of popular government, a republic is more likely than a democracy to control majority factions, partly because democracies are by their very nature inclined toward instability. Also, republics allow for representation and increased size of population and territory. These last two factors are considered below.

8. Republics make it possible to have elected representatives, and good ones can refine the factious spirit that might spread among the majority.

    a. Large republics are more likely than small republics to elect good representatives for two reasons:

        i. Regardless of their size, all republics need the same number of legislators in order to avoid the clubbiness of too few and the confusion of too many. But in a large republic, there will be more options to fill those seats with qualified people.

        ii. Since the size of the constituency is greater in the large republic, it will be less susceptible to deception by unworthy candidates. (Is it harder to fool 100,000 people than 10,000?)

        iii. However, on this as on other points, one must strive for the mean. If the constituency is too large, the representative will not be sufficiently aware of local conditions. If the constituency is too small, the representative will be too tied to local conditions and unable to see the larger picture or pursue the national interest. The Constitution forms a "happy combination" that refers "great and aggregate interests" to the federal Congress and "local and particular" interests to the state legislatures. (Is there one optimum ratio of representative to be represented for a national legislature, and another optimum for state legislatures? And is this a guarantor that the states are "closer" to the people?)[15]

9. Republics make it possible to increase the size of the citizenry and territory, and larger republics make it less likely that majority factions will form.

    a. The larger the society, the greater the variety of parties and interests. (Did Madison prefer a pluralistic society?)

    b. The greater the diversity of interests in society, the less likely a majority will have a single passion or interest. Put differently, majorities in large societies are more likely to be coalitions of various interests than a monolithic force of one interest. (Is this also an obstacle for forming majorities around a single public good?)

    c. The larger the number of citizens and territory, the more difficult it will be for those who could form a factious majority to discover one another and come together. (Does this still hold in today's society of telecommunications, electronic media, and supersonic jets?)

10. The Union is more likely to control the effects of faction than are the states composing it.

a. Members of Congress are more likely to possess the enlightened views and virtuous sentiments needed to override local prejudice. (If "Cato" had a localistic "small town" bias, did Madison suffer from a cosmopolitan bias?)

b. The greater variety of parties in the Union as a whole will prevent any one party from outnumbering the others. For example, a factious leader may be able to take over one state but not the Union; a religious sect may become a factious majority in one region, but other sects will prevent its spread; a particular fad or disruptive element or wicked group is less likely to take over the whole system than a part of it.

11. "In the extent and proper structure of the Union, therefore, we behold a republican remedy for the diseases most incident to republican government." Madison fully considered the extent of the Union, but he did not go as far in addressing its "proper structure" (i.e., its compound nature); a matter which is introduced in point 10 and continued in *The Federalist No. 51.*

B. *The Federalist No. 51*
and the Principle of the Compound Republic

1. Madison continued the theoretical discussion of *No. 10*, shifting attention from controlling minority and majority factions to controlling all factions and government itself. At the end of the fourth paragraph, he noted: "A dependence on the people [i.e., on the republican idea of popular consent] is, no doubt, the primary control on the government; but experience has taught mankind the necessity of auxiliary precautions" (i.e., extra safeguards).

2. Madison identified three "auxiliary precautions": limited government, framed by laws; divided government, with one "department" (i.e., branch) checked by another; and a compound republic, providing the double security of two sets of limited and divided governments (i.e., federal and state).

3. All three precautions are governed by the same policy of "checks and balances." As Madison noted in paragraph five: "This policy, of supplying by opposite and rival interests, the defect of better motives, might be traced through the whole system of human affairs, private as well as public." (Historians of science find this view of the political world similar to Newton's view of the universe. What do you think?)

4. In a classic statement of human nature, Madison explained the need for auxiliary precautions (see the middle of paragraph four):

a. Ambition must be made to counteract ambition. (Why did Madison single out ambition?)[16]

b. If men were angels, no government would be necessary. If angels governed men, no controls on government would be necessary. (How does this compare with Hamilton's view in *The Federalist No. 6*, paragraph three?)

c. In framing a government of men over men, one must first empower the government to control the people, and then oblige it to control itself. A dependence on the people is the best control over the government, but other safeguards are necessary.

C. *The Federalist No. 37* and the Task of Forming a Compound Republic

1. Madison addressed the difficulties of forming a compound republic.[17]

2. The first challenge is to insure a proper balance among three seemingly contradictory principles:

a. Energetic government, which seems to require concentrating power in a single hand;

b. Stability, which seems to require a long duration in office, and

c. Republican liberty, which seems to require widely distributing power among many hands holding office for short periods of time.

3. The second set of challenges is the task of deciding the proper distribution of authority between general and state governments, and among legislative, executive, and judicial branches.

4. The final set of challenges has to do with mediating the differences between large and small states, and among other combinations of states (e.g., North vs. South, and East vs. West).

D. *The Federalist No. 39* and the New Federalism

1. In this essay, Madison finally got down to the specific ways in which the Constitution establishes a government that is both republican and federal.

2. In the first six paragraphs, Madison offered a specific definition of republican government and, in textbook fashion, showed how the new government is fully republican in form.

3. Madison then took on the charge that the framers should have "preserved the *federal* form, which regards the Union as a *Confederacy* of sovereign states; instead of which they have framed a *national* government, which regards the Union as a *consolidation* of the States." (Recall the way these terms were used in 1787: "federal" and "confederal" were synonyms referring to the lateral relations among states.)

4. Madison's answer is a perfect combination of campaign rhetoric and political theory. The new Constitution, explained Madison, keeps the federal element of interstate relations and simply adds to it a national element. The result, Madison cleverly concluded, "is, in strictness, neither a national nor a federal Constitution, but a composition of both."

5. Madison's answer nicely elaborates the Constitution as a compound of federal and national elements:

a. The ratification of the Constitution is a federal act, with the people electing delegates and the delegates voting on the Constitution, both as members of their respective states.

b. The source of powers for the new government is partly federal and partly national, with the House of Representatives elected nationally, the Senate elected by the states (i.e., federally), and the president elected by an electoral college which accumulates a national majority on a state-by-state basis.

c. The operation of the new government is national, because it acts directly on the individual citizen.

d. The extent or scope of the new government is federal, because it is supreme not over all things but only with regard to the enumerated powers granted to it, while the states remain supreme within their respective sphere.

e. Finally, the amendment process is neither wholly federal, nor wholly national, requiring special majorities of both the Congress and the states.[18]

Conclusion

Federalism occupies a critical position in *The Federalist*, both as a campaign document and a serious work of political thought. In one master stroke, Madison preempted the federal principle, taking it away from the sole preserve of Antifederalist opposition, while at the same time redirecting it toward the goals of building a new nation and expanding the republic. In this effort, Madison provided a bridge from the way federalism had been defined to the way federalism is understood today.

The Logic of *Federalist No. 10*

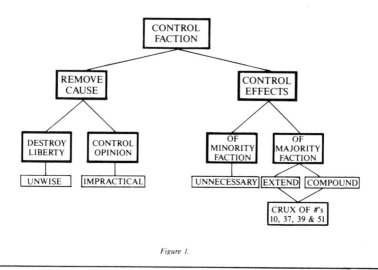

Figure 1.

NOTES:

¹Article 7 of the proposed Constitution requires the "ratification [consent] of the conventions [not legislatures] of nine States [i.e., over two-thirds of the thirteen states]" to establish [i.e., bring into effect] the Constitution.

²For a full account, see John P. Kaminski, "New York: The Reluctant Pillar," in *The Reluctant Pillar: New York and the Adoption of the Federal Constitution*, ed. Stephen L. Schechter (1985; Albany, N.Y.: New York State Bicentennial Commission; 1987).

³Then, on 8 November 1788, Thomas Greenleaf, the Antifederalist printer, advertised the first pamphlet of . . . *Letters From the Federal Farmer to the Republican*, considered then and today to be one of the best Antifederalist commentaries.

⁴Many commentaries on the Constitution were written under pseudonyms, both to protect the author and to make full use of available symbols. Heroes of the Roman Republic were popular choices, because many were well-known symbols of republicanism. (Plutarch's *Lives of the Noble Romans* was widely read at that time.) Publius Valerius established stable republican government after the overthrow of Tarquin, the last Roman king. The choice of this hero was undoubtedly Hamilton's since he had used that pseudonym nearly ten years earlier.

⁵*The Federalist No. 1*, at 6–7. All quotes from *The Federalist* are from the Jacob E. Cooke edition (Middletown, CT: Wesleyan University Press, 1961), now distributed in paperback edition by Harper & Row.

⁶As quoted in John P. Kaminski and Gaspare J. Saladino, eds., *The Documentary History of the Ratification of the Constitution, Commentaries*, Volume I (Madison, WI: State Historical Society of Wisconsin, 1981), p. 487. This excellent series presents the commentaries on the Constitution in chronological order and with useful annotations and footnotes.

⁷Piecing together this context is not as difficult as it might seem. *The Documentary History* noted above is arranged in chronological order, so one can simply look up *The Federalist No. 1* and begin reading the previous documents looking for cross-references.

⁸Constitutionalism is the belief that society should be governed by laws, of which the Constitution is the most fundamental.

⁹*Sic.* There were few established rules of standard spelling in the eighteenth century.

¹⁰In the language of the day, popular government had two species: a republic in which governmental decisions were made by the people's representatives; and a democracy in which governmental decisions were made by the people directly (as at an open-air meeting).

¹¹The heading is taken from Herbert J. Storing, *What the Anti-Federalists Were For* (Chicago: The University of Chicago Press, 1981). This slim paperback reviews Antifederalist political thought and introduces the multi-volume collection of Antifederalist writing, *The Complete Anti-Federalist*, edited by Storing.

¹²Hamilton sets out the theoretical argument for a large, compound republic in *The Federalist No. 9*. John Jay, often forgotten in his role as "Publius," wrote the more politically persuasive version in a pamphlet entitled *An Address to the People of the State of New York*, signed by "A Citizen of New-York," and published on April 15, 1788.

¹³Number 10 was the first essay that Madison wrote, but, in the reader's mind, it was still the tenth essay written by "Publius." Since Hamilton had spoken of factions in Number 9, and since factionalism was generally accepted as a major danger facing republics, Madison might well have decided to focus on factions as a way of beginning his own case while appearing to continue the argument set out in the previous essay. Madison's discussion of factions in *No. 10* followed Hamilton's analysis in *No. 9*. The two men approached the problem of factionalism from different directions: Hamilton pointing out that the power of the federal government may be used to break the violence of faction; Madison arguing that the nature of the extended republic is such as to render remote, if not impossible, the creation of a dangerous faction. Both men were writing against the conventional political wisdom that factions were an inescapable disease of republican government, often associated with Charles Louis Secondat, Baron de Montesquieu, the author of *The Spirit of the Laws* and the leading philosopher of government of the eighteenth century. Madison did not mention Montesquieu in *The Federalist No. 10*; Hamilton quoted him against himself in *No. 9* to defend the idea that the Constitution created a confederate republic, a form of republic proof against the dangers of faction.

¹⁴Suggestion: Compare factious behavior with the laws and cases on seditious behavior as threats to the public safety.

¹⁵The Constitution specifies in Article I, Section 2 that the number of representatives in the House of Representatives cannot be more than one for every 30,000 people. This means there cannot be two per 30,000, but there could be one per 100,000, reflecting the framers' fear of localism. In 1929, Congress fixed the number of representatives at 435, and the ratio has steadily increased to one to over 500,000. How does this compare with the ratios for your state legislature?

¹⁶Since the time of the ancient Greeks, political philosophers have focused on ambition (the desire to achieve something important and win lasting recognition for it) as the single most important motivation for entering the world of politics.

¹⁷It was common practice up to the Civil War to refer to the federal government as the "general" government, and the term has much to recommend it. It suggests a government of general scope, avoids the status element in the term "central" government, and nicely sidesteps the choice between "federal" and "national" government.

¹⁸Readers interested in identifying other occurrences of terms like "federal" and "national" in *The Federalist* can consult Thomas S. Engeman, Edward J. Erler, and Thomas B. Hofeller, eds., *The Federalist Concordance* (Middletown, CT, 1980; paperback ed., Chicago: University of Chicago Press, 1988), which lists all key words in their contextual occurrences.

Alexander Hamilton and New York's Ratification *

JACOB E. COOKE and JOHN HENRY MACCRACKEN
Lafayette College

Historians disagree on Alexander Hamilton's role in New York's ratification of the Constitution. Writing a century or so ago, Henry Cabot Lodge contended that Hamilton "overcame by open debate" a "very large" and "carefully disciplined" Antifederalist majority. "Tried by the severest debate, that of winning votes," Lodge wrote, "Hamilton's victory is of the highest rank in the annals of modern oratory."[1] Writing in the 1950s, Broadus Mitchell, in his landmark biography of Hamilton, echoed this praise. "Hamilton's leading part in persuading the New York State Convention," Mitchell concluded, "was his foremost political exploit."[2] Linda DePauw, author of the standard monograph on New York's ratification, disagrees. "Hamilton's oratorical display," she writes, "had no appreciable effect on the men who were to vote on the Constitution."[3]

Who is right? Ultimately, the issue is unresolvable, since there is no way to determine precisely the effect of Hamilton's spirited defense of the Constitution on its ratification by the New York convention. To argue otherwise, one would have to ascertain how many (and precisely whose) opposition votes he changed and, a yet more difficult assignment, eliminate other causal considerations that might have contributed to the switch in votes that brought New York into the Union. Granted the insuperability of such problems, is it not still possible to contend that without Hamilton's skill in debate and off-the-floor negotiations the solid Antifederalist majority might have held fast, or at least for a much longer time? Again, we cannot know for sure. Such larger questions aside, there can be no doubt that Hamilton's role at the New York

*Conference paper presented at "New York's Ratification of the United States Constitution," Federal Hall, New York City, May 20 and 21, 1988.

convention is both an important chapter in the story of his own public career and a prominent feature of the political drama played out in Poughkeepsie in the summer of 1788.

Certainly no member of the convention that assembled in the small New York village was better prepared than Hamilton. Over the preceding year much of his time had been given over first to fashioning the proposed Constitution and then to defending it, activities that are too well known to warrant repetition here. His single most important contribution was also the single most historically significant exposition of his political thought—*The Federalist*. Although these essays presumably did not influence many of the delegates at the New York convention (or elsewhere for that matter), they did provide a storehouse of ready-made material for Hamilton's participation in debate.

Hamilton attended the gathering in Poughkeepsie as a delegate from New York City, one of a small band of Federalists chosen in an election that gave the Antifederalists a solid majority of forty-six representatives as opposed to only nineteen for their opponents. The election appeared to be an unequivocal mandate for New York's rejection of the Constitution. If the Antifederalists heeded the voice of their constituents and also remained united (indeed even if they lost ten or more seemingly assured votes), how could New York be brought into the Union? Even if every Federalist were a Demosthenes and every Antifederalist a mute, by what legerdemain could such a decisive majority be turned into a minority?

Having little choice but to display a facade of optimism, Federalist leaders, professed to believe that the miracle would be wrought by their oratorical prowess. And their debating skill, along with their intellectual and educational superiority, did give them an impressive advantage. The most distinguished members of the Federalist delegation and its undisputed leaders were John Jay, leader of the revolutionary movement in New York, statesman and diplomat, and Robert R. Livingston, the state's chancellor and a personally imposing New York blueblood of "polished wit and classical taste."[4] But Hamilton, recognized even by his personal detractors as a man of intimidating brilliance and dazzling oratorical prowess, became the star of the show. "He generally spoke with much animation and energy and with considerable gesture," wrote James Kent, who was in Poughkeepsie to observe the convention's proceedings. "His language was clear, nervous, and classical. His investigations penetrated to the foundation and reason of every doctrine and principle which he examined, and he brought to the debate a mind filled with all the learning and precedents applicable to the subject."[5]

Hamilton's effectiveness was offset, however, by certain disadvantages. For one thing, he had offended the supporters of Governor George Clinton, among whom virtually all the Antifederalists could be numbered, by a slashing attack on the governor published in July of the preceding year. In an attempt to counter Clinton's effective and popular campaign against the deliberations of the Constitutional Convention then sitting in Philadelphia, Hamilton accused the governor of undermining public confidence in that body's deliberations (which, being secret, Clinton should not have known about) and, implicitly, of demagoguery.[6] It is likely, too, that Robert Yates and John Lansing, Jr. (more likely Lansing, who openly aired the issue during the Poughkeepsie debates) had shared with some of their partisans an account of Hamilton's ill-advised speech at the Philadelphia Convention on June 18, 1787, in which he had recommended the subversion of state sovereignty and a national government closely modelled on England's. Alluding to Hamilton's alleged affinity for monarchy, Antifederalist Charles Tillinghast commented that "you would be surprised, did you not know the man, what an *amazing Republican* Hamilton wishes to make himself be considered. *But he is known.*"[7] It may well also be that Hamilton diminished his influence by the very means that he often sought to exercise it: an intellectual approach that made his remarks sometimes appear to be lectures in political philosophy. George Clinton, for example, commented on one occasion that Hamilton was serving up "a second Edition of Publius well delivered,"[8] and Melancton Smith, prominent Antifederalist leader remarked that Hamilton "like Publius [has] much to say [—] not very applicable to the subject."[9]

The acknowledged leader of the large Antifederalist contingent was the state's governor, George Clinton, who predictably was elected president of the convention. As such (and perhaps because of personal preference), Clinton seldom took part in debate, though his die-hard opposition to unconditional ratification of the Constitution was unquestioned. To Hamilton, who distrusted the governor more than any other Antifederalist delegate, Clinton's opposition was not only unquestioned but irrational, perverse, and irreversible. "The collective view of his [Clinton's] conduct," Hamilton wrote a year later, "will admit of no other supposition than that he has entertained a project for erecting a system of STATE POWER unconnected with, and in subversion of the union."[10]

Leadership in debate was assumed by lesser Antifederalist luminaries who, as Linda Grant DePauw comments, were "mostly country lawyers who had no greater distinction than a few terms in the state legislature."[11] Their principal leaders were Robert Yates and John Lansing, Jr., who as members of New York's three-man delegation to the Philadelphia Convention of 1787 had vigorously opposed its handiwork; Gilbert Livingston, kinsman of the chancellor [Robert R. Livingston]; Samuel Jones of Queens County; and Melancton Smith of Dutchess County. Smith was the unofficial floor leader of the Antifederalist forces.

More important than the leadership of the Antifederalists and their commanding majority, however, was one possibly fatal flaw: their awareness, though seldom avowed, that if the requisite number of states ratified and if a new union was formed, New York would have to join. From the outset, this knowledge subtly undermined the sincere conviction of influential Antifederalist leaders that conditional amendments should be the irreducible condition of New York's ratification. And to the modern student, as I have said elsewhere, it is a situation "that makes the formal proceedings of the convention appear . . . mere shadowboxing. . . ."[12]

But in June 1788 this was by no means apparent to the Federalists at Poughkeepsie. Neither New Hampshire nor Virginia had as yet ratified the Constitution and until one or the other did, thus establishing the new government, that document's New York opponents might contrive a swift and emphatic rejection, adjournment without action or, at least, a conditional ratification. As Hamilton and his fellow Federalists saw the issue, stalling tactics were called for. To this end, on June 19, the third day of the convention, Robert R. Livingston introduced a motion, drafted by himself and Hamilton, that the Constitution be considered clause by clause before any "question general or particular shall be put. . . ."[13] To the surprise of some of their fellow partisans, the Antifederalists readily accepted the motion. Why this willingness to allow their opponents to engage in delaying tactics that could only jeopardize their own position? Perhaps Robert Yates spoke for them when he explained that "fully relying on the steadiness of our Friends, we see no danger in this mode and we come into it to prevent the Opposition from charging us with Precipitation."[14] Or was the real reason the awareness of influential Antifederalist leaders of the dangers of New York's precarious position should the proposed union go into effect and their consequent unwillingness to push for outright rejection (which they might at the very outset have accomplished)?

Hamilton prudently decided that his antagonists were prepared to use their large majority to block ratification and that he and other Federalist leaders must exert all the persuasiveness they could muster in order to overcome such perverseness. Accordingly, he addressed the Convention twenty-six times, far more often than any other Federalist delegate.[15] (Indeed, between them, Hamilton and his principal antago-

nist, Melancton Smith, monopolized more than half the debate.)[16] And
Hamilton's performance, whether or not he won over many or any of
his opponents, was one of the finest of his career. Avoiding the acri-
moniousness that often accompanied his public disputes, the intemper-
ateness of his defenses against personal attacks, and the abrasiveness
of the tactics by which he sometimes sought to win converts (as at the
Constitutional Convention), Hamilton's manner was conciliatory, cooperative, and courteous. His well-crafted speeches were dispassionate
appeals to reflection and reason. Above all, they were effective rejoinders
to Antifederalists' fears and anti-Union biases, which Hamilton acknowledged to be sincere and well-intentioned, though misplaced and
unfounded.

He announced this approach at the outset of his first speech at
the convention. Affirming that he believed the "weaknesses of the Union
to be real, and pregnant with destruction, "he went on to reassure his
opponents that "however weak our country may be, I hope we shall
never sacrifice our liberties," adding somewhat disingenuously: "If
. . . on a full and candid discussion, the proposed system shall appear
to have that tendency, for God's sake, let us reject it! . . . No arguments
drawn from embarrassment or inconvenience ought to prevail upon us
to adopt a system of government radically bad. . . ."[17] Having demonstrated that his sole object, like that of his opponents, was to secure
the best possible government, Hamilton promptly alluded to what he
knew was the most vulnerable point in the Antifederalists' position. "We
must consider," he said, "whether we, as a State, could stand alone."
And, then, as if his audience might not understand him: "every prudent man will consider . . . that a rejection of the Constitution may involve most fatal consequences."[18]

Such appeals aside, Hamilton's speeches set forth two major
themes: (1) the conformity of the proposed Constitution to true republican principles; and (2) the insubstantiality of the Antifederalists' apprehension that the new government would undermine the power, per-
quisites, and ultimately the sovereignty of the states, creating in their
place a political behemoth, a "consolidated" government. Returning
to these themes time and again, Hamilton also sought to refute other
arguments raised by the Antifederalists—such as the insufficiency of
representatives in the House, the aristocratic nature of the Senate, the
dangers of an allegedly unlimited power to tax, and the absence of
safeguards for the citizenry's fundamental civil rights.

Hamilton's insistence that the Constitution exemplified and guaranteed republicanism represented a shift in focus. At the Constitutional

Convention he had stressed the necessity of a stable government immune to the volatile whims of the populace, and in *The Federalist*, he had urged adoption of an energetic one. Now he emphasized the "truly republican principles" exemplified by the proposed Constitution. "The establishment of a republican government," he remarked, "is an object of all others the nearest to my own heart"; the only issue in dispute was "the means of accomplishing this great purpose."[19] His definition of a republic was the same as it had been at the Constitutional Convention and in *The Federalist*, and it was one on which most informed citizens of the eighteenth century, including most of the delegates assembled in Poughkeepsie, agreed. It has to be understood, first of all, in terms of what it was not. It was to be distinguished from a monarchy, from an aristocracy, and, above all, from democracy, a government in which, to use Hamilton's words, "the whole power of the government [is] in the people . . . whether exercised by themselves," or by popular assemblies directly and solely accountable to them.[20] And a "pure democracy," Hamilton explained in what he accepted as an axiom of political philosophy, "never possessed one feature of good government." Its "very character was tyranny"; its "figure deformity."[21] By contrast, what was a republic? It was, Hamilton answered, "a mixed government" combining the three traditional modes. Consequently, the government proposed by the Constitution was "*a representative democracy*,"[22] but one based on a finely calibrated separation of powers. At the Poughkeepsie convention Hamilton turned to that doctrine time and again in order to assure his Antifederalist opponents that the Constitution provided protection against both usurpation by any one branch of government and encroachments by the Union on the rights of the people.

Hamilton's insistence that the Constitution was constructed on republican principles was, as noted earlier, one of the two major themes that he emphasized. The second was the security afforded state governments, which would continue to exercise important, essential, and extensive powers. Hamilton's manifest purpose was to answer the Antifederalists' repeated charge that the basic flaw of the Constitution was the threat it posed not only to the powers of the states but to their very existence. How could their abolition serve the interests of the Union, Hamilton asked? "It can derive no advantage from such an event," he replied. "But, on the contrary, would lose an indispensable support, a necessary aid in executing the laws. . . ." The states, he insisted, "are absolutely necessary to the system. Their existence must form a leading principle in the most perfect constitution we could form."[23] Dismissing the possibility of annihilation of the states as "fantastical,"[24] Hamilton repeatedly contended that, to the contrary, their "natural strength and resources . . . will ever give them an important superiority over the general government. If we compare the nature of their different powers," he continued, "we shall find the advantage entirely on the side of the states."[25] Why was this so? "In whatever direction the popular weight leans," he argued, "the current of power will flow: Wherever the popular attachments lie, there will rest the political superiority."[26] Hamilton's reassurances were not inconsistent with views that he had long held. What he wisely chose not to share with Antifederalist delegates was his fear that the powers reserved to the states might render nugatory the powers conferred on the government of the Union. But, then, Hamilton's goal in the Poughkeepsie debates was not so much to spell out his own political creed as to alter what he viewed as his opponents' myopic refusal to discern the advantages of union.

Nevertheless, Hamilton neither obscured nor misrepresented his own views. Although intent on persuading the delegates at Poughkeepsie that under the proposed Constitution the state governments would remain secure and sometimes enjoy superior authority to that of the general government, he also insisted that in particular cases national supremacy was not only desirable but imperative. It was essential, Hamilton said, to grant the federal government powers "in all respects and in every degree, equal to . . . [the] objects" specifically committed to its care and to assure its command of the resources requisite to such objects. To what extent should these resources be used? Hamilton's reply: "Reason says as far as possible [national] exigencies can require; that is, without limitation. A constitution cannot set bounds to a nation's wants. . . . The contingencies of society are not reducible to calculations: They cannot be fixed or bounded, even in imagination."[27] Hamilton's Antifederalist opponents could scarcely have escaped awareness of the implications of his argument, though they curiously chose not to harp on them, but it would have made no difference. On this issue Hamilton was adamant, even at the expense of alienating the opposition. "The local interests of a state ought in every case to give way to the interests of the Union," he remarked in another speech. "For when a sacrifice of one or the other is necessary, the former becomes only an apparent, partial interest, and should yield. . . . There must be a perpetual accommodation and sacrifice of local advantage to general expediency."[28]

In defending the powers committed to the national government, Hamilton was expressing a long-held and consistent conviction; in stressing the necessity and desirability of state powers he was perhaps bowing to expediency. But throughout his remarks he insisted that the Antifederalists were conjuring up imaginary dangers to defeat a plan of government that in fact was designed to safeguard the rights of the people and to preserve the integrity of the states. Of these alleged perils he exasperatedly commented: ". . . the danger is too distant; it is beyond all rational calculations."[29] At the same time he sought to allay such irrational apprehensions by the sage conclusion: "Constitutions should consist only of general provisions: The reason is that they must necessarily be permanent, and that they cannot calculate for the possible changes of things."[30]

Did Hamilton convince even a handful of Antifederalists? What effect, overall, did he have on the outcome of the convention? Had prizes been awarded for superiority in debate, Hamilton would have won first place. But the convention was not primarily a debating contest, and it is arguable that the formal debates—including Hamilton's role in them—had no effect on the outcome. Writing to Washington on the last day of June, John Jay observed that "there is no reason to think that either party has made much impression on the other"[31] and Hamilton himself told James Madison on July 2 that "our arguments, confound but do not convince."[32] If the arguments of Hamilton and other Federalist leaders did not convince the requisite number of Antifederalists to adopt the Constitution, what then was responsible?

It would be plausible to assume that ratification of the Constitution by New Hampshire (news of which reached Poughkeepsie on June 24) and Virginia's assent (announced to the New York convention on July 2) were of crucial importance. As the ninth state to ratify, New Hampshire assured the launching of a new government; Virginia's ratification greatly enhanced the possibility of its success. Although New Hampshire's ratification made that of New York seem inevitable, few Antifederalist delegates appeared to think so. On the day following New Hampshire's decision, Chancellor Livingston informed his opponents that "it had become evident that the circumstances of the country were greatly altered, and the ground of the present debate changed. . . He presumed the Convention would consider the situation of their country. He supposed, however, that some might contemplate disunion without pain."[33] Livingston's rebuke had no discernible effect except to unite his opponents. John Lansing, Jr., spoke for them when he replied that "I presume I shall not be charged with rashness, if I continue to insist that it is still our duty to maintain our rights. We acknowledge that our dissent cannot prevent the operation of the government: since nine states have acceded to it, let them make the experiment. . . . We ought not . . . to suffer our fears to force us to adopt a system which is dangerous to liberty."[34]

It is, however, difficult to believe that Virginia's decision had no effect on the Antifederalists in Poughkeepsie. So long as that state refused its assent, New York Antifederalists could assume with some confidence that they could make their approval of the Constitution conditional upon the acceptance of amendments. If two such large and populous states did not ratify the Constitution, how could the Union under the Constitution succeed? Could these two states, whose geographical positions made them all the more important, not dictate the terms of their accession? Conversely, once the crucial state of Virginia ratified, did not New York's refusal to do so become an ideological luxury? Certainly the Federalists thought so. As Hamilton confided to James Madison on June 27, only a few days before Virginia's affirmative decision, "our only chance of success depends on you. There are some slight symptoms of relaxation in some of the [Antifederalist] leaders; which authorises a gleam of hope, if you do well; but certainly I think not otherwise."[35] Gilbert Livingston, a prominent Antifederalist floor leader, also referred to the issue. Explaining his last-minute vote for ratification without accompanying conditions, Livingston commented that such action "considering our *present* situation with respect to our sister states, [is] the wisest and best measure, we can possibly pursue."[36] The effect of Virginia's ratification on New York Antifederalists cannot be proved because so few of them even alluded to the issue, much less conceded how critical it was. Following the Virginia decision, however, there was a subtle change in the proceedings at Poughkeepsie, as some members—notably Chancellor Livingston on the one side and Melancton Smith and Gilbert Livingston on the other—exchanged personal attacks of a kind that previously had only rarely surfaced during the formal debate.[37]

In any event, the Antifederalists tried to act as if nothing had changed, and to all outward appearances remained confident of the solidarity of their commanding majority. Thus, on July 10, three days following the end of the convention's scrutiny of the text of the Constitution section by section, John Lansing, Jr., announced the strategy by which the Antifederalists had, all along, intended to foil the Federalist hopes of ratification without crippling conditions. This took the form of what Lansing called "a plan of amendments, or a new arrangement." Specifically, Lansing proposed three types of amendments—"1st Explanatory, 2d Conditional, and 3d Recommendatory."[38] The Federalists were willing to accept all but the second type; as they saw the issue, conditional amendments were the equivalent of no ratification. On July 11, the day following introduction of Lansing's plan, John Jay countered with a motion (drafted by Hamilton) for ratification accompanied by the stipulation "that such parts of the said Constitution as may be doubtful ought to be *explained* [emphasis added] and that whatever amendments may be deemed useful, or expedient ought to be *recommended*."[39] [emphasis added] The battle was now joined; for the next two weeks, the opposing sides engaged in a contest of thrust and parry, modifying their positions while not changing their fundamental disagreement: conditional versus outright ratification. To the Federalists, the most disquieting aspect of this protracted dispute was the solidarity displayed by the large Antifederalist majority; the greatest problem the Constitution's opponents faced was their constantly gnawing apprehension that the hard reality of perilous isolation might cause hitherto firm "Antis" to cave in.

It was during these last weeks of the debate that Hamilton made his most important contribution to New York's ratification. He did so by repeatedly insisting that it was inadmissible for the New York convention to make "any restrictions or conditions whatever."[40] His insistence also carried the unmistakable implication that the high price of conditional ratification was New York's economic isolation and possible strangulation, thus appealing to waverers among the otherwise solid Antifederalist majority who all along had feared they must in the end surrender principle to expediency.

On July 23, the white flag was raised by Samuel Jones, an influential Queens county Antifederalist, who "moved that the words *upon condition* in the form of ratification, should be obliterated, and that the words *in full confidence* should be substituted."[41] Melancton Smith agreed. In a speech affirming his commitment to the Antifederalist cause while supporting Jones's motion, Smith, in an oblique expression of confidence in his antagonists, particularly Hamilton, observed that Federalist leaders in the New York convention had insisted that Congress would not admit New York into the Union on the basis of a conditional ratification. It was thus imperative that his Antifederalist colleagues count on amendments in the mode prescribed by the Constitution itself, relying on the support of New York Federalists, men of such prominence that their ideas would have "vast weight in the national councils."[42] Jones's motion carried by a margin of two votes (31 to 29). After additional days of sparring, the official vote on the formal form of ratification was cast—the Constitution won, this time by a vote of thirty to twenty-seven. Twelve Antifederalists had changed their votes. Why? Whatever the underlying reasons, the immediate precipitant was the switch in votes of Melancton Smith, Samuel Jones, and other prominent leaders who at last openly accepted what they all along had perceived they must eventually acknowledge: the unacceptability and impracticability of an independent New York State.

Ratification was accompanied by approval of a circular letter to the governors of the states recommending that a general convention be called to consider amendments to the Constitution. The denouement of the political debate at Poughkeepsie was appropriate: the circular letter was the idea and product of the two Federalist leaders who had done most to secure ratification—Hamilton and Jay. But was not the compromise that ended the impasse a ruse, designed to save face for Antifederalists who, already having made one major concession by dropping their demand for conditional amendments, were unwilling to make another openly? Within months the recommendation for a general convention to consider amendments was not taken seriously even by the Antifederalists. Had they not realized all along that, once the Constitution was adopted, a second convention was highly unlikely? Surely Hamilton and John Jay (who had arranged the compromise and persuaded the Federalists to support it) knew so. In sum, Hamilton's greatest contribution to New York's ratification may have been not his oratory but his role in persuading fellow Federalists to approve a face-saving compromise that had no chance of success.[43]

NOTES

[1]*Alexander Hamilton* (new ed., New York, 1980), 74, 75.

[2]*Alexander Hamilton*, 2 vols. (New York, 1957, 1962), 1:430 (hereafter cited as Mitchell, *Hamilton*).

[3]Linda G. DePauw, *The Eleventh Pillar: New York and the Federal Constitution* (Ithaca, NY, 1966), 200 (hereafter cited as DePauw, *Eleventh Pillar*).

[4]James Kent, *Memoirs and Letters*, edited by William Kent (Boston, 1898), 294.

[5]*Ibid.*, 305.

[6]"To the Daily Advertiser," July 21, 1787, in Harold C. Syrett *et al.*, eds., *Papers of Alexander Hamilton*, 27 vols. (New York, 1961-1987), 4:229-232 (hereafter cited as *Hamilton Papers*).

[7]Quoted in George Dangerfield, *Chancellor Robert R. Livingston of New York: 1746-1813* (New York, 1960), 259.

[8]Clinton to John Lamb, June 21, 1788, quoted in DePauw, *Eleventh Pillar*, 201.

[9]Smith to Nathan Dane, June 28, 1788, in Edmund C. Burnett, ed., *Letters of Members of the Continental Congress*, 8 vols. (Washington, 1921-1936), 8:757.

[10]*Hamilton Papers*, 5:299.

[11]DePauw, *Eleventh Pillar*, 186.

[12]Jacob E. Cooke, *Alexander Hamilton* (New York, 1982), 60.

[13]*Hamilton Papers*, 5:13.

[14]Yates to George Mason, June 25, 1788, quoted in DePauw, *Eleventh Pillar*, 195.

[15]Mitchell, *Hamilton*, 1:439.

[16]DePauw, *Eleventh Pillar*, 198.

[17] *Hamilton Papers*, 5:16.

[18] *Ibid.*, 17.

[19] *Ibid.*, 104, 67.

[20] *Ibid.*, 150. For Hamilton's somewhat different definitions of "democracy" see *ibid.*, 69, 82, 100.

[21] *Ibid.*, 38–39.

[22] *Ibid.*, 150.

[23] *Ibid.*, 160.

[24] *Ibid.*, 84–85.

[25] *Ibid.*, 71.

[26] *Ibid.*, 101–102.

[27] *Ibid.*, 97–98.

[28] *Ibid.*, 70. See also *ibid.*, 72, 83, 103.

[29] *Ibid.*, 38.

[30] *Ibid.*, 118.

[31] H.P. Johnson, ed., *The Correspondence and Public Papers of John Jay*, 4 vols. (New York, 1891), 3:346.

[32] *Hamilton Papers*, 5:140.

[33] Jonathan Elliot, ed., *Debates in the Several State Conventions on the Adoption of the Federal Constitution. . .*, 5 vols. (Philadelphia, 1859), 2:322 (hereafter cited as Elliot, *Debates*).

[34] *Ibid.*, 325.

[35] *Hamilton Papers*, 5:91.

[36] *Country Journal* (Poughkeepsie), July 29, 1788, quoted in DePauw, *Eleventh Pillar*, 253–254.

[37] For examples of such exchanges see Elliot, *Debates*, 2:382–410.

[38] *Ibid.*, 2:410.

[39] *Hamilton Papers*, 5:149.

[40] For an example of Hamilton's argument on this issue, see *ibid.*, 157–158.

[41] Elliot, *Debates*, 2:412.

[42] This summary of Smith's speech is a close paraphrase of DePauw's account (*Eleventh Pillar*, 242–243) based on the *Independent Journal*, July 28, 1788, which is also the source of the phrase quoted.

[43] For a concurring analysis, though one that emphasizes the role of Jay over that of Hamilton, see Richard B. Morris, "John Jay and the Adoption of the Federal Constitution in New York: A New Reading of Persons and Events," *New York History* 63 (1982): 132–164.

For Further Reading

Alexander Hamilton's role in the New York Ratifying Convention is best followed in Harold C. Syrett *et al.*, eds., *The Papers of Alexander Hamilton*, 27 vols. (New York, 1961–1987), especially volume 5, which includes all of Hamilton's own speeches (as well as his correspondence during this period). The proceedings as a whole are printed in Jonathan Elliot, ed., *Debates in the Several State Conventions on the Adoption of the Federal Constitution. . .*, 5 vols, (Philadelphia, 1859), especially volume 2. This edition will be replaced by the New York volume of Merrill Jensen, John P. Kaminski, Gaspare J. Saladino, and Richard Leffler, eds., *The Documentary History of the Ratification of the Constitution and the Bill of Rights*, 9 vols. to date of 17 projected (Madison, WI, 1976–   ). The standard monograph on the New York convention is Linda G. De Pauw's *The Eleventh Pillar: New York and the Federal Constitution* (Ithaca, NY, 1966), an exemplary study that effectively refutes a number of long-standing interpretations. Biographies of Hamilton perforce include an account of the part he played at the convention. Of these, the most useful are Broadus Mitchell's *Alexander Hamilton*, 2 vols. (New York, 1957, 1962), especially volume 1, and John C. Miller, *Alexander Hamilton: Portrait in Paradox* (New York, 1959). Although I tried to avoid repetition, reliance on my own biography of Hamilton (New York, 1982) was inescapable. A restudy of the subject of Hamilton's part in the New York ratification controversy, however, led me to revise some of the principal ideas that I set forth in my earlier work.

The Long Island Representatives at New York's Ratifying Convention*

ROBERT ERNST
Professor Emeritus, Adelphi University

On June 17, 1788, after eight states had ratified the federal Constitution, and while conventions were in session in New Hampshire and Virginia, fifty-two representatives gathered on the ground floor of the new stone courthouse in Poughkeepsie for the opening of the New York ratifying convention. Governor George Clinton, hostile to the Constitution, was elected to preside. Forty-six of the sixty-five delegates were Clintonians. Two men carried the burden of the Antifederalist case: John Lansing, Jr., the mayor of Albany and a former delegate to the Confederation Congress who (with Robert Yates) had walked out of the Federal Convention in Philadelphia, and Melancton Smith, currently a delegate to the Confederation Congress. Smith was the Clintonians' chief political organizer and spokesman.

Of the eleven Long Islanders in the convention, all the Suffolk County delegates had been signers of the Association of 1774 adopted by the First Continental Congress, which committed them to oppose British policy, and they all had been active in the Revolution. Among them was Thomas Tredwell, perhaps the most ardent Clintonian of the group; the governor had referred to him as a friend as early as 1776. Tredwell had inherited a house and considerable land in the Fort Salonga area of Smithtown, including what is now the Sunken Meadow State Park. He attended the College of New Jersey (later Princeton), where he developed a taste for the classics, and graduated in 1764, the year

*Conference paper presented at "New York's Ratification of the United States Constitution," Federal Hall, New York City, May 20 and 21, 1988.

before the Stamp Act. He married Ann Hazard, the daughter of a prosperous merchant, became a lawyer, and served as Smithtown's overseer
of highways and later as an assessor.

The Revolutionary War galvanized Tredwell into a frenzy of patriotic activity. He served on a committee to cooperate with other Suffolk
towns in the election of delegates to the First Continental Congress,
organized military resistance at Smithtown, and was a delegate to all
four provincial congresses. After the British invasion of Long Island,
he and his family fled, and his home became headquarters for Whig
whaleboatmen who crossed Long Island Sound from Connecticut for
plundering raids. As a delegate to the New York constitutional convention at Kingston in 1777, he was one of two members to vote against
the new constitution because he did not consider it democratic enough.
He was one of the fifteen members of the Council of Safety, a provisional government until the state legislature met, and he was a Suffolk
representative in the assembly from 1777 to 1782. To Alexander Hamilton he was "a sensible and honest man" and one of five assemblymen
who had influence.[1]

After the war Tredwell sold his 450 acres of "Sunken Meadow
neck" and moved to New York City, returned to Long Island about 1786,
settling in Huntington. He had served since 1778 as a probate court judge
from 1778 until his resignation in 1787, when he became the first surrogate of Suffolk County.[2]

Tredwell had politics in his blood. In 1786 he was elected to the
state senate and served until 1789. He disapproved the work of the
Federal Convention and, as an active Antifederalist county committeeman, distributed party propaganda as he traveled throughout Suffolk in 1788. In the words of John Smith of Mastic, Tredwell portrayed
"the dredful consiquences that will follow this adoption of the Con-
stitutioon in as high coulers [colors] as the Prophet Daniel did the
distress of the Babilonians previous to their destruction."[3]

In addition to Tredwell, Governor Clinton had other Long Island
friends, including Nathaniel Lawrence of Queens, whom he asked to
make certain personal introductions, and Samuel Jones, also of Queens,
one of the few former Loyalists who ever got close to Clinton. Later
Jones was called "the leading and strong man" among the "friends
of the governor." Like most of the delegates at Poughkeepsie, the Long
Islanders were silent participants; with the minor exceptions of Lawrence and Stephen Carman of Queens, it is clear that the only vocal
Long Islanders were Tredwell and Jones.[4]

Samuel Jones was the most important of the four Queens delegates. Born at Fort Neck (now Massapequa) in the Town of Oyster Bay,

he studied law under the celebrated William Smith, and after admission to the bar in 1760 developed an extensive and lucrative practice, won a reputation as a legal scholar, and in 1771 served as special counsel to New York City. By marrying Cornelia Haring (Herring) of a wealthy old Dutch family in Manhattan he acquired and developed valuable real estate. Great Jones Street is named after him and Cornelia Street after his wife.[5]

According to the sketch of Jones in the *Dictionary of American Biography*, his association with Judge William Smith and his connections through marriage "led him to espouse the cause of the colonists." In fact, Jones did not support the colonists but sympathized with the Tories. He was one of the conservative members of New York City's Committee of Sixty in 1774, and although appointed the next year to its successor Committee of 100, he was doubtful about its prospects, failed to attend meetings, and was replaced. Early in the war he quietly practiced law; after the surrender of Long Island he was dispossessed of a farm he had bought on the ground that it was rebel property, since the mortgagor was a rebel. His misfortune was compounded when the state legislature disbarred him.[6]

Readmitted to practice in 1786, he won repute as a real estate lawyer, his legal scholarship embellishing this distinction. He collaborated with Richard Varick, the recorder of New York City, in codifying the laws of New York State, but he did most of the work himself.[7]

His rapid rise to political prominence after the Revolution is remarkable because he was the only Loyalist to win a place in the trusted inner circle of Governor Clinton. In 1786, Queens County voters elected him to the state assembly, where he sponsored repeal of New York's anti-Tory laws. Although in this respect he followed the lead of Hamilton and Jay, he strenuously supported their political opponent, Clinton, and marshalled downstate Antifederalists in 1788. His weight was felt well beyond Queens County. Accused of controlling the Kings County assemblymen, he was also a member of the New York County Antifederalist Committee, and by maintaining active residences in New York City and Oyster Bay, he was the only candidate for the Poughkeepsie convention to be listed on tickets in two counties. He lost in New York but won in Queens.[8]

As an assemblyman Jones played a creative role. He introduced various bills to revise and consolidate the laws of the state, abolish entails, and regulate elections. He voted to tax arrears more effectively and to suppress vice and immorality. By opposing a motion to permit sentences of as many as thirty-nine lashes in a single day, he showed a humane spirit when it came to corporal punishment.[9] After the federal Constitution was signed, Jones, believing that the Federal Convention had exceeded its powers, tried to assure New York's right to propose amendments.[10]

In the Poughkeepsie convention Jones, Tredwell, and Peter Lefferts of Kings County were Long Island members of a bipartisan committee to consider amendments offered by John Lansing, Jr. When the committee met, John Jay, one of its members, complained of being faced "by a complete set of propositions in a dictatorial manner for their passive acquiescence." The committee dissolved in frustration, but it is significant that Jones, like Melancton Smith, also a member, was said to have "discovered a disposition somewhat moderate."[11]

Even so, Jones was bent on limiting the power of Congress as set forth in the Constitution. At the outset of debate on the election of senators and representatives, he opposed giving Congress the power to change the time, place, and manner of holding elections. Fearing that the states would be deprived of an essential right, he offered an amendment precluding Congress from making or altering any state election regulations.[12] His motion, with an addition by Lansing, was accepted by the committee of the whole and later incorporated into the instrument of ratification. Jones proposed another amendment declaring that the power of Congress to establish post offices and post roads was not to be construed as extending to the building or repair of highways in any state without its consent. Although accepted by the committee of the whole, this proposal was not included in the final instrument of ratification.[13]

Among the silent Long Island delegates were the two Federalists from Kings County. Judge Lefferts had had no previous political experience. He had been a lieutenant in a Flatbush militia company, and when the British landed on Long Island in August 1776, the Americans set his house and grain on fire to deny shelter and forage to the advancing enemy. Scion of an old Dutch family, he became a trustee of the Reformed Dutch Church of Flatbush and was one of the organizers of Erasmus Hall Academy in 1786. Between 1784 and his death in 1791 he was a judge of the Court of Sessions and Common Pleas of Kings County.[14] The other Federalist from Kings was Peter Vandervoort, who had been chosen by Brooklynites in 1753 as one of five trustees to defend their patent from New York City's encroachments. When the British controlled Long Island he joined the flood of refugees to Connecticut but returned to Brooklyn after the war, and in 1785 was appointed sheriff of Kings County, a post he held when elected to the Poughkeepsie convention.[15]

The four Queens County delegates, all Antifederalists, had won a clear though not overwhelming victory. Their greatest strength was in the populous towns of Oyster Bay and North and South Hempstead, and it seems likely that Samuel Jones's influence among moderate voters had tipped the balance in their favor.[16] Stephen Carman, who, according to one scholar, had come from a family "thoroughly saturated with loyalism," was an Antifederalist committeeman and an assemblyman who had voted to censure the Philadelphia Convention for exceeding its powers.[17] John Schenck of Manhasset was a former Loyalist, had become a county judge in 1784, had served in the assembly in 1787, and would serve again in the twelfth session of 1788-89.[18] Nathaniel Lawrence of South Hempstead had left the College of New Jersey for military service in a North Carolina unit at Valley Forge; he was captured and held prisoner by the British for nearly two years until exchanged. He received his college degree in 1783, studied law with Egbert Benson and James Kent, became a captain in the New York County militia, and in 1787 married the daughter of a Princeton trustee and justice of the New Jersey Supreme Court. Only twenty-eight when elected to the Poughkeepsie convention, he had had no previous political experience, but he was ambitious. Described as "very wary & cold blooded for a young Man," he was a moderate Antifederalist and one of the founders of the Federal Republican Club to foster a second federal convention.[19]

In addition to Tredwell, Suffolk County sent four others to Poughkeepsie. Henry Scudder, a Huntington trustee from 1771 to 1774, had been a Smithtown militia officer who spied behind the British lines, fled to Connecticut, then recrossed Long Island Sound to make sketches of Fort Salonga, making possible its destruction by an American raid. After the war he resumed his post as Huntington trustee, and when elected to the ratifying convention was an Antifederalist county committeeman.[20] John Smith was the son of Judge William Smith, Lord of the Manor of St. George, who served on Brookhaven's revolutionary committees, in the provincial congress of 1775 and in the state senate until 1783. The younger Smith, a militia lieutenant, supplied money and intelligence to the American resistance while managing his father's estate during the British occupation. He was seized by the British and swore loyalty to the Crown, but he soon violated his oath, quit Long Island, and participated in raiding expeditions. After the war he was elected to the state assembly where he voted with the antislavery reformers. An active Antifederalist committeeman in Suffolk, he nevertheless voted against censuring the Philadelphia Convention.[21]

David Hedges had been for many years deacon of the Bridge Hampton church and had officiated in the absence of a pastor during the war. Supervisor of the Town of Southampton for twenty years, he was elected to New York's fourth provincial congress in 1777. A member of the state assembly from 1787 to 1789, he supported a bill to suppress vice and immorality and a measure to include actors in a bill to punish "rogues, vagabonds and other disorderly persons." Like Smith, he was unwilling to criticize the Philadelphia convention, yet was a member of the Antifederalist county committee.[22] The youngest Suffolk delegate was the studious Jonathan Nicoll Havens, who had graduated from Yale in 1777 and returned that year with his refugee family to their home on Shelter Island. He was chosen a trustee of the local Presbyterian church, succeeded his father as town clerk in 1783, and served as town supervisor from 1785 to 1793. Elected to the assembly in 1786, he was a fiscal conservative who voted against the issuance of state bills of credit. A moderate Antifederalist, he opposed censuring the Philadelphia Convention, supported Governor Clinton, and, like the other Suffolk delegates, was a county committeeman.[23]

Of the Suffolk representatives the most outspoken was Thomas Tredwell. Early in July he moved four amendments, all revealing his aversion to centralized power: the first would have denied to Congress the power or right to declare war without a two-thirds vote in both houses. (In substance this was later proposed as an amendment by the convention.) A second would have limited the Constitution's prohibition of state *ex post facto* laws only to crimes and require that it not be construed to prevent calling public defaulters to account. (In substance this was made part of the convention's instrument of ratification.) A third would have precluded Congress from laying a poll tax. (In substance this became another of the convention's proposed amendments.) The fourth Tredwell proposal, rejected by the convention, would have required publication of federal receipts and expenditures at least once a year.[24]

Tredwell had a sharp tongue. On July 16, the day after Melancton Smith had moved for a conditional ratification of the Constitution, Tredwell objected to Judge William Hobart's motion for an adjournment. He did not "mean to be warm," he said, but considering that the motion was made by a Federalist, he thought it an "affront" to the convention. It should have come "from our side of the house," he argued; "we know the minds of our constituents—they will not accept without amendment." Federalist James Duane retorted that Tredwell treated the House "like two armies. . . . He speaks of his constituents

[as] my brethren—my fellow citizens—whom I love;'' his observations were "indecent and tend to irritate."[25] Jay claimed to pity the Long Islander who, he said, was "almost consumed." Despite Federalist pleading, the convention refused to adjourn.[26]

At some time, probably late in the proceedings, Tredwell composed a long address but never offered it on the floor, probably because many of his ideas had been expressed by others, and another lengthy speech would fall flat.[27] In his undelivered remarks, Tredwell regretted that the framers of the Constitution had not adequately ensured free elections, proper representation, a free press, and trial by jury in both civil and criminal cases.[28] These were, he wrote:

> The rocks on which the Constitution should have rested; no other foundations can any man lay, which will secure the sacred temple of freedom against the power of the great, the undermining arts of ambition, and the blasts of profane scoffers. . . .[29]

The defenders of the Constitution, he maintained, had been more concerned with power than with freedom. Despite the "strongest assertion that there are no wolves in our country," he wrote, "if we see the footsteps in every path, we should be very credulous and unwise to trust our flocks abroad and to believe that those who advised us were very anxious for their preservation."[30] The Constitution departed widely from the principles and faith of 1776, "when the spirit of liberty ran high, and danger put a curb on ambition." Individual rights were unprotected; there was no assurance of the preservation of the state governments. "Our lives, our property, and our conscience," Tredwell affirmed, "are left wholly at the mercy of the legislature, and the powers of the judiciary may be extended to any degree short of almighty." The provision for ratification by merely nine states was "a flagrant violation of public faith."[31]

Tredwell wished that the framers had been more concerned about the freedom of religion, and he decried the continued importation of slaves under the Constitution. The slave trade, "a stain to the commerce of any civilized nation," had, he asserted, "blackened half the plains of America with a race of wretches made so by our cruel policy and avarice, and which appears to me to be already repugnant to every principle of humanity, morality, religion, and good policy."[32]

In opposing the new federal framework, he argued that dual sovereignty was absurd, like two circles with a single circumference. Although a republican form of government was guaranteed by the Constitution, its substance was swallowed up by the federal government, for the states would be made completely dependent on the bounty of Congress.[33]

> We may now surrender, with a little ink, what it may cost seas of blood to regain; the danger of Ambition is now pointed at the fair bosom of Liberty, and to deepen and complete the tragedy, we, her sons, are called upon to give the fatal thrust.[34]

In words that reflected the Puritan heritage of Long Island, Tredwell characterized the proposed federal system as "founded in sin and reared up in iniquity," and capped by a "most iniquitous breach of the public faith." If it went into operation, the people would be "justly punished with the total extinction of their civil liberties."[35] Tredwell was the conscience of a skeptical constituency, rural people of New England origin who had emerged from the Revolution determined to maintain personal freedom, to mistrust power, and to place their faith in government close to the electorate.

Lacking Tredwell's intense fervor, Samuel Jones of Queens nevertheless spoke forcefully about taxation, contracts, and the law. He worried over the extent of the federal taxing power, believing that Congress could not tax "fairly & properly." He disapproved the Constitution's ban on the impairment of contracts by the states. He asked: "What is the Extent of the word *Impair*? It can not be defined," to which Alexander Hamilton sneered, "The word Impair is an English word and means to weaken or injure."[36]

An acknowledged expert on the law, Jones criticized the Constitution's Article III on the judicial power, and he predicted a clash of jurisdictions between federal and state courts. It could not be determined, he contended, whether states or the federal government had jurisdiction. Of the United States Supreme Court, he declared that new courts "should be erected with great Caution." "All men love power," he affirmed. "Without restrictions there would be a Contest for Power —and the Great National Court must swallow the others."[37]

Determined to preserve the state courts from federal encroachment, Jones submitted on July 5 ten amendments relating to the judicial power: providing that Congress could create only appellate courts; limiting common law appeals from New York courts only to those by writ of error; prohibiting U.S. Supreme Court judges from holding other federal or state offices; limiting federal judicial power in controversies over land grants; excluding federal suits against states; excluding criminal prosecutions in cases involving a state; providing a presidential review commission in case an individual were "aggrieved" by a Supreme Court decision; and finally, denying enlargement or extension of the jurisdiction of federal courts.[38] These resolutions, in substance, were adopted.

After learning of Virginia's acceptance of the Constitution, Jones began to worry that the Confederation Congress would reject a conditional ratification. On July 11, when Jay moved that the convention ratify with certain explanations and recommendatory amendments, Jones was not on the floor. His absence inspired speculation. "Several Gentlemen have told me that Mr. Jones is very much terrified," wrote an observer in Poughkeepsie; "this day he was absent on account of sickness, though I conjecture political sickness."[39] Jones was tormented by conflicting desires—for amendments, yet for keeping New York in the Union. He thought the Constitution should be ratified, but he did not wish to vote against his fellow Clintonians; moreover, if the Antifederalists held out for conditional ratification they would be blamed for the loss of New York City as the seat of Congress. His wife, a native of the city, where they both had Federalist friends and owned valuable property, had urged him as early as January to be "by all means . . . a fed[e]ral and vote for the Constitution . . . dont be obstinate for government must soon take place or there will be great Confusion in the City[;] let it not be your fa[u]lt."[40]

In a probably influential letter, Antifederalist Samuel Osgood observed to Melancton Smith and Jones that in all the states where amendments had been recommended, the members of the state conventions who also had been in the Philadelphia convention had "not dared to disagree to such Amendments; they are therefore compleatley [*sic*] committed. . . ." The opponents of the Constitution ultimately would succeed in obtaining amendments, and as there was now so little danger in accepting the Constitution it was expedient to ratify. Moreover, if New York insisted on conditional ratification, the Antifederalists would be blamed for the removal of Congress from New York City.[41] Undoubtedly this letter reinforced the argument of his wife six months earlier.

Meanwhile at Poughkeepsie, amid "complicated proceedings and political maneuvers," Federalists buttonholed Antifederalists off the floor but to no avail.[42] On July 14 Melancton Smith moved to amend Jay's motion for unconditional ratification so that it would conform to Lansing's earlier proposals for amendments. A Federalist motion to adjourn was easily defeated, with Tredwell, John Smith, Scudder, Lawrence, and Carman (all Long Islanders) voting nay. Jones, however, voted for adjournment, as did Havens of Suffolk and Schenck of Queens. These three were the only Antifederalists voting with the Federalists.[43]

To his Antifederalist colleagues, Jones seemed immobilized. "Mr. Jones it is said is so much intimidated by the Threats of the Federalists that he does not any more take an active part," wrote Abraham Lansing.[44] It appears, however, that Jones and Smith already had reached crucial decisions. The Queens delegate's intention to approve the Constitution was known in New York City on July 20, when Antifederalist strategist David Gelston was reported as predicting that Jones's conduct would be approved by both parties in the city. State Senator Ezra L'Hommedieu believed that most city residents thought it expedient to ratify the Constitution and that, in general, people in the southern part of the state agreed.[45]

On July 17 Melancton Smith proposed to the convention that since ten states had ratified, New York should do so as well and append a bill of rights, explanatory amendments, and a circular letter urging the other states to join in calling for another convention. Like Jones, Smith had become convinced that Congress would not accept a conditional ratification, and announced that he would not vote for any form of conditional ratification. The Antifederalists were dismayed. They caucused and rejected Smith's proposal that New York ratify but reserve the right to withdraw from the Union, and on July 19 Smith withdrew his plan.[46]

Four days later, during the debate on Lansing's proposal that New York ratify the Constitution "upon condition" that certain amendments be accepted, Jones moved that the words "upon condition" be struck out and replaced by the phrase "in full confidence." Smith supported Jones's new wording.[47] So did Gilbert Livingston and Zephaniah Platt, two of Smith's Dutchess County colleagues.[48]

Jones's motion was adopted by the close vote of 31 to 29. The Antifederalists were stunned, but the measure was supported by all the Long Island delegates except two Suffolk men—David Hedges, who probably had left the convention early, and Thomas Tredwell.[49]

As amendments were discussed on July 24 and 25, Tredwell objected to the words "in confidence" in the preamble to the proposed bill of rights and offered to change his mind if the amendments were, as he put it, "properly secured." He therefore moved for reconsideration. Jones could not see how a change of wording could provide greater protection to the individual. "It stands better as it is," he remarked, to which the Suffolk delegate retorted, "as it stands not a single right remains." To him the proposed amendments still encompassed "the most unwarrantable donations of power."[50] Although the convention accepted

Tredwell's motion to reconsider the preamble, the final version, even when amended, included the words "in Confidence that the Amendments . . . will receive an early and mature Consideration."[51]

One of these amendments would prohibit Congress from calling the militia from one state into service in another for more than six weeks without the consent of the legislature. Nathaniel Lawrence of Queens had argued strongly for it. Giving Congress full command of the militia, he affirmed, was a "source of much uneasiness" to New Yorkers.[52]

Samuel Jones was responsible for a large number of amendments. His motion that Congress levy no excise except on "ardent spirits" was readily accepted by the convention.[53] All of his ten resolutions offered on July 5 protecting the legal authority of the states and severely limiting federal judicial power were adopted and in substance became amendments.[54]

On July 25 the convention unanimously resolved to send a circular letter to the state legislatures recommending another federal convention.[55] The next day the delegates accepted a bill of rights, a form of ratification, and fifty-five amendments. All the "impressions" relating to the judicial power asserted in the ratification instrument originated with Jones, as did all but one of the proposed amendments relating to the judiciary. With the exception of Tredwell, the lone Long Island holdout, and the absent Hedges, the Long Islanders—Federalists Lefferts and Vandervoort of Kings; Antifederalists Jones, Lawrence, Carman, and Schenck of Queens; and Havens, Scudder, and John Smith of Suffolk voted for the amendments and the form of ratification.[56]

On July 26, New York finally ratified the Constitution by a vote of 30 to 27, the closest of any of the ratifying conventions yet held. This narrow majority was achieved by the defection of twelve delegates from the Antifederalist ranks, including four from Queens and three from Suffolk. Excepting Tredwell, no delegate from counties below Dutchess and Orange voted against ratification. The Long Islanders represented areas close enough to New York City to anticipate benefits from a federal government located permanently, as they hoped, in that city, a government that could regulate foreign and interstate commerce and pay the United States debt. In general, they expected a second constitutional convention to propose amendments that would overcome their objections to the Constitution as it stood. Major credit for the final decision must be assigned to Melancton Smith, the influential Dutchess County delegate who had been born in Jamaica, Long Island, and who had extensive mercantile and legal business in New York City, and Samuel Jones, a close collaborator who found the formula that succeeded. Although some delegates who switched sides explained their motives, the Long Island representatives left no personal correspondence to illuminate their specific concerns. We must accept their votes as their voices; their seven Antifederal votes, together with four from Dutchess and one from Washington County, provided the Constitution's margin of victory in New York State.[57]

NOTES

[1]Timothy Tredwell's will, June 2, 1747, photocopy, Long Island Collection, Smithtown Library; Virginia Malone, "News of Long Ago," *Smithtown News*, January 22, 1970; will of Mary Tredwell, February 29, 1772, contemporary copy, Long Island Collection, Smithtown Library; James McLachlan, *Princetonians 1748-1768: A Biographical Dictionary* (Princeton, 1976), 468-469; *Biographical Directory of the American Congress, 1774-1961* (Washington, D.C., 1969), 1727; Benjamin F. Thompson, *History of Long Island* (New York, 1918), 2: 279; William S. Pelletreau, comp., *Records of the Town of Smithtown, Long Island, N.Y.* (Smithtown, N.Y., 1898), 108-110; Henry D. Sleight, *Town Records of Smithtown* (1929), 1:401; Peter Force, *American Archives*, 4 ser., 2:351-358, 1288, 4:383-439, 6:1299-1443; Henry Onderdonk, Jr., *Revolutionary Incidents of Suffolk and Kings Counties* (1849, reissued, Port Washington, 1970), 17, 21, 22, 25-28; Gary Monti, "Prejudice and Pressure: Divided Loyalties, and the New York Act of Attainder of October 22, 1779" (MA thesis, Adelphi University, 1985), 162; *Papers of Alexander Hamilton*, Harold C. Syrett and Jacob H. Cooke, eds., (New York, 1962), 3:139, 140.

[2]Pelletreau, *Smithtown*, 334-335; McLachlan, *Princetonians*, 469-470; Thomas Tredwell to Gov. George Clinton, n.d., but received March 30, 1787, Misc. MSS, T., NYHS.

[3]*Biographical Directory*, 1727; Stepehen L. Schechter, ed., *Reluctant Pillar: New York and the Adoption of the Federal Constitution* (Troy, N.Y., 1985), 87, 201; E. Wilder Spaulding, *New York in the Critical Period, 1783-1789* (New York, 1932), 240; John Smith to David Gelston, n.d., John Smith Misc. MSS, NYHS. Schechter (*Reluctant Pillar*, 87) gives the date as April 23-27, 1788.

[4]*Public Papers of George Clinton, First Governor of New York*, eds., Hugh Hastings and J.A. Holden (Albany, 1911), 1:241, 5:714-715; Nathaniel Lawrence to John Lamb, July 3, 1788, Lamb Papers, Box 4, NYHS; Edward Countryman, *People in Revolution: the American Revolution and Political Society in New York, 1760-1790* (Baltimore, 1981), 268; Jabez D. Hammond, *History of Political Parties in the State of New York* (Albany, 1842), 1:10.

[5]Thompson, *History of Long Island*, 3:529; Sidney I. Pomerantz, *New York: An American City, 1783-1803* (New York, 1938), 108; William S. Pelletreau, *Historic Homes and Institutions and Genealogical and Family History of New York* (New York, 1907), 3:190; "Memoirs of Samuel Jones," *New York Legal Observer*, 11, September 1853, in Samuel Jones Papers, Box 2, NYPL.

[6]Durward V. Sandifer, "Samuel Jones," *DAB*, 10:197-198; Carl Becker, *History of Political Parties in the Province of New York, 1760-1776* (Madison, Wis., 1909), 168, 197, 198; Thomas Jones, *History of New York during the Revolutionary War*, Edward Floyd Delancey, ed. (New York, 1879), 2:41-42; Pomerantz, *New York: An American City*, 108; Alfred F. Young, *Democratic Republicans of New York: The Origins, 1763-1797* (Chapel Hill, 1967), 50. The legislature's acts of disbarment occurred in 1779 and 1781.

[7]Thompson, *History of Long Island*, 3:530; *DAB*, 10:197-198. Jones's new commission, dated April 29, 1786, enabling him to resume practice, is in the Samuel Jones Papers, Box 2, NYPL. From 1789 to 1796 Jones himself was the Recorder. See his commission, dated September 29, 1789, *ibid.*, Box 1. Jones later was a state senator (1791-1799). He drafted the law creating the office of state comptroller (1796) and was appointed by Governor Jay as the first comptroller; he served from 1796 to 1799.

⁸Pomerantz, *New York: An American City,* 89, 108; Young, *Democratic Republicans,* 50; New York State Assembly, *Journal,* Eleventh Session, 90, 95; Countryman, *People in Revolution,* 267; New York *Daily Advertiser,* February 20, 1788, cited in Schechter, *Reluctant Pillar,* 87. Benjamin Thompson (*History of Long Island,* 3:9–530) claimed that Jones was the "intimate friend" of Clinton and instructed the governor's nephew, DeWitt, in his law office. For Jones as a candidate in two counties, see Schechter, *Reluctant Pillar,* 190.

⁹New York State Assembly, *Journal,* Ninth Session, 9, 62, 70, and Tenth Session, 95.

¹⁰The assembly rejected his motion. *Ibid.,* Eleventh Session, 48 (January 31, 1788); Schechter, *Reluctant Pillar,* 74–75, 165–166; Steven R. Boyd, *The Politics of Opposition: Antifederalists and the Acceptance of the Constitution* (Millwood, N.Y., 1979), 35–36.

¹¹New York *Daily Advertiser,* July 15, 1788; *Papers of Alexander Hamilton,* Harold C. Syrett and Jacob E. Cooke, eds. (New York, 1961–1987), 5:156, quoting the *Daily Advertiser,* July 16, 1788.

¹²This was on June 25, 1788. Jonathan Elliot, ed., *Debates of the several State Conventions on the adoption of the Federal Constitution* (2nd ed., Philadelphia, 1836), 2:325–326.

¹³John McKesson, Notes of the New York Ratifying Convention, July 1, 3, 1788, [microfilm], NYHS.

¹⁴Teunis R. Bergen, *Genealogy of the Lefferts Family, 1650–1878* (Albany, 1878), 83–86; Thomas M. Strong, *History of Flatbush, in Kings County, Long-Island* (New York, 1942), 142.

¹⁵Henry R. Stiles, *History of the City of Brooklyn* (Brooklyn, 1870), 3:526–527; Bergen, *Genealogy of the Lefferts Family,* 31.

¹⁶See Linda Grant DePauw, *The Eleventh Pillar: New York State and the Federal Constitution* (Ithaca, 1966), 251–252; Young, *Democratic Republicans,* 95; Schechter, *Reluctant Pillar,* 94.

¹⁷Spaulding, *New York in the Critical Period,* 236; New York State Assembly, *Journal,* Eleventh Session, 45–46 (January 29, 1788). Carman must have pleased his constituents: he served twenty-one terms in the assembly. Stephen C. Hutchins, *Civil List and Constitutional History of the Colony and State of New York,* for the year 1882 (Albany, N.Y., 1883), 289–90, 292–93, 295–305.

¹⁸Henry Onderdonk, Jr., *Queens County in Olden Times* (Jamaica, N.Y., 1865), 71; Schechter, *Reluctant Pillar,* 198.

¹⁹Richard A. Harrison, *Princetonians 1776–1783: A Biographical Dictionary* (Princeton, 1981), 425–429; Nathaniel Hazard to Alexander Hamilton, September 30, 1791, *Papers of Alexander Hamilton,* 9:247. Lawrence was again in the assembly in 1791 and 1792, and again in 1795 and 1796. He was appointed attorney general in 1792 and became district attorney in 1795. He died of tuberculosis in 1797.

²⁰Schechter, *Reluctant Pillar,* 200; Spaulding, *New York in the Critical Period,* 240; Sleight, *Town Records of Smithtown,* 1:277; Onderdonk, *Revolutionary Incidents,* 28, 105; Luise Weiss, *Reflections on 1788: Long Island and the Constitution* (Middle Country Public Library, Centereach, N.Y., 1987), 6–7, citing Cynthia Q. Hendrie, "Henry Scudder: A Hero of Great Cow Harbor" (Huntington Historical Society, Huntington, N.Y., 1976), 48–49; *Public Papers of George Clinton,* 4:199, 424; Peter Ross, *History of Long Island from its Earliest Settlement to the Present Time* (New York, 1902), 1:715.

²¹Harold D. Eberlein, *Manor Houses and Historic Homes of Long Island and Staten Island* (1928; Port Washington, N.Y., 1966), 104–105; R.M. Bayles, "Brookhaven," in [W.W. Munsell], *History of Suffolk County . . .* (N.Y., 1882) 66, 69; Osborn Shaw, "Town of Brookhaven," in Paul Bailey, ed., *Long Island: a History of Two Great Counties, Nassau and Suffolk* (N.Y., 1949), 1:286, 287; *Biographical Directory of the American Congress* (1971 edition), 1716; Spaulding, *New York in the Critical Period,* 240; Frederic G. Mather, *Refugees of 1776 from Long Island to Connecticut* (1913; Baltimore, 1972), 571; Peter Force, ed., *American Archives,* 4th ser., 4:438; Thomas Jones, *History of New York*

during the Revolutionary War (New York, 1879), 1:292–293; *Public Papers of George Clinton*, 4:127, 5:616, 6:403; New York State Assembly, *Journal*, Eighth Session, 53, 86, 120. Smith was unsympathetic toward the foreign-born in New York City. (*Ibid.*, 178.) He was in the assembly, 1784–94 (except 1786) and 1798–1800, was a congressman to 1804 and United States senator, 1804–1813. In 1814 President Madison appointed him marshal of the southern district of New York. Smith died in 1816.

²²Henry P. Hedges, *Centennial and Historical Address, delivered at Bridgehampton, L.I., July 4th, 1876* (Sag Harbor, 1876), 10–11, 18; Jeanette E. Rattray, *East Hampton History including Genealogies of Early Families* (East Hampton, N.Y., 1953), 374–375; [Munsell], *History of Suffolk County*, 33; New York State Assembly, *Journal*, Ninth Session, May 3, 1786, and Eleventh Session, 40–41, January 24, 31, 1788.

²³*Biographical Directory of the American Congress*, 1088; Brooks M. Kelley, *Yale, a History* (New Haven, 1974), 78, 86; Jacob A. Mallmann, *Historical Papers of Shelter Island and Its Presbyterian Church* (New York, 1899), 69, 70; *Public Papers of George Clinton*, 7:19; Onderdonk, *Revolutionary Incidents*, 91; Ralph G. Duvall, *History of Shelter Island from its Settlement in 1652 to the Present Time* (Shelter Island Heights, N.Y., 1932), 71; New York State Assembly, *Journal*, Ninth Session, March 3, 6, 10, 1786; E[benezer] Sage to Jonathan Nicoll Havens, March 12, 1786, Dering Collection, East Hampton Library, East Hampton, N.Y.; St. Patrick [Jonathan Nicoll Havens] to John Smith, April 5, 7, 1788, Misc. MSS., John Smith of Mastic, L.I., NYHS; Spaulding, *New York in the Critical Period*, 240.

²⁴*Ibid.*, 407; *Papers of Alexander Hamilton*, 5:190. Apparently these amendments were offered on July 2. Additional Antifederalist amendments were moved on July 4, 5, and 7. Elliot's *Debates*, 2:407–410.

²⁵Gilbert Livingston, Notes on the New York State Constitutional Convention, 1788, Abraham Yates, Jr. Papers, NYPL.

²⁶*Ibid.*; Elliot's *Debates*, 2:411.

²⁷DePauw, *Eleventh Pillar*, 197. The speech was sent by Tredwell to Jonathan Elliot after the first volume of the 1830 edition of the *Debates* had appeared and was printed in the third volume. It is also in the second edition (1836), 2:396–406, which I used.

²⁸Elliot's *Debates*, 2:397.

²⁹*Ibid.*, 399.

³⁰*Ibid.*, 401.

³¹*Ibid.*, 401–402.

³²*Ibid.*, 402.

³³*Ibid.*, 403.

³⁴*Ibid.*, 404.

³⁵*Ibid.*, 405.

³⁶John McKesson Notes, June 30, July 3, 1788, microfilm, NYHS.

³⁷*Ibid.*, July 4, 1788.

³⁸Elliot's *Debates*, 2:408–409; McKesson Notes, July 5, 7, 1788, NYHS.

³⁹David S. Bogart to Samuel Blatchley Webb, July [misdated June] 11, 1788, *Correspondence and Journals of Samuel Blatchley Webb*, W.C. Ford, ed. (New York, 1893–1894), 2:105; Schechter, *Reluctant Pillar*, 108.

⁴⁰Schechter, *Reluctant Pillar*, 108; DePauw, *Eleventh Pillar*, 242. For the quotation from Cornelia Jones to Samuel Jones, January 27, 1788 (misdated 1787), in Misc. MSS., Jones, C., NYHS, I am indebted to Harrison Hunt of the Nassau County Museum Reference Library.

⁴¹Samuel Osgood to M. Smith and S. Jones, July 11, 1788, photocopy from the files of *The Documentary History of the Ratification of the Constitution and the Bill of Rights 1781–1791* (University of Wisconsin–Madison), which was kindly supplied by editor John Kaminski. DePauw, *Eleventh Pillar*. 252, stated that the original letter was

located in the National Park Service Collections, Federal Hall Memorial, New York City, but on inquiry I learned that it could not be found.

[42]DeWitt Clinton to Charles Tillinghast, July 19, 1788, DeWitt Clinton Papers, Columbia University Libraries; Charles C. Tillinghast to John Lamb, June 21, 1788, Lamb Papers, Box 5, NYHS; James M. Hughes to John Lamb, June 18, 1788, *ibid.*

[43]Schechter, *Reluctant Pillar*, 108–109; McKesson Papers, July 17, 1788, NYHS; *New-York Journal and Daily Patriotic Register*, July 22, 1788.

[44]Abraham G. Lansing to Abraham Yates, Jr., July 20, 1788, Abraham Yates, Jr. Papers, NYPL.

[45]Ezra L'Hommedieu to John Smith, July 20, 1788, Misc. Papers, John Smith of Mastic, NYHS. L'Hommedieu, who relayed Gelston's opinion as well as stating his own, had been a Suffolk assemblyman from 1777 to 1783 and senator from the southern district since 1784.

[46]Schechter, *Reluctant Pillar*, 109–110; DePauw, *Eleventh Pillar*, 226.

[47]Gilbert Livingston Notes, July 23, 1788, Abraham Yates, Jr. Papers, NYPL.

[48]*Independent Journal*, July 25, 1788; DePauw, *Eleventh Pillar*, 243.

[49]Schechter, *Reluctant Pillar*, 111; DePauw, *Eleventh Pillar*, 247; Gilbert Livingston Notes, July 24, 1788, Yates Papers, NYPL. The reason for Hedges's absence is unknown.

[50]Gilbert Livingston Notes, July 24, 25, 1788, Yates Papers, New York Public Library; *New-York Journal*, July 26, 1788.

[51]John McKesson Notes, July 25, 1788, microfilm, NYHS.

[52]*New-York Journal*, July 26, 1788.

[53]*Ibid.*

[54]DePauw, *Eleventh Pillar*, 293–302. The only proposed amendments concerning the judicial power not originated or presented by Jones related to an impeachment court.

[55]Elliot's *Debates*, 2:413. The circular letter had been composed by Jay, Lansing, and Melancton Smith, though Jay was mainly responsible for the draft. John Smith of Suffolk probably was absent on July 25, but his vote on July 23 supporting Jones's motion suggests that he had decided to vote with the Federalists, which he did on the final vote on July 26.

[56]Elliot's *Debates*, 2:413.

[57]It must be added that none of the proposed amendments that had originated with Jones and Tredwell were accepted by the First Federal Congress in 1789, although other recommendations in New York's instrument of ratification were incorporated in what eventually became the federal Bill of Rights. These related to the free exercise of religion, peaceable assembly, a free press, the right to bear and keep arms, due process of law, prohibition of unreasonable search and seizure, excessive bail, cruel and unusual punishment, and guarantees of grand jury indictments, speedy and impartial jury trials and the rights of the accused. The text of the New York instrument of ratification is conveniently available in DePauw, *Eleventh Pillar*, 293–302. Four other states had similarly stressed the need for immediate amendments.

New York City Merchants and the Constitution: A Fragile Consensus *

CATHY MATSON

University of Tennessee-Knoxville

Few public observers in New York in early 1788 felt obliged to analyze closely the social and economic interests which formed coalitions to support or to oppose the Constitution. As the date approached when city residents would elect delegates to the Poughkeepsie ratifying convention, generalization and exaggeration supplanted appeals to particular public constituencies. Federalists were happy to be characterized as "the very respectable citizens," the "monied interest," the "better sort," or the "high prerogative Gentlemen."[1] A typical characterization was that Federalists included the "generality of landed, commercial and legal minds" in New York.[2] Federalist denigrated Antifederalists as "the common people," "the insubstantial members of the state," and "men of small property."[3] They called Antifederalists the "politically inept" debtors, the "Blockheads and Bankrupts" who had "as good a Vote as a better Man."[4]

But Antifederalist Clintonians were equally skilled at polarizing the constitutional discussion and appropriating positive labels for their opposition to the proposed document. In less generous moments they associated Federalists with the "speculator interest" or "paper securities defrauders."[5] They insisted that Federalists sought "consolidation" for "the aggrandizement of a few over the many," while they, the opponents of the Constitution, represented "the liberty, property, and every social comfort in the life of the yeomanry."[6]

It was this association of the yeoman or "agrarian interest" with constitutional opposition which became rooted in the public mind by

*Conference paper presented at "New York and the Ratification of the U.S. Constitution," Federal Hall, New York City, May 20 and 21, 1988.

1788 as well as in subsequent historiography. The corollary to this generalization held that the largest constituency of Federalists were from "the Mercantile Interest."[7] Even prominent Clintonians like Thomas Tredwell, who had played a major role in building the state's authority, believed the major interests supporting or disputing the Constitution could be reduced to those of "the navigating and the non-navigating individuals" in New York.[8] And Robert R. Livingston hinted at the confidence Federalists felt about merchant support when he announced in his opening remarks at Poughkeepsie that it was not necessary to "touch on the declining state of our commerce; nor will I remind you of our national bankruptcy . . . and the private misery it causes; nor will I wound your feelings by a recapitulation of the insults we daily receive from nations," who reap the benefits of American commerce. "These topics," he continued, "have been frequently touched; they are on every man's mind." The failure to secure a national revenue from an impost; continuing foreign depredations against American commerce; ineffectual settlement of disputes in the interior; and counterproductive divisions among the states over the regulation of commerce: these economic problems were too well known, said Livingston, to require elaboration.[9] The election of two "old-line" merchants of the pre-Revolutionary generation—Nicholas Low and Isaac Roosevelt—to represent New York City at Poughkeepsie seemed to underscore this reasoning. Low and Roosevelt were silent yet solid visual testimony that at least five-sixths of the city's merchants stood behind the proposed Constitution by 1788.[10]

But did merchants give their unquestioning support to the Constitution during the months it was framed and debated? Was Alexander Hamilton justified in claiming that "the commercial interest" had "a natural attachment to union?"[11] Is it true that "merchants were particularly opposed to Clintonian policies,"[12] or that the Antifederalist "Clintonians were scarcely interested in commerce?"[13] In fact, while most merchants supported the Constitution by 1789, not all merchants had a " natural attachment to union" throughout the 1780s. Generalizations about one commercial interest—or one agrarian interest—do not capture the social complexity of shifting political coalitions during the 1780s, nor do they reflect the public discourse engendered in the process of advancing new interests during and after the Revolution. Indeed, the Revolutionary generation had grasped opportunities to dissect intellectually the social structure of the sovereign states and then rebalance politically its many interests into more satisfying arrangements. In addition, although the process of stabilizing the American republican experiment during the 1780s divided along the recognizable lines of nationalists and state leaders, the two political constituencies had no fixed and formulaic characteristics with respect to wealth, status, and economic specialization.

In the case of merchants who experienced new economic opportunity, and nurtured it in the public discourse of the Revolution, their apparently unified "commercial interest" was in fact many particular interests. In seeking to represent and serve these diverse interests between 1783 and late 1786, merchants had to be convinced that nationalists— and then Federalists—offered the best protection for their property and future prosperity. Until then, they preferred to pursue their interests in a popular, attentive state government rather than the Confederation Congress. Nationalists were aware that significant numbers of merchants hesitated to adopt their goal of a centralized political economy; but more than one prominent nationalist in New York realized that convincing the majority of the commercial community about the necessity of federal union provided significant leverage for winning over other groups of New Yorkers.[14]

Who were the early nationalists among the ranks of city merchants, and who were the reluctant nationalists who held attachments to state and local sovereignty over economic developments? What issues divided city merchants early in the decade and what issues drew them together by mid-1788? Precision in answering these questions is impossible, given the dearth of contemporary narrative reflections by merchants. But impressionistic information hinting at the existence of certain popular assumptions, as well as the commercial records of the port of New York, indicate the bases for divisions and realignments among merchants. A preliminary examination of merchants' correspondence, legislative records, and newspapers during the 1780s and the New York City Directory for 1786[15] suggests that one important division New Yorkers made was between the "great" or "dry goods" merchants, and the "lesser" or "West Indies" merchants. These labels of comparative success and places of trade, and their implications for the types of commodities and trading patterns among the city's merchants, cannot be measured systematically; there are no extant lists of income or profits and few wills and inventories. Indeed, part of the present argument is based on contemporary evaluations of merchants and the subjective political choices they made during the stormy 1780s. Moreover, these relative distinctions were made under shifting economic conditions during the Revolutionary and post-Revolutionary years.

Dry goods wholesalers traded in British and European markets. It was a received wisdom that they held a great share of the city's wealth; from 1784 to 1787, over three-fourths of the value of New York's imports originated from English ports, and although much of it was carried in English vessels, New York's dry goods merchants captured an increasing share of this bilateral traffic.[16] These "great" merchants kept account books showing heavy activity in the exchange of commodities between New Yorkers and outsiders; they owned at least one ship or large numbers of shares in many vessels; they regularly corresponded from the port of New York with foreign merchants; and they enjoyed eminent reputation among other city residents.[17]

Given this, it was hard to escape the impression that dry goods merchants were the most privileged of New York's commercial elite in other ways as well. Some seemed to enjoy an easy return to normalcy after the Revolution. Others accumulated ever greater fortunes in commerce and real estate under the aegis of reconstituted political authority. The recently evacuated city seemed to offer more opportunities to them than to other merchants to purchase vacated and confiscated real estate; to consolidate special areas of consumer demand; and to reestablish ties with distant correspondents. Although we know the approximate size of fortunes for only a few great merchants in 1786, we can avail ourselves of inferential evidence from contemporary observers about their reputations, and comparative information from their accounts and correspondence about the number of voyages they made, amounts of goods they sold, or ships they owned. This information, taken together, distinguishes these merchants as a group who created the networks of political patronage, calculated marriages, and amassed economic fortunes; they formed an economic elite held in either deferential awe or unconcealed contempt by the city's former residents and new immigrants during the 1780s.[18]

Moreover, their marriage alliances with the great trading firms of London, Bristol, or Philadelphia, and their political affinities with the pre-Revolutionary "court" elites on both sides of the Atlantic, reinforced the public perception during the 1780s that many of New York's most secure commercial leaders were closely allied to a "British interest" influencing every port of the English-speaking world. This composite of English merchants and their agents in New York, as well as the ex-Loyalists who lingered in the port or actively sought reintegration in commerce, seemed to be not only conspicuously wealthy, but also politically suspect. As one struggling merchant remarked, if government served the special interests of the most economically privileged it could not simultaneously create opportunity for the expectant trader of modest means; if those special interests were British, or allied with the former enemy, the Revolution itself would not realize its fullest potential.[19] The "British interest" provided a focus for general frustrations, a focus as conspicuous for its recent attachment to the enemy as for its visible material success. Indeed, some commentators continued to believe that ex-Loyalists were more likely than other merchants to be very successful.[20]

This latter perception had more value for political ideology than it did in commercial reality. The city directory for 1786 lists 320 resident "merchants."[21] To these we can add at least 102 who do not appear in the directory but were residents engaged primarily in wholesale importing and exporting.[22] Among these 422 were 101 (24 percent) whose outstanding success in trade cannot be disputed. These 101 included 37 ex-Loyalists and 64 former Patriots, indicating that a superior postwar economic position in the city had no apparent causal connection to earlier choices about whether to oppose or support the independence movement. Moreover, these 101 ex-Loyalists and former Patriots shared concerns about particular issues during the 1780s, largely because their prior advantages and reputations required protection from rising or new commercial interests. Together, their majority sponsored petitions to recharter the Chamber of Commerce; organized and directed the Bank of New York, a public auctioning system, and insurance and financial brokerage firms; and accumulated large quantities of Revolutionary securities.[23]

Yet despite their homogeneity of interests, based on great property, eminent traders also divided into two general groupings along the lines of their trading patterns. Among the thirty-seven eminent ex-Loyalist merchants, nineteen were dry goods wholesalers with England, and most others were involved in trading patterns which took in the trans-Atlantic flaxseed trade to Ireland, or the lucrative wine trade from Southern Europe. We can identify only two prominent ex-Loyalists with connections to the bilateral trade with the West Indies; one other traded primarily along the American coastline.[24] Thus, although wealth alone was not a major cause for political divisions among New York's merchants, the association of ex-Loyalists with British trade and the "British interest" living in America may have carried great popular weight and that it facilitated the association of dry goods importers as a whole with congressional nationalists' goals of reintegrating ex-Loyalists and conducting negotiations with England for commercial treaties.

In contrast to the great merchants, the majority of "lesser merchants" found power and advantage to be more elusive. Although this group traded everywhere in the Atlantic networks, they were distinguished by their wholesale trade with the West Indies and ports of the North American coastline, as well as their regular communications with the New York region's commercial farmer-exporters. More often than not, these lesser merchants were grain brokers and exporters, or provisioning merchants to the British and French West Indies. Their lines of communication often extended far into the interiors of Connecticut, New Jersey, and the Hudson River valley where they gathered small quantities of surpluses for export through New York City. Only a few ventured in European grain markets, the western fur trade, or Far Eastern voyages.[25]

There were many more lesser merchants than wealthy ones. While we can readily identify only fourteen as ex-Loyalists (compared to thirty-seven eminent merchant ex-Loyalists), there were forty-seven former Patriot merchants of modest fortune and stature in 1786 (compared to sixty-four eminent former Patriots). There were, in addition, thirty-nine lesser merchants in New York in 1786 who were there in the 1770s but to whom we cannot assign a Revolutionary political affiliation. And there were another ninety-six lesser merchants who were probably in New York before the Revolution, although evidence is unclear.[26] Finally, forty-seven lesser merchants were definitely new to the city after 1783 and sixty-seven were probably new residents. Among this latter group of 114 were immigrants from New England, Ireland, and Germany, as well as the sons of merchants in other states who wished to extend family commercial liaisons by transplanting offspring or marrying them into New York's trading families. Of these 289 lesser merchants (about three-fourths of the total list), a few rose out of the ranks of mechanics and ship captains to positions as merchants, but research indicates that fewer still of these merchants rose from the ranks of lesser merchants to the status of great merchants.[27]

Most of these merchants will remain forever obscure as economic actors and political beings. However, among those for whom we can reconstruct a modest profile, certain important characteristics in their trading patterns may help to explain their attachment to state sovereignty in the first years of American independence. This category comprises the forty-seven lesser merchants who were former Patriots and, to some degree, the thirty-nine lesser merchants known to be in New York City before and after the Revolution. Among the forty-seven, not one lesser merchant ex-Patriot is known to have traded primarily to England; only one was in the Irish flaxseed trade; only four took in ports in southern Europe and New England on the way to and from England. The overwhelming majority of these forty-seven traded bilaterally with the West Indies or multilaterally with the West Indies and coastal American ports, while a few of them traded in a triangle between New York, the West Indies, and Holland. Among the thirty-nine lesser merchants whose revolutionary politics are unclear, nineteen traded exclusively or primarily in the Caribbean after 1783. To the extent that we can trace other names in the more obscure population of lesser merchants, trading patterns are similar.[28]

Lesser merchants' trading patterns may have been linked to a widening perceptual gulf between themselves and great traders, and a corresponding attachment to state policies which promoted their special needs while simultaneously interfering with the interests of great traders. Lesser merchants were no less ambitious than their eminent peers; in fact, the great success of some West Indies traders must have inspired many lesser merchants to enter this arena. And, no doubt, the initial euphoria about expanding markets and rising fortunes, which even preceded the Peace of Paris in 1783, infected all merchants regardless of their relative advantages. But these aspirations may also help explain a heightened sense of the economic distinctions and uneven political entitlement which became evident in the glutted New York City markets by early 1784. Some lesser merchants returned after 1783 to ruined property and the loss of vital linkages to commercial correspondents, forcing them to confront a fragile postwar economy in a weakened personal condition. Others had fewer initial advantages and a slower rate of success; in addition to many normal daily and seasonal disappointments, lesser merchants had fewer hedges against long-term adversity than had more prosperous merchants. Whether former residents or new immigrants, they had less starting capital and fewer pre-Revolutionary liaisons abroad, and often had to rely on more troubled (or less lucrative) markets than the eminent traders. In the scanty surviving notations about bankruptcies, the greatest proportion came from the ranks of lesser merchants.[29]

Lesser merchants appear to have had more at stake in winning and shielding American political independence than their eminent colleagues had. State sovereignty was the ideological focus of revolutionary optimism about eradicating the systemic problems of imperial authority for rising or expectant traders; one such problem was making government attentive to their particular concerns about local and regional development. State sovereignty over commerce also offered the real prospect of local control over trade regulations and governmental purse strings. Here, then, was the basis for temporary alliances between lesser merchants and small domestic traders. Lesser merchants were more sensitive than the great dry goods importers to the problems which local retailers, shopkeepers, and itinerant peddlers had in collecting debts or satisfying consumer demand for scarce domestic goods. Whereas great wholesalers employed clerks to collect debts, keep accounts, and make transactions with inland retailers and shopkeepers, lesser merchants were far more likely to perform these tasks themselves.

The stature and wealth of lesser merchants also was often comparable to that of domestic traders, making it increasingly difficult to enforce deferential—or even respectful—behavior between men of commerce and men of petty exchange. As Revolutionary experiences had taught people of all economic positions, the power of mobility, as well as the mobility of power, New Yorkers were increasingly willing to accept the existence of an ill-defined spectrum of fortune, implicitly questioning whether they should grant privileged status to a "commercial interest" which included the most eminent traders.[30] Moreover, the presumed antagonisms between an "agrarian interest" and a "commercial interest" were muddied during the 1780s as New Yorkers discussed the future of recognizably prosperous commercial farmers, on the one hand, and staples exporters in the port city who shared farmers' concerns about international grain prices and markets in the West Indies, on the other hand. In effect, the traditional line between agrarian and commercial interests was blurred when members of each group acted as partners of an exporting enterprise in which distinctions of wealth and stature often did not exist.[31] Moreover, although the association of wealth with political rights would fade only slowly (until the challenges of industrialization and the restructuring of class relations in the nineteenth century), the political language of liberty and rights, and the economic experiences of the Revolution with unregulated prices and wages, had unleashed a tendency in new propertied interests to seek and win power in state governments. The same discussions and experiences elevated the political expectations of lesser merchants while simultaneously drawing attention to their relative handicaps in commerce.

By the 1780s, the term "lesser merchant" implied a certain distance from the most successful traders. Although associated with activities in markets outside the state, these city residents were neither conspicuously wealthy nor attached to the eminent trading families of the pre-war generations. Immigration from other states and from foreign nations brought public attention to new merchants and younger sons just getting a start in commerce. It also brought attention to the growing number of non-specialists and merchants who handled their own retail establishments or distributed their own goods to the interior as a hedge against middlemen's fees and frauds. While great merchants were associated with vast tracts of speculative real estate and the accumulation of Revolutionary paper securities which would eventually pay lucrative interest, lesser merchants invested in lesser enterprises; they secured their reputations through more cautious, small-scale investments in state development projects, state currency and loan offices, and the state bank.[32]

The opportunities afforded by political independence for immigrants or ambitious sons, especially due to the hypothetical vacancies in trade left by merchants who became Loyalists or were ruined by the war, did not necessarily mean that few in the "West Indies interest" could rise to positions of prominence by the late 1780s; most observers believed that the merchant elite was still dominated by "old wealth" in dry goods importing. These perceptions tended to reinforce antipathy to the "British interest" and the distance of lesser merchants from nationalist goals in the first years of political independence. Indeed, the contrast between lesser merchants' struggles to succeed in commercial ventures, and the perceived rewards flowing into dry goods wholesalers' coffers, ran counter to the lesser merchants' understanding of independence and liberty. Although Americans had dissolved their attachments to the British empire. their former enemy now seemed to be slipping back into the city as well as legislating as a foreign nation against the opportunities of free Americans.[33]

The debate over congressional requests for a national impost in the early 1780s underscored the division between great and lesser merchants. Dry goods importers connected to British markets and English firms consistently supported the campaign for the impost. They hoped that the revenue from this 5 percent tax on imports would secure domestic finances, redeem paper securities issued during the Revolution, and bolster America's reputation abroad.[34] Many of them were members of the New York City Chamber of Commerce, which did little to obscure its interest in linking the revenue from a national impost with redeeming the paper securities and speculative bonds they held. In their 1784 petition for recharter, signed by some forty former Loyalists and conservative Whigs who were mostly among the wealthiest city merchants, the Chamber of Commerce appealed for more congressional powers over international and interstate trade. Subsequent statements by chamber members requested that Congress be invested with powers "to counteract the late Restrictions" of foreign nations and to "bring to a speedy end the commercial jealousies which destroy the mutual benefits of trade among the states."[35] Many merchants were soothed by the pledges of John Jay and Robert R. Livingston to establish a modest, uniformly enforceable tax on imports, which would eventually give way to international reciprocity.[36]

In 1781, Congress's request for an impost met with general approval in New York's State legislature, although evidence suggests that legislative representatives understood it to be a temporary expedient to be administered by state appointees.[37] After failing to secure the amendment's approval by all the states as required under the Articles of Confederation, Congress revived its appeal for an impost in 1783. By then, many New Yorkers were less clear about approval: a political division over the impost was apparent in the state government and "out of doors." Opponents of what they viewed as the nationalist proposal were led by a group of primarily lesser merchants connected to provisioning the West Indies; they demanded state control over import revenues. Together with a few early manufacturers, coastal traders, and many commercial farmers in temporary legislative power, they denied the nationalist prediction that sovereign state legislation would result in thirteen mutually annihilating policies. Clintonians were convinced that Congress never would get all the states to agree to uniform legislation, and commerce would not wait for dawdling politicians. A state impost, they argued, would be less onerous for New Yorkers than a national one, and it would discriminate against British or neighboring state merchants with differential duties, thereby boosting "infant traffic." Incidental national expenses still could be covered by the familiar remedy of specific requisitions; power over the purse strings would be held locally and thus be more responsive to shifting commercial opportunities.[38] The state, too, could be more sensitive to the needs of particular clusters of interest, while a centralized national revenue would serve anonymous special interests from afar. Through 1786 these arguments contributed to the defeat of the national impost proposal, and the popular success of a state impost in its place.[39]

Alignments over the impost debate were tied to international commercial circumstances, as well as British policies, during the 1780s. The depression of the mid-1780s, occasioned both by the failure of agricultural export prices to keep up with creditors' demands for payment for costly imported manufactures and by the inability to manufacture products for export, caused lesser West Indies merchants and coastal traders to suffer more bankruptcies, more currency shortages, more interrupted markets than transatlantic traders. Lesser merchants also recovered more slowly after 1785 from the depression's first shocks than dry goods merchants who could expand their credit temporarily.[40]

Early in 1783, the British Parliament's discussion about future commercial relations with America raised other serious problems. That discussion culminated in a series of Orders in Council that effectively reinstituted restrictive mercantile constraints, defeating hopes for the commercial reciprocity that Americans had hoped to gain. The most important orders restricted trade between British West Indies possessions and America to provisions, tobacco, and naval stores, and specified that only British vessels could enter British ports. Within a year, a series of import duties were placed on many commodities entering British ports.

Dry goods merchants who often used British vessels and shuttled between England and New York expressed far less concern than lesser West Indies traders whose normal uncertainties were exacerbated by the British restrictions. Some of the West Indian traders felt entirely shut out of rising opportunities.[41]

While some lesser West Indies merchants reasoned that if British ministers could be persuaded to remove their lamentable barriers, America's "commercial republicanism" would flourish, others were less sanguine.[42] These observers believed that the states would have to retaliate. The Orders in Council directly affected New York's primary markets for agricultural exports, the West Indies. Moreover, rather than encouraging slower importation of British manufactured goods, the orders encouraged the "British interest" to import to excess and glut city markets with "unnecessaries." Lesser merchants pointed angry fingers of protest at "monopolists" and "fortune engrossers" who were well-known ex-Loyalists. In republican rhetoric reminiscent of the 1770s, they blamed dry goods importers for chronic credit and currency crises; this excessive importation did not correspond to consumer demand or the public welfare, but merely introduced more luxury spending.[43] "British agents," agreed an anonymous resident, had put the country "in an uproar."[44]

Although the depression and British commercial aggression began to draw many merchants closer to supporting nationalist proposals for a unified America, significant numbers of merchants in New York during 1784 and 1785 did not take part in this shift.[45] Lesser merchants trading with the West Indies and coastal ports were joined by some of the great merchants who also concentrated their commerce southward in support of state legislation designed to overcome some of the worst effects of the depression and to create more favorable conditions of trade in response to the Orders in Council. Lesser merchants' arguments against the "British interest" and a national impost had a certain appeal to prominent West Indies traders who grew impatient with both congressional friendship toward Britain and Congress's apparent obsession with creating stable centralized finances before securing the commercial means to obtaining a revenue foundation.

Among the 101 wealthiest merchants, the 64 known former Patriots were more diverse in trading patterns and goods than their ex-Loyalist peers. Of these, 11 had established liaisons with English dry goods traders and 5 were primarily involved in the Irish flaxseed trade by 1786. Moreover, there were only 2 coastal traders in this group of 64, which also reflects their preference for high-risk ventures. But 16 of these merchants traded exclusively with the West Indies, 12 traded with the West Indies and touched at coastal ports, and 7 traded between New York and Holland or southern Europe.[46] Unless some of these traders were sufficiently prosperous to spurn the irritations of the Orders in Council, they probably had grounds to challenge British interferences with their trade. At particular moments, then, many of the wealthiest West Indies merchants were likely to subordinate their identity with all eminent merchants and nationalists, and to link their economic interests to lesser merchants of the "West Indies interest." The "West Indies interest" linked the mixture of former Patriotism and trade with non-English areas to political policies that emanated from the local and state level. Under circumstances which curtailed the fullest possible competitive advantages of so many city merchants, the "British interest" may have loomed as a positive evil not only to the lesser merchants for whom the economic stakes were higher but also to the great West Indies traders who anticipated uninhibited benefits from political independence.[47]

Thus, many wealthy West Indies traders joined lesser merchants in blaming the host of "foreigners" in their midst for the gluts of British goods which seemed to worsen under the Orders in Council. Together, they prevailed upon state policymakers to find a suitable response. An open, or reciprocal, trading relationship with England depended upon balancing too many international factors out of American control, including the ascendance of mercantile Parliamentarians. Moreover, nationalists in the Confederation Congress clung to the hope of negotiating international commercial reciprocity and thus failed to produce any immediate response to the British legislation which satisfied American merchants. But the individual states' sovereignty also prevented any one of them from negotiating to reopen the British West Indies; their thirteen distinct jurisdictions gave them little weight in world opinion.

Thus, although with little direct effect, the Clintonians of New York resorted to the indirect remedy of state discrimination against British ships and goods, a remedy which was tailored to benefit the merchants who were perceived to be most adversely affected by the Orders in Council.[48] From 1785 to 1787 a double tonnage duty was placed on British ships entering New York ports; in the same years, the neighboring states of New Jersey and Connecticut were subject to additional discriminatory legislation. In 1787 the state exempted many goods of American origin from import taxes while placing a duty of 25 percent on all foreign goods entering the city and an additional 2.5 percent *valorem* rate on British goods.[49] In late 1784 the state legislature placed duties on luxuries which British merchants or eminent ex-Loyalists usually carried into the city: southern European wines, English watches, carriages, and buckles; it also initiated a policy of protectionism for American manufactures such as iron tools and agricultural implements.[50] Lesser merchants in the New York State Assembly supported this legislation.[51] At the same time, some of them exercised a degree of control over preventing the imposition of certain regulations on the grain trade, and over retaining state-appointed positions as tidewaiters, port collectors, and weigh masters—positions which allowed them to grant informal favors to commercial farmers' agents and fellow lesser merchants.[52]

The legislation passed by the state to raise revenues, discriminate against competitive commerce, and protect infant manufactures produced a substantial state impost. In 1786 and 1787, the impost yielded nearly one-half of the state's total revenue. Connecticut alone may have paid nearly one-third of the impost, primarily because New York was a preferred port for the sister state's merchants; large amounts of the impost were paid by New Jersey, Vermont, and Massachusetts merchants.[53] But in the context of the widespread controversy beginning in 1781 about congressional proposals for a national impost, the state's measures were particularly troublesome to New York's own nationalists. The Chamber of Commerce immediately condemned the state impost, for it did not "promote all the commercial interests" of the city and encouraged "the scandalous practice of smuggling" from the West Indies.[54] Throughout the city, great merchants, regardless of the type of trade they conducted, tended to support a national impost as opposed to state remedies, because they wished to prevent a tax on the real estate holdings they were acquiring with accumulated capital—a rumored alternative for raising national funds. Now, in the face of state discriminatory legislation against the British, they also wanted to prevent higher duties on British vessels and goods for which they could be the responsible importing merchants.[55] The depression itself was laid at the feet of the Clintonians: because of the state's misguided policies—and not because of wider international causes—"a flourishing and successful commerce" was thwarted and trade was, instead, "daily on the decline."[56]

Other issues reinforce the generalization that before 1786 Clintonians included a large number of the West Indies and coastal traders, new entrants to trade, marginal venturers, and merchants associated with exporting grain from the interior. One of these issues was paper money. Long a matter of contention in the colonial and Revolutionary periods, it loomed again between 1785 and 1787. The state senate was the locus of statewide opposition to paper money and legal tender provisions, and representatives from New York City in both the assembly and senate consistently opposed it *en bloc*.[57] Despite the permanent departure of colonial Delanceyites, many New York City representatives to the senate and assembly in the 1790s upheld the conservative position that paper money was a violation of individual contracts and a menace to public financial stability.[58] The chamber's merchant members applauded attempts to defeat the paper money emissions.[59]

But many merchants endorsed the Clintonian emissions of paper money in 1784, 1785, and 1786.[60] Less established traders—including some of the state's grain exporters or dealers in small quantities of exportable farm surpluses—needed easier means of making domestic payments. They found paper money a useful device for extending short-term credit to the interior, paying taxes, and providing a medium of exchange in general. Thus, although they had a minimal legislative voice, private correspondence and petitions to the legislature suggest that lesser merchants preferred the state's modest emissions of paper money during 1785–86 to the hard money position of merchants in the Chamber of Commerce and among the nationalists generally. Moreover, they supported the establishment of a state loan office to convert their modest sums of paper securities and wartime pay certificates into more reliable state notes. Their correspondence indicates support for this state assumption of the Revolutionary War debt as a means to bolster the credibility and security of New York, as well as to secure their individual fortunes. State control over returning economic stability was a necessary antidote, they argued, to the "speculators," "monopolizers," and "grand brokers" who favored nationalist centralized finance.[61] "A Spartan" wrote in 1786 that the more natural division of interests in New York was not between agriculture and international commerce, but between those of modest property throughout the state and those who wished to protect great fortunes. He assured readers that merchants of modest property shared the commercial farmer's interest in establishing a circulating medium of exchange, and that together they were opposed to the "British interest" in the city.[62]

Similar arguments arose over the founding of a bank in New York. By 1784 traditional preoccupations with providing a landed security for currency was waning rapidly.[63] Instead, those who favored banks to facilitate exchange, discounting, and conversion of Revolutionary obligations were more and more inclined to accept the propriety of specie and paper securities banks. Lesser merchants in the Clintonian camp were no enemies of banking; rather, they based their criticisms of nationalists on the political abuses and factionalism that a centralized, distant institution would engender. They were less alarmed by the prospect of a state specie bank than a national one, and warned the public that the state project would be undermined by more powerful—and more sinister—nationalist forces.[64]

Public commentary about the Bank of New York, established in 1784, reflected these lines of distinction. "Be not deceived," said one observer, "by the names of a few Whig characters who appear among [the state bank's promoters]." Regardless of the state bank's intentions to serve the general welfare, "the real agents are behind the curtain."[65] The "real agents," as subscribers to the state bank soon discovered, were nationalists who quietly purchased large blocks of bank shares and, by late 1784, appear as the bank's directors. Still, there is evidence from the extant subscription list that the bank's initial group of about 220 supporters consisted mostly of returning pre-Revolutionary merchants, and a sprinkling of New England and Philadelphia immigrant merchants, most of them of modest fortunes. Their goals were to facilitate local development projects and state financial stability. The struggle, said "Censor," was between merchants who sought protection of their property by more centralized national means, and merchants who did not act in the interest of "private emolument," but joined with "the farmer and the honest trader" to create banks grounded on modest incomes and the public welfare.[66]

Over the period between 1783 and 1786, then, the state government established popular and effective policies for retiring the Revolutionary War debt, collecting revenue, emitting paper money, establishing conservative local banking, and initiating modest protectionism. For many lesser merchants, Clintonian policies stood in stark contrast to the nationalists' agenda. And it seems likely that they shared certain beliefs about the appropriateness of state economic control, at least temporarily, with the well-established West Indies traders. The relative distinctions based upon success in postwar commerce, however, were not sufficient to sustain clearly diverging interests between great and lesser merchants. Nor were the depression and the Orders in Council sufficient to sustain an alliance between great and lesser West Indies and coastal traders who tried to retain control over state sovereignty in economic affairs. Between 1786 and 1788, general opinion shifted toward the nationalists—so much so that the Constitution was overwhelmingly approved in the southern counties of New York. Among the swing group were many lesser merchants who had not been reliable nationalists in the early postwar period, but who became Federalists by 1788. Why did this happen?

Lesser merchants were not, as a group, catapulted suddenly into the ranks of the well-to-do. If some of them rose rapidly in wealth and status by the end of the decade, many more did not. However, there was a sudden shift in certain economic conditions after the mid-1780s which helps to account for some lesser merchants' altered political perceptions. After 1785, West Indies merchants expressed fewer concerns about the British exclusion of American ships at West Indies ports. Commercial farmers' exportable grain surpluses began to rise in quantity and quality after a difficult period in mid-decade. Urban craftsmen and rural household manufacturers required merchants' services in transporting their goods to neighboring states. By 1786, French West Indies ports were also opened to American provisioners. By 1787, lesser merchants who turned their attention to transporting grain and other commodities from the hinterlands and processing them for export expressed optimism about the "mutual interests" of producing and consuming Americans everywhere.[67]

While the domestic economy was clearly on the rebound, however, international markets were still hampered by the traditional twin evils of extensive foreign regulation and rising lawlessness. Nationalists had warned New Yorkers that their own illicit trade in the Caribbean was only self-annihilating. After an initial postwar decline, smuggling increased to obvious—and irritating—levels; opinion also grew that inept Clintonian port officials promoted this illicit trade, with a consequent loss of revenue from duties. Prosperous eminent West Indies merchants—and no doubt many lesser West Indies merchants as well—began to abandon the Clintonians as it became more evident that the state government could not effectively stifle the costly economic competition of such unvirtuous traffic.[68]

Lesser merchants also began to reevaluate state discrimination against British traders and goods. Although the state impost had produced over half of the state's revenue, the number of entering British vessels at New York continued to rise until it reached over one-third of all vessels entering in 1788.[69] Small traders also grew skeptical about whether New York's discrimination against its sister states of New Jersey and Connecticut was in fact keeping them subordinate to New York's commercial interests. Rumors insisted that goods which would be naturally transported overland to New York City were being diverted to places where duties were lower or smuggling easier. Loss of these exportable commodities and of state revenues made some lesser merchants reevaluate the wisdom of New York's commercial discrimination. Thus, state supporters grew sensitive to the Federalist charges that Clintonians were merely self-interested. "Men of great Influence and very leading Characters in the State," wrote a Baltimorean, were "actuated by a dread of the loss of their *own* Popularity—not the Liberties of their Country."[70] "A train of collectors of impost and excise, tide-waiters and bailiffs," added a Bostonian, acquired "immense property . . . by our exertions and . . . converted [it] to their particular benefit." New Yorkers, he insisted, had "a system which increases their relative importance only by weakening and depressing their neighbors." Even as the commercially significant members of society they had proved "unworthy our confidence."[71] Added to this loss of reputation, another blatant economic fact made New York's merchants reevaluate the wisdom of state sovereignty. As coastal traders expanded their carrying trade to South Carolina and Virginia, the burden of other states' taxes on their commerce increased. On the eve of the September 1786 Annapolis Convention, the combined effect of lost markets in the north and higher duties in the south drove lesser traders to consider whether it was not wise to support nationalists' calls for a "uniform system of commerce" under "the federal principle."[72]

For those city merchants who still opposed the idea of union in early 1788, rumors in May and June that the predominantly Federalist southern counties might sever ties to the northern ones if the Constitution was not ratified struck fear in the hearts of the most ardent Clintonians.[73] New Yorkers as a whole had various reasons to dread the prospects of the southern counties joining the union without the rest of the state, but the state's West Indies grain and provisions exporters were very firm about the dangers they faced. They would lose "natural markets" for grain in the interior of New York and possibly those of New England, rice from the Carolinas, and wheat from the Delaware valley. And if the national union did not accept the southern counties' secession, merchants would be prey to the discrimination of a powerful central government directing the trade of neighboring states. Without exports from New Jersey and Connecticut, New York's commerce with the West Indies, and its sources of hard currency for international trade, would shrivel to insignificance.

Many established wholesalers already were convinced that a Federalist union would secure uniform commercial opportunities and America's international reputation. In the months leading up to New York's ratification convention they tried to win over the younger, marginal, and still rising merchants of New York to their view. They drew on precedents for lesser traders' more precarious advantages and insisted that lesser merchants would fall more easily should opportunities for external markets narrow in the future. But few lesser merchants needed convincing by early 1788, as they contemplated the risks of sustaining state sovereignty in the face of neighboring states rapidly ratifying the Constitution and prophesying their commercial strength under uniform federal policies. As "An American" put it, without union New York would "be placed, as it were, between the upper and nether millstones, and find herself an alien among her father's children."[74] By July, many prominent Antifederalists were switching their loyalty to the Constitution; outside the state ratifying convention a few lesser merchants lamented the collapse of the Federal Republican Committee's campaign to defeat the Federalists.[75]

Although Melancton Smith threw his support to the Federalists by July, he tried early in the convention to state the Antifederalist position in the most compelling terms. "[T]o understand the true commercial interests of a country," he said, "not only requires just ideas of the general commerce of the world, but also and principally, a knowledge of the productions of your own country and their value, what your soil is capable of producing[,] the nature of your manufacturers and the capacity of the country to increase both. . . . [It] requires something more than an acquaintance with the abstruse parts of the system of finance. It calls for a knowledge of the circumstances and ability of the people in general, a discernment how the burdens imposed will bear upon the different classes." Smith described a "middling class" of New Yorkers who were neither "poor and indifferent to government" nor "in the habit of profuse living." They were of "substantial circumstances" "arrived at by frugality and attention to the public good."[76] John Williams agreed that the wealthiest inhabitants of New York were not the best rulers, for they had promoted the "dissipation and luxury," of "foreign commodities which have. . . . deluged our country;—which have loaded us with debt."[77] Other Antifederalists spoke out against commercial "monopolies," the centralized banking plan which Hamilton hinted at, and relinquishing the power of the purse to a new national government.[78]

Antifederalist arguments about the nature and location of power appealed to many lesser merchants for most of the 1780s, when it still seemed appropriate—and feasible—to reconstruct the new republic's economy on a foundation of state sovereignty. But by 1787, specific Antifederalist proposals rang hollow to merchants. Arguing against Federalist fiscal plans—especially the national impost—the best solution they mustered for retaining state power of the purse was that Congress should resort to the cumbersome system of specific requisitions when financial needs arose. Requisitions, they argued, could be tailored to draw larger proportions of sums from the state's wealthy citizens.[79] At the convention John Williams, Melancton Smith, and John Lansing, Jr., argued against a state excise on manufactures because it would hit the "middling class" of mechanics and small entrepreneur and developers hardest. But not one of them argued openly for the protective legislation just beginning to mark the future of state and federal involvement in manufactures. Their vision of development tended to see citizens spreading across the new western counties, modest internal improvements along waterways, and the traditional pursuits of farming and commerce. With the exception of Robert R. Livingston, Antifederalists and Federalists alike approached tentatively even the discussion of home manufactures.[80]

However appealing the Antifederalist program was to an "agrarian interest" in 1788, it no longer offered ambitious lesser merchants the kind of state sovereignty they sought. It was a vision with insufficient international commercial scope and excessive attention to outmoded perspectives about domestic development. Federalist delegates such as Livingston offered the alternative of a symbiotic relationship between city and country, with a vast territory of mutually supportive manufacturing, commercial farming, and merchant exporting activities. Union, they argued, would be positive, protective, promotive, and inclusive of all economic interests.[81]

In sum, although the gaps in the historical record do not permit us to assign precise numbers to Clintonian or nationalist merchants, we can speculate, on the basis of known members of the merchant community and the political choices they expressed, that there were, between 1783 and 1786, political struggles between Clintonians and nationalists over issues of crucial importance to merchants. These were, in turn, the result of economic struggles based upon difference within the merchant community about internal and external markets, the manner in which trade should be conducted, and general beliefs about who ought to pursue commerce in the name of the American consumer. If some merchants were convinced of the Confederation's weaknesses early on, others defended for a time the benefits which the state bestowed upon them under the Confederation. Robert R. Livingston and other Federalists were entitled to express confidence that most of the commercial interest supported a Federalist union by 1788, but many merchants had not shared a nationalist perspective through the 1780s. We might close with a query about subsequent years: is it sufficiently clear that Federalist discourse and politics in the new nation continued to attract the majority of merchants? Or, under the pressure of new circumstances, did important divisions develop within the merchant community once again after 1789? At stake was whether Federalists could, and would, promote and protect the economic activities which proponents of union had advocated in order to secure the Constitution, or whether ratification in 1788 contained a rather more fragile consensus.

NOTES

¹See, e.g., items in the *Hudson Gazette*, Mar. 13, 20, 1788; and Henry Oothoudt to John McKesson, April 3, 1788, McKesson Papers, The New-York Historical Society.

²Alexander Hamilton, "Conjectures about the New Constitution," Sept. 17-30, 1787, in Harold Syrett, Jacob E. Cooke, and Barbara Chernow, eds., *The Papers of Alexander Hamilton*, 27 vols., (New York, 1961-87), 4:275. Hamilton frequently remarked about the "good will of the commercial interest throughout the states" for the Constitution and linked this interest with "men of property"; *ibid.*

³For example, Robert Yates to George Mason, June 25, 1788, Emmet Collection, New York Public Library.

⁴Lewis B. Morris to General Webb, Feb. 7, 1788, in W.C. Ford, ed., *The Correspondence and Journals of Samuel Blatchley Webb*, 3 vols. (New York, 1894), 3:93.

⁵Item in the *Hudson Gazette*, Mar. 20, 1788.

⁶Items in the *New York Journal*, Mar. 4, Apr. 30, 1788.

⁷Constable, Rucker, and Company to John Gray and Thomas Blount, Nov. 30, 1787, in Alice B. Keith, ed., *The John Gray Blount Papers*, 2 vols. (Winston-Salem, NC, 1952), 1:360.

⁸Thomas Tredwell to the New York Ratifying Convention, July 2, 1788, in Jonathan Elliot, ed., *The Debates in the Several State Conventions on the Adoption of the Federal Constitution*, 5 vols. (Philadelphia, 1876), 2:396.

⁹Robert R. Livingston to the New York Ratifying Convention, June 19, 1788, in *ibid.*, 2:210-211.

¹⁰For generalizations, see Jackson Turner Main, *The Antifederalists: Critics of the Constitution, 1781-1788* (Chapel Hill, NC, 1961), 270; for information about the Cuylers, Bayards, Schuylers, Morrises, VanCortlandts, Ten Broecks, Van Rensselaers, and others who were linked in their commerce and were avid supporters of the Constitution, see Alfred F. Young, *The Democratic-Republicans of New York: The Origins, 1763-1797* (Chapel Hill, NC, 1967), 79-82.

¹¹Alexander Hamilton, *The Federalist No. 35*, in Jacob E. Cooke, ed. and intro., *The Federalist* (Middleton, CT, 1961), 215-222, at 219. See also *The Federalist Nos. 1, 11, 12, 37*, in *ibid.*, 3-7, 65-79, 231-239 (No. 37 is by Madison but echoes Hamilton's arguments).

¹²Jackson Turner Main, *The Upper House in Revolutionary America, 1763-1788* (Madison, WI, 1967), 139.

¹³E. Wilder Spaulding, *New York in the Critical Period, 1783-1789* (New York, 1932), 28. See also Main's reference to a similar view in the work of Thomas Cochran, in *The Antifederalists*, 242. In general, see Young, *Democratic-Republicans*, 69-71, 77 n. 60, 143.

¹⁴Cathy Matson and Peter Onuf, *A Union of Interests: Politics and Economy in Revolutionary America* (Lawrence, KS, 1990), chaps. 3, 5.

¹⁵In the absence of systematic customs and census materials, the best information on merchants during the 1780s derives from an eclectic array of contemporary references, including merchants' own reflections in correspondence and newspapers, oaths, political and legal records for the city and state, and newspaper information on the nature of commerce, prices, voyage patterns, and descriptions of the various economic interests affecting the life of the city. The most certain information includes that on entrances and clearances, tonnage, state revenues, and the size of the merchant community. Footnotes which follow will indicate the ways specific sources are used; the composite of information is in the author's possession.

¹⁶In most cases, the term "dry goods" referred to finished manufactures, primarily textiles, metal and earthenwares, and small fineries. On the value of imports, see "Letter from John Lamb" Jan. 10, 1789, in *American Museum*, V (Mar. 1789), 230 and items

from New York, d. Mar. 19, 1789, *ibid.*, VII (Jan. 1790): 52; and *ibid.*, (June, 1790), 311. On tonnage, see Robert G. Albion, "New York Port in the New Republic, 1783-1793," *New York History* 21 (1940): 388-403, at 392-3, where he gives summaries of annual average tonnage imports for the decade 1783-1792 and notes that 45 percent arrived from Britain and its possessions; 31 percent from British and foreign West Indies; 19 percent from foreign West Indies; 14 percent from British West Indies; and 26 percent from coastal trade. The remaining 10 percent derived from Southern European and coastal trade with Connecticut and New Jersey, which were not accounted for in other figures. The latter states will figure importantly in the grievances of lesser merchants after 1784.

[17]The pool of "great merchants" for this study does not include those who held residence in an adjacent state, and who thus may have held different views about the impost, banking, and trade in general. New Jersey and Connecticut merchants tended to be earlier, and more committed, Federalists than New Yorkers. The total also excludes city residents whose retailing, auctioning, brokering, distilling, or manufacturing activities occupied more time and investment than international wholesaling. Finally, the total excludes those with the appellation "gentlemen merchant," implying they held large amounts of real estate or aspired to gentrify; this group includes many Livingstons, Morrises, and Van Dams, as well as other "gentlemen merchants" whose activities centered less on commerce than on a combination of money-lending, real estate investment, and the law. Moreover, Main's analysis of the upper house shows that while many of the Crugers, Waltons, Beekmans, Schuylers, and others began as merchants in the pre-Revolutionary years, they and their offspring often removed their activities and fortunes from the city after the war; see *Upper House*, 55-9, 135-6, 141, 142, 276nts.

[18]See information compiled from merchants' correspondence and accounts in Cathy Matson, "From Free Trade to Liberty: The Reshaping of Dissenting Economic Ideas in New York City, 1620-1790," chap. 8 and appendices, mss. in preparation.

[19]Young, *Democratic-Republicans*, 79.

[20]See, e.g., [Anon.], *A Few Salutary Hints Pointing Out the Policy and Consequences of Admitting British Subjects to Engros Our Trade and Become our Citizens, to Those Who Either Risqued or Lost Their All in Bringing About the Revolution* (New York, 1786).

[21]David Franks, publ., *The New York Directory for 1786* (New York, 1786), 45-77.

[22]See notes 15 and 18.

[23]For the Bank of New York, brokers, and insurance leaders see Franks, *New York Directory*, 45-77, 90, and *idem.*, *New York Directory for 1787* (New York, 1787), 50-55. For auctions, see *Laws of the State of New York Comprising the Constitution and the Acts of the Legislature Since the Revolution, from the First to the Fifteenth Session, Inclusive* (New York, 1792), in microfilm, *Records of the States of the United States*, comp. and ed., William Sumner Jenkins (Washington, DC, 1949), B.2, reel 6, 9th sess., chap. 17, Mar. 21, 1786, p. 18. The act to incorporate the Chamber of Commerce is at *ibid.*, 7th sess., chap. 30, Apr. 13, 1784, p. 32-37.

[24]See notes 15 and 18.

[25]This series of generalizations is based on information described in notes 15 and 18. For the remaining sixty-eight merchants (23 percent) there is very little to identify. They may or may not have been in New York City before and during the Revolution; may or may not have been Loyalists; and may or may not have even stayed in the city after 1786. No doubt many of them lived a precarious existence sharing wharf space, commissioning small amounts of goods on the ships of established merchants, and most often diversifying their trade goods and patterns to a much further extent than wealthy and reputable peers. Bankruptcy records are not a useful guide in measuring business failures in the 1780s, especially since they do not include merchants who could not afford legal fees to recover debts; nevertheless, many in this third, marginal group no doubt assumed the title "merchant" for only a short period.

²⁶As a whole, these two groups comprise merchants whose surnames and commercial linkages suggest pre-Revolutionary residency and post-Revolutionary resumption of trade in the city. The second group of ninety-six includes some merchants who may have been sons or nephews of mature pre-Revolutionary traders, or merchants with common surnames.

²⁷On immigration, see e.g., Robert East, *Business Enterprise in the American Revolutionary Era* (New York, 1938), 235–237, and Spaulding, *New York in the Critical Period*, 30–31.

²⁸Patterns of trade can be ascertained with a modest degree of certainty by combining information on the names of ships, ownership registration, references in merchants' correspondence to each other's ships, and the records for entrances and clearances which specify duties paid on goods which come from the various areas of trade. Of course, there may have been additional ports of call which any particular voyage would not indicate, and there were most likely many fraudulent entries at New York for the goods on board particular ships. This smuggling may have been greater among the merchants who appear to have been coastal merchants in most of their trade; their records of merely American ports of call—especially in the cases of southern states—may have hidden clearances from foreign West Indies and other ports.

²⁹See *Journal of the Assembly of the State of New York*, in microfilm, *Records of the States of the United States*, comp. and ed., William Sumner Jenkins (Washington, DC, 1941), A. lb reel 4, 8th sess., Feb. 11, 1785, p. 32; Apr. 27, 1785, p. 181–82; and 9th sess., Mar. 24, 1786, p. 100–101, for bankruptcies and general comments about the conditions of Lawrence Marston, Thomas Armstrong, Thomas Miller, Stephen Grossfield, John Turner, Henry Sickels, J. and A. Anthony, Benjamin Cole, and other lesser merchants. See also the items in the *New York Morning Post*, Mar. 10, 1785, and the *New York Packet*, Apr. 21, 1785. For hints that the interests of the lesser merchants were not only distinguishable from those of great merchants, but from the interests of mechanics, artisans, and others as well, see the series of essays by Antifederalists "Cato," "Brutus," "Cincinnatus," and "A Countryman" in the *New York Journal*, from Sept. 27, 1787, to Feb. 14, 1788.

³⁰The difficulties of enforcing deference were compounded by the confusion of titles. Those who had been referred to generally as "merchants" before the revolution are increasingly divided into "merchant tailors," "merchant druggist," merchant ropemakers, or into grocers, general store owners, and merchant craftsmen.

³¹A contemporary view of the mutuality of interests can be found in John Jay's very popular tract, "A Citizen of New York," *An Address to the People of the State of New York* (New York, 1788), 6–15.

³²East, *Business Enterprise*, appendix A; Frank, *New York Directory for 1786*, 90; and Matson, "From Free Trade to Liberty," chap. 8.

³³See the perceptions in older works such as Thomas E.V. Smith, *The City of New York in the Year of Washington's Inauguration* (New York, 1889), 119, and Rufus Griswold, *The Republican Court, Or American Society in the Days of Washington* (New York, 1856), 414–415. Their evaluations seem to correspond well to merchants' writings about themselves during the 1780s.

³⁴See, e.g., entries referring to the Council of Revision, *Journal of the Assembly*, 8th sess., Mar. 14, 1785. Senators supporting the impost who were associated with, or were, great merchants included Parks, Allison, Webster, Palmer, Floyd, Roosevelt, Duane, Paine, Haring, and Ten Broeck in 1783; by 1785, Whiting, Russell, Vrooman, Taylor, and Gardiner added their voices of agreement.

³⁵For the legislature's response to the petition to the chamber and the incorporation law, see *Laws*, 7th sess., chap. 30, Apr. 13, 1784, p. 32–37. See also Minutes of the Chamber of Commerce, Feb. 15, May 16, 1785, New York Public Library; and item, *New York Packet*, Nov. 10, 1785. For an example of merchants desiring a national impost as a step toward redeeming securities see the great merchant, Robert C. Livingston's Letter Book, The New-York Historical Society.

[36]Sidney Pomerantz, *New York: An American City, 1783–1803* (New York: Columbia University Press, 1938), 179 n. 54, 180 n. 55; and Matson, "From Free Trade to Liberty," chap. 8 and appendices.

[37]For the earliest approval of the national impost, Nov. 21, 1781, and for the legislature's declaration of support for more congressional powers, see the list of papers presented by Thomas Tredwell to the state ratifying convention, June 27, 1788, in Elliot, *Debates*, 2:238–240.

[38]"Philo-Patria," *New York Journal*, Sept. 24, 1786. Antifederalist delegates to New York's ratifying convention would also express a preference for requisitions.

[39]For elaboration of this argument see Cathy Matson, "Liberty, Jealousy, and Union: The New York Economy in the 1780's," in Paul Gilje and Bill Pencak, eds., *New York in the Age of the Constitution*, (Charlottesville: University Press of Virginia, forthcoming). See also Young, *Democratic-Republicans*, 47–50, 77 n. 60, 137–140.

[40]On the depression and its effects on marginal producers and lesser merchant exporters, see Richard B. Morris, *The Forging of the Union, 1781–1789* (New York, 1987), chap. 6: and Matson and Onuf, *A Union of Interests*, chap. 3.

[41]Henry B. Dawson, "The Motley Letter," *Historical Magazine*, 2nd ser., 9 (Mar. 1871): 157–201.

[42]See the correspondence for 1784–1788 of merchants Ebenezer Stevens, Samuel Hake and Samuel Hake, Jr., Solomon Townshend, and Edward Goold, all at The New-York Historical Society; and the many references in the correspondence of the Beekman family to business with less eminent merchants like Peter Curtenius, Steven Sayers, Charles McEvers, and William Goforth, in Philip L. White, ed. and transcr., *The Beekman Mercantile Papers, 1746–1799*, 3 vols. (New York, 1956), esp. vol. 2.

[43]Item, *New York Journal*, Sept. 28, 1786.

[44]Item d. Mar. 7, 1786, *New York Gazetteer*, repr. in Apr. 1, 1786, *Independent Gazetteer* (Philadelphia).

[45]For growing nationalist influence and their persistent appeals for stronger central government, see the excellent introduction and notes in John P. Kaminski and Gaspare J. Saladino, eds., *Commentaries on the Constitution, Public and Private*, vol. 1, Feb. 21 to Nov. 7, 1787, printed in their series, *Documentary History of the Ratification of the Constitution*, (Madison, WI, 1976–), 13:11–43.

[46]See notes 15 and 18.

[47]*Ibid.*; in addition, see examples from the correspondence of merchants indicated in note 45.

[48]Albion, "New York Port in the New Republic," 388–403; Pomerantz, *An American City*, 147–159; and Merrill Jensen, *The New Nation, A History of the United States During the Confederation, 1781–1789* (New York, 1950), 197–199.

[49]For the duties, see *Laws*, 7th sess., chap. 10, Mar. 22, 1784, 11–17; chap. 52, May 3, 1784, 158–160; 8th sess., chap. 7, Nov. 18, 1784, 10–15; 8th sess., chap. 34, Mar. 15, 1785, 188; chap. 53, Apr. 4, 1785, 213. For the discrimination against Connecticut and New Jersey, see *Laws*, 10th sess., chap. 81, Apr. 11, 1787, 144–156, under which act "foreign" was interpreted to mean the sister states as well as England. See also Charles Lincoln, *Messages from the Governors, Comprising Executive Communications to the Legislature*, 2 vols. (Albany, 1909), 2:201; and *Journals of the Assembly*, 8th sess., Mar. 30, 31, 1785, 126, 130.

[50]The capstone of New York's protectionist legislation is at *Laws*, 11th sess., chap. 72, Mar 12, 1788, 168–172; it was a tax of 8 percent on certain enumerated imports above the other standing duties. For protectionist arguments in general, see, e.g., *Journal of the Assembly*, 11th sess., Jan. 11, Feb. 27, 1788, 7, 94–95.

[51]See Matson, "From Free Trade to Liberty," chaps. 8–9, for specific manufactures promoted, and for perceptions about the mutual interests of manufacturers and merchants, 1785–1787; and see Thomas Earle and Charles Congdon, ed., *Annals of the General Society of Mechanics and Tradesmen in the City of New York, 1785–1880* (New York, 1882), 12, 14.

[52] For the names of lesser merchants who held these positions the original lists were compared to the positions listed in the annual city directories, especially those for 1786 and 1787. For the legislative and public discussion about commercial exports of grain and other agricultural products, see Matson, "From Free Trade to Liberty," chaps. 8–9.

[53] See items in the *New York Packet*, Mar. 23, 1786; and the *Hudson Gazette*, June 28, 1787; and Matson, "Liberty, Jealousy, and Union."

[54] The impost discussion has received much attention from historians. For a summary of the debate in New York with respect to the congressional requests and the rising nationalist sentiment for centralized import duties, see Cathy Matson, "American Political Economy in the Constitutional Decade, 1781–1791," in R.C. Simmons, ed., *The U.S. Constitution: the First 200 Years* (Manchester, U.K., 1989), 16–35. The discussion reached a peak in New York in 1786, when Clintonians again defeated the impost and allowed that the state impost be paid in state paper money. The vote was 33 to 22; in 1787 the legislature voted again to defeat the national impost, 33 to 19, and added the requirement that the governor appoint impost collectors. See also *Journal of the Assembly*, 6th sess., Mar. 10, 1783, 151; 9th sess., Apr. 13, 1786, 134–5; and 10th sess., Feb. 15, 1787, 51–52.

[55] Comments by the Council of Revision, *Journal of the Assembly*, 8th sess., Mar. 14, 1785, 88.

[56] Item in the *New York Packet*, Nov. 10, 1785, reporting on the repetition of Nov. 3 by the Chamber of Commerce.

[57] For an example of public opposition to paper money, see item d. Feb. 13, 1786 from New York, repr. in the *Independent Gazetteer* (Philadelphia), Feb. 25, 1786. For senate opposition, see the Chamber of Commerce Minutes, Feb. 15, May 16, 1785.

[58] See for example, the *Journal of the Assembly*, 9th sess., Feb. 15, 17, 21, 1786, 41–42, 43, 49–50; Mar. 30, 1786, 110–115; and 8th sess., Mar. 17, 1785, 95, for arguments about paper money, state assumption of the debt, and legal tender provisions. Opponents included Duer, Boyd, Dongan, Troup, Arndt, John Livingston, Harper, Gardiner, Thomas, and Youngs. See also Main, *Upper House*, 135, 141–142, 276nts.

[59] Chamber of Commerce Minutes, Feb. 13, 1786. See also item in the *Country Journal and Poughkeepsie Advertiser*, Feb. 23, 1786.

[60] For New York's main paper money bills, see *Laws*, 9th sess., chap. 40, Apr. 18, 1786, 61–78; 9th sess., chap. 21, Mar. 31, 1786, 21–23; and 10th sess., chap. 94, Apr. 20, 1787, 188–189.

[61] See the examples in the *Independent New York Gazette*, Dec. 6, 1783; and *New York Journal*, Dec. 16, 1784, Sept. 15, 1785; the *New York Packet*, Dec. 13, 1784, Jan. 2, Mar. 9, 1786; and the *Daily Advertiser*, Feb. 23, 1786. For lesser merchants' correspondence, see note 45.

[62] "A Spartan," *New York Packet*, Feb. 16, 1786; item in *ibid.*, May 25, 1787; and item in *Hudson Gazette*, June 1, 1786. Lesser merchant support for paper money in the assembly included Sears, Goforth, Evert Bancker, Denning, Stagg, Malcolm, Vanderbilt, Cooper, Townsend, and J. Smith; in all, forty-seven members of various socio-economic status in the legislature supported paper money in 1786.

[63] For the traditional debate on funding paper money with land, as it developed in New York, see Matson, "From Free Trade to Liberty," chap. 3. For the awareness that landed security was no longer a basis of banking, see, for example, item in the *New York Journal*, Mar. 25, 1784. Main, *Antifederalists*, 165–167, 268–270, makes the point that paper money was almost always associated with the states' interiors and farmers, a point this author would dispute; however, he also argues that in New York paper money was clearly a Clintonian issue, which leaves room for including some lesser merchants among the group of supporters in 1784, 1785, and 1786. Interestingly, commercial farmers of Connecticut and New Jersey were both paper money advocates *and* constitutional supporters; lesser merchants involved in grain exporting may have coincided in their views of economic necessity and political choices.

[64]Of course, there were exceptions. Nationalists supported land banks in some cases, although the support of merchants like Jeremiah Wadsworth and Peter Colt for specie banks represented the more traditional position. State-oriented merchants supported specie banks, although merchants like John Stevens, Stephen Sayer, and some of the Livingstons continued to insist on landed security for banking. See, for example, the discussion in East, *Business Enterprise*, 197–198.

[65]Anonymous article in the *Independent Gazette*, Mar. 11, 1784.

[66]The subscription list is reprinted in East, *Business Enterprise*, 327–9; the generalizations in this paragraph are derived from comparing this list with the author's other information about lesser merchants in the city. The quote is from "Censor," *New York Packet*, Jan. 21, 1790.

[67]On the revival of grain export markets and domestic small-scale production, see Matson and Onuf, *A Union of Interests*, chap. 5. On the French West Indies, see Albion, "New York Port," 392–393.

[68]On the rise of smuggling and lesser merchants' growing despair of establishing legitimate trade under Clintonian auspices, see the names of merchants and ships in Bryan Edwards, *The History, Civil and Commercial, of the British Colonies in the West Indies*, 2nd ed., 2 vols. (London, 1793-1794), 2: chap. 4. In general, see Jacques Pierre Brissot de Warville, *New Travels in the United States of America, in 1788*, 2 vols. (orig. publ., Paris, 1791; repr., New York, 1919), 1:463.

[69]See "Letter from John Lamb," Jan. 10, 1789, in *American Museum*, V (Mar. 1788), 230–233.

[70]"Extract of a letter from Baltimore to a Gentleman in This City," d. Dec. 12, 1787, *Connecticut Journal*, Dec. 26, 1787. See also, Oliver Ellsworth speech in the Connecticut Convention, d. Jan. 7, 1788, *ibid.*, Jan. 14, 1788. For the response of these states to New York's discrimination—free ports and stronger nationalism—see Matson, "Liberty, Jealousy, and Union."

[71]"To the Honorable Richard Henry Lee, Esq.," Dec. 24, 1787, *Connecticut Courant*. See also, "Landholder," [Oliver Ellsworth], essay VIII, Dec. 24, 1787, *ibid.*

[72]For the southern duties and their effects on New York trade, see the Letterbook of Anthony Lispenard Bleecker, correspondence for 1784-1787, at The New-York Historical Society.

[73]John Jay to George Washington, May 29, 1788, in Henry P. Johnston, ed., *The Correspondence and Public Papers of John Jay*, 4 vols. (New York, 1891), 3:335-6; Abraham Yates to Abraham G. Lansing, May 28, 1788, Yates Papers, New York Public Library; and Hamilton to James Madison, June 8, 1788. See also "An American," May 13, 27, 1788, *New York Packet*; and Robert R. Livingston's speeches, June 19, 25, 1788, at the ratifying convention, in Elliot, *Debates*, 2:210-211, 274-275. For evidence of some lesser merchants still resisting federal union in mid-1788, see Joseph Barrell to Nathaniel Barrell, Dec. 20, 1787, in Sandeman-Barrell Papers, Massachusetts Historical Society; Hugh Ledlie to John Lamb, Jan. 15, 1788, The Lamb Papers, The New-York Historical Society; and Aedanus Burke to Lamb, June 23, 1788, in *ibid.*

[74]"An American," May 13, *New York Packet*.

[75]For club members John Lamb, Charles Tillinghast, Melancton Smith, Marinus Willett, Samuel Jones, James H. Hughes, among others, all of whom were lesser merchants, see Lamb Papers, Box 5, The New-York Historical Society.

[76]Melancton Smith speech, June 21, 1788, in Elliot, *Debates*, 2:245, 246.

[77]John Williams speech, June 21, 1788, in *ibid.*, 2:240. See also John Williams, "An Extract from a Letter," Jan. 29, 1788, *Albany Federal Herald*, Feb. 25, 1788.

[78]Speeches of Williams, June 25, 27, Governor Clinton, June 28, and Lansing, June 28, all in Elliot, *Debates*, 2:330-331, 338-340, 359, 371-372.

[79]Speech of John Lansing, Jr., June 28, in *ibid.*, 2:372-374.

[80]On excises, see *ibid.* On manufactures, see the contrast between speeches of Williams, June 25, and Robert R. Livingston, June 23, in *ibid.*, 2:331–333, 274–275. See also Robert R. Livingston speech of June 27, in *ibid.*, 2:341–344. The awakening of manufacturing interests—especially as they emerged from lesser merchants' and middling craftsmen's perceived economic needs—is developed at more length in Matson and Onuf, *A Union of Interests*, chap. 8.

[81]Mutuality of economic interests had been Hamilton's earlier argument in, for example, *The Federalist Nos. 1 and 12* (seconded by Madison's *The Federalist No. 37*); at the convention in New York he once again emphasized such a foundation of government; see his speeches of June 21, 24, and 25, in Elliot, *Debates*, 2:267–268, 300–306, and 316. Also see Robert R. Livingston's speeches of June 23, and 27, in *ibid.*, 2:274–9, 341–344; James Duane's speech of July 1, in *ibid.*, 2:379; and John Jay's speech of July 1, in *ibid.*, 2:380–381.

The Role of Newspapers in New York's Debate Over the Federal Constitution *

JOHN P. KAMINSKI

University of Wisconsin–Madison

The Founding Fathers had a deep appreciation for newspapers—they had served the Revolutionaries well in the struggle for independence and were expected to serve an equally important role in the debate over the proposed new form of government. This expectation was fulfilled as the public debate over the ratification of the Constitution was largely conducted in America's newspapers.

At the time the Constitutional Convention adjourned in September 1787, there were about ninety-five newspapers published in the United States. Most were weeklies, a few biweeklies, triweeklies, and dailies, none of which were published on Sundays.

Only about a half-dozen newspapers throughout the country maintained a blatantly Antifederal posture on the Constitution, while another half-dozen or so remained neutral to the point where they printed a goodly amount of Antifederalist literature. The remaining eighty newspapers were patently Federalist, printing a large percentage of items in favor of the Constitution.

New York mirrored the other twelve states. In New York City the *New York Journal* was ardently Antifederalist, while the *New York Morning Post* was basically neutral. All other nine New York newspapers—especially the four in upstate New York—strongly favored the new Constitution.

---

*Conference paper presented at "New York and the Ratification of the U.S. Constitution," Federal Hall, New York City, May 20 and 21, 1988.

By 1787 American newspapers had created a primitive news service system. Assisted by the post office's policy of free postage, printers exchanged their newspapers with each other and regularly reprinted essays, news items, and fillers. Some popular items were reprinted thirty, forty, or even fifty times. Occasionally, the reprinting newspaper cited its source, but more commonly only the dateline appeared to tell the reader where the item had originated. Political partisans knew how the newspaper exchange system worked, and they used it to their advantage. For example, Tench Coxe, one of the most prolific Federalist writers in America, had his essays printed in Philadelphia. He would then send several copies to James Madison, then serving as a Virginia delegate to Congress in New York City, asking Madison to forward the articles to Virginia for republication and to give a copy to Alexander Hamilton who, if he felt it appropriate, could have the essays reprinted in New York. Hamilton himself sent several numbers of *The Federalist* to Benjamin Rush in Philadelphia asking that they be published in that city's newspapers. "Perhaps," Hamilton wrote, "even if they are not wanted with you, it might be well to give them a passage through your papers to your more Southern neighbors."[1] Thus, even though UPI, AP, and other news services did not exist, American politicians and printers knew how best to disseminate information throughout the country.

It is only a mild exaggeration to say that the newspaper campaign to ratify the Constitution was under way even before the Constitutional Convention met. Although articles favoring a stronger central government had appeared occasionally in newspapers throughout the 1770s and 1780s, once Congress officially sanctioned the Constitutional Convention in February 1787, a full-fledged campaign began to adopt whatever the grand Convention might propose. Newspapers in Philadelphia, Boston, and New York City printed and reprinted numerous articles warning Americans "that unless an energetick, permanent continental government is speedily established, our liberties will be set afloat in the confusion that will inevitably ensue.—At present we . . . are every day tottering on the brink of civil dissention. . . . It would be better to embrace almost any expedient rather than to remain where we are."[2] Another article marvelled at the doings in Philadelphia: "Whatever measures may be recommended by the Federal Convention, whether an addition to the old constitution, or the adoption of a new one, it will, in effect, be a revolution in government, accomplished by reasoning and deliberation; an event that has never occurred since the formation of society."[3]

Shortly after the Convention adjourned, David Humphreys, a trusted aide to George Washington, wrote to his chief: "The well affected have not been wanting in efforts to prepare the minds of the citizens for the favorable reception of whatever might be the results of your Proceedings. . . . Judicious & well-timed publications have great efficacy in ripening the judgment of men."[4] Stationed in New York City, Henry Knox, the Confederation's Secretary at War, wrote the Marquis de Lafayette: "The minds of the people at large were fully prepared for a change without any particular specification."[5] The printers of the Lansingburgh, (Troy, N.Y.) *Northern Centinel* later admitted in their newspaper that they "conceived it a duty incumbent on them to prepare the minds of their readers" for the reception of the new Constitution.[6] Thus, even before the Constitution was published, newspapers had performed an important service in the ratification debate. Previously, whenever Congress proposed amendments to the Articles of Confederation, the public was suspicious of the attempt of the central government to grasp more powers. Now, due to the extensive and favorable publicity given the Convention in the newspapers, there was a general, widespread predilection to accept whatever the Convention ultimately proposed.

The partisan debate over the Constitution in New York newspapers began several months before the debate in other states. In February, March, and April 1787 three New York City newspaper items advocated dividing the country into three or four separate confederacies which in turn would be united by a loose federal alliance.[7] They maintained that the United States was a mixture of different climates, customs, and interests that would never be able to accommodate each other. Furthermore, the writers accepted Montesquieu's principle that republics could not exist over large territories without eventually degenerating into despotisms. A "West Chester Farmer" totally disagreed, suggesting that the states be reduced to the status of "civil corporations" and that their laws should be null and void if they conflicted with the laws of the central government.[8] Another nationalist, signing himself "A Well Wisher to the United States of America," recommended that no state law go into effect "without the Assent of Congress first," the pet scheme of James Madison at the Constitutional Convention.[9] A writer in the *Albany Gazette* on June 21, 1787, decried "the prevailing rage of excessive democracy—this fashionable contempt of government." The Convention, he argued, must propose a new form of government that would restore the people's respect for authority. It was time, he said, "for politicians to begin to consider mankind *as they are* and not *what they ought to be*." "Let no one suppose," he continued, "that I am an enemy to freedom—I am a friend to liberty, and to secure it inviolate to the people, would wish to banish licentiousness.—But let them know, that without a sacred regard to the laws—a reverential submission to authority—an impartial and sometimes a severe administration of justice—this invaluable jewel, this boasted liberty will be inevitably lost.'' These were general arguments about the need to create either a stronger central government or to break up the ineffective conglomerate Confederation into efficient sub-confederacies.

The trigger that apparently set off the newspaper debate in New York over the Constitution was the departure of two New York delegates, Robert Yates and John Lansing, Jr., from the Constitutional Convention. On their way home to Albany, the two Clintonians stopped in New York City and, in all likelihood, conferred with Governor George Clinton, telling him that the Constitutional Convention was up to no good. Supporters of a strengthened central government interpreted their departure as a sign that New York's Clintonians had rejected the idea of cooperating with the other states in strengthening Congress. When most rational nationalists would have been totally disheartened at this abdication by New York, Alexander Hamilton took this opportunity to go on the offense. On July 21 Hamilton, also temporarily home from the Constitutional Convention, attacked Governor Clinton in an anonymous article published in the *Daily Advertiser.* Clinton, Hamilton charged, reprobated in public company the appointment of delegates to the Constitutional Convention ''and predicted a mischievous issue.'' Clinton's attitude was ''That the present confederation is, in itself, equal to the purposes of the union.'' Hamilton, however, maintained ''that the general government is fundamentally defective; that the very existence of the union is in imminent danger.'' The derogatory remarks by Clinton against the Convention before its results were known proved that the governor was more attached ''to his *own power* than to the *public good*, and furnishes strong reason to suspect a dangerous predetermination to oppose whatever may tend to diminish the *former*, however it may promote the *latter.*''

Six later ''A Republican,'' writing in the *New York Journal,* without admitting that Clinton had been disrespectful of the Convention, defended the governor's right to speak out.[10] Any attempt to limit free speech was said to be ''high treason against the majesty of the people.'' This exchange set the tone for much of the newspaper debate in New York as Federalists attacked the unwillingness of the Clintonians to give up any of either their own power or the state of New York's peculiar mercantile advantages. Antifederalists, on the other hand, denounced their aristocratic opponents for wanting to overturn the principles of the Revolution.

Beginning on September 21 in the *Daily Advertiser* and the *New York Packet*, the Constitution was printed in nine of the state's eleven newspapers within a two-week period. Three days after the first printing of the Constitution, New York's first newspaper commentary on it appeared in the *Daily Advertiser*. The Constitution, it said, would "render us safe and happy at home, and respected abroad." Adoption of the new form of government would "snatch us from impending ruin" and provide "the substantial basis of liberty, honor and virtue." It was "the duty of all honest, well-disposed men, friends to peace and good government . . . to cultivate and diffuse . . . a spirit of submission" to the Constitution; which, although not perfect, was "much more so than the most friendly and sanguine expected."

Three days later, on September 27th, the first of seven essays by "Cato" appeared in the *New York Journal*. "Cato" called on freemen to be prudent and cautious in considering the Constitution—"if you are negligent or inattentive, the ambitious and despotic will entrap you . . . and . . . you, and your posterity, may never be freed." "Beware how you determine—do not, because you admit that something must be done, adopt anything—teach the members of that convention, that you are capable of a supervision of their conduct." If the Constitution were found defective, another convention could consider amendments. The Constitution should be adopted if it were found acceptable, but if it were judged to be dangerous, freemen were urged to "reject it with indignation—better to be where you are, for the present, than insecure forever afterwards."

Four days later, on October 1st, "Caesar" attacked "Cato" as a demagogue. "Caesar" asked, "shall we now wrangle and find fault with that *excellent whole*, because, perhaps, some of its parts *might have been* more perfect?" Then he warned "Cato" and other Antifederalists that it would be wiser to accept George Washington willingly as the first president under the Constitution than to have the former commander-in-chief lead another army to establish the Constitution by force.

This kind of give-and-take persisted throughout the entire debate over the Constitution. From our perspective, the arguments may look insubstantial, but they kept the public's interest high. Readers looked forward to the next "Cato," the next "Caesar," the next "Cincinnatus." Who would get the better of whom?

But these were not the only political essays to appear in newspapers, broadsides, and pamphlets. Starting on the 18th of October 1787, several remarkable series of essays appeared in the New York press. First, sixteen essays by the Antifederalist "Brutus" appeared in the *New York Journal;* then eighty-five numbers of "Publius," *The Federalist;* followed by an insightful Antifederalist pamphlet by "Federal Farmer"; and finally two smaller pamphlets published in April 1788 by "A Citizen of New York" and "A Plebeian." These essays are generally regarded, not only as the finest products of the "newspaper war" over the Constitution, but as enduring American contributions to political thought and constitutional law. That they all originated in the New York newspapers bespeaks the importance of those papers to the ratification controversy.

It is appropriate here to digress so that we may consider the question of authorship of these anonymous essays. Around 1900, Paul Leicester Ford, a prominent scholar of early American history, published two collections of eighteenth-century essays and pamphlets on the debate over the Constitution.[11] These compilations were valuable contributions to the literature, and they have been widely cited for almost 100 years. Ford's volumes, however, were not totally without fault. He went out of his way to identify the authors of various pseudonymous essays. According to Ford, Elbridge Gerry was "A Columbian Patriot," George Clinton was "Cato," Alexander Hamilton was "Caesar," Robert Yates was "Brutus," Melancton Smith was "Plebeian," and Richard Henry Lee was "Federal Farmer." Little or no evidence exists for any of these attributions; for over fifty years now, historians have been attacking some of them. For example, Charles Warren, not Elbridge Gerry, was "A Columbian Patriot."[12] Yet, at least half of the current references to "A Columbian Patriot" still cite Gerry as the author.

Linda Grant DePauw in *The Eleventh Pillar* disputed Clinton's authorship of "Cato," while Jacob Cooke in an article in the *William and Mary Quarterly* rejected the claim that Hamilton was "Caesar."[13] Morton Borden and William Jeffrey, Jr., rejected Robert Yates's authorship of the "Brutus" essays.[14]

By far the most controversial and long-lived debate over the authorship of a pseudonymous essay has centered around the *Letters from the Federal Farmer*—probably the single best Antifederalist statement during the entire ratification debate.

Thirty-five years ago, William W. Crosskey first questioned Richard Henry Lee's authorship, but he gave no corroborating evidence. Fifteen years ago, Gordon Wood substantiated his argument against Lee's authorship, but put forth no alternative author. Most scholars today have adopted Wood's position—Lee was not "Federal Farmer," but we do not know who was.[15]

In 1987, Robert H. Webking (University of Texas–El Paso), published an article in the *William and Mary Quarterly* attributing the essay to Melancton Smith.[16] Webking's entire thesis, however, rests and, I believe, falls upon one fact alone—that Melancton Smith in the New York Convention in June and July 1788 used many of the same arguments published by "Federal Farmer" eight months earlier.[17]

Webking maintains that only "Federal Farmer" and Smith make the same arguments—and that no other Antifederalists took the same position. This, however, is just not true. Webking relies on Herbert Storing's *The Complete Anti-Federalist* as his source of Antifederal literature, but recent scholarship suggests that *The Complete Anti-Federalist* might be about ninety percent incomplete.[18] Furthermore, even when Storing's volumes do contain similar Antifederalist arguments, Webking either ignores them or disputes their importance.

I would like to suggest a better condidate for the author of the *Letters from the Federal Farmer*. My best guess is that the author was Elbridge Gerry.

Elbridge Gerry left Philadelphia after the Constitutional Convention adjourned and arrived in New York City by September 20. While in New York, he conversed with other opponents of the new government—men such as Richard Henry Lee, Arthur Lee, and William Grayson of Virginia; Nathan Dane of Massachusetts; Abraham Clark of New Jersey; and Governor Clinton, John Lamb, Melancton Smith, Abraham Yates, Jr., and Samuel Jones of New York. Of all these men, it seems as if Gerry was the most likely to have been "Federal Farmer."

Gerry was one of the three delegates to the Constitutional Convention who had refused to endorse the proposed Constitution. As such he was expected, and he himself planned, to give the reasons for his actions. On October 18, Gerry wrote to his close friend James Warren, Speaker of the Massachusetts Assembly, stating that he was going to write a short letter to the Massachusetts legislature outlining his objections to the Constitution to be followed later by a lengthier address giving the reasons for his opposition.[19] Gerry wrote his short letter to the legislature on October 18, but his promised address never appeared. Possibly Gerry believed that he had fulfilled his obligation by anonymously publishing his reasons for opposing the Constitution.

An analysis of Gerry's letter to the Massachusetts legislature and the "Federal Farmer" letters indicates that the former was either a summary of or an outline for the latter.[20] All of the issues raised in the letter were developed in the pamphlet. Furthermore, the style, tone, and wording of the pieces are quite similar. For instance, on the first page of the pamphlet, "Federal Farmer" stated that the new Constitution retained "some federal features" but was "the first important step" toward a "consolidated government." Gerry, in his letter to the legislature, wrote that the proposed Constitution "has few, if any *federal* features. . . ." Despite his objections and his refusal to sign the Constitution, Gerry stated in his letter that he would support the Constitution if it were ratified; while the "Federal Farmer" wrote (much to the chagrin of some Antifederalists) that "every good citizen will acquiesce" to the new Constitution even if it were adopted without amendments. Melancton Smith was in no such frame of mind in the fall of 1787. New York Antifederalists were in a strong position, and Smith steadfastly maintained that ratification should not occur unless amendments were first accepted.

Other aspects of the "Federal Farmer" tend to confirm Gerry's authorship. All of the positions taken by "Federal Farmer," both in his first and second pamphlets, appear to be perfectly consistent with Gerry's stance in the Constitutional Convention; while several references by "Federal Farmer" indicate that he had information about what had transpired during the secret meetings of the Convention. On several occasions, "Federal Farmer" showed his sectional bias by favorably picturing New England, while characterizing the South as "a dissipated aristocracy." Numerous references to the state constitutions, particularly those of Massachusetts and New York, confirm Gerry's statement that the newly proposed federal Constitution was "neither consistent with the principles of the Revolution or of the constitutions of the several states."

If, indeed, Elbridge Gerry was the "Federal Farmer," it remains to be explained why he refused to disclose his identity. By the time the "Federal Farmer" letters were written, Gerry had already been severely censured for his role in the Constitutional Convention. Renewed attacks, even by Gerry's friends, surfaced when his letter to the legislature was published on November 3, 1787—about the time when the "Federal Farmer" pamphlet was published in New York. Obviously Gerry was not eager to open the door for further abuse by acknowledging his authorship. He and other Antifederalists already suspected that Federalists were tampering with their mail, and therefore no private disclosure of his authorship to his friends should be expected in Gerry's correspondence. Furthermore, Gerry himself, in his letter to Warren, stated that the authorship of anonymous pieces against the Constitution was "a Matter of no consequence to the public, the Sentiments are in many respects just."[21]

Finally, two New York incidents dealing with newspapers should be noted. With exclusively Federalist newspapers established in the Hudson River Valley, Antifederalist leaders in Albany realized the difficulties they faced in their effort to elect Antifederal delegates to the state convention. Consequently, they urged New York City Antifederalists to assist them in establishing an Antifederalist printer in the Albany area. On January 31, 1788, Abraham G. Lansing, the coordinator of Antifederalist activities in the Albany area, wrote New York Congressman Abraham Yates, Jr., that the printers of the Lansingburgh *Northern Centinel* planned to move their newspaper to Albany and change its name to the *Federal Herald*. Lansing did not wish them well, hoping that "they will return to their original Insignificance."[22]

Charles R. Webster and his brother, George, were already printing the *Albany Journal* twice a week, and Charles Webster alone printed the *Albany Gazette* with a circulation of almost 800 in Albany, Montgomery, Clinton, and Columbia counties as well as in the principal towns of New Hampshire and Vermont. Lansing told Yates, "It is the sincere wish of our Friends that some Person would set himself down here and disconcert these White Livers by publishing an impartial paper." Perhaps, he suggested, fellow New York City Antifederalist Melancton Smith could prevail upon Thomas Greenleaf, printer of the ardently Antifederal *New York Journal* "to send one of his Journeymen to set up a printing office here." Such an establishment "would meet with Encouragement."

This initial proposal lay fallow for a month. Finally, on March 1, Abraham Lansing, his brother John, the former delegate to the Constitutional Convention, Jeremiah Van Rensselaer, and four other members of the Albany Antifederalist Society wrote to Melancton Smith about the need to establish an Antifederal newspaper in upstate New York.[23] "We daily experience Inconveniences," they wrote, "from the partiality of the printers in this part of the State whose papers are constantly filled with pieces in Favor of the new Constitution and whenever any are inserted against it, which is always done with Reluctance, they are accompanied with others to counteract their Effects." Serious consequences were expected from this biased policy as "the people are prevented from forming a proper Judgment on the occasion."

To solve the problem, the committee reasserted "the utmost Importance to have an impartial printer" in Albany. They promised 200 subscribers in the Albany area with assurances that more subscriptions would come in from other counties. Abraham and John Lansing, as well as Peter W. Yates, all promised to subscribe for six issues of the newspaper.

The Albany committee pleaded with Smith to send a printer "up without Delay with his press." Albany Antifederalists would, if necessary, "advance him a sum of Money on account, immediately on his arrival." They proposed to call the new newspaper the *Albany Register.*

Secrecy was important in this endeavor. If upstate newspaper printers got wind of the attempt to establish an Antifederal competitor in
Albany, they might refuse to publish any items against the new Constitution. The committee begged Smith to respond "as early as possible."

On March 2, Abraham Lansing again wrote to Abraham Yates enclosing a copy of the Albany committee's letter to Melancton Smith.[24]
Lansing told Yates that "Our Friends here are . . . exasperated against"
Charles Webster and they are "under such apprehension that he will
deceive us when his services should be most wanted."

On March 23 Abraham Lansing received a letter from John Lamb,
chairman of the New York City Republican Society—a group heavily
involved in distributing Antifederalist literature throughout the state and
New England. Lamb's letter, dated March 9, was not encouraging.[25] The
delay in hearing from their New York City allies convinced Albany Antifederalists to seek out a printer directly. On March 23, the Lansing
brothers responded to the letter they had just received from Lamb.[26]
"Despairing of receiving any Aid from New York we have made explicit
Arrangements here which we have every Reason to suppose will answer
our purpose. We therefore wish you not to persist in engaging the
printer."

Albany Antifederalists had procured Robert Barber, a former
journeyman printer with Charles Webster. Antifederalist leaders in the
Albany area then sent letters to prospective subscribers throughout the
upper Hudson River Valley.

Albany Antifederalists had hoped that Barber could begin publishing the *Albany Register* by the 1st of September, but on September 1,
Barber travelled south to New York City to buy a printing press, type,
and the other items needed to publish a newspaper. The first issue of
the *Register* did not appear until October, two months after the state
had ratified the Constitution.

The most serious incident involving newspapers in the entire country
occurred in New York City. Throughout the ratification debate, Antifederalist printer Thomas Greenleaf's *New York Journal* had been a
thorn in the Federalists' side. Federalist leaders, though, realized that
any attack on Greenleaf before New York's ratification would be interpreted as an attack on freedom of the press. Consequently, Greenleaf
was allowed to continue unmolested.

According to some Federalists, Greenleaf's scurrility reached its
height on July 24, 1788, when he ridiculed the Federalist procession held
the preceding day in New York City. Federalists, however, did nothing
to Greenleaf because the state convention was still meeting in Poughkeepsie and the fate of the Constitution, perhaps the fate of the country,

hung in the balance. Two days later, however, at 9:00 P.M., news arrived in New York City that the convention had ratified the Constitution. Joy and relief filled the air as bells tolled and cannon boomed until midnight.

With the stroke of the clock, a Federalist mob spontaneously formed with the intention of attacking Greenleaf's home, which also housed his print shop. Between one and three A.M., 500 men gathered at the printer's house. Awakened by the noise, Greenleaf armed himself with two pistols, threw open a window, and asked, "Gentlemen, what do you want?" The leader of the mob shouted, "God damn him, break down the door—by God down with it." Then followed a shower of rocks upon the house. Greenleaf, again at the window, vowed to protect his property, warning his assailants, "Gentlemen, I am armed." At that point, four men charged the door, while others smashed the windows. Greenleaf fired into the mob, wounding a sailor in the left hand. The shot only infuriated the mob, which had by this time procured axes that were being used to tear down the door. Greenleaf then fired point-blank at one of the axe-wielding rioters, but the pistol flashed in the pan, thus probably saving the life of one assailant, and perhaps indirectly saving Greenleaf's life.

The mob, sensing that Greenleaf was out of ammunition, advanced and broke into the house. Having no further defense, Greenleaf escaped through the rear of the building. The intruders entered the print shop, destroyed much of the type, and carried off other material.

The mob, finishing at Greenleaf's, marched on to the homes of Governor Clinton and John Lamb. In both cases, the mob played the rogue's march, but no violence occurred.[27]

Federalists and Antifederalists naturally viewed the attack on Greenleaf differently. Federalists, while openly condemning the violence, claimed that Greenleaf himself was the instigator. The virulence of the *New York Journal* had so incensed the public that vengeance was inevitable. Antifederalists, however, pictured the attack as another step in their opponents' plan of repression. Greenleaf himself stated that he had repeatedly received threats against his life and property. He believed that the July 27th attack was not motivated by his satirical report of the federal procession three days earlier; rather, the sacking was planned by Federalist leaders with the intention of destroying "the usefulness of his paper." Other Antifederalists agreed with Greenleaf's assessment. Eleazer Oswald in Philadelphia asked for deliverance from God "If these be *the dawnings* of the new federal government."[28]

Why, then, did Federalists, after achieving their unexpected victory in Poughkeepsie, find it necessary to resort to violence? Was it, as their leaders suggested, the vengeance of the people finally let loose, or was there a more insidious purpose?

New York's ratification of the Constitution was achieved at a tremendous cost. Federalists, outnumbered in the state convention by over two to one, were forced to acquiesce in a circular letter to the states that called for a second constitutional convention, which was to draft amendments to the proposed Constitution. New York Federalists, therefore, had won only a partial victory—some Federalists both in and out of the state believed it a Pyrrhic victory.

In the anticipated struggle over a second convention and amendments, Federalists used the mob to intimidate Greenleaf in an effort to neutralize his press. In this effort, Federalists were abundantly successful. Even though Greenleaf declared that he would not be intimidated, the *New York Journal* was cut back from a daily to a weekly, and Greenleaf's editorial policies moderated noticeably. By taking these drastic measures against Greenleaf, Federalists demonstrated that the Antifederalist press in New York had been abundantly successful in persuading readers throughout the state that the new Constitution needed amending before it could be considered safe. Newspapers had, in fact, played a major role in the ratification debate.[29]

NOTES

[1]Hamilton to Rush, November 21, 1787, Harold C. Syrett, ed., *The Papers of Alexander Hamilton* (New York, 1962), 4:832–33.

[2]*Massachusetts Centinel*, June 30, 1787, in John P. Kaminski and Gaspare J. Saladino, eds., *Commentaries on the Constitution: Public and Private* (Madison, Wis., 1981), 1:148–49. The five-volume set of *Commentaries* is part of *The Documentary History of the Ratification of the Constitution* edited by Merrill Jensen, John P. Kaminski, and Gaspare J. Saladino and published by the State Historical Society of Wisconsin.

[3]*Pennsylvania Herald*, June 20, 1787, *Commentaries*, 1:35

[4]Humphreys to Washington, September 28, 1787, *Commentaries*, 1:261–62.

[5]Knox to Lafayette, October 24, 1787, *Commentaries*, 1:441–42.

[6]*Albany Federal Herald*, March 31, 1788. The printers had moved to Albany and changed the name of their newspaper.

[7]*New York Daily Advertiser*, February 23, March 24, and April 2, *Commentaries*, 1:54–59.

[8]*New York Daily Advertiser*, June 8, *Commentaries*, 1:128–30.

[9]*Observations on the Articles of Confederation* . . ., July 27, 1787, *Commentaries*, 1:180–81.

[10]For Hamilton's attack on Clinton and "A Republican's" response, see *Commentaries*, 1:136–40.

[11]*Pamphlets on the Constitution of the United States* . . . (Brooklyn, N.Y., 1888) and *Essays on the Constitution of the United States* . . . (Brooklyn, N.Y., 1892).

[12]Charles Warren, "Elbridge Gerry, James Warren, Mercy Warren and the Ratification of the Federal Constitution," *Massachusetts Historical Society Proceedings* 54 (1930–32):142–64.

[13]DePauw, *The Eleventh Pillar: New York State and the Federal Constitution* (Ithaca, N.Y., 1966), 283–92; and Cooke, "Alexander Hamilton's Authorship of the 'Caesar' Letters," *William and Mary Quarterly*, 3rd ser., 17 (1960):78–85.

[14]Morton Borden, ed., *The Antifederalist Papers* (East Lansing, Mich., 1965), 42. Borden bases his rejection of Robert Yates as the author on an incorrect premise that Yates's "Sydney" essays are obviously inferior to "Brutus." The "Sydney" essays, however, were written by Abraham Yates, Jr. William Jeffrey, Jr., "The Letters of 'Brutus'— a Neglected Element in the Ratification Campaign of 1787-1788," *University of Cincinnati Law Review* 40 (1971):644–46.

[15]For a summary of this debate, see *Commentaries* (Madison, Wis., 1983), 3:14–18.

[16]Robert H. Webking, "Melancton Smith and the *Letters from the Federal Farmer*," *William and Mary Quarterly*, 3rd ser., 44 (1987):510–28.

[17]This is an important point. Many Antifederalists used the "Federal Farmer's" arguments because he was widely accepted as the most logical of the Antifederal essayists. What must be done, however, to establish any credence of authorship is to show that the private and public statements of a person expressed before the publication of the "Federal Farmer" pamphlet coincide with the ideas expressed in the pamphlet.

[18]Herbert J. Storing, ed., *The Complete Anti-Federalist* (7 vols., Chicago, 1981).

[19]*Commentaries*, 1:407.

[20]For Gerry's letter to the Massachusetts legislature, see *Commentaries*, 1:546–50. For "Federal Farmer's" pamphlets, see *Commentaries*, 3:14–54; and *Commentaries*, 5 (1990).

[21]Gerry to Warren, October 18, *Commentaries*, 1:407.

[22]Lansing to Yates, January 31, 1788, Yates Papers, New York Public Library.

[23]Lansing et al. to Smith, March 1, 1788, *ibid*.

[24]Lansing to Yates, March 2, 1788, *ibid*.

[25]Lamb's letter of March 9, 1788, has not been found.

[26]Lansing and Lansing to Lamb, March 23, 1788, Lamb Papers, The New-York Historical Society.

[27]*New York Journal*, August 7, 1788.

[28]*Independent Gazetteer*, July 30, 1788.

[29]See also, on this subject, John T. Alexander, *The Selling of the Constitutional Convention: A Study in News Management* (Madison, Wis., 1990).

Newspapers and Magazines of New York State

(1787–1788)

GASPARE J. SALADINO
University of Wisconsin–Madison

CITY OF ALBANY

The Federal Herald
February 11–April 14, 1788
Moved from Lansingburgh where it had been *The Northern Centinel, and Lansingburgh Advertiser.* Moved back to Lansingburgh after the issue of April 14, 1788. *Type:* Weekly (Monday). *Owners:* Thomas Claxton and John Babcock until April 7, 1788. John Babcock after that date. *Office:* No. 47, State Street. *Motto:* The Press is the Cradle of Science, the Nurse of Genius, and the Shield of Liberty. *Price:* Probably $1.25 per annum (see Lansingburgh *Northern Centinel* below). *Party:* Federalist.

The Albany Gazette
Type: Weekly (Thursday). *Owner:* Charles R. Webster. *Office:* No. 36, State Street (on the north side), near the English Church. *Motto:* Open to All Parties (until August 1788). *Price:* $1.50 per annum. This newspaper was issued in conjunction with *The Albany Journal* (see below), and, if both newspapers were taken, the cost for both was $2.25 per annum. *Party:* Federalist.

The Albany Journal: or, The Montgomery, Washington and Columbia Intelligencer
Established January 26, 1788
Type: Semi-weekly (Monday and Saturday) until March 31, 1788; weekly (Monday) with the issue of March 31. *Owners:* Charles R. Webster and

George Webster. *Office:* No. 36, State Street (on the north side), near the English Church. *Price:* $1.50 per annum. This newspaper was issued in conjunction with *The Albany Gazette* (see above), and, if both newspapers were taken, the cost was $2.25 per annum. *Party:* Federalist.

The Albany Register

Established October 1788

Type: Weekly (Monday). *Owner:* Robert Barber. *Office:* Maiden Lane, four doors west of the Market. *Price:* $1.50 per annum. *Party:* Antifederalist.

HUDSON, COLUMBIA COUNTY

The Hudson Weekly Gazette

Type: Weekly (Thursday; with the issue of April 15, 1788, Tuesday). *Owner:* Ashbel Stoddard. *Office:* Near the City Hall; after January 3, 1788, corner of Main and Third Streets. *Party:* Federalist.

LANSINGBURGH, THEN ALBANY COUNTY

The Federal Herald

Moved from Albany after issue of April 14, 1788. First issue printed in Lansingburgh was that of April 28. *Type:* Weekly (Monday). *Owners:* John Babcock and Ezra Hickok. *Office:* King and Hoosack Streets. *Motto:* The Press is the Cradle of Science, the Nurse of Genius, and the Shield of Liberty. *Price:* Probably $1.25 per annum (see *Northern Centinel* below). *Party:* Federalist.

The Northern Centinel, and Lansingburgh Advertiser

May 21, 1787–January 15, 1788

Until the issue of October 15, Lansingburgh in the title was spelled (Lansingborough). Moved to Albany and was established as *The Federal Herald* with the issue of February 11, 1788 (see above). *Type:* Weekly (Monday; with issue of November 13, 1787, Tuesday). *Owners:* Thomas Claxton and John Babcock. *Office:* King Street, between Hoosack and South Streets; with the issue of September 10, 1787, corner of King and North Streets. *Motto:* The Press is the Cradle of Science, the Nurse of Genius, and the Shield of Liberty. *Price:* $1.25 per annum (accepts country produce as well as cash). *Party:* Federalist.

NEW YORK CITY

The American Magazine ...

December 1787–November 1788

Type: Monthly (issued the first day of each month). *Owner:* Noah Webster. *Printer:* Samuel Loudon; with the issue of March 1788, Samuel and John Loudon. *Office:* No. 5, Water Street, between the Coffee House and the Old Slip. *Motto:* Science the guide, and truth the eternal good. *Price:* $.25 per issue; $1.25 for six months; and $2.50 per annum. *Party:* Federalist.

The Daily Advertiser: Political, Historical, and Commercial
(After October 17, 1787, *The Daily Advertiser.*)
Type: Daily (except Sunday). *Owner:* Francis Childs. *Office:* The New Printing Office, near the Coffee House; with the issue of May 1, 1787, New Printing Office, No. 22, Hanover Square; and with issue of May 1, 1788, No. 190, Water Street, corner of King Street. *Motto:* The Noblest Motive is the Public Good (dropped with the issue of October 17, 1787). *Price:* 4 pence per issue; $6.00 per annum. *Party:* Federalist.

The New-York Gazetteer; and, Public Advertiser
(Last known issue was that of August 16, 1787.)
Type: Semi-weekly (Monday and Thursday). *Owners:* George Carroll and John Patterson; with the issue of May 7, 1787, John Patterson. *Office:* No. 32, Maiden Lane; with the issue of March 8, 1787, No. 16, Water Street, below the Coffee House, the opposite side. *Price:* $3.00 per annum. *Party:* Unknown.

The Impartial Gazetteer, and Saturday Evening's Post
Established May 17, 1788
Name changed to *The Impartial Gazetteer* on August 9, 1788; and changed again on August 16 to *The Impartial Gazetteer, and Saturday Evening Post*. Became *The New-York Weekly Museum* after September 13, 1788 (see below). *Type:* Weekly (Saturday, 5:00 P.M.). *Owners:* John Harrisson and Stephen Purdy, Jr. *Office:* No. 3, Peck's Slip. *Price:* $1.25 per annum. *Party:* Unknown.

The Independent Journal: or, The General Advertiser
(With the issue of December 29, 1788 it became *The New-York Daily Gazette.*) *Type:* Semi-weekly (Wednesday and Saturday). *Owners:* John M'Lean; with the issue of July 2, 1788 John and Archibald M'Lean. *Office:* No. 231, Queen Street; with the issue of May 2, 1788, No. 41, Hanover Square; and with the issue of June 18, 1788, Franklin's Head, No. 41, Hanover Square. *Party:* Federalist.

The New-York Journal, and Weekly Register
On November 19, 1787 it became *The New-York Journal, and Daily Patriotic Register* (the Thursday paper for country subscribers remained

The New-York Journal, and Weekly Register). When it became a weekly again with the issue of July 31, 1788, it assumed its original title. *Type:* Weekly (Thursday, through November 15, 1787); daily (except Sunday) with issue of November 19, 1787 (a weekly edition published on Thursday for country subscribers). It became a weekly (Thursday) again with issue of July 31, 1788. *Owners:* Thomas Greenleaf (with issue of January 18, 1787). *Office:* No. 25, Water Street, four doors from the Old Coffee House. *Motto:* Here Truth Unlicens'd reigns; and dares accost e'en Kings themselves, or Rulers of the Free! [James Thomson, *Liberty*, Part I, "Ancient and Modern Italy Compared" (London: 1734–1735), lines 365–366.] *Price:* $2.00 per annum for the weekly; and $6.00 per annum for the daily. *Party:* Antifederalist.

The New-York Morning Post, and Daily Advertiser
Changed on October 6, 1788 to *The Morning Post, and Daily Advertiser.* *Type:* Daily (except Sunday). *Owner:* William Morton. *Office:* No. 22, Water Street, opposite the Coffee House; early in May 1788, No. 231, Queen Street. *Price:* 4 pence per issue; 6 pence per issue after mid-June 1787. *Party:* Neutral. (But leaned toward Antifederalist.)

The New-York Museum
Established May 23, 1788
Type: Semi-weekly (Tuesday and Friday). *Owner:* John Russell. *Office:* No. 84, Water Street, near Peck's Slip. *Motto:* Multum in Parvo [Much in little; a great deal in a small compass]. *Price:* $2.50 per annum. *Party:* Unknown.

The New-York Packet
Type: Semi-weekly (Tuesday and Friday). *Owners:* Samuel and John Loudon. *Office:* No. 5, Water Street, between the Coffee-House and the Old Slip. *Motto: Tros Tyriusque Nobis Nullo Discrimine Agetur. Virg.* [I shall act impartially toward all, Virgil, *The Aeneid*, I, 574]. *Price:* One paper, $2.00 per annum; two papers, $3.00 per annum. *Party:* Federalist.

The New-York Weekly Museum
Established September 20, 1788 as a continuation of *The Impartial Gazetteer*, see above.
Type: Weekly (Saturday). *Owners:* John Harrisson and Stephen Purdy, Jr. *Office:* No. 3, Peck's Slip. *Price:* $1.25 per annum. *Party:* Unknown.

POUGHKEEPSIE, DUTCHESS COUNTY

The Country Journal, and the Poughkeepsie Advertiser
(With the issue of September 30, 1788 the title was changed to *The Country Journal, and Dutchess and Ulster County Farmer's Register*).
Type: Weekly (Wednesday; after January 22, 1788, Tuesday). *Owner:* Nicholas Power. *Office:* Next door to the tavern of Mr. Thomas Poole, and nearly opposite the tavern of Captain Stephen Hendrickson, a few rods south of the Court House. *Motto:* In my Free Page let different Works reside, / Tho' Party's hostile Lines those Works divide; / Party! Whose murdering Spirit I abhor / More subtly cruel, and less brave than war. [With the issue of September 30, 1788, the following became a second motto: "Venerate the Plough."] *Price:* $1.50 per annum (takes produce in payment). *Party:* Federalist.

EXPLANATORY NOTE

The newspapers and the one magazine listed above were published at some time between February 21, 1787—the day the Confederation Congress asked the states to appoint delegates to the Constitutional Convention—and July 26, 1788—the day that the New York Convention ratified the Constitution. Also included is *The Albany Register* which began publication in October 1788, but which Albany Antifederalists had tried to establish in February and March 1788.

The standard bibliography for newspapers is Clarence S. Brigham's *History and Bibliography of American Newspapers, 1690–1820* (2 vols., Worcester, Mass., 1947). A supplement to this work is in the *Proceedings* of the American Antiquarian Society, LXXI, Part I (1961), 15–62. The researcher should also examine Paul Mercer, *Bibliographies and Lists of New York State Newspapers: An Annotated Guide* (Albany, 1981); Edward Connery Lathem, comp., *Chronological Tables of American Newspapers, 1690–1820: Being a Tabular Guide to the Holdings of Newspapers Published in America Through the Year 1820* (Barre, Mass., 1972); and Library of Congress Catalogs, *Newspapers on Microfilm, United States, 1948–1983* (2 vols., Washington, D.C., 1984). The Readex Corporation has put eighteenth-century American newspapers on either microcard or microfilm. Catalogs may be obtained from the company itself.

Pseudonyms Used in the Newspaper Debate over the Ratification of the United States Constitution in the State of New York, September 1787–July 1788

GASPARE J. SALADINO
University of Wisconsin–Madison

Introduction

The debate over the ratification of the Constitution during the years 1787 and 1788 precipitated an avalanche of the finest and most prolific political writing in American history. The Constitution was debated at every level, but most particularly in newspapers, pamphlets, and broadsides. This was not the first time that Americans had resorted to these vehicles in such large measure to express their political opinions; they had done so in their struggle against British imperial rule before 1776. That debate set the stage for the debate over the Constitution.

The state of New York was one of the three great centers of the debate on the Constitution—the other two being the states of Massachusetts and Pennsylvania. Most important, these three states had the largest numbers of newspapers. At one time or another, from September 17, 1787 to July 26, 1788, thirteen newspapers and one magazine were published in the state of New York. These fourteen publications printed some of the most influential pieces for and against the Constitution that appeared anywhere in the United States. In most instances, writers of articles signed themselves with pseudonyms, a time-honored practice that probably reached its peak during the debate over the Constitution. According to Douglass Adair, pseudonyms were the "norm" during the years of the American Revolution and the early Republic.

The pseudonyms in this list were selected from articles that, for the most part, discuss the provisions and purposes of the Constitution at some length, or that relate to essays that did. Those used in the campaign for the election of state ratifying convention delegates do not appear here unless the articles also include a substantial discussion of the Constitution. The newspaper articles are in the files of *The Documentary History of the Ratification of the Constitution,* Department of History, the University of Wisconsin–Madison, or in some of the eight volumes already published by that project.

Almost every one of the writers sheltered by a pseudonym expressed his views on the Constitution strongly. In this list, supporters of the Constitution have been labeled "Federalists," opponents, "Antifederalists." These labels are commonly used by present-day students of the debate over the ratification of the Constitution. In the eighteenth century, however, these terms had different meanings. The "Antifederalists" of the ratification debate did not apply that term to themselves; it was fastened to them by the advocates of the Constitution. These advocates wanted to portray themselves as "federalists," not "nationalists" (proponents of a powerful central government), a more apropos label. "Antifederalists" believed themselves to be the true "federalists," those who wanted to divide the powers of government between the states and the central government, with the scales tipped in favor of the former. "Antifederalists" considered the government under the Articles of Confederation to be "federal" in structure. Those writers who did not take sides in their articles have been described as "impartial," rather than "neutral." The Constitution was too important an issue for anyone to remain truly neutral.

Pseudonyms were employed for a variety of reasons. The freedom of the press had not yet become firmly established. Some writers evidently wanted to cloak their identities because politics were sometimes rough and tumble and highly personal. Duelling was still fairly common. For example, the fiery Antifederalist newspaper publisher, Eleazer Oswald of Philadelphia, seemed to be constantly on the verge of fighting duels. Other writers probably wanted to wait for the most opportune political moment before they went public. On the other hand, some authors chose pseudonyms that they had used before, or sobriquets by which they were known so that their readers would readily recognize them. Occasionally, the language that they employed plainly identified the writers. Pseudonyms were intended to express a particular point of view; readers were expected to know exactly where writers stood simply by the pseudonyms. Some pseudonyms, however, such as **Cato**, had such a powerful and positive image that both sides used them.

Many of the pseudonyms, used by both Federalists and Antifederalists, came from the classical world, or were based upon the Greek and Latin languages. According to Richard M. Gummere, the years 1787 and 1788 marked "a time when the influence of the classics was at its height" in America. The study of Greek and Latin, he said, peaked by 1789. Meyer Reinhold, another classicist, wrote that a "cult of antiquity" flourished in eighteenth-century America; he described these years as the "golden age of the classical tradition in America." The resort to classical pseudonyms was just one of the many manifestations of the "cult of antiquity." People in many walks of life used the classics as their authority, as a means of guiding their lives; the study of the classics was one of the principal roads taken in the pursuit of "civic virtue." At no time in American history have people more consciously mimicked the ancients.

Many of the pseudonyms, used by both Federalists and Antifederalists, came from the classical world, or were based upon the Greek Federalists and Antifederalists sought to portray themselves as republicans; failure to do so would have been courting political disaster. So strong was this feeling that one Antifederalist, **Sidney**, even took his pseudonym from Algernon Sidney, a leading and martyred player in the failed republican movement of seventeenth-century England.

Federalists also employed *noms de plume* that had a distinctly nationalistic or patriotic flavor; these choices emphasized the nation—America. On the other hand, Antifederalists chose pseudonyms that were localist, that were associated with the state of New York. A number of pseudonyms denoted the occupations of authors, or the groups to which they were appealing. This was especially true of the frequent use by Antifederalists of such terms as "countryman" and "farmer." This homespun quality was clearly one that Antifederalist writers tried to project; the simple folk, particularly the sturdy yeoman farmers, were the principal supporters of the Antifederalist cause. Federalists, however, keenly aware of the importance of shaping public opinion, did not allow Antifederalists to monopolize either these pseudonyms or those that were localist in tone. Both sides also battled over the use of the term "federalist." Bluntly put, they pulled few punches; the stakes were too high.

To discover the meanings and origins of the pseudonyms, biographical and classical dictionaries, foreign- and English-language dictionaries, encyclopedias, bibliographies, documentary collections, histories, biographies, and historical monographs were consulted. Most important were the classical and biographical dictionaries, though at times they differed on even the most essential facts. These dictionaries were supplemented by a number of Latin and English dictionaries. The most informative English ones were Dr. Samuel Johnson's *A Dictionary of the English Language* (first printed in 1755) and the multivolume, unabridged *Oxford English Dictionary*. Also useful were dictionaries on the origins and meanings of first names and reference works on eighteenth-century English literature. Monographs on political and classical thought provided the historical context that made the search more meaningful. The selected bibliography at the end lists the works that were most helpful. Lastly, Frank M. Clover, Professor of Ancient History at the University of Wisconsin–Madison, graciously answered questions on a variety of subjects.

Alexander the Great (Antifederalist)

This item, published in the Poughkeepsie *Country Journal* on April 22, 1788, was an Antifederalist satire regarding the Federalist argument that encouraged people to support the Constitution because it was drafted and advocated by great men. The writer saw no reason why he, too, should not use a "pompous" pseudonym, like those employed by Federalist writers.

America (Federalist)

This article was written by Noah Webster, the editor of the New York *American Magazine*, and printed in the New York *Daily Advertiser* on December 31, 1787. It was an answer to the "Dissent of the Minority of the Pennsylvania Convention"—a document that explained why the minority had voted against ratification of the Constitution on December 12. (This document had been reprinted in three New York City newspapers before **America** answered it.) **America** attacked the dissenters for trying to disturb the peace of the United States, and he made a strong plea for "our Federal Union." Webster was also **Giles Hickory** (below). (See also **A Citizen of America**, below.)

The pseudonym, **America**, clearly appealed to a sense of national feeling, rather than pride in and identification with a single state. When

Webster established his *American Magazine* in December 1787, he intended that it be a national magazine; articles were to be cast in a decidedly nationalistic tone.

An American (Federalist)

This essay was published in the *New York Packet* on May 27, 1788, about a week before the convening of the New York ratifying convention. It urged New York to remain in the Union because it would benefit economically. (See **America**, above, for the meaning of this pseudonym.)

Americanus (Federalist)

This series of seven essays was printed in the New York *Daily Advertiser* between November 2, 1787 and January 21, 1788. Written by John Stevens, Jr., of New Jersey, five of these articles criticized **Cato** (below), while the others attacked the "Dissent of the Minority of the Pennsylvania Convention" (see **America**) and the October 10, 1787 letter of Virginia Governor Edmund Randolph to the Speaker of the Virginia House of Delegates in which he explained why he had not signed the Constitution as a member of the Constitutional Convention. (Like the "Dissent," Randolph's letter had been reprinted in New York City just before **Americanus** replied to it.) **Americanus** scored Antifederalists for their "blind attachment to a party, or to the local interests of a narrow district." Unlike **Cato**, he believed that a republic could exist over a large territory like the thirteen states. **Americanus** obviously considered himself a citizen or resident of America, not just a single state.

A Baptist (Antifederalist)

This item, printed in the *New York Journal* on November 30, 1787, criticized the Baptist churches belonging to the Philadelphia Baptist Association for supporting the Constitution which did not guarantee the freedom of religion. The Association consisted of churches from the middle states, including New York.

Brutus (Antifederalist)

This series of sixteen essays was printed in the *New York Journal* between October 18, 1787 and April 10, 1788. The authorship of these essays has not been determined. Among those seriously suggested as authors are Melancton Smith, Thomas Tredwell, Abraham Yates, Jr., and Robert Yates. These articles, along with the pamphlets of the **Federal Farmer** (below), are among the finest expressions of Antifederalist thought printed anywhere in the United States. In particular, **Brutus** believed that the Constitution destroyed the sovereignty of the states and that a bill of rights was needed to protect the rights and liberties of the people. He was also a defender of republican government which, he believed, the Constitution endangered. *The Federalist* by **Publius** (below) was, in part, initiated as a response to **Brutus**.

The pseudonym was probably a reference to Marcus Junius Brutus, a leader of the conspiracy against Julius Caesar that resulted in Caesar's assassination, in the hope of restoring the republic. Brutus, a firm republican, is said to have acted out of patriotic reasons in opposition to the dictatorship of Caesar. He was also known for his moral earnestness and independence. Brutus' second wife was Porcia, the daughter of Cato the Younger. She inherited her father's firm republican principles, and she knew beforehand of the plot against Caesar. (See **Cato** and **Caesar**, both below.)

Another possibility is Lucius Junius Brutus, a founder of the Roman Republic who was consul in 509 B.C., after he helped to destroy the monarchy of Tarquin, the last king of Rome. Brutus loved the Republic so much that he put his two sons to death because they conspired to restore the Tarquins. He died fighting to retain the Republic.

Brutus, Junior (Antifederalist)

This article was published in the *New York Journal* on November 8, 1787. **Brutus, Junior,** sought to answer those Federalist arguments that had not been answered by, among others, **Brutus** (above). The identity of **Brutus, Junior,** has not been determined, but passages and references from his essay resemble some found in the **Federal Farmer's** first pamphlet (below).

Caesar (Federalist)

Two articles signed **Caesar,** in answer to **Cato** (below), were published in the New York *Daily Advertiser* on October 1 and 17, 1787. These essays have long been ascribed to Alexander Hamilton, but the editors of *The Papers of Alexander Hamilton*, among others, have questioned this attribution.

The reference is to Caius Julius Caesar whom Cato the Younger had so long resisted; the author of these essays made that clear in his first one. There has been much historical controversy over Caesar's true role and nature. The author of the **Caesar** essays obviously had Plutarch's Caesar as his model. Plutarch's Caesar, according to Douglass Adair, was a man of genius who sought absolute power and who wanted to be the greatest man in Rome. He was an honorable man, a man brave in battle, a man who yearned for distinction. Caesar passionately believed that he was born to accomplish great things. He disdained money-making, but he distributed his wealth effectively among his followers. Adair says that Alexander Hamilton admired these qualities in Caesar and considered him "the greatest man that ever lived."

Caesar was a man of extraordinary achievements. In the fifth decade B.C., he defeated Pompey and his followers (among them Cato the Younger) in a bitter civil war and became dictator of Rome. In this position, Caesar unified the Roman Empire after a century of strife and worked for the benefit of Rome and the Empire. He was a lawgiver and an advocate of good government and economic development. He established libraries, passed agrarian laws, improved housing, built aqueducts, drained marshes, enlarged harbors, and dug canals. He also secured the boundaries of the empire, pacified the provinces, and formed commercial colonies. In 44 B.C., a group of conspirators, disgusted with Caesar's increasing power, assassinated him, hoping to restore the Republic.

Caledonia (Antifederalist)

This item was printed in the *New York Journal* on April 22 and 25, 1788. Caledonia is the Latin name for Scotland. The article argued against ratification of the Constitution by describing the disadvantages to Scotland when it joined with England in 1707 to form Great Britain. In short, the Constitution would establish a consolidated government to the detriment of the states.

Cato (Antifederalist and Federalist)

This series of seven articles was printed in the *New York Journal* between September 27, 1787 and January 3, 1788. **Cato** was among the first major attacks upon the Constitution printed in the United States. Federalists attributed the articles to New York Governor George Clinton, a major Antifederalist leader. This attribution, long accepted by historians, has been challenged in recent years by some scholars. **Cato** was a strong advocate of a bill of rights and a defender of republican government, endangered, he believed, by the Constitution. In particular, he thought that a republic could not exist over a large territory.

This pseudonym was probably taken from Marcus Porcius Cato Uticensis (Cato the Younger), a longtime opponent of Caius Julius Caesar (above) and a supporter of republican principles. (Uticensis means of or belonging to the city of Utica.) His opposition to Caesar came to a head in the fifth decade B.C., when he joined forces with Pompey against Caesar. After Pompey's death, Cato fled with his army to the city of Utica in Africa, where he was pursued by Caesar. Facing certain defeat in 46 B.C., he committed suicide. Before he died, however, Cato asked his followers to make peace with Caesar. The great orator, Cicero, defended him in a pamphlet. Caesar replied in a pamphlet entitled *Anticato*, but overstated his case and made Cato a martyr. Cato became the rallying cry for republicans, and in some historical works, he came to personify godlike virtue.

The pseudonym was first used by English radical Whigs, John Trenchard and Thomas Gordon, who published 138 essays between 1720 and 1723, mostly attacking the policies of the ministers of George I. Among other things, the essays discussed the nature of virtue, the values of political liberty, the justice of tyrannicide, the evils of tyranny, and the essential nature of the freedom of the press and religion. The essays were widely read and reprinted in colonial America. Americans cited **Cato** most often on matters concerning the freedom of the press and religion, the evils of standing armies in peacetime, and the nature of the British empire. Bernard Bailyn says that the letters were quoted so often that they gave rise to a "Catonic image" that was central to the political theory of colonial America.

This pseudonym was also used by a Federalist writer (or writers) who published items in the Poughkeepsie *Country Journal* on December 12 and 19, 1787 (supplement) and July 8, 1788. In the article of July 8, **Cato** called upon the opponents of the Constitution to accept it and to put aside the idea of a civil war similar to the conspiracy of Catiline against the consuls of Rome. Cato was an opponent of Catiline and voted for his execution, as well as for the execution of the other conspirators. Catiline died in battle in 62 B.C.

That both sides could adopt **Cato** as a pseudonym is perhaps best illustrated by an event in English history—the performance and publication of Joseph Addison's play, *Cato, A Tragedy* in 1713. English Whigs and Tories both claimed *Cato* and its lofty phrases about liberty. Addison portrayed Cato as a public man of the highest moral character and personal honor who emphasized the role of liberty and religion. Even Trenchard and Gordon were probably influenced in their choice of the pseudonym because of the enormous popularity of Addison's play. In America, this play was performed as early as 1736, and its popularity peaked in the 1760s and 1770s. In 1778, it was performed at Valley Forge before General George Washington, who greatly admired Cato the Younger. Washington hoped that the play would be a morale booster. By 1800, at least eight editions of *Cato* were printed in the United States.

Cincinnatus (Antifederalist and Federalist)

This series of six Antifederalist essays, printed in the *New York Journal* between November 1 and December 6, 1787, was written by Arthur Lee of Virginia, a revolutionary patriot who was stationed, at this time, in New York City as a member of the Confederation Board of Treasury. The essays were addressed to James Wilson, Esq., of Pennsylvania and were political, philosophical, and personal responses to his speech of October 6 to a public meeting in Philadelphia. Wilson's speech, the most influential Federalist statement on the principles of the Constitution, had been reprinted in New York.

The pseudonym is probably taken from Lucius Quinctius Cincinnatus who lived in the fifth century B.C. The consul Minucius' forces had been surrounded by the Aequians and Volscians, and Cincinnatus was called upon to serve as dictator and to rescue Minucius and his army. At the time that Cincinnatus was approached, he was ploughing his own fields, even though he was a member of the patrician order. Cincinnatus rescued Minucius, left his post as dictator about two weeks after he had been given it, and returned to his farm. He was considered the savior or deliverer of his country. Americans often compared George Washington to Cincinnatus.

A Federalist author, writing for the Lansingburg *Northern Centinel* on October 15, 1787, also used this pseudonym. He painted a dismal picture of life during the Confederation and demonstrated how the Constitution would improve that life. He attacked Antifederalists as party men trying to hold on to their offices. **Cincinnatus** said that he was a soldier during the Revolution who, after the war, had "retired to private business." He had nothing to gain from the Constitution; he only wanted the United States to be able to rival the other nations of the world.

A Citizen (Antifederalist, Federalist, and Impartial)

This pseudonym was employed by Federalists, Antifederalists, and some who did not take sides. Only one example of each will be given.

An Antifederalist writer attacked **Medium** (below) in the *New York Journal* on November 24, 1787, for not being tougher on Federalists. On January 31, 1788, a Federalist writer in the *Hudson Gazette* took issue with some Antifederalist objections. On March 3, 1788, an impartial observer, writing for the Albany *Federal Herald*, asked people to think carefully about the Constitution; he was of no party. He described himself as a citizen of New York "entitled to the privileges, and immunities thereof in life, liberty and property." Among other things, he was apparently a freeman or freeholder who had the right to vote. A "citizen" could also be "a townsman; a man of trade; not a gentleman," according to lexicographer, Samuel Johnson.

A Citizen of America (Federalist)

Published in the New York *Daily Advertiser* on February 19, 1788, this essay was a strong plea for union and an energetic government. Noah Webster, who had published **America** (above) in the *Daily Advertiser*, had used this pseudonym as a pamphleteer in October, 1787, before he moved from Philadelphia to New York City.

A Citizen of New-York (Federalist)

This pamphlet, written by John Jay and entitled *An Address to the People of the State of New-York on the Subject of the Constitution*, was offered for sale on April 15, 1788. John Jay reviewed the inadequacies of the Articles of Confederation and the economic hardships of the 1780s. The Constitutional Convention, he said, was called to establish "a national government, *competent to every national object.*" The Constitution, the product of its deliberations, was not perfect, but another convention would not do better. New York was asked to ratify the Constitution for several reasons: it would benefit economically; it would appease its neighbors who had already ratified; and it would remain part of the Union because nine other states would definitely ratify.

On September 26, 1787, the New York *Daily Advertiser* published an article under this pseudonym that listed more than thirty possibilities for the first president of the United States under the Constitution. John Jay was not among those listed.

A Country Federalist (Federalist)

This pseudonym was used by Federalist James Kent (later Chancellor of New York) in the Poughkeepsie *Country Journal* on December

19, 1787 (supplement) and January 9, 1788. Since many country or rural people opposed the Constitution, Kent tried to demonstrate that some country folk could support the Constitution. Kent was in the process of publishing an abridgement of *The Federalist* (see **Publius**, below) in the *Country Journal*. (For the meaning of the term "federalist," see the **Introduction**.)

A Countryman (Antifederalist)

This series of six "letters" was printed in the *New York Journal* between November 21, 1787, and February 14, 1788. Written by Antifederalist Hugh Hughes, a farmer and an old Revolutionary patriot, the essays were entitled (beginning with number II) "Letters from a Gentleman in Dutchess County, to his Friend in New-York." The friend was possibly Antifederalist leader John Lamb to whom many Antifederalist essays were sent before they were printed in the *New York Journal*. (For example, see **Expositor**, below.) Hughes also wrote **Expositor**. (See also **A Son of Liberty**, below.)

A Countryman (Antifederalist)

This collection of five "letters" was printed in the *New York Journal* between December 6, 1787, and January 17, 1788. They were written by DeWitt Clinton, a nephew of Governor George Clinton and a native of rural New Britain in Orange County. DeWitt Clinton, then only eighteen years old, was reading law with Antifederalist leader Samuel Jones. In his fourth "letter," the youthful DeWitt sarcastically remarked that the only thing that he had learned from *The Federalist* (see **Publius**, below) was "that it is better to be united than divided."

A Countryman (Federalist)

This pastoral allegory was printed in the New York *Daily Advertiser* on March 5, 1788, supporting the decision of the Constitutional Convention to abandon the Articles of Confederation in favor of a new Constitution. Federalists were demonstrating that they, too, could use such a pseudonym.

Curtiopolis (Federalist)

This article, addressed to the New York legislature that was meeting to consider (among other things) the calling of a state ratifying convention, was printed in the New York *Daily Advertiser* on January 18, 1788. It was a Federalist spoof on the numerous Antifederalist objections to the Constitution.

The meaning of the pseudonym is uncertain, but perhaps it is related to **Curtius** (below). Curtius (or Curtii) is the name of a Roman clan related to the mythological hero, M. Curtius. Perhaps Curtiopolis wanted to indicate some sort of kinship with **Curtius,** who had also published material on the Constitution in the *Daily Advertiser.* ''Polis'' is a common suffix for a Greek name.

Curtius (Federalist)

This series of three articles, addressed to the citizens of New York, was published in the New York *Daily Advertiser* between October 18 and November 3, 1787 (supplement). The articles supported the Constitution and were critical of the essays of **Cato** and **Brutus** (both above).

This pseudonym appears to have been taken from the name of a mythological hero—M. (perhaps Marcus) Curtius. In the myth, a chasm opened suddenly in the Roman Forum. An oracle told M. Curtius that the Republic of Rome could survive and prosper only when the chasm was filled by something precious. M. Curtius believed that Rome's finest treasure was a gallant, courageous, and armed citizen. Whereupon, armed and on horseback, he threw himself into the chasm and it closed over him. He had saved the Republic. At the point where M. Curtius had filled the chasm, the place came to be called the *Lacus Curtius.* (Other traditions, however, suggest other reasons for this name.)

D--- (Federalist)

This item, printed in the New York *Daily Advertiser* on December 12, 1787, rejected a statement that originated in a Philadelphia newspaper claiming John Jay opposed the Constitution. **D---** labeled the statement as an Antifederalist misrepresentation.

Democritus (Antifederalist)

This group of three essays was printed in the *New York Journal* on December 14, 21, and 28, 1787, as an answer to **The Examiner** (below). The author attacked **The Examiner** for criticizing republican writers, and he satirized Pennsylvania Federalists Benjamin Rush and James Wilson. Both men were attacked for mouthing religious platitudes and for making the Constitution appear to have been divinely inspired. This pseudonym was probably taken from a Greek philosopher of the fourth and fifth centuries B.C. who was known as "the laughing philosopher." He ridiculed the follies and vanities of mankind. In politics, he was a democrat. In Latin, "democritus" means one who is selected from the commons.

Detector (Antifederalist)

The writer of this item, printed in the *New York Journal* on October 25, 1787, found or detected a paradox. Some Massachusetts printers insisted that writers of essays attacking the Constitution identify themselves. Yet the Massachusetts Constitution declared that the liberty of the press was "essential to the security of freedom in a state," and, therefore, should not be restrained.

Dick a Dick (Antifederalist)

On March 7, 1788, the Philadelphia *Independent Gazetteer* printed a brief article stating that Arthur Lee of Virginia, a member of the Confederation Board of Treasury in New York City, had declared that four-fifths of the people of Virginia were Antifederalists. Several days later, three New York City newspapers printed items denying that Lee had made such a declaration. On March 29, **Dick a Dick**, writing for the *New York Journal*, questioned the authenticity of the denial and challenged Lee, who had just returned to New York from Virginia, to come forward with his denial. **Dick a Dick** probably means from one man to another, or man to man.

A Dutchess County Farmer (Federalist)

This article, printed in the Poughkeepsie *Country Journal* on February 26, 1788, criticized Robert Yates and John Lansing, Jr.—the two New York delegates who had left the Constitutional Convention early and who had published a letter explaining why they had done so. **A Dutchess County Farmer** accused them of being influenced by **Cato** (i.e., Governor George Clinton). Evidently, the writer's use of the description "farmer," was an effort to demonstrate that not all farmers were Antifederalists. (See **A Dutchess County Rifleman**, below.)

A Dutchess County Rifleman (Antifederalist)

Printed in the Poughkeepsie *Country Journal* on April 8, 1788, this article defended Robert Yates and John Lansing, Jr., against the attack of **A Dutchess County Farmer** (above). The writer possibly used "rifleman" as a synonym for "militiaman," the citizen soldier. Antifederalists often criticized the Constitution because it gave the central government control over the state militias. State control over their militias was a precious right to the Antifederalists and not one to be relinquished.

The Examiner (Federalist)

This series of five essays was published in the *New York Journal* between December 11, 1787, and January 4, 1788. The author was physician Charles McKnight who used a variety of medical terms in the essays and who was given to personal invective. A physician is, of course, one who examines or looks into the nature and condition of a person's body. McKnight, then, does not appear to have tried very hard to hide his identity. In his first essay, **The Examiner** announced his intention to examine or investigate the writings of several Antifederalists. Among others, **The Examiner** attacked **Cato, Brutus**, and **Democritus** (all above).

Democritus (above) knew the identity of **The Examiner** because he referred to him as "Dr. Sawney M'Foolish." "Sawney" was a derisive name for a Scotsman, and McKnight was Scotch-Irish. **The Examiner** was also called a poor man's Jonathan Swift. (See **A Friend to Common Sense**, below.)

Expositor (Antifederalist)

This series of two articles, written by Hugh Hughes, was published in the *New York Journal* on January 24 and 31, and February 7 and 28, 1788. These "expositions" or explanations of the Constitution were written with a strong sense of irony. Antifederalist leader John Lamb personally oversaw their publication. Lamb divided up the essays so as to excite "the curiosity of People to see the Remainder." Hughes was also **A Countryman** (above). (See also **A Son of Liberty**, below.)

Fabius (Federalist)

Several articles signed **Fabius** appeared in these two newspapers: *Albany Journal*, February 9, 11, 18, and 23, 1788; and Albany *Federal Herald*, March 17, 1788. The reference is to Quintus Fabius Maximus Verrucosus who was variously consul, censor, dictator, pontifex, and augur of Rome in the third century B.C. He is best known for his actions against Hannibal in the second Punic War. Fabius avoided pitched battles with Hannibal and tried to wear him down. He became known as Cunctator, "the delayer," and the Shield of Rome. A patrician of the old order, he was also noted for his courage. Americans often referred to George Washington as the American Fabius.

Federal Farmer (Antifederalist)

This writer published two pamphlets, in the form of letters, that were first advertised for sale on November 8, 1787, and on May 2, 1788. The first set of five letters, addressed to the "Republican," was entitled *Observations Leading to a Fair Examination of the System of Government Proposed by the Late Convention* . . . , while the second set, consisting of thirteen letters, was called *An Additional Number of Letters from the Federal Farmer* . . . . The "Republican" was probably Governor George Clinton, who was known to some Antifederalists under that sobriquet. It is also believed that Clinton used the pseudonym **The Republican** in his own defense in the *New York Journal* on September 6, 1787, against charges made by Alexander Hamilton (New York *Daily Advertiser*, July 21) that he was an opponent of the Constitutional Convention.

The *Letters* are perhaps the best expression of Antifederalist thought printed in America. In particular, the **Federal Farmer** attacked the Constitutional Convention for establishing a consolidated or national government and for failing to provide for a bill of rights. The **Federal Farmer** supported what he considered to be a truly "federal" government, a government in which the power of the states was paramount. By describing himself as a "farmer," he was appealing to the group from which Antifederalists drew their greatest strength. The **Federal Farmer** was himself too erudite to have been a simple yeoman farmer.

For a long time, historians believed that Richard Henry Lee, a Virginia congressman in New York City when the first set of letters was written, was the author, but recently several scholars have seriously challenged this attribution. These scholars have not suggested someone in Lee's place, although it appears from comments made by New York Antifederalist Hugh Hughes in a private letter that the writer was probably a New Yorker. Certainly, the arguments employed by the **Federal Farmer** were popular in New York Antifederalist circles at the time.

A Federalist (Federalist)

This writer published an article in the Poughkeepsie *Country Journal* on April 22, 1788, supporting a strong energetic government. (For the meaning of the term "federalist," see the **Introduction**.)

The Federalist

See **Publius** (below).

A Friend to Common Sense (Antifederalist)

This article, published in the *New York Journal* on December 19, 1787, criticized **The Examiner** (above) for trying to be an American Jonathan Swift. Swift, a supremely gifted satirist, had written in support of the Tory ministry of Queen Anne (1702–1714).

A Friend to Good Government (Federalist)

This article, printed in the Poughkeepsie *Country Journal* on April 8 and 15, 1788, discussed both sides of the issue, but came down on the Federalist side.

Giles Hickory (Federalist)

This series of four articles was published in the monthly New York *American Magazine* in December 1787, and January, February, and March, 1788. The articles, the first of which denied the need for a bill of rights, were written by the *Magazine*'s editor, Noah Webster. Webster thought that a bill of rights was unnecessary against the encroachments of the elected representatives of the people. The people surrendered their sovereignty to their elected representatives who were drawn from the educated upper classes. Webster also wrote under the name **America** (above).

The name "Giles" is from the Greek *aegis*, meaning "goatskin"; in other words, "a shield that protects." In Greek mythology, "aegis" was a shield or breastplate worn variously by Zeus, Athena, and Apollo. Hickory is a tough, elastic wood that was used in the making of canes and rods (switches). The hickory rod was an instrument of the schoolmaster. In his second essay, Webster used the analogy of the schoolmaster and the rod, stating that "A proper degree of respect for the man and his laws, would prevent a thousand hard knocks." Webster himself had been a schoolmaster and, with his recently published grammars, readers, and spellers, was becoming the "schoolmaster to America."

Honestus (Antifederalist)

This article, printed in the *New York Journal* on April 26, 1788, criticized a wide variety of mechanics and artisans who were in favor of the Constitution. They would do better to stick to business, not politics, said **Honestus**. In Latin, "honestus" means to be full of honor, or honorable; to be regarded with honor; distinguished, noble, virtuous.

Lather (Federalist)

This satire, published in the New York *Daily Advertiser* on October 24, 1787, ridiculed the Antifederalists who would leave office or the state because of the "new unconstitutional Constitution." **Lather** spoofed the Antifederalist notion of *"State Sovereignty"* by writing about *"City Sovereignty"* and *"Street Sovereignties."* He also hoped that Congress would create the office of *"Shaver General"* in the Northwest Territory for "some worthy disgusted Patriot." Antifederalist leaders John Lamb and George Clinton both held the rank of brigadier general, and both (especially Lamb) had been patriots. (See also **Roderick Razor**, below.)

A Lover of Truth (Antifederalist)

This article was printed in the *New York Packet* on October 30, 1787, correcting a report that George Mason, a Virginia delegate to the Constitutional Convention, had been treated contemptuously by the mayor and corporation of the town of Alexandria, Va., for refusing to sign the Constitution.

A Lover of Truth and Decency (Antifederalist)

This item, published in the *New York Journal* on March 18, 1788, criticized Federalists for their criticisms of the Antifederalist, **Rough-Hewer** (below).

A Lunarian (Federalist)

The printer of the New York *Daily Advertiser* was asked to print this article from "a correspondent in the Moon." He did so on December 20, 1787. **A Lunarian** attacked Antifederalist writers because their articles lacked substance and were of such huge dimensions that they floated up to the moon like balloons. Moreover, these Antifederalist writers appear to have come under the influence of the moon.

A Man of No Party (Impartial)

These two articles, printed in the New York *Daily Advertiser* on October 19 and 20, 1787, attacked both Federalist and Antifederalist authors.

Marcus (Federalist)

This item was printed in the New York *Daily Advertiser* on October 15, 1787. **Marcus** listed, in a format resembling the verse form, the principal occupations and classes in society and explained why it was in the "interest" of each to support the Constitution.

The pseudonym is perhaps taken from Marcius, the Roman seer whose prophetic verses were discovered in 213 B.C. The verses were preserved in the Capitol (i.e., temple) along with the prophetic Sibylline Books.

Medium (Impartial)

This writer, whose article appeared in the *New York Journal* on November 21, 1787, criticized both Federalists and Antifederalists for intemperance and obstinacy. True to his name, **Medium** took a moderate, or middle course. (See **A Citizen**, above.)

Observer (Federalist)

This article, printed in the *New York Journal* on January 1, 1788, attacked **Democritus** (above), who had criticized **Observer's** friend, **The Examiner** (above). **Observer** admitted that Dr. Charles McKnight was **The Examiner**. For another Federalist article signed **An Observer**, see the Lansingburgh *Northern Centinel*, October 22, 1787.

One of the Nobility (Antifederalist)

This Antifederalist satire, published in the *New York Journal* on December 12, 1787, spoofed Federalists and their principles. Federalists were attacked for opposing liberties and for not trusting the people. **One of the Nobility** used the term "Republican or Anti-foederal pieces," implying that Federalists were not republicans.

P. Valerius Agricola (Federalist)

This article, a Federalist statement on why the Constitution should be ratified, was printed in the *Albany Gazette* on November 8 and December 6, 1787. The writer prefaced his essay with this quotation from Joseph Addison's *Cato, A Tragedy: "My* BANE *and* ANTIDOTE *are both before me!"* He planned to continue the essay after December 6, but no continuation has been found in the extant issues of the *Albany Gazette*. (It may have appeared on December 27, an issue that is not extant.) The first part of **P. Valerius Agricola** was printed in the *Albany Gazette* the week before that newspaper reprinted the first number of *The Federalist* by **Publius (Valerius Poplicola)** (below).

No person with the name P. Valerius Agricola appears to have existed. The name is a contrived one; the Valerian clan did not use the cognomen "Agricola." Valerius was an ancient and celebrated patrician clan in Rome. Publius Valerius Poplicola (see **Publius,** below) was of this clan. In early times under the republic, this clan was at the forefront in advocating the rights of plebeians. Agricola means peasant, or farmer, or countryman. There is the possibility that Agricola may also have referred to Gnaeus Julius Agricola, the father-in-law of the historian, Tacitus. Agricola, as governor of Britain, was noted for his moderation and equity and for bringing the Latin language and civilization to Britain. He became so famous for his public and private virtues that a jealous Domitian, Emperor of the Roman Empire, ordered him to return to Rome and probably had him poisoned in A.D. 93.

Philopoemen (Impartial)

This article, printed in the New York *Daily Advertiser* on November 16, 1787, was critical of James Wilson's speech of October 6 before a Philadelphia public meeting and of the critics of that speech. Both sides, it said, were excessive. **Philopoemen** called for a "cool, disinterested and discreet examination" of the Constitution. He wanted his readers to come up with as "peaceable and unanimous a determination as the subject admits, and our situation requires." (For Wilson, see **Cincinnatus,** above.)

The name was perhaps taken from Philopoemen of Megalopolis who lived in the second and third centuries B.C. He was a distinguished soldier who loved agriculture and the country life, living simply and prudently. Philopoemen was hipparch and general of the Achaean Confederacy; he restored the military efficiency of the Confederacy. Philopoemen killed the tyrant of Sparta and made that powerful military state tributary to the league. When the league came under the control of Rome, he did not resist Rome militarily, but fought all encroachments on the liberties of the people. After his defeat and death at the hands of Dinocrates of the Messenians, he became a great hero to his people and statues were erected to him throughout the cities of the league. He was known as "the last of the Greeks."

Philo-Publius (Federalist)

Philo-Publius (an admirer of **Publius**, below) was William Duer, the secretary of the Confederation Board of Treasury, a New York businessman, and a close friend of Alexander Hamilton. Duer wrote four brief articles that were originally intended to be part of *The Federalist*. Duer's lackluster efforts were printed in the New York *Daily Advertiser*, October 30 and December 1; *New York Packet*, November 16; and New York *Independent Journal*, November 28.

Plain Truth (Federalist)

Published in the Albany *Federal Herald* on March 31, 1788, this article tried to set the record straight on some alleged misrepresentations made by Antifederalists.

A Plebeian (Antifederalist)

A Plebeian, one of the common people, was the author of a pamphlet entitled *An Address to the People of the State of New York: Showing the Necessity of Making Amendments to the Constitution, Proposed for the United States, Previous to Its Adoption*. The pamphlet appeared in New York City on April 17, 1788. **A Plebeian** is generally believed to be Melancton Smith; there is no hard contemporary evidence indicating that Smith was the author, although some historians have compared the pamphlet to other things that Smith wrote or said. Melancton Smith was a man of considerable property, hardly a plebeian, but he knew that many of the opponents of the Constitution in New York could be classified plebeian. In fact, he addressed himself to "the common people, the yeomanry of the country," who would be the biggest losers if the Constitution was adopted without amendments. **A Plebeian** dismissed most of the Federalist arguments in favor of the Constitution and reviewed many of the Antifederalist arguments for amendments. The pamphlet contains a postscript attacking John Jay's **A Citizen of New-York** (above), which had appeared a couple of days earlier.

Poor S---m (Federalist)

This article, printed in the *New York Packet* on February 12, 1788, complained about the hard times which the adoption of the new Constitution would alleviate.

A Public Creditor (Federalist)

Writing for the New York *Daily Advertiser* on December 20, 1787, **A Public Creditor** posed numerous questions to **Brutus** and **Cato** (both above) concerning finances. He insisted that the Constitution would protect public creditors and private property.

Publius (Federalist)

The Federalist, written by **Publius** and addressed to the people of the state of New York, was published in eighty-five numbers between October 27, 1787, and May 28, 1788. All but the last eight first appeared in one or the other of these New York City newspapers—the *Independent Journal*, the *New York Packet*, the *Daily Advertiser*, and the *New York Journal*. The *Independent Journal* and the *New York Packet* eventually published every essay. On March 22, 1788, a volume was printed with the first thirty-six essays, and on May 28, a second volume contained the remaining essays, including the last eight which appeared for the first time.

The Federalist was written by Alexander Hamilton, John Jay, and James Madison (of Virginia). The authorship of sixty-nine of the eighty-five essays is definite. Hamilton wrote fifty—Nos. 1, 6–9, 11–13, 15–17, 21–36, 59–61, and 65–85; Madison, fourteen—Nos. 10, 14, 37–48; and Jay, five—Nos. 2–5, 64. The most recent scholarship has concluded persuasively that Madison apparently wrote the remaining disputed essays —Nos. 18–20, 49–58, and 62–63.

The first number, written by Hamilton, announced the purposes of the series: to demonstrate the necessity of "UNION," to outline the weaknesses of the Articles of Confederation, and to enumerate the nature and benefits of the new Constitution. **Publius** also answered the objections of Antifederalists, especially **Brutus** (above). But *The Federalist* was more than just a series of superlative political documents designed to convince the people of New York that the Constitution should be ratified. In November, 1788, Thomas Jefferson described *The Federalist* as "the best commentary on the principles of government which ever was written," and in May 1790 he was moved to say that "descending from theory to practice there is no better book than the Federalist."

Alexander Hamilton, who initiated the series, had first employed the pseudonym **Publius** in the fall of 1778. At that time, he wrote three newspaper articles attacking Samuel Chase of Maryland for using secret congressional information in order to corner the flour market because Congress was planning to buy flour for the French fleet.

The pseudonym was taken from Publius Valerius Poplicola (or Publicola), who in the sixth century B.C. led a successful revolt (along with Lucius Junius Brutus) against the monarchy of Tarquin, the last king of Rome, and established a republic in its place. One of the first consuls of the Republic, Publius is credited with establishing a stable and just government. He adopted laws that supported the Republic and the liberties of the people. One law stated that anyone who tried to make himself king could be killed. Another gave both patricians and plebeians the right to appeal decisions of magistrates. The Roman cognomen, Publicola, or Poplicola, means "one who courts the people," hence, "a friend of the people." The historian Plutarch says that Publicola means "people-lover."

The projection of men like Hamilton, Madison, and Jay (especially Hamilton who chose the pseudonym) as "people-lovers" was clearly a misrepresentation. The government created by the Constitutional Convention was an attempt to curb the "excesses of democracy," to place restraints upon the people and their principal protectors—the state governments. The misrepresentation was compounded by entitling the series *The Federalist*. The essays probably should have been called *The Nationalist*, or to use one of Hamilton's earlier pseudonyms, *The Continentalist*.

A **Querist** (Antifederalist)

This article, printed in the *New York Journal* on November 24, 1787, asked questions about the meaning of certain provisions of the Constitution.

A **Real Federalist** (Antifederalist)

This writer, whose article was printed in the Poughkeepsie *Country Journal* on March 11, 1788, attacked Federalists (supporters of the Constitution) for wrongfully applying that label to themselves. He said that the supporters of the Constitution were out to destroy "the *federal league"* established by the Articles of Confederation in which the sovereignty of the states was paramount. The supporters of the Constitution, he inferred, were really nationalists because the Constitution destroyed the power of the states. Antifederalists, the opponents of the Constitution, believed they were the true federalists. (For more on the term "federalist," see the **Introduction**.)

A Republican (Antifederalist)

This item, a criticism of James Wilson's October 6 speech before a Philadelphia public meeting, was printed in the *New York Journal* on October 25, 1787. (See **Cincinnatus**, above, for Wilson's speech.) The author is unknown, but George Clinton was referred to as the "Republican." (See **Federal Farmer**, above.) Republican, according to some opponents of the Constitution, was also a synonym for Antifederalist. Antifederalists often insisted that they, not the Federalists, were the true republicans. Another article, which was critical of the Constitution for not having a bill of rights, appeared under this pseudonym in the *New York Journal* on December 27, 1787.

Roderick Razor (Federalist)

This Federalist satire, printed in the New York *Daily Advertiser* on December 11, 1787, attacked Antifederalists who would lose their state offices when the Constitution was adopted. **Roderick Razor** was willing to accept a "snug birth" [sic] in one of **Lather's** (above) "*Street Sovereignties.*" He also ridiculed the major Antifederalist arguments on the Constitution (i.e., bill of rights, standing armies, etc.) and the Antifederalist reliance on Montesquieu.

It is possible that the pseudonym was taken from Englishman Tobias Smollett's picaresque novel, *The Adventures of Roderick Random* (1748).

Rough–Hewer (Antifederalist)

Rough–Hewer was Abraham Yates, Jr., of Albany, but no articles about the Constitution have been found under this pseudonym. Yates often published articles in the Albany newspapers, and a number of issues of those papers are no longer extant. However, he may have written some essays on the Constitution under that name because several Federalist writers attacked **Rough–Hewer**. The pseudonym definitely fits Yates's aggressive and passionate style; he was forever trying to cut things down, or to hack them to pieces. The pseudonym may also have been an attempt to convince people that he was a man of humble origins, like most Antifederalists. Such was not the case, however, despite his apprenticeship to a shoemaker as a boy. Yates also used the pseudonym **Sidney** (below).

Rusticus (Antifederalist)

This article, published in the *New York Journal* on May 23, 1788, was written by someone who lived in the small town of Goshen in Orange County. In Latin, "rusticus" means someone who lives in the country. Another possibility is L. Junius Arulenus Rusticus, who was tribune of the plebeians in A.D. 66. **Rusticus** attacked the Revolutionary War records of some members of the Constitutional Convention.

Senex (Federalist)

This item was found in the *Pennsylvania Journal* of March 12, 1788, which reprinted it from a no longer extant issue of the *Albany Journal*. **Senex** attacked **Rough-Hewer** (and others like him) for abusing the freedom of the press. In Latin, "senex" means an aged man or a gentleman.

Sidney (or Sydney) (Antifederalist)

Sidney was Abraham Yates, Jr., of Albany. Because some issues of the *Albany Gazette* are missing, we may not have all of the articles that he printed in opposition to the Constitution. Those essays signed **Sidney** that do exist are in the Poughkeepsie *Country Journal*, February 5 and March 11, 1788 (both reprinted from the *Albany Gazette*), and in the *Albany Gazette*, February 21 and March 13, 1788. While the New York convention was meeting, the *New York Journal*, on June 13 and 14, published a lengthy article (signed **Sydney**) comparing the New York State Constitution with the United States Constitution paragraph by paragraph, concluding that the latter absorbed all of the state's powers. (On October 18, 1787, the *New York Journal*, in an extraordinary issue, published a brief item signed **Sidney** that was clearly in Yates's style.) Yates also used the pseudonym **Rough-Hewer** (above).

The pseudonym was a reference to Algernon Sidney (or Sydney) (1622–83), one of the principal republican thinkers in England. His magnum opus, *Discourses on Government*, was published after his death. According to Caroline Robbins, the *Discourses* became a "textbook of revolution" in colonial America. Sidney was executed for plotting to overthrow Charles II in order to restore a republic. He met death like a martyr and was looked upon as such by later generations. Sidney fixed sole power in Parliament and the people; he preached that men had a right and a duty to rebel if their liberties and rights were threatened, and that tyrants had to be destroyed. Like Yates, Sidney was an aggressive and passionate man.

A Slave (Federalist)

This article was printed in the *New York Journal* on October 25, 1787. It was a response to an Antifederalist satire printed in the Philadelphia *Independent Gazetteer* on October 6. The writer in the *Gazetteer* had itemized what was wrong with the Constitution, under the heading "*blessings* of the new-proposed government." **A Slave**, in turn, drew up a list of what he thought was right with it. **A Slave** was answered by **A Son of Liberty** (below).

A Son of Liberty (Antifederalist)

This article, printed in the *New York Journal* on November 8, 1787, answered **A Slave** (above) point-by-point. **A Son of Liberty** signed his article from Orange County, where Hugh Hughes, a former Son of Liberty, had once lived. The Sons of Liberty were secret political organizations that resisted British imperial policy before the American Revolution. The organization in the colony of New York, led by (among others) John Lamb, was among the most radical and violent of all of these organizations. According to Alfred Young, the leaders were "upstart" merchants and mechanics, while the rank and file consisted of mechanics, journeymen, laborers, and sailors. In New York City, the principal supporters of Governor George Clinton during the 1780s were the remnants of the leadership of the Sons of Liberty. Most of the Liberty Boys went over to the Federalists; they needed the Constitution to rescue them economically.

A Spectator (Antifederalist)

This essay, printed in the *New York Journal* on May 2, 1788, asserted that only nine states would ratify the Constitution; the other four would not. Therefore, it would be impossible to put the new government into operation unless amendments were added to the Constitution.

Suilbup (Antifederalist)

This article, printed in the *Albany Gazette* on February 21, 1788, was an Antifederalist satire that praised **Rough–Hewer** (above) and his allies. **Suilbup,** which is **Publius** (above) spelled backwards, attacked the great and the well-born as well as the Constitution for favoring aristocratic government.

Timoleon (Antifederalist)

This article was published in an extraordinary issue of the *New York Journal* on November 1, 1787. The writer attacked the excessive powers of Congress and the lack of a bill of rights. The pseudonym is taken from Timoleon, a Corinthian who liberated Syracuse (in Greek Sicily) from the tyrant Dionysius II in the fourth century B.C. After this victory, he began a program of political and social reconstruction and a crusade against the tyrants of other Sicilian states whom he eventually crushed. Timoleon brought peace and prosperity to Sicily.

Timon (Federalist)

This article, addressed to the farmers of the state of New York, was published in the New York *Daily Advertiser* on March 22, 1788. The writer said that the Constitution would give America respect at home and abroad. The pseudonym was possibly taken from Timon of Athens, a famous misanthrope who secluded himself almost entirely from the world. Plutarch mentioned him in his life of Mark Antony, and Shakespeare wrote a play entitled *Timon of Athens.* Another possibility is the Greek philosopher who lived in the third and fourth centuries B.C. This Timon expressed bitter satire in his poems and plays and was a skeptic in his philosophy.

A True Federalist (Antifederalist)

This item, printed in the *New York Journal* on March 25, 1788, was supposedly written by Eleazer Oswald, the publisher of the Philadelphia *Independent Gazetteer.* The article was addressed to Postmaster General Ebenezer Hazard, stationed in New York City, attacking him for disallowing newspapers postage-free delivery so that they could be exchanged by printers. In particular, this practice hurt the dissemination of Antifederalist material. (For this Antifederalist writer's use of the term "federalist," see the **Introduction.**)

BIBLIOGRAPHY

Adair, Douglass, "A Note on Certain of Hamilton's Pseudonyms," *William and Mary Quarterly*, 3rd ser., 12 (1955): 282–97. An excellent discussion, although not related to the debate over the ratification of the Constitution, of why Hamilton chose these pseudonyms—"Phocion," "Tully," "Camillus," and "Pericles." Adair emphasizes the importance of Plutarch.

Bailyn, Bernard, *The Idealogical Origins of the American Revolution*. Cambridge, Mass.: Harvard University Press, 1967.

The Classick Pages: Classical Reading of Eighteenth-Century Americans. Edited by Meyer Reinhold. University Park: The Pennsylvania State University, 1975.

DePauw, Linda Grant, *The Eleventh Pillar: New York State and the Federal Constitution*. Ithaca, N.Y.: Cornell University Press, 1966.

A Dictionary of Greek and Roman Biography and Mythology. Edited by William Smith. 3 vols., London: John Murray, 1873.

The Documentary History of the Ratification of the Constitution. Volumes XIII–XVI. Commentaries: Public and Private, 21 February 1787 to 31 March 1788. Edited by John P. Kaminski and Gaspare J. Saladino. Madison: State Historical Society of Wisconsin, 1981–1987. The fifth and last volume is forthcoming. In addition to containing many of the articles discussed in this list, these volumes include the evidence used to identify some of the writers who used the pseudonyms.

The English Libertarian Heritage: From the Writings of John Trenchard and Thomas Gordon in The Independent Whig and Cato Letters. Edited by David L. Jacobson. Indianapolis and New York: Bobbs–Merrill, 1965.

Gummere, Richard M., *The American Colonial Mind and the Classical Tradition: Essays in Comparative Culture*. Cambridge, Mass.: Harvard University Press, 1963.

Harper's Dictionary of Classical Literature and Antiquities. Edited by Harry Thurston Peck. New York: Harper and Bros., 1897.

The Jonathan David Dictionary of First Names. Edited by Alfred J. Kolatch. New York: Perigree Books, 1980.

Lempriere's Classical Dictionary of Proper Names Mentioned in Ancient Authors Writ Large. Edited by F.A. Wright. 3rd. ed. London and Boston: Routledge and Kegan, 1984. This volume, based upon many earlier classical and mythological dictionaries, was published at the end of 1788.

The Oxford Classical Dictionary. Edited by N.G.L. Hammond and H.H. Scullard. 2nd ed. Oxford: Clarendon Press, 1970. The finest of the classical dictionaries.

Plots and Characters in the Fiction of Eighteenth-Century English Authors. Volume II, Henry Fielding, Tobias Smollett, Laurence Sterne, Samuel Johnson, and Oliver Goldsmith. Edited by Clifford R. Johnson. Hamden, Conn., and Folkestone, Kent, Eng.: Archon Books/Dawson, 1978.

[Plutarch], *Plutarch: The Lives of the Noble Grecians and Romans.* Translated by John Dryden and revised by Arthur Hugh Clough. New York: The Modern Library, [1932]. According to Meyer Reinhold, "no other Classical author was as popular [as Plutarch] in seventeenth and eighteenth century America. . . . Copies of his works, especially the *Lives*, were to be found everywhere in early American libraries." Plutarch discussed, in glowing terms, many of the characters described in this list of pseudonyms.

Reinhold, Meyer, *Classica Americana: The Greek and Roman Heritage in the United States.* Detroit: Wayne State University Press, 1984. This volume has very extensive notes and an excellent bibliography.

Robbins, Caroline, *The Eighteenth-Century Commonwealthman: Studies in the Transmission, Development and Circumstance of English Liberal Thought from the Restoration of Charles II until the War with the Thirteen Colonies.* Cambridge, Mass.: Harvard University Press, 1961.

[Webster, Noah], *Bibliography of the Writings of Noah Webster.* Compiled by Emily Ellsworth Ford Skeel and edited by Edwin H. Carpenter, Jr., New York: New York Public Library, 1958.

Young, Alfred, *The Democratic Republicans of New York: The Origins, 1763-1797.* Chapel Hill: The University of North Carolina Press, 1967.

The Federalist Express

GASPARE J. SALADINO

University of Wisconsin–Madison

Five states—Delaware, Pennsylvania, New Jersey, Georgia, and Connecticut—ratified the United States Constitution with overwhelming majorities by January 9, 1788. Then, the Massachusetts convention adopted, on February 6, by a vote of 187 to 168 and recommended amendments to the Constitution. On April 26, the Maryland convention ratified by a vote of 63 to 11, and Federalists defeated an Antifederalist attempt to recommend amendments. Only two more states were needed to ratify. The South Carolina convention was scheduled to meet on May 14; the Virginia, New York, and New Hampshire conventions on June 2, 17, and 18, respectively; and the North Carolina convention on July 21. Rhode Island had not even called a convention, but that did not matter much to supporters of the Constitution. To them, Rhode Island was a small, insignificant state with a long, colorful history of dissent; moreover, they held, "Rogue Island" in contempt, especially for its financial policies that favored debtors. Its vote was no longer needed as it had been under the Articles of Confederation, when the adoption of amendments to that constitution required a unanimous vote of the states.

Most Americans believed that the conventions of South Carolina and New Hampshire (whose first session had adjourned in February) would adopt the Constitution, bringing the total number of ratifying states to nine. Federalists appeared to have a slight majority in the Virginia convention, while Antifederalists had a majority of 46 to 19 in the New York convention. If the American Union under the new Constitution was to be viable, however, both Virginia and New York, two large and influential states, would have to be part of it. If Virginia ratified, New York would have little choice but to adopt the Constitution; it was in no position to defeat the Constitution by itself. Therefore, New York Antifederalists, led by John Lamb of New York City, corresponded with Virginia Antifederalists (as well as with those in the other states that had not ratified) and asked them to try to prevent ratification, unless amendments were made a condition of ratification.[1] This Antifederalist movement eventually failed, but New York Federalist leaders, who were aware of the strength of their adversaries and of what they were trying to do, were much concerned. Consequently, they paid particular attention to the progress of ratification in Virginia and New Hampshire (especially the former), and they made provision to rush the news of favorable votes on ratification (and favorable votes only) from Richmond and Concord to the New York convention in Poughkeepsie. Federalist leaders in the New York convention also developed a strategy to delay a vote on ratification until news was received from these two states.

Communication Established

The idea for establishing a rapid means of communication with the New Hampshire and Virginia conventions appears to have originated with convention delegate Alexander Hamilton, a New York City lawyer, although Rufus King, a former Massachusetts convention delegate who had moved temporarily to New York City, and Henry Knox of Massachusetts, the Confederation Secretary at War stationed there, helped him to establish the express systems. Knox, who had correspondents all over the United States, often acted as a conduit for information about state and national politics. He was especially active during the debate over the ratification of the Constitution. Not only were these three men political allies, but they were also close personal friends. For example, in April 1788, Hamilton, Knox, and Knox's wife were sponsors at the Anglican baptism of King's first child.

On May 19, Hamilton wrote James Madison, a Federalist leader and a Virginia convention delegate, "We think here that the situation of your state is critical. Let me know what you think of it. I believe you meet nearly at the time we do. It will be of vast importance that an exact communication should be kept up between us at that period; and the moment *any decisive* question is taken, if favourable, I request you to dispatch an express to me with pointed orders to make all possible diligence, by changing horses &c. All expences shall be thankfully and liberally paid." Virginia's ratification was absolutely necessary, reasoned Hamilton, because New York Governor George Clinton, "truly the leader of his party," was so "inflexibly obstinate" that Hamilton counted "little on overcoming opposition by reason." Only the ratification of nine states "may shake the firmness" of Clinton's adherents.[2]

(Clinton and Hamilton had been especially bitter enemies since the summer of 1787 when Hamilton, writing anonymously for the *The Daily Advertiser* [New York], had accused Clinton of opposing the Constitutional Convention which was then in session.[3] On June 8, Hamilton, who already knew that South Carolina had ratified on May 24 and had recommended amendments, repeated his request to Madison. Hamilton was fearful that the Antifederalists might adjourn the New York convention without voting in order "to *see how the government works and to act according to circumstances*." He considered them as "hostile to the Union."[4]

Madison's reply to Hamilton's May 19 letter has not been found, while his June 16 reply to Hamilton's June 8 letter says nothing about setting up an express system. Madison, however, was obviously amenable to Hamilton's recommendation, since both men corresponded regularly while the Virginia and New York conventions were in session. When New Hampshire ratified, Hamilton sent that news by special messenger to Madison in Richmond, and when Virginia ratified, Madison dispatched an express rider to New York.

On the 4th and 10th of June, Rufus King, who had journeyed to Boston from New York, wrote John Langdon, the president of New Hampshire and a state convention delegate, asking him to forward the news of New Hampshire ratification to Hamilton in Poughkeepsie, since that information "will have the most important Influence on the decision of New York." King requested that Langdon hire an express rider to carry the news to William Smith, a merchant in Springfield, Massachusetts, from which point Smith would have another rider take it to Hamilton. "Any Expence which you may incur," concluded King, "shall be cheerfully repaid."[5] On June 12, King wrote Hamilton that the express had been established and that the prospects for ratification in New Hampshire were good. He thought that the Antifederalists in the New York convention would be "greatly perplexed" by the news of New Hampshire ratification.[6] Four days later, King wrote Henry Knox that he had "not forgotten the necessity of communicating the Decision of N Hampshire (if favorable) to Poughkeepsie."[7]

The arrangements to have the news taken from Springfield on to Poughkeepsie had already been made by Henry Knox. These last arrangements were apparently completed in late May or early June because, on June 3, Hugh Williamson, a North Carolina delegate to the Confederation Congress, had heard that "There is a Line of Communication established by which we are told the New Yorkers at Pokepsie for I think they are to sit there, may hear within 40 Hours what is done in New Hampshire."[8]

On June 6, Alexander Hamilton, wanting to make certain that he received the news of New Hampshire's ratification, or perhaps unaware of the actions of King and Knox, wrote John Sullivan, the president of the New Hampshire convention, requesting "that the instant you have taken a decisive vote in favor of the Constitution, you send an express to me at Poughkeepsie. Let him take the *shortest route* to that place, change horses on the road, and use all possible diligence. I shall with pleasure defray all expenses, and give a liberal reward to the person. As I suspect an effort will be made to precipitate us, all possible safe dispatch on your part, as well to obtain a decision as to communicate the intelligence of it, will be desirable." Hamilton also hoped for "a speedy decision" in the convention; this would be a *"great advantage"* to New York Federalists. By his actions, Hamilton had provided for a second express rider from the New Hampshire convention.[9]

While these express systems were being created, the newspapers of New York State, both Federalist and Antifederalist, were filled with extracts of letters from Virginia reporting on the debates in the Virginia convention at Richmond and speculating on the chances of ratification. Moreover, members of the Virginia convention and others, both Federalists and Antifederalists, were writing their friends in New York and neither side was entirely optimistic. The mailbags of the postriders and the mail pouches carried by the stagecoaches must have been bulging with letters and newspapers.

New Hampshire Ratifies

On June 21, the New Hampshire convention, meeting in Concord, ratified the Constitution by a vote of 57 to 47, thereby becoming *"The Ninth and sufficient Pillar Raised"* in the "grand FEDERAL EDIFICE." With "great pleasure and satisfaction," John Langdon wrote Hamilton, giving the vote and telling him that his letter was being sent to William Smith in Springfield who would forward it to Hamilton in Poughkeepsie.[10] Langdon also sent letters to Rufus King and George Washington. In his letter to Washington, he described New Hampshire's ratification as "the Key Stone in the great Arch."[11] At 1:00 P.M., the exact time that the Constitution was ratified, John Sullivan wrote to Henry Knox by another express rider.[12]

On Sunday, June 22, John Langdon's express rider passed through the Massachusetts town of Worcester, "on his way to the westward." The rider reached William Smith's house in Springfield on June 23, at 5:00 A.M., and Smith "immediately" forwarded "the agreable information" to Poughkeepsie. "LAUS DEO!!," rejoiced Springfield's newspaper, as it informed its readers that it had learned of New Hampshire's ratification from an "*indisputable* authority." According to Philip Schuyler, Hamilton's father-in-law and a Federalist leader, Smith's express rider arrived in Poughkeepsie on June 24, at noon.[13] It had taken seventy-one hours to get the news from Concord to Poughkeepsie.

No report has been found announcing the arrival of Sullivan's express, but Sullivan's letter of June 21 to Knox was received in Poughkeepsie, as Knox docketed the letter: "From Poughkeepsy." Furthermore, Sullivan wrote Hamilton that he had received the express rider's bill which he had paid. Sullivan regretted that the express rider had lamed his horse, but he indicated that Hamilton's instructions had been carried out faithfully. Sullivan's rider took a more northerly route that included Northampton and Pittsfield, Massachusetts.[14] On June 25, *The Hampshire Gazette* of Northampton reported that on the evening of June 23 a rider from Concord arrived in Northampton with the news of New Hampshire's ratification, and on June 26 *The Berkshire Chronicle* of Pittsfield announced "the erection of the NINTH PILLAR in the fabrick of FREEDOM and UNION."

Soon after John Langdon's letter was received in Poughkeepsie on June 24, Philip Schuyler, acting for Alexander Hamilton, wrote James Madison and enclosed a copy of Langdon's June 21 letter to Hamilton. Schuyler told Madison that "Unless the adoption [by] New Hampshire should alarm the fears of those in opposition in the convention here, they will I apprehend persevere in the intention which they have decidely [*sic*] evinced of adoption predicated on previous Amendments, and those such as would render the new Government very little, If any more energetic than the present."[15] The information from New Hampshire probably lifted Hamilton's spirits a little because the day before he had received a pessimistic letter from Madison, in which Madison had indicated that the prospects for ratification in Virginia were "critical." In his reply of June 25, Hamilton told Madison: "Our chance of success here is infinitely slender, and none at all if you go wrong. The leaders of the Antifederalists finding their partisans somewhat squeamish about rejection, are obliged *at present* to recur to the project of conditional amendments. We are going on very deliberately in the discussion and hitherto not without effect." Two days later, he reminded Madison about the New Hampshire news and said: "We eagerly wait for further intelligence from you, as our only chance of success depends on you. There are some slight symptoms of relaxation in some of the leaders; which authorises a gleam of hope, if you do well: but certainly I think not otherwise."[16] Outwardly, however, Hamilton probably appeared more optimistic; Antifederalist convention delegate Christopher P. Yates of

Montgomery County noted that "Federalists appear much elated." In Albany, another Antifederalist said that Federalists there "plume themselves much," but that they had "not proceeded to any public demonstrations of Joy."[17]

Antifederalists in the New York convention were unimpressed. Christopher P. Yates and Henry Oothoudt of Albany County saw no changes in the resolution of their compatriots. Governor George Clinton of Ulster County, the president of the convention, said that the news of New Hampshire's ratification "has not had the least Effect on our Friends.[18] The opinions of these three men were verified by Daniel Huger, a South Carolina delegate to the Confederation Congress who was visiting in Poughkeepsie. Huger said that the news "made no impression on the Convention at all."[19] On June 25, Robert R. Livingston of New York County, the state chancellor and a Federalist leader, reminded the convention that "since the intelligence of yesterday, it had become evident that the circumstances of the country were greatly altered, and the ground of the present debate changed." Melancton Smith of Dutchess County (the Antifederalists' convention manager) and John Lansing, Jr., of Albany County summarily dismissed his arguments. Their feelings had not changed.[20] In private, however, Smith's views were changing. He hoped that some of the leading Antifederalists would show more "moderation" and "calmly . . . consider the circumstances in which we are, and to accommodate our decisions to those circumstances." Smith was beginning to reconsider the Antifederalists' caucus' agreement that the Constitution not be ratified without previous amendments.[21] Since "the principal labor of managing the Controversy" lay with him, Smith's growing moderation (along with that of Samuel Jones of Queens County) would splinter the Antifederalists and eventually result in the ratification of the Constitution by the New York convention.

At about 2:00 A.M. on June 25—fourteen hours after the news from New Hampshire had reached Poughkeepsie—an express rider left carrying Schuyler's letter to Madison and a copy of Langdon's June 21 letter to Hamilton. He arrived in New York City at noon, a ten-hour ride. A half hour later, Langdon's letter was read in the Confederation Congress. At the same time, Virginia's three congressional delegates, Edward Carrington, John Brown, and Cyrus Griffin, wrote to Madison, enclosing the Schuyler and Langdon letters. If Madison was absent from the Virginia Convention, the letters were to be turned over to another delegate, Governor Edmund Randolph. Abraham Yates, Jr., a New York delegate to Congress and a diehard Antifederalist, was disturbed that the news of New Hampshire's ratification "bread [*sic*] such an inattention to the Business" of Congress. So committed was Yates to previous amendments that he believed New York should stay out of the Union, even if twelve states ratified.[22]

Cyrus Griffin, who was also the president of Congress, gave the Schuyler and Langdon letters to express rider Colonel David Henley, a former Continental Army officer. Griffin and the other Virginia delegates to Congress thought it best to use an express rider because the news was "critical" to Virginia. At 1:00 P.M. on June 25, Colonel Henley "sat off, *express*, for Virginia, with the *joyful tidings*." Henry Knox predicted that the news of New Hampshire's ratification would "probably reach" the Virginia convention in Richmond on June 29 or early the following day.[23]

At 2:00 P.M., the churchbells of New York City "were sat a ringing, which incessantly rang until 7 in the evening. Many citizens were rejoiced on this occasion; to testify which bottles of choice *nectar* were *quaffed—and, at that hour, the guns were fired*." The "discharge of cannon" was "attended by repeated huzzas from a large concourse of citizens" and the "federalism" of the citizens was evident "by the visible marks of satisfaction in almost every countenance."[24]

Virginia Ratifies

Colonel Henley reached Philadelphia on June 26 and was described by one newspaper as an "express to Mr. Maddison of Virginia, from the President of Congress." According to Philadelphia merchant, Thomas Willing, Henley had beaten the post from New York by two hours. Willing hoped that Henley's news would give "fresh courage" to the Federalists in Richmond. At 10:00 or 11:00 A.M. on June 27, Colonel Henley reached Baltimore, and early on the morning of the 28th ("two hours before day") he arrived in Alexandria, where news had been received the previous night that the Virginia convention, on June 25 at 2:30 P.M., had ratified the Constitution and that it would recommend amendments.[25] (The convention recommended amendments on the 27th, after the express rider had left.) Virginia had become the tenth pillar in the federal edifice.

At Alexandria, Colonel Henley "met an express bound to New-York"—"This interesting circumstance rendered" his "further pursuit fruitless."[26] Colonel Henley forwarded the New York and New Hampshire letters to James Madison, while he probably received a copy of the preliminary Virginia form of ratification and a letter from Madison to Hamilton from the express rider. Madison received the New York and New Hampshire letters in Richmond on June 29, two days after the

Virginia convention had adjourned.[27] It had taken eight days to get the news of New Hampshire's ratification from Concord to Richmond.[28] Henry Knox's prediction that the news would reach Richmond on the 29th had proved to be correct.

Colonel Henley remained in Alexandria on June 28 and took part, along with George Washington who lived nearby, in the festivities celebrating the news of Virginia's and New Hampshire's ratifications. Washington described the scene in Alexandria: "The cannon roared, and the Town was illuminated . . . as *magnificent* a dinner as Mr. Wise could provide (to which this family were invited and went), was displayed before the principal *male* inhabitants of the Town; whose Ears were saluted at every quaff with the melody of federal Guns." Henley was evidently one of the "Genteel Strangers" who dined with Washington and his family and friends at John Wise's tavern on Royal Street.[29]

On June 29, Colonel Henley started back for New York City. Henley reached Philadelphia between 6:00 and 7:00 P.M. on June 30, with the news of Virginia ratification and "all the bells in the city were rung, and continued till twelve o'clock that night."[30] In the morning of the same day, the printer of *The New-York Journal, and Daily Patriotic Register* predicted that the news of a vote on "the final question" in the Virginia convention (which he thought would be taken on June 25) would arrive in New York City on the evening of July 1, "at [the] farthest."

Soon after the news of Virginia's ratification reached Philadelphia, a stage coach left that city and arrived in New York City on the evening of July 1. "A passenger of veracity" on that stage told some people that Virginia had adopted the Constitution. One newspaper printer hoped that the post expected the next day would "bring a confirmation of the above very important information."[31]

At 2:37 A.M. on July 2, Colonel David Henley arrived in New York City "with the same zealous expedition he went," having brought "the tidings" of Virginia's ratification "to the anxious expectants."[32] According to General Samuel Blachley Webb, a merchant, "at the dawning of the day all the Bells of the City began and Rung for four hours at the Suns riseing we were saluted with Ten—Twenty four pounders which made noise sufficient to awaken the most drowsy, in short the whole day has been devoted to amusement."[33] On this day, the news of Virginia's ratification appeared in three New York City newspapers— *The Daily Advertiser, The Independent Journal: or, the General Advertiser*, and *The New-York Journal, and Daily Patriotic Register.* The publisher of the *Independent Journal*, who had printed the news in the morning, also published (later that day) a one-page broadside supplement that included the vote on ratification (incorrectly stated), the preliminary Virginia form of ratification, and this paragraph at the end: "A letter from Richmond advises, 'that a motion for previous amendments was rejected by a majority of EIGHT; but some days would be passed in considering subsequent amendments, and these, it appeared, from the temper of the Convention, would be RECOMMENDED.' " The printer was able to print this information because of what had just been received in the post.[34] Henry Knox was pleased that the Virginia amendments, as in the case of Massachusetts, would only be recommendatory.[35] Between the 3rd and 5th of July, five more New York City newspapers printed the preliminary Virginia form of ratification, without the extract of the Virginia letter.[36] On the 9th and 10th of July, respectively, *The Daily Advertiser* and *The New-York Journal, and Weekly Register* printed the text of the Virginia convention's recommendatory amendments that were included in that convention's final form of ratification.[37]

Express to Poughkeepsie

Almost immediately after the Virginia news was received early on the morning of July 2, Colonel William Smith Livingston, a New York City lawyer whose former law office had been near Alexander Hamilton's on Wall Street, left for Poughkeepsie, a distance of about eighty miles. Colonel Livingston changed horses twice en route and, despite "the ruffness of the road," he arrived in Poughkeepsie at about 12:30 P.M. The ride had taken between nine and ten hours. The Poughkeepsie newspaper reported that the ride had "been performed on this occasion with more expedition than has hitherto been known on that road"; the ride had been "an act of comtemplation" [*sic*]. An eyewitness, who was interviewed decades later, said that, after dismounting from his "powerful bay horse," Colonel Livingston delivered "a sealed package" to the doorkeeper of the New York convention. The package, said the eyewitness, included a dispatch from Edmund Pendleton, the president of the Virginia convention, and a letter from James Madison to Alexander Hamilton.[38]

Colonel Smith's entrance into the convention coincided, ironically, with a speech by Governor George Clinton. A New York City newspaper described his arrival this way: "while the Governor was speaking, Col. Livingston, who arrived at Poughkeepsie in 9 hours and 1–4 from this city, made his appearance in the Convention Chamber, with the interesting intelligence of the ratification of Virginia, which occasioned such a buz through the House, that little of his Excellency's Speech was heard."[39]

Philip Schuyler wrote Stephen Van Rensselaer, his son-in-law and patroon of a vast manor in Albany County, congratulating him "on this very Important Occasion with all that satisfaction which arise in the heart." Schuyler hoped that the news "will have a proper influence on the minds" of Antifederalists who "will not sacrifice their Country to the Obstinacy of certain desperadoes." On the other hand, Antifederalist convention delegate Cornelius C. Schoonmaker of Ulster County trusted that "our Deliberations will not in the least be Affected or Changed, in consequence of the States of New Hampshire & Verginia Acceeding to the Constitution," while DeWitt Clinton, the governor's nephew and an observer and reporter at the convention, remarked that the news had made "no impressions upon the republican members." An anonymous Antifederalist noted that "the antifederal party took no more notice of it than if the most trifling occurrence had been mentioned."[40]

Outside the convention that afternoon, "a respectable number of Federalists, whose exultations on the happy news from Virginia, were too great to be confined to their own breasts, had a meeting to congratulate each other, fired ten cannon in honor of the ten adopting States, and with three huzzas sent the welcome news to their friends in the country."[41]

Nicholas Power of *The Country Journal, and the Poughkeepsie Advertiser* printed a broadside of the preliminary Virginia form of ratification and the extract of the Richmond letter under the heading "POGHKEEPSIE/July 2d, 1788. JUST ARRIVED/BY EXPRESS." On July 8, Power also published the form and the New Hampshire convention's recommendatory amendments in his newspaper, and on the 15th and 22nd he printed the text of the Virginia convention's recommendatory amendments.[42]

The news of Virginia's ratification was received in Albany in the afternoon of the 3rd of July, and this time the city's Federalists "assembled to demonstrate their joy." From 4:00 P.M. "until sunset" the bells of the city rang, and ten cannon were fired "with three huzzas between each shot." The next day, the 4th of July, the city's Antifederalists met and burned the Constitution early in the morning, and later that morning they joined with the Federalists in celebrating the 4th.[43]

In the New York convention, the news of Virginia's ratification was crucial to the success of the Federalist cause, although it was not until July 26 that the convention finally ratified the Constitution. The complex story of the maneuvering that took place, in the three weeks after the convention learned that Virginia had ratified, is told elsewhere and the details need not be repeated here.[44]

The key Antifederalist players in the unfolding drama were Melancton Smith and Samuel Jones, who realized that previous amendments did not have a chance and who knew that the Confederation Congress would not accept any conditional ratification.[45] On the Federalist side, the leadership, especially John Jay and Alexander Hamilton, became conciliatory and expressed their willingness to accept recommendatory amendments. On July 25, the committee of the whole house ratified the Constitution by a vote of 31 to 28, and the next day the final vote on the engrossed ratification with recommendatory amendments was 30 to 27. The Federalists then made one more important conciliatory gesture. They agreed to a circular letter, mainly the work of John Jay, that was to be forwarded to all of the states. The letter, which the convention adopted unanimously, called for a second constitutional convention to consider the amendments to the Constitution that had been proposed by several state ratifying conventions.

The outcome was extraordinary. The delaying tactics of the Federalists and their conciliatory attitude had worked perfectly. They had remained unified; all nineteen of them, representing southern counties, supported ratification, although Richard Morris of New York did not vote. They had also effectively used the threat of secession by the southern counties (which included populous and commercial New York City) if the Constitution were not ratified. On the final day, twelve Antifederalists, including Melancton Smith, Samuel Jones, and Gilbert Livingston of Dutchess County, voted with the Federalists. Seven of the twelve came from the Long Island counties of Queens and Suffolk that were tied economically to New York City. Nevertheless, the crossover of twelve Antifederalists did not ensure ratification of the Constitution. The Federalists were also victorious because eight Antifederalists, including George Clinton (as the convention's president), did not vote on the last day. Governor Clinton, however, had rejected ratification on the 25th. With respect to Clinton, Henry Knox noted: "a precise history of his conduct is difficult to be written and must be left to time to explain." Some of the eight abstaining Antifederalists probably left Poughkeepsie before the vote, while others absented themselves from the convention chamber when the vote was taken.[46]

Reflecting on the events of the convention, Morgan Lewis, a New York City lawyer, astutely observed to a correspondent that "You are doubtless much surprised to find that this State has adopted the Constitution contrary to all Expectation. I believe it has not any where been controverted with more Heat, and, on the Part of its Opponents, more illiberality [sic]. At the Commencement of the Session the Difference was 46 to 19 and yet, a[ltho'] a variety of palliatives and Expedients suggested by the Ingenuity of a few leading characters, to embarrass the Business, they have given a full unequivocal & unconditional Ratification—Great Merit is certainly due to the Gentln. who advocated it in Convention; And they are, I believe, much indebted for their Success, to Virginia, and an Apprehension of a separation of the southern part of the State." And Aaron Burr, another perceptive New York City lawyer, wrote: "I think it is a fortunate event and the only one which could have preserved peace; *after the adoption by ten States,* I think it became both politic and necessary that we should also adopt it."[47]

NOTES

[1]For the efforts that New York Antifederalists made to cooperate with Antifederalists in other states in May and June 1788, see Linda Grant DePauw, *The Eleventh Pillar: New York State and the Federal Constitution* (Ithaca, N.Y., 1966), 205-6, 211-14; Steven R. Boyd, *The Politics of Opposition: Antifederalists and the Acceptance of the Constitution* (Millwood, N.Y., 1979), 126-35; and *The Documentary History of the Ratification of the Constitution*, ed. Merrill Jensen, John P. Kaminski, Gaspare J. Saladino et al. (Madison, Wis., 1976–), vol. 9 (*Ratification of the Constitution by the States: Virginia [2]*), forthcoming.

[2]*The Papers of Alexander Hamilton*, ed. Harold C. Syrett and Jacob E. Cooke, 27 vols. (New York, 1961-1987), 4:649-50.

[3]See the *The Daily Advertiser* (New York) [NYDA], July 21 and September 15 (both Hamilton), and "A Republican" (Clinton), *The New-York Journal, and Weekly Register* [NYJWR], September 6. On November 19, Thomas Greenleaf, the publisher of the *Journal*, began to print his newspaper as *The New-Journal, and Daily Patriotic Register*. On Thursdays, however, the newspaper was issued as *The New-York Journal, and Weekly Register*. This Thursday issue had the widest circulation and the most important essays appeared in it.

[4]*Hamilton Papers*, ed. Syrett, 5:3-4. By the 8th of June, at least six New York City newspapers had printed the news of South Carolina's ratification of the Constitution.

[5]King Papers, The New-York Historical Society [Nhi].

[6]*Hamilton Papers*, ed. Syrett, 5:5.

[7]Knox Papers, Massachusetts Historical Society [Mhi].

[8]Williamson to John Gray Blount, Blount Papers, Duke University; and Rufus King to Alexander Hamilton, June 12, *Hamilton Papers*, ed. Syrett, 5:5.

[9]*Ibid.*, 5:2.

[10]The original letter written by Langdon has not been found. Philip Schuyler had a copy of it made on the verso of a letter that he wrote to James Madison on June 24. Both letters are in the Madison Papers at the Library of Congress. Langdon's letter is printed in *Hamilton Papers*, ed. Syrett, 5:34. For the publication of Schuyler's letter, see note 15, below.

John Sullivan and Tobias Lear, George Washington's secretary who was visiting family and friends in New Hampshire, put the time of ratification at 1:00 P.M. (Sullivan to Alexander Hamilton, June 21, Knox Papers, Mhi, and Lear to Washington, June 22, Washington Papers, Library of Congress [DLC]), while *The New-Hampshire Spy* (Portsmouth), June 24, said it was 2:00 P.M.

[11]King Papers, Nhi; and Washington Papers, DLC.

[12]Knox Papers, Mhi.

[13]*Thomas's Massachusetts Spy: Or, The Worcester Gazette,* June 26; Smith to John Langdon, June 23, Langdon/Elwyn Papers, New Hampshire Historical Society; *The Hampshire Chronicle* (Springfield), June 25; and Schuyler to Stephen Van Rensselaer, June 24, in Stan V. Henkels, Auction Sale Catalog No. 1125 (January 23, 1915), page 16, item no. 108.

[14]Sullivan to Hamilton, July 10, *Hamilton Papers,* ed. Syrett, 5:148–49

[15]*The Papers of James Madison,* ed. William T. Hutchinson, William M.E. Rachal, Robert A. Rutland et al. (Chicago and Charlottesville, Va., 1962-), 11:171.

[16]*Hamilton Papers,* ed. Syrett, 5:80, 91.

[17]Christopher P. Yates to Abraham Yates, Jr., June 27, and Abraham G. Lansing to Abraham Yates, Jr., June 29, Abraham Yates, Jr., Papers, New York Public Library [NN].

[18]Yates to Abraham Yates, Jr., June 27, and Oothoudt to Abraham Yates, Jr., June 27, Abraham Yates, Jr., Papers, NN; and Clinton to Lamb, June 28, Lamb Papers, Nhi.

[19]Abraham Yates, Jr., to George Clinton, June 27, Yates Papers, NN.

[20]DePauw, *The Eleventh Pillar,* 208-9.

[21]To Nathan Dane, June 28, Dane Papers, Beverly Historical Society, Beverly, Mass.

[22]NYJWR, June 26; Carrington, Brown, and Griffin to Madison, June 25, *Madison Papers,* ed. Rutland, 11:180; and Yates to Abraham G. Lansing, June 25, Yates Papers, NN. The express rider was identified only as "Mr. Kelsey," who was probably Jonas Kelsey of Poughkeepsie, a brother-in-law of prominent Federalist Lewis DuBois. Kelsey was apparently a horse trader. (The information on Kelsey was provided by Dr. Thomas E. Burke, then a member of the staff of the New York State Commission on the Bicentennial of the United States Constitution.)

The Confederation Congress took no official action on New Hampshire's ratification until July 2, the day after it received official word from that state's president, John Langdon. On July 2, Congress appointed "a committee to examine" the ratifications of the Constitution by the nine states and to "report an act to Congress for putting the said Constitution into operation in pursuance of the resolutions of the late Federal Convention." Congress did not adopt an ordinance for calling the elections of representatives and senators to the first Congress under the Constitution and the first president of the United States until September 13. (See *The Documentary History of the First Federal Elections, 1788-1790,* ed. Merrill Jensen, Robert A. Becker, Gordon DenBoer et al., 4 vols. [Madison, Wis., 1976-1989], 1:23-143.)

[23]NYJWR, June 26; *The Pennsylvania Packet, and Daily Advertiser* (Philadelphia) [PP], June 27; and Knox to Jeremiah Wadsworth, June 29, Wadsworth Papers, Connecticut Historical Society [CtHi]. Colonel Henley, who like Henry Knox was a native of Massachusetts, had been given one of his commands in the Continental Army by General George Washington and had married a resident of Alexandria, Va., in 1782. He had recently served on a three-man commission that helped to settle Virginia's claims against Congress for the expenses that the state had incurred during the Revolution protecting the frontier against Indians. In the 1790s, Colonel Henley was an agent for Secretary Knox's War Department.

[24]NYJWR, June 26; and *The New-York Packet* [NYP], June 27. Immediately below its account, the *Packet* also reported that the city's tradesmen and mechanics "are preparing for a GRAND PROCESSION" to celebrate the adoption of the Constitution by nine states. This procession, which was put off several times, eventually took place on July 23, when both the ratification of the Constitution by ten states and the 4th of July were celebrated. By that time, Federalist leaders were in control of an event in which thousands took part. For the description of this procession, see Sarah H.J. Simpson, "The Federal Procession in the City of New York," *New-York Historical Society Quarterly Bulletin* 9 (1925): 39-57; Whitfield J. Bell, Jr., "The Federal Processions of 1788," *ibid.*

46 (1962): 29–37; and Richard Leffler, "The Grandest Procession," *Seaport: New York's Historical Magazine* 31 (1987–1988): 28–31.

[25]PP, June 27; Willing to William Bingham, June 29, Gratz Collection, Historical Society of Pennsylvania [Phi]; Samuel Smith to Tench Coxe, June 27, Coxe Papers, Series II, Correspondence and General Papers, Phi; Stephen Austin to Jeremiah Wadsworth, June 25, Wadsworth Papers, CtHi; and George Washington to Charles Cotesworth Pinckney, June 28, *The Writings of George Washington From the Original Manuscript Sources, 1745–1799*, ed. John C. Fitzpatrick, 39 vols. (Washington, D.C., 1931–1944), 30:9. The arrival time of "two hours before day" was given by George Washington. An anonymous New York letter writer, who claimed that he got the information from Henley himself, gave the time as 1:00 A.M. (*The Massachusetts Centinel* [Boston] [MC], July 5).

[26]NYJWR, July 3.

[27]No letter dated June 25 adressed from Madison to Hamilton (informing him of Virginia ratification) has been located, although it is unlikely that Madison did not write to Hamilton. The editors of the *Madison Papers* believe that a letter signed by Madison and dated June 25, whose address page had been detached, is the one that Madison wrote to Hamilton (11:177–78).

Madison's letter, in which he says that he had just received the dispatches from Poughkeepsie, is undated and the editors of the *Madison Papers* have placed it under June 30 because it was postmarked on that day (11:184). However, according to another Virginia convention delegate, David Stuart of Fairfax County, the dispatches arrived on the 29th (to Harry Innes, June 29, Innes Papers, DLC).

[28]Eight days from Concord to Richmond was good time. For example, the post from Boston to Richmond, a route shorter by about seventy miles, took thirteen days. (See MC, June 14.)

[29]Washington to Tobias Lear, June 29, Jonathan Bayard Smith Papers, 1:69, DLC; Henry Knox to Jeremiah Wadsworth, July 2, Wadsworth Papers, CtHi; and *The Maryland Gazette; or, the Baltimore Advertiser*, July 8 (reprint from the no longer extant *The Virginia Journal, and Alexandria Advertiser* of July 3).

[30]*The Independent Gazetteer; or the Chronicle of Freedom* (Philadelphia), July 1; and *The Independent Journal: or, the General Advertiser* (New York) [NYIJ], July 2. At 9:00 P.M. on June 30, Daniel Humphreys, the publisher of *The Pennsylvania Mercury and Universal Advertiser*, wrote the printer of *The New-Haven Gazette, and the Connecticut Magazine* [NHG] that the news of Virginia ratification had "just arrived" (NHG, July 3).

[31]NYDA and NYIJ, July 2.

[32]NYJWR, July 3; and *The Country Journal, and the Poughkeepsie Advertiser* [PCJ], July 8. The time of arrival of 2:37 A.M. was given by the *Country Journal*. The *New-York Journal, and Weekly Register* of the 3rd of July placed the time at 3:00 A.M., while Henry Knox, Samuel Blachley Webb, and Thomas Goadsby (a merchant) said it was 2:00 A.M. (Knox to Wadsworth, July 2, Wadsworth Papers, CtHi; Webb to Catherine Hogeboom, July 2, Webb Papers, Yale University Library [CtY]; and Goadsby to Kirkman, Holmes, and Company, [July 2], Hancock Papers, Baker Library, Harvard Graduate School of Business Administration, Harvard University).

[33]Webb to Catherine Hogeboom, July 2, Webb Papers, CtY.

[34]The writer of the Richmond letter has not been identified. The *Independent Journal's* one-page broadside supplement was reprinted from a broadside that had been printed by William Goddard, the publisher of *The Maryland Journal, and the Baltimore Advertiser*, on June 28 or soon thereafter. Goddard struck off his broadside after he had received (on the evening of June 28) an express from Alexandria sent by Colonel Gabriel P. Van Horne, a stagecoach operator. Goddard's broadside has not been located, but it is mentioned in his newspaper for July 1.

[35]Knox to Jeremiah Wadsworth and to Henry Jackson, July 2, Wadsworth Papers, CtHi; and MC, July 5.

[36]NYDA, NYJWR, and *The New-York Morning Post and Daily Advertiser*, July 3; NYP, July 4; and *The Impartial Gazetteer, and Saturday Evening's Post*, July 6. Three newspapers, *The New-York Journal, and Weekly Register*, July 3, *The Daily Advertiser*, July 4, and *The Independent Journal: or, the General Advertiser*, July 5, also printed the recommendatory amendments of the New Hampshire convention.

[37]These amendments were part of the Virginia convention's final form of ratification.

[38]Philip Schuyler to Stephen Van Rensselaer, July 2, Henry Ford Museum Bicentennial Collection, Edison Institute, Greenfield Village and Henry Ford Museum, Dearborn, Mich. [MiDbEI]; Cornelius C. Schoonmaker to Peter Van Gaasbeek, July 2, Roosevelt Collection, Franklin Delano Roosevelt Library, Hyde Park [NHpR]; DeWitt Clinton to Charles Tillinghast, Clinton Papers, Columbia University Libraries [NNC]; NYJWR, July 3; PCJ, July 8; and Edmund Platt, *The Eagle's History of Poughkeepsie From the Earliest Settlements, 1683-1905* (Poughkeepsie, 1905), 58-59. The interview of the eyewitness, which is published in Platt's volume, was conducted by historian Benson Lossing (1813-1891). This eyewitness gave the arrival time of Colonel Livingston at about noon. *The Country Journal, and the Poughkeepsie Advertiser* and Cornelius C. Schoonmaker said it was 12:30 P.M., while Philip Schuyler put it at about 1:00 P.M. The estimates about the length of time that the trip took also varied. DeWitt Clinton said that it took nine hours, *The Daily Advertiser* (New York), July 8, nine and one-quarter, Schuyler nine and three-quarters, *The Country Journal*, nine and fifty-three minutes, and the eyewitness under ten. *The Country Journal* also stated, that not counting the time for "the stoppages on the road," the actual riding time was seven and one-quarter hours.

[39]NYDA, July 8.

[40]Schuyler to Stephen Van Rensselaer, July 2, Henry Ford Museum Bicentennial Collection, MiDbEI; Schoonmaker to Peter Van Gaasbeek, July 2, Roosevelt Collection, NHpR; Clinton to Charles Tillinghast, July 2, Clinton Papers, NNC; and MC, July 16. The part of the DeWitt Clinton letter quoted here was printed as an anonymous extract of a letter in *The New-York Journal, and Daily Patriotic Register* on the 7th of July. During the convention, the nineteen-year-old Clinton kept Charles Tillinghast of New York City—Antifederalist leader John Lamb's son-in-law—regularly informed about that body's actions. Throughout the debate over the ratification of the Constitution, Lamb and Tillinghast regularly provided Thomas Greenleaf, the publisher of the *Journal*, with Antifederalist material. Clinton himself also sent information about the convention directly to Greenleaf.

[41]NYDA, July 8.

[42]Power's broadside was similar to the one that had been printed by the publisher of *The Independent Journal: or, the General Advertiser* (New York) on the same day.

[43]*The New-York Journal, and Daily Patriotic Register*, July 14, and *The Connecticut Courant, and Weekly Intelligencer* (Hartford), July 14.

[44]See DePauw, *The Reluctant Pillar*, 214-64; and John P. Kaminski, "New York: The Reluctant Pillar," in *The Reluctant Pillar: New York and the Adoption of the Federal Constitution*, ed. Stephen L. Schechter (Troy, N.Y., 1985), 106-17. In 1987 this volume was reissued by the New York State Commission on the Bicentennial of the United States Constitution.

[45]Any Antifederalist hope that Congress might accept a conditional ratification was dashed on July 24. On that day, John Lansing, Jr., an Antifederalist leader from Albany County, moved that the form of ratification should contain the right of New York to secede from the Union if amendments were not adopted within a certain period of time. Whereupon, Alexander Hamilton read to the convention a letter dated July 20 from James Madison, who was answering a Hamilton letter of the 19th. Madison told Hamilton that Congress would not accept a conditional ratification by New York, in which the state

reserved "the right to recede" from the Union if amendments proposed by the New York convention were not decided upon in five or seven years. Lansing's motion was defeated the next day, 31 to 28 (*Madison Papers*, ed. Rutland, 11:188, 189; DePauw, *The Eleventh Pillar*, 244–45; and Kaminski, "New York: The Reluctant Pillar," 112–13).

[46] Knox to George Washington, July 28, Washington Papers, DLC.

[47] Lewis to Tench Coxe, July 29, Coxe Papers, Series II, Correspondence and General Papers, Phi; and Burr to Richard Oliver, July 29, *Political Correspondence and Public Papers of Aaron Burr*, ed. Mary-Jo Kline and Joanne Wood Ryan, 2 vols. (Princeton, N.J., 1983), 1:33.

Constitutional Celebrations in New York State July–September 1788

GASPARE J. SALADINO
University of Wisconsin–Madison

New York City
(Manhattan)
July 2, 2:00–3:00 A.M.

An express rider arrived announcing that the Virginia Convention had ratified the Constitution on June 25. The bells of the city were rung for four hours. At 5:00 A.M. ten guns (twenty-four pounders) were fired in honor of the ten states that had ratified the Constitution. The entire day was "devoted to amusements." (See *New-York Journal*, July 3; and Samuel B. Webb to Catherine Hogeboom, July 2, in Worthington Chauncey Ford, ed., *Correspondence and Journals of Samuel Blachley Webb* [3 vols., New York, 1893–1894], 3: 110.)

Poughkeepsie
Dutchess County
July 2, 12 Noon (approximately)

Colonel William Smith Livingston arrived from New York City, after a ride of less than ten hours, and reported that Virginia had ratified the Constitution. A group of people gathered before the courthouse (corner of Main and Market streets); they marched around the building several times. At night, a small bonfire was lit. (See Edmund Platt, *The Eagle's History of Poughkeepsie from the Earliest Settlements, 1683–1905* [Poughkeepsie, 1905], 59.)

City of Albany
Albany County
July 4, 9:00 A.M.

Antifederalists left Hilton's Tavern, marched to the site of Fort Frederick, and burned the Constitution. At 11:00 A.M. a procession of Federalists (and some Antifederalists) marched from the city hall to the city tavern where Federalists dined. At 6:00 P.M. a procession of 800–1,000 went to Fort Frederick where Federalists erected a "federal tree" on the spot where the Constitution had been burned. Ten cannon for the ten ratifying states were fired. On the procession's return, a "fracas" broke out between Federalists and Antifederalists; about eighteen people were hurt; Federalists were victorious; several Antifederalists were taken prisoner; and Hilton's Tavern was badly damaged. (See *Collier's* [*Litchfield*, Conn.] *Weekly Monitor*, July 7; *New York Daily Advertiser*, July 10; *New-York Journal*, *Connecticut Courant*, and *The Vermont Gazette*, July 14; and *New York Packet*, July 15.)

Brooklyn
Kings County
July 4

Thirteen Federalists attended a dinner at Dawson's Tavern in the town of Brooklyn. (See New York *Impartial Gazetteer*, and New York *Daily Advertiser*, July 5, 1788.)

Frederickstown
then Dutchess County
now Kent in Putnam County
July 4

Antifederalists met for entertainment at the house of Matthew Patterson, Esq., and thirteen muskets were fired. About sixty Federalists met at Mr. Phillips' tavern for dinner; there were thirteen discharges of cannon. (Ten discharges had been fired before dinner.) (See Poughkeepsie *Country Journal*, July 22, 29.)

City of Hudson
Columbia County
July 4

A military parade took place; thirteen discharges of cannon were fired; and dinner was served at Mr. Gordon's tavern. Armed force was used against some Antifederalists who tried to interfere with the entertainment. (See *Hudson Weekly Gazette*, July 8.)

Jamaica
Queens County
July 4

Bells were rung; thirteen muskets were fired; and an elegant dinner, attended mostly by Federalists, was served. (See *New-York Packet*, July 8.)

Kingston
Ulster County
July 4

"A cold collation was provided, in the true REPUBLICAN *stile*" at Mr. Elmendorf's tavern. Thirteen discharges of cannon were fired. (See *New-York Journal*, July 12.)

Lansingburgh
then Albany County
now in Troy, Rensselaer County
July 4

An elegant dinner took place at Mr. Platt's tavern. (See Albany *Federal Herald*, July 7.)

New York City
(Manhattan)
July 4

Military exercises were held at "The Fields" (now City Hall Park); cannon were discharged from the ship *Hamilton*; the Society of the Cincinnati met at City Hall; the Society attended Colonel William Duer's oration at St. Paul's Church; the society dined at the city tavern; the military officers who were not members of the society dined at Beekman's Hall on Cortlandt Street; and a rocket display was launched on Long Island opposite the city. (See New York *Impartial Gazetteer*, and New York *Daily Advertiser*, July 5.)

Federalists postponed their massive celebration to July 10, then to July 22, and finally to July 23 (see below).

Poughkeepsie
Dutchess County
July 4

A thirteen-gun salute was fired. There were gatherings under "an elegant and fanciful arbor" and at the governor's quarters which were attended by members of the New York convention. Antifederalists had their dinner at Hendrickson's Tavern; while Federalists had theirs at Poole's Tavern. (See Poughkeepsie *Country Journal*, July 8; and New York *Daily Advertiser*, July 9.)

New York City
(Manhattan)
July 23

The Federalists of New York City wanted to celebrate the adoption of the Constitution by ten states at the annual festivities for the 4th of July, but not wanting to offend the New York Convention which had not yet ratified the Constitution, they postponed their celebration to the 10th, then the 22nd, and ultimately the 23rd. Between 8:00 and 10:00 A.M. a huge procession of the trades, occupations, professions, and officials of the city was organized at "The Fields" (now City Hall Park). The procession, consisting of about 5,000 people and viewed by about 20,000, marched a-mile-and-a-half down Broadway to Great Dock Street, thence through Hanover Square, and Queen, Chatham, Division, and Arundel Streets. At Bullock Street, the procession turned left and marched a few blocks to the farm or orchard of alderman Nicholas Bayard. Included in one of the ten divisions was a thirty-two-gun frigate called *The Hamilton* which had a crew of more than thirty sailors and marines. At Nicholas Bayard's, about 6,000 people dined at ten tables (each 440 feet long) in a specially-built structure that had been designed by Major Pierre L'Enfant. After the banquet, the procession went back over its route and came to a halt at 5:30 P.M. The cost of the procession and the banquet was estimated at between $20,000 and $25,000. (See the New York *Daily Advertiser*, and the New York *Independent Journal*, August 2; Samuel B. Webb to Catherine Hogeboom, July 20, Ford, ed., *Webb Correspondence*, 3: 112; and Sarah H.J. Simpson, "The Federal Procession in the City of New York," The New-York Historical Society *Bulletin* 9: (1925), 39–56.)

THE NEW YORK CONVENTION
RATIFIED THE CONSTITUTION ON JULY 26,
BECOMING THE ELEVENTH STATE TO DO SO.

Newburgh
then Ulster County
now in Orange County
July 26, 4:00 P.M.

The news of ratification arrived in Newburgh. There was a salute of eleven guns, and eleven toasts were drunk. (See *New-York Packet*, August 1.)

New York City
(Manhattan)
July 26, 9:00 P.M.

The news of ratification arrived in New York City. Bells were rung; and cannon were discharged from the fort and the ship *Hamilton*. Merchants at coffeehouses "testified their joy by repeated huzzas." People went to the homes of the city's delegates to the New York convention and gave three cheers. They also "drank freely of the *Federal Bowl*." After midnight, a mob wrecked the press of Thomas Greenleaf, the editor of the Antifederalist *New-York Journal*. (See New York *Independent Journal*, July 28, extra; *New-York Packet* and *New-York Weekly Museum*, July 29; and *New-York Journal*, August 7.)

New York City
(Manhattan)
July 28

The city's delegates to the New York convention returned home, and at night an eleven-gun salute was fired before the house of each delegate. (See *New-York Packet* and New York *Daily Advertiser*, July 29.)

Ballston
then Albany County
now in Saratoga County
July 30

A dinner was held at the house of Captain Uriah Gregory. Eleven toasts were made by the musketeers of Capt. Gregory's company. (See Albany *Federal Herald*, August 4.)

Red Hook
Dutchess County
August 6

A number of gentlemen met at the house of Mr. Thomas Swart. The day was spent "in a sociable and harmonious manner, smoaking the Calumet of Peace, and burying in oblivion all distinctions of party." (See Poughkeepsie *Country Journal*, August 12.)

City of Albany
Albany County
August 8, 11:00 A.M.

A procession of the trades, professions, occupations, and officers of the city was formed in the fields near Watervliet. The procession was led by Major General Philip Schuyler, who carried the Constitution on horseback. It moved through Watervliet, Market (now Broadway), and State streets to the "FEDERAL BOWER" near the site of old Fort Frederick. The bower (or arbor) was 145 feet in length and 44 in breadth. People sat down at eleven tables "plentifully covered with substantial American cheer." After dinner the procession formed again, and went down State Street into Pearl Street, and then to Columbia, Market, and Court streets, arriving at the pasture south of Fort Orange. (When the procession had reached Green Street, a number of Antifederalists attacked the procession but were routed by the charge of some "lighthorse.") (See Joel Munsell, *The Annals of Albany* [10 Vols., Albany, 1850–1859], 1: 331–35. Munsell obtained this information from an account published in the *Albany Gazette*, August 28. The *Gazette*'s report was reprinted in the *New-York Packet*, September 5, 9, and the New York *Daily Advertiser*, September 6, 8.)

Flushing
Queens County
August 8

The inhabitants of Queens County met in a "splendid and beautiful colonnade, erected on the green" in the center of the town of Flushing. The colonnade was constructed of "pillars, covered with sprigs of the fir and yew trees." A dinner was served, and there were eleven discharges of cannon. An oration was delivered by John Mulligan, a student at Columbia College. (See New York *Daily Advertiser*, August 13.)

Dover
Dutchess County
August 11

The celebration took place at The Federal Village on the estate of Major Henry G. Livingston, in Dover. An elegant entertainment was provided at Messrs. Gregorys' Federal Store in said village. There were eleven toasts and discharges of cannon. About 500 people sat at eleven tables and partook of roast ox which was supplied by Major Livingston. (See Poughkeepsie *Country Journal*, August 19.)

Hurley
Ulster County
August 12

The inhabitants of Hurley and the adjacent towns (Federalists) attended at the house of Captain Cornelius DuBois, where eleven toasts were drunk. Each toast was followed by the discharge of cannon. (See Poughkeepsie *Country Journal*, August 26. This account was published by specific request of the town of Hurley.)

Saratoga District
then Albany County
now in Saratoga County
August 13

A meeting took place at the house of Mr. Ezekiel Ensign. A military procession was formed. There were eleven discharges of cannon, and eleven toasts were drunk at a dinner. (See Albany *Federal Herald*, August 18.)

Waterford
then Albany County
now in Saratoga County
August 13

The inhabitants of the Half-Moon District assembled at Waterford where there was a procession of military men and men from various occupations. About 500 people had dinner on the plain on the west side of town. It was "a truly American feast" held under "a beautiful bower erected for the purpose." Eleven toasts were drunk, each followed by a discharge of cannon. (See Albany *Federal Herald*, August 25.)

Smithtown
Suffolk County
August 14

The inhabitants of Smithtown and many from Huntington, Islip, and Brookhaven met at the Smithtown Church and heard an address by Jeffrey Smith. A dinner, consisting of "an excellent cold collation," was held on the green next to the church. In the evening there was a procession of young ladies and gentlemen, followed by "the exercise of dancing." Indians and Negroes "had what they would eat," and the rest was distributed to the poor. (See New York *Daily Advertiser*, September 2.)

Schenectady
then Albany County
August 15

A "bower" was erected at the house of Mr. Robert Mostyn. The company drank eleven toasts under the bower. (See *The Pennsylvania Mercury and Universal Advertiser*, September 4, which reprinted it from the *Albany Gazette*, August 21.)

New York City
(Manhattan)
September 17

This was the first anniversary of the signing of the Constitution by the members of the Constitutional Convention. A salute of eleven cannon was fired by the American brig *Federalist*, Captain George Bright. The brig was beautifully decorated with the flags of foreign nations, and eleven toasts were drunk. (See New York *Daily Advertiser*, September 18.)

EXPLANATORY NOTE:

At almost all of these celebrations, toasts were drunk and cannon or muskets were fired. The number of toasts or firings at the 4th of July celebrations was either ten (for the states that had ratified the Constitution) or thirteen (for the states in the Union). At the celebrations of New York's ratification, the number was invariably eleven since New York was the eleventh state to ratify the Constitution.

For more on these processions, especially the one in New York City, see Sarah H.J. Simpson, "The Federal Procession in the City of New York," The New-York Historical Society *Bulletin* 9 (1925): 39–56; Whitfield J. Bell, Jr., "The Federal Processions of 1788," The New-York Historical Society *Quarterly* 46 (1962): 5–40; John P. Kaminski, "New York: The Reluctant Pillar," in Stephen L. Schechter, ed., *The Reluctant Pillar: New York and the Adoption of the Federal Constitution* (Troy, N.Y., 1985), 112–13; and Linda Grant DePauw, *The Eleventh Pillar: New York State and the Federal Constitution* (Ithaca, N.Y., 1966).

In citing New York newspapers and magazines, the auther has adopted a shortened form for each. For the full titles, see the author's "Newspapers and Magazines of New York State, 1787–1788," in this volume.

A Supplement to "A Guide to Sources for Studying the Ratification of the Constitution by New York State"*

GASPARE J. SALADINO
University of Wisconsin–Madison

The Bicentennial of the United States Constitution has precipitated the publication of an avalanche of scholarly articles and monographs and primary source materials that have significantly enhanced the depth of our knowledge and understanding of the Revolutionary generation and the American Founding. Historians, political scientists, and lawyers have all made important contributions. The emphasis, in keeping with the present scholarly fashion, has been upon "ideology and political culture"—a trend that began in the late 1960s with the writings of Bernard Bailyn and Gordon S. Wood.[1] Consequently, the study of the practical politics in the making of the Constitution and its ratification by the states has been slighted. When compared to the vast general literature on the American Founding, the number of articles and monographs produced on the stories of ratification in the states is minimal. In short, the emphasis has been on what men said rather than what they did and why they did it.

This article deals primarily with the secondary and primary material that has been printed since 1985, with a few allusions to earlier material that did not appear in this writer's original article.[2] The emphasis is on the scholarly literature, although some popular works will also be considered.

General Works, Encyclopedias, Bibliographies, and Anthologies

Several general works have appeared since 1985 that have contributed much to our knowledge and understanding of the Revolutionary generation and the American Founding. In 1987 the late Richard B. Morris, the dean of historians of the Confederation Period, published his long-awaited *The Forging of the Union, 1781–1789*, a volume in the "New American Nation Series," of which he was also co-editor. This work supplants but does not supersede Merrill Jensen's *The New Nation: A History of the United States During the Confederation, 1781–1789* (New York, 1950) as the standard account of the Confederation.[3] Morris gives the most balanced picture to date of this rich, varied, and complex period in which the future of the American nation was determined. He focuses squarely on the creation of the American nation. His footnotes are a superb guide to the primary sources, to the classic historical studies of the nineteenth- and early-twentieth centuries, and to the most recent scholarship in such diverse fields as demography, ecology, historical geography, political theory, legal and military history, diplomacy, and black, women's, and Native American studies. A solid survey on constitution making, which is also a good guide to recently published primary sources and scholarly monographs, is Richard B. Bernstein's and Kym R. Rice's lavishly illustrated *Are We to Be a Nation? The Making of the Constitution* (Cambridge, Mass., and London, 1987). Intended as a companion guide to the New York Public Library's exhibition on the Bicentennial of the Constitution, *Are We to Be a Nation?* places particular emphasis on the intellectual and constitutional background of the American Founding. The most comprehensive account of this background, however, is Forrest McDonald's *Novus Ordo Seclorum: The Intellectual Origins of the Constitution* (Lawrence, Kan., 1985).[4]

Other useful works on the intellectual and theoretical framework of the Founding published since 1985 are: J.G.A. Pocock, *Virtue, Commerce, and History: Essays on Political Thought and History, Chiefly in the Eighteenth Century* (Cambridge, 1985); Jack P. Greene, *Peripheries and Center: Constitutional Development in the Extended Politics of the British Empire and the United States, 1607–1788* (Athens, Ga., 1986); Ralph Lerner, *The Thinking Revolutionary: Principle and Practice in the New Republic* (Ithaca, N.Y., 1987); John Phillip Reid, *The*

Constitutional History of the American Revolution: The Authority to Tax (Madison, Wis., 1987); Edmund S. Morgan, *Inventing the People: The Rise of Popular Sovereignty in England and America* (New York and London, 1988); Thomas L. Pangle, *The Spirit of Modern Republicanism: The Moral Vision of the American Founders and the Philosophy of Locke* (Chicago, 1988); John Phillip Reid, *The Concept of Liberty in the Age of the American Revolution* (Chicago, 1988); and John Phillip Reid, *The Concept of Representation in the Age of the American Revolution* (Chicago, 1989).

One of the principal scholarly monuments to the Bicentennial of the Constitution is the *Encyclopedia of the American Constitution*, ed. Leonard W. Levy, Kenneth L. Karst, and Dennis J. Mahoney, 4 vols. (New York and London, 1986). This work, under the chief editorship of one of the most prolific historians of the Constitution and the Bill of Rights, has approximately 2,100 articles written by 262 lawyers, historians, and political scientists. Lawyers comprise the largest group of contributors. The articles, which run from a few sentences to 6,000 words, fall into the following categories: doctrinal concepts of constitutional law (55%), people (15%), judicial decisions (15%), public acts (i.e., laws, treaties, etc.) (5%), and historical periods (10%). Each article is followed by a brief, selected bibliography in which the entries are arranged alphabetically by author with the date of publication prominently displayed.

This comprehensive work is supplemented by two other encyclopedias, both published by Charles Scribner's Sons, that cover a smaller number of topics in lengthy articles that are followed by brief bibliographic essays. These two works are: the *Encyclopedia of American Political History: Studies of the Principal Movements and Ideas*, ed. Jack P. Greene, 3 vols. (New York, 1984); and the *Encyclopedia of the American Judicial System: Studies of the Principal Institutions and Processes of Law*, ed. Robert J. Janosik, 3 vols. (New York, 1987). The encyclopedia edited by Greene has ninety articles written by such experts as Jack N. Rakove on the "Articles of Confederation"; Leonard W. Levy on the "Bill of Rights"; Lance Banning on "The Federalist Papers"; and J.G.A. Pocock on the "English and European Political Inheritance." Janosik's encyclopedia has eighty-eight articles and is divided into the following categories: legal history; substantive law; institutions and personnel; process and behavior; constitutional law and issues; and methodology.

In the last few years, several fine historiographical and bibliographical essays have been published. In the order of the date of publication, they are: Jack P. Greene, *A Bicentennial Bookshelf: Historians Analyze the Constitutional Era* (Philadelphia, 1986); Richard B. Bernstein, "Charting the Bicentennial," *Columbia Law Review* 87 (1987): 1565–1624; Patrick T. Conley, "Posterity Views the Founding: General Published Works Pertaining to the Creation of the Constitution; A Bibliographic Essay," in *The Constitution and the States: The Role of the Original Thirteen in the Framing and Adoption of the Federal Constitution*, ed. Conley and John P. Kaminski (Madison, Wis., 1988); and Peter S. Onuf, "FORUM, Reflections on the Founding: Constitutional Historiography in Bicentennial Perspective," *William and Mary Quarterly*, 3rd ser., 46 (1989): 341–75. Greene reviews, in his thirty-one page pamphlet done under the auspices of the Friends of the Independence National Historical Park, the literature published through 1986 on (1) the making and ratification of the Constitution, (2) "ideology and political culture," (3) state and national politics, before, during, and after ratification, (4) the economy, society, and diplomacy, (5) biographies, and (6) documentary collections. Greene promises an addendum to his pamphlet that will cover the historical literature through 1987.[5] Bernstein is concerned primarily with the material published in conjunction with the Bicentennial. He describes and critiques the one-volume and multivolume compilations on the framing and ratification of the Constitution and the multivolume editions of the papers of the Founding Fathers. Much of his essay amounts to a series of analytical book reviews of scholarly monographs and the literature aimed at the general reader. Conley's essay is a supplement to a series of essays on the ratification of the Constitution in each of the thirteen states. The individual authors include bibliographies on the individual states, while Conley deals with the general works (primary, secondary, historiographical, and bibliographical) on the Constitution, with a strong emphasis on constitution making and political and constitutional thought. Onuf reviews the literature of the republican synthesis, the works that have challenged this synthesis, the renewed interest in the nature of the Confederation Period, the revitalized interest "in the efforts of constitutional reformers to construct—and conceptualize—a workable federal system," and the debate (between 1787 and 1789) over the kind of the government created by the Constitutional Convention.

Kermit L. Hall, a leading scholar of constitutional and legal history, has edited *A Comprehensive Bibliography of American Constitutional and Legal History, 1896-1979*, 5 vols. (Millwood, N.Y., 1984). This well-indexed bibliography, which runs to over 68,000 entries, is divided into constitutional and legal subjects, chronological periods, geographical areas, governmental institutions, and biographical studies. For each item, Hall gives the inclusive dates covered by the author. ABC–Clio, a database located in Santa Barbara, Calif., has published a single-volume bibliography edited by Suzanne Robitaille Ontiveros that is entitled *The Dynamic Constitution: A Historical Bibliography*. Its most compelling feature is the large number of scholarly articles that have been abstracted for the reader's convenience.[6]

In January 1988 the Federal Justice Research Program of the Office of Legal Policy in the U.S. Department of Justice published the *Bibliography of Original Meaning of the United States Constitution*. Directed by Bernard H. Siegan, the faculty and students of the University of San Diego School of Law culled a variety of primary and secondary works "to provide sources of historical information for judges, scholars, litigants, and others interested in the meaning of the Constitution, as understood by its authors." At the time this volume was printed, the Department of Justice was headed by Attorney General Edwin Meese III, one of the principal exponents of the constitutional theory that the judges of the Supreme Court should interpret the Constitution according to the "original intent" (or "original intention") of the Framers.

The books read by the Founding Fathers are discussed in two pamphlets: Jack P. Greene, *The Intellectual Heritage of the Constitutional Era: The Delegates Library* (Philadelphia, 1986); and Robert A. Rutland, *"Well Acquainted with Books": The Founding Framers of 1787, With James Madison's List of Books for Congress [1783]* (Washington, D.C., 1987). Both authors also print bibliographies of scholarly monographs on political theory, American and European constitutionalism, the intellectual background of the American Revolution, the philosophers, historians, and theorists read by the Founding Fathers, the legal treatises read by them, and their classical learning. On the Framers' reading in the law, the reader should also consult *Imported Eighteenth-Century Law Treatises in American Libraries, 1700–1799*, ed. Herbert A. Johnson (Knoxville, Tenn., 1978); and Jenni Parrish, "Law Books and Legal Publishing in America, 1760–1840," *Law Library Journal* 72 (1979): 355–452.

In the last couple of decades, the anthology of scholarly articles has become a favorite and useful means of disseminating knowledge, and the Bicentennial of the Constitution has produced several fine ones. In fact, some of the best writing on the Constitution in the last two or three years has been done in anthologies that are concerned with such topics as republicanism, constitutionalism, federalism, liberty, civic virtue, political thought and economy, the structure of government, and "the theoretical underpinnings of the Revolutionary Generation." In their order of publication, these anthologies are: *Beyond Confedera-*

tion: Origins of the Constitution and American National Identity, ed. Richard Beeman, Stephen Botein, and Edward C. Carter II (Chapel Hill, N.C., 1987); *Constitutionalism and Rights*, ed. Gary C. Bryner and Noel B. Reynolds (Provo, Ut., 1987); *The Bill of Rights: A Lively Heritage*, ed. Jon Kukla (Richmond, 1987); *The Framing and Ratification of the Constitution*, ed. Leonard W. Levy and Dennis J. Mahoney (New York and London, 1987); *Conceptual Change and the Constitution*, ed. Terence Ball and J.G.A. Pocock (Lawrence, Kan., 1988); *The American Founding: Essays on the Formation of the Constitution*, ed. J. Jackson Barlow, Leonard W. Levy, and Ken Masugi (New York, Westport, Conn., and London, 1988); *Essays on Liberty and Federalism: The Shaping of the U.S. Constitution*, ed. David E. Narrett and Joyce S. Goldberg (College Station, Tex., 1988); *Toward a More Perfect Union: Six Essays on the Constitution*, ed. Neil L. York (Provo, Ut., 1988); and *Principles of the Constitutional Order: The Ratification Debates*, ed. Robert L. Utley, Jr. (Lanham, Md., 1989). Two other anthologies outline the story of ratification in each of the thirteen states—*The Constitution and the States*, ed. Conley and Kaminski; and *Ratifying the Constitution*, ed. Michael Allen Gillespie and Michael Lienesch (Lawrence, Kan., 1989). In the Conley-Kaminski volume, John P. Kaminski has published a briefer version of his article on New York ratification that first appeared in *The Reluctant Pillar* and which was discussed in this writer's "A Guide to Sources" in the same volume. The title of Kaminski's later version is: "Adjusting to Circumstances: New York's Relationship with the Federal Government, 1776-1788."

In the second volume of *[Collected Essays on] United States Constititonal and Legal History*, 20 vols. (New York, 1987), Kermit L. Hall has reprinted from scholarly journals twenty-eight of some of the best articles on the formation and ratification of the Constitution that were printed between 1908 and 1981. Two of the articles relate to New York: Robin Brooks, "Alexander Hamilton, Melancton Smith, and the Ratification of the Constitution in New York," *William and Mary Quarterly*, 3rd ser., 24 (1967): 339–58; and Staughton Lynd, "Abraham Yates's History of the Movement for the United States Constitution," *ibid.* 20 (1963): 223–45.

Printed Primary Sources

A. Constitutional Convention

In the year of the Bicentennial of the Constitution, James H. Hutson (with the assistance of Leonard Rapport) produced the *Supplement to Max Farrand's The Records of the Federal Convention* (New Haven,

1987). In conjunction with this volume, Yale University reissued Farrand's first three volumes, first printed in 1911. Hutson incorporates into his volume (1) the documents that Farrand had printed in his supplementary fourth volume in 1937, (2) the notes of New York delegate, John Lansing, Jr., that Joseph R. Strayer had published in 1939, and (3) a multitude of additional letters, diaries, journals, and notes of debates. The new material is incorporated into the two indexes that Farrand had published, a general index and an index by clauses of the Constitution. Hutson also discusses, at length, the integrity of James Madison's notes of debates, concluding that Madison had not doctored his notes, as others had claimed.[7] Hutson reiterates his earlier findings concerning the questionable authenticity of New York delegate Robert Yates's notes which were altered when they were published by Citizen Edmond Genet in 1821.[8] A facsimile edition of the 1821 edition of Yates's was printed in 1987 by the Linn–Henley Research Center of the Birmingham (Ala.) Public Library as the *Bicentennial Edition of the Secret Proceedings and Debates of the Convention Assembled at Philadelphia, in the Year 1787, for the Purpose of Forming the Constitution of the United States of America.* The volume has an introduction by John Charles Armor and a name and place index to Yates's notes which was not part of the original edition. Another valuable publication of the records of the Constitutional Convention is *1787: Drafting the U.S. Constitution,* ed. Wilbourn E. Benton, 2 vols. (College Station, Tex., 1986). Benton takes the notes of debates by James Madison, Rufus King, John Lansing, Jr., Robert Yates, and James McHenry and rearranges them by article, section, and clause of the Constitution.[9] The Farrand–Hutson arrangement is chronological.

B. Ratification of the Constitution

The Bicentennial has produced a large number of documentary collections, both single-volume and multivolume. The student of the debate and fight over ratification in New York would profit from any of them because each has many documents that were published in New York, which, along with Massachusetts and Pennsylvania, was one of the three principal centers for the publication of articles, broadsides, and pamphlets on the Constitution. On the Federalist side, for example, New York contributed *The Federalist* by "Publius" (Alexander Hamilton, John Jay, and James Madison) and a pamphlet by "A Citizen of New-York" (John Jay); while on the Antifederalist side there were two pamphlets by the "Federal Farmer" and one by "A Plebeian" and the essays of "Cato," "Brutus," and "A Countryman."

Since 1985, the most outstanding collection of documents published on the debate over the ratification of the Constitution is *The Founders' Constitution*, ed. Philip B. Kurland and Ralph Lerner, 5 vols. (Chicago, 1987), a monumental work that runs to about 3,200 large, double-columned pages. The editors seek "to recover an 'original understanding' of those who agitated for, proposed, and argued over, and ultimately voted for or against the Constitution of 1787." In short, they are concerned with ideas, not politics, economics, or social forces. They have collected documents from well over 100 printed sources and organized them according to (1) the phrases in the Preamble to the Constitution, (2) the articles, sections, and clauses of the Constitution, and (3) the first twelve amendments to the Constitution. The bulk of the documents chosen cover the years 1787 to 1791, but there are others that go as far back as 1531 (Niccolo Machiavelli, *Discourses on the First Ten Books of Titus Livius*) and as far forward as 1836 (the U.S. Senate's reception of petitions for the abolition of slavery). At the end of each group of documents, the editors list additional readings of documents. Since the volumes are organized by subjects, the editors have supplied no subject index. They have, however, included brief indices of constitutional provisions, authors, and documents; and a table of judicial cases. In the first volume, which has also apeared in paperback, the editors have provided introductions to each of the seventeen major themes that they have located in the Preamble to the Constitution, such as the popular basis of political authority, the right of revolution, republican government, separation of powers, rights, equality, and securing the republic.

One of the sources used by Kurland and Lerner is *The Documentary History of the Ratification of the Constitution*, ed. Merrill Jensen, John P. Kaminski, Gaspare J. Saladino et al. (Madison, Wis., 1976–). In 1986, this documentary history published the fourth volume in its series entitled *Commentaries on the Constitution: Public and Private*. This chronological series presents the day-to-day regional and national debate on the Constitution by drawing together the most widely reprinted newspaper and magazine articles, the most widely circulated pamphlets and broadsides, and a multitude of private and public letters. The fourth volume takes the story to 31 March 1788 and extends the publication of "Brutus" through number 15 and *The Federalist* by "Publius" through number 75. Many New York documents are also printed in the appendix entitled "The Controversy over the Post Office and the Circulation of Newspapers." Michael Kammen, who has reviewed all four volumes of *Commentaries* for *New York History*, captured the essence of the series when he reviewed the first volume. He said: "There is much in this volume to interest New Yorkers. Some of the material, such as Alexander Hamilton's letters, has recently been printed elsewhere; but here it is set amidst substantively congruent documents. We can see, as never before, the dialogues that occurred betwen New Yorkers and writers in other states. . . . The intermingling of public and private documents works marvelously well for many reasons. We can compare the rhetoric designed to persuade with ruminations reflecting doubt or apprehension. We can compare assertions and predictions with what actually came to pass.''[10]

In the last four years, at least six one-volume compilations have appeared, all of which are available in paperback. They are: *The Anti-Federalist: An Abridgement by Murray Dry, of The Complete Anti-Federalist Edited, with Commentary and Notes, by Herbert J. Storing* (Chicago and London, 1985);[11] *The Essential Antifederalist*, ed. W.B. Allen and Gordon Lloyd (Lanham, Md., 1985); *The Origins of the American Constitution: A Documentary History*, ed. Michael Kammen (New York, 1986); *The Antifederalist Papers and the Constitutional Convention Debates*, ed. Ralph Ketcham (New York, 1986); *The American Constitution, For and Against: The Federalist and Anti-Federalist Papers*, ed. J.R. Pole (New York, 1987); and *Federalists and Antifederalists: The Debate Over the Ratification of the Constitution*, ed. John P. Kaminski and Richard Leffler (Madison, Wis., 1989).

Each of the compilations is introduced by a general interpretative or historical essay, and, with the exception of Kammen's volume, which includes many private letters, these compilations print documents of the public debate over ratification. Each volume, the Allen–Lloyd one excepted, has a brief index. In those compilations that print Federalist arguments, *The Federalist* is overly represented. Kammen and Ketcham also provide the reader with annotated bibliographies of secondary readings on the Constitution, while Pole has a brief list of readings.

The principal differences among the compilations, however, may be found in the manner in which the documents are organized. Because of this fact, the reader will be able to see the documents of New York ratification in a different context in each of these volumes, thereby obtaining a different perspective. Dry's abridgement of Herbert J. Storing's seven-volume work, the most heavily annotated of the compilations, follows Storing's original organization with the writings of the major authors, such as the "Federal Farmer" and "Brutus," appearing first and the rest of the documents by state. The Allen–Lloyd volume is divided into four subject chapters: the origin of Antifederalist thought; the Antifederalist views of federalism; the Antifederalist views of republicanism; and the Antifederalist support of capitalism and democracy.

The documents printed by Kammen cover the period 1776 to 1789; the first chapter deals with the genesis of the Constitution and the last with its implementation. The second chapter includes the private correspondence of the Founding Fathers, with the bulk of the letters coming from the Federalist side. The third chapter consists of selections from *The Federalist*; while the fourth has selections from the writings of several Antifederalists, especially "Brutus" and the "Federal Farmer." The first half of Ketcham's volume includes selections from the debates in the Constitutional Convention, while the second consists of documents dealing with the debate over the ratification of the Constitution. He also provides a table giving the Federalist answers (almost entirely from *The Federalist*) to the Antifederalist essays that he prints.

In the first half of his volume, Pole publishes the writings or speeches of several Antifederalists, while in the second half he prints selections from *The Federalist*. The Kaminski–Leffler compilation is divided into six chapters and within each chapter the Antifederalist and Federalist arguments are grouped together, with the former preceding the latter. The chapter headings are: the Constitution and the nature of republican government, the House of Representatives, the Senate, the Presidency, the Judiciary, and the Bill of Rights.

About two-thirds of the third volume of *The Documentary History of the First Federal Elections, 1788–1790* (Madison, Wis., 1986), edited by Gordon DenBoer and Lucy Trumbull Brown, includes documents on the elections of representatives, senators, and presidential electors in New York State in 1788 and 1789. These elections are an extension of the ratification story because one of the principal issues was concerned with amendments to the Constitution. In fact, the New York Convention would not have ratified the Constitution had there not been the promise of both a bill of rights and structural amendments. A large portion of the documents for this neglected period has never been published. The fourth and last volume, which was published in 1989, is largely concerned with the general history of the first presidential election, in which many New York documents are included.[12]

Another forthcoming publication also deserves mention. In two or three years, the prestigious Library of America is scheduled to publish Bernard Bailyn's two-volume edition on the debate over the ratification of the Constitution. In addition to printing selections from many of the major serialized essays, such as "Publius," "Brutus," "Centinel," and "An Old Whig," Bailyn will include pamphlets and broadsides, a significant number of private letters, and substantial excerpts from the debates of the various state conventions.

The Federalist

The best edition of *The Federalist*, which consists of eighty-five essays written by Alexander Hamilton, John Jay, and James Madison, remains Jacob E. Cooke's edition, first printed by the Wesleyan University Press of Middletown, Conn., in 1961. It is still available in both clothbound and paperbound editions. Except for the last eight essays, which first appeared in the second volume of the book edition published by John and Archibald McLean in May 1788, Cooke prints the essays from the newspapers in which they were first published in 1787–88. He also collates the texts of the essays with the texts from three book editions by these printers, John and Archibald McLean (1788), George F. Hopkins (1802), and Jacob Gideon (1818). In 1980 the Wesleyan University Press printed *The Federalist Concordance*, edited by Thomas S. Engeman, Edward J. Erler, and Thomas B. Hofeller, and eight years later the University of Chicago Press reissued this concordance in both clothbound and paperback editions. The paperback sells for about one-third the price of the hardbound edition.

Several other editions of *The Federalist* published in recent years are also valuable because each has features that will benefit the student of that seminal work. In 1986 Mentor Books reissued in paperback Clinton Rossiter's 1961 edition, which is based on the McLeans' text. Rossiter includes a brief introduction, a synoptical table of contents, a superb analytical index, and a list of his choices of the twenty-one best essays. He also collates *The Federalist* with the Constitution, which he reproduces as an appendix. He places relevant page numbers of *The Federalist* next to the clauses of the Constitution.[13]

In 1987 several printing houses reissued editions of *The Federalist*. The Johns Hopkins University Press reprinted a paperback version of the second edition of Roy P. Fairfield's collection of fifty numbers of *The Federalist*. The first and second editions had originally been published by Doubleday and Company as an Anchor paperback; the second Anchor edition, which had been updated and printed in 1981, is the one reprinted by the Hopkins Press. This volume includes a substantial, well-footnoted introduction, and 125 footnotes to the text of the essays. It has a bibliographical appendix of the important books and articles about *The Federalist* printed by 1981, and a chronological listing of all the editions of that work published in the English language and in foreign languages from 1788 to 1981.[14] Bantam Books reissued in paperback Garry Wills's 1982 edition of *The Federalist*. Wills, who uses Jacob E. Cooke's text, views the authors of essays as great teachers and outlines their principal themes and arguments. He also has a glossary of terms which had different meanings in the eighteenth century and a brief bibliography of works on *The Federalist* that includes his full length study of this work—*Explaining America: The Federalist* (New York, 1981).[15] The major feature of Isaac Kramnick's edition of *The Federalist* in the "Penguin Classics" (paperback) is an historical intro- duction of seventy pages that also has an analysis of the arguments used in the debate over the Constitution. Kramnick used the McLeans' text.[16] Global Affairs Publishing printed Michael Loyd Chadwick's edition of *The Federalist* in clothbound and paperback and it issued an accom- panying students' guide.[17] Lastly, Basil Blackwell published the second edition of English political scientist Max Beloff's *The Federalist or, the New Constitution* that first appeared in 1948.[18]

Several fine monographs and articles about *The Federalist* have ap- peared since 1984. In the order of publication, they are David F. Ep- stein, *The Political Theory of The Federalist* (Chicago and London, 1984); Albert Furtwangler, *The Authority of Publius: A Reading of The Federalist Papers* (Ithaca, N.Y., and London, 1984); Morton White, *Philosophy, The Federalist, and the Constitution* (New York and Ox- ford, Eng., 1987); *Saving the Revolution: The Federalist Papers and The American Founding*, ed. Charles R. Kesler (New York and London, 1987); and Daniel Walker Howe, "The Political Philosophy of *The Fed- eralist*," *William and Mary Quarterly*, 3rd ser., 44 (1987): 485–509, and "The Language of Faculty Psychology in *The Federalist Papers*," in *Conceptual Change and the Constitution*, ed. Ball and Pocock, 107–36. (For additional studies on *The Federalist* published after 1984 and for those published before that date, see *The Constitution and the States: The Role of the Original Thirteen in the Framing and Adoption of the Federal Constitution*, ed. Patrick T. Conley and John P. Kaminski [Madi- son, Wis., 1988], 320–22.)

David F. Epstein, challenging Gordon S. Wood and J.G.A. Pocock,[19] asserts that *The Federalist* demonstrates that the ideal of republican vir- tue and republican civil humanism was not lost with the adoption of the Constitution. The pursuit of one's self-interest could be honorable and benefit the common good. Albert Furtwangler reassesses *The Fed- eralist* "by looking closely at their form—by recognizing the literary strategies that shape their arguments and the conventions of political journalism which give meaning to the series as a whole." Philosopher Morton White examines "the epistemology, the ethics, the philosophy of history, [and] the theory of human nature" enunciated by "Publius."

"Publius" was an ideologist and a pragmatist; therefore, by studying the philosophy of *The Federalist*, one can better understand the pragmatist. White concludes that *The Federalist* is "a philosophical hybrid, an offspring of Lockeian rationalism in morals and Humeian empiricism in politics."

According to editor Charles R. Kesler, the fourteen essays in *Securing the Revolution* emphasize *The Federalist*'s lesson in constitutionalism: "the need for a permanent form of government anchored in a written constitution to protect man's unalienable rights, and to serve the public good; and the inculcation of man's duties under but also *to* the Constitution." Kesler emphasizes the civility of "Publius" in the debate over ratification; "Publius" was the "fountainhead of civic education." Daniel Walker Howe believes that to understand the crucial terms (interest, balance, reason, passion, and virtue) used by "Publius," we must examine "the theory of eighteenth-century faculty psychology"—"the study of human powers." Since this discipline was in a state of flux, "Publius" cleverly portrayed self-interest as an "intermediate motive," brief and passionate, but also long-term and rational. In so doing, "Publius" appealed to the educated opinion of the late eighteenth century upon whom the Enlightenment had had its impact.

Useful background material to the writing of *The Federalist* has been provided by Richard B. Morris in his popular but learned *Witnesses at the Creation: Hamilton, Madison, Jay, and the Constitution* (New York, 1985). In this group biography, Morris demonstrates how the early careers of each man prepared him to write parts of *The Federalist*. He describes how each sought to strengthen the central government during the 1780s; how Hamilton and Madison pursued their goals in the Constitutional Convention; and how each fought to get the Constitution ratified. This is not a book about *The Federalist*, only about the men who wrote it and why they did so, but as such it illuminates what they said.

Another item of interest on *The Federalist* is James G. Wilson's "The Most Sacred Text: The Supreme Court's Use of *The Federalist Papers*," *Brigham Young University Law Review* 1985: 65–135. Wilson discusses the Court's use of *The Federalist*, legal texts (e.g., Joseph Story and James Kent), historical monographs, and the papers of the Founding Fathers, and he provides a table indicating the frequency of their use by decade since 1790. It should also be noted that the Bernard H. Siegan's bibliography on "original intent" (mentioned above) has numerous references to *The Federalist* taken from the Jacob E. Cooke edition.

Lastly, the New York State Commission on the Bicentennial of the United States Constitution has granted a subvention to The Center for the Study of the American Constitution, at the University of Wisconsin–Madison, for a volume entitled *The Response to The Federalist: Contemporary Commentaries on a Political Masterwork, 1787–1788* (Madison, Wis., forthcoming, 1990).

Secondary Accounts of Ratification

The Bicentennial has not produced an abundance of scholarly books and articles that concentrate on the story of ratification in New York, but several good articles have appeared on some aspects of the ratification. In the *William and Mary Quarterly*'s special issue on "The Constitution of the United States," Robert Webking published an article in which he argues that Melancton Smith was the author of the *Letters from the Federal Farmer to the Republican*. He compares Smith's speeches in the New York Convention with the "Federal Farmer's" writings and finds similarities "in general thrust, specific points, and reasoning." Smith also had the time, intellect, background, and moderate temperament to have written these superlative Antifederalist essays.[20]

In 1988, David E. Narrett examined a major Antifederalist concern, "the preservation of liberty—the right of individuals to govern themselves and to be protected from arbitrary or despotic power." This concern was a great unifying concept for Antifederalists who defended middle-class values and who sincerely believed that the Federalists sought to establish an aristocratic government. In particular, Antifederalists attacked the Constitution's principle of representation; Congress was not big enough, thereby endangering liberty. They also feared Congress' power to tax and its control of the military. Narrett rejects the assertion that the Bill of Rights was "a fair compromise" between Federalists and Antifederalists. The structure of government, the major reason for their opposition to the Constitution, was not changed by that document. Although Antifederalists were in general agreement on these matters, Narrett uses Melancton Smith, George Clinton, and Abraham Yates, Jr., to demonstrate that there were differences in degree among them. Smith was the most accommodating and the Yates the most radical.[21]

The next year, Cecil L. Eubanks presented both sides of the debate on the Constitution. The debate was between two different views of republican government based upon class and two different notions of political economy. The Antifederalists, epitomized by Melancton Smith, were popular whigs who were localist and middle class and who strove for equality of opportunity in all areas of life. They extolled the independent and agrarian way of life and placed the yeoman on a pedestal. They feared and hated the aristocratic and consolidated government established by the Constitution. The Federalists, exemplified by Alexander Hamilton, were conservative whigs who wanted to enourage commerce and to protect property against democracy and who had a vision of a vast commercial empire. Only a powerful national government, dominated by a natural aristocracy of learning, could guaranteed these ends. "All told," states Eubanks, "the power of events and the expediency of self-interest were the major reasons for New York's approval" of the Constitution. Virginia had ratified and New York's southern counties had threatened to secede. Antifederalists were divided and some of the leaders (Melancton Smith and Samuel Jones) were accommodating because they hoped for amendments. And Federalists were conciliatory on amendments.[22]

Bernard Friedman and Robert F. Jones published articles on Hugh Hughes and William Duer—the first a popular whig or Antifederalist, the second a conservative whig or Federalist. Friedman seeks to rescue Hughes, an old Son of Liberty, from the dustbin of history. Hughes's "personal history," states Friedman, "incorporates a good deal of the common experience of that middling stratum of urban tradesmen and entrepreneurs from whose ranks came the radical leadership in New York." Hughes was a man who had suffered economic adversity before the Revolution because he had overextended himself in an era when risk taking was necessary for success. He hated the old elitist families and opposed ratification of the Constitution. The national government established by the Constitution endangered individual rights. Hughes sincerely believed that ordinary human beings were capable of governing themselves.[23]

Jones demonstrates that William Duer, a close friend and associate of Alexander Hamilton, was the prototype of an extreme conservative whig. He advocated a national government from which he could personally benefit economically. Throughout the 1780s, Duer supported every measure that would increase the power of Congress. Unlike Hamilton, he was not interested in establishing a virtuous republic; he was not a "disinterested" patriot. The pursuit of "individual happiness" was the most powerful motivating force in his life. Duer was among those individuals who made "profitable use of the circumstances of the moment."[24]

Members of the aristocratic elite were not the only ones who looked after their own economic well-being. Graham Russell Hodges's study of New York City cartmen shows how this large group of freemen joined with merchants and mechanics to support a strong national government. Cartmen also advocated economic regulation and policies that would foster the economic growth of New York City. During the 1780s this group received lucrative contracts from the city government run by Federalist James Duane. In the great parade of July 23, 1788 celebrating the ratification of the Constitution, there were 300 cartmen in the eighth division. (This division also included artisans representing many crafts.) The alliance with the city's economic and political elite broke down in the 1790s when the cartmen realized that they were not being treated as equals, especially with respect to political offices.[25]

Paul A. Gilje, in his work on mobs, demonstrates how the ideology and rhetoric of the Revolution gave artisans an enhanced sense of their worth and how the procession of July 23 increased this feeling. One of the ways in which artisans had been given a strong sense of their value to the community was their organization into mobs by both conservative and popular whigs in order to voice opposition to British imperial policy. Mobs were well-controlled, short-lived, and generally nonviolent, and they brought the entire community together. They were an expression of the immediate will of the people. In time, however, the economic and political elite looked upon mobs as a danger to the Republic and all mob action became illegitimate.[26]

A last article published on New York's ratification of the Constitution is Robert Ernst's group portrait of Long Island's delegates to the New York Convention. Except for those from Kings County, these delegates were Antifederalist even though all but one voted to ratify the Constitution. In fact, seven of the twelve Antifederalists who voted for ratification came from Long Island. They changed their minds because of the Island's proximity to New York City, which would benefit both politically and economically from the Constitution. Moreover, they believed that a second constitutional convention would be called to consider the amendments proposed by the state ratifying conventions. Ernst devotes the most space to Long Island's two most important delegates— Samuel Jones of Queens County and Thomas Tredwell of Suffolk County.[27]

New York State Commission on the Bicentennial of the United States Constitution

The Commission has sponsored and supported many activities and publications, but only some of the publications done under its immediate direction will be considered. Among these is *New York and the*

Union (the present volume) that, among other things, reprints the items on New York's ratification of the Constitution that first appeared as *New York Notes.* Included are biographical sketches of Egbert Benson, Aaron Burr, James Duane, William Duer, Alexander Hamilton, John Jay, John Lansing, Jr., Robert R. Livingston, Gouverneur Morris, Philip Schuyler, and Robert and Abraham Yates, Jr. Also included are such topical contributions as *The Federalist*; Clintonism and the New Federalism; New York newspapers and magazines; pseudonyms used by New York essayists in the newspaper debate over ratification; and New York constitutional celebrations. (*New York and the Bicentennial*, a companion volume to *New York and the Union*, is a useful sourcebook for planning commemorative activities and an account of the Commission's history and programs.)

The pamphlet, *Community: Birthplace of Popular Consent, A Salute to New York's Bicentennial Towns*, ed. Shirley A. Rice (Interlaken, N.Y., 1988), has an article by Carol Kammen on the contributions made by the towns to the growth of constitutional government and two lists of the bicentennial towns and counties; it also reprints the New York State town and county acts of 1788.

A forthcoming publication, *World of the Founders: Community Life in New York at the Time of the Constitution*, edited by Stephen L. Schechter and Wendell Tripp, "will examine the social, economic, cultural, and political milieu of the ratification period" in Newtown, L.I., New York City, the manors of the Hudson and Mohawk valleys, Poughkeepsie, Albany, and the new frontier communities of Western New York. The contributors, who are acknowledged experts on these subjects, are: Stefan Bielinski, Kenneth R. Bowling, Thomas E. Burke, Leo Hershkowitz, Jacob Judd, Jessica Kross, and William H. Siles. For example, Kross's article on Newtown is an extension of her book, *The Evolution of an American Town: Newtown, New York, 1642–1775* (Philadelphia, 1983). Her introduction to that volume contains a strong plea for more studies of New York towns, similar to those that have been made for so many New England towns. The article by Bielinski, also a strong advocate of community studies, is an elaboration of a small part of his earlier essay, tracing Albany's growth from a trading post in the 1620s to a prosperous commercial center in 1800.[28] Bowling has written a doctoral dissertation at the University of Wisconsin–Madison on the first United States Congress (1968) and has published articles on that body and the attempts to establish a national capital in the 1780s and 1790s; he will publish a book-length study of the subject with the George Mason University Press in 1990. Judd has edited and compiled four volumes of the papers of the Van Cortlandt Family of Cortlandt Manor (1976–1981), while Siles has completed a doctoral dissertation at the University of Massachusetts–Amherst on the Genesee Country from 1788 to 1800 (1978).

Another forthcoming book, edited by Stephen L. Schechter and Richard B. Bernstein, entitled *Contexts of the Bill of Rights*, will consider the first ten amendments to the United States Constituton, in the adoption of which New York played a prominent role. Articles will cover such topics as the British and American antecedents of the Bill of Rights, the late eighteenth-century meanings of each of the rights, and a history of the Bill of Rights from the Constitutional Convention through its ratification by the states. A bibliographic essay will discuss the primary sources and the historical literature on the Bill of Rights, concentrating on the years 1787 to 1791. The contributors to this volume are Donald Lutz, John P. Kaminski, and Gaspare J. Saladino.

Conclusion

The studies made in recent years have improved our understanding of why New York ratified the Constitution, even if the unfolding story is becoming more complex. This is not surprising because the society and politics of New York were so diverse. This diversity has fascinated scholars who are paying greater attention to the role of socio-economic classes, social and cultural institutions, and communities. Without an understanding of the class and economic conflicts that permeated New York society, we cannot begin to comprehend the lives of New Yorkers. The common man, to the chagrin of the elites, was making his presence felt. For example, a publication that examines the class and economic conflicts in New York is *Authority and Resistance in Early New York*, a collection of essays on seventeenth- and eighteenth-century New York edited by William Pencak and Conrad Edick Wright and published by the New-York Historical Society in 1988. The essays cover such topics as religion, women, ethnic groups, the poor and poor relief, pirates, riots, and freemanship. In addition, *World of the Founders* will take the community approach to enhance our understanding of New York society.

Some significant work has been done on political groups and individual politicians. David E. Narrett's sophisticated treatment of the Antifederalists and the concept of liberty reinforces the notion that this was not a monolithic group. Robert F. Jones's study of William Duer demonstrates that Duer was not the typical Federalist, but that he did represent a more extreme aspect of Federalism. Robert Webking has given Melancton Smith an even greater role in the debate over the ratification of the Constitution, expanding upon the work done earlier by Robin Brooks on Smith. And Robert Ernst has rescued the Long Island delegates to the New York Convention from obscurity.

A closer study has also begun to be made of the richness of the political ideas and theories employed in the debate over the ratification of the Constitution in New York State. Cecil L. Eubanks, for instance, has made a good start in analyzing this debate, but he barely tapped its prolific sources. A comprehensive examination probably will not be possible until *The Documentary History of the Ratification of the Constitution* publishes its volumes on New York in its series, *Ratification of the Constitution by the States*. Nevertheless, that project has given the student of New York a good head start with the publication of four of the five volumes in another series, *Commentaries on the Constitution: Public and Private*. New York, as Michael Kammen has demonstrated, is especially well represented in these four published volumes. In particular, we still do not fully understand the relationship of "Publius" (*The Federalist*) to other essayists in New York.[29]

Nevertheless, the gains made during the bicentennial bode well for the future of ratification studies in New York State; that is, if the euphoria and energy generated by the bicentennial are not entirely extinguished.

NOTES:

*This essay does not consider articles that have appeared in historical journals since mid-1989. The author wishes to thank Richard B. Bernstein, Shirley A. Rice, Stephen L. Schechter, and Wendell Tripp for their helpful recommendations concerning both style and content. Thomas E. Burke and Stefan Bielinski graciously provided materials that were unavailable to the author. Lastly, the author is indebted to computer programmer and operator Charles D. Hagermann, to the circulation, reference, acquisition, and cataloguing departments of the library of the State Historical Society of Wisconsin, Madison, and to the reference departments of the Memorial and Law libraries of the University of Wisconsin-Madison. For the study of the ratification of the U.S. Constitution in New York State, the reader will also profit from a perusal of the author's bibliographic essay on the Bill of Rights published in *Contexts of the Bill of Rights* (see below).

¹Bailyn, *Ideological Origins of the American Revolution* (Cambridge, Mass., 1967); and Wood, *The Creation of the American Republican, 1776-1787* (Chapel Hill, N.C., 1969). In its July 1987 issue, devoted to the Constitution, the *William and Mary Quarterly* [WMQ] paid tribute to Wood's seminal work when it invited historians to comment upon it, and a dozen prominent members of the profession responded. Their comments and Professor Wood's reply are published as: "FORUM, *The Creation of the American Republic, 1776-1787*: A Symposium of Views and Reviews," WMQ, 3rd ser., 44 (1987): 549-640.

²See "A Guide to Sources for Studying the Ratification of the Constitution by New York State," in *The Reluctant Pillar: New York and the Adoption of the Federal Constitution*, ed. Stephen L. Schechter (Troy, N.Y., 1985), 118-39. In 1987 this volume was reissued by the New York State Commission on the Bicentennial of the United States Constitution.

³Morris, who died in March 1989, himself praised Jensen's book in a foreword that he wrote for a reprint edition of it made by the Northeastern University Press of Boston in 1983. He described it as "a classic," while in *The Forging of the Union* he labeled it "magisterial."

⁴McDonald's other two major works on the Constitution are: *We the People; The Economic Origins of the Constitution* (Chicago, 1958); and *E Pluribus Unum: the Formation of the American Republic, 1776-1790*, 2nd ed. (1965; Indianapolis, 1976). See also McDonald and Ellen Shapiro McDonald, *Requiem: Variations on Eighteenth-Century Themes* (Lawrence, Kan., 1988)—a collection of essays on a wide variety of subjects, such as the intellectual world of the Framers, warfare as a cultural ritual, the Constitution and the separation of powers, Shays's Rebellion, and John Dickinson and the Constitution. Chapter 7, "The Constitutional Principles of Alexander Hamilton," is a distillation of part of Forrest McDonald's *Alexander Hamilton: A Biography* (New York, 1979).

⁵Greene's discussion in the section on "ideology and political culture" is particularly full. For several historiographical articles on republicanism, one of the principal issues treated by Greene, see Robert E. Shalhope, "Toward a Republican Synthesis: The Emergence of an Understanding of Republicanism in American Historiography," WMQ, 3rd ser., 29 (1972): 48-80, and Shalhope, "Republicanism and Early American Historiography," *ibid.* 39 (1982): 334-56; Isaac Kramnick, "Republican Revisionism Revisited," *American Historical Review* 87 (1982): 629-44; and Linda K. Kerber, "The Republican Ideology of the Revolutionary Generation," *American Quarterly* 37 (1985): 474-95. Also useful is Jeffrey J. Crowe, "Beyond the Republican Synthesis: Reinterpreting the Constitution," *North Carolina Historical Review* 64 (1987): 320-26. Crowe's essay is a review of *Beyond Confederation: Origins of the Constitution and the American National Identity*, ed. Richard Beeman, Stephen Botein, and Edward C. Carter II (Chapel Hill, N.C., 1987).

[6]For a useful bibliography of bibliographies, the reader should consult Francis Paul Prucha, *Handbook for Research in American History: A Guide to Bibliographies and Other Reference Works* (Lincoln, Neb., 1987).

[7]Hutson extended his analysis of the documentation on the Constitution to include the state ratifying conventions and the first Congress under the Constitution in his article: "The Creation of the Constitution: The Integrity of the Documentary Record," *Texas Law Review* 65 (1986): 1–39. Another outgrowth of Hutson's work on the Convention is his "Riddles of the Federal Constitutional Convention," WMQ, 3rd ser., 44 (1987): 411–23.

Richard B. Bernstein reviews the books, mostly popular, that were published on the Constitutional Convention in 1987 in his "Charting the Bicentennial," 1610–12, 1614–18. One of the works he considers is Elizabeth McCaughey's *Government by Choice: Inventing the United States Constitution* (New York, 1987)—the companion volume to the New-York Historical Society's exhibition on the Bicentennial. Bernstein characterizes this slender volume as one of those volumes which offers "the hope of building bridges between the scholarly community and a more general audience." The most recent works on the Convention and the ideological background of the Framers are discussed in Peter S. Onuf's "Reflections on the Founding," 346–64.

A book on the Constitutional Convention that deserves particular mention here is: Calvin C. Jillson, *Constitution-Making: Conflict and Consensus in the Federal Convention of 1787* (New York, 1988). Employing sophisticated techniques of roll-call analysis, Jillson demonstrates that the compromises in the Constitutional Convention were the result of both philosophical principles and economic and political interests. On voting patterns, see also Robert A. McGuire and Robert L. Ohsfeldt, "An Economic Model of Voting Behavior over Specific Issues at the Constitutional Convention of 1787," *Journal of Economic History* 46 (1986): 79–111.

[8]Hutson's original article is "Robert Yates's Notes on the Constitutional Convention of 1787: Citizen Genet's Edition," *Quarterly Journal of the Library of Congress* 35 (1978): 173–82.

[9]In 1941 Arthur Taylor Prescott rearranged Madison's notes by subject in *Drafting the Federal Constitution: A Rearrangement of Madison's Notes Giving Consecutive Developments of Provisions in the Constitution of the United States, Supplemented by Documents Pertaining to the Philadelphia Convention and to the Ratification Processes, and Including Insertions by the Compiler* (University, La., 1941).

[10]*New York History* [NYH] 64 (1983): 77–79. See also his reviews of volumes 2 to 4 in NYH 65 (1984): 395–97; 66 (1985): 332–33; and 68 (1987): 428–29. Kammen highlights what is valuable in the volumes for the study of New York ratification.

[11]Herbert J. Storing's *The Complete Anti-Federalist* was published in seven volumes by the University of Chicago Press in 1981.

[12]*The Documentary History of the First Federal Elections, 1788–1790*, ed. Merrill Jensen, Robert A. Becker, Gordon DenBoer et al., 4 vols. (Madison, Wis., 1976–1989). For an article that demonstrates that New York Federalists and Antifederalists carried their bitter fight over ratification of the Constitution into the first presidential election, see Tadahisa Kuroda, "New York and the First Presidential Election: Politics and the Constitution," NYH 69 (1988): 319–51.

[13]*The Federalist Papers: Alexander Hamilton, James Madison, and John Jay* (New York and Scarborough, Ontario, 1961).

[14]*The Federalist Papers: A Collection of Essays Written in Support of the Constitution of the United States*, 2nd ed. (Baltimore and London, 1981).

[15]*The Federalist Papers by Alexander Hamilton, James Madison and John Jay* (Toronto, New York, London, Sydney, and Auckland, 1982).

[16]*The Federalist Papers: James Madison, Alexander Hamilton, and John Jay* (Harmondsworth, Middlesex, Eng., 1987).

[17] The Federalist: A Collection of Essays, Written in Favor of the Constitution of the United States, as Agreed upon by the Federal Convention, September 17, 1787, by Alexander Hamilton, John Jay, and James Madison (Springfield, Va., 1987).

[18] The Federalist or, the New Constitution, 2nd ed. (New York, 1987).

[19] See Wood, The Creation of the American Republic; and Pocock, The Machiavellian Moment: Florentine Political Thought and the Atlantic Republican Tradition (Princeton, N.J., and London, 1975).

[20] "Melancton Smith and the Letters from the Federal Farmer," WMQ, 3rd ser., 44 (1987): 510–28. In his article, "Charting the Bicentennial," Richard B. Bernstein presents additional evidence supporting Webking's thesis that Smith was the "Federal Farmer" (pp. 1593n–94n). A second article that supports Smith's authorship (and one that summarily rejects the authorship of Richard Henry Lee) is Joseph Kent McGaughy, "The Authorship of The Letters from the Federal Farmer, Revisited," NYH 70 (1989): 153–70.

[21] "A Zeal for Liberty: The Anti-Federalist Case against the Constitution in New York," in Essays on Liberty and Federalism: The Shaping of the U.S. Constitution, ed. Narrett and Joyce S. Goldberg (College Station, Tex., 1988), 48–87. Narrett published a briefer version of his article under the same title in NYH 69 (1988): 285–317.

[22] "New York: Federalism and the Political Economy of Union," in Ratifying the Constitution, ed. Michael Allen Gillespie and Michael Lienesch (Lawrence, Kan., 1989), 300–40.

[23] "Hugh Hughes, A Study in Revolutionary Idealism," NYH 64 (1983): 229–59. It should be noted that Professor Friedman did not use the Hugh Hughes Papers in the Library of Congress; had he done so he would have discovered Hughes's significant role in the ratification story in New York. Some of that story can be pieced together by examining the first three volumes of Commentaries on the Constitution: Public and Private in The Documentary History of the Ratification of the Constitution.

[24] "Economic Opportunism and the Constitution in New York State: The Example of William Duer," NYH 68 (1987): 357–72.

[25] New York City Cartmen, 1667–1850 (New York, 1986); and "Legal Bonds of Attachment: The Freemanship Law of New York City, 1648–1801," in Authority and Resistance in Early New York, ed. William Pencak and Conrad Edick Wright (New York, 1988), 226–44. The essays in the Pencak–Wright volume are based upon papers given in 1984 at a conference held at the New-York Historical Society and entitled "New York and the Rise of American Capitalism."

For the great procession of July 23, see Sarah H.J. Simpson, "The Federal Procession in the City of New York," New-York Historical Society Quarterly Bulletin 9 (1925): 39–57; Whitfield J. Bell, Jr., "The Federal Processions of 1788," New-York Historical Society Quarterly 46 (1962): 29–37; and Richard Leffler, "The Grandest Procession," Seaport: New York's History Magazine 31 (1987–1988): 28–31.

[26] The Road to Mobocracy: Popular Disorder in New York City, 1763–1834 (Chapel Hill, N.C., 1987); and "Republican Rioting," in Authority and Resistance, ed. Pencak and Wright, 202–25. Also useful on the role of artisans in New York society is Sean Wilentz, Chants Democratic: New York City & the Rise of the American Working Class, 1788–1850 (New York and Oxford, Eng., 1984).

Studies on some other classes and groups, although not directly related to the ratification of the Constitution, also deserve mention. On the poor of New York City, see Robert Emmet Cray, Jr., Paupers and Poor Relief in New York City and Its Rural Environs, 1700–1830 (Philadelphia, 1988), and "Poverty and Poor Relief: New York City and Its Rural Environs, 1700–1790," in Authority and Resistance, ed. Pencak and Wright, 173–201. On Loyalists, see Philip Ranlet, The New York Loyalists (Knoxville, Tenn., 1986); and Joseph S. Tiedemann, "Patriots by Default: Queens County, New York, and the British Army, 1776–1783," WMQ, 3rd ser., 43 (1986): 35–63, "Loyalists and Conflict Resolution in Post-Revolutionary New York: Queens County as a Test Case," NYH 68 (1987): 27–43, and "A Revolution Foiled: Queens County, New York, 1775–1776," Journal of American History 75 (1988): 417–44.

[27]"The Long Island Delegates and the New York Ratifying Convention," NYH 70 (1989): 55–78. For another essay on the Long Island delegates, see Luise Weiss, "The Election of Long Island Delegates to the New York State Convention to Consider the Federal Constitution," *Long Island Historical Journal* 1 (1988): 71–80. See also a pamphlet by Weiss, *Reflections on 1788: Long Island and the Constitution* (Centerreach, N.Y., 1987).

[28]"The People of Colonial Albany, 1650–1800: The Profile of a Community," in *Authority and Resistance*, ed. Pencak and Wright, 1–26. Bielinski is the Director of the "Colonial Albany Social History Project," a service program of the Division of Research and Collections of the New York State Museum, Albany. By November 1986 the project had a computer database with more than 6,500 individual biographical cases. For an historiographical article that Bielinski has written on community studies for eighteenth- and nineteenth-century New York, see "From Gates to Ellis to Benson to Ryan: A History of Social History in New York State," *New York State History Network* 4 (Fall 1982): 4–11.

Those studying communities might also profit from William E. Nelson's "The Eighteenth Century Constitution as a Basis for Protecting Personal Liberty," in *Liberty and Community: Constitution and Rights in the Early American Republic*, ed. Nelson and Robert C. Palmer (New York, London, and Rome, 1987). Nelson is concerned with the manner in which governments encouraged economic growth and how they provided for the distribution of the benefits of that growth within the community. It was hoped that all would gain from economic growth, although some would gain more than others.

[29]For further recommendations of work that might be done to improve our understanding and enhance of knowledge of the ratification story in New York State, see this writer's earlier essay in *The Reluctant Pillar*, ed. Schechter, 146–47.

III. New York Participants in the Making of the Constitution, 1787–1789

Egbert Benson

(1746–1833)

WYTHE W. HOLT, JR.

University of Alabama School of Law

Egbert Benson's public career led him to the office of the attorney general for New York State and membership in the United States House of Representatives. He worked for ratification of the Constitution and took a prominent role in shaping the new nation's judiciary. Benson served on the New York State Supreme Court and as chief judge of the Second Circuit Court of Appeals.

Egbert Benson was born of Dutch ancestry in New York on June 21, 1746. He took a classical course at King's College (now Columbia University), graduating in 1765. Benson then chose the bar, studying law in the office of one of the colony's foremost attorneys, John Morin Scott. Benson was one of a group of King's College students who became lawyers, remained close friends, and, usually, political allies, and led distinguished lives. The most notable of this group and Benson's closest friend within it was John Jay, later chief justice of the United States. Others in the group included Robert R. Livingston, chancellor of New York from 1777 to 1801; Gouverneur Morris, one of the principal drafters of the U.S. Constitution; and the Loyalist and legal educator Peter Van Schaack.

Commencing his law practice in New York City upon his admission to the bar in January 1769, Benson discovered the business there "trifling."[1] He managed to save enough money to begin a modest career of land speculation, but his income remained insecure and eventually he "saw [an] Opening elsewhere."[2] In 1772, he relocated to Red Hook in Dutchess County, about 80 miles north.

Benson soon found there such business as would "afford [him] something more than a comfortable subsistence."[3] He seems to have established a practice in real estate and general litigation, much like most country lawyers of his time. His most famous student and his eulogist, the learned James Kent, thought him an orderly, deliberate, and discerning lawyer, with an acute mind well steeped in the learning of the English common law. Kent's highest praise was reserved for Benson's mastery of fundamental ideas. "He was more distinguished than any man among us, Hamilton alone excepted," Kent remembered, "for going, in all researches, to the reasons and grounds of the law, and placing his opinion on what he deemed to be solid and elementary principles."[4]

Public Career

Benson was also desirous of public service, and—like many of his precocious generation—circumstances, connections, and personal merit soon rewarded him well along those lines. The commencement of the rupture with Great Britain caused him, in Jay's words, to "Devote [himself] to his Country and to what he thought his Interest."[5] Thus, although Benson was a conservative, he nevertheless became an organizer of the Dutchess County revolutionary committee. "It followed, of course," said Kent, "that his knowledge of law and of the enlightened principles of civil liberty, and his practical and business talents, would carry him forward rapidly to places of high public trust."[6]

State leaders quickly recognized Benson's abilities. At the age of thirty, Benson became the first attorney general of the independent state of New York, serving ably in that capacity from 1777 to 1789. He was elected almost simultaneously to the assembly of the first state legislature, where he became a prized legislative resource, drafting "almost every important bill that passed the assembly during the war."[7] He became a confidant and advisor of George Clinton, governor from 1777 to 1794. He left the state legislature when elected to the Continental Congress in 1781, serving with desultory attendance into 1788.

In 1777, the New York legislature appointed Benson one of its commissioners to present its claims to jurisdiction over Vermont, and in 1784 named him a commissioner to oppose before a special national tribunal the claims of Massachusetts to a large portion of western New York. General George Washington came also to repose much confidence in Benson's administrative competence, making him (among other appointments) commissioner to oversee the departure of British and Loyalist forces from New York in 1783.

Not much is known about Benson's law practice during these full years of public service. He did appear in 1784 as counsel in one of the most important cases of the time, *Rutgers* v. *Waddington*. Benson's opposing counsel, the brilliant young Alexander Hamilton, convinced the court to review the applicability of a New York statute under the law of nations, and to find it inapplicable under that law. At the time, *Rutgers* "was generally considered to be a direct attack upon the power of the legislature,"[8] and it is today considered to be one of the important decisions developing notions of judicial review.

Benson and his widening circle of important friends strongly supported the efforts by their younger colleague and emerging leader, Hamilton, to obtain stronger and more centralizing powers for what they saw as the beleaguered government of the United States. A convention had met in Hartford in November 1780, where Benson as one of the two New York delegates met with delegates from the New England states and joined in proposals to strengthen congressional powers. At Washington's urging in January 1786, the Virginia legislature called for a convention of state delegates to discuss the deterioration of commerce in the midst of a worsening depression. New York's two attending delegates at the ensuing Annapolis Convention in September 1786 were Hamilton and Benson, the latter serving as its secretary. Commissioners from only four other states appeared, and they adopted Hamilton's draft *Report* calling for a general convention to meet in Philadelphia in May 1787, to revise the Articles of Confederation.

When the Philadelphia Convention produced a Constitution granting to the national government the centralizing strength he had long hoped for, Benson was arduous and untiring in his advocacy of the new plan. His motion in the New York Assembly calling for a state ratifying convention was adopted on January 31, 1788. Benson's attempt to become a delegate to that convention was defeated in Antifederalist Dutchess County. (Benson had been the only nationalist to represent that county in the legislature since 1782.) However, upon the adoption of the Constitution, Benson was elected to the first Federal Congress, one of six New York members of the House of Representatives, and was reelected to the Second Congress. He was the fourth lawyer admitted to practice before the United States Supreme Court in 1790.

The House of Representatives drew fully upon Benson's experience as draftsman and lawyer, commissioner and administrator. Kent reports that he "drew the bills organizing the executive department of the government."[9] He served on several committees which dealt with the jurisdiction and structure of the new national court system. His wisdom and his ability to craft a compromise were relied upon in debate and in committee. Perhaps Benson's most important contribution as a national legislator, however, resulted in the failure to amend the Judiciary Act of 1789 two years after its enactment.

The Judiciary Act

The Judiciary Act of 1789, which established and organized the third branch of the national government, displeased Benson and the other Federalists who desired to maximize the powers of the government, since it contained many restrictive compromises approved by those suspicious of the breadth and vagueness of the constitutional grant of authority to the judiciary. Cases involving constitutional issues or issues of federal law, for example, were to be tried in state courts, not in federal courts. Benson and his friends grudgingly accepted the act, however, since it was necessary to appease opponents of the Constitution during the tense period in which the shaky new national government was becoming established. At the same time, two significant nationalizing features were secured in the 1789 act. First, all important national legal problems could eventually be heard before a national court, since appeals were allowed to the United States Supreme Court from the state courts in cases involving issues of constitutional or federal law. Second, federal courts were numerous and scattered throughout the nation, thus bringing the majesty and the reality of the new national government to the doorsteps of all the people. The compromises embodied in the act, then, were acceptable ones in the minds of Benson and his friends.

To those of Benson's views, the 1789 compromise was threatened by the proposal which Attorney General Edmund Randolph presented in late 1790 for a complete revision of the judiciary. Randolph shrewdly saw as fundamentally disruptive to the Union the possibililties of summary reversal by the Supreme Court of carefully considered state court decisions on important constitutional issues. State judges, already jealous of their prerogatives and suspicious of the potentially broad jurisdiction of the new national courts, would, Randolph thought, erupt in indignant opposition to Supreme Court decisions reversing them in controversial cases. Randolph proposed completely to separate state court jurisdiction from the jurisdiction of the national courts, leaving it to the decision of the litigants at the commencement of litigation whether a case involving both state law issues and national constitutional issues would occur in state or federal court. If they chose to leave important constitutional issues in state court, Randolph's proposed revision would have kept the case there, cutting off any possibility of later review by the Supreme Court.

Those of Benson's persuasion severely distrusted the state courts, and thought it would be fatal to the Union for a state court to have the final word on any important constitutional issue. However, they could not express their distrust directly, for fear of exciting the very animosity and opposition they were attempting to avoid. They had to cast about for an acceptable alternative way of expressing their views. Benson put his drafting ability together with his negotiating talent to discover an ingenious vehicle.

In order to dramatize the dangers of making important changes in the compromise Judiciary Act of 1789, Benson on March 1, 1791, laid before the Congress a constitutional amendment which would in effect have eliminated the lower federal courts, rendering the state supreme courts into the lowest level of national court. Many Americans in 1787 and 1788 had predicted a national court structure with only a few courts created by Congress; they expected the state supreme courts to become the national courts of first instance. Benson's twist, however, was to demonstrate the restrictions inherent in such an arrangement, leading to a great deal of control by the federal government over the state judiciaries. His amendment would have given to Congress the power to regulate all the national jurisdiction which the state supreme courts would be given. Moreover, state high court judges' salaries would be paid by Congress, not by the state legislatures. Finally, in states where existing high court judges did not have lifetime tenure, Congress would be enabled to create a state court with such a feature; and all state officers "in the administration of justice," including supreme and inferior judges and "ministerial" as well as judicial personnel, would be considered national officials subject to the power of Congress to give them "such farther duties as they shall deem proper for that purpose."[10]

Benson's proposal made apparent the divisiveness that would be produced by any drastic change in the compromises already reached over the national judiciary. As a result, both his amendment and Randolph's proposal were buried in committee, never to emerge. In the minds of Benson and his Federalist friends, this action preserved the Constitution by eliminating potentially fatal wrangling over the power of the judiciary. The Judiciary Act of 1789 remained essentially intact until the end of John Adams' troubled administration, when the Federalist party, hedging against the loss of the presidency and Congress to a Jeffersonian party they believed would destroy the Constitution, passed a strongly centralizing Judiciary Act of 1801. Benson would play an important role then, too.

Service on the Bench

After he left Congress in 1793, Benson returned to full-time law practice, but only for a short while. The New York legislature created a fifth position on the state supreme court, and the appointment was given in January 1794 to Egbert Benson. Kent joined his mentor on the court in 1798. It was an important time for the growth of commercial law in New York, and Benson's seven years on the court saw a steady development of jurisprudence, so much so that thirty years later Kent, reflecting on the commencement of his service, observed: "We had no law of our own & nobody knew what it was."[11] Benson most often chose to join the opinion of a colleague rather than to pen his own, so his great influence was chiefly felt behind the scenes. Kent does relate, however, that Benson drew up rules of practice for the court which proved a most useful reform.

Service to the national government always beckoned. President Washington wanted to name him a commissioner under the 1794 treaty that John Jay had negotiated with Great Britain, to adjudicate the thousands of claims by British merchants for unpaid debts incurred by colonial Americans before the Revolution. He was promised an appointment to the Supreme Court following such difficult service, but Benson declined the commission post, since he would have to give up his seat on the New York Supreme Court, and he was unwilling to trust that Washington's successor would honor the understanding. However, he soon accepted a commission more to his liking and consonant with his experience as boundary negotiator, under another, less controversial portion of the Jay Treaty—to decide the disputed northern boundary of Maine. He spent much time in this endeavor from 1796 to 1798.

Benson was still a justice of the New York Supreme Court when, in February 1801, President Adams was casting about for good lawyers who were also good Federalists to fill the sixteen new national circuit court judgeships created by the Judiciary Act of 1801. The Federalists felt that only by retaining control of a more powerful national judiciary could they even hope to repel the assaults on the Constitution which they expected the Jeffersonian Republicans to attempt. At the urging of Federalist members of Congress, Adams appointed Benson to be chief judge of the newly created Second Circuit, encompassing New York, Vermont, and Connecticut. The court sat for eighteen months before it was eliminated by repeal of the 1801 act, accomplished by the Jeffersonians in 1802 as their first important legislation upon assuming control of the executive and legislative branches of the government. Repeal also destroyed the supposedly life-tenured judgeships of the 1801 act.

The Federalists, and particularly the circuit judges, were furious at what they took to be a blatantly unconstitutional act. Bloody revolution was called for by some because of this attack on the Constitution. One of the circuit judges, Richard Bassett, published a "judicial" opinion declaring the repeal to be unconstitutional. However, when the Federalist justices on the Supreme Court decided not to oppose the repeal, the circuit judges (among whom Benson was a leader), joined by many Federalist lawyers, tried but failed to mount an effective counterattack. Their protest to Congress was dismissed out of hand by the Jeffersonian majority in February 1803, and the matter was laid uneasily and bitterly to rest.

Benson retired to private life and practice, except for a short stint in the House of Representatives in 1813. With Morris, Jay, and other old Federalist friends, he grimly opposed the War of 1812. He served as a regent of the State University of New York from 1787 to 1802, and as a trustee of his alma mater (now reorganized as Columbia College) from 1804 to 1815. He was founding president of The New-York Historical Society from 1805 to 1815. He received honorary doctorates from Union, Harvard, and Princeton. He moved from Red Hook to Poughkeepsie and then to Jamaica, nearer New York City, passing his lengthy old age in contemplative retirement and "invincible"[12] bachelorhood, regaling his friends with his disputatiousness and sense of humor, zealously supporting the causes of the Dutch Reformed Church and of Dutch Americans, publishing short tracts and learned diatribes, but "almost unknown and forgotten by the profession which he once so greatly adorned."[13] He died in August 1833 at age eighty-seven, his mind "vigorous & active till the day of his death."[14]

NOTES

[1]Egbert Benson to David Van Schaack, March 10, 1773, Egbert Benson Papers, The New-York Historical Society.

[2]*Ibid.*

[3]*Ibid.*

[4][James Kent,] "James Kent's Essays on Egbert Benson," in [John D. Gordan, III, ed.,] *Egbert Benson: First Chief Judge of the Second Circuit (1801-1802)* (New York: Second Circuit Committee on the Bicentennial of the United States Constitution, 1987), 56.

[5]John Jay to Peter Van Schaack, June 16, 1783, in Richard B. Morris, ed., *John Jay: . . . Unpublished Papers*, 2 vols. to date (New York: Harper & Row, 1975 & 1980), 2:542.

[6]Kent, "Benson," 56.

[7]*Ibid.*

⁸David A. Nourse, "Egbert Benson—Lawyer and Justice of the New York Supreme Court," in [Gordan,] *Egbert Benson*, 30.

⁹Kent, "Benson," 57.

¹⁰Linda Grant DePauw *et al.*, eds., *Documentary History of the First Federal Congress of the United States of America*, vols. 1-6 to date (Baltimore and London: The Johns Hopkins University Press, 1972-1986), 3:768-70.

¹¹James Kent to Thomas Washington, October 6, 1828, quoted in Nourse, "Benson," 33.

¹²Kent, "Benson," 58.

¹³*Ibid.*, 57.

¹⁴*Ibid.*, 58.

For Further Reading

Julius Goebel and Joseph H. Smith, eds., *The Law Practice of Alexander Hamilton*, vols. (New York: Columbia University Press, 1964); Richard B. Morris, ed., *John Jay: . . . Unpublished Papers*, 2 vols. to date (New York: Harper & Row, 1975 & 1980); essays by James Kent, David A. Nourse, and Wythe Holt, in [John D. Gordan, III, ed.,] *Egbert Benson: First Chief Judge of the Second Circuit (1801-1802)* (New York: Second Circuit Committee on the Bicentennial of the United States Constitution, 1987); Stephen L. Schechter, ed., *The Reluctant Pillar: New York and the Adoption of the Federal Constitution* (1985; Albany: N.Y. State Bicentennial Commission., 1987); Max M. Mintz, *Gouverneur Morris and the American Revolution* (Norman: University of Oklahoma Press, 1970); John Bassett Moore, *History and Digest of the International Arbitrations to which the United States Has Been a Party . . .,* 6 vols. (Washington: Government Printing Office, 1898), vol. 1. This essay was also based upon original research by John D. Gordan, III (used with kind permission), and by Wythe Holt.

George Clinton:
The Nationalist
Turned Inside Out *

JOHN P. KAMINSKI
University of Wisconsin–Madison

George Clinton is an enigma. He and his counterparts from Massachusetts and Virginia—John Hancock and Patrick Henry—were the most popular governors in Revolutionary America, and yet little is known about the three of them because most of their personal papers have not survived. Without documents—the raw material from which history is written—historians tend to overlook individuals and events or, worse, invent or repeat myths. Such has been the case with George Clinton. Because of his stance on the Constitution, Clinton has the reputation in history of being a radical who opposed and was despised by the more conservative Hamiltonians.

Elected governor of New York seven times, Clinton was probably the most effective and best liked of the wartime governors. Despite his popularity, divisive partisanship lay just below the surface while the seemingly united New York Whigs—both conservatives and radicals—fought for their very lives against the British and their Tory and Indian allies.

Throughout the war, Governor Clinton advocated a strengthened Congress that could wage war more effectively. When the war ended, however, Clinton reassessed his state's position within the Confederation and concluded that a dramatic change needed to take place. He no longer favored a stronger Congress, but intended to rely on a strong

*A conference address presented at "George Clinton in Retrospect," September 23, 1989, Kingston, N.Y.

state government, invigorated with an independent source of revenue—the state impost.

In March 1787, George Washington wrote to James Madison expressing his disbelief in the change that had occurred in New York. "It is somewhat singular that a State (New York) which used to be foremost in all foederal measures, should now turn her face against them in almost every instance."[1] To use the new terminology of the time, New York had become "antifederal." How could such a transformation have occurred? The people, for the most part, were still the same, and George Clinton still sat as governor. What had changed so federally minded a state?

This study examines George Clinton, the public figure. Because most of his personal papers and many of his public papers were destroyed in the disastrous 1911 fire at the New York State Library in Albany, much of what we know about Clinton comes from what others said about him and from the events that surrounded him. To know George Clinton, one must know the history of New York during his time. The man and the state were inexorably intertwined for over forty years. In answering the age-old biographer's question: "Does the man make the times or do the times make the man," it is clear that George Clinton—the public man—was predominantly a product of his times.

* * * *

In 1768, as the conflict between Parliament and the colonies intensified, New York's royal governor Henry Moore dissolved the Whig-controlled assembly and ordered new elections. Ulster County freeholders, overlooking members of the governor's party, such as Cadwalader Colden, Jr., the lieutenant governor's son, chose instead two radicals, forty-year-old Charles DeWitt of Kingston and the twenty-eight-year-old lawyer George Clinton of New Windsor.

When the new assembly convened in New York City in October 1768, George Clinton found himself strangely out of place. A member of the Whig, anti-Parliament party, which was dominated by the Livingston family, he could expect to play only a minor role in the dramatic events that were anticipated. The new legislator's expectations were reduced even further when it was discovered that the DeLanceys (the Livingstons' conservative counterparts and adversaries) had won control of the assembly for the first time in a decade. Although opposed to Parliament, Clinton still swore allegiance to the Crown and to the royal governor. But, when the inevitable anti-Parliamentary issues came before the assembly, Clinton invariably sided with his Ulster County colleague, and with Philip Schuyler, Abraham Ten Broeck, Philip Livingston, and Pierre Van Cortlandt, who served as the nucleus of the anti-government party.

Since Parliament's actions alienated most colonists, even the DeLanceys endorsed petitions for relief. In turn, a disgruntled Governor Moore again dissolved the assembly, whereupon Ulster County re-elected its two Whig assemblymen. George Clinton returned to New York City a more confident man—a leader of the gentry, standing second in command only to the aristocratic Philip Schuyler. The young Clinton had served a short apprenticeship; he was eager to be involved—he was ready to lead. Unfortunately for the young Ulsterite, the Whigs were so outnumbered that little could be done to further the revolutionary effort. While other colonies advanced toward independence, the conservative Delanceys stood firm. Despite his minority position, the hot-blooded Clinton persevered and came to be regarded as the leader of the radicals in the New York assembly. His anti-government voting record was even more consistent than Philip Schuyler's. But when Lieutenant Governor Colden prorogued the assembly on January 27, 1770, Clinton quietly left the charged atmosphere of New York City and went back home to the relative tranquility of New Windsor, where he bided his time.

When the assembly reconvened in January 1775, Clinton reassumed his leadership role. In a vote on the proposals recommended by the Continental Congress, the Delanceys narrowly defeated the radicals by a vote of 11 to 10. Although professing loyalty to his sovereign, Clinton warned the assembly "that the time was nearly come, that the colonies must have recourse to arms, and the sooner the better."[2] Called to order by the chair, the outspoken Whig apologized and the house proceeded with business. When a motion was proposed exempting New York from all internal taxes levied by Parliament, the Ulster firebrand argued that Parliament had no right whatsoever to tax the colonies. This kind of radicalism did not go unnoticed. When a popularly elected provincial congress was called to replace the conservative assembly, Ulster freeholders overwhelming elected George Clinton as one of their three delegates. It was this radical assembly that appointed Clinton to the Second Continental Congress "to meet the Delegates from the other Colonies, and to concert and determine upon such measures as shall be judged most effectual for the preservation and reestablishment of American rights and privileges, and for the restoration of harmony between Great Britain and the Colonies."

Not enamored with legislative duty in Philadelphia, Clinton nevertheless dutifully joined the radical forces. According to the Tory chronicler Thomas Jones, Clinton "took an active part, was violent and decisive against Great Britain, he ridiculed all terms of accommodation, condemned all thoughts of reconciliation, and even, in an enthusiastic speech, went so far as to wish a poniard [a dagger] in the heart of George the tyrant of Britain, and would gladly contribute towards a handsome reward to any person who would perform so religious, so glorious, and so patriotic an act."[3] This extreme rhetoric continued to gain notoriety for the thirty-six-year-old congressman—so much so that the New York Committee of Safety, serving during the recess of the provincial congress, appointed Clinton brigadier general of the Ulster and Orange county militia.

General Clinton returned home eager to assume his command. According to Jones, Clinton was "in full power, as absolute and despotic in Ulster, as the French King in France, and as cruel and arbitrary as the Grand Turk. He tried, condemned, imprisoned, and punished the Loyalists most unmercifully. They were by his orders tarred and feathered, carted, whipped, fined, banished, and in short, every kind of cruelty, death not excepted, was practised by this emissary of rebellion in order to compel them (those within his jurisdiction) to obey, conform to, and execute the laws, rules, and recommendations of Congress."[4] New York, Clinton realized, was in a life-and-death struggle. Those unfriendly to the cause were considered the enemy and were treated accordingly.

General Clinton's primary concern for the next two years was to fortify the Hudson Highlands and to block the river from British navigation. "To me," he reported to the New York convention, "it appears a Matter of the utmost Importance that the River should be obstructed which being effectually done will be [of] more real advantage to the United States than 10,000 Men [in] the next Campaign & it is more than likely would change the seat of War."[5] He constructed two forts, guarded the passes through the Highlands, ran a huge iron chain across the river, and stationed two armed vessels in the Hudson immediately above the chain. Repeatedly he responded to the urgent appeals from the state convention and from Commander-in-Chief George Washington by calling out the militia. When the militia hesitated in turning out, Clinton spurred them on: "The season is approaching when in all probability you may be called upon to defend your County ag't the Attacks of a Tyrannical ministry and it will reflect great Dishonour on a County so forward in every other Respect in the Cause of Liberty to be found so extremely negligent in so important a Matter."[6] When this gentle prodding failed, Clinton was quick to recommend to his colonels that company commanders be punished if they failed to furnish their quota of men.[7] On those numerous occasions when bad news arrived, he consoled his men by saying that "we must learn to bear the sound of bad as well as good news; indeed, it would be unreasonable to expect the chance of war always in our favour."[8]

By the summer of 1777, Clinton was pleased to report to the New York convention that the posts in the Highlands "are in so respectable a state of defence, as to promise us security against any attack on that quarter. This, together with the several obstructions in Hudson's river, has probably induced General Howe [the British commanding general in New York City] to alter his original plan, and to adopt another."[9] Washington and the Continental Congress were so pleased with Clinton that on March 25, 1777, the New Yorker was elected Continental commandant of the Highlands posts with the rank of brigadier general in the Continental Army. Clinton would retain this rank throughout the war. He modestly accepted the commission, telling Washington that "as early in the present contest I laid it down as a maxim not to refuse my best, though poor services, to my country in any way they should think proper to employ me, I cannot refuse the honor done me in the present appointment."[10]

Unlike the earlier temporary peacefulness in the Highlands, the British steadily advanced in the southern parts of the state. The New York convention regularly moved from town to town, trying to keep one step ahead of the advancing British army. While fleeing, the convention drafted and, on April 20, 1777, adopted the state's first constitution. Most New Yorkers approved their new charter, but John Jay, its principal author, knew that "unless the government be committed to proper hands, it will be weak and unstable at home, and contemptible abroad." Jay could think of no better person to fill the three-year position of governor than Philip Schuyler.[11] As the gubernatorial election approached, the state committee of safety made its recommendations to the county committees. Philip Schuyler was the consensus candidate for governor and George Clinton for lieutenant governor.[12]

Despite these recommendations, Clinton was elected both governor and lieutenant governor. Obviously disappointed, the aristocratic Schuyler hoped that "Gen. Clinton's having the chair of Government will not cause any divisions amongst the friends of America. Altho' his family and connections do not entitle him to so distinguished a predominance; yet he is virtuous and loves his country, has abilities and is brave." Schuyler pledged his loyalty and hoped that Clinton would receive, the "support, countenance and comfort" of "every patriot."[13]

General Clinton was notified of his election on July 9, 1777. Two days later he responded. If left to his own wishes, he told the council of safety, he would accept neither office, but he felt duty-bound to accept "the Free Suffrages of the Public." He readily declined the lieutenant governorship and told the council it could expect him to attend and take the oath of office as soon as he could safely leave his military post.[14]

Word traveled quickly of Clinton's election. Lieutenant-Colonel Alexander Hamilton, Washington's principal aide, wrote to Clinton's immediate military superior, Major General Israel Putnam, "It is regretted that so useful an officer is obliged to leave the posts under his superintendency at a time like this."[15] General Washington wrote the New York council of safety that "The appointment of General Clinton to the Government of your State, is an event, that, in itself, gives me great pleasure, and very much abates the regret I should otherwise feel for the loss of his Services in the Military line. That Gentleman's Character is Such, as will make him peculiarly useful at the head of your State, in a Situation so alarming and interesting, as it at present experiences."[16]

Among others, the Reformed Dutch Church of Kingston congratulated Clinton on his election—"the highest Honor the Subject of a free State can possess." The church was "uniformly attached to the cause of America" and believed that "Religion and morality" justified this "glorious revolution." The ministers admonished Clinton to use "vigilance, impartiality and firmness" in preserving inviolate the state constitution and the rights of the people.[17]

The governor-elect thanked the Dutch ministers for their support and agreed with them "in thinking that the Constitution gives the fairest Promises of Happiness." Clinton vowed "to preserve inviolate and thereby secure to the People those Civil and religious Liberties which it [the state constitution] has with the utmost Liberality and Wisdom been attentive to establish and guard."[18] In responding to a committee of Kingston gentlemen, Clinton promised "under the double Tie of Gratitude & Duty . . . faithfully to discharge the important Trust reposed in me by strictly adhering to the Principles of the Constitution so wisely calculated to secure the Rights & promote the Happiness of a free People."[19] Alexander Hamilton perhaps summed up the feelings of most New Yorkers: "Governor Clinton will do all in his power to promote objects, in which the state he Commands in is so Immediately Concerned."[20]

Throughout the remainder of the Revolution, New York continued to be the theater of battle, while New York City and the six lower counties remained occupied by British forces. Repeated threats of an invasion up the Hudson from New York City forced the state to keep up its guard. Despite Clinton's assurances about the security of the Highlands, Forts Clinton and Montgomery were captured in October 1777 by the British after a valiant defense by the outnumbered garrisons.

Governor Clinton assumed command of the defenses himself and barely escaped capture only by crossing the Hudson under cover of darkness. The northern invasion by General John Burgoyne's army from Canada sent shivers throughout the state, but the American victory over Burgoyne at Saratoga was perhaps the turning point in the war.

Obviously the most frustrating and disconcerting problem the governor faced was the defense of the frontier. For three years the entire perimeter of the state—in particular, the Mohawk River Valley—was under the constant threat of attack from enemy bands of 50 to 500 men, consisting of British regulars, Loyalists, and the hostile tribes of the Iroquois. No one knew exactly where or when these brutal raids would occur. The uncertainty and complete vulnerability of settlers created near panic situations. Seemingly coming out of nowhere, the enemy would swarm down on isolated farms and villages, killing, mutilating, and scalping the men who would not swear allegiance to the king; burning homes and outbuildings; and taking women, children, and the elderly as prisoners to Canada. The raiders destroyed vast quantities of grain and ran off with large numbers of cattle and horses. The Continental Army and the state militia were deprived of much needed provisions because these farms could not be properly protected. Many farmers on the frontier left their homes and fields as they brought their families to the safety of the interior. Only sporadically would the American forces and their Indian allies meet a raiding party and do battle. The New York government's inability to provide protection for these frontier settlers weighed heavily on Governor Clinton. Endless petitions were submitted to him for troops to be stationed at various frontier locations. Over and over, the governor in turn sought assistance from General Washington only to be refused or to have reinforcements delayed because of needs elsewhere.

Adding to the military difficulties facing the governor, the state was expected to supply the Continental Army and French navy with provisions, clothing, arms, ammunition, and pay. When the army was not well provided for, the soldiers would desert or mutiny. To compound all of these problems, the governor had to safeguard families and communities from their hostile Loyalist neighbors as well as occasional bands of roving *banditti* and marauding soldiers. The governor often felt inadequate to the demands made upon him and the state. On more than one occasion he wanted to resign.

A logical answer to New York's and the country's problems seemed to be to strengthen Congress under the newly proposed Articles of Confederation. Many New Yorkers, including Governor Clinton, advocated a stronger Congress with an independent revenue not derived from voluntary contributions made by the states. On February 13, 1778, Alexander Hamilton wrote his friend Governor Clinton a remarkable letter.[21] Hamilton, serving as aide-de-camp to Washington at Valley Forge, decried the lack of representation in Congress. Not only was Congress poorly attended—it lacked the wisdom and courage it had shown earlier: "Folly, caprice a want of foresight, comprehension and dignity, characterise the general tenor of their actions. . . . Their conduct with respect to the army especially is feeble indecisive and improvident. . . . they have exposed the army frequently to temporary want, and to the danger of a dissolution, from absolute famine. . . . If effectual measures are not speedily adopted, I know not how we shall keep the army together or make another campaign."

Congress had suffered "the present falling off" because "the great men who composed our first councils" had taken positions in the army or as civil officers of their states. "The only remedy then," according to Hamilton, "is to take them out of these employments and return them to the place, where their presence is infinitely more important." Hamilton acknowledged the importance of the state governments, but in his judgment, "it is infinitely more important to have a wise general council; otherwise a failure of the measures of the union will overturn all your labours for the advancement of your particular good and ruin the common cause. You should not beggar the councils of the United States to enrich the administration of the several members. . . . How can the common force be exerted, if the power of collecting it be put in weak foolish and unsteady hands?" Only through a strong and effective Congress could the war be won.

Hamilton felt uneasy, he wrote, about putting these bold thoughts on paper. He would confide only "to those in whom I may place an entire confidence." It was time, he admonished, "that men of weight and understanding should take the alarm, and excite each other to a proper remedy." Hamilton, himself, felt unable to accomplish much; he could only "hint" at the problems. It was up to Clinton to take the lead. New York was generally better represented in Congress than the other states, but the governor should try to get John Jay, Robert R. Livingston, and Philip Schuyler appointed. Much more importantly, Clinton should use his influence to give "the alarm to the other states, through the medium of your confidential friends." "Indeed," Hamilton pleaded, "it is necessary there should be a change. America will shake to its center, if there is not."[22]

The busy governor responded to Hamilton on March 5, a month after the New York legislature had unanimously adopted the Articles of Confederation. Though Clinton signed the act adopting the Articles on February 16, he believed them to be defective. If Congress were strengthened beyond the provisions of the Articles, "even their Want of Wisdom but too Evident in most of their Measures wou[l]d in that Case be less Injurious." Could our soldiers "subsist on Resolves," Clinton satirically lamented, "they wou[l]d never want Food or Cloathing. Resolves are most Powerful Expedients. They are to fill, to Cloath, to Feed, & pay our Armies, at least this is the Language which the late Conduct of our Masters speak."²³ Hamilton was pleased to see that the governor's "ideas" corresponded exactly with his. As spring neared, however, Hamilton felt more "melancholy" than ever. The army, he said, was adequate to assure victory in the next campaign, but the weakness of Congress "will, in all probability, ruin us." Hamilton told the governor that he dwelt "upon the faults of Congress because I think they strike at the vitals of our opposition [to Britain] and of our future prosperity, and with this idea I cannot but wish that every Gentleman of influence in the country should think with me."²⁴ Clinton was of the same mind.

In early August 1780 delegates from the states of New Hampshire, Massachusetts, and Connecticut met in Boston to discuss efforts to coordinate activities and to strengthen Congress's powers. The delegates called another convention to meet in Hartford in November 1780, and New York was invited to attend. Governor Clinton transmitted the invitation to the legislature, declaring that the powers of Congress had to be increased. In September the legislature appointed three delegates to the proposed conference. Philip Schuyler, one of the delegates, wrote his son-in-law that "A Spirit favorable to the common cause has pervaded almost both houses, they begin to talk of a dictator and vice dictators, as if it was a thing that was already determined on. I believe I shall be sent with Instructions to propose that a Dictator should be appointed."²⁵ The convention met in November 1780 and proposed that George Washington be given dictatorial powers. Congress should also be given the power to levy tariffs to pay the interest on the public debt and should have coercive power to force the states to comply with its dictates. Furthermore, the delegates advocated that Congress be vested with wide implied powers as opposed to the expressly limited powers specified in the Articles of Confederation. These proposals went far beyond what Clinton had advocated, and he was worried that they might endanger republican government.

The dreadful financial and military situation facing the country encouraged Congress in February to propose a federal tariff—the impost of 1781—of five percent on all goods imported, to be earmarked to pay the interest and principal on the public debt. New York acted swiftly and ratified the impost on March 19. Eleven other states adopted the federal tariff, but Rhode Island refused. Because the Articles of Confederation required that all amendments to the Articles be adopted by all thirteen state legislatures, the impost died.

Although the military prospects had brightened after Yorktown in October 1781, the country was still in a financial morass. Governor Clinton wrote John Hanson, president of Congress, in November 1781 expressing his concerns. New York, he said, was completely federal: "I trust there can be no higher Evidence of a sincere Disposition in the State to promote the common Interest, than the alacrity with which they passed the Law for grant'g to Congress a Duty on Imports, and their present Proffer to accede to any Propositions which may be made for rendering the Union among the States more intimate, and for enabling Congress to draw forth & employ the resources of the whole Empire with the utmost Vigor." The governor admitted that the state had few resources at present to pay its federal taxes, but, he predicted, when the British evacuated New York City and peace was established, New York would be prosperous. Clinton assured the president that New York at that time would "chearfully consent to vest" Congress "with every power requisite to an effectual Defence against foreign Invasion & for the Preservation of internal Peace & Harmony." "As an Individual," Clinton could not "forbear declaring my Sentiments that the Defects in the Powers of Congress are the chief Source of present Embarrassm'ts, and as a Friend to the Independence & True Interests & Happiness of America, I could wish to be indulged in expressing an earnest Desire that Measures might be taken to remedy these Defects."[26] Consequently the New York legislature, meeting in special session in July 1782, resolved that Congress be given additional taxing authority and that a general convention be called to revise the Articles of Confederation. These resolutions were forwarded to Congress, but New York congressman Ezra L'Hommedieu informed Clinton that they would not have the desired consequences because "but very few States seem disposed to grant further Powers to Congress."[27] After being considered by various committees, a congressional committee in September 1783 recommended that action on the resolutions be postponed. The following month, Governor Clinton wrote to George Washington that he was "fully persuaded unless the Powers of the national Council are enlarged & that body better supported than it is at present all their Measures will discover such feebleness & want of Energy as will stain us with Disgrace & expose us to [the] worst of Evils."[28]

Whether George Clinton was totally committed to strengthening Congress toward the end of 1783 is uncertain. It seems that sometime in 1783 or early 1784 Clinton's attitude toward Congress changed. A number of factors contributed to this alteration.

Most New Yorkers believed that their state had shouldered an inordinately large share of the burden of the Revolution. The southern counties, including New York City, had been occupied by the British for virtually the entire war. The occupying force posed a constant threat to the rest of the state; therefore, New Yorkers always had to be ready to counter any British maneuvers. New York also had to contend with Burgoyne's invasion in 1777 and with the repeated raids on the frontier. At no time during the war was the state free from conflict or the seemingly impossible job of provisioning the contending armies.

Throughout the war, Vermont served as a constant irritant to New York. New York's claim to Vermont was disputed by New Hampshire and Massachusetts. In 1777 Ethan Allen and his Green Mountain Boys declared Vermont to be an independent state. New York appealed to Congress for support, but got no relief. The Vermonters even hinted that they would join forces with the British if Congress or New York attempted to restore the latter's rule. Some New England states were pleased with Vermont's independence, which would add another state to their congressional bloc while diminishing the power of the despised Yorkers. In an attempt to ameliorate New York, Congress continually delayed a definitive decision on the matter, but the delaying tactic only irritated New Yorkers, particularly those New Yorkers who owned land in Vermont. As the Vermonters gained strength, they became more aggressive. Settlers with land titles from New York were dispossessed, and, if they balked, they were banished by authority of the Vermont legislature. Those who refused to leave were imprisoned. Appeals were made to the New York legislature, but the state did not have the resources to add Vermont to its list of enemies at that time. Governor Clinton thoroughly despised the Vermont separatists and stated that he had evidence that their leaders were guilty of treasonable dealings with the British. If Congress refused to act in supporting New York's just claims, Clinton vowed, he would seize his state's rightful property by force of arms. New York's congressional delegation reported to the governor on April 9, 1784, that Congress is determined "not to do any thing about that matter, expecting that in Time we shall be obliged to consent that [Vermont should] . . . become a seperate State."[29] Congressmen believed that "the flames of Civil War will be kindled in that Country in the course of four or five months."[30]

New Yorkers also felt threatened and betrayed by Congress on the matter of the state's western lands. In February 1780 New York's legislature ceded its western lands beyond the state's present borders to Congress. Congress gratefully accepted this first cession by any of the states. As peace neared, however, Massachusetts, under its 150-year-old charter, claimed most of the land in present-day western New York. This demand, made on the floor of Congress, evoked no hostile reaction from anyone but New Yorkers. Congress recommended that the case be settled by the cumbersome judicial machinery provided by the Articles of Confederation. The case dragged on for almost four years when agents for New York and Massachusetts finally agreed to a settlement. New York would retain jurisdictional control over the land, but Massachusetts would retain the property rights. The state of New York had just lost the value of a huge section of its land; Massachusetts had gained a windfall.

As the war wound down, New York's legislature passed resolutions calling for the state to raise 500 soldiers who would occupy the Northwest posts at Niagara and Oswego when the British evacuated them under the provisions of the Treaty of Peace. Since the Articles of Confederation prohibited states from having peacetime standing armies, New York requested special dispensation from Congress for these troops. Furthermore, since New York was embarrassingly bereft of funds, the legislature asked Congress to provide immediate subsistence to the troops but to charge these expenses against the state's account with the Confederation.

Alexander Hamilton, New York's delegate to Congress, did not submit these resolutions to Congress. Instead, Congress passed its own resolutions calling for 700 soldiers from Massachusetts, New Jersey, Connecticut, Pennsylvania, and New York to garrison the forts. New York felt threatened. What was Congress trying to do by sending "foreign" troops into New York? New York's new delegates to Congress, Charles DeWitt and Ephraim Paine, warned Governor Clinton about possible attempts to seize the state's northwestern lands: "Upon the whole Sir it is our opinion that the utmost Vigilence ought to be exercised to prevent any encroachment on our Territory as we are to expect no protection otherwise than from our own arms." Three weeks later Paine wrote that "it appears to be the general Sense" of Congress "that the western Country ought to be Considered as belonging to the united States in Common." Consequently, Paine concluded, "it is high time for our State to tak[e] the Same measures as though it was Sorounded with open and avowed Enemies." On June 4, Charles DeWitt repeated the warning: "I hope the Legislature have taken every precaution respecting the W. Territory. I believe Sir a Plan is formed and perhaps wrought into System to take that Country from us."[31]

Governor Clinton also saw the danger Congress posed to the state's revenue. Congress and nationalists throughout the country opposed New York's policy of confiscating Loyalist estates. The peace treaty prohibited such confiscations in the future and called upon the states to compensate those Loyalists who had lost property. Clinton would not hear of such compensation to Loyalists who had wreaked such havoc during the war or who had lived in safety and relative luxury behind British lines. Not only did the state benefit financially from the confiscations, but many of the large manors had been or would soon be broken up after they had been seized by the state. This parcelling out of tracts satisfied Clinton's republican principles.

Finally, there was the newly proposed federal tariff—the impost of 1783. On March 15, 1783, the legislature repealed its earlier approval of the impost of 1781. The new state impost was expected to be the cornerstone of New York's recovery program. As such, it could not be surrendered to federal use. Annual income from the state impost during the Confederation years ranged between $100,000 and $225,000, and represented from one-third to over one-half of the state's annual income. Such an income would allow the legislature to levy little or no real estate taxes. The governor saw the benefits to be derived from this horn of plenty. After all the ill treatment the state had received from its neighbors and from Congress, why should New York give up its most valuable asset? Perhaps the time had come, Clinton must have thought, not to strengthen Congress, but to build a stronger New York.

NOTES

[1]March 31, 1787, Robert A. Rutland et al., eds., *The Papers of James Madison* (Chicago, 1975), 9: 343.

[2]Thomas Jones, *History of New York During the Revolutionary War* (2 vols., New York, 1879), 2: 328.

[3]*Ibid.*

[4]*Ibid.*, 327–28.

[5]November 1776, Harold Hastings, ed., *Public Papers of George Clinton . . .* (10 vols., New York and Albany, 1899–1911), 1: 430.

[6]To Colonel Charles DeWitt, New Windsor, January 9, 1776, *Public Papers*, 1: 217.

[7]To Colonels Pawling and Snyder, Fort Montgomery, April 27, 1777, *Public Papers*, 1: 745.

[8]To John McKesson, *Public Papers*, 1: 241.

[9]*Public Papers*, 2: 298.

[10]Quoted in E. Wilder Spaulding, *His Excellency George Clinton, Critic of the Constitution* (New York, 1938), 71.

[11]Henry P. Johnston, ed., *The Correspondence and Public Papers of John Jay* (4 vols., New York, 1891), 1: 141.

[12]Kingston, June 2, 1777, *Public Papers*, 1: 855–56. The committee of safety was composed of John Jay, Charles DeWitt, Zephaniah Platt, Mathew Cantine, and Christopher Tappen. (Tappen was Clinton's brother-in-law.)

[13]To John Jay, Fort Edward, July 14, 1777, Johnston, 1: 146–47.

[14]Fort Montgomery, July 11, 1777, *Public Papers*, 2: 105–6.

[15]Harold C. Syrett, *et al.*, eds., *The Papers of Alexander Hamilton* (27 vols., New York, 1961–1987), 1: 297.

[16]August 4, 1777, John C. Fitzpatrick, ed., *The Writings of George Washington from the Original Manuscript Sources, 1745–1799* (39 vols., Washington, D.C., 1931–1944), 9: 15.

[17]August 2, 1777, *Public Papers*, 2: 161–62.

[18]August 4, 1777, *Public Papers*, 2: 175–76.

[19]August 1777, #13433, New York State Library.

[20]To Major General Israel Putnam, New York, November 9, 1777, Syrett, 1: 357.

[21]*Public Papers*, 2: 860–64.

[22]*Ibid.*

[23]Syrett, 1: 436.

[24]Valley Forge, March 12, 1778, Syrett, 1: 439.

[25]To Alexander Hamilton, September 16, 1780, Syrett, 2: 433.

[26]Poughkeepsie, November 24, 1781, *Public Papers*, 7: 520–22.

[27]Philadelphia, September 11, 1782, *Public Papers*, 8: 38.

[28]Poughkeepsie, October 14, 1783, *Public Papers*, 8: 257–58.

[29]Annapolis, April 9, 1784, Edmund C. Burnett, ed., *Letters of Members of the Continental Congress* (8 vols., Washington, D.C., 1921–1936), 7: 487.

[30]Richard Dobbs Spaight to the Governor of North Carolina, Annapolis, April 30, 1784, *ibid.*, 509–10.

[31]*Ibid.*, 487–88, 504–5, 545.

George Clinton: Political Professional in the New York Governorship *

GERALD BENJAMIN
State University of New York at New Paltz

The parade down Pennsylvania Avenue in the nation's capital was several miles long. The casket, covered with flowers, passed before the Capitol. The Congress adjourned for the occasion, and the vice president, senators, and representatives assembled on the Capitol steps to pay their respects. The remains were then brought by train and boat to New York City, where over forty thousand people visited the casket while it lay in state at City Hall. Then it was brought up the Hudson on the Navy gunboat "Wasp," escorted by a flotilla of other gunboats and submarines. Nineteen-gun salutes were fired in New York City and again and again as the flotilla passed Yonkers, Tarrytown, West Point, Newburgh, and Esopus. In Kingston there was another military parade. In the Dutch Churchyard uptown —after an invocation and committal service was read—a volley was fired; there was still another nineteen-gun salute, taps was sounded, and then all present entered the church to continue the ceremonies.[1]

Thus, in 1908, almost a century after he died, George Clinton, Ulster County's "greatest gift to America and to the cause of liberty" finally came home to rest.[2] That occasion (1908) was also the 250th anniversary of the establishment of the City of Kingston, a proud center of liberty and democracy—in the Revolution, throughout its history, and today.

As we walk past the old Dutch Church cemetery daily, going about our business, we may tend to overlook the importance of George Clinton, resting quietly here, to life in New York and the United States. Yet the scope of that ceremony in 1908 dramatizes Clinton's stature in

*A conference address presented at "George Clinton in Retrospect," September 22, 1989, Kingston, N.Y.

American history. Here we celebrate a life and contribution of a truly great state and national leader. George Clinton believed in federalism and the vital role of state and local government in American life. He was a revolutionary general of the first rank, the longest serving governor in New York history, and a key figure in the formation of the state party system and the democratization of the state political system. He was a formidable actor in the formative years of the Republic, a champion of the Bill of Rights, and a vice president of the United States.

Clinton was also the longest-serving county clerk in Ulster County history. He held the job for fifty-three years, from 1759 to 1812. Interestingly, Clinton got his initial clerkship from the British governor, George Clinton, a distant relative; our George Clinton had connections. Our George Clinton also may have set a record for dual officeholding. He remained county clerk while in the colonial assembly, the army, the governorship, the state legislature, and the vice presidency. He was a professional politician.

Like Clinton's contemporaries, modern Americans tend to undervalue political skills, to dismiss "mere politicians." Describing a person as a "professional politician" is not great praise. Yet Clinton's life and work serve to remind us that democratic politics well practiced can be a high art, that political skills are special skills, providing to those blessed with them an opportunity for leadership and greatness in both ordinary and extraordinary times. This essay argues that George Clinton's special skills were political, that he was our first great professional politician as governor of New York, and Clinton's life and career demonstrate the critical importance of such skills for successful public leadership in New York.

Historically, New York's governors may be divided into two groups: those who emerged from privileged elite backgrounds, who were "born great," to steal a phrase from Shakespeare's *Twelfth Night*, and those who fought to the top from more humble beginnings, who "achieved greatness" over the course of long and determined public careers.[3]

George Clinton, of course, was the first of the latter group, those "who achieved greatness." The nineteenth-century historian of New York's political parties, Jabez Hammond, who knew Clinton, described him as ". . . the manufacturer of his own fortune."[4] Clinton's was quintessentially an American story. His career was based upon public service, military and civilian, and his fortune upon real estate ownership and speculation. For him, as for others of his station, the Revolution provided opportunities for leadership that in an earlier time simply would not have been available. Though not fully self-made, George Clinton was clearly self-improved, and he was surely upwardly mobile.

George Clinton was a "man's man" in a time when only men voted. One historian described him as the most "masculine" of New York's revolutionary leaders: he was big, rugged—a military officer while still in his teens. Later, Clinton made his living on and off the land. He got out into the woods, and he was comfortable with people, all kinds of people.[5]

The future governor was not a stranger to the New York elite, tied to it as he was by his marriage to Cornelia Tappan and then to her extended family, the Livingstons and the Wynkoops. Kinship networks were central to Hudson Valley politics. But George Clinton was not of the elite. His was not the right family; not the right education; not the right church. His origins were comfortable, but not especially rich. His connections were good, but not especially central.

Clinton gained his first political office, the county clerkship, by appointment. After all, being reasonably well situated still counted for something. What has not been generally understood is the importance of this base in Ulster County for George Clinton's political career. In Clinton's time, clerks paid the expenses of their office—including the salaries of assistants—out of the fees they collected, while retaining the balance as personal income. From the tenacity with which Clinton held this post, we may deduce that these fees provided a part of the financial base from which he could pursue a grander political career. Then as now, incumbency was a partial substitute for personal wealth for the political professional.

George Clinton soon entered electoral politics, and in the electoral arena he had special advantages, perhaps unique for his time in New York. Clinton had the ability to mediate between the elite and the electorate, an electorate that was not the unpropertied mass, but the lesser men of property, the 100-pound freeholders who could vote for governor under the state constitution. Clinton communicated with those accustomed to ruling, but sprang from the same roots as those who were ruled. There was an identity between Clinton and the electorate.

Both experience and scholarship tell us that people vote for candidates who are "like them," but admired for being only slightly "better"—better qualified, better public speakers, or better proponents of strongly held views or interests.[6] In the campaign, the candidate struggles to make a connection, to find an identity with the voter, and the voter, asked to offer trust, seeks that identity, too. Physically big, authoritative, accustomed to leadership, experienced in the colonial assembly, firm in his views, good at listening to others, an Irishman (being Irish then as now was no disadvantage in New York State or Ulster County politics—though Clinton was Scotch-Irish, and, of course, Protestant)—Clinton was a man with whom each of those (relatively few) voters would be comfortable.

The key word is "comfort." Clinton was comfortable for the voters, and they were comfortable with him. And yet he was also a man who, as a result of career and character, was widely known. He had what we today would call name recognition, but what a political observer of the time described as having ". . . a stronger hold on the affections of the people, than any other citizens of the state."[7] Thus, he automatically exuded authority and commanded respect in the circles that counted for something in New York politics.

Interestingly, George Clinton was not a person who came to the governorship because of extraordinary achievement in another area of life. Clinton was a good general, but not a great hero. He was a good lawyer, but not a great one like his mentor William Smith the younger. He speculated in land, but achieved neither spectacular fortune nor spectacular failure. He lacked a brilliant mind like that of his great adversary, Alexander Hamilton. He was not a great orator or writer. Some of the controversy among historians about the authorship of the Antifederalist "Cato" letters is based in the belief that Clinton just was not the type of man who was likely to write such pieces.[8] Even admiring contemporaries like Elbert Herring, who was offered a glowing eulogy before the George Clinton Society in 1813, found in Clinton no ". . . shining qualities, that dazzle the blind."[9]

George Clinton was a man of action, a public man, a successful professional politician, and an office holder for his entire adult life. His success was based upon a shrewd understanding of people, a capacity for getting them to do what he wanted them to do while retaining his position and power. As Gouverneur Morris remarked after his death, ". . . [H]e . . . studied mankind, not in books, but in the world; not in the closet, but in the camp; and practically knew what reliance . . . [was] . . . to be placed on reason, what resource could be derived from hope and fear."[10]

In sum, George Clinton's great skills were political skills. And judging by results, he used them well. Though not expected to win in 1777, he captured a governorship designed by New York's conservative elite to be held by the elite. When Clinton emerged victorious, his defeated patrician opponent, Philip Schuyler, wryly remarked: ". . . he has played his cards better than was expected. . . . [H]is family and connections do not entitle him to such distinguished a predominance."[11]

And Clinton kept winning. In a state full of ambitious and able men, he was unopposed in 1780, faced minimal opposition in 1783, and was unopposed in 1786. This absence of substantial opposition is itself a testimony to George Clinton's political stature and skill. He survived a tough election in 1789, when the Federalists ran Judge Robert Yates, a member of Clinton's own party, against him to split the Republican vote. And 1792 was a very tough year, too, pitting Clinton against John Jay. There arose the Macomb land sales issues, charges of possible theft of election returns by the Clintonians, and suspected massive vote fraud by the Federalists.

Clinton, who played hardball politics to win the governorship, served that term (1792–1795) under a cloud, retired (for health reasons, he claimed) for the next six years, but then came back and won again in 1801.

George Clinton did all this in a shifting environment of an expanding and growing electorate. Partial returns for the unoccupied area of the state in 1777 showed 3,762 votes recorded. In 1792 there were 12,353 votes for governor. In 1801, the year of Clinton's last victory, there were 45,651 votes recorded. The electorate was doubling and redoubling, yet within this volatile political environment, Clinton kept winning.

The governor's coalition changed as political parties emerged and alliances shifted. Clinton started with a base in Ulster and Orange, with the Federalists strong on the east bank of the Hudson and, after it was liberated in 1783, in New York City. But by 1801, the governor was carrying Westchester, Dutchess, and New York City, while in the western counties, settlers of English (not Scotch–Irish or Dutch) stock from Federalist New England were bringing their Federalist sentiments with them.

In the later years, incumbency helped, too. Clinton was first mildly "anti-establishment," but after he won they sought to join him. Those who wanted to buy land and build canals and roads and acquire status and position, sought out the durable governor. In 1792, for example, the Livingstons joined him, as did many rich prominent New York City Federalists. The state government, after all, monopolized certain scarce resources.

No matter how many former adversaries came over, the governor continued to remember and reward his friends. According to one observer, ". . . all [Clinton's] appointments seem to have been, and no doubt were, well calculated to sustain himself and his party against the weight of character and influence of his opponents."[12] He did not make appointments alone, but his domination of nominations before the council of appointments was unchallenged until the early 1790s.

The "who should nominate?" question, critical to the council's role in the state constitutional system, bedeviled Jay, and later Clinton. But even with actual control of the power of nomination in the governor's hands, perhaps such a council to ratify appointments (long since abandoned in New York) was not a bad idea. It assured that political appointments would be used at least in some measure for purposes other than building a personal organization for the governor.

Building political parties is a more effective means than building personal support groups to assure and sustain a competitive party system offering real choice for the electorate. Perhaps out of necessity—he faced constant and vigorous opposition—Clinton was an early party builder, and knew the importance of party in mobilizing the electorate. The key to his success, however, remained the governor's identity with the broader electorate. The property qualification remained, but more and more men qualified, and Clinton was one of them.

But gathering power and retaining it are not ends in themselves. What distinguishes the great governors from those who are merely good is their use of power and the ends they seek. In this connection, political leadership at its highest level entails not only the art of compromise, but the art of knowing when not to compromise. It includes having priorities, knowing what may be sacrificed, and what may not. George Clinton had priorities, knew them, and pursued them.

Another reason we remember our governors is for their capacity to respond to a crisis. Some men, Shakespeare also says, ". . . have greatness thrust upon them." George Clinton was our best crisis governor.

During the Revolution and after, Clinton was a single minded leader, supporting the ideas of liberty and independence. Over the course of the war, his intolerance for Loyalists became legendary. Clinton sincerely believed, however, that harsh treatment of Loyalists was necessary. Under the most difficult circumstances, with more than half the state's population and wealth dominated or threatened by the enemy, Clinton needed to lead New Yorkers in revolution. A key element of this task was to preserve the people's commitment to the Revolution—if necessary, by using the power of the government against those unwilling to make that commitment. "[W]ho shall tell," Gouverneur Morris wrote at his death, ". . . his exertions to quench the spark of conspiracy, to control the struggles of faction, to resist the inroads of invasion, to repel the ravages of plundering foes, to squeeze, from the indigence of an exhausted people, supplies for the starving continental army. . . ."[13]

Throughout the crisis, the governor kept the goal of winning always in sight. He did not like taxes, but pressed for them. Clinton's popularity declined, Alexander Hamilton acknowledged in a letter to Robert Morris in 1782, in part because of ". . . vigorous execution of some necessary laws that bore hard upon the people, and severity of discipline among the militia."[14]

The governor made hard choices. With uncertainty and selfish ambition rampant, in the face of the pervasive fear of the retribution that the British would exact if the war was lost, Clinton held together a socially and economically diverse coalition, convinced them of their interdependence, and helped reinforce their new common identity as Americans. Literally everything was at stake. Clinton was solid, and Washington, with good reason, relied upon him.[15]

After the war, Clinton's priorities shifted to serving his constituency. More ordinary politics, the politics of getting and keeping power, dominated these more ordinary times. If he had lived during the end of the eighteenth rather than at the end of the nineteenth century, the legendary Tammany ward boss George Washington Plunkett would have liked Clinton, for the governor was no reformer. He was little interested in such causes as the abolition of slavery or relief for the poor. The reasons were simple: Many of the 100-pound freeholders in the Hudson Valley owned slaves, and the poor did not vote. This first "popular" governor responded not to all the people, but to that portion of the people who could vote.

Thus, not surprisingly, Clinton's program involved giving his voters and his big money supporters the services they wanted—such as roads and canals to get their produce to market (and not incidentally, to produce opportunities for speculative profit), and subsidies for the public education of their children—while avoiding taxing their real property to pay for them. Little wonder that the governor wanted to keep in effect New York's excise taxes on all goods that moved through the port of New York, a key reason he opposed a stronger central government after the Revolution was won. Little wonder, too, that selling vast tracts of state land appeared to the governor to be a strategy by which New Yorkers could not lose: It produced the money to pay for other services without land taxes, providing potentially great opportunities for the speculators in his circle, and could even be justified as a fast way of encouraging upstate settlement and development. But by 1792, the governor's postwar efforts to meet citizens' expectations of government, while at the same time avoiding the taxes they hated, put him at risk with these very same citizens, for they disliked the resulting atmosphere of scandal in the state's politics.

Additional measures of a governor's legacy include the effectiveness of his advocacy for the state in the larger national political system, and of his guardianship of the prerogatives of the governor's office within the state political system. It is in the first of these areas, if anywhere, that George Clinton's record falls short. Clinton's efforts to protect New York's territorial integrity in Congress against the Vermont secessionists failed, as did his opposition to the adoption of the Constitution on the grounds that it would be bad for New York. The Poughkeepsie convention's vote to ratify the Constitution was perhaps his most spectacular failure.

With regard to executive-legislative relationships, there was a real balance in New York in the eighteenth century (a balance to which we are only now just returning after a long period of executive predominance). George Clinton's surviving papers contain evidence that the eighteenth-century New York governor not only sent messages to the legislature, but received them from each house. This is a lost practice (one rooted in British colonial practice and, ultimately, out of the English constitution), but one we might profitably consider resuming today. Certainly Clinton seemed comfortable with the executive-legislative balance in the first constitution. He was no institutional reformer either, perhaps because he could make the system work so well with the powers he already had.

In his 1782 letter to Robert Morris, Alexander Hamilton also wrote of Clinton: "The preservation of his place is an object to his private fortune as well as his ambition; and we are not to be surprised, if instead of taking a lead in measures that contradict a prevailing prejudice, however he may be convinced of their utility, he either flatters it or temporizes; especially when a new election approaches." In other words, Hamilton regarded Clinton as a professional politician whose principal goal was reelection, who would not do the unpopular, however important his judgment told him it might be, if it threatened reelection.

Hamilton was right. Clinton was a professional politician for whom reelection was a high priority. But, for a governor in a democratic society, sensitivity to reelection may well produce a sense of accountability. It may also support a political strategy of accommodating and responding to diverse interests, helping to create an identity of interests, and thus allowing the political system to respond to social needs.

George Clinton's well honed political skills were essential in holding together the coalition in New York that supported the Revolution during its most fragile time and in its most critical location. Later, these same skills were essential in launching state government in circumstances of unprecedented difficulty. Clinton's career as governor was not without its flaws, but fundamentally it demonstrated that he knew the importance of two essentials of politics: priorities and persistence. When the opportunity arose, George Clinton proved that, again in Shakespeare's terms, he was "not afraid of greatness." He seized leadership gladly and demonstrated again and again that he knew how to use power, both to keep power and to get things done. It is thus particularly appropriate that, during the bicentennial of the making of the U.S. Constitution, we rediscover George Clinton as a great politician and a great governor.

NOTES:

[1]James Austin Holden. "Reinterment of Governor Clinton at Kingston," in George Clinton, *Public Papers of George Clinton, First Governor of New York* (Albany and New York: State of New York, 1899-1914) 10: 1009-1010.

[2]Benjamin M. Brink, chairman of the exercises during the Clinton reinternment in Kingston, *ibid.* at 1013.

[3]*Twelfth Night*, Malvolio speaking, Act II, scene 5, line 158.

[4]Jabez Hammond. *History of Political Parties of the State of New York* (Cooperstown, 1846), 4.

[5]The best general account of Clinton and his career is still E. Wilder Spaulding, *His Excellency George Clinton* (New York: Macmillan, 1938; reprinted in 1964 by Ira J. Friedman, Inc., also of New York). For this summary I also drew heavily upon Alfred F. Young, *The Democratic Republicans of New York* (Chapel Hill: University of North Carolina Press, 1967) and Edward Countryman, *A People in Revolution* (Baltimore: Johns Hopkins University Press, 1981).

[6]For an insightful account of how modern candidates seek to establish identity with voters see Richard Fenno, *Homestyle* (Boston: Little Brown, 1981).

[7]Hammond (1846), 4.

[8]See Gaspare J. Saladino, "Pseudonyms Used in the Newspaper Debate Over the Ratification of the United States Constitution in the State of New York, September 1787-July 1788," reprinted in this volume, at 298-325.

[9]Elbert Herring, "An Oration on the Death of George Clinton. . . . May 20, 1812" (New York) in the collection of the New York State Library.

[10]Gouverneur Morris, "Eulogy at the Request of the New York City Common Council," May 19, 1812. In the collection of the New York State Library, 7.

[11]Spaulding (1938), 93.

[12]Hammond (1846), 33.

[13]Morris (1812), 12.

[14]Harold Syrett, ed., *The Papers of Alexander Hamilton* (New York: Columbia University Press, 1962), 3: 137-138.

[15]John P. Kaminski, "The Governor and the Commander-in-Chief," unpublished paper prepared for the New York State Commission on the Bicentennial of the U.S. Constitution Conference, "George Clinton in Retrospect," Kingston, New York, September 23, 1989, reprinted in this volume at 408-422.

The Governor and the Commander in Chief: A Study in Admiration and Friendship*

JOHN P. KAMINSKI
University of Wisconsin–Madison

In *The Democratic Republicans of New York*, Alfred Young likened George Clinton to Andrew Jackson. The democratic leanings of the New Yorker presaged those of the future seventh president. During his presidency, Jackson was often called "The Second Washington." Surprisingly, despite the Clinton–Jackson and the Jackson–Washington comparisons, no one has compared George Clinton with George Washington. Although such a comparison does not readily leap forward, there are, in fact, many similarities between the men—similarities that first made Washington and Clinton admirers of each other and then life long friends. Even after they took up totally different positions on the new Constitution in 1787, Washington and Clinton remained on the best of terms. While the Constitution and later issues related to it caused Washington to become estranged from other long time friends—first George Mason, then Thomas Jefferson and James Madison—the first president and New York's first governor remained close.

George Washington and George Clinton both were born into the middling gentry. They were trained as surveyors; and, although they did not intend to follow surveying as their primary careers, they used the

*A conference address presented at "George Clinton in Retrospect," September 22, 1989, Kingston, N.Y.

knowledge gained from surveying later when they had the opportunity to speculate in land. Both men fought for the British on the frontier with their colonial militia during the French and Indian War. This military experience served them well in the Revolution.

To a certain extent, Washington and Clinton improved their social and financial situations through marriage. Martha Custis and Cornelia Tappen were quiet—almost reticent—and were willing to stay in the background as their husbands became dominant military and political figures. Neither wife was a beauty, and both had recurring health problems. They remained apart from their husbands during much of the war years. The most conspicuous familial difference between the two men was that Washington had no children of his own (Martha had a son and a daughter from a previous marriage), while Clinton had six children—five daughters and a son. The governor demonstrated his respect and admiration for the commander-in-chief by naming his only son George Washington Clinton and his fourth daughter Martha Washington Clinton.

The revolutionary struggle with Great Britain presented opportunities to Washington and Clinton as it did to many other gentry. Both men probably would have become political leaders within their counties had no conflict occurred with the mother country. The imperial and intra-colonial conflicts, however, thrust both men forward, first on the state and then the national levels. These self-made men typified many others of the gentry who filled the political vacuum created during the Revolution.

Washington and Clinton each served in their colonial assemblies. As the hostility with Great Britain heightened, they were elected to the Second Continental Congress; indeed, the two men first met in this body. In mid-June 1775, Washington was appointed commander-in-chief of the American army. On his journey northward to take command in Massachusetts, Washington stopped and addressed the New York legislature. The legislature asked for assurance that he would resign his commission after the conclusion of hostilities. Washington told the New Yorkers that becoming a soldier did not relieve him of his duty as a citizen. He promised the legislature that he would relinquish his authority as commander-in-chief as soon as it became expedient. George Clinton admired this American Cincinnatus who left his farm to serve his country in time of need. No doubt Clinton felt honored as he hosted the country's new leader for dinner on the evening before Washington left New York City. Six months later, Clinton, like Washington, was thrust into a military command as the legislature appointed him brigadier general of the Ulster and Orange county militia.

Washington and Clinton had limited military service before the Revolution. Both men readily conceded their inadequacies. Neither demonstrated military genius during the Revolution. In fact, the American army had generals far superior in tactics and strategy to Washington (for instance, Benedict Arnold and Nathanael Greene), and the New York militia had better officers than Clinton (Alexander McDougall, James Clinton, and Marinus Willett). Subordinates could be more daring on the battlefield, but Washington and Clinton could not afford the luxury of risk-taking themselves.

But neither Washington nor Clinton was excelled as a leader of men. They had a special quality, a rare ability to inspire devotion and confidence—to give men the willingness to endure deprivation and the faith to persist in seemingly endless campaigns against enormous odds.

Washington and Clinton knew what it was like to lead an army without the necessary resources. Throughout the war, their armies suffered from a scarcity of men, money, food, and materiel. Theirs was usually a defensive war. Often, the enemy even had the advantage of surprise on its side. But throughout the long eight-year war, Washington and Clinton maintained a strict adherence to the supremacy of civil authority over the military. They also adamantly recognized the rights of private citizens—whether Patriots or Tories—despite the needs of the army. On numerous occasions Washington and Clinton refused to allow their armies to plunder the countryside for food and supplies. They believed that the army must be subject to the rule of law even when it was in desperate need, otherwise the Revolution would be fought in vain as one despotism would merely replace another. When the inevitable unsanctioned plundering occurred, each man was quick to investigate and administer justice.

Throughout their military careers Washington and Clinton were criticized—the former more than the latter. Cabals arose that conspired to replace the commander-in-chief and the governor. Clinton, like Washington, stoically accepted these intrigues, believing that all "Men in public Life" have "political Enemies" who drop hints to their disadvantage. "Enmity like this," he felt, was not "Evidence of your abilities, nor does it mark the want of Integrity." He was confident that "Friends will not readilly believe any Thing to your Disadvantage."[1] Fortunately for the war effort, both men weathered these storms and persevered.

Washington, born in 1732, was seven years older than Clinton. During the Revolution, the two men developed a brotherly relationship with Clinton assuming the role of a younger brother who greatly admired his heroic older sibling, while Washington grew to rely on the support he knew Clinton would always be willing to give. Both men were sternly inflexible when they believed they were right. Neither man was gregarious nor noted for his humor. They both had hot tempers that seldom flared. Those unfortunate enough to be the recipient of their ire, however, were pitiable. Both men were awesome figures who towered above the ordinary person. Each stood over six feet tall and was well built; their military bearing and excellent horsemanship commanded respect.

Although well educated for the time, neither Washington nor Clinton had extensive formal education. They were fond of books. Each had his own personal collection, and Clinton was a dues-paying member of the New York City lending library.[2] Though both men were intelligent and thoughtful, neither was a scholar nor a philosopher. They dealt in solid, practical realities, whether on the farm, on the battlefield, in a legislative assembly, or when serving as chief executive. Despite their pragmatism, or perhaps because of it, they had a strong belief in constitutional government. Whatever their personal preferences and whatever was most expedient, they believed that they had a duty to protect the constitution under which they served. Their personal and public correspondence, although voluminous, consisted primarily of short letters directed to a specific point. General Alexander McDougall, in apologizing for a lengthy, rambling epistle, wrote that "I am informed my Friend Governor Clinton likes short Letters. He will in future have them so."[3] For their formal speeches, they relied heavily on drafts from dedicated advisors. Both men were hesitant about public speaking and not very good at it.

Washington and Clinton were ardent republicans—they despised monarchy and believed that the establishment of an American monarchy threatened the fundamental principles that they had fought for during the war. Washington repeatedly rejected suggestions that he become the new nation's first king, while Clinton and his followers believed, with some justification, that their opponents were too sympathetic to the idea of monarchy. Both had serious misgivings about the Society of the Cincinnati—the hereditary association of continental army officers formed in 1783. Washington required extensive alterations in that organization before he accepted the position of president general, a position he reluctantly held until his death. George Clinton was named vice president of the New York chapter of the society, but stepped down after one term because he saw the society as aristocratic.

Although both men were greatly admired by the people, they had a strong distaste for demagoguery and mobocracy. On two occasions—Shays's Rebellion in Massachusetts in 1787 and the New York City doctors' riots in April 1788—Clinton called out the militia to suppress violence. Washington, too, expressed his revulsion at Shays's Rebellion and the courthouse burnings in backcountry Virginia. During the winter of 1786–87 he feared that there were combustibles in every state ready to be ignited by a single spark. As president, Washington did not hesitate to raise an army to suppress the Whiskey Rebellion in 1794, thus asserting the dominance of the federal government.

Both men actively speculated in land—an honorable activity at the time—while they eschewed the less respected practice of speculating in either commodities or financial securities. They took their ownership of land seriously and dealt harshly with squatters or delinquent renters.

Their mutual interest in land brought Washington and Clinton together. In the fall of 1782, Washington had a rare opportunity unfold for him. For over twenty years, "with little or no prospect of success," he had tried to buy a parcel of land completely encircled by his plantation. Now this land seemed obtainable in the form of a trade "*Tract for Tract.*" But first, Washington had to buy a 376-acre farm near Alexandria, Virginia. Notifying Washington of the availability of the land, the owner's agent told Washington that other purchasers would eagerly buy this farm. Because of his interest, however, Washington would be given the first option to purchase the property. The commander-in-chief was advised to act quickly. Unfortunately, as was so often the case, Washington was cash-poor, and it looked as if this once-in-a-lifetime opportunity might slip through the general's fingers. At this point, the frugal governor stepped forward and offered a £ 2,000 loan. Washington was greatly appreciative. This would not be the last time that an investment in land brought the two men together.[4]

George Clinton was elected governor of New York in June 1777. During his first winter in office, he was already besieged with requests from his militia colonels for food and clothing to see the state troops through the arduous winter. The governor also received urgent messages from General Washington and from a committee of Congress in mid-February 1778 appealing for provisions for the Continental Army, then languishing at Valley Forge. According to Washington, the army was in a "dreadful situation." "It is more alarming than you will probably conceive," Clinton was told. "For some days past, there has been little less, than a famine in camp."[5] Something had to be done to provide sustenance for the troops, the congressional committee pleaded. The alternatives were "Mutany, Desertion, a Spirit of Depredation & Plunder ending at last in a total Dissolution perhaps of our whole Army."[6] Judging from Clinton's previous service, the congressional committee hoped that the governor would "amply supply our Deficiency." General Washington told Clinton that he expected "every thing within the compass of your power, and that the abilities and resources of the state over which you preside, will admit.'' In particular, the army needed cattle ''to be at camp in the course of a month.'' Governor Clinton quickly replied that New York was in a peculiar situation. ''Having been long the seat of war, it has been ravaged, plundered & greatly exhausted.'' American armies in both New England and in the Middle States drew upon New York for provisions, as did the enemy forces in New York City and the southern counties. ''Notwithstanding these Difficulties,'' Clinton ordered that 100 head of cattle and 150 barrels of salt pork be sent to Valley Forge ''without a Moment's Delay.'' The governor assured Congress and General Washington that the state of New York was committed to ''the American cause'' while the ''attachment the People have to the commander-in-chief, will excite them to the most vigorous Exertions for the Relief of his army.'' Clinton could not promise to deliver more provisions but he assured Washington ''that our most Strenuous Endeavours to procure them shall not be wanting.''[7] Within a week, the governor informed Washington that another 1,700 barrels of salt pork were on the way. General Washington thanked Clinton: ''The readiness with which you comply with all my requests in prosecution of the public service has a claim to my warmest acknowledgments.''[8]

Throughout the war, supplying the troops with food, clothing and pay remained a serious problem. By mid-1780, Washington's profoundest fears about an army mutiny materialized. The Connecticut troops in Washington's army, now stationed at Morristown, New Jersey, demanded to go home. After some tense moments the mutiny was quelled, but Philip Schuyler, in camp with Washington, realized that ''we have too much reason to apprehend that it will shew itself soon and more seriously unless provisions arrive.'' Officers went on bread-and-water rations so that the troops could have the last of the meat.[9] Washington feared that similar uprisings might spread to the Continental troops in New York at West Point and Fort Schuyler.

On January 1, 1781, the Pennsylvania Line stationed at Morristown mutinied. Several officers were killed and wounded in a vain attempt to suppress the uprising. The troops paraded with arms, seized the division's artillery, and marched toward Philadelphia to present their grievances to Congress. Officers, watching for an opportunity to regain control, accompanied the troops, hoping to keep them from plundering the countryside.

Washington feared that the entire war effort had reached a devastating crisis. Would all the discontented troops disobey their officers? Would there be wholesale desertions? On January 4, Washington reported to Clinton that the Continental officers in command of the highland forts on the Hudson could not guarantee their commands. The commander-in-chief needed the governor's assistance. If the Continental troops revolted, only the New York militia could be counted on to protect the forts. If the militia failed to fill the breach, the forts would easily fall because, with the Hudson entirely free of ice, the way was open for a major British assault from their New York City stronghold. If the forts fell, the British would control the Hudson, thus dividing New England from the rest of the states—their favorite plan since the beginning of the war. "Under these circumstances," Washington believed "it indispensably necessary" that Governor Clinton stay as near the forts as possible. The governor's "influence with the militia would give a spring to their exertions," and Clinton's advice "would be of infinite service." Washington asked Clinton to forgo the legislative session about to convene in Albany and visit him at headquarters. The next day Clinton responded that he would immediately attend the commander-in-chief and that during this alarming situation, he would unhesitatingly render Washington "every assistance in my Power."[10]

On January 13 Washington wrote Clinton that the Pennsylvania mutiny had worsened. British emissaries within the soldiers' ranks had been discovered fomenting the discontented troops, and the troops refused to turn over the conspirators to the officers for prosecution. It seemed that unless the soldiers' demands were met, they might go over to the enemy. The situation looked desperate as Washington readied a detachment of Continental troops to march from the New York forts to suppress the mutineers. How much support, Washington asked, could he expect from Clinton and the New York militia? The governor responded that 1,000 men could be assembled within three or four days. Some could reach West Point on the day that they were called up to service; most would be there the following day.[11] A grateful Washington responded the next day: "I had the honor last night to receive Your Excellency's Letter . . . and am happy to inform you that there probably will be no occasion to march the Detachment, nor consequently to call the Militia to our aid." A committee of Congress had reached an accommodation with the rebellious soldiers.[12]

Within days of the settlement of the Pennsylvania Line's mutiny, the New Jersey troops rebelled. Washington refused to tolerate any more insubordination. Immediately he ordered a detachment of Continental troops from the highland forts "to compel the mutineers to unconditional submission, to listen to no terms while they were in a state of resistance, and on their reduction to execute instantly a few of the most active, and most incendiary Leaders." Washington hoped that the troops from New York would "do their duty," but, in any case, he preferred "any extremity to which the Jersey Troops may be driven" rather than take part in another compromise that would only encourage more mutinies. Civil liberties, Washington said, would be endangered if armed soldiers could dictate "terms to their country."[13]

On January 26 Governor Clinton reported to Washington that he was forced to leave the Highlands because of a threatened insurrection among the troops in Albany. "I think it my Duty, therefore, to be near them & prevent if possible the Spirit of Discontent from spreading." If, during the governor's absence, Washington needed the support of the New York militia, Clinton authorized the commander-in-chief to call upon the brigade's colonels directly. An application to Clinton in Albany "might be attended with too much Delay."[14] By the end of the month, however, the governor reported, "The Spirit of Discontent which had reached the Troops" in Albany "has subsided and I am in Hopes a Repetition is not to be apprehended."[15]

From May through the fall of 1782 the governor and the commander-in-chief toured the state. Starting at West Point and ending at Kingston, the two men viewed the devastation wreaked throughout New York. The governor already knew the high price New Yorkers had paid supporting the war effort; the commander-in-chief came now to realize fully the sufferings New Yorkers had endured.

As the war wound down and the army suffered through another winter with shortages of food, clothing, and pay, the chances of mutiny actually seemed to increase. With a treaty of peace imminent, the troops wanted to go home. Less threatened by the British, Congress felt it could renege on promises made to the army. The combination of events seemed explosive. Major William North, Baron Von Steuben's twenty-eight-year-old aide-de-camp, typified most soldiers: "I am heartily sick of the War." Congress should surely do something for the army—but Congress, in North's judgment, had "no honor."[16] Major Nicholas Fish, a twenty-four-year-old veteran of seven years of combat, knew not what to expect:

> I think public Justice is at this moment become indispensable, and will prove the only means of keeping the Army together.
>
> Should Congress continue deaf to the voice of Justice, and the real interest of the Country, by withholding pay from the Troops, & perservering in their iniquitous system of parsimony, I am apprehensive we shall be reduced to the sad alternative of dismissing them, or disbanding the Army; should the latter be preferred, I am well assured that no other can ever be raised and then farewell to the Liberties and Independence of this Country.[17]

As the commander-in-chief waited for the definitive peace treaty to arrive, he realized that he sat on a powder keg at his headquarters in Newburgh, New York. If he disbanded the army, he might encourage a new British offensive that would prolong the war. But Washington knew that his officers and men were disgruntled. Fears of another mutiny loomed in the general's mind. Such fears materialized in March 1783 when a number of officers plotted to blackmail Congress into meeting its commitments for back pay and retirement benefits. The army would not disband if Congress did not fulfill its obligations. Hearing about the plot, Washington summoned the officers together and deftly stifled the conspiracy.

Three months later, the army had become so serene that the general felt at ease taking time off for private business. For three weeks, from July 18 to August 5, Washington and Governor Clinton toured upstate New York looking for land to invest in. They traveled more than 750 miles together throughout the frontier making a list of potential tracts. Later the governor made bids on the property. The first two bids—at Saratoga Springs and the area on which Fort Schuyler stood—were rejected. Finally Clinton purchased 6,071 acres on the Mohawk River between present-day New Hartford and Clinton, a few miles southwest of Utica. Washington complimented Clinton on the "advantageous terms in the purchase . . . you certainly have obtained it amazingly cheap."[18]

Although the land was shared equally, Clinton paid for it with his own money, charging Washington seven percent annual interest on his debt. In December 1783 Washington arranged for over $2,000 owed to him by the Confederation government to be transferred from the federal treasury to Clinton as the first installment on his debt. A second payment was made in April 1785. In November 1786 Washington informed Clinton that he was "endeavouring by the sale of Land, to raise money to pay for my Moiety of the purchase on the Mohawk River," and the following June Washington paid the balance of $840.[19]

From the very beginning of the business venture, Washington deferred to Clinton, asking that the governor "take the trouble of doing with my moiety the same as you would do with your own at all times and in all respects."[20] In late 1795, because of the difficulty of getting deeds signed by both Clinton in New York and President Washington either at the capital in Philadelphia or at home at Mount Vernon, Washington gave Clinton the power of attorney "in the management and sale of the Lands in which we are jointly interested."[21] On February 28, 1796, Washington wrote Clinton asking what lots remained unsold in their joint venture. A week later Clinton informed his partner that they still owned seven lots consisting of 1,446 acres valued at over five dollars per acre. Clinton recommended that the land not be sold. "The soil is good and in proportion to the rapid settlement of that Part of the Country the value of those Lands continue to increase."[22] The speculative partnership had been profitable for both men. With almost twenty-five percent of their land still available, the investment had already returned a handsome profit. The two old surveyors had done well as a team.

During this three-week trip in 1783, Clinton and Washington probably got to know each other very well personally. The two men had plenty of time to reminisce and to discuss the future. They each looked forward to the day that they could relinquish their commands and return to the more placid rural life. No longer would it be the commander-in-chief and the governor. It would be two friends tied together by mutual business interests and by a strong patriotic desire to see the fulfillment of the republican experiment they had been so instrumental in bringing about. But all too soon their brief escape ended and they returned to their responsibilities. The conclusion of the war lay in sight.

On April 8, 1783, Washington notified Governor Clinton that official word had just been received "announcing a Certainty of the glorious Event of a general Peace." The commander-in-chief could now start to think about retirement—about fulfilling the promise he had made eight years earlier to the New York Assembly. When, he thought, should he step down? How would the ceremony take place—in person or by letter? Should he write a farewell address? If so, to whom should it be addressed and who should be asked for advice?

Washington decided to announce his retirement in a formal letter to the state executives in which he would also give his advice to the fledgling nation. He would leave the final plans for the ceremonial retirement to Congress. The commander-in-chief now began a thoughtful period of time during which he prepared his farewell address—perhaps the most important letter of his career—an address he himself styled as his legacy to his country.

Less than a week after he informed Clinton of the official news of the peace, Washington wrote to the governor seeking advice on the country's peacetime military establishment. Washington wanted to recommend to the states that a peacetime army be maintained, but he knew that, as commander-in-chief, he was treading on thin ice. Would war-weary Americans—always wary of a peacetime standing army and the dangers it posed to liberty—welcome a sitting general's recommendations for a perpetual military establishment? Despite these apprehensions, Washington knew that America needed a strong defense—the system of state militias had so many shortcomings that a new system had to be devised. Governor George Clinton was the man to whom Washington turned for advice on this sensitive subject.

Three days after Washington wrote his letter requesting advice, Clinton responded.[23] Characteristically, he expressed his inadequacy to address so important a topic. With that necessary qualifier, the governor plunged in.

Clinton believed that a regular, ongoing American army was absolutely necessary to man the frontier posts and to guard the country's magazines. This garrisoning army would "by no means be sufficient for Defence in case of War." But Americans would never accept the kind of standing armies then in vogue in Europe. By the same token, the revolutionary experience had "abundantly evinced that it is hazardous and expensive to the last Degree to leave the Defence of a Country to its Militia." Consequently, America needed a new kind of military establishment—an army ready at a moment's notice to take to the field, yet an army under civilian rule that could "be most speedily reduced to Order and Consistency."

To provide for such an army, Governor Clinton proposed that "a sufficient number of Officers . . . be retained in Service" at the end of the war. Each officer would retain his rank, and promotions and the filling of vacancies would regularly occur. The officers would be paid only when they were on active duty, but they would "be entitled to certain Encouragements of the negative kind such as exemptions from serving in the Militia or in any of the burthensome Offices of Society, together with some such positive Distinctions (if any should be necessary) as would not tend to give the most distant Cause of Jealousy or Apprehension among the most scrupulous Republicans." These benefits would have to be significant enough to convince the officers to remain in the army "and be at the Call of their Country."

To guarantee a steady supply of qualified new officers, Clinton proposed that one college in every state establish a professorship, offer courses, and grant degrees in military science. A distinguished army officer would make annual visits to inspect the course offerings and "report to the proper Office." All vacancies in the army should be filled from graduates with these degrees—no commission should be conferred upon anyone without a sufficient number of the required military courses.

The governor also recommended that all army officers should serve on active duty on a rotating basis. Every officer should at one time or another serve at the western posts. In this way the officers would gain active experience without "the Mischiefs which in Time of Peace might arise from too long a continuance in Command at fixed Posts."

It was of special importance, the governor advised Washington, that "In all our Peace Arrangements we ought, I conceive, to have an Eye to the Support of the foederal Union as the first and principal Object of national Concern. Influenced by this Consideration I would prefer an Establishment (however feeble it might appear) that is calculated to maintain that intimate Connection between the different States which gave us Success in War and upon which I am persuaded our Happiness and Importance will depend in Peace; and it is this which would induce me to wish to preserve even the name of a *Continental Army* as well as to cherish that Sense of military Honor which is so nearly allied to public-Virtue as not to admit of Distinction; but which from the peculiar Situation of our Country may otherwise be too soon extinguished."

Although the peace treaty had been signed, British forces still occupied New York City and the southern counties. The commander-in-chief and Governor Clinton both looked forward to the day American forces would reenter the city. On May 6, Washington, Clinton, and British commander Sir Guy Carleton met at Tappen, New York, to discuss the British evacuation. At this meeting Carleton only agreed to withdraw from Westchester County. For the next six months the governor communicated sporadically with Carleton to plan the exchange of power. Neither the Americans nor the British wanted to see violence break out during that delicate period of time when power was transferred from the departing British to the incoming American forces; consequently, a slow and orderly evacuation occurred. As the time for British withdrawal neared, Governor Clinton wrote General Washington to ask that the New York Continental troops in Westchester County be moved forward close to New York City. The governor also requested, "if there should be no impropriety in it," that these troops "be subject to my Direction while they remain there."[24] Washington, appreciative of all the support he had received from the governor, happily informed his friend that the troops would be moved forward and that it struck him "very forcibly" that Clinton should have command. Washington informed General Henry Knox, then commanding the American forces outside New York City, that Knox and the governor should coordinate the plan to enter the city.[25] On November 25, the long-anticipated day arrived. General Knox and the army secured the city, and notified Washington and Clinton that the formal entry could proceed. The commander-in-chief and the governor, side by side on horseback, escorted by a body of Westchester light cavalry, led the procession. Eight long years of exile had ended. Civil government had been restored. In honor of the glorious event, a song was composed and sung to the tune "He comes! He comes!"[26]

> They come! they come! the Heroes come!
> With sounding fife, with thund'ring drum,
> Their ranks advance in bright array,
> The Heroes of AMERICA.
>   He comes! 'tis mighty WASHINGTON!
> Words fail to tell all he has done;
> Our Hero, Guardian, Father, Friend!
> His fame can never, never end.
>   He comes! he comes! 'tis CLINTON comes!
>   Justice her ancient seat resumes.
> From shore to shore let shouts resound,
> For Justice comes with Freedom crown'd.
>   She comes! the white rob'd Virgin, Peace,
> And bids grim War his horror cease;
> Oh! blooming Virgin with us stay,
> And bless, oh! bless AMERICA.
>   Now Freedom has our wishes crown'd,
> Let flowing goblets pass around,
> We'll drink to Freedom's Fav'rite Son,
> Health, Peace, & Joy to WASHINGTON.

That evening Governor Clinton expressed his gratitude to Washington and his officers at a grand dinner at Fraunces' Tavern. A couple of days later, the governor hosted another gala dinner at Cape's Tavern honoring Washington and the French minister, the Chevalier de Luzerne.

The time for Washington to leave New York had arrived. Congress, meeting at Annapolis, awaited the formal resignation of their army's commander-in-chief. The governor bade his comrade-in-arms—his friend—goodbye, not knowing if they would ever see each other again. For Washington and his officers it was an emotional farewell. He would miss them all. But perhaps most of all, he would miss the man he had relied upon throughout the war, the man he had learned so much about as they traveled through upstate New York together, the man who had become a dear friend.

Washington resigned his commission to Congress on December 23, 1783. He was back home at Mount Vernon in time for Christmas. Three days later, after all of the excitement had died down, the former commander-in-chief wrote a brief letter to the governor.

"I am now a private Citizen on the banks of the Powtowmack, where I should be happy to see you if your public business would ever permit, and where in the meantime I shall fondly cherish the remembrance of all your former friendship.

"Altho I scarcely need tell you how much I have been satisfied with every instance of your public conduct, yet I could not suffer Col. Walker . . . to depart for N. York, without giving your Excellency one more testimony of the obligations I consider myself under for the spirited and able assistance, I have often derived from the State under your Administration. The Scene is at last closed. I feel myself eased of a load of public Care. I hope to spend the remainder of my Days in cultivating the affections of good Men, and in the practice of the domestic Virtues; permit me still to consider you in the Number of my friends, and to wish you every felicity."[27]

NOTES:

[1]To Gouverneur Morris, Poughkeepsie, June 23, 1779, Harold Hastings, ed., *Public Papers of George Clinton . . .* (10 vols., New York and Albany, 1899-1911), 5:101.

[2]George Clinton Account Book, August 5, 1790, at 35, New York State Archives.

[3]To George Clinton, Headquarters, Peekskill, March 24, 1779, *Public Papers*, 4: 664-65.

[4]George Washington to Lund Washington, to George Clinton, and to Robert Morris, Newburgh, November 21, 1782, December 18, 1782, January 8, 1783, John C. Fitzpatrick, ed., *The Writings of George Washington from the Original Manuscript Sources 1745-1799* (39 vols., Washington, D.C., 1931-1944), 25: 361-64, 451-52, 26:19.

[5]George Washington to George Clinton, Valley Forge, February 16, 1778, Fitzpatrick, 10: 469.

[6]Congressional Committee to George Clinton, Camp near Valley Forge, February 17, 1778, *Public Papers*, 2: 766-67.

[7]To James Reed, to Congressional Committee, to George Washington, Poughkeepsie, February 24, 1778, n.d., March 5, 1788, *Public Papers*, 2: 799-800, 823-24, 866.

[8]Middlebrook, May 3, 1779, *Public Papers*, 4: 796.

[9]Philip Schuyler to George Clinton, Morristown, N.J., May 26, 1780, *Public Papers*, 5: 760-61.

[10]George Washington to George Clinton, New Windsor, January 4, 1781; George Clinton to George Washington, January 5, 1781, *Public Papers*, 6: 547-51.

[11]*Public Papers*, 6: 571-73.

[12]January 16, 1781, Fitzpatrick, 21: 113-14.

[13]George Washington to George Clinton, New Windsor, January 1781, *Public Papers*, 6: 592-93; to Robert Howe, West Point, January 22, 1781, Fitzpatrick, 21: 128-29.

[14]George Clinton to George Washington, Poughkeepsie, January 26, 1781, *Public Papers*, 6: 597-98.

[15]To George Washington, Albany, January 31, 1781, *Public Papers*, 6: 603.

[16]To Benjamin Walker, Schuykill, February 4, 1783, #13703, New York State Library.

[17]Nicholas Fish to Henry Glen, Camp Ver Planks Point, September 11, 1782, Misc. Mss., Library of Congress.

[18]Mount Vernon, November 25, 1784, Fitzpatrick, 27: 501.

[19]Mount Vernon, November 5, 1786, June 9, 1787, Fitzpatrick, 29: 53, 230.

[20]Mount Vernon, April 20, 1785, Fitzpatrick, 28: 134.

[21]George Clinton to George Washington, Greenwich, December 17, 1795, Washington Papers, Library of Congress.

[22]George Clinton to George Washington, Greenwich, March 7, 1796, Washington Papers, Library of Congress.

[23]Poughkeepsie, April 17, 1783, *Public Papers*, 8: 144-47. The published letter is incorrectly dated April 7 and is very badly transcribed. The manuscript recipient's copy, dated April 17, is in the Washington Papers at the Library of Congress.

[24]To George Washington, Poughkeepsie, October 14, 1783, Washington Papers, Library of Congress.

[25]George Washington to George Clinton, Rocky Hill, October 23, November 2, 1783, Fitzpatrick, 27: 205, 228.

[26]*New Hampshire Gazette*, December 27, 1783; printed from the original (with slight variations from the *New Hampshire Gazette* printing) in the *New York Journal*, November 26, 1787.

[27]Mount Vernon, December 28, 1783, Fitzpatrick, 27: 287-88.

First Ladies of New York State: The Constitutional Era

Introduction

MARGARET GORDON–COOKE AND SHIRLEY A. RICE
New York State Bicentennial Commission

The population of New York State in the constitutional era is estimated at approximately 300,000, nearly three-quarters of whom were women and children. Their contributions to the development of the Empire State have recently earned the belated but welcome attention of scholars, authors, and educators as they re-examine the events that led first to independence and then to the establishment of our state and national governments.

Alexander Hamilton, John Jay, George Clinton, and other state and national leaders all shared their domestic and political lives with perceptive and industrious women from influential families—women like Elizabeth Schuyler Hamilton, Sarah Livingston Jay, and Cornelia Tappen Clinton. The bicentennial of the United States Constitution has stimulated renewed interest in the lives of both the men *and* women of this period.

These essays introduce New Yorkers to this state's first two "First Ladies": Cornelia Tappen Clinton (1744–1800) and Sarah Livingston Jay (1756–1802). Between 1777 and 1804, George Clinton served seven terms as governor of New York, after which (and after his wife's death) he became the nation's third vice president. John Jay, the first chief justice of the United States, resigned that office in 1795 to accept election as New York's governor, a post to which he was reelected in 1798. For more than twenty-five years, the political, military, diplomatic, and constitutional milestones of Clinton's and Jay's lives intersected in a series of often exhilarating, often bewildering, and sometimes dismaying events for their wives and families.

Cornelia Tappen Clinton rarely, if ever, travelled beyond the boundaries of New York State, preferring the roles of wife, mother, and homemaker expected of women of her time. As the state's first "First Lady," she entertained persons as prominent as George Washington and the Marquis de Lafayette. A traditional, well-to-do matron, she excelled in the domestic sphere, shunning the public life that her position offered.

In stark contrast, we might characterize Sarah Livingston Jay as a member of the eighteenth-century equivalent of the international "jet set." Young, beautiful, and socially adroit, she accompanied her husband to Europe during his tenure as the American minister plenipotentiary to Spain in 1779 and as peacemaker (together with Benjamin Franklin and John Adams) at Paris in 1782. She continued this role during Jay's difficult tenure as the Confederation's secretary for foreign affairs from 1784 to 1789.

Although far from typical in the courses of their lives, these women shared a range of experiences common to all American women of the late eighteenth century. They managed households, cared for the ill, gave birth to (and buried) several children, and suffered from the loneliness imposed by a series of military conflicts. In addition, they often anguished over stinging public criticism of the political and diplomatic decisions advanced by their husbands.

Cornelia Clinton and Sarah Jay lived at a time in the history of the Atlantic world when women played vigorous, often unprecedented roles in their nations' political and intellectual lives—despite the "conventional wisdom" that women were constitutionally incapable of exercising power. For nearly three-quarters of the eighteenth century, Russia was ruled by female sovereigns. Catherine the Great, for example, reigned with unchallenged authority from 1762 to 1796. Elsewhere, Portugal's Queen Marie ruled from 1777 to 1816, and Maria Theresa succeeded to the Austrian throne after her husband's death, wielding power for forty years. Keen protectors of their own monarchies, all shared an interest in the negotiations that followed the close of hostilities between the United States and Great Britain. That women wielded political power in some monarchies (albeit solely by birth or inheritance) but were denied a direct voice in public life in other monarchies and in virtually all republics was an irony that was not lost on such forthright women as Catherine Macaulay Graham and Mary Wollstonecraft. The work of recent scholars such as Linda K. Kerber has shown that arguments such as Wollstonecraft's, whose pathbreaking *A Vindication of the Rights of Woman* was published in London in 1797, found a receptive audience among the women of the American republic.

In sum, Cornelia Clinton and Sarah Jay, along with thousands of their contemporaries, bequeathed a legacy of personal sacrifice and steady devotion to the founding of our state and our nation.

Cornelia Tappen Clinton

(1744–1800)

MARGARET GORDON–COOKE
New York State Bicentennial Commission

Cornelia Tappen was born into an established and influential family in Ulster County, New York, her Dutch ancestors having arrived in New Netherland in the seventeenth century.

Cornelia's mother, Tjaatje (Charity) Wynkoop (1710–1793), was the daughter of Cornelius Wynkoop, Jr., and Barbara Mathyson. The Wynkoop name signifies "wine-buyer" or "wine-merchant." The family first appeared in America in 1642; Peter Wynkoop settled in Rensselaerswyck (Albany) as "Commissioner Superintendent of Wares & Merchandise" for the patroon, Jeremias Van Rensselaer.

Cornelia's father, Petrus Tappen (1716–1748), was the son of Christoffel and Cornelia (Vas) Tappen. He was born in Kingston and was a descendant of Jurian Teunisse Tappen, a glassmaker, who immigrated from Holland to America in the early 1600s. Petrus Tappen was an eminent, substantial landholder of the Kingston corporation.

Tjaatje Wynkoop and Petrus Tappen were married July 2, 1736, by Domine Petrus Vas at the Reformed Dutch Church of Kingston. Their first son, Christoffel (1737), their second son, Pieter (1738), and their first daughter, Cornelia (1740), all died in infancy, victims of the high eighteenth-century mortality rate. The Tappens' fourth child, Christoffel (1742–1826), became a trustee of Kingston and a clerk of the corporation and was a member of the New York Provincial Congress from 1775–1777. The youngest Tappen, Petrus (1748–   ), was born barely five months after his father's unfortunate early death. He became a noted Ulster County physician and also dabbled in politics.

Cornelia (1744–1800), the Tappens' second daughter, was named after her grandmother, perpetuating the eighteenth-century custom of naming their infants after grandparents, aunts, uncles, and deceased siblings. At the age of twenty-six, Cornelia married George Clinton (1739–1812), then a young lawyer, part-time surveyor, and member of the New York General Assembly. Less than eight years later, he became New York State's first elected governor, and Cornelia its first "First Lady."

The Early Years

On Wednesday evening, February 7, 1770, George Clinton and Cornelia Tappen, in the company of Anthony Hoffman and Jannitje Wynkoop, left the village of Kingston and travelled by sleigh to East Camp (now Germantown). There, they were married by the Reverend Gerhard Daniel Koch, pastor of the Reformed Dutch Church.

This marriage allied George Clinton to both the Tappens and the Wynkoops, families of considerable political influence in Ulster County. Furthermore, both families were ardent opponents of the Crown and Parliament and were to become Patriots in the American Revolution.

George Clinton's parents, Colonel Charles Clinton (1690–1773) and Elisabeth Denniston Clinton, immigrated to America from Dublin in 1729. Of the Clinton's first three children, Catharine, (1723–1762), James (1726–1729), and Mary (1728–1729), only Catharine survived the outbreak of measles on board ship shortly after their departure from Dublin. Their ship, the *George and Anne*, dropped anchor at Cape Cod, Massachusetts October 4, 1729, and the Clintons spent their first winter there.

The following year the family moved to Ulster County, New York, and named their homestead, "Little Britain." It was here that four more sons, Alexander (1732–1758), Charles, Jr. (1734–1779), James (1733–1812), and George (1739–1812) were born. George was named for his distant cousin and royal governor of New York, (1743–1753), who showed a special interest in his namesake, and appointed him clerk of the Court of Common Pleas of Ulster County. George served in this capacity in person or through a deputy from 1759 to his death in 1812.

After their marriage, the Clintons moved to their new home at New Windsor. Their farm was located on a hillside that commanded a superb southerly view of the rugged Hudson highlands. The newlyweds apparently enjoyed decorating their first residence. They shopped in New York City for paint, sheet iron for the fireplaces, English superfine tiles, paper for the walls, and pots and kettles for the kitchen. The Clintons' first two children were born at New Windsor: Catharine, on November 5, 1770, and Cornelia, on June 29, 1774.

Times were prosperous for the young Clintons; Cornelia maintained her home and cared for her husband and children. George busied himself with farming and milling, pursued his law practice, and spent several months a year representing Ulster County in the New York General Assembly. By 1775, Clinton was devoting most of his time to public service. On December 19 of that year, the New York Committee of Safety appointed him brigadier general of the Ulster and Orange county militia in response to the threat of impending hostilities with Great Britain.

The War Years

During the Revolutionary War, Cornelia and her family remained in close touch with the general. His headquarters, from which he commanded both militia and Continental Army troops, was located within several miles of their homestead at New Windsor. When conditions permitted, Cornelia accompanied her husband on inspection tours of nearby military installations.

In September of 1776, the British burned New York City, destroying 1000 homes. The refugees fled north to Patriot-held Hudson River counties and moved in with relatives and friends, straining already tight provisions and housing.

Like other military wives, Cornelia supplied her husband with fresh linen and personal items, and the children often packed gifts of butter, tea, and snuff to send to the general. His monthly salary of $125.00 allowed them to maintain a relatively comfortable standard of living.

Letters from home kept General Clinton informed of daily activities. John McKesson, a family friend, advised him of Cornelia's presence at church in New Windsor, and concluded with news of the children. "Caty is well, tho' her Eyes are weak" he wrote, and "Cornelia is the best girl I ever saw at her age."

In July of 1777, George Clinton took the oath of office as New York State's first chief executive, making Cornelia Tappen Clinton the first "First Lady." The burdens of statesmanship contributed to their already heavy wartime responsibilities. Having moved to Poughkeepsie, Cornelia occupied the Crannell house from 1778 to 1783.

Hardship Continues

Cornelia Clinton grieved for her neighbors as the enemy set fire to Kingston in October of 1777, demolishing every house. For days, unburied bodies lay in the streets. Survivors drove the remaining livestock to the interior, and made efforts to secure the harvest before raiding parties could carry it off. With two children and sixty head of sheep and cattle to care for, Cornelia abandoned her furniture, but managed to save vital crops of buckwheat, potatoes, turnips, and cabbage. General Clinton considered moving his family to Connecticut as the situation grew more alarming. Adding to the toll of battle injured, an epidemic of smallpox swept through the region early in 1778.

During this period, Cornelia became fast friends with Martha Washington, as General George Washington and Major General George Cinton devised defensive plans for the expected British invasion through New York's waterways. The wartime hardships were keenly felt by the mistresses of farms, taverns, and shops, as inflated paper currency replaced hard specie and military service drew fathers, husbands, and sons away from home. The labor-intensive life style of the late eighteenth century was shifted to the women, who assumed responsibility for the survival of their families on meager rations, restricted commerce, and a soldier's salary of four dollars a month.

In spite of these discouraging conditions, Cornelia Clinton and other New York women contributed to the ever-increasing demands of the military by weaving cloth, collecting lead for ammunition, brewing rum, operating mills, and farming.

At Home in New York City

After the war, Cornelia and George Clinton moved to New York City in 1784, where they occupied a house at No. 10 Queen (later Pearl) Street. The Clintons maintained their friendship with General and Mrs. Washington, to whom they sent lime and balsam trees, ivy, corn, and peas for their plantation at Mount Vernon, Virginia.

In 1785, the Clinton's sixth and last child, Maria, was born. Alexander Clinton, the governor's nephew, also resided at No. 10 Queen Street, and served as the governor's personal secretary.

Many of the Revolution's most important figures lived within a few blocks of their East Ward neighborhood—Alexander and Elizabeth Schuyler Hamilton; John Jay and his wife, Sally Livingston Jay; Mr. and Mrs. Alexander McDougall; and William and Kitty Duer, among others. These families faced new challenges when confronted with the political and economic dilemmas spawned by the deterioration of the Articles of Confederation. Old allies became enemies as the struggle for approval of the United States Constitution reached its zenith in New York in July of 1788. Now in his eleventh year as governor, George Clin-

Portrait of Mrs. George Clinton
by Thomas Bluget de Valdenuit.
Charcoal and chalk on paper, 1797.
Courtesy Munson-Williams-Proctor Institute
Photo by G.R. Farley

ton led the Antifederalists, the opponents of ratification, who dominated
the New York ratifying convention at Poughkeepsie. With New York
City a Federalist stronghold, Cornelia Clinton seldom socialized with
his former comrades and their wives, but relied on her large, close-knit
family for companionship. She taught the girls knitting and embroi-
dery and instructed them in household management.

On July 26, 1788, the political drama at the Dutchess County Courthouse was resolved in favor of ratification, and New York celebrated
its role as the "eleventh pillar of the federal republic." Cornelia heard
the cannons' salute from the Battery and listened to the simultaneous
ringing of churchbells throughout the city.

New York City: First Federal Capital
The Inner Circle

The Washingtons and Clintons frequently dined together and often
attended the John Street Theater, where "The Old Soldier" and "A
School for Scandal" were popular with New York audiences. Governor
and Mrs. Clinton hosted a formal dinner for the new president prior
to the inaugural festivities, and joined hundreds of other New Yorkers
at an inaugural ball that followed the April 30, 1789, oath-taking ceremonies at Federal Hall.

From 1791 to 1794, the Clintons resided at Government House, built
at Bowling Green to house the president of the United States when New
York City was the first federal capital. It was never occupied by President and Mrs. Washington, however, who lived at No. 3 Cherry Street,
a house built by Walter Franklin during their time in New York City.

The Clintons spent leisure time at a farm purchased from James Rivington in a suburb known as Greenwich. Located on the banks of the Hudson in "The Burgomasters' Bowery," the farm appealed to the Clintons with its rustic appearance, its cottage-like dwellings, its orchards, and its view of the river.

Obligations Fulfilled

A little more than three months after their daughter, Cornelia, married "Citizen" Genet, twelve year-old Martha Washington Clinton, Cornelia's fifth child, died. It appears that Cornelia took great comfort from visits to the Greenwich farm, and a grandson, born in November of 1795, helped to fill the void.

In 1795, after eighteen years of public service, George Clinton temporarily retired. From 1795 until 1800, he was able to spend a substantial amount of time with his family at Greenwich where he attended to personal matters and recouped his health.

Late in the fall of 1799, Cornelia became very ill. Her physician, Dr. Young, held out hope for recovery, but she died on March 15, 1800, at the age of fifty-six. George Clinton, "the aged governor," was deeply affected by the loss of his "dearest wife." During their thirty-year marriage, she had been a devoted wife and mother.

Cornelia Clinton did not seek to exploit her position and did not appear to relish the public role that was occasionally thrust upon her. She entertained when necessary, but was most comfortable when surrounded by her immediate family and close friends. As a contemporary observed, she was "not showy, but a kind, friendly woman," more than fulfilling the obligations expected of women in the constitutional period. Had she lived for another decade, Cornelia could have claimed an expanded role by virtue of George Clinton's two terms as vice president of the United States in the administrations of Thomas Jefferson and James Madison.

Sarah Livingston Jay

(1756–1802)

SHIRLEY A. RICE
New York State Bicentennial Commission

Sarah (Sally) Van Brugh Living-
ston, the eighth of thirteen children, was born to William Livingston
and Susannah French Livingston in Elizabethtown, New Jersey, in 1756.
Livingston was a major figure in the politics of colonial New York and
New Jersey. He and his wife raised their large family at their Elizabethtown home, "Liberty Hall." Sally spent her adolescence on this comfortable rural estate overlooking the Elizabeth River.

Sally's parents made certain that she and her sisters received the
prescribed education for well-to-do young women of the time. Such
education included proficiency in reading, writing, and arithmetic; religious instruction; and training in the "accomplishments"—needle-
work, music, dancing, and drawing. Sally also listened with youthful
curiosity to the discussions about rebellion and independence that preoc-
cupied her father, who represented New Jersey in the Continental Congress and also was the state's first governor.

Livingston's colleagues and fellow patriots included John Jay, a
talented attorney, and Alexander Hamilton, then a student at King's
College; Jay and Hamilton often sought the counsel of their distinguished host, and the companionship of his attractive daughters. On
April 28, 1774, Sally Livingston and John Jay exchanged wedding vows
in the great parlor at Liberty Hall. She was seventeen; Jay, twenty-eight.

The first years of marriage separated the young couple. Sally remained at Elizabethtown while Jay played a growing role in the colonists' efforts to deal with their worsening relations with Great Britain.

Jay was the principal author of New York's first state constitution, served on revolutionary committees, and shuttled between east coast cities while serving as a delegate to the Continental Congress.

Eventually, British troops threatened Liberty Hall. On November 29, 1777, Catherine (Kitty) Livingston reported to Sally, who was then living in Philadelphia, that "everything [had been] carried off [including] hinges, locks, and panes of glass."

Voyage to Europe

In October of 1779, Sally accompanied her husband to Europe, where as American minister plenipotentiary to Spain he pursued efforts to secure a military alliance for the United States and loans to support America's war effort. They left their three-year-old son, Peter Augustus Jay, with Sally's parents in Elizabethtown and embarked on the *Confederacy*.

On the first leg of their journey, Sally spent lazy shipboard afternoons writing long letters to family and friends. To her sister Kitty, she wrote:

> Where is the country where Justice is so impartially administered, industry encouraged, health and smiling plenty so bounteous to all as in our favored country? And are not those blessings, each of them resulting from or matured by freedom, worth contending for? What have I to do with politicks! Am I not myself a woman, and writing to Ladies?

A gale forced the *Confederacy* to put in at Martinique for repairs; while waiting for the voyage to resume, Sally toured the sugar mills on the island. Further delays required the Jays to charter passage on the *Aurora*, which departed St. Pierre for Cadiz, on the southern coast of Spain, in December, 1779.

The Mission to Spain

Arriving in Cadiz in January of 1780, the Jays began preparations for the overland journey to Madrid. Sally, now pregnant with their second child, combed the markets in Cadiz for hams, chocolate, sugar, and household supplies, and supervised the packing.

Their small party led a mule train northward toward Xeres. With them was Brockholst Livingston, Sally's brother, who acted as Jay's personal secretary, and Peter Jay Munro, their young nephew.

Jay's assignment was plagued by the lack of funds, poor communications with the Continental Congress, Spanish duplicity, and the per-

A diplomat's wife in Paris
Artist: Alonzo Chappel

sonal animosity of Brockholst Livingston, who sought to undermine Jay's efforts. On August 28, 1780, Sally wrote a poignant letter to her mother reporting a family tragedy:

> On monday the 22nd day after the birth of my little innocent, we perceived that she had a fever, but were not apprehensive of danger until the next day when it was attended with a fit. On wednesday the convulsions increased, and on thursday she was the whole day in one continued fit, nor could she close her little eyelids until fry-day morning the 4th of August at 4 o'clock, when wearied with pain, the little sufferer found rest. . . .

Snubbed by the court of Charles III, worrying about the family's strained finances, and grieving over the death of four-week-old Susan, Sally suffered both indignation and despair.

Paris

In 1782, the Jays welcomed reassignment to Paris, where John was to serve, with Benjamin Franklin and John Adams, as a key member of the American team of diplomats negotiating a peace treaty to end the Revolutionary war. Having buried an infant daughter in Madrid and given birth to another, Sally had directed her full attention to her household. Now, the new mission promised reunion with other Americans in the diplomatic corps and an introduction to the celebrated ambience of the French capital.

Sally gave birth to a third daughter, Ann (Nancy), while the complex negotiations dragged on, culminating in the Treaty of Paris. When the treaty was concluded in late 1782, Sally saluted the happy news with this series of thirteen toasts, one for each state of the American republic, as was customary in the Revolutionary period:

The United States of America,
may they be perpetual

The Congress

General Washington and
the American Army

The United Netherlands and all
other free States in the world

His Catholic Majesty and all other
Princes and Powers who have
manifested Friendship to America

The Memory of the Patriots
who have fallen
for their Country—
May kindness be shown to their
Widows and Children

The French Officers and Army
who served in America

Gratitude to our Friends and
Moderation to our Enemies

May all our Citizens be Soldiers,
and all our Soldiers Citizens

Concord, Wisdom and Firmness to
all American Councils

May our Country be always
prepared for War,
but disposed to Peace

Liberty and Happiness
to all Mankind.

Sally also savored the diversions of life in Paris in the 1780s, including witnessing the Montgolfier brothers' balloon ascensions and dining with Dr. Benjamin Franklin, who entertained with demonstrations of the properties of magnetism. Sally also read in popular French literature, ordering among other books the novel *Evelina*, and had the children inoculated against smallpox.

Finally, John Jay completed his duties as peace commissioner. Sally was overjoyed at the prospect of returning home; she and her husband had not seen Peter Augustus Jay for nearly five years.

Return to New York, 1784–1795

On their return to America in 1784, John Jay began to build a square, three-story stone residence at No. 8 Broadway in New York City. The Jays eagerly embraced the society of long-absent family and friends. Sally's circle included Elizabeth Schuyler Hamilton, Cornelia Tappen Clinton, Kitty Duer, and Alice DeLancey Izard. Meanwhile, Maria (born in 1782) and Ann were enrolled at the celebrated Moravian school in Bethlehem, Pennsylvania, where "were educated a large proportion of the belles who gave the fashionable circles of New York . . . their inspiration. . . ."

Sally supervised the household affairs, directing the work of the family's servants and slaves. Among them was Benoit, whom the Jays had purchased in Martinique, and who had accompanied them to Spain and to France.

Sally and her overworked staff had to cope not only with frequent Jay and Livingston family visits, but also with Sally's responsibilities as the wife of the Confederation's new secretary for foreign affairs. John Jay had been named to the most prominent post under the Confederation; in effect, he was the chief of state, dealing with foreign ministers, state and local government officials, Congressmen, and other dignitaries. Sally's at-home entertaining each Thursday thus assumed something of an official character, as well as a manner befitting the dignity of the republic. These responsibilities continued, although to a lesser degree, once the new government authorized by the Constitution went into effect. Even when John Jay, now the nation's first chief justice, was away from home riding circuit, Sally continued to fulfill her social obligations.

During one particularly difficult time in 1786, Sally Jay was drawn into the heart of one of her husband's most challenging and frustrating assignments. Jay had long sought to persuade Don Diego de Gardoqui, the Spanish minister to the United States, to come to an agreement by which American citizens could use the Mississippi River and the port of New Orleans without having to swear allegiance to the Spanish throne. Gardoqui refused, thinking instead to persuade Jay to give up American claims to the Mississippi in return for undefined Spanish trade concessions. Gardoqui also thought that, by showering attentions and presents on Jay's wife, he could enlist Sally's support in this venture. Sally remained immune to Gardoqui's blandishments.

Throughout this time, Sally remained interested in her husband's work and on occasion was able to assist him. When Jay was ill, for example, he would dictate letters for her to write to friends and colleagues. During Jay's frequent absences while riding circuit and, for an entire year in 1794–95, while acting as a special diplomat to Great Britain, Sally once again assumed the full range of responsibilities for running the household, including its finances—even though she was deeply distressed by her husband's acceptance of yet another diplomatic assignment separating him from his wife and children (including William, born in 1789, and Sarah Louisa, born in 1792).

First Lady of New York State, 1795–1801

John Jay's return to New York in 1795 delighted his family. It was Jay's last diplomatic mission. A local political development also meant that Jay could give up the arduous and frustrating duties of circuit-riding, his principal responsibility as chief justice.

In 1792, without ever campaigning for the post, Jay was almost elected governor of New York—an office which he regarded as both more useful and more honorable than that of chief justice of the United States. Only last-minute chicanery at the polls and in counting the votes by the supporters of Governor George Clinton kept the Republican governor in office. Jay accepted his defeat philosophically. Three years later, while he was abroad completing negotiations for what has become known as the Jay Treaty, he was elected governor on Clinton's retirement, again without having campaigned or declared his candidacy. Jay thankfully resigned the office of chief justice to become governor.

Jay's election as governor in 1795 opened a new chapter in Sally's life as well. The Jays continued to maintain their home in New York City and rented temporary quarters in Albany when in 1797 that city became the capital of the state. Sally continued to entertain weekly on Thursday evenings, and the Jays attended other receptions hosted by prominent neighbors.

Last Years

At the turn of the century, John Jay determined to retire from public life. The Jays yearned for a future free from the heavy responsibilities they had borne for nearly thirty years. Sally's health, however, began to fail rapidly.

Despite her decline, John and Sally Jay began to realize their long-delayed desire for a country homestead. A comfortable farmhouse, surrounded by an array of outbuildings, slowly emerged on a rural tract long owned by the Jay family in Bedford, Westchester County. Early in 1801, they took possession. They were able to enjoy it together only for little more than a year.

On May 28, 1802, with her husband at her side, Sarah Livingston Jay succumbed to a long-standing illness. She was just forty-six; her youngest child, Sarah Louisa, was a girl of ten.

A vivacious and intelligent woman, Sally cherished her family and was a devoted and caring mother. The lessons of the years abroad and the challenges encountered at home had seasoned the privileges of birth and tempered the character of the woman whose untimely death was mourned by all who knew her.

Without hesitation, she adopted an international life that held more pitfalls than praise, travelled thousands of miles under the most primitive conditions, negotiated the minefields of politics and diplomacy, and mastered the intricacies of the life of Paris salons. She remained to the end a beloved wife and companion.

Sally is interred in the Jay family vault at "The Locusts," Rye.

"Mine is an Odd Destiny": Alexander Hamilton* (1755–1804)

JOANNE B. FREEMAN

Alexander Hamilton is perhaps the least known and most misunderstood of our nation's founders. When remembered at all, he is charged with being a monarchist, anxious to install George Washington as America's first king; an elitist, pandering to the well-born at the expense of the common man; an egotist, willing to make any sacrifice for power, prestige, and glory; a corrupt financier, willing to intrigue with political supporters for their profit and his. Some of these charges are false. Others are merely exaggerated. But none of them captures the truth behind this pivotal figure in our nation's history.

The story of Alexander Hamilton is an American "success story." Penniless and orphaned when he arrived in America, within twenty years he was one of the most powerful and influential members of America's new government—the nation's first secretary of the treasury. His success grew from his own particular talents—his brilliance, his boldness, his limitless energy. However, these same abilities, taken too far, brought about his downfall. In the end, Hamilton had no one to blame for his destiny but himself.

Hamilton's main contribution to America was his vision for its future. An immigrant to American shores, he was unhampered by state loyalties, enabling him to view America as one unified nation with a great and glorious destiny. His fight to implement his vision attracted

*This essay is based on an exhibition entitled "Alexander Hamilton: First Secretary of the Treasury," developed for the Museum of American Financial History, John Herzog, director. The exhibition was produced by Joanne B. Freeman, historian/curator, and Lou Storey, exhibition designer, and was displayed at the United States Customs House from September 12, 1989 to December 15, 1989.

controversy, acclaim, and powerful political opponents. Those who did not share his convictions accused him of a string of unpardonable crimes. But in the end, Hamilton's vision of America's destiny proved more prophetic than his opponents'. The story of his accomplishments is the story of the emergence of the American nation.

I. The Making of a Treasury Secretary
"My Ambition is Prevalent"

Alexander Hamilton spoke sparingly, if at all, of his youth. He was born in the British West Indies on January 11, 1755. His father, James Hamilton, the fourth son of a Scottish lord, came to the Indies seeking a fortune in trade. Lazy and careless with his money, he was soon reduced to poverty. His mother, Rachel Faucette, was the daughter of French Huguenot immigrants to the islands. She was fleeing an abusive husband when she met James. The two lived together for many years, but never married; their two sons, James and Alexander, were illegitimate.

By the age of thirteen, Hamilton was orphaned, penniless, and desperate to advance his station. To a close friend, he confessed:

> I contemn the grov'ling . . . condition of a Clerk or the like, to
> which my Fortune, &c. condemns me and would willingly risk my
> life tho' not my Character to exalt my Station,

adding in a revealing statement, "my Ambition is prevalent." Anxious to provide the promising youth with a formal education, friends contributed money to pay his passage to America.

Arriving in the colonies in 1772, Hamilton began to prepare for college. To meet college admission requirements, he compensated for his lack of formal schooling with a year of intensive study in a New Jersey preparatory school. By 1773, older than many of his fellow students and anxious to advance, Hamilton demanded entrance to the College of New Jersey (now Princeton University) on the condition that he could progress through the courses as quickly as he chose. The college refused the unusual request, but King's College (now Columbia University) accepted the boy on his own terms.

While still a student, in 1774, Hamilton wrote two pamphlets in response to several by "A Westchester Farmer," a pen name for Samuel Seabury, a powerful, middle-aged Loyalist. Seabury criticized the Continental Congress for restricting trade with Great Britain; instead, he urged the colonies to trust in their "mother country." In a pamphlet entitled *A Full Vindication of the Measures of the Congress, from the Calumnies of their Enemies . . .*, Hamilton responded by defending the Congress, and vindicating the colonies' claims against the British Parliament. This pamphlet and its sequel, *The Farmer Refuted*, reveal the beginnings of many of Hamilton's later convictions and his strong identification with the colonies' struggles.

Within two years of his arrival, Hamilton was an impassioned participant in the colonies' struggle with their mother country—at first in print, and soon thereafter in person, with his enlistment in the army. Yet, despite all his accomplishments, Hamilton never completely escaped the stigma of his birth. His dubious origins gave political opponents ample material for gossip. More important, Hamilton's origins profoundly influenced his character, his actions, and his view of the world —an influence which he felt to the end of his days.

"A Member of the General's Family"

The Revolutionary War provided Hamilton with his formal introduction to the American nation. As aide-de-camp to General George Washington, Hamilton had his first opportunity to view the American struggle on a national level. He experienced firsthand the flaws inherent in the weak Confederation Congress. As a member of the general's military family, he mingled with America's political and military elite. And in Washington himself, Hamilton encountered the unquestioned symbol of America.

Hamilton's military career began while he was still a student in New York. In 1776, his commitment to the American cause and his craving for glory led him to seek the position of Captain of the Artillery Company of New York. Characteristically anxious to excel, he bought his men uniforms with his own funds and spent a considerable sum on his own dapper uniform. A veteran officer who encountered Hamilton during the war described him as "a youth, a mere stripling, small, slender, almost delicate in frame, marching . . . with a cocked hat pulled down over his eyes, apparently lost in thought, with his hand resting on a cannon, and every now and then patting it, as if it were a favorite horse or plaything." His small stature and intense nature led fellow soldiers to later dub him "The Little Lion."

In March of 1777, Commander in Chief George Washington invited Hamilton to join his military family as an aide-de-camp. Washington probably received high recommendations from some of Hamilton's more influential friends; he may have witnessed the performance of Hamilton's company, described as a model of discipline. Washington was continually desperate for aides who could "write a good Letter, write quick, are methodical, and diligent." In Hamilton, he found much more.

From 1777 to 1781, Hamilton assisted Washington in the arduous task of organizing a war. Along with a handful of other aides, Hamilton was "confined from morning till eve, hearing and answering . . . applications and letters," as Washington himself described his aides' duties. Hamilton's work at Washington's side taught him about the American nation, developed his many talents, and gave him an intimate knowledge of the mind and personality of George Washington. Washington, in turn, learned of the temperament and talents of his "most confidential aide." Quickly earning a reputation as a young man with a promising future, Hamilton launched his career as a public figure while working at Washington's side. The meeting of the grave older general and the proud impulsive youth marked the start of a relationship that would affect not only the future of these two men, but of the American nation as well.

Although Hamilton's duties as Washington's aide were formidable, Hamilton sometimes had his mind on less weighty matters. He once joked with fellow aide John Laurens:

> I empower and command you to get me . . . a wife. . . . Take her description—She must be young, handsome . . . well bred . . . chaste and tender. . . . But as to fortune, the larger stock of that the better.

When Elizabeth Schuyler, daughter of the wealthy and influential General Philip Schuyler, came to camp in 1780, Hamilton found what he had been looking for. Down-to-earth and sweet-tempered, Betsey quickly captured Hamilton's attentions; one aide described Hamilton as "a gone man." The two were married on December 14, 1780. Elizabeth proved to be a strong stabilizing force in Hamilton's life.

Despite his happiness with his new wife, Hamilton was not content; his military ambitions were unfulfilled. Hamilton wanted a field command. For a solid year, he pleaded with Washington to grant him a chance to "raise my character as a soldier above mediocrity." In February of 1781, frustrated, weary, and feeling slighted, Hamilton had a brief argument with Washington, and used it as his excuse to leave. To a friend, he wrote:

The Great man and I have come to an open rupture. Proposals of accommodation have been made on his part but rejected. . . . He shall for once at least repent his ill-humor.

As Hamilton prepared to leave headquarters, he began to worry about his future. Anxious to further his reputation and make his ideas known, he began studying in earnest to construct a report on the nation's finances. In a forty-five page letter to Superintendent of Finance Robert Morris, Hamilton discussed national credit, manufacturing, and the future of the American nation. In his letter, Hamilton predicted: " 'Tis by introducing order into our finances—by restoring public credit—not by gaining battles, that we are finally to gain our object." Morris later praised Hamilton's "performance," noting him as a man "of genius and abilities."

Despite Morris's praise, Hamilton still craved the chance to prove himself as a soldier. Desperate for military glory, he played his last card by sending his commission to Washington, formally resigning his rank. Washington finally acquiesced, giving Hamilton a field command at Yorktown. Hamilton made the most of his moment on the battlefield; in a "frenzy of valour," he drilled his men in direct line of fire of the enemy. Hamilton's successful capture of a vital British position contributed to the surrender of Cornwallis at Yorktown in October of 1781, and the end of the Revolutionary War.

"A Member of the Convention"

With the ending of the Revolutionary War, Hamilton turned his thoughts to the future. Convinced of the need for a strong national government capable of uniting thirteen squabbling states into a respected nation, he began campaigning for change. His efforts contributed to the calling of the Federal Convention of 1787, where the form of America's new government would be debated and decided. As a delegate from New York, Hamilton vigorously argued for his beliefs. But the other two delegates from his state, John Lansing, Jr., and Robert Yates, resisted his nationalism. Their continued opposition made Hamilton virtually useless at the Convention.

Hamilton's appointment to the Federal Convention of 1787 followed years of consistent efforts to promote a stronger national government. A delegate to the Annapolis Convention the year before, Hamilton had drafted the final address calling for a future convention to consider reform of the American government. With the meeting of the Federal Convention, Hamilton's hopes were realized.

On June 18, 1787, in reaction to what he saw as the convention's hesitancy in strengthening the national government, Hamilton presented his plan for a new American government. According to some accounts, his speech lasted six hours. Throughout his address, he promoted a strong national government, headed by a strong executive. Hamilton's ideas proved too radical for the Convention; a fellow delegate remarked that his speech was "praised by every body, but he has been supported by none."

"Under the Signature of Publius"

Hamilton proved himself after the Convention, during the fight to ratify the new Constitution in New York. With America's destiny at stake, he exerted his full energies to convincing New York—and, indirectly, other states as well—to adopt the Constitution and put the American republic on its feet. Hamilton soon became New York's strongest activist in the struggle for ratification. To support what he felt was the only hope for the future of America, he planned *The Federalist*—a series of anonymous newspaper articles explaining and defending the new Constitution, published under the name "Publius." He invited John Jay of New York and James Madison of Virginia to assist him in writing. The essays were written in great haste; the printer frequently stood by the writer's side, taking the manuscript as soon as pen lifted from page. Eventually collected in book form and circulated around the nation, *The Federalist* earned its authors a national reputation. The work remains the finest commentary on the American Constitution.

The three authors of *The Federalist* divided responsibility for the topics to be covered in the essays; each man wrote on subjects he felt most strongly about. All three men recognized the importance of the success of the American experiment. Hamilton eloquently expressed this sentiment in his stirring introduction to *The Federalist No. 1:*

> It has frequently been remarked that it seems to have been reserved to the people of this country, by their conduct and example, to decide the important question, whether societies of men are really capable or not of establishing good government from reflection and choice, or whether they are forever destined to depend for their political constitutions on accident and force. . . . [T]he crisis at which we are arrived may with propriety be regarded as the era in which that decision is to be made; and a wrong election of the part we shall act may . . . deserve to be considered as the general misfortune of mankind.

Hamilton's contributions to *The Federalist* primarily dealt with the benefits of the Constitution to the American economy, the importance of an energetic executive, and the role of the judiciary. In his fifty-one essays, Hamilton expressed many of his heartfelt convictions about the structure of the American government and the American nation. In his essays concerning the president, for example, he declared his belief in the need for a strong, "energetic" executive:

> Energy in the executive is a leading character in the definition of good government. . . . A feeble executive implies a feeble execution of the government. A feeble execution is but another phrase for a bad execution; and a government ill executed, whatever it may be in theory, must be, in practice, a bad government. [*The Federalist No. 70*].

While discussing the effect of the Constitution on the American economy, Hamilton revealed both his vision for America's future, and his recognition of the importance of finance to the survival of the nation. In *The Federalist No. 30*, he asserted that "money . . . is the vital principle of the body politic." Without proper means of financing the national government, Hamilton questioned how the government could "ever possess either energy or stability, dignity or credit, confidence at home or respectability abroad."

In *The Federalist No. 78*, when speaking of the role of the federal judiciary, Hamilton defined courts of justice as "the bulwarks of a limited Constitution against legislative encroachments." If the Constitution is perceived as "a fundamental law," then it is the

> proper and peculiar province of the courts . . . to . . . ascertain its meaning as well as the meaning of any particular act proceeding from the legislative body. . . . If there should happen to be an irreconcilable variance between the two, . . . the Constitution ought to be preferred to the statute, the intention of the people to the intention of their agents.

Nine years later, in 1796, Hamilton tested these principles while acting as special counsel for the government in the "carriage tax" case—the first case in which the Supreme Court ruled on the constitutionality of an act of Congress.

Hamilton's contributions to *The Federalist* remain the most comprehensive, and arguably, the most eloquent statement of his political convictions. Yet, *The Federalist* had little direct effect on the ratification campaign; debate over the Constitution continued in New York. Days before the state convention's final vote on ratification, merchants and tradesmen anxious for improved trade organized a parade, hoping to influence the convention in favor of the Constitution. Included in the parade was the frigate "Hamilton," featuring a wooden statue of Hamilton as its figurehead, holding the Constitution aloft. Hamilton was celebrated as New York's foremost supporter of the Constitution, and the man most responsible for adding the state to the new United States of America. His role in the struggle for ratification made him a national figure. But the most difficult task lay ahead—the challenge of putting the new government in motion.

II. Alexander Hamilton: Secretary of the Treasury
"Very Busy and Not a Little Anxious"

With the inauguration of George Washington as America's first president, the nation wondered who he would choose to serve in the major posts of the new government. Economic ruin threatened, making the position of treasury secretary particularly vital and destined for controversy. On September 11, 1789, Washington filled the key position; he nominated thirty-four-year-old Alexander Hamilton, his former aide and long-standing colleague, to become America's first secretary of the treasury, head of the nation's largest and most important government department. Hamilton faced an economic crisis that threatened the very survival of the American experiment. But by the time he resigned in 1795, his controversial financial plans had succeeded in setting the American republic on a firm foundation, earning it respectability and honor at home and abroad.

Underlying Hamilton's economic plans was his clear, heartfelt vision of America's destiny; a nation honored among nations, prosperous and industrious, with a strong national government directed by a strong executive, and stabilized by the support of the wealthy and powerful. This vision pervaded all of Hamilton's actions while serving as treasury secretary, whether he was directly involved with the nation's finances, or asserting himself on matters far removed from his official role as treasury secretary.

The unstructured nature of the new government gave the aggressive treasury secretary frequent opportunities to influence public policy beyond the sphere of finance. Washington usually asked all of his Cabinet secretaries for opinions on important matters, ignoring the division between government departments. This policy led to competition among secretaries, and eventually, to open dissension.

Hamilton was always more than happy to give his advice, requested or not. In one letter, written to Washington long before Hamilton had even been nominated for the office of treasury secretary, Hamilton offered counsel on presidential etiquette. To maintain the dignity of the office, Hamilton recommended ceremonies and formalities to set the president somewhat above the other branches of government. His advice reflects his continuing campaign for a powerful executive, and the tendencies that Secretary of State Thomas Jefferson would later label "aristocratical."

Hamilton's persistent efforts to influence wide-ranging government policy had their effect. Much to his opponents' chagrin, he soon became the unofficial leader of the government.

Hamilton's first major undertaking as treasury secretary was to create a plan for "an adequate provision for the support of public credit," as the congressional request phrased it. Before delivering his first major report, Hamilton confessed to his sister-in-law, Angelica Church: "You may imagine that . . . I am very busy and not a little anxious." His anxiety was well-founded. The *Report Relative to a Provision for the Support of Public Credit*, submitted on January 14, 1790, was Hamilton's first attempt to articulate his economic and political policies, and his many recommendations supported his desire for promoting respect for the new nation, and for a strengthened national government. One of his most controversial recommendations proposed that the national government assume responsibility for all the states' debts, linking creditors to the national government. Congress took seven months to approve Hamilton's controversial report, making it the main point of discussion for its entire second session.

Hamilton faced fierce opposition to his plan for national assumption of state debts. By July of 1790, he was desperate; failure of his plan could mean the collapse of America's credit and finances, and ultimately the collapse of the nation. Secretary of State Thomas Jefferson, meeting Hamilton by chance one day, saw the treasury secretary's anxiety. He arranged a dinner between Hamilton and Representative James Madison of Virginia, the chief opponent of the plan. The dinner resulted in a political deal. Madison agreed to stop working against assumption, and to find other votes for the measure. In exchange, Hamilton would work to move the nation's capital from New York to Philadelphia for a period of ten years, and from there, to a spot on the banks of the Potomac River between Virginia and Maryland.

The second main feature of Hamilton's financial plan was the creation of a national bank. Hamilton hoped to promote stability through national financial security, active circulation of money, and investment in the government through purchase of bank stock. Opposition to Hamilton's report focused on its constitutionality; the Constitution did not specifically empower the government to charter the bank. Most of Washington's advisors supported this view, and Washington prepared to reject the bill. However, he allowed Hamilton the chance to defend his proposal.

Hamilton's defense argued that the Constitution contained the implied power to charter a bank. He found the source of this implied power in the "necessary and proper" clause of Article I, section 8. As he put it, the Constitution gave the government the power

> 'to make all laws, necessary & proper for carrying into execution the foregoing powers & all other powers vested by the constitution in the government of the United States, or in any department or officer thereof.' To understand the word [necessary] as the Secretary of State does, would be to depart from its obvious & popular sense, and to give it a restrictive operation; an idea never before entertained. It would be to give it the same force as if the word absolutely or indispensably had been prefixed to it.

With his *Opinion on the Constitutionality of an Act to Establish a Bank*, Hamilton not only convinced Washington to approve the bank bill; he established the principle of "broad construction" of the Constitution, furthering his fight for a strong national government.

The capstone of Hamilton's financial plan was his *Report on the Subject of Manufactures*. In this report, he revealed the full scope of his vision for the future of America. To Hamilton, the nation would survive only if it fostered industry as well as agriculture and commerce. Support industry, and the character of the entire nation would change; America would be a prosperous industrial power, with industrious, hardworking citizens. Congress, finding Hamilton's report too radical in its implications, rejected it.

Hamilton's vision of an industrial nation led by a strong national government clashed with Secretary of State Thomas Jefferson's dream of an agrarian republic headed by a far less powerful federal government. The two men were destined for conflict. Even their temperaments seemed opposite. Hamilton, aggressive, direct, and combative, was faced with the seemingly retiring, indirect Jefferson. By 1793, each man was convinced that the other aimed at nothing less than the corruption of the nation. Their fierce opposition brought about the beginnings of political parties in America.

The conflict between Hamilton and Jefferson soon spread into the newspapers. Each man supported a newspaper defending his particular views. The pro-Hamilton *Gazette of the United States* launched a vicious attack on Jefferson in a series of articles written by Hamilton. The Jeffersonian *National Gazette*, in turn, published a defense of Jefferson penned by Jefferson's supporter James Madison. The sight of two of the government's leading figures reduced to public brawling amazed the public and infuriated President Washington. The dispute soon made front-page news.

Weary of the constant bickering and embarrassed by the public nature of the conflict, Washington wrote to both Jefferson and Hamilton, pleading with them to attempt a reconciliation. Both men responded in essentially the same manner. Each accused the other of instigating the dispute, and refused to stop until the other party did so first. The public battle eventually ended, but only with Jefferson's resignation in 1793.

Jefferson was not the only government official to oppose Hamilton. Adversaries continually attacked Hamilton and his policies, charging him with corruption, and calling for investigations into his conduct. The constant attacks sometimes drove the defensive treasury secretary to extremes. Hamilton wrote countless angry responses to charges against him, publishing them in leading newspapers. He also was known simply to lose his temper, a dangerous character flaw in the age of dueling. When Representative John Francis Mercer of Maryland charged Hamilton with corruption and bribery, their conflict almost led the two men to fight a duel.

However, Hamilton never wavered in his struggle for what he perceived as the public good. When, in 1794, farmers in western Pennsylvania rebelled against an excise tax on whiskey, Hamilton viewed it as a challenge to national honor and stability. He strongly advised Washington to send troops to Pennsylvania to crush the rebellion. Secretary of War Henry Knox was absent on family business, so Hamilton took on the additional position of acting secretary of war. Despite his duties in both departments, Hamilton applied to Washington for permission to accompany the expedition, a sign of his continued craving for military glory. Washington consented. The insurrection was eventually suppressed without any bloodshed.

Throughout Hamilton's career as treasury secretary, Elizabeth Hamilton carried the full weight of managing the household on limited finances; one friend praised her as being a better financier than her husband. By 1794, their growing family consisted of five children, plus an adopted orphan child, and the family was expecting a new addition in the near future. When Hamilton set out to help suppress the Whiskey Rebellion, he once again sacrificed his family's interests to the public good. In a letter to his children, he tried to reassure them that "there will be no fighting and of course no danger. It will only be an agreeable ride which will I hope do me good." Elizabeth later suffered a miscarriage due to her fears for Hamilton's safety.

With the successful defeat of the Whiskey Rebellion, Hamilton was ready to retire. To his sister-in-law Angelica, he wrote:

> Our finances are in a most flourishing condition. Having contributed to place those of the Nation on a good footing, I go to take a little care of my own; which need my care not a little.

Hamilton formally retired on January 31, 1795. President Washington bade farewell to his secretary with a glowing tribute: "In every relation which you have borne to me I have found that my confidence in your talents, exertions, and integrity, has been well placed." Hamilton's resignation was regretted by many; in honor of his accomplishments, New York granted him the freedom of the city.

III. The Mischief of Faction

"Malicious Intrigues to Stab Me in the Dark"

Scandal and intrigue set the tone of Hamilton's life in the years following his service as treasury secretary. As the leader of the Federalists, Hamilton was the prime target of all those who opposed his party. Political adversaries attacked his public reputation and exposed his private life at every opportunity, driving the thin-skinned Hamilton to embarrassing public confessions and rash outbursts in defense of his wounded honor.

Without an official role in the government, yet desperate to steer the course of the nation, Hamilton resorted to intrigue to make his influence felt. Throughout John Adams's presidency, Hamilton acted as a secret prime minister, consulted in private by Adams's Cabinet members on almost every major government decision. But the boldness and daring that at times seemed genius became recklessness, bordering on self-destructiveness. Frustrated by his inability to direct government policy, angered at the attacks on his reputation, and wanting to strike back at political opponents, Hamilton went too far. His unwise maneuvering destroyed his party and brought his political career to ruin.

One of Hamilton's best-known mistakes occurred while he was still serving as treasury secretary. In 1791, the attractive Maria Reynolds had come to Hamilton begging for financial aid, and had quickly provided the opportunity for much more. As Hamilton later described it:

> I took the bill out of my pocket and gave it to her. Some conversation ensued from which it was quickly apparent that other than pecuniary consolation would be acceptable.

The trap was sprung when Maria's husband began to demand blackmail payments in exchange for secrecy. Hamilton's adulterous affair with Maria continued for over a year, until Hamilton finally put an end to it.

Political opposition brought the old affair to light in 1797, along with added charges of financial corruption. To defend his public reputation, Hamilton published *Observations on Certain Documents Contained in No. V & VI of "The History of the United States for the Year 1796," in which the Charge of Speculation Against Alexander Hamilton Late Secretary of the Treasury, is fully refuted. Written by Himself.* In the pamphlet, he explained that

> the charge against me is a connection with one James Reynolds for purposes of improper pecuniary speculation. My real crime is an amorous connection with his wife.

He then went on to describe his adulterous affair in great detail, explaining that his payments to Reynolds were not illegal speculation, but blackmail. The publication of Hamilton's confession to adultery created a great scandal, not only in America, but abroad as well. On the effect of the scandal on Hamilton's political career, a fellow politician remarked:

> Hamilton is fallen for the present, but if he fornicates with every female in the cities of New York and Philadelphia, he will rise again. For purity of character, after a period of political existence, is not necessary for political patronage.

This prophecy proved correct, for the "Reynolds Affair" did not remove Hamilton from the political arena. Throughout John Adams's

Alexander Hamilton

presidency, Hamilton acted as a secret prime minister to Adams's Cabinet. The secretaries regularly consulted Hamilton on important matters of state. Adams was largely unaware of the range of Hamilton's influence, but he grew to distrust increasingly the ambitious New York lawyer. Their conflict led to the eventual destruction of the Federalist party. Many years later, Adams recalled, ". . . all the sovereignty then existing in the nation was in the hands of Alexander Hamilton . . . I was as President a mere cipher."

Adams's dislike and distrust of Hamilton was evident in 1798, when war threatened with France. President Adams called George Washington out of retirement to become commander-in-chief of the American army. Hamilton, still anxious for military glory, wanted the position of inspector general, or second-in-command. The weary Washington planned to spend most of his time at Mount Vernon, overseeing the army in absentia; for all practical purposes, the second-in-command would be in control. John Adams strongly resisted Hamilton's appointment, but Washington's insistence won Hamilton the position. The post eventually proved frustrating for Hamilton; without many men to command and with no actual war to fight, he spent most of his time on trivial details.

In 1800, when Adams realized the full extent of Hamilton's influence on his Cabinet, he flew into a rage. Forcing the resignation of all of Hamilton's supporters, he accused Hamilton of leading a British faction, and called him a "Creole Bastard." In frustration and anger,

Hamilton wrote *Letter From Alexander Hamilton Concerning the Public Conduct and Character of John Adams, Esq., President of the United States*. In this pamphlet, he explained for forty-five pages why Adams was "unfit . . . for the office of Chief Magistrate." Hamilton made a grave error by publishing this pamphlet. Not only did it divide and destroy his political party, but it effectively ended his political career. Fellow Federalist Robert Troup commented: "Hence he is considered as an unfit head of the party."

Hamilton's attack on John Adams divided his party during a presidential election, throwing victory to the Republicans. In an unforeseen complication, however, vice-presidential candidate Aaron Burr and presidential candidate Thomas Jefferson received an equal number of votes, throwing the tie into the U.S. House of Representatives to be decided. Faced with the unpleasant choice of Burr or Jefferson for president, Hamilton mustered what little political clout he still possessed and began an active letter-writing campaign, trying to sway the election toward Jefferson. Although he violently opposed Jefferson, he feared Burr far more:

> If there be a man in the world I ought to hate it is Jefferson. With Burr I have always been personally well. But the public good must be paramount to every private consideration.

Hamilton's efforts, though great, had little influence.

With the election of Thomas Jefferson as president, Hamilton's political ascendancy ended. At the thought of Jefferson's leadership of the nation, Hamilton said: "Reflecting men must be dismayed at the prospect before us."

"Mine is an Odd Destiny"

With the turn of the century, Hamilton ended the days of his youth. Impatience and arrogance gave way to tolerance, and eventually resignation. Turning his attentions to his wife and eight children, he began building a home. In the fall of 1799, Hamilton had purchased a tract of land in upper Manhattan. There, he built "The Grange," named after the ancestral Hamilton estate in Scotland. Dividing his time between his downtown office and his "country home," Hamilton made the three-hour round trip several times each week.

This was a bittersweet time for Hamilton, despite the comfort he found in his domestic life; he felt the nation's destiny slipping beyond his reach, moving toward a goal alien to his dreams. In despair, he confided to long-time friend Gouverneur Morris:

> Mine is an odd destiny. Perhaps no man in the U[nited] States has sacrificed or done more for the present Constitution than myself. . . . Yet I have the murmurs of its friends no less than the curses of its foes for my reward. What can I do better than withdraw from the Scene? Every day proves to me more and more, that this American world was not made for me.

Despair set the tone for Hamilton's private life as well. In November of 1801, Hamilton's eldest son Philip fought a duel with one of his father's political opponents. Mortally wounded, the nineteen-year-old boy died in great agony. Philip's death tortured Hamilton; he considered his son "the eldest and brightest hope of my family." Overwhelmed with grief, Hamilton collapsed at the funeral while standing beside his son's grave. Soon thereafter, his eldest daughter, Angelica, went mad due to the shock of her brother's death. One of Hamilton's close friends remarked: "His countenance is strongly stamped with grief."

Nonetheless, Hamilton still cared passionately for the future of his country, and thought that, perhaps at some future point, he might prove useful to the nation he had helped to build. This opportunity never came.

For fifteen years, Hamilton opposed Aaron Burr. Although the two men socialized, and frequently practiced law together, Hamilton felt that Burr was a threat to the nation; once in power, he would place his own ambitions above the public good:

> Burr . . . is sanguine enough to hope every thing—daring enough to attempt every thing—wicked enough to scruple nothing. From the elevation of such a man heaven preserve the Country!

By 1804, Burr was frustrated with Hamilton's constant opposition. When he heard that Hamilton had supposedly insulted him at a social function, he seized upon the opportunity to confront Hamilton and set the stage for a duel.

Burr had read a letter in *The Albany Register* that quoted Hamilton declaring that Burr was "a dangerous man, and one who ought not to be trusted with the reins of government." The author of the letter then revealed that he "could detail . . . a still more despicable opinion which General Hamilton has expressed of Mr. Burr." Burr wrote to

Hamilton demanding an explanation for the "more despicable opinion" Hamilton had apparently expressed. Hamilton, in accordance with the rules of the code *duello*, asked Burr to state a specific remark which had given offense; he would then be willing to defend it, or to apologize. Burr felt that Hamilton was evading his demand. He and Hamilton both selected seconds to serve as intermediaries, and their correspondence continued for almost two weeks.

Although Hamilton later delivered the original apology that Burr had requested, by this point Burr had lost patience. He now demanded a blanket apology for all of Hamilton's remarks over their many years of opposition. Hamilton replied through his second that "while he was prepared to meet the particular case fully and fairly he thinks it inadmissible that he should be expected to answer at large as to anything that he may possibly have said in relation to the character of Colonel Burr, at any time or upon any occasion." He could not give Burr the apology he wanted. A specific date and meeting place were chosen, and each man began to plan for the possibility of his death at the hand of the other.

In the last days before the duel, Hamilton wrote a statement explaining his conduct and motives. Despite religious and moral conflict over participating in a duel, Hamilton's concern with his personal honor, combined with his hopes for his future, compelled him to accept the challenge:

> what men of the world denominate honour, imposed on me (as I thought) a . . . necessity not to decline the call. The ability to be in future useful . . . would probably be inseparable from a conformity with public prejudice in this particular.

Yet, loath to fire on another man in cold blood, and recognizing that he may have given Burr grounds for a challenge, Hamilton stated that he would withhold his fire, leaving the ultimate outcome of the duel entirely in Burr's hands.

On the morning of July 11, 1804, Hamilton and Burr met on the dueling ground at Weehawken, New Jersey. At the word "present," two shots rang out. Hamilton's shot struck a tree branch over Burr's head. Burr's bullet struck Hamilton in the abdomen lodging in his spine. After suffering in great pain for more than a day, Hamilton died at the age of forty-nine on July 12, at 2:00 in the afternoon, surrounded by family and friends.

Courtesy of the Chase Manhattan Archives

Hamilton's death left his family $55,000 in debt. Most of this sum was incurred while building "The Grange." To provide financial relief for the widow and her eight children, friends formed a trust fund. Among the trustees of Hamilton's estate were former secretary of the treasury and family friend Oliver Wolcott, and leading New Yorkers such as Gouverneur Morris and Rufus King. Although a substantial sum of money was raised, it was not sufficient to provide much relief for the family's financial problems.

On the day of Hamilton's funeral, a solemn procession wound through the streets of lower Manhattan, ending at Trinity Church, Hamilton's final resting place. Bells tolled throughout the city, and ships in the harbor fired salutes. At the funeral, Hamilton's friend and colleague Gouverneur Morris delivered the eulogy, concluding: "I charge you to protect his fame—it is all he has left."

IV. Conclusion

During his brief and crowded life, Alexander Hamilton accomplished much. He fought in the Revolutionary War, serving as an invaluable aide to Washington, and winning a critical victory at Yorktown. He took part in the creation of the American Constitution, and fought to include New York in the new Constitutional government. His actions as treasury secretary saved the United States from financial ruin, and left his imprint on the identity of the American nation. Yet, when he died, Hamilton could not see the scope of any of his achievements. In his eyes, the success of the American experiment was still in doubt. Perhaps his driving ambitions, always inducing him to strive for more, prevented Hamilton from feeling satisfaction with any of his accomplishments; there was always more to achieve. Perhaps the ascendancy of Thomas Jefferson to the office of president convinced Hamilton that all of his hard-earned victories would now come to nothing, undone by his old political opponent.

Yet, despite his doubts, Hamilton's influence on the history of the United States is irrefutable. His efforts and energy contributed to the establishment of a government, of precedents in policy, and of a national identity which continue to the present day. When Hamilton died, the nation mourned the passing of a leader in the creation of the United States. But only the passage of time has shown the true value of the efforts of Alexander Hamilton.

For Further Reading

Caldwell, Lynton K. *The Administrative Theories of Alexander Hamilton and Thomas Jefferson*, 2nd ed. (New York: Holmes & Meier, 1988)

Frisch, Morton J., ed. *Selected Writings and Speeches of Alexander Hamilton*. Washington, D.C.: American Enterprise Institute for Public Policy Research, 1985.

McDonald, Forrest. *Alexander Hamilton, A Biography*. New York: W.W. Norton & Company, 1979.

Miller, John C. *Alexander Hamilton, Portrait in Paradox*. New York: Harper & Row, Publishers, 1959.

_____ . *The Federalist Era*. New York: Harper & Row, Publishers, 1960.

Mitchell, Broadus. *Alexander Hamilton*. 2 vols. New York: The Macmillan Company, 1957, 1962.

_____ . *Alexander Hamilton, A Concise Biography*. New York Oxford University Press, 1976.

Morris, Richard B., ed. *Alexander Hamilton and the Founding of the Nation*. New York: The Dial Press, 1957.

John Sloss Hobart: Forgotten Patriot

(1738–1805)

RICHARD W. STREB

Teachers College, Columbia University (Retired)

John Sloss Hobart's public life spanned forty years—from 1765, when he became a leader of the Sons of Liberty on Long Island—to his death in 1805, when he was a United States District Judge for the District of New York. During his public career, he was a member of the fourth provincial congress, the body that drafted the New York Constitution of 1777, and served on the committee of the provincial congress that approved the Declaration of Independence at White Plains in 1776. He was an associate judge of the first New York Supreme Court and held that post for almost twenty years, until 1798, when he reached the mandatory retirement age of sixty. The state legislature then elected Hobart to the United States Senate to fill the seat left vacant by the retirement of Philip Schuyler. Hobart held that office from January until April 1798 when he resigned. Late in 1798, President John Adams nominated him to the United States District Court and the Senate confirmed him. He held that post until his death at the age of sixty-seven.

Early Life

Peter Hobart, John Sloss Hobart's great-grandfather and the founder of the Hobart family in America, arrived about 1650 and settled in Hingham, Massachusetts. He was the first pastor of the church in Hingham. His son David, a farmer, gradually added to the family's land holdings. David's son Noah chose the religious life and became the pastor of Christ Church (Congregationalist) in Fairfield, Connecticut. John was born and raised in Fairfield.

On his mother's side, John Sloss Hobart was descended from John Sloss, a well-to-do merchant from Fairfield. The Sloss family had been in America for four generations and were so well-established in Connecticut that Noah Hobart removed willingly from Hingham to Fairfield, where the Slosses arranged for his pastorate. John Sloss's greatest legacy to his namesake was a large piece of land called Eatons Neck, which he had bought in 1710. When John Sloss died in 1720, his will (now in the Fairfield County Courthouse) declared: ''I give unto my daughters Sarah, Ellen, and Deborah all my Manor of Eaton or Eaton's Neck lying upon Long Island in the Province of New York, each of them, one third part to them and their heirs forever—if any dye without heirs of their bodies the survivor shall have that their part.'' Ellen Sloss, the middle daughter of John Sloss and the mother of his namesake, was the only one of the three daughters to have children; thus, when she died in 1754, all the land passed to John, her oldest son.

John had an ordinary childhood. He had a younger brother and sister, who were his earliest playmates. The only real excitement in their lives came with the occasional Indian war, for then men would be drilling and making all the necessary provisions for prolonged absence. The people in the community would give the departing militia a rousing send-off, with flags waving and crowds cheering (and some weeping), and martial music filling the air. Hobart studied with a tutor and then enrolled at the local academy. In 1754 he entered Yale College, from which he was graduated in 1757 at the age of nineteen.

The Land and the Landholder

When Hobart finished college, he chose to start a life of his own on Eatons Neck, the land he had inherited three years before. For the next twenty years Eatons Neck was his home, and it was from Eatons Neck that he set out to begin his public service to the American Revolution. It is thus appropriate to review the history of this beautiful and unusual territory.

Eatons Neck is a heavily wooded headland jutting into Long Island Sound north of the village of Northport. At one time it was an island—and occasionally still is during severe storms which hit at high tide—but it is now connected to the mainland by a narrow strip of land. That three-mile strip is now Asharoken Village, named for the best-known Indian chief during the early days of English settlement. Theophilus Eaton, founder and governor of the New Haven colony (now part of present-day Connecticut), obtained the fifteen hundred acres of land from the Matinecock Indians in 1646 and gave his name to the land. The deed transferring the land to him, one of the earliest on Long Island, is preserved in the Huntington Town records. The real purpose of Eaton's purchase was to block further Dutch expansion on Long Island and keep a toehold there for the British. When Eaton died, the land passed to his daughter, Hannah, and her husband, William Jones. In 1662, a Hartford Indian fighter named Robert Seelye bought the property and in turn sold it for a nice profit to George Baldwin, who built the first house on the land and began to fence it with a view to raising cattle. During Baldwin's forty-year tenure, Governor Thomas Dongan, with the approval of Parliament, declared Eatons Neck a Royal Manor, one of only five such Manors on Long Island. Dongan's action conferred unusual governmental and legal privileges on the owner of Eatons Neck. The land was only partly developed when John Sloss bought it in 1710.

John Sloss Hobart was the real developer of Eatons Neck; he experimented with various crops and had a successful cattle business underway when the American Revolution began. Some reports indicate that his holdings included thousands of head of cattle; he also raised sheep and processed both leather and wool on his manor. He incurred such heavy debts during the Revolution and suffered such serious losses from the British occupation that he was forced to sell the entire manor in 1788. Robert Watts purchased the land from Hobart as an exercise in real estate speculation and then sold it to the famous Gardiner family in 1792, recouping a handsome return on his investment. The Gardiners kept the land until 1863.

Soon after Hobart finished college, he began to study law in New York City. He met, fell in love with, and married Mary Grinnell (some newspapers spelled her name Greenill) and planned and began to build a substantial two-story manor house on the west side of Eatons Neck facing Huntington harbor. The house, surrounded by a beautiful garden framed by boxwood, lasted for generations, eventually serving as the home of the Gardiner family while they lived at Eatons Neck. Two of the bricks from this house are in the time capsule buried on the grounds of Northport High School (to be excavated in the year 2000).

Hobart and his bride moved into the home on Eatons Neck in 1763 and settled into the comfortable life of the landed gentry. The Long Island gentry were closely affiliated with and closely resembled their counterparts in New England, both in the pattern of their daily lives and in their political thinking. They were also like English Whigs, mixing farming with trade and adopting forward-looking views about limiting parliamentary power.

In the 1760s, religious leaders such as Hobart's father Noah were losing status and power and no longer were the only recognized leaders in colonial society. Lawyers and gentlemen with some legal training were joining the ranks of the colonial elite, and John Sloss Hobart benefited from this trend, "a gentleman and a lawyer." From the beginning of his time at Eatons Neck he evinced great interest in new ideas about agriculture and experimented with new crops and new processes of tilling the soil. His correspondence with John Jay documents these efforts.

Public Life I: Resistance to the British

John Sloss Hobart entered public life as one of the many colonial politicians rallying in the mid-1760s to oppose what they deemed British tyranny. British Chancellor of the Exchequer George Grenville had proposed, and Parliament had adopted, new policies of taxation and regulation of trade designed to compel the colonists of British North America to assume partial responsibility for the huge war debt Britain had amassed during the Seven Years' War (1756–1763). Grenville's program included the Sugar Act, the Stamp Act, and the Quartering and Currency Act. The colonists claimed that these taxes and other measures violated a basic principle of the English constitution and the rights of Englishmen: no taxation without representation.

Hobart became a leader of the local chapter of the "Sons of Liberty" and served on the Committee of Correspondence for Huntington and Suffolk County. The colonists' boycott of English goods led to the repeal of the Stamp Act; at the same time, however, Parliament enacted the Declaratory Act reaffirming its power to legislate for the colonists "in all cases whatsoever"—an ominous measure overlooked by the celebrating colonists.

Grenville's successor, Charles Townshend, proposed measures of his own that exacerbated relations between the colonists and the mother country. Not only did Parliament impose new taxes on tea, glass, lead, paper, and other products, and not only were these taxes to be collected by resident commissioners independent of colonial governors. Parliament conferred on these officials sweeping enforcement powers that, in the colonists' view, trampled upon their rights under the English constitution. The leaders of the boycott that had defeated the Stamp Act resumed their activities and reinstated boycotts, and violence broke out in many places. Customs officials were tarred and feathered, ships were burned, tea thrown into the sea, and property destroyed. These acts of resistance spread a state of general unrest.

By this time Hobart was a justice of the peace for the village of Huntington; in 1770 he was elected to the committee of correspondence and charged with keeping in touch with the rest of the county and with New York City. He was beginning his entry into American politics, where he would meet and become a colleague of many national figures.

On June 21, 1774, the Town Board of Huntington adopted the Huntington Declaration of Rights. The scholarly consensus is that the Huntington politicians acted independently of similar actions in New York City in May and in East Hampton on June 21, and that these actions also anticipated the First Continental Congress, which first met in Philadelphia in September. Hobart played a key role in the framing and adoption of this radical statement, which was strong evidence of the growing militancy of the resistance offered by many New Yorkers to British rule.

The Huntington Declaration set forth seven points expressing the townsmen's outrage at the British decision to close the port of Boston and denouncing the Townshend duties as unconstitutional violations of the essential rights of British subjects. The declaration also provided for the appointment of a committee of two to execute the principles adopted and to seek unity locally and elsewhere in resisting British violations of constitutional rights.

Hobart was not a delegate to the First Continental Congress but did serve on the committee that chose the Long Island representatives, who were committed to the principles of the Huntington Declaration. They were outnumbered by the three New York City leaders, who were, by contrast, highly conservative and resisted open defiance of British authority.

Hobart served in all four of the provincial congresses that governed New York from May 1775 through May 1777, after the adjournment of the colonial assembly on April 3, 1775. In 1776–1777, he spent his energy trying to delay or prevent the British from occupying Long Island. He took his wife to Connecticut, where she would be safe from capture, and in effect abandoned his property and home. Among his many tasks were those of organizing and providing ammunition to troops engaging the British; recommending officers for regiments he helped to organize; gathering and evaluating information about British forces and their movements (in other words, spying for the Revolution); and serving as a clearinghouse for processing and investigating reports of those New Yorkers who had violated the non-trade association rules about dealing with the enemy and determining appropriate punishments for recalcitrants and Loyalists. Somehow he also found time to report often to the provincial congresses on conditions on Long Island; indeed, his seven long reports constitute a valuable contemporary history of the Revolution on Long Island.

In June 1776, Hobart asked permission for a leave to protect his cattle from British attacks. His efforts to defend his property were doomed to failure, for that very month General Sir William Howe and Admiral Sir Richard Howe, skirting Eatons Neck, entered New York harbor with 31,000 soldiers under their command, including 8,000 Hessians. These soldiers were bivouacked on Staten Island and Long Island. By 1783, when the British finally evacuated New York City, Hobart's cattle and sheep had been killed to feed the British, his home was a ransacked shell, his furniture was either gone or destroyed, and his land had returned to its original state.

Hobart was on the committee of the provincial congress that approved the Declaration of Independence on behalf of New York. While he was in White Plains with his fellow delegates, his neighbors in Huntington celebrated the news, as reported by the town records for July 23, 1776: "Yesterday freedom and independence of the 13 United Colonies was with beat of drums proclaimed at several places by parade, by reading the Declaration of the General Congress together with the Resolution of our Provincial Congress thereupon." The residents of Huntington also burned George III in effigy and drank thirteen toasts to the American cause.

Huntington eventually became the northern headquarters for the British forces occupying Long Island; the town's residents were forced to gather in the center of the town and pledge their allegiance to George III. For the rest of the Revolutionary War, supporters of American independence on Long Island conducted hit-and-miss raids against British ships and supplies. Thousands of refugees fled to Connecticut or to safer places in other parts of New York.

Hobart continued his efforts for the American cause during the next three years. Among other things, he developed a plan (at the request of General George Washington) to drive the British from Long Island; planned, found, and delivered aid to refugees from the British occupation; and spied out and reported on conditions on Long Island. He also played an important role in the deliberations of the fourth provincial congress on the adoption of the 1777 Constitution. At long intervals, he was granted brief leaves to visit his family and to look after their welfare.

Public Life II: Judge, Revolutionary Leader, Federalist

In May of 1777, the New York Supreme Court was established. John Jay became its first chief justice, and was then succeeded by Richard Morris. The associate justices were Robert Yates and John Sloss Hobart. Hobart held this post for twenty years, retiring only when he reached the mandatory retirement age of sixty. Upon his death, Chancellor James Kent observed, "He was a faithful and discerning judge during the time he remained on the bench." Hobart, however, always believed that he did not have enough training in the law to assume such responsibilities. He wrote, "I entered with great diffidence upon the functions of the office, not having been educated in the profession of the law."

In 1778, a committee on government for the Southern District (including the counties of Kings, New York, Queens, Richmond, Suffolk, and Westchester) was established to provide for the care of any land freed from British control until such time as the regular government could conduct business. The committee had the authority to deal with any British authority to expedite the withdrawal progress. Hobart served on this committee with Judge Egbert Benson, who became his closest friend. On November 25, 1783, the day when the British evacuated New York City, Hobart and his fellow committee members rode into New York City four abreast, immediately behind General Washington and Governor George Clinton. Hobart was also present for the moving farewell which Washington paid to his officers at Fraunces Tavern on December 4, 1783.

Hobart was chosen as a delegate to the Annapolis Convention of 1786 and was elected to the New York ratifying convention which met at Poughkeepsie in June and July of 1788 to consider the proposed Constitution. A strong Federalist, he joined with John Jay, Richard Morris, Alexander Hamilton, Robert R. Livingston, Isaac Roosevelt, James Duane, Richard Harison, and Nicholas Low in their successful effort to secure New York's adoption of the Constitution, in the process renewing his friendships with some of his allies and forging new friendships with others.

From 1789 until 1798 Hobart occupied himself with his work on the state supreme court, although he was able to join with thousands of New Yorkers on April 30, 1789, in hailing the inauguration of President George Washington at Federal Hall in New York City. As the United States entered a period of growth, stability, and prosperity, the work of the state courts grew accordingly.

Senate Interlude

Philip Schuyler's resignation from the United States Senate coincided with Hobart's retirement from the New York Supreme Court. He was nominated as Schuyler's replacement and secured a large majority in both houses of the state legislature. Although Hobart appreciated the signal honor, he had doubts that he could afford the move from New York to Philadelphia. In his letter accepting election, he provided a moving and honest description of his financial plight, concluding, "I therefore go without hesitation, in obedience to the commands of the Senate and Assembly, to take a seat in the Senate of the Congress of the United States, relying firmly on the experience I have already had, that the legislature of my own State will not suffer an old servant to drink the bitter cup of poverty and distress in the evening of life."

He served from January 11 through April 16, 1798. During that time he introduced one bill, to establish a lighthouse on Eatons Neck, and secured its enactment. The structure was designed by James McComb, a Scotsman who was one of the two architects of New York's City Hall. The lighthouse stands to this day, on a hill surrounding ten acres overlooking Long Island Sound and the coast of Connecticut. This landmark building has been entered on the National Register of Historic Structures; the U.S. Coast Guard base on the site is one of the busiest in the United States.

The U.S. District Court

Hobart resigned from the Senate because, as he had feared, he could not afford to continue; in addition, his wife's health was failing and he wanted to be with her. Apparently Governor Jay played a key role in securing his appointment as a United States District Judge for the District of New York. Hobart met the tests which the nervous Federalists applied to ensure that the federal bench would be staffed by reliable Federalist judges should the Jeffersonian Republicans capture the presidency and the Congress in the 1800 elections. Judge Egbert Benson's courtroom adjoined Judge Hobart's, and the two men continued and strengthened their friendship. Hobart served with distinction until his death in 1805.

Personal Affairs and Death

Hobart was listed as an official donor to the Revolution and thus received some payment of compensation, but the money was worthless and he had no way to restore his estate to its former glory. As early as 1777, Hobart's prosperity had dissolved and he was living as a relatively poor man. If he expected that his circumstances would restore him to his former wealth at the end of the Revolution, he was mistaken. In 1788, as noted above, he was forced to sell Eatons Neck at a loss, and he never recovered his former status. In 1780, when he was chosen a delegate to the Hartford Convention (convened to find ways to check rampant inflation), he tried to resign the appointment because he could not afford to continue; Governor Clinton found legal means to make allowances for him as a judge and encouraged him to stay. Similar embarrassments plagued him for the rest of his life.

Soon after the new Constitution was adopted and the new government went into operation, John Jay advised Hobart on some investment opportunities in New York property. Hobart engaged in modest speculations in foreclosures and sheriff's sales but the surviving evidence suggests that these efforts did not change his financial situation. With Jay's help he purchased a small farm on Throg's Neck—a piece of land jutting from the Bronx mainland into Long Island Sound. Hobart built a small house on this property, describing it in a letter to Jay as a manse. On the house's completion in 1794, Chief Justice Jay sent Hobart two silver candlesticks as a housewarming gift. This small house served the Hobarts as their home for the rest of their lives. Mary died in 1803, and Hobart, suffering from declining health and spirits, followed her in 1805. The grief-stricken Benson commissioned a marble plaque which he installed in Hobart's courtroom in New York's City Hall. It read as follows:

> His birth at Fairfield in Connecticut, his father the pastor of the church there. A judge of the Supreme Court of this state from 1777 to 1798 "when he attained the age of Sixty Years."—afterwards, in the same year, appointed Judge of the District Court of the United States within this district: and continued in that trust to his death in 1805
>
> As a man—firm
>   As a citizen—zealous
>   As a judge—distinguishing
>   As a Christian—sincere
>
> This tablet is placed to his memory by One, to whom he was "As a friend—as close as a brother."

Commemorating John Sloss Hobart: Personal Reflections

Mary Voyce, a retired school teacher in Huntington, spent many years trying to save John Sloss Hobart from the obscurity into which his name had fallen. Because of her long and inspiring efforts, the Town of Huntington finally named a beach after him; the beach traditionally known as Sand City is now Hobart Beach.

Inspired by Mary Voyce's efforts, I organized high school students into research teams to rediscover Hobart. One of the projects they undertook was to find the missing marble plaque that Judge Egbert Benson had set up in Hobart's memory. When the executive director of the New York City Art Commission told the students that there were no available staff members to search for the plaque, the students started a petition drive in their local community, Northport, where they gathered 2,000 signatures. The students presented the signed petitions to Larry Delany, then the Suffolk County Democratic chairman. Delany called Mayor Robert F. Wagner of New York City, described the situation, and secured a promise of aid from the mayor.

The ensuing hunt for the plaque determined that it had been taken down in 1837 when the new U.S. Court House opened; at that time, the second floor of City Hall underwent a facelift, which transformed the two courtrooms into the Governor's Room, intended to be used by governors of the state as an office when they were in New York City. The plaque was stored in the basement of City Hall and then sent to a new city storage space on 34th Street. It remained there until the Sixth Avenue elevated railroad was built in the 1870s. There the trail ended. The search ordered by Mayor Wagner finally located the plaque in the basement of City Hall. The New York City Council agreed, after extensive lobbying by the students, to turn the plaque over to Northport High School in exchange for a payment of one dollar. The plaque now has been placed on the wall at the entrance to the school auditorium, a constant reminder of the town's local Revolutionary hero.

One more mystery remains to be solved: Where was Hobart buried? He left no diary and no will. No descendants survived to keep a family record. All the New York City newspapers covered his funeral but none recorded his burial place. Working with students, I have checked the burial records in Fairfield, Connecticut, and am certain that his remains are not there. Possibly exploration of the records of the Congregational Church or of contemporary cemeteries in Brooklyn may turn up added leads. The Daughters of the American Revolution have offered a reward for anyone who finds Hobart's grave.

In his *History of Long Island*, Benjamin Thompson provided a fitting characterization of Hobart:

> Although not a lawyer he was a man of sound education and excellent understanding. His deportment was grave, and his countenance austere; yet he was a warm-hearted man, and universally respected for his good sense, his integrity, his pure moral character, and patriotic devotion to the best interests of his country. He possessed the entire confidence of the public councils of the state, and on all fitting occasions this confidence was largely and freely maintained.

For Further Reading

Booth, Mary L. *History of the City of New York*. New York: 1880.

Dexter, F.B. *Yale Biographies and Annuals*, 2nd Series (1745–1763).

Huntington Town Records, vols. 1, 2, 3. Town Hall, Huntington, Long Island, New York.

Mather, F.G. *The Refugees of 1776 from Long Island to Connecticut*. Albany, N.Y.: 1913.

Thompson, Benjamin. *History of Long Island*. New York: 1913.

An Ecological Study for Eatons Point. vol. 1. Wallace, McHarg, Roberts, and Todd. Prepared for Otto Paparazzo Associates, Inc.

Abundant primary source materials can be consulted at the New-York Historical Society, New York City, and in the John Jay collection of the the Columbia University Library, New York City.

Hugh Hughes
(1727–1802)

BERNARD FRIEDMAN

Indiana University
Purdue University at Indianapolis

The life and revolutionary career of Hugh Hughes offers an exemplary case study in the making of an Antifederalist. Hughes's earlier years as an aspiring tradesman, his bankruptcy in the aftermath of the French and Indian War and subsequent affiliation with the radical Liberty Boys in New York, his several strenuous and frustrating tours of duty as a deputy quartermaster general in the Continental Army, and then his latter years as a country schoolmaster seeking financial restitution from a seemingly indifferent national government, all would seem to have contributed to the shaping of a political outlook which can best be described as laissez-faire liberalism. Hughes was ever wary of government as an instrument of a privileged class, or aristocracy, and ever ready to argue that the people were quite capable of managing their separate affairs in a manner conducive to the public interest. Hughes was not a systematic thinker, nor always consistent, but he mirrors in just such respects the naive idealism of that Revolutionary generation.

Early Life

Hugh Hughes was born on April 20, 1727, the youngest of the three sons of Hugh and Martha (Jones) Hughes. According to family tradition, the elder Hughes had run away to America at the age of nine, and had then been joined by his Welsh parents in Pennsylvania, where the family took up a tract of land in the heavily Welsh district of Upper Merion, in what was then Philadelphia County. The errant son in due course inherited the family farm, "Walnut Grove," as it came to be called, but not before pursuing the trade of tanner in Philadelphia. The younger Hugh Hughes was trained to the same craft, presumably by his father, just as his older brother, John, was to begin his rise in life as a baker, indicative in both instances of a family situation of clearly middling means.[1]

Hugh Hughes's arrival in New York is first heralded by his marriage to a Charity Smith of that city in 1748. His name appears in the rolls of the freemen of the city in 1752 as practicing the trade of "Currier," and then shortly afterwards as "one of the Corn Measurers of this City" appointed by the Common Council. A decade later, advertisements in the local press informed the public that "Hugh Hughes . . . has a Tan-Yard, and Currying Shop, in Ferry Street, near Peck's Slip, where the Business is carried on as usual." It would appear that Hughes had risen into the ranks of the artisan entrepreneurs of the city, that element from whom would soon be recruited the vanguard leadership of the revolutionary movement in New York. Hugh Hughes's collapse into bankruptcy in the next several years suggests the general state of the provincial economy in the wake of the French and Indian War and makes more understandable the widespread reaction against the Grenville program among that class of "inferior burghers" in New York whose prospects and expectations seemed most threatened by that legislation. Hughes, in any case, chose to become involved with the Sons of Liberty in New York and engaged actively in their vigorous resistance to the Stamp Act of 1765, even if he was obliged to play his part covertly by virtue of the threat of imprisonment for indebtedness which then hung over him.[2]

It was during this period of virtual house arrest that Hughes embarked upon a second career as a schoolmaster, offering another example of the type of learned tradesman characteristic of the era. Indeed, it was partly in consequence of Hughes's broad-ranging intellectual interests that he was at this time drawn into a dispute with Benjamin Franklin over payment for scientific equipment which the latter had procured for Hughes in England. Hughes claimed that he had not ordered "a 10th part" of the consignment, as the printer, James Parker, informed Franklin, adding as well that the latter was very much displeased with Franklin's alleged capitulation to the Stamp Act. Hughes's irritation with Franklin may well have been magnified by his unhappiness with his brother, John Hughes, who had accepted the post of stamp master for Pennsylvania at the recommendation of Franklin, with whom the latter had been long associated in the politics of that province. Some twenty-odd years later, Hugh Hughes would recall his misgivings about Franklin in a number of the pieces he wrote opposing the ratification of the federal Constitution in New York.[3]

Revolutionary Career

Hughes's financial difficulties kept him in the background of the resistance movement until the outbreak of armed rebellion relieved him of the necessity of remaining publicly incognito. He was employed at that critical junction in some sort of intelligence network (indeed his letters were signed the "Intelligencer") involving Samuel and John Adams in Massachusetts, to whom he passed along a mixture of hard fact and opinion about the state of affairs in New York. It was probably Sam Adams who assisted Hughes in securing an appointment as a deputy quartermaster general for the New York district in 1776, an appointment which carried with it the rank of colonel in the Continental Army. Hughes served two terms with the quartermaster, resigning for the first time in the spring of 1778, when a reorganization of the department under a new head, General Nathanael Greene, suggested to Hughes that his position had been downgraded. It may very well have been the case that Hughes was reacting more to the grinding difficulties of the job than he was to this imagined slight. In the summer of 1780, Hughes was again called upon to resume the post of deputy quartermaster general by still another quartermaster general, Colonel Timothy Pickering, and would appear to have remained with the department "till sometime in 1783." Hughes's wartime letter books (which are available in The New-York Historical Society) document the extraordinary pressures that went with the assignment, pressures which Hughes would seem to have withstood with his ego bruised but his revolutionary idealism relatively intact.[4]

The Quartermaster Department was widely regarded by contemporaries as riddled with corruption, which makes it all the more indicative of the character of Hugh Hughes that he left the service still in financial arrears, and in part because he had allowed himself to stand security for some of the debts incurred by the department in his jurisdiction. He was to expend considerable time and effort in later years seeking repayment from an unable and then unwilling national government. This may have perhaps contributed to his notably negative opinion of politicians who were too removed from their constituents. His political attitudes were shaped even more by a middle class predilection for free trade and a level playing field in the game of life. Barely two years after the conclusion of hostilities, Hughes was sounding a warning that it was "*absolutely requisite* . . . to continually guard against power, for once Bodies of Men, in Authority, get Possession, or become invested with Property or Prerogative, whether it be by Intrigue, Mistake, or Chance, they rarely relinquish their claim, even if found in Iniquity itself."[5]

Hughes was giving expression in this last utterance to more than a general opinion about mankind; he was reacting specifically to the resurrection of genteel political influence in New York City in the previous few months. Hughes had been one of a slate of "warm and hot headed whigs," as Robert R. Livingston described them, who had been elected by the freemen and freeholders of the city to serve in the first peacetime state assembly.[6] As was Hughes, the radical Whigs had been refugees from their port city since the British occupation in the late summer of 1776. In the intervening years, they had quite naturally attached themselves to the cause of the upstate maverick, George Clinton, who had successfully challenged the old ruling families in winning election as governor of New York in 1777. The alliance with the Clintonians carried over into the immediate postwar years as a mutual opposition to an emerging coalition of Whig and Loyalist patricians. But in moving toward the upstate Clintonians on such broadly ideological grounds, the radical Whigs seem to have forgotten the longstanding conflict of interests between the city and the rural hinterlands. In the subsequent election of state assemblymen, the radical slate, which had swept to victory in New York City in the previous year, went down to defeat, and so ended the very brief electoral career of Hugh Hughes.

Hughes offers some further insight into that loss of rapport on the part of the old Liberty Boys with their former constituency of urban artisans and shopkeepers in his response to the struggle that was waged by the Society of Mechanics which had been established in the city to acquire a charter from the assembly in 1785. Hughes had by this time settled down to schoolteaching on a farm near Yonkers, in Westchester County. This farm was rented from one of his old friends from among the Liberty Boys, General John Lamb, whose connections with the Clinton faction had been recently firmly cemented by his appointment as collector of customs for the port of New York. These men, although of common backgrounds, had drifted away from their old associations, as is documented in Hughes's lukewarm support of the Society of Mechanics. The producer class was undoubtedly the salt of the earth, but nonetheless Hughes was, in principle, "not greatly in favour of corporate Bodies" inasmuch as they were the beneficiaries of special privilege by government. It seemed to Hughes that the mechanics might better safeguard their long-term interests by "attend[ing] properly to the education of their children'' who would thus be less susceptible to the wiles of political demagogues ''as well as render them more truly respectable.''[7]

Constitutional Era Politics

Thus was the stage set for Hughes to join forces with John Lamb and a surviving remnant of the old radical leadership of New York City in actively opposing the ratification of the federal Constitution. Both Lamb and Hughes viewed the Constitution as a vehicle for the restoration of a privileged order in America. Writing under the pseudonyms of ''A Countryman from Dutchess County'' and ''Expositor'' in two series of letters carried in the *New-York Journal* in the late months of 1787 and into early 1788, Hughes argued strenuously that the delegates to the Constitutional Convention had in the first instance violated their trust by proposing an entirely new system of government, and that their work posed a threat to the rights and liberties of all Americans. These pieces exhibit a certain shrillness of tone and vindictiveness that may bespeak his own narrowed circumstances, but they are finally the expression of an uncompromising and all too abstract democratic idealism.

Hughes immediately set the tone of the letters by insinuating that the Constitution was the work of an inner group of ''artful and designing members, who have long envied the great Body of the People of the United States, [and] the Liberties they enjoy.'' How else to explain a system of government which vested ''unlimited Powers . . . in a haughty Senate, and a hungry Monarchy [the presidency], both of which may be continued as long as exorbitant Grants of Land, Contracts, Places, Pensions, and every Species of Bribery and Corruption, have an influence.''[8] Hughes was invoking here an image of a distant government organized on the principle of patronage and plunder, much like the portrayal of Britain by the Sons of Liberty before the Revolution.

If Hughes was somewhat carried away in his aspersions to ''insidious'' characters seeking to undermine ''the rights of Mankind,'' he was nonetheless reasoning from an established opinion about the role of government. As he was to remark some years later, the ''Genius'' of the American people was such ''that a very great Majority . . . are as easily governed, if I may use a Phrase that I don't approve, as any People in the World,'' which was to say that the least government was the best.[9] That there was an element of contradiction in these opposing strictures of ungovernable governments and self-governing individuals is simply a measure of the democratic optimism inspired by the emancipation of an American middle class from the restraints of both imperial regulation and a hierarchial social order.

Hughes's democratic convictions come through with particular force in his condemnation of the Framers of the Constitution for their acceptance of slavery. Here was tangible "Proof of their being Enemies to the Rights of Mankind." A dozen years earlier, on the occasion of Lord Dunmore's proclamation offering freedom to slaves who enlisted in the British forces, Hughes had spoken out in favor of offering some "gleam of hope" to those "poor desponding sufferers." "I don't like those half pac'd Sons of Liberty that only want Freedom for themselves," he had remarked to Sam Adams, "if we contend for Liberty, let us show we are worthy of it, by diffusing the blessings of it to the whole human Race, within our Influence. . . ."[10] But if Hughes was thoroughly sincere in his detestation of slavery, he nonetheless used the occasion of the debate over the Constitution to settle an old score with Benjamin Franklin. The latter was singled out, along with John Dickinson, as having betrayed his own earlier stated opposition to slavery. Hughes disposed of Dickinson with a relative economy of means, citing the latter's famous "Letters from a Pennsylvania Farmer" as evidence of his earlier forebodings about slavery, but reserved his harshest comments for Franklin, whom he castigated severely as a thoroughly duplicitous individual. He documented his case against Franklin by citing a letter of 1764 in which the latter betrayed a willingness to accept an Anglican episcopate in the colonies as the price for ending proprietary government in Pennsylvania. Hughes charged also that Franklin had been likewise ready to countenance a standing army in America, if that was what it took to make Pennsylvania over into a royal colony. Hughes's final allegation regarding Franklin's lukewarm adherence to Whig principles was the familiar claim that the latter had been too ready to accept the Stamp Act in 1765. In that connection, Hughes asserted he had personally read a letter *"of the Doctor's own Writing"* wherein Franklin, in his capacity as a deputy postmaster, served notice on the printer of the *New-York Gazette*, John Holt, that it would be in his better interest to curtail publication of letters attacking the Stamp Act.[11] There still obviously remained within Hughes an unresolved legacy of bitter memories.

Having exorcised the devil, Hughes settled down in his later communications to the *Journal* to a more impersonal assessment of the Constitution. His views were almost entirely conditioned by his overriding fear of an abuse of the powers of government rather than by a consideration of the validity of such powers. Accordingly, he pointed to the lack of "a substantial bill of rights," which was of course a favorite theme of the Antifederalists. The legislature, as laid down by the Framers, Hughes argued further, was not based upon "an equitable representation." The terms of legislative office, he held, needed to be reduced in length by half, and succession in office had to be limited to avoid the dangers of an entrenched class of officeholders. In Hughes's opinion, the three branches of the proposed federal government were not sufficiently separated, nor was this government confined to "its proper objects." What he meant by the latter can be surmised by his insistence that the states be left "sovereign and independent with respect to their internal police," and by the restrictions he would have placed upon the central government with respect to a standing army and a federally managed militia force. As might be expected, Hughes regarded with some suspicion the "supreme law of the land" clause in the Constitution which he found unjustifiably ambiguous as written. Hughes thought, however, that some such provision could serve a useful purpose. He suggested in this last respect the imposition of some higher authority outside the national government itself—in his view the people—to determine the constitutionality of the ordinary enactments of the Congress. Hughes returned again to the issue of slavery, insisting in his usual heated rhetoric that a properly moral system of government could not continue "drenching the bowels of Africa in gore, for the sake of enslaving its free-born innocent inhabitants."[12]

Hugh Hughes's Antifederalism was grounded in a deep distrust of central government as lending itself too readily to the machinations of men of wealth and position. The designs of such men could be better countered at the local levels of government where legislators were more directly accountable to the people. Too much government was in any event a hindrance to the economic and social advancement of a people who were better left alone to pursue their own separate interests. In this last regard there was a measure of the mystical in Hughes's reliance upon a special Providence that would reconcile personal advantage with the public good. That Hughes's personal experience did not conform to such expectations is probably beside the point. He was in the grips of an irresistible middle class faith in the possibilities of human betterment.

Later Career

Hughes's late years were spent in a continuing vain effort to secure reimbursement from the newly strengthened national government for his service-related expenditures. He made one last attempt following the installation of a Republican administration in 1801, visiting the new national capital on the Potomac bearing the gift of a privately printed volume of documents vouching for his claims.[13] Hugh Hughes died on March 15, 1802, a few weeks after his return from the District of Columbia. He had lived just long enough to witness a revival of democratic sentiment in the United States, but under the auspices of a slaveowning planter elite.

NOTES:

[1]The family background is provided in Ellwood Roberts, ed., *Biographical Annals of Montgomery County, Pennsylvania* (2 vols., N.Y., 1904), 1:282–286.

[2]See the *New York Gazette*; or *The Weekly Post Boy*, Oct. 7, Dec. 30, 1762, for the above-mentioned advertisement. Hughes's financial difficulties are recounted in a series of letters from James Parker to Benjamin Franklin which are to be found in Leonard Labaree, et. al., ed., *The Papers of Benjamin Franklin* (New Haven, 1959–   ) for the years 1765 and 1766. For Hughes's covert activities as a Son of Liberty see Francis Bernard to Henry Conway, Jan. 19, 1766, "The Fitch Papers," *Connecticut Historical Society Collections* (1920), 384–385.

[3]Hughes's dispute with Franklin is covered in the Parker–Franklin correspondence cited above as also in a letter from John Holt to Franklin, October 2, 1771, *Franklin Papers*, 18:225–227. For John Hughes's problems as a stamp master and beyond, see Edmund S. and Helen Morgan, *The Stamp Act Crisis: Prologue to Revolution* (N.Y., 1963), 301–324.

[4]The "Intelligencer" letters are to be found in the Samuel Adams Papers, New York Public Library (NYPL). Hughes's exchange of letters with General Greene are in *The Papers of General Nathanael Greene* (Richard Showman, ed., Chapel Hill, 1976–   ), 2:307–313, 342–343, 352–353, 373–375. Hughes's wartime letter books consist of nineteen manuscript volumes of varying lengths which are a rich source of information about the operations of the Quartermaster Department during the Revolution.

[5]Hughes's continuing postwar attempts to gain reimbursement from the new government is documented in *The Memorial and Documents in the Case of Colonel Hugh Hughes . . .Respectfully Submitted to Congress by the Memorialist*, Washington City, 1802. Hughes to Charles Tillinghast, March 7, 1785, Lamb Papers, The New-York Historical Society (NYHS).

[6]Robert R. Livingston to John Jay, Jan. 25, 1784, as quoted in Alfred F. Young, *The Democratic Republicans of New York: The Origins, 1763–1797* (Chapel Hill, 1967), 31–32.

[7]Hughes to Tillinghast, March 7, 1785, Lamb Papers, NYHS. It should be noted that there is some confusion about Hughes's whereabouts in the years immediately after the close of the Revolution. The Census of 1790 definitely places him in Westchester County, but Hughes used the pseudonym of a "Countryman from Dutchess County" in some of his Antifederalist pieces of late 1787–early 1788. The "Biographical Gazetteer of New York Federalists and Antifederalists" compiled by Stephen L. Schechter, which appears in Stephen L. Schechter, ed., *The Reluctant Pillar: New York and the Adoption of the Federal Constitution* (Troy, N.Y., 1985), notes that Hughes was resident in Dutchess County in April, 1788, but "planning to move to a farm in Yonkers owned by John Lamb whose children he had been tutoring."

[8]*New York Journal*, Nov. 21, 1787.

[9]Hughes to Tillinghast, Aug. 19, 1794, Lamb Papers, NYHS.

[10]*New York Journal*, Nov. 21, 1787; for the earlier statement, Hughes to Sam Adams, Dec. 22, 1775, Samuel Adams Papers, NYPL.

[11]*New York Journal*, Nov. 23, Dec. 3, 1787.

[12]*New York Journal*, Dec. 15, 1787, Jan. 22, Feb. 14, 1788. See especially the January 22 essay which is the most constructive in the series.

[13]*The Memorial and Documents in the Case of Colonel Hugh Hughes . . .*

John Jay and the Creation of the American Republic

(1745-1829)

RICHARD B. BERNSTEIN
New York State Bicentennial Commission

For twenty-seven years, from 1774 through 1801, John Jay was active in the politics of New York and the United States. During those years, he compiled a record of public service which, for breadth and significance, equals that of any of the well-known "Founding Fathers," such as George Washington, Thomas Jefferson, Alexander Hamilton, and James Madison. Although Jay was not as original a thinker or as eloquent a writer as the more famous leaders of the Revolutionary generation, he, too, was indispensable to the creation of an American nation and national identity and the development of American constitutionalism.[1]

Jay was born in New York City on December 12, 1745. He was descended from French Huguenots who had journeyed to the New World to escape the French religious wars of the seventeenth century. Jay's awareness of his ancestors' persecution at the hands of French Catholics was a source of his distrust for the Catholic Church and a stimulus of his deep religious faith. He attended King's College, was graduated in 1763, and, after four years of clerking for prominent New York attorney Benjamin Kissam, was admitted to the New York bar in 1768. In April 1774, he wed Sarah (Sally) Livingston, the daughter of William Livingston, a leading figure in the politics of New York and New Jersey. Although some of Jay's adversaries derided the marriage as one of political convenience and social climbing, John and Sally remained devoted to each other.

In September 1774, after serving on several local committees opposed to British colonial policy, John Jay was elected as a delegate representing the province of New York at the First Continental Congress in Philadelphia. In keeping with his earlier caution on this issue, Jay aligned himself with the more conservative delegates at the Congress, such as "Dictator" John Rutledge of South Carolina and James Duane of New York, who urged moderation and conciliation in dealing with the British government's colonial policy. At the close of the Congress, Jay signed the Non-Importation Association and prepared the Congress's Address to the People of Great Britain. As Richard B. Morris has noted, these steps "propelled him at once into the front line of Whig propagandists."[2]

The next year, Jay represented New York at the Second Continental Congress, where again he became a principal member of the moderate wing urging compromise of the colonists' disputes with Great Britain. In the summer of 1775, backing the moderate delegates' plea for one last appeal for compromise to King George III over the heads of Parliament, Jay prepared the first draft of what came to be called the "Olive Branch Petition." Jay's colleagues deemed his draft too dutiful, conceding too many points to the mother country; as a result, John Dickinson of Pennsylvania prepared the actual petition—although even Dickinson's version was too conciliatory for leading radicals in Congress such as John Adams of Massachusetts. The Olive Branch Petition failed in its purpose, as George III refused even to receive it. This failure made an American bid for independence all but inevitable.[3]

Jay had returned to New York to accept election as a delegate to New York's provincial congress by the time in 1776 that the Second Continental Congress voted to adopt Virginia delegate Richard Henry Lee's resolution declaring "that these united colonies are, and of right ought to be, free and independent states." Thus, he never got the chance to put his name to the Declaration of Independence. And it is uncertain whether Jay would have signed the Declaration had he been present, as he was the author of the New York provincial congress's resolution depriving the colony's delegates of the authority to vote for independence. Once the Second Continental Congress *had* voted for independence, however, Jay willingly accepted the result. The provincial congress, transforming itself into the "Convention of the Representatives of the State of New York," voted on July 9, 1776, to endorse the Declaration of Independence and align New York with the other rebellious colonies as part of the new United States of America. Jay was a principal architect of this decision. Having sincerely sought conciliation with Britain to the last full measure, Jay recognized his quest's futility and never looked back. He became an uncompromising advocate of punitive measures against New York's Loyalists and chairman of the state's Committee for Detecting and Defeating Conspiracies.[4]

In May 1776, the Second Continental Congress had adopted a resolution suggesting to the people of each colony that they frame new charters of government. John Jay was a leading member of the committee of the revolutionary convention appointed to prepare a new constitution. Working with the committee's other members—including Robert and Abraham Yates, James Duane, Robert R. Livingston, and Gouverneur Morris—Jay was the leading framer of the New York constitution, which the revolutionary convention promulgated on April 20, 1777.

The New York Constitution of 1777 was a pathbreaking charter of government. Although, like many of the other states' revolutionary constitutions, it provided for a relatively weak governor, it was the first to require that the governor be elected directly by the voters of the state. Moreover, the governor was given the power to appoint officials (shared with a council of appointment) and to veto legislation (shared with a council of revision); his veto power was not absolute, however, as the legislature could override it by a two-thirds vote. Jay also included in the new constitution a provision guaranteeing complete religious toleration "without discrimination or preference" and "to all mankind"—although with caveats aimed directly at the state's Catholic population. Last, the New York constitution was the first state constitution to provide for a judiciary, although its exact structure was left to the discretion of the new state's legislature. John Adams, the leading theorist of Revolutionary constitutionalism, declared that the New York constitution was "by far the best Constitution that had yet been adopted."[5]

Jay was chosen the first chief justice of New York under the 1777 constitution, but soon afterward returned to the Continental Congress as a New York delegate. In 1779, he was chosen president of the Congress. The next year, he began the first of several important diplomatic missions for the fledgling nation. Jay sailed to Spain to seek an alliance and military and economic aid for the United States, but languished for months in idleness and frustration. The Spanish were not interested in American independence; they were cool to the possibility of a new and potentially powerful rival for domination of the Americans. Although Spain eventually did declare war on Great Britain, it did so more as a matter of European power politics than of sympathy for the American cause. Jay's mission thus was a failure, through no fault of his own.

Jay's next diplomatic mission was far more successful. He was chosen as a member of the five-man American delegation to negotiate treaties of peace ending the American War of Independence. Two commissioners never took part in these negotiations: Thomas Jefferson of Virginia never managed to join his colleagues in Europe, and Henry Laurens of South Carolina was captured by the British and spent most of 1782 and 1783 as a prisoner in the Tower of London. Thus, Jay, John Adams, and Benjamin Franklin were on their own in dealing with representatives of the great powers of the western world.[6]

The three commissioners were beset with difficulties of all sorts. The Confederation Congress had adopted instructions restricting their freedom to negotiate without prior consultations with the French, and the French were all too willing to sell the Americans out in exchange for concessions from the British. Moreover, Jay had constantly to act as mediator between the irritable and suspicious John Adams and the elderly, convivial, and trustingly Francophilic Benjamin Franklin. Jay won the respect of both of his colleagues, and played a key role in the commissioners' decision to break their instructions and enter into direct, separate negotiations with the British. The critical step was Jay's decision, taken on his own initiative, to send an emissary to Lord Shelburne, the British prime minister. The French, confronted with a *fait accompli*, had no choice but to accept.

The Treaty of Paris of 1783 is a cornerstone of American national identity. Under the terms of this treaty, Great Britain was compelled to recognize the independence of the United States—a point insisted upon by John Jay as a prerequisite to any treaty. In addition, the treaty provided that the British would cede all territory between the Allegheny Mountains (the prewar border of British North America) and the Mississippi River; this cession more than doubled the size of the United States. As a result of long and bitter arguments about the issue of compensation for Loyalists who had had their property confiscated by the revolutionary state governments, the Treaty provided that the United States and the individual states would not hinder the efforts of Loyalists to recover debts owed to them or property seized from them. This clause was a foundation for several later state judicial decisions embodying the doctrine of judicial review.

Jay returned home "covered with honor," as John Adams declared. At the end of 1784, the Confederation Congress chose him as the new secretary for foreign affairs—a post not provided for in the Articles of Confederation. As a condition of accepting this office, Jay demanded that the Confederation Congress relocate to New York City, so that he could be near his wife and family. Congress consented to the move, and Jay held this post for five years.

As secretary for foreign affairs, Jay was in perhaps the best position of anyone in the United States to appreciate the problems facing the new nation and the inadequacies of its form of government. Indeed, due to the recurring difficulty that the Confederation Congress had in convening a quorum, Jay found that he was often *the* government of the United States. He maintained the diplomatic correspondence of the nation with foreign powers and with American diplomats abroad, including John Adams in London and Thomas Jefferson in Paris.

Faced with a British trade war against the United States, with Spanish and French indifference, and with the Confederation's difficulties in asserting its authority, collecting needed funds, and enforcing the Treaty of Paris, Jay began to fear that the Articles of Confederation were too weak and fragile to succeed as an instrument of government. He was a consistent and open advocate of reform—but he was uncertain as to the correct way to proceed to remedy these problems. He knew that the Articles' requirement of unanimous consent of the thirteen states to any proposed amendment doomed any prospect of granting the Confederation the powers it needed to protect American interests. Yet he was wary of any attempt to circumvent the procedures formally established by the Articles.

In the spring and summer of 1786, Jay unwittingly provoked a controversy that crystallized the problems of the Confederation and the defects of the Articles. He entered into formal negotiations with Don Diego de Gardoqui, the Spanish envoy, to secure a commercial treaty with Spain and American rights of navigation and access to the Mississippi River. Spain controlled the port of New Orleans and thus could strangle American trade on the Mississippi; moreover, Spanish authorities frequently demanded of American ships that their captains and crews swear fealty to Spain as a condition of access to New Orleans and the Mississippi.

Gardoqui underestimated Jay, and overestimated the likelihood that his blandishments and gifts could turn the head of Sally Jay and thus work indirect influence on her husband. But Gardoqui's hints of a favorable commercial treaty with the United States in exchange for American renunciation of rights to the Mississippi intrigued the secretary for foreign affairs. He asked the Confederation Congress for permission to make this concession, reasoning that the promised commercial treaty was worth the price and that the pressure of American population growth in the western territories someday would force the Spanish to recognize American rights to the Mississippi. But delegates from the five southern states were outraged. James Monroe of Virginia attacked Jay's honesty and patriotism; even more level-headed southerners, such as James Madison of Virginia, were appalled. Congress voted to approve Jay's recommendation, but the five southern states voted in a bloc against the proposition, thereby conveying the message that they could prevent the adoption of any treaty that Jay might negotiate. The Jay–Gardoqui talks fizzled as a result.[7]

Difficulties at home and abroad continued to mount in late 1786 and early 1787, and Jay kept up his informal campaign of letter-writing to such leading American politicians as Alexander Hamilton and George Washington. On January 7, 1787, Jay penned a one-sentence prescription for a new American government: "Let Congress legislate—let others execute—let others judge." Jay's mastery of the doctrines of separation of powers and checks and balances had been evidenced in the New York Constitution of 1777; now he believed that some such formula was vital to any revision of the government of the United States.

The pressures of his duties to the Confederation and the hostility of the New York legislature to friends of a stronger general government barred Jay from taking part in the Federal Convention of 1787. Still, he kept lines of communication open to many of the leading participants, and at least one idea of his found its way into the Constitution— his recommendation that only a native-born American be eligible for the office of commander-in-chief of the armed forces (a function assigned to the president). In addition, his handiwork in the New York Constitution of 1777 exerted a powerful influence on the structure of government embodied in the United States Constitution. For example, the grant of veto power to the president with the possibility that this veto can be overridden by a two-thirds vote of both houses of Congress comes directly from the New York Constitution of 1777.[8]

When the new Constitution was released to the public in September of 1787, Jay enlisted in the ranks of its supporters. He was generally respected and admired—so much so that Antifederal propagandists put out a false rumor that Jay opposed the new charter of government. Jay worked actively for the Constitution in all the ways open to him. He and Alexander Hamilton planned a series of newspaper essays defending and explaining the Constitution; the two New Yorkers were later joined by James Madison, a Virginia delegate to the Confederation Congress. Writing under the pen name "Publius," they produced a series of eighty-five essays later collected in book form as *The Federalist*. Illness permitted Jay to write only five essays as "Publius" (Nos. 2–5 and 64); these essays focused on the virtues and necessity of Union, which could be protected only by a government at least as strong as that outlined in the proposed Constitution, and on the Senate's role in adopting treaties. In the spring of 1788, he gathered his resources to write a brief pamphlet, *An Address to the People of the State of New-York*, which became the single most popular and influential pro-Constitution publication.[9]

Jay was one of the few Federalist candidates for the New York ratifying convention to win election. During the convention's sessions in June and July of 1788, Jay was the conciliator and coalition builder among the outnumbered Federalist delegates. While Alexander Hamilton and Robert R. Livingston fought the polemical battles on the convention floor with Antifederalists Robert and Abraham Yates, John Lansing, Jr., and Melancton Smith, Jay worked to find grounds of compromise and enable Antifederal delegates to switch sides without losing face. At the climax of the convention, Jay helped to frame the critical compromise that ensured the delegates' 30–27 vote to ratify the new charter. He drafted a circular letter to the other states' legislatures recommending amendments to the Constitution and requesting a second convention to consider amendments. Madison was shaken and appalled by the letter, but Jay correctly suspected that the second-convention movement was stillborn.[10]

During the difficult transition period from the Articles of Confederation to the Constitution, Jay stayed at his post as secretary for foreign affairs, relinquishing it only when Thomas Jefferson returned from France to take up his duties as secretary of state. President George Washington offered Jay his choice of government posts in the new government. Jay declined the office of secretary of state, preferring to become the new nation's first chief justice. The Senate unanimously confirmed Jay and his fellow appointees in the fall of 1789, but the federal court system did not really begin its work until early 1790.

Historians have unfairly neglected the work of the Supreme Court and the lower federal courts under Chief Justice Jay, preferring to celebrate the Court's "golden age" under Chief Justice John Marshall. Of course, in its first year, the Supreme Court had little enough to do, as it was primarily an appellate court and thus had to wait for cases to work their way up the federal judicial pyramid. The justices made their most important contributions while "riding circuit," that is, sitting as judges of the U.S. circuit courts, the principal federal trial courts under the Judiciary Act of 1789. This statute created three circuits—Eastern, Middle, and Southern. Each had its own circuit court which would sit twice a year in each state; the judges of that court would be two justices of the Supreme Court and the federal district judge of that state. These courts were one of the principal points of contact between the people of the United States and their new government. "Court day" would be a time of formal ceremony; the presiding justice would deliver a charge to the newly appointed federal grand jury—and to the people assembled to see the new court in operation—explaining the principles of the Constitution and the federal laws. Thus, as Ralph Lerner has written, these courts served as "republican schoolmasters" to the new nation.[11]

Among the principal decisions of the circuit courts on which Chief Justice Jay served were the 1791 Connecticut case striking down a provision of that state's debtor relief statute which violated the Treaty of Paris, and the 1791 Rhode Island decision striking down that state's tender money laws as violations of the Constitution's clause prohibiting the states to impair the obligations of contract. Chief Justice Jay and his colleagues also asserted the power of judicial review of acts of Congress in considering a new law requiring the circuit courts to rule on the claims of those seeking pensions for service in the Continental Army, subject to review by the secretary of war. Jay found a saving construction of the statute that enabled him to avoid having to strike it down as a violation of separation of powers. In a related case in Pennsylvania, Justices James Wilson and John Blair and U.S. District Judge Richard Peters ruled for the Middle Circuit that the law was unconstitutional on the ground that Jay indicated.[12]

Jay's most famous opinion as chief justice was that in *Chisholm v. Georgia* (1793), in which he held that citizens of one state (or subjects of a foreign country) could sue the government of another state without that state's consent. This decision, which violated the reassurances of the Constitution's supporters in 1787–88, stunned the nation and led to the Eleventh Amendment. Ratified in 1798, this was the first constitutional amendment to overturn a decision of the Supreme Court and the only one to limit the powers of the federal judiciary.[13]

Equally significant was the justices' unanimous decision in the spring of 1793 not to accede to a request by President Washington and Secretary of State Jefferson for an opinion on the constitutionality of the president's Neutrality Proclamation and measures to be taken under it. The Court politely, but firmly, reminded the president that its power extended only to actual cases and controversies; therefore, it could not issue advisory opinions. This precedent still stands.[14]

In 1794, President Washington prevailed upon Chief Justice Jay to act as a special envoy to Great Britain to negotiate a new treaty covering such issues as the debts owed by American citizens to British subjects and Loyalists. Abroad for more than a year, Jay returned home with a treaty that inflamed party sentiment already divided along the lines of friendship to Britain or France. It was said that Jay could have walked the length of the United States by the light of bonfires burning him in effigy. Nevertheless, Jay's Treaty, as historians call it, was ratified. It eased tensions between the United States and Great Britain, but exacerbated factional divisions that led ultimately to the formation of organized political parties.[15]

Jay also discovered on his return that he had been elected governor of New York. The chief justice had grown to dislike the exhausting system of circuit riding and, in 1792, had allowed his name to be put forward as a candidate for governor of his home state. The forces supporting Governor George Clinton stole the election on that occasion. In 1795, without Jay's knowledge, his friends put his name forward again, and he was elected without having done a thing to advance his candidacy. To accept this new post, and to escape the onerous and thankless job of chief justice, Jay resigned from the Court. Six years later, in 1801, President John Adams nominated him for the office of chief justice to succeed Oliver Ellsworth. The Senate swiftly confirmed him. Again, Jay had not sought this honor—this time, however, he courteously turned down the appointment, explaining his dislike of the chief justice's responsibility to ride circuit and his inclination to retire from public life.

In his final months as governor of New York, Jay performed one last public service. The Federalist Party was facing defeat in the presidential election of 1800, and a desperate Alexander Hamilton proposed that Jay call the state's legislature back into special session to rework New York's method of choosing presidential electors. Hamilton's proposal, if adopted, would have given Federalists a chance to win at least five of New York's electoral votes, thereby giving the Federalist ticket a fighting chance. Jay refused to lend his support to the measure, thus making possible the first peaceful transition of power from one political party to another.[16]

In 1801, his second term as governor concluded, Jay retired from public life. His hopes for a happy retirement were shattered by the sudden death of his wife in 1802. He lived quietly, consoling himself with ever deeper immersion in religious matters, until his death in 1829 at the age of eighty-four. Perhaps he drew comfort from the labors of Chief Justice Marshall to establish the authority and prestige of the federal judiciary. Marshall was building on foundations of national unity and federal judicial power that Jay had helped to establish.

NOTES:

[1]See generally Richard B. Morris, *John Jay, the Nation, and the Court* (Boston: Boston University Press, 1967); Richard B. Morris, *Seven Who Shaped Our Destiny: The Founding Fathers as Revolutionaries* (New York: Harper & Row, 1973), 150–188; Richard B. Morris, *Witnesses at the Creation* (New York: Holt, Rinehart & Winston, 1985); Frank Monaghan, *John Jay* (Indianapolis: Bobbs-Merrill, 1935); George Pellew, *John Jay* (Boston: Houghton Mifflin, 1898). Two editions of Jay's papers are available: Henry P. Johnston, ed., *The Correspondence and Public Papers of John Jay*, 4 vols. (New York: Putnam, 1893), and Richard B. Morris and Ene Sirvet, eds., *John Jay: Unpublished Papers*, 2 vols. of 4 projected (New York: Harper & Row, 1976-).

[2]Morris, *Seven Who Shaped Our Destiny*, 173.

[3]On the Olive Branch Petition, see Richard B. Bernstein with Kym S. Rice, *Are We to Be a Nation?* (Cambridge, Mass.: Harvard University Press, 1987), 18–20; Morris, ed., *John Jay: Unpublished Papers*, 1: 147–154.

[4]Morris, *Seven Who Shaped Our Destiny*, 183–185.

[5]John Adams, quoted in Bernstein with Rice, *Are We to Be a Nation?*, 56. On the New York constitution and Jay's role in its creation, see Morris and Sirvet, eds., *John Jay: Unpublished Papers*, 1: 389–418; Willi Paul Adams, *The First American Constitutions* (Chapel Hill, N.C.: University of North Carolina Press, 1980), 83–86; William A. Polf, *1777: The Political Revolution and New York's First Constitution* (Albany: New York State Bicentennial Committee, 1977); Bernard Mason, *The Road to Independence: The Revolutionary Movement in New York* (Lexington: University of Kentucky Press, 1966), chap. 7.

[6]The best account is Richard B. Morris, *The Peacemakers: The Great Powers and American Independence* (New York: Harper & Row, 1965), supplemented by Morris and Sirvet, eds., *John Jay: Unpublished Papers,* II, *passim*. See also Richard B. Morris, *The American Revolution Reconsidered* (New York: Harper & Row, 1967), chap. 3.

[7]On the Jay–Gardoqui talks, see Bernstein with Rice, *Are We to Be a Nation?*, 84–85 & 297 n. 7.

[8]See Charles Warren, *Congress, the Constitution, and the Supreme Court*, rev. ed. (Boston: Little, Brown, 1935), 1–40, esp. 30–34.

[9]See generally Richard B. Morris, "John Jay and the Adoption of the Federal Constitution in New York: A New Reading of Persons and Events," *New York History* 63 (1982): 132–164; Morris, *Witnesses at the Creation*. The context of Jay's activities is ably presented in Linda Grant DePauw, *The Eleventh Pillar: New York State and the Constitution* (Ithaca, N.Y.: Cornell University Press, 1966), and Stephen L. Schechter, ed., *The Reluctant Pillar* (Troy, N.Y.: Russell Sage College, 1985). The *Address* is available in Johnston, ed., *Correspondence and Public Papers*, 3: 294–319, and in Paul L. Ford, ed., *Pamphlets on the Constitution of the United States* (Brooklyn, N.Y.: privately printed, 1888), 67–86; it has also been reprinted in Richard B. Bernstein, ed., *Defending the Constitution* (Mount Vernon, N.Y.: A. Colish, 1987).

[10]Morris, "John Jay and the Adoption of the Federal Constitution in New York," *passim*.

[11]See Ralph Lerner, *The Thinking Revolutionary* (Ithaca, N.Y.: Cornell University Press, 1987), 91–136.

[12]These cases will be discussed in the forthcoming vol. 4 of Morris and Sirvet, eds., *John Jay: Unpublished Papers*. See generally Morris, *John Jay, the Nation, and the Court*.

[13]See generally Clyde Jacobs, *The Eleventh Amendment and Sovereign Immunity* (Westport, Conn.: Greenwood Press, 1973); Morris, *John Jay, the Nation, and the Court*, 49–70.

[14]Morris, *John Jay, the Nation, and the Court*, 45–46.

[15]See generally Samuel Flagg Bemis, *The Jay Treaty: A Study in Commerce and Diplomacy*, rev. ed (New Haven: Yale University Press, 1955); Jerald A. Combs, *The Jay Treaty* (Berkeley: University of California Press, 1970); Morris, *John Jay, the Nation, and the Court*, 92–96.

[16]Morris, *John Jay, the Nation, and the Court*, 100–101.

Rufus King
(1755–1827)

GRAHAM R. HODGES
Colgate University

Rufus King was born on March 24, 1755, in Scarboro, Maine, then part of Massachusetts. He was the eldest son of Captain Richard King, a successful merchant, and his first wife, Isabella Bragdon King. Young Rufus was educated at Dummer Academy in South Byfield, Massachusetts. He later entered Harvard, graduating in the class of 1777. Although his father was a strong Loyalist, King became a Patriot. After the occupation of Boston in 1775, he wrote, "America spurns the production of the petty tyrant and treating it with deserved contempt, stands firm upon the pillars of Liberty, immovable as Heaven, and determined as fate. One kindred spirit catches from man to man."[1] At Harvard, King showed a deep interest in law, history, and oratory, while following the events unfolding at Lexington and Concord. After graduation, he studied law at Newport under Theophilus Parsons, and gained brief military experience as aide to General Glover in the failed expedition to Rhode Island. He became a member of the bar in 1780 and opened his practice in Newburyport.

In 1784, he was elected by the Massachusetts legislature as a delegate to the Continental Congress in Trenton, New Jersey. He prepared a resolution on March 16, 1785, proposing that there should be neither "slavery nor involuntary servitude" in the Northwest Territory, a phrase later incorporated into the Ordinance of 1787. A confirmed nationalist, he urged all states to contribute to federal expenses and attempted to persuade Pennsylvania to provide Congress with a five percent impost.

Constitutional Era Activities

King originally was opposed to any major changes in the Articles of Confederation. He described the Annapolis Convention of 1786 as a failure, perhaps not realizing that Alexander Hamilton had deliberately framed its report in order to secure the calling of a wider convention in Philadelphia. Without much optimism, King wrote James Bowdoin on September 17, 1786, of the plans for a general revision of the Articles: "Foreign nations had been notified of this convention . . . the Friends to a good federal government through these states . . . had to look to it with anxiety and hope; the History of it will not be more agreeable to the former, than it must be seriously painful to the latter."[2] Soon rumblings of Shays's Rebellion prompted a change of heart, and King moved from support of internal revision of the Articles to favoring a stronger central government. He worried, "Are our Countrymen incapable of a free government—or does all this originate from the defect of the federal Constitution?"[3] As Shays's Rebellion closed down the courts in Springfield, Massachusetts, King wrote, "It will be humiliating indeed if the Blood and Treasure expended so gloriously by our country should establish our Disgrace and furnish just grounds of exultation to the Advocates of Tyranny and Despotism."[4] He urged Massachusetts Governor Bowdoin to declare a state of insurgency against Shays and his men, supporting further federal enlistments as a means to stem future rebellions. As Robert Ernst has argued, King feared anarchy, and Shays's Rebellion jolted his mind onto a more nationalistic path.[5]

King was one of five members of the Massachusetts delegation to the Philadelphia Convention, the only New Englander to be present on opening day, May 25, 1787. Already noted for his oratory, King deeply impressed William Pierce of Georgia, to whom history owes much for his capsule portraits of delegates. Pierce described King as "ranked among the Luminaries of the present Age."[6] At Philadelphia, King acted as conciliator, as watchdog for protocol, and as a firmer Federalist than all save Hamilton. Pragmatic, King noted impracticalities in motions regarding taxation, on presentation of proposals and ballots, and executive power over the judiciary. He stood strongly on the side of judicial review. After listening to William Paterson's brilliant presentation of the New Jersey Plan, King remarked succinctly that the Convention should make up its mind whether it favored confederacy or a new national government. On June 19, King, after the Convention was belabored by the nationalist oratory of Hamilton, was able to move successfully that the New Jersey Plan be declared inadmissible, and that the Virginia Plan, favoring the larger states, be reported by the Committee of the Whole.

Unlike Hamilton, who admitted a desire to dissolve state governments, King was capable of merging state powers with the national. He argued the states lacked peculiar powers of the national, describing the states as "they were dumb, for they could not speak to any foreign Sovereign whatever. They were deaf, for they could not hear any propositions from such Sovereign. They had not even the organs or faculties of defence or offense, for they could not of themselves raise troops, or equip vessels, for war. . . . A Union of the states is a union of the men composing them, from which a national character results to the whole."[7] Countering the opposition of Luther Martin of Maryland, King defended the urge to create a new government. Unless the members seized the time, "Farewell to the Freedom of our Government—our military Glory will be tarnished, and our boasts of Freedom will be the scorn of the Enemies of Liberty."[8]

Though ostensibly in favor of retaining state powers, King argued vehemently for representation solely on the basis of population, rather than Benjamin Franklin's wise plans to offer equality in the Senate and proportional representation in the House. In response to Franklin, King was "filled with astonishment that if we were convinced that every man in America was secured in all his rights, we should be ready to sacrifice this substantial good to the phantom of State sovereignty."[9] King's position polarized the Convention while framing the spectrum of debate over representation.

King was most forceful over the issue of slavery and the slave trade. He couched his arguments in moral attacks upon the slave trade itself. The importation of slaves was a "most grating circumstance," which caused northern states to necessarily defend the south, increasing its dangers without compensation. Moreover, exported slaves should be taxed, "to enable the General Government to defend their masters." King hoped for a time limit on the slave trade, for "He could never agree to let them be imported without limitation and then be represented in the National Legislature. . . . Either slaves should not be represented, or exports should be taxable."[10] Later, King refuted southern arguments for placating slaveholders, by announcing that omission of a tax on slaves would create an "inequality that could not fail to strike the commercial sagacity of the Northern and middle states."[11] King thus enunciated a theory which would resound through the succeeding decades and form important impulses behind the Missouri Compromise of 1820; if the South expected favorable federal treatment, it must offer benefits, not impose deference, upon the North and West.

King's positions were often taken seriously in Philadelphia. Though not as extreme generally as Hamilton, King occasionally outdid him, calling, for example, for a twenty-year term for presidents. His more prudent views were incorporated in the final document, which he proudly signed. King upheld the principles of the separation of powers, a strong and independent executive, and a strong general government. He helped restrict the importation of slaves and influenced the Convention to secure the sanctity of contracts from state action. His reputation grew with his steady championship of nationalism. Though he had an important job to do insuring ratification of the new Constitution in Massachusetts, King seemed ready for the national stage.

King's national career almost lost him his local prominence in Massachusetts. Only a quick return to Newburyport earned him a seat at the state ratification convention. Devoted to his expectant wife in New York, King considered delaying his appearance even though allies pleaded, "You have no idea how much depends upon your presence!"[12]

As did New York, Pennsylvania, Virginia, and the Carolinas, Massachusetts suffered from a division between a Federalist mercantile elite centered in coastal cities, trading towns, and prosperous farmers, and a backwoods-and-farmer Antifederalism which feared increased powers of creditors, disliked lawyers and moneyed men, and acted in a long tradition of violence and mobbing. Massachusetts needed to placate such populism, still aroused over the stern suppression of Shays's Rebellion.

King eloquently presented Federalist positions over representation and terms of office, and explained the thorny issues of the three-fifths' clause, which he described as the "language of all America." Despite his efforts, Antifederalists seemed in charge, especially by using the tactic of discussing the Constitution clause by clause. King waited cautiously, answering pointed attacks with "a superior Lustre. His speeches are clear, cool, nervous [animated], pointed and conclusive."[13]

King was at the center of Federalist councils in Boston, corresponding with James Madison in Virginia. He was fairly pessimistic about the Constitution's chances, deploring the Antifederalist method of vetoing each clause: "If the opposition was grounded on any precise points, I am persuaded that it might be weakened, if not overcome. . . . The opponents affirm to each other that they have an unalterable majority on their side."[14] King's gloominess continued as Federalists considered tacking amendments on the proposed Constitution to satisfy the opposition.

Finally, King and his allies hit upon what turned out to be a popular scheme. They had Governor John Hancock present a motion ratifying the new Constitution with the recommendation of several amendments, several of which were later incorporated into the Bill of Rights. When that proposal passed by the narrow vote of 187–168, King jubilantly wrote Madison that popular support in Massachusetts was insured, without which the new Constitution would have stalled badly. King remained in Newburyport until final ratification on February 6, 1788.

Post–Constitutional Activities

While King served as a Massachusetts delegate, his growing nationalism and affiliation with Hamilton brought him closer to New York City. King became a New Yorker soon after the new federal government organized. On March 30, 1786, he had married Mary Alsop, the daughter of a wealthy New York merchant. King then moved to New York and abandoned the practice of law. Within a month, he was elected to the New York Assembly, and then was chosen by the state legislature (with the quiet but firm support of Governor George Clinton) to be the first United States Senator from New York. When, as required by the Constitution, the Senators drew lots to begin the system of staggered elections and terms, he gained a six-year term while the other senator from New York, General Philip Schuyler, received a two-year term. In the Senate, he became a key and articulate proponent of Secretary of the Treasury Alexander Hamilton's fiscal program, specializing in discussions of maritime law and commercial matters. He was elected in 1791 as a director of the Bank of the United States and to a second senatorial term in 1795. Washington nominated King to be minister plenipotentiary to Great Britain in 1796, where he served with distinction until 1803. Nominated a Federalist vice-presidential candidate in 1804, he and presidential nominee C. C. Pinckney were crushed by Jefferson and Clinton; the election of 1808 saw a repeat of this debacle at the hands of Madison and Clinton, with Pinckney and King winning only the New England states.

In 1813, King, an opponent of the War of 1812, returned to the Senate. After the burning of Washington, D.C. by British forces, however, he strongly supported the war effort. His revived popularity prompted Federalists to nominate him for president in 1816, but he was trounced by James Monroe, again winning only New England. King was the last presidential candidate of the disintegrating Federalist Party. In his last years, he served in the House of Representatives, and was especially regarded for his opposition of slavery into Missouri. He died in 1827, a victim of gout and exhaustion.

NOTES:

[1]Rufus King to Robert Soutgate, undated, circa June, 1775, as quoted in Robert Ernst, *Rufus King, American Federalist* (Chapel Hill: University of North Carolina Press, 1968), 17. Ernst's work remains the definitive biography of King. See also Charles R. King, ed. *The Life and Correspondence of Rufus King*, 6 Vols, (New York, 1894–1900), 1:8–10.

[2]King to James Bowdoin, September 17, 1786 as quoted in Ernst, *Rufus King*, 81.

[3]King to Elbridge Gerry, August 5, 1786, King Papers, The New-York Historical Society (NYHS).

[4]King to Theodore Sedgwick, September 29, 1786, Massachusetts Historical Society, as quoted in Ernst, *Rufus King*, 83.

[5]Ernst, *Rufus King*, 90.

[6]William Pierce, "Characters in the Convention of the States Held at Philadelphia, May 1787," in Max Farrand, ed. *Records of the Federal Convention of 1787*, 4 vols. (rev. ed., New Haven: Yale University Press, 1937), 3:87.

[7]Farrand, ed., *Records of the Federal Convention*, 1:323–24.

[8]*Ibid*, 1:332.

[9]*Ibid*, 1:490.

[10]*Ibid*, 1:208.

[11]*Ibid*, 2:373.

[12]Nathaniel Gorham to Rufus King, December 12, 1787, King Papers, NYHS.

[13]Quoted in Ernst, *Rufus King*, 127.

[14]Quoted in *ibid*, 127.

John Lamb
(1735–1800)

GRAHAM R. HODGES
Colgate University

John Lamb was born in New York City on January 1, 1735, the son of Anthony Lamb, a noted optician and instrument maker, and his Dutch wife. Anthony Lamb originally came to America as a transported felon, convicted in association with the notorious burglar, Jack Shepard. Although Shepard was hanged, Anthony Lamb's youth and inexperience earned him a reduced sentence of exile. He served his time in Virginia before moving to New York. There, he became involved in local politics as overseer of the fire engines.

Although not formally educated, John Lamb learned several languages, including Dutch, French, and German, and entered his father's trade. He later encountered the hurly-burly of local popular politics through his father's post with the fire department. By the age of twenty-five, John Lamb had established himself as a liquor merchant, an occupation he followed throughout the American Revolution. On November 13, 1755, he married Catherine Jardine, a Huguenot immigrant, with whom he had three children. Lamb's avocation was military history, and his linguistic abilities allowed him to study important works of military science. He became noted as a forceful speaker and an assertive political writer much concerned about the protection of American liberties from the Crown.

Revolutionary Era Activities

As the turmoil over the revenue acts of the 1760s unfolded, Lamb quickly became a leader of popular demonstrations. Along with fellow merchants Isaac Sears, Joseph Allicotte, and Alexander MacDougall,

Lamb formed the Sons of Liberty, composed of disaffected merchants, mariners, rowdy apprentices, and slaves. Lamb wrote a number of pamphlets, broadsides, and petitions opposing the Stamp Act of 1765, the focal point of local grievances. He established committees of correspondence to communicate with Sons of Liberty in other cities and visited Philadelphia and Baltimore to encourage resistance against the revenue acts and the agents of the British government. Particularly effective in street organizing, Lamb led the riots of November 1765 in New York which destroyed the home of Lieutenant Governor Cadwallader Colden. During the next few years, Lamb was important in republican rituals and political organizing among the aroused artisan electorate. In 1769 he publicly denounced the colonial assembly for subservience to the British governor. The same year, Sears, Lamb, and the other Liberty Boys were highly visible in their support of the imprisoned Alexander MacDougall.

In 1775, upon learning of the battles of Lexington and Concord, Lamb and Sears led the Liberty Boys in seizing the customs house and the military storehouse in New York City. Lamb and Sears immediately organized a mob to seize guns and ammunition. As the city toppled into chaos, Sears and Lamb were observed "calling out the people every Day to the Liberty Pole," the symbol of anti-British, revolutionary struggle.[1]

Commissioned a captain in General Montgomery's army in 1775, Lamb rose in the ranks despite his superior's distrust. Montgomery noted that Lamb had a "restless genius" which "has been used to haranguing his fellow-citizens in New York and cannot restrain his talent here,"[2] suggesting the presence of popular radicalism in the Continental army. Wounded and captured in Canada, Lamb was paroled in 1776. Freed during an exchange of prisoners, he rapidly rose to colonel, then to brigadier general by the close of the war. He served with General George Washington, forming an alliance which would last through periods of political opposition.

Elected to the New York legislature in 1784 as a popular Whig, he soon earned a major patronage plum as collector of customs for the port of New York. Clearly aligned with Governor George Clinton, Lamb's activities required mixing with future Federalists as well as Clintonians. Cooperating with the emerging Federalist coalition led by Alexander Hamilton, Lamb took part in the effort to create the Bank of New York in 1784, and invested in land speculation in northern New York with future Federalists. In other ways he supported Clintonian programs. Although personally opposed to slavery, he did not push abolitionist efforts in the mid-1780s because of the opposition of upstate Clintonian slaveowners. Along with Marinus Willet and Isaac Sears, he demanded that James Rivington, the Tory publisher of the *Royal Gazette*, cease business in 1784. Lamb and other former Liberty Boys led general efforts to harass Tories left in New York and purchased a sizable amount of confiscated Loyalist land in the city and upstate.

Constitutional Era Activities

Lamb's efforts to combat the ratification of the proposed Constitution on behalf of the Clintonians were greatly hampered by the general support of the new government in New York City. Even with his powerful post as collector of customs for the port of New York, Lamb had few allies and was generally shunned by better New York society. For example, his name does not appear on Mrs. John Jay's extensive dinner invitation lists of New York City society in 1787 and 1788. The weakness of Antifederalism in New York caused Lamb to be soundly defeated by Jay as a delegate to the Poughkeepsie convention to consider ratification of the Constitution. Consolation from delegate John Lansing, Jr., brought little succor. Lansing wrote Lamb, "Dispairing of receiving any aid from New York we have made explicit arrangements here which we have every reason to suppose will answer our purpose."[3] Undeterred, Lamb helped Antifederalist activity in several ways. He and his allies formed the New York City Antifederal Committee, which, among other things, collected and republished many of the most influential Antifederal publications, such as Samuel Bryan's "Centinel" essays. The Committee also reprinted and distributed 1,700 copies of Mercy Otis Warren's "Observations on the New Constitution . . . by a Columbian Patriot." Lamb also renewed his Liberty Boy correspondences with opponents of general governments in other states, sending letters to friends in North Carolina, New Hampshire, Virginia, South Carolina, and Maryland. A letter to Nathaniel Peabody of New Hampshire is typical:

> While we see in common with our Brethren of the other states, the Necessity of making alterations in our present existing federal Government: We cannot but apprehend that the one proposed in its room, contains in it principles dangerous to public Liberty and Safety. . . . We are anxious to form a Union with our Friends in other States, and to manifest to the Continent, and to the World, that our Opposition to this Constitution does not arise from an

impatience under the restraint of good government, from local or state attachments, from interested motives or party Spirit—But from the purer sentiments of the love of Liberty, an Attachment to republican Principles, and an adherence to those Ideas which prevailed at the commencement of the late Revolution.[4]

Such letters often arrived far too late to influence events in other states. Though several states had already ratified the new Constitution before hearing from Lamb, that fact did not arrest his hopes. Even after New York's ratification of the Constitution, Lamb, Marinus Willet, and Melancton Smith, following an Antifederalist strategy, attempted to diminish its importance, and formed an association to demand a second federal convention to revise the newly adopted government. Though ineffective at first, this coalition formed the nucleus of the Clintonian, later Democratic-Republican Party in New York City. In the 1790s, Lamb's street-level techniques would earn important political bonuses for the Republicans.

Washington, whom Lamb described as the sole trustworthy Federalist, attempted to ease dissension in New York by preserving Lamb's incumbency as collector of the port, a post more lucrative each year. Lamb earned more than $8,000 in 1792 alone. Washington's move showed nonpartisanship, rewarded a well-known Patriot, and undermined Antifederalist activity in the city. Less favorable was Lamb's treatment at the hands of a Federalist mob shortly after the ratification parade in early July 1788. The mob marched on Lamb's home after sacking Thomas Greenleaf's printing shop. Lamb was well prepared for the mob, having already secured his house, barricading the front hall and stairway and extinguishing the lights. Lamb and three relatives waited with rifles. After the mob realized how well the house was defended, they left the home unmolested. Lamb's critics doubtless relished the sight of the old Liberty Boy under attack.

Later Life

In the tumultuous 1790s, Lamb, though slowed by gout, played an important role in the emergence of the Republican Party. He was active in support of the French revolutionary emissaries, especially "Citizen" Genet, and regularly received French naval officers, to the horror of Federalists. Lamb also maintained his close contact with George Clinton and lent his patronage to support the governor's reelections.

In 1797 Lamb's career was rocked by the announcement that an employee had embezzled a substantial portion of the customs receipts. As collector, Lamb was responsible for the sums, and most of his property was sold at auction to satisfy the losses. He died in poverty on May 31, 1800.

NOTES:

[1] R.R. Livingston to his wife, May 3, 1775, Livingston Papers, New York Public Library, as quoted in Paul Gilje, *The Road to Mobocracy: Popular Disorder in New York City, 1763-1834* (Chapel Hill, 1988), 60-61.

[2] Richard Montgomery to General Phillip Schuyler, November 24, 1775, *Papers of the Continental Congress, 1774-1789*, National Archives Microfilm, M 247, Reel 179, Item 169, 445.

[3] John Lansing, Jr. to John Lamb, March 23, 1788, John Lamb Papers, The New-York Historical Society (NYHS).

[4] John Lamb to Nathaniel Peabody, May 18, 1788, John Lamb Papers, NYHS, as quoted in Linda Grant DePauw, *The Eleventh Pillar: New York State and the Federal Constitution* (Ithaca, 1966), 205.

John Lansing, Jr.
(1754–1829)

GRAHAM R. HODGES
Colgate University

Born into one of Albany's most prominent families, John Lansing, Jr., participated in the most significant events that occurred in eighteenth-century New York. He served in the Revolution under General Philip Schuyler, in the Continental Congress, in the New York State Assembly, and, with Robert Yates and Alexander Hamilton, represented New York at the Constitutional Convention in 1787. In later life, he became state chancellor and a regent of the University of the State of New York.

John Lansing was born in Albany, New York, on January 30, 1754, the son of Gerrit Jacob and Jannetje Waters Lansing. He studied law with Robert Yates in Albany and James Duane in New York City and was admitted to practice in Albany in 1775. During the first years of the Revolution, he served as General Philip Schuyler's military secretary, a post he filled with his characteristic thoroughness and hard work, earning a distinguished reputation.

Although he humorously wrote Richard Varick in 1780 that "the air becomes infected when a number of politicians assemble,"[1] Lansing prepared for a career in politics. Though Schuyler favored the young lawyer, Lansing sided with the dominant party of Governor George Clinton. Clinton oversaw Lansing's initial successes as a member of the New York Assembly from 1780 until 1784 and again in 1786 and 1788, serving as speaker his last two years. As a Clintonian assemblyman, Lansing spearheaded the movement to alleviate debtor distress. At the close of the 1787 session, he read a list of prisoners confined by their creditors, ten of whom had debts totaling *L* 24. All of the members then contributed a day's pay, a gesture that released the prisoners.

Lansing was a member of Congress in 1784 and 1785. In 1786, he served with Robert Yates as a commissioner to settle a territorial dispute with Massachusetts. During this period he grew prosperous, obtaining 40,000 acres of confiscated Tory lands and eventually accumulating more than $7,000 in public securities. Nonetheless, he depended upon his law practice and public emoluments to support a growing family.

He married Cornelia Ray of New York City in 1781; the couple had ten children, five of whom survived infancy. In 1786, Clinton appointed him mayor of Albany, a post replete with sizable patronage rewards. Later, Lansing would refuse high public office in order to pursue a prosperous law career in Albany. By the mid-1780s, Lansing enjoyed a solid legal reputation. Alexander Hamilton described him in 1782 as "a good fellow and a good practitioner of law, but his friends mistook his talents when they made him a statesman. He thinks twopence upon plate a monstrous tax."[2] Soon, Hamilton would find him a formidable foe.

The Constitutional Convention

Following Governor Clinton's wishes, the state assembly appointed Lansing, along with his ally, Robert Yates, and the nationalist New York City attorney Hamilton to attend the Philadelphia meeting in May, 1787, for "the express purpose of revising the Articles of Confederation and reporting to Congress and to the several Legislatures alternatives and Provisions therein, as shall, when agreed to in Congress and confirmed by the several states, render the Federal Constitution adequate to the exigencies of government."[3] If Hamilton regarded the latter clause as a wide-open opportunity to discard the Articles of Confederation and replace them with a more centralized government, Lansing and Yates felt bound by the limitations of the assembly's orders. The New York delegation soon split over these interpretations.

Lansing first attended the Constitutional Convention on June 2. William Pierce of Georgia, who prepared thumbnail sketches of each delegate as they arrived, characterized Lansing as "a practicing Attorney at Albany, and Mayor of that Corporation. he has a hisitation in his speech, that will prevent his becoming an orator of any eminence;—his legal knowledge I am told is not extensive nor his education a good one. He is however a man of good sense, plain in his manners and sincere in his friendship. He is about 32 years of age."[4] James Madison regarded Yates and Lansing as representatives sent by Governor George Clinton to curb Hamilton's nationalist tendencies, describing the pair as a "clog on their colleague."[5]

When the Convention opened on May 25, 1787, it quickly became apparent to Yates (who briefed Lansing on his arrival) that much more was at work than revision. As Governor Edmund Randolph presented the Virginia Plan, the delegates were assured at first that only an enlargement of the Confederation's authority was necessary to insure "common defense, security of liberty and general welfare."[6] What followed startled the upstate members of the New York delegation; the fourteen resolutions proposed would demolish the Articles of Confederation and replace them with a strong centralized government. A bicameral legislature, only half of which was to be selected by the people, a powerful national executive, and a judiciary with far-reaching powers were the principal elements of the new plan. Though the Virginia Plan clearly suggested an entirely new government, a vote to consider it passed overwhelmingly on May 30. Connecticut demurred, while New York divided. This was the first of many occasions in which Hamilton lost to his fellow delegate, a circumstance which would be exacerbated by Lansing's arrival and which would lead to controversial withdrawals from the Convention by both New York factions. Nonetheless, the delegates' decision to go forth meant a commitment to a national government in some form, replacing the Articles of Confederation.

As Yates and Lansing watched, the Virginia Plan became the basis of the Convention's work in the succeeding weeks. The plan would award many powers to a strong national government and provide the south with representation based on its total population, including slaves. As Madison, Hamilton, and other nationalists attempted to rush the proceedings, Lansing tried to delay votes in order to let alternative measures develop. When William Paterson of New Jersey proposed a federal system that would preserve state power, Lansing was enthusiastically supportive. Some historians regard him as one of the authors of the resulting "small states" plan.

On June 16, 1787, Lansing spoke before the Convention in support of Paterson's New Jersey Plan. He argued that a federal plan, flowing from the respective state governments, was preferable to the consolidated plan, which would "ultimately destroy or annihilate the state governments." Furthermore, he voiced his doubts that New York would even have sent a delegation to consider the second. It was vain, he believed, to create a government that the people would oppose. The states would never "sacrifice their essential rights to a national government." Contemporary opinion held that granting additional power to Congress was acceptable; to exceed that "will be fruitless." While the Articles of Confederation spoke of a union, it never meant a "consolidation," a term that encapsulated Antifederalist anxiety over the Virginia Plan.

Lansing's words were carefully considered and transcribed by Yates, Hamilton, Madison, and Rufus King.[7] It now became clear to Lansing, Hamilton, and the remainder of the Convention that New York's delegation was hopelessly split, a situation that became more pronounced with each vote. Hamilton, embarrassed by his inability to control the delegation, found it expedient to leave Philadelphia temporarily. On June 20, Lansing informed the Convention that he was not authorized to accede to a system that would annihilate the states' governments and that the Virginia Plan "was declarative of such extinction,"[8] words that anticipated his next crucial step.

Chronology of John Lansing's Amendment Strategy at the Ratifying Convention

July 7, 1788

Lansing reads a bill of rights "to be prefixed to the Constitution."

July 10, 1788

Lansing submits an Antifederalist compromise that specifies three kinds of amendments to the proposed Constitution: (1) explanatory, including a bill of rights; (2) conditional, providing for limitations on the military, fiscal, and political powers of the national government; and (3) recommendatory, to be considered by the first federal Congress under the Constitution.

July 19–23

The convention considers Lansing's conditional ratification plan. On July 23, he calls for New York to ratify the Constitution "upon condition" that amendments be accepted. Later, the phrase, "upon condition," is replaced by Samuel Jones's key substitution, "in full confidence."

July 24

Lansing's next ratification proposal includes the right of New York to secede from the Union if certain amendments are not adopted within a number of years. It is rejected by a vote of 31–28 on July 25.

July 25

With Lansing's urging, a circular letter to the other states is prepared, stressing the necessity for a general convention to consider certain amendments.

July 26

The New York convention votes to ratify unconditionally the proposed Constitution by a margin of three votes, and the circular letter is approved unanimously.

Lansing recommends a list of twenty-five amendments, some of which are subsequently adopted in 1791. The first American constitutional provision of the phrase, "due process of law," is found in Lansing's list and is later expressed in Amendment V of the Bill of Rights.

On July 10, 1787, Yates and Lansing quit the Convention, convinced that their presence was inappropriate. In a letter of explanation to Governor Clinton, they outlined what would become the Antifederalist position on the new Constitution. They argued that they were appointed to revise the Articles of Confederation, not abandon it for a new document. They disapproved of the "consolidation" of the United States into one national state, for it would subvert the constitution of New York and destroy state sovereignty. Such a national union was impractical—too large to control, defend, or enforce its own laws—its government too expensive.[9] On that note, the Clintonians departed.

The Ratification Debate in New York State

New York was not scheduled to vote for its ratification convention delegates until the spring of 1788. However, as soon as the proposed Constitution made its appearance, a war of words began in the state's newspapers. Anonymous essays were written by Hamilton, John Jay, and James Madison and later published in book form as *The Federalist*. Hamilton's political strategy called for delaying New York's considerations until events in other states forced the Clintonians' hand.

Though many New Yorkers were discomfited by Lansing's failure to remain at the Philadelphia Convention, Governor George Clinton selected him to organize the opposition to the Constitution. Lansing initially ran a low-key campaign. On April 26, 1788, Lansing and several other Albany Antifederalists, including Robert Yates, publicly announced their reasons for opposition. In a statement issued in the *New York Journal*, they reiterated the argument that the Constitution proposed a "consolidated," not a federal government. The new plan, they warned, granted extensive control over the lives, liberties and properties of every citizen. Tax monies, they feared, would be diverted to the treasury of the United States. The new government was empowered to organize a standing army, "the bane of a republican government."[10] It lacked a bill of rights, and the executive would hold powers equal, if not superior to, a European monarch. Citing its many defects, the signers made clear that passage of the new Constitution would be tantamount to revocation of the Revolution. The Articles of Confederation needed revision, they admitted, but reform was preferable to adoption of a defective Constitution.

On February 1, 1788, the New York legislature agreed to consider the new Constitution. The ratifying convention held its first meeting on June 17. Chancellor Robert R. Livingston opened the proceedings with extensive remarks in support of the Constitution. Livingston also demanded point-by-point consideration of the document, a strategy that worked to the Federalists' advantage. The next day, Lansing began the Antifederalist defense of the Articles of Confederation. Shifting his position slightly, Lansing countered Federalist criticism of the Articles' inability to provide for defense and domestic tranquility by arguing that reform and expanded congressional power short of that conferred by the Constitution would remedy these faults. It was wrong, he argued, to abandon the present system of government to the possibility of greater tyranny. He closed by denying that Antifederalist strategy was determined by self-interest.

Over the next few weeks, Hamilton and Lansing offered opposing arguments, Lansing joining Melancton Smith as principal proponents of their philosophies. Lansing argued for broad dissemination of political rights, and demanded that states retain the power of recall and rotation over representatives and senators. In response to Chancellor Livingston's criticisms, he pronounced an American political truism. "Local interests," he stated, "will ever prevail in the general government, in a greater or lesser degree. It was on this presumption that the small states were induced to join themselves to the Union."[11]

After Hamilton responded by pointing out the virtues of the compromise by which small states were guaranteed power through the House of Representatives, Lansing brilliantly articulated Antifederalist fears of the powers of the new Constitution. It stripped the states of sovereignty, he maintained, rendering them unnecessary.

As the debate continued, the Antifederalist position was undermined by news of New Hampshire's ratification, putting the Constitution into effect. Now only Virginia, New York, North Carolina, and Rhode Island remained uncounted. A week later, Virginia's Federalists overcame the eloquent opposition of Patrick Henry to ratify the Constitution with recommendatory amendments. Undaunted, Lansing maintained his opposition and argued that New York "ought not adopt a system which is dangerous to our liberty."[12] Lansing provoked Federalist fears by noting that dissolution was a possibility if the Constitution were forced upon an unwilling people. Over the next few weeks, he continued his assault by arguing against federal revenue plans, insisting upon debt reform, and, in a final gesture, seeking conditional ratification contingent upon passage of a bill of rights. On July 23, the Convention defeated Lansing's last attempts to preserve the right of New York to withdraw from the union if, after a period of years, a bill of rights was not attached. The vote for ratification took place on July 26, 1788, with victory gained by the narrow margin of three votes (30 to 27). Lansing, an Antifederalist to the end, voted against ratification.

Post-Constitutional Politics

In 1790, Lansing was recommended for, but declined, the post of United States senator from New York. He subsequently was appointed a judge of New York's supreme court and in 1801 became chancellor, a post he held with distinction until his retirement in 1814. Though always a Clintonian Antifederalist, he had earned the respect of Federalists, who supported Lansing for governor in 1804.

Later, Lansing became a regent of the University of the State of New York. In 1821, he caused a furor by publishing Robert Yates's *Secret Proceedings and Debates of the Convention . . . in Philadelphia in 1787.* The book attacked the Constitution as the product of a cabal led by Hamilton and Madison, prompting the latter to publish his own version. Lansing's notes at the Philadelphia Convention were not published until 1939.

In December 1829, John Lansing disappeared during an evening stroll in New York City; he was never found. Murder was assumed and the case remains unsolved.

Summary

Lansing best articulated the Antifederalist position in the debates over the Constitution. Clear-minded and forceful, he was nearly as successful as Hamilton in presenting his views. If Hamilton and Madison were geniuses who created a visionary government of the future, Lansing ably articulated the political truths of his time.

NOTES:

[1]John Lansing to Richard Varick, September 5, 1780, Varick Papers, The New-York Historical Society.

[2]Quoted in Alfred F. Young, *The Democratic-Republicans of New York: The Origins, 1763-1797* (Chapel Hill, 1967), 40.

[3]Max Farrand, ed., *Records of the Federal Convention* 4 Vols. (New Haven, 1911), 3:580.

[4]*Ibid.,* 3:90.

[5]Quoted in Richard B. Morris, *The Forging of the Union, 1781-1789* (New York, 1987), 275.

[6]Farrand, *Records,* 1:18.

[7]See *Ibid,* 1:249, 257, 263; for later recollections see Robert Yates, *Secret Proceedings and Debates of the Convention* (Albany, 1821), and for Madison, see *New York Commercial Advertiser,* August 10, 1821.

[8]*Farrand, Records,* 1:336, 341 and 3:190.

[9]Herbert J. Storing, *The Complete Anti-Federalist,* 7 Vols. (Chicago, 1981), 2:16-18.

[10]*New York Journal,* April 26, 1788.

[11]*Ibid.,* 299.

[12]*Ibid.,* 2:413.

Chancellor Robert R. Livingston: Judge, Diplomat, and Advocate of the Constitution*
(1746–1813)

Eugene A. Gaer, Esq.

On April 30, 1789, the revolutionary era in American history came to a vivid conclusion when George Washington was inaugurated first president under the new federal Constitution. A statue on the steps of Federal Hall on Wall Street—the site of a building which in 1789 was also New York City Hall—still reminds visitors of the scene: the new president, already regarded as the symbol of the new nation, solemnly swearing to "preserve, protect and defend the Constitution of the United States" before a crowd of his fellow citizens. But who was it who administered the oath? There was as yet no national government, much less a chief justice to head the unformed federal judiciary.

New Yorkers may be proud to learn that the oath was administered by New York's chancellor, Robert R. Livingston, a judge and diplomat who played a significant role throughout the revolutionary and early national period, even though often overshadowed by more brilliant, if less socially prominent, contemporaries. One of Livingston's distinctions was his role in New York's ratification of the Constitution.

Chancellor Livingston—the title "chancellor" is always prefixed to his name to distinguish him from other Robert Livingstons who were also prominent in our early history—was born in 1746 into one of the most eminent families of the province of New York. Like their close

*Reprinted from *Bicentennial Minutes* (Albany, N.Y., 1988), with the kind permission of the New York Bar Foundation.

relatives, the Van Rensselaers, Beekmans and Schuylers, the Livingstons controlled vast tracts of land in the Hudson Valley and in unsettled areas west of the Hudson, and were not above speculating in lands seized from Tory sympathizers. Indeed, one curious aspect of New York's role in the Revolution was the adherence of these great aristocrats to the cause of liberty and independence, even while steadfastly maintaining semi-feudal rights over their own tenant farmers.

When the aristocratic families held together, they were usually able to dominate New York politics. When they splintered, the reverberations were felt throughout the political system. Thus, the party system in the province, and later the state, of New York owed less to differences between social classes than to differences within an aristocracy where each family often had multiple interests in land, commerce, finance, and the law.

Livingston was graduated from King's College (now Columbia University), where he distinguished himself as a student exponent of American "liberty." After an unstructured apprenticeship, he was admitted to the bar in 1768 and for a few years practiced in partnership with his later rival, John Jay, the future governor and first chief justice of the United States.

In 1775, Livingston was sent to Philadelphia as one of New York's delegates to the Continental Congress. The next year, he was chosen to serve with Thomas Jefferson, John Adams, Benjamin Franklin, and Roger Sherman on the committee charged with drafting the Declaration of Independence. Unfortunately, a chain of circumstances prevented Livingston from being present either when the Declaration was voted on or when it was signed.

During the central part of the Revolutionary War, Livingston was at least as active in local New York politics as in national. In early 1777, he was a member of the Kingston convention which adopted the first constitution for the independent state of New York. Livingston helped draft that constitution and was soon chosen chancellor of the new state.

The position was an unusual one, reflecting an attempt to adapt the traditional legal system of the English monarchy to the new circumstances of a revolutionary state. Under the English system, certain important judicial powers (called "equity jurisdiction") could be exercised only by a high official called the chancellor, who presided over the specialized chancery court. In colonial New York, the governor had usually served as chancellor *ex officio*, deciding equity cases himself.

When the revolutionary convention drafted the new state constitution, one of its primary concerns was to limit the broad powers which the governor had exercised as an agent of the British Crown. For that reason, a separate chancery court was established for the state, to be presided over by a chancellor equal in rank to the chief justice of the state supreme court. Besides judging cases, the chancellor served, along with the governor, chief justice, and other supreme court justices, on the council of revision, which had the power to veto laws passed by the legislature.

Livingston was to hold the office of chancellor for twenty-four years, during much of which time he combined it with other significant public office. From the fragmentary surviving records, it appears that the chancellor held court sporadically wherever he happened to be—in New York City, Albany, or at Clermont, his estate in what is now Columbia County. Almost no reported decisions or rulebooks have survived from Livingston's chancery court, particularly from the period before 1785.

In the late 1770s, sitting as chancellor was not Livingston's most important task—helping to win the Revolution was. Without resigning his judicial post, Livingston returned to the Continental Congress in 1778. In 1781, he was elected the first secretary for foreign affairs under the Articles of Confederation. Before that time, foreign affairs had been managed by a committee of the Congress.

Consolidating foreign policy in the hands of one secretary should have provided greater unity and coherence to the new nation's international relations. However, as at other stages in his career, Livingston was overshadowed by his collaborators and nominal subordinates: Benjamin Franklin in France, John Jay in Spain, and John Adams in The Netherlands. Thus, Livingston exercised only limited diplomatic powers. Once independence appeared certain, Livingston recognized that his two offices could not easily be reconciled. He therefore resigned the foreign affairs post in June 1783, although he returned to Congress again in 1784 and 1785.

The mid-1780s are a controversial period in American history. For some historians, they represent the "critical period" in our history, when petty bickering within and among the states almost caused the enterprise of independence to founder. For others, the Articles of Confederation represent a lost opportunity for America to have developed very differently as a far more decentralized and (perhaps) democratic society than it became.

Historians have debated over what political and social forces may have been responsible for the new federal Constitution of 1787. Some see it as primarily directed at alleviating American weaknesses in international relations, but the extensive attention given to domestic issues indicates that the Framers must have had broader goals. Others stress that it was a conservative document, designed to dampen revolutionary excesses, but find it difficult to explain why many prominent opponents of ratification were landowners. One well-known theory attempts to reconcile these contradictions by stressing that the Constitution appealed especially to speculators in currency and bonds issued by the states, who wanted a strong national government capable of insuring payment of these issues. As this fiscal policy would arguably harm the landed interests, many of them became Antifederalists.

These theories offer few clues as to why Livingston should have supported ratification. As a state court judge, he must have been unenthusiastic about the establishment of a competing federal judiciary. As one of the leading landowners of New York (who had little investment in paper property), he had nothing to gain from the fiscal policies associated with the Federalists. Indeed, in later years, Livingston was aligned with the party of Thomas Jefferson and George Clinton, which absorbed the bulk of the Antifederalists of the ratification period.

Nonetheless, in the crucial New York debate over ratification, Livingston joined with his rivals, Hamilton and Jay, to support the Constitution. Certainly, one special perspective was his former post as head of the American foreign service, where he felt keenly embarrassed by the continuing lack of power of the new nation in international relations. Only the adoption of a stong federal government, he believed, could require Great Britain, France, and other European powers to accord the United States respect as a sovereign, if not equal, power on the international scene.

Livingston expressed his feelings in an address on July 4, 1787, to the New York Society of the Cincinnati (an organization of Revolutionary War veterans) while the Constitutional Convention was meeting in Philadelphia. He condemned contemporary states for giving insufficient offices to those with "abilities & education," as well as the "leisure to attend to the affairs of government." With respect to foreign policy, he asked:

> Who [can deny] that we are, at this moment, colonies for every purpose but that of internal taxation of the nation from whom we vainly hoped our swords had freed us?

In the ratification convention which met in Poughkeepsie in June 1788, Livingston represented Federalist New York County rather than Columbia, where a Livingston family split permitted an Antifederalist landslide. His pro-ratification views were a distinct minority; however, as chancellor, Livingston was entitled to give the keynote speech. Livingston is credited with the parliamentary strategy of having the entire Constitution considered as a single document before any vote would be taken on any individual portions. It is thought that if individual portions had been voted on separately, the Constitution may have been defeated before pressure could build up for ratification. However, because the opponents had their own reasons for delay, Livingston's proposal was adopted.

At the convention, Livingston, working closely with Hamilton and Jay, was most successful in negotiating behind the scenes with wavering delegates. It is doubtful that Livingston's speeches to the convention, which were generally marked by a haughty aristocratic tone, could have been very effective in bringing over avowedly Antifederalist delegates elected by ordinary farmers and workers.

Livingston's most distinguished biographer, George Dangerfield, theorizes that New York's ultimate vote for ratification resulted neither from debates nor backroom negotiation, but from the realization (once word arrived that New Hampshire and Virginia had voted for ratification) that New York would be desperately isolated if it failed to go along. In addition, there was widespread fear that the southern counties (*i.e.,* Long Island, Westchester and the present New York City), would form their own state to avoid being shut out from the commerce of the ratifying states. Thus, the New York convention, faced with the inevitable, ratified the Constitution by a vote of 30 to 27 (with other "yes" votes probably in reserve). As one of the three leaders of the ratification cause at Poughkeepsie, Livingston is entitled to a generous measure of credit for this result.

Aside from being allowed to preside at Washington's inauguration, Livingston received no honors from the new administration. Although Hamilton was named secretary of the treasury and Jay chief justice, Livingston was passed over for major federal office. Very likely, it was resentment at such preference for his old colleagues, rather than any deeper motivations, which led Livingston to move politically toward the old Antifederalists as they regrouped into the Republican Party. In the 1791 contest for a seat in the United States Senate, Livingston supported the ambitious young lawyer, Aaron Burr, over the aristocratic General Philip Schuyler, who also happened to be Hamilton's father-in-law. Moving further into opposition to the Washington administration, Livingston, in 1795, was a vigorous opponent of the conciliatory trade treaty which Jay had negotiated with the British.

Jefferson's election in 1800 at last provided Livingston an opportunity to serve in the national government and to perform what many consider his greatest public service. Appointed Minister to France, it was Livingston who in 1803 received Napoleon's surprise offer to sell the vast Louisiana territories. In an era of slow communication, it may have taken months for Livingston to consult with his superiors about whether to accept. Rather than risk delay, Livingston, largely on his own, signed the treaty of purchase, an act which he predicted would enable "the United States to take their place among the powers of the first rank."

A short time later, Livingston retired from political life. He continued to perform notable public service as a patron of scientists and inventors, most notably of Robert Fulton, whose steamboat, *Clermont*, was named for Livingston's estate.

But of all events in Livingston's life, perhaps none deserves to be remembered so well, in this bicentennial year, as the brief moment on April 30, 1789, when he stood on the balcony of New York City Hall at the focal point of all eyes in America and proclaimed: "It is done. Long live George Washington, President of the United States."

For Further Reading

Dangerfield, George. *Chancellor Robert R. Livingston of New York, 1746–1813*. New York: Harcourt, Brace and Co., 1960.

Gouverneur Morris:
New York's "Other Delegate"
(1752–1816)

CALVIN JILLSON AND GEORGE RUIZ
Louisiana State University

Born in what is now the Bronx, Gouverneur Morris (1752–1816) attended King's College (now Columbia University), studied law with William Smith, and was elected to the third New York provincial congress.

As an author, with John Jay, Robert R. Livingston, and others, of New York State's first constitution, he exerted a profound influence on state government. Morris later represented Pennsylvania at the Constitutional Convention in 1787, where he adopted and espoused the Federalist principles of another New Yorker, Alexander Hamilton.

A term as minister plenipotentiary to France was capped by an appointment to fill an unexpired term (1800–1803) as United States Senator from New York. His long career in state and national affairs marks him as one of the most important figures of his day.

When, on January 31, 1752, Gouverneur Morris was born on the family manor at Morrisania, across the Harlem River from Manhattan Island, New York was a colony of eighty thousand inhabitants. Gouverneur's father, Lewis Morris, Jr., was a well-respected jurist and member of the provincial legislature. Gouverneur's mother, the former Sarah Gouverneur, was descended from a long line of French Huguenots who settled in New York following the revocation of the Edict of Nantes in 1685.

Lewis Morris evidently had great hopes for his son for, in his will, written four years before his death in 1764, he wrote, "It is my desire that my son, Gouverneur Morris, may have the best education that is to be had in England or America." In 1764, after three years at the New Rochelle Academy, Morris, then only twelve years old, was enrolled at King's College (now Columbia University) in New York City. During his four-year tenure at King's, Morris pursued a classical course of study, with particular emphasis on philosophy, literature, and languages. An excellent student, Morris was selected to deliver the commencement address at his graduation. He chose as his topic, "Wit and Beauty."

Soon after graduation, Morris apprenticed himself in the law office of William Smith, an old family friend, widely regarded as one of the best legal minds in the colonies. Besides gaining excellent preparation in the law, Morris incorporated much of Smith's conservative ideological posture into his own world view. Admitted to the New York bar in 1771 at age nineteen, Morris fully expected to establish a long and lucrative private practice.

In Morris's young life and new career, as in the lives and careers of so many of the bright and visible young men of his generation, public responsibilities overwhelmed private plans. As political and economic relations between the colonies and the mother country continued to deteriorate through the early 1770s, young incendiaries from Samuel Adams's Boston to Christopher Gadsden's Charleston pushed for confrontation. Morris and many members of the New York and Philadelphia commercial communities, dependent as they were on trade with Britain, were, on the other hand, only just beginning painfully slow and thoroughly conservative paths to revolution. Initially, Morris was convinced that reconciliation with Great Britain was in the best interest of the colonies. Specifically, he urged a settlement of all differences with the Crown as the only way to avert the ultimate evil, "mobocracy." Morris tried to alert his countrymen to the dangers that might accompany revolutionary upheaval. He said, "I see, and I see it with fear and trembling, that if the disputes with Britain continue, we shall be under the worst of all possible dominions. We shall be under the dominion of a riotous mob."

Nonetheless, by May 1776, relations between the two sides were so strained that the Continental Congress directed the various colonies to override royal institutions and to establish forms of government as they saw fit. In the third provincial congress of New York, Morris took the lead in satisfying this directive. At the age of twenty-six, Morris was one of the principal delegates, (the others including John Jay, Robert R. Livingston, both thirty years old, and Abraham Yates, Jr.), to be charged with drafting the New York constitution. Further, in an eloquent and impassioned speech before his fellow assemblymen, Morris called for independence, arguing that British actions had so impinged the dignity and liberty of Americans that no other alternative existed but to sever all ties between the two nations. Morris's change of heart was indicative of a larger shift of opinion in New York in favor of American independence. Indeed, less than a week after the Continental Congress issued the Declaration of Independence in July 1776, the New York provincial congress expressed its full support for the action taken in Philadelphia.

Following the adoption of New York's new constitution in April 1777, Morris was selected as a delegate to the Continental Congress. His new colleagues honored him with important committee assignments from the very beginning. In October 1778, Morris was entrusted with the task of drawing up the first instructions ever sent to an American diplomat. Earlier that year, General George Washington had relayed to Congress a copy of a parliamentary bill sponsored by Lord North which appeared to concede the colonial claim to exclusive power over internal taxation and to provide for the appointment of commissioners to deal with the Americans. Suspecting the sincerity of this proposal, Morris prepared a report which declared that the United States could not deal with England until the British military was withdrawn and American independence acknowledged. This report was unanimously adopted by Congress and subsequently became the basis of the peace negotiations which culminated in the 1783 Treaty of Paris.

While Morris's reputation as a statesman and intellect of the first rank continued to grow in Philadelphia, in New York the perception grew that he had neglected the interests of his constituents. This discontent was ultimately manifested in the New York State Assembly's decision to reject him for Congress. Undaunted by this setback and still determined to remain active in the critical public debates then occurring, Morris moved to Philadelphia and began work on a series of essays published under the pseudonym, "An American." In these essays, Morris focused primarily on issues of national finance, banking, trade, and commerce. While Gouverneur Morris's financial expertise was already well known to leading nationalists in and around Congress, these essays greatly strengthened his reputation.

When Robert Morris (no relative, but a close friend) was appointed by the Congress to the new position of Superintendent of Finance, he quickly appointed Gouverneur Morris to be his chief assistant. Together the Morrises worked to establish public confidence in the credit of the United States, and, with the modest sum of four hundred thousand dollars, they established, and the Congress incorporated, the "Bank of North America." The struggle to equip, feed, and otherwise fund Washington's Continental Army during the waning years of the war and then to reconstruct the new nation's wartorn economy "induced [both Morrises] to wish that Congress may be possessed of much more authority than has hitherto been delegated to them." Thus, over the course of the 1780s, Gouverneur Morris and a growing cadre of young nationalists centering on Congress came increasingly to favor centralization of authority in the national government.

Morris's advocacy of a strong national government flowed directly from the three basic premises of his political philosophy: (1) that human nature is intrinsically selfish and should be subject to constraint, (2) that the institution of private property formed the basis of society, and (3) that a nation's property owners ought to control that nation's government. Morris saw the role of government as aiding in the expansion and safeguarding of property through the steady and predictable enforcement of laws of contract and the equally swift and certain punishment of crimes. At bottom, it was first Britain's and then the states' suppression of popular liberty to such a degree as to threaten free commerce that underlay Morris's movement from a stance of Loyalism through a final position of American nationalism. As Morris prepared to attend the Federal Convention as a delegate from Pennsylvania, the key question for him was whether the American public had matured sufficiently since 1776 to accept the institution of a national government powerful enough to establish and maintain the kind of political stability that Morris thought necessary to promote economic expansion.

Morris in the Convention

The Constitutional Convention met in Philadelphia from May 25 to September 17, 1787. For nearly all of that time the delegates struggled over control of the proposed government, over the proper relationship between the state and national governments, and over the nature of an effective and safe relationship between the departments of a government in the republican form. Gouverneur Morris was one of the Convention's dominant figures. The New Yorker owed his seat in the Pennsylvania delegation to the power of his friend and fellow delegate Robert Morris. Though he was absent for the entire month of June, having returned to Morrisania to attend to pressing personal matters, he spoke more frequently than any other member of the Convention and often took the lead at critical points in the debate. Yet, Morris's positive influence in the Convention was limited by both the content of his views and by the manner in which he pressed them. William Pierce, a delegate from Georgia, wrote a penetrating character sketch of every delegate that attended the Convention. Pierce's description of Morris, while striking and even entertaining, shows how Morris was viewed by his colleagues in the Convention. Pierce says that

> Mr. Gouverneur Morris is one of the Genius's in whom every species of talents combine to render him conspicuous and flourishing in public debate: —He winds through all the mazes of rhetoric, and throws around him such a glare that he charms, captivates, and leads away the senses of all who hear him . . . But with all these powers he is fickle and inconstant, —never persuing one train of thinking,—nor even regular.

While the first delegates to gather in Philadelphia awaited the arrival of a quorum, Morris met daily with the members of the Virginia delegation and others from Pennsylvania to discuss and adjust a plan of government written by James Madison and to map strategy for the upcoming debates. Madison recorded that Morris took a characteristically strong and uncompromising role in these discussions:

> Previous to the arrival of a majority of the States, the rule by which they ought to vote in the Convention had been made a subject of conversation among the members present. It was pressed by Gouverneur Morris and favored by Robert Morris and others from Pennsylvania, that the large States should unite in firmly refusing to the small States an equal vote. . . . The members from Virginia, conceiving that such an attempt might begat fatal altercations between the large & States . . . discountenanced & stifled the project.

Once Madison's Virginia Plan was adopted as the Convention's working agenda on May 29, Morris joined Hamilton and Madison in spearheading the nationalists' early move to put the Convention on record in favor of a "national and supreme" government with proportional representation in both the House and the Senate. Yet with only one day of substantive debate completed, Morris left Philadelphia on May 31, not to return until July 1. During his long absence the Convention bogged down and nearly disintegrated over the critical issue of representation. The large states, principally Massachusetts, Pennsylvania, and Virginia, continued to demand that seats in both the House and Senate be distributed among the states on the basis of population, while the smaller states, such as New Jersey, Delaware, and Maryland, held out for an equal vote in the Senate. Upon his return to Philadelphia, Morris found his closest allies near despair. One contemporary source records:

> When Morris returned to the convention, he went to Robert Morris' house, where Washington was staying, and learned that everyone was despondent in the belief that the convention was about to dissolve in failure and that Hamilton was preparing to leave. At the request of those present, Gouverneur went to see Hamilton.

Morris made two long and impressive speeches on July 2 and 5. Neither speech was effective in the sense of rallying a majority behind the proposals that they contained, but together they provide great insight into Morris's distinctive understanding of the relationship between social class structure and the appropriate design of political institutions in the new nation.

Although Morris took a recognizably Lockean view of the origins of government, he took a rather distinctive view of its purposes. Like most men of his age, he believed that government was created to protect life, liberty, and property. But unlike Jefferson, who had replaced property with the pursuit of happiness in the Declaration of Independence, Morris declared property to be the very basis of government. Morris argued that

> though Life and liberty were generally said to be of more value, than property. An accurate view of this matter would nonetheless prove that property was the main object of Society. The savage State was more favorable to liberty than the Civilized; and sufficiently so to life . . . It was only renounced for the sake of property which could only be secured by the restraints of regular Government.

The national government should provide stable currency, credit, banking, and trade structures. Individuals would then be free to pursue their private interest in wealth, property, and status to their own and their communities' benefit. Like Madison, Morris believed that self-interest was the motive that most frequently moved men both in and out of government. Rather than depending on public virtue, in words very similar to those that Madison would later use in *The Federalist No. 10*, Morris argued that "one interest must be opposed to another interest. Vices as they exist, must be turned against each other."

Morris departed most clearly from Madison and most of his contemporaries, however, in describing the interests and vices that he thought
needed to be balanced to secure the social peace that economic and political stability required. Madison saw the American society as composed
of such a multiplicity of interests that the sheer size of the new nation
would make it difficult for majorities to form, let alone to seize government for oppressive purposes. Within government, power would be
limited, divided, and dispersed in a system of intricate checks and balances. Morris, on the other hand, saw the basic divisions in society much
more simply. Danger, he thought, came from the very rich and the very
poor. Morris warned his colleagues not to "Give the votes to people
who have no property . . . they will sell them to the rich." The rich presented quite a different problem. They were too powerful effectively to
be denied the opportunity and influence to do harm. Morris noted a
basic social fact:

> The rich will strive to establish their dominion & enslave the rest.
> They always did. They always will. . . . Let the rich mix with the
> poor and in a Commercial Country, they will establish an Oligar-
> chy. Take away commerce, and the democracy will triumph. Thus
> it has been all the world over.

If class conflict was the key problem facing the new nation, Morris was prepared with a set of institutional proposals to deal with it.
Morris opened his remarks of July 2 by asking "What is the object [of
the Senate]?" He answered that its role was "to check the precipitation, changeableness, and excesses of the first branch [the House]. Every
man of observation had seen in the democratic branches of the State
Legislatures, precipitation; in Congress, changeableness. in every department excesses agst. personal liberty private property & personal safety."
Many delegates undoubtedly agreed with all of this. Yet, characteristically, the solution that Morris offered to these problems went far beyond
what anyone other than Hamilton could anticipate with equanimity.

Notes taken by Robert Yates provide the clearest statement of Morris's views. Morris argued, "The second branch ought to be composed
of men of great and established property—*an aristocracy*. Men, who
from pride will support consistency and permanency. . . . Such an
aristocratic body will keep down the turbulency of democracy." Madison
recorded Morris as arguing that "The Checking branch (the Senate)
must have a personal interest in checking the other branch. . . . It must
have great personal property, it must have the aristocratic spirit, it must

love to lord it thro' pride. . . . The proper security agst them is to form them into a separate interest. The two forces will then controul each other.'' But Morris and others in the Convention were aware that senators, no matter what their social status, if selected through popular elections, or for brief two-, three-, or four-year terms, were often no more independent, wise, or stable than their colleagues in the lower house. Therefore, Morris proposed that ''The aristocratic body . . . should be for life.'' Although Morris's proposal for permanency and stability in government deriving from life tenures in office received little support, he did not abandon the principle.

When the Convention turned to issues of executive selection, tenure, and powers, Morris was firmly opposed to the majority's preference for a weak executive to be chosen by the legislature and to be ineligible to a second term. Morris argued on July 17 that ''ineligibility . . . tended to destroy the great motive to good behavior, the hope of being rewarded by a re-appointment. It was saying to him, make hay while the sun shines.'' Therefore, when, two days later, Virginia's James McClurg proposed that the President serve ''during good behavior,'' Morris ''expressed great pleasure in hearing it. This was the way to get a good Government. . . . He was indifferent how the Executive should be chosen, provided he held his place by this tenure.''

Morris's reasoning in this instance, as in the case of the life tenure for the Senate, was grounded in a class analysis of the American society. Morris argued that ''the Executive Magistrate should be the guardian of the people, even of the lower classes, agst. Legislative tyranny, against the Great & the wealthy who in the course of things will necessarily compose—the Legislative power.'' Morris was, however, unsure that any republican executive could fulfill this critical mission. Therefore, Morris supported Madison's proposal of July 21 to join the executive and the judiciary in a revisionary power over acts of the legislature, though both worried, in Morris's words, that ''The interest of our Executive is so inconsiderable & so transitory, and his means of defending it so feeble, that there is the justest ground to fear his want of firmness in resisting encroachment.'' This concern for strength in the executive led Morris on August 15 to propose ''the expedient of an absolute negative in the Executive'' because ''Encroachments of the popular branch of the Government ought to be guarded agst.''

Morris's role in the Convention cannot be fully understood with reference only to his political views. His personality and style were as distinctive and, to many, as disconcerting as his ideas. Morris, though capable of the most inspired rhetoric, had little time for the kind of stylized courtesy with which legislators, then and now, treat each other. As a result, Morris could, and frequently did, insult and alienate both his friends and his enemies. For example, with the Convention foundering over the issue of representation, and Morris just returned from New York, he assured his colleagues that

> He came here as a Representative of America; he flattered himself he came here in some degree as a representative of the whole human race. . . . He wished gentlemen to extend their views beyond the present moment of time; beyond the narrow limits of place from which they derive their political origin. . . . We must look forward to the effects of what we do. These alone ought to guide us.

This impressive statement of Morris's commitment to the general interests of America is characteristic of his high-flying rhetorical style. Equally characteristic of this style was the scarcely veiled iron fist beneath the velvet glove. Morris followed his call that members of the Convention act as "Representatives of America" with a dire warning to those delegates still demanding equality for each state in the Senate. Morris warned that

> This Country must be united. If persuasion does not unite it, the sword will. He begged that this consideration might have its due weight. The scenes of horror attending civil commotion cannot be described, and the conclusion of them will be worse than the term of their continuance. The stronger party will then make traytors of the weaker; and the Callows and Halter will finish the work of the sword.

Morris's unrestrained rhetoric also directed its withering fire toward the very friends upon whose cooperation his effectiveness in the Convention depended. Morris's southern colleagues, including Madison, Washington, and Charles Pinckney of South Carolina, must have been stunned to hear the cutting indictment of their societies that he delivered on August 8. Morris invited his southern colleagues to "Compare the free regions of the Middle States, where a rich and noble cultivation marks the prosperity & happiness of the people, with the misery & poverty which overspread the barren wastes of Va. Maryd. & the other States having slaves." The sense of outrage that the delegates of Maryland and Virginia must have felt in hearing their states described as "barren wastes" overspread with "poverty & misery" would certainly have been shared by the delegates of South Carolina and Georgia when Morris went on to declare on August 8 that

> The admission of slaves into the Representation comes to this: that the inhabitants of Georgia and S.C. who goes to the Coast of Africa, and in the defiance of the most sacred laws of humanity tears away his fellow creatures from their dearest connections & dam(n)s them to the most cruel bondages, shall have more votes in a Govt. instituted for the protection of the rights of mankind, than the Citizen . . . who views with a laudable horror, so nefarious a practice.

Finally, Morris also took a very dim view of the political, social, and economic impact that the new West was likely to have on the America that he wished to build. Morris was prepared to deny the West representation in Congress and any possibility of eventual statehood. The West would be ruled by and for the Atlantic seaboard. Morris's role in the Convention, as he interpreted it, was essentially to defend the present and future supremacy of the commercial states against the agricultural interests of the South and West. On July 13 only two weeks after he had returned to the Convention, Morris summarized his view of the dangers inherent in the regional characteristics and conflicts that he saw in the new nation. He concluded:

> The consequence of . . . a transfer of power from the maritime to the interior & landed interest will he foresees be such an oppression of commerce, that he shall be obliged to . . . provide some defence for the N. States agst it. . . . If the Southn. States get the power into their hands, and be joined as they will be with the interior Country they will inevitably bring on a war with Spain for the Mississippi . . . [every] thing was to be apprehended from their getting power into their hands.

For Morris, as for Hamilton and for many of the nationalists from the middle states and New England, the grandeur of the future "American Empire" lay in the trading states of the Atlantic coast, rather than in the agricultural areas of the South and the West.

The Post-Convention Years

Morris was unique among his contemporaries in that not only was he actively involved in the American Revolution but he also played a leading role in another event which was to change the destiny of humankind—the French Revolution. Initially sent to Paris by Robert Morris to negotiate personal business matters, Gouverneur Morris quickly and purposefully ingratiated himself with many of the leading figures in French politics and society. At the time of Morris's arrival in 1789, France stood on the brink of domestic turmoil. A bad harvest and an industrial depression acted in concert to exacerbate peasant demands for tax relief and bourgeois demands for social equality. In addition, credit extended to the Americans by the French government during the previous decade had left the country near bankruptcy.

Morris did not hesitate to offer both solicited and unsolicited advice to the French inner elite. Specifically, he proposed a program of moderate social reform which would result in a limited monarchy, a hereditary senate, and a national assembly elected in the urban districts by married adult males and in the rural areas on the basis of property qualification. However, much to Morris's chagrin, the French Estates-General failed to enact his reform program and adjourned without seriously addressing the issues of the impending revolution. As the crisis deepened, Morris became more convinced than ever that some form of monarchy must be preserved if France were to restore domestic stability. In the months ahead, Morris watched in horror as political opposition turned into social revolution. Morris's worst fears for the American Revolution more than a decade earlier, that it would deteriorate into a vicious "mobocracy," were in his view, realized as the Bastille fell, the King and many of his family were killed, and Robespierre's terror gripped Paris and the nation.

Needless to say, Morris's close ties to the French monarchists, even during the Revolution's moderate early stages, did little to bolster his already tattered republican credentials back home. Indeed, when President Washington formally submitted Morris's name as his nominee for minister plenipotentiary to France, the accusations of Morris being a "monarch man" surfaced once again. However, largely out of deference to Washington, the Senate confirmed Morris on January 12, 1792, by a vote of sixteen to eleven.

If Morris's relationship with the royal government had at times been strained, his relationship with the leaders of republican France was intolerable from the beginning. In fact, by May 1793, relations had so soured that Morris was forced to retreat to a twenty-acre country estate at Seine–Port, twenty-seven miles from Paris. The republican government, convinced that Morris was secretly designing plans for their ouster, anxiously awaited the first available opportunity to request his recall.

That opportunity came with Washington's rejection of Citizen Genet as French minister plenipotentiary to the United States. In retaliation, the French government promptly declared Morris *personna non grata*. Thus ended Morris's mission in France.

Morris departed France, not for home, but for Britain, where he spent the late 1790s in the successful pursuit of private business opportunities. Morris's decade in Europe did not weaken his political stature at home. When Morris arrived back in New York in 1799, the Federalists controlled the New York Assembly and the Federalist administration of President John Adams was still in power. Morris was almost immediately named to fill out the remaining three years (1800–1803) of a term in the United States Senate, where he frequently acted to obstruct the Jefferson administration's policies. Nonetheless, though a staunch Federalist, Morris could no more be an unthinking and automatic party man any more comfortably in 1800 than he could have in 1787 or in 1775 and 1776. Theodore Roosevelt, the future president, who wrote a life of Morris in 1888, indicated that during Morris's service in the Senate he remained "both too independent and too erratic to act always within strict party lines." By the end of Morris's Senate term, New York had fallen into Republican hands, and he was not reappointed. Morris retired to his beloved Morrisania, where he spent the final decade of his life in apparent comfort, pleasure, and happiness. Morris's last years were highlighted by the frequent visits of his lifelong friend and neighbor John Jay, by the taking in 1809 of a wife, the former Anne Cary Randolph of Virginia, and by the birth of a son in 1813. On November 6, 1816, at the age of sixty-four, Gouverneur Morris died after a brief illness.

Philip Schuyler:
An Unsung Founding Father
(1733-1804)

DON R. GERLACH

The University of Akron

Military commander, provincial assemblyman, state senator, United States senator, and heir to a family fortune that placed him among the Hudson Valley's wealthiest residents, Albany's Philip Schuyler exerted a profound influence on the affairs of New York State. His commitment to the principles of Federalism was shared by his son-in-law, Alexander Hamilton. Together, they worked for New York's ratification of the United States Constitution.

Announcing the death on November 18 of Philip Schuyler, the *Albany Gazette* of November 22, 1804 called him "eminent for his useful labours, in the military and civil affairs of our country. Distinguished by strength of intellect, extensive knowledge, soundness and purity of moral and political principles—He was a practical, not a theoretical statesman; an active, not a visionary patriot—He was wise in devising, enterprising and preserving in the execution of plans of great and public utility." The *Albany Register* of November 23, 1804, by contrast, barely cited his death and burial, a typical response for a Republican paper to a notable Federalist whose own partisanship followed him to his grave. The eulogy of the Federalist *Gazette* included an assessment which came closest to an estimate of the man. In the past thirty years, the unknown author wrote, there had been little public business in which Schuyler had not taken some part, "contributed some aid or influence." His public life had been "one uninterrupted scene of interesting engagement and active pursuit. A prime agent in all important affairs. . . ."[1]

Early Life

Born on November 10, 1733, at Albany, Schuyler was the fourth-generation scion of one of New York's oldest and most prosperous families whose kinship included Van Cortlandts, DeLanceys, Livingstons, and Van Rensselaers. Founders of the Schuyler line in America put down roots in New Netherland about 1650. Typically Dutch, they engaged in trade, expanded their land holdings, and made their way into the circles of local and provincial government.

Young Schuyler was left fatherless at the age of seven; his rearing passed to his mother, an aunt, and his paternal grandfather. After war broke out between Britain and France in 1754 over claims to the Ohio country, Schuyler was commissioned a captain in the militia. In 1755 he married Catharine Van Rensselaer, whose family was the Claverack branch of the patroonal clan. Subsequently, he served with John Bradstreet, whose army quartermaster work took Schuyler to England in 1761–1762 to settle Bradstreet's accounts. His family growing apace, the young Schuyler worked to enlarge and develop his Saratoga estate and other land holdings. Governor Sir Henry Moore promoted him to colonel in the militia in 1767, and in 1768 Schuyler won his first election to the provincial assembly.

A proud partisan and reluctant rebel, he served in the New York provincial assembly as the American Revolution developed from a series of protests against imperial measures into a determined clash of arms. Sent to the Continental Congress, he was appointed a major-general in June 1775. For two years he commanded the Northern Army. After 1777, he served as an Indian commissioner, a collector of intelligence and supplies for Washington, a constant advisor to the Virginian (as in the planning of the Sullivan–Clinton expedition against the Iroquois), a member of Congress, and leader of two of its committees to headquarters in 1779 and 1780, where he labored to raise men and supplies for the commander-in-chief. His commitment and service to the patriot cause were recognized even by the enemy, who attempted to kidnap him from his Albany house in August 1781.

Advocate of Reform

Schuyler's experiences in the army, in Congress, and in the New York State Senate (to which he was first elected in 1780) led him to see the necessity of a national union stronger than was provided under the Articles of Confederation. As early as 1778, for example, he spoke in Congress for the army's interests and plunged into efforts to deal with

problems of finance, currency depreciation, and other ways of supporting the Continental Army. He insisted that Congress should devise a
real plan for remedying fiscal evils like currency depreciation instead
of using stopgap measures. He promoted the provision of land grants
and adjustment of salaries for military personnel and urged the reform
of the quartermaster and commissary departments. He also pressed for
New York's adjustment of western land claims in order to satisfy states
like Maryland, which would not ratify the Articles of Confederation
until they were assured that the western domain was surrendered by the
states to the nation.

As a member of the New York State Senate in 1780, Schuyler
pressed for sending delegates to the Hartford Convention where efforts
might be made to propose measures to "give Vigor to the governing
Powers, equal to the present Crisis. . . ."[2]

In another effort to strengthen the Union for the sake of the war
effort, Schuyler in 1780 began to urge the New York legislature to settle
its disputed claims with the people of the Hampshire Grants, thus paving the way for the new state of Vermont, gaining support for the Continental Army, and strengthening the defense of American frontiers. Unfortunately, Governor George Clinton prevented the surrender of New
York's claims to the Vermont territory by threatening to prorogue the
legislature, preferring to delay the issue and allow the Continental Congress to grapple with it. For Schuyler, provincial interests should give
way to the national welfare. Thus he worked for a Union with enlarged
powers that would include loyal Vermonters who might be enlisted in
the common cause against the British. In that he failed, until 1791, when,
as a United States Senator under the new Constitution, he was able to
support the entry of Vermont as the fourteenth state.

As the War for Independence ground toward its conclusion,
Schuyler became convinced that the states must part "with so much
of their sovereignty, respectively, as would enable the governing power
to draw forth the strength and resources of the country." The cause of
independence would be lost "unless another system of government is
adopted" with "a fund for the redemption of common debts. . . ."[3]
In February 1781, just before the Articles of Confederation became effective, he prompted the New York legislature to propose their alteration by the enlargement of national powers. Congress and the states did
not respond. As he explained to Henry Van Schaack in 1787, "the politicians of this state seldom, if ever, drew with those of the eastern states.
I wished to eradicate the injurious jealousy which prevailed between them
and us. Impelled by these sentiments, I proposed . . . that a Convention should be held, the ostensible object of which would be to devise

more efficient means for prosecuting the war, but the real one to form such a tacit compact as has long subsisted between what we call the New England States. . . . But my plan was too bold to meet with success from timid politicians and such as still regarded with jealous suspicion the people of New England. In short, I failed."[4] By early 1781, Schuyler had cemented an alliance with his son-in-law, committed nationalist Alexander Hamilton. The coincidence of their views, abilities, and energies proved to be a basis for one of the most remarkable and influential associations in all of American history.

In March 1781, Schuyler and Egbert Benson induced the New York legislature to approve an amendment to the Articles of Confederation authorizing a 5 percent national impost as requested by Congress. Schuyler believed that there also should be "Additional articles" to enlarge congressional power. In 1782, Schuyler supported the nationalist interest by winning passage of a New York law incorporating the Bank of North America—a statute deemed necessary when members of Congress doubted their own powers of incorporation. And in July 1782, partly through Schuyler's influence as a state senator, the legislature elected Hamilton a delegate to Congress and requested it to call a "general Convention . . . especially authorized to revise and amend The Confederation," subject to ratification by state legislatures.[5]

In 1787, Schuyler attended the New York State Senate from late January until April 21. His arrival at New York City on January 25 prompted Governor Clinton to report that "now I suppose the Senate Rooms will ring with malevolent Rhapsody and feigned Patriotism, hitherto it has been blessed with singular Harmony."[6] Clinton's sentiment reflected the growing division between his opponents and supporters— and subsequently those of the proposed Constitution. Part of the division was revealed in the legislature's choice of delegates to the Confederation Congress—and in the battle over Schuyler's and Hamilton's proposal to instruct those delegates to ask Congress for a general convention to revise the Articles of Confederation. The Clintonians later checked the influence of Hamilton by choosing Robert Yates and John Lansing, Jr., as his fellow delegates to the Philadelphia Convention— and by refusing to select five delegates, as Schuyler proposed in the state senate. Schuyler complained to Henry Van Schaack of the narrow interests of Clinton's "junto, the principles of which are a state impost, no direct taxation, keep all power in the hands of the legislature, give none to Congress."[7]

Whatever impact the Schuyler–Hamilton alliance might have had at the Philadelphia Convention in 1787 was partially negated when Hamilton's fellow New York delegates left the session, protesting that the drafting of a new constitution violated their instructions to revise the Articles of Confederation. New York was therefore deprived of a vote in the Convention. Only Hamilton was a committed nationalist. Lansing, who, for his wartime association with Schuyler as the general's aide and secretary, and subsequently as his attorney, might have been expected to share Schuyler's views, had come to be of a different mind.

When the work of the Philadelphia Convention was completed, Schuyler was ready to join Hamilton in efforts to promote the ratification of the Constitution. Asked in 1832 by Hamilton's widow what her husband's and "father's agency in adopting the Constitution" had been, Chancellor James Kent recalled dining with them at Schuyler's Albany house in October 1787: "General Schuyler was full of lively, spirited, and instructive reflection, and he went into details, showing in his usual calculating manner, the great expense and complicated provisions of our local financial systems, and the order, simplicity, and economy that would attend one national system of revenue."[8] He might also have added that Schuyler successfully battled motions introduced by Abraham Yates, Jr., in the New York State Senate to delay passage of a resolution to call the state ratifying convention, and then visited the Poughkeepsie convention during the period June 24–July 25 where he lent his aid in persuading Antifederalist delegates to agree to ratification.

Unfortunately, little evidence of Schuyler's influence at Poughkeepsie remains. His presence as a spectator there is documented, as is his correspondence with James Madison relaying news to Virginia of New Hampshire's ratification. It was on the day that news arrived of New Hampshire's approval that Schuyler also observed (to Henry Van Schaack, June 24, 1788) that "Should Virginia reject, I fear the Anties [here] will follow their example."[9] But the news from Virginia on July 1 was positive.

Meantime, Schuyler informed his son, John Bradstreet Schuyler, that he had intended to return to Albany June 26, but friends urged him to remain at Poughkeepsie in hopes he might render his country "some aid." The New Hampshire ratification, he thought, "will be the Means of ultimately bringing this state into the union," but he had "no reason to conclude that It is attended with such effect as to induce the Convention to adopt the Constitution, otherwise than with previous amendments." Many people had probably voted for Antifederal delegates "either from misapprehension, or were led to it by the arts & insinuations of interested and designing Men." Forbearance and conciliation might yet win the cause, and when the debates were published and read "the candid will acknowledge that those of the Chancellor [Robert

R. Livingston,] Messrs. Jay Harrison & Hamilton ought to have caused conviction." Convinced that when James Duane would speak "he also will do justice to the Cause," Schuyler thought that Hamilton's eloquence was greatest; his "elevated sentiments" and correct judgment reached the heart. Alas, there were too many who labored under prejudice.[10]

When the Poughkeepsie convention's committee of the whole voted 31 to 28 on July 25 to adopt the Constitution with explanatory and recommendatory (but not conditional) amendments, including a bill of rights, Schuyler was satisfied that final ratification would follow. His instincts were confirmed the next day when the convention voted to ratify by a vote of 30 to 27. "Thus perseverance, patience and abilities have prevailed against numbers and prejudice"—the very qualities that much of his own life exemplified.[11]

The First Federal Elections

On August 8, 1788, as Albany celebrated the ratification with a procession, refreshments, and toasts, Philip Schuyler, on horseback, carried the Constitution fastened to a staff, following a body of light-horse and musicians. As the city's ranking citizen, it was fitting that he should do so, accompanied by another of his sons-in-law, Stephen Van Rensselaer, the "last patroon," who guided an "elegant plough" followed by farmers, brewers, printers, and other craftsmen and tradesmen.[12] Less pleasurable was the wrangle that arose in the New York legislature between December 11, 1788 and March 3, 1789 over the selection of presidential electors and United States senators.

At the outset, the state senate battled over an answer to Governor Clinton's opening address. Schuyler, voting with the majority, refused to support Clinton's proposal that "the exercise of different powers would be suspended until" the Constitution was further revised "by a General Convention of the States."[13] By votes of 10 to 8, Schuyler won senate approval for legislative procedures to choose the state's senators and presidential electors. In both instances, he proposed that each house nominate these officers. If their choices agreed, the nominees would be elected. If not, each house would choose one of the nominees of the other house for the Senate; and in the case of the eight presidential electors, each would choose four of the other's nominees. However, Clintonians in the assembly, wanting a joint ballot in the case of disagreements, so effectively thwarted these schemes that New York was unable to cast votes in the first presidential elections or to select its senators in time for the opening of the first Congress. Fortunately, there was no such disagreement to delay the popular election of New York's members of the federal House of Representatives.

Although Federalists failed to unseat the Clintonians in the state's April 1789 elections, their own control of the state senate enabled them to block assembly objections to their election bill. Earlier, in February, the assembly also rejected Schuyler's senate bill whereby each house might choose half of New York's presidential electors. His attempt to mollify the Clintonian assembly also failed. Although the senate approved an assembly resolution requesting Congress to call another convention to amend the Constitution, the election issue remained deadlocked, and on March 3, the legislature adjourned to the first Tuesday of January 1790, unless called sooner by the governor.

Finally, Governor Clinton did summon the legislature into special session to select senators. Meeting during July 6–16, 1789, the first selection proposal was vetoed by the Council of Revision. The council ruled that the procedure calling on each house to select one senator from the other's nominees would violate the constitutional requirement that *both* houses act together on both offices. Then, on July 15, 1789, the senate received the assembly's resolution that James Duane and Philip Schuyler be chosen senators. After a recess for suitable caucusing, Philip Livingston moved approval of the election of Duane, but John Williams tried to postpone the matter until the next morning. Williams proposed the standard Clintonian device whereby each house sitting separately should nominate two senators. If they failed to agree, they should then cast joint ballots, the larger number of assemblymen thereby being able to outvote the smaller number of senators. Schuyler and the senate rejected Williams's motion, 11 to 9. When the motion to elect Duane failed 10 to 9, John Vanderbilt moved approval of the assembly's resolution to elect Schuyler. That carried 13 to 6, thus clearing the way for another battle which revealed legislative divisions over the candidacy of Ezra L'Hommedieu and Rufus King.

A newcomer to New York from Massachusetts, King had only just been elected to the state assembly, and he was evidently considered to be more acceptable to Clintonians than was Ezra L'Hommedieu. Although the Senate rejected substituting King for L'Hommedieu, when it elected L'Hommedieu, 11 to 7, all "no" votes came from the men who had supported Schuyler; and all six senators who had voted against Schuyler voted in favor of L'Hommedieu. This result indicated that while Clintonian Antifederalists were more cohesive than their opponents, Federalists were united for Schuyler but divided on the candidacy of King and L'Hommedieu.

The assembly, however, rejected L'Hommedieu's candidacy and proposed Rufus King. Upon this, the senate voted 11 to 8 for King. Of those who favored King, nine had supported Schuyler, one was Schuyler himself, and one (Jacobus Swartwout) had opposed Schuyler. The eight who opposed King included three who favored Schuyler and five who had opposed him—an indication of both general partisanship and particular personal attractions and aversions. Together, Schuyler and King proved to be more harmonious in their views and votes than some of King's supporters may have expected. During Schuyler's two years in the Senate, he and King agreed eighty-four times in ninety-one roll-call votes. Together, they supported Hamilton's fiscal program which proved to be the single most important accomplishment of the Federalist Era.

Senator Schuyler

Schuyler served as a United States senator from July 1789 to March 1791. He drew a two-year term (the first Senate established staggered terms so that a third of its members would stand for election every two years) and then failed of reelection because partisan maneuvers supplanted him with Aaron Burr in 1791. Largely unnoticed and unheralded, his Senate record is nonetheless significant, for it demonstrates that great men and great deeds depend upon the support and involvement of others of only proportionately lesser rank in fame, activity, and ability.

The First Congress (1789–1791) was the most important in our history for its implementation of the Constitution through legislation and the establishment of precedents. As a senator, Schuyler participated in the establishment of executive departments, confirmation of Hamilton's appointment as secretary of the treasury, enactment of the secretary's fiscal program, passage of the Judiciary Act of 1789, and submission of the first amendments to the Constitution. In this latter case, he and Rufus King helped defeat the addition to the Second Amendment of a long-winded diatribe against standing armies—a reflection of his and other Federalists' belief in national defense, which prompted their opponents to accuse them of militarism.

In a variety of other business, Schuyler's influence was wielded with varying degrees of importance. Especially remarkable was his simultaneous service in both New York and United States Senates until March 1790, when the New York State Senate voted to exclude national officials from that body. First in significance was Schuyler's aid to Hamilton in developing and enacting a fiscal program. The secretary of the treasury's January 1790 report on the public credit was partly based on his father-in-law's "endless calculations," made to discover how to refinance the debt and make it manageable.[14] Together they successfully opposed James Madison's proposal to discriminate in favor of original holders of the debt, but Schuyler and others did disagree with the secretary who wanted to balance the assumed debt against national resources and so reduce the Confederation's promise of 6 percent interest on its certificates of indebtedness. Whereas others argued that 4 percent was sufficient, Schuyler, Rufus King, and Robert Morris were opposed to any reduction of interest lest the national honor be compromised. In the end, Hamilton persuaded them to accept three kinds of interest-bearing certificates: 6 percent certificates on the principal of the debt, 3 percent certificates on the arrears of interest thereon, and 6 percent certificates which would bear no interest for the first ten years. However, Schuyler won his point inasmuch as it was calculated that, with the appreciation of certificates, the overall interest would amount to 6 percent for the entire funding.

In other instances, crusty William Maclay of Pennsylvania testified to Schuyler's considerable influence on behalf of Hamilton's program. In March 1790, for example, Maclay complained of an appropriations bill because it lacked particulars. Schuyler and Robert Morris, he said, called for the third and last reading of the bill as soon as it had passed a second reading, "for they said the Secretary wanted to make remittances to Europe. They got what they wanted. . . ." Another instance involved delaying passage of the bill to relocate the federal capital and legalize President Washington's choice of the capital site after he had exceeded statutory requirements on boundaries. In this instance, Maclay acidly but aptly averred that "Schuyler is the supple-jack of his son-in-law Hamilton."[15] Hamiltonian supporters like Schuyler postponed the bill, obliging Washington to approve chartering the First Bank of the United States *before* they would pass the capital measure—an effective power-play that countered Jefferson's and Madison's connivance with the president to demand legalization of his boundary action by threatening to veto the bank bill.

In other action, Senator Schuyler supported Federalist policy. He favored taxation such as the whiskey excise, the admission of Vermont as the fourteenth state (long a bone of contention with Governor George Clinton, who had hitherto blocked Schuyler's moves for New York concessions on land claims), the addition of another regiment to the United States Army for the protection of the frontiers, and a national militia law (which was not enacted until 1792).

Later Years

For most of the remainder of his life, Schuyler proved to be as active in state government as in national, battling the Antifederalists and Jeffersonian Republicans in the interest of building a stronger national republic. From 1792 to 1797 he again served in the New York State Senate, and led the work of two inland lock and navigation companies for improving river transportation with locks and segments of canals for the benefit of both the state and nation. Replaced by Aaron Burr as a United States senator, Schuyler enjoyed the revenge of supplanting Burr in 1797.

By 1804, when his beloved Hamilton was killed by their mutual foe, Schuyler was in decline, and few patriots of the Revolution were still in public service. "In a constellation so reduced, so thinly scattered," as his eulogist observed, "the extinction of a single star seems to create an immense void."[16] Few of his contemporaries could claim so long a record of dedicated service to the emerging republic or commitment to the cause of independence and the national interest.

NOTES:

[1] *The Albany Gazette*, Nov. 22, 26, 1804; *The Albany Register*, Nov. 23, 1804. New York State Library, Albany, N.Y.

[2] *New York State Senate Journal*, Sept. 23, 1780. New York State Library, Albany, N.Y.

[3] Jared Sparks, ed., *Correspondence of the American Revolution*. 4 vols. (Boston, 1853), 3: 212-214.

[4] Henry Van Schaack, *Memoirs of the Life of Henry Van Schaack* (Chicago, 1892), 152-153.

[5] *New York State Senate Journal*, July 22, 1782. New York State Library, Albany, N.Y.

[6] George Clinton to Dr. Tappen, Jan. 26, 1787. L.W. Smith Collection, Morristown National Historical Park.

[7] Henry C. Van Schaack, *Life of Peter Van Schaack* (New York, 1842), 151.

[8] William Kent, ed., *Memoirs and Letters of James Kent, LL.D.* (Boston, 1898), 278-331.

[9] Alexander Flick, ed., *History of the State of New York*. 10 vols. (New York, 1933-1937), 5: 55.

[10] Schuyler to John B. Schuyler, June 26, 1788 (copy from original by E.W. Schuyler). Union College Library, Schenectady, N.Y.

[11] Schuyler to Peter Van Schaack, July 25, 1788. New York State Library, Albany, N.Y.

[12]Cuyler Reynolds, comp., *Albany Chronicles: A History of the City Arranged Chronologically* (Albany, 1909), 372–373.

[13]*New York State Senate Journal*, Dec. 11, 1788. New York State Library, Albany, N.Y.

[14]Forrest McDonald, *Alexander Hamilton: A Biography* (New York, 1979), 160; cf. Harold C. Syrett *et al.*, eds., *The Papers of Alexander Hamilton*. 27 vols. (New York, 1961–1987), 6: 62.

[15]Charles A. Beard, ed., *The Journal of William MacLay, United States Senator from Pennsylvania, 1789–1791* (New York, 1927), 215–216, 390.

[16]*The Albany Gazette*, Nov. 26, 1804. New York State Library, Albany, N.Y.

For Further Reading

Don R. Gerlach, *Philip Schuyler and the American Revolution in New York, 1733–1777* (Lincoln: University of Nebraska Press, 1964).

_____ , *Proud Patriot: Philip Schuyler and War of Independence, 1775–1783* (Syracuse, N.Y.: Syracuse University Press, 1987).

_____ , *Twenty Years of the "Promotion of Literature"*: *The Regents of the University of the State of New York, 1784–1804* (Albany, N.Y.: State University of New York Press, 1974).

Forrest McDonald, *Alexander Hamilton: A Biography* (New York: W.W. Norton and Company, 1979).

Broadus Mitchell, *Alexander Hamilton: Youth to Maturity, 1755–1788* (New York: The Macmillan Co., 1957).

_____ , *Alexander Hamilton: The National Adventure, 1788–1804* (New York: The Macmillan Co., 1962).

Alfred F. Young, *The Democratic Republicans of New York: The Origins, 1763–1797* (Chapel Hill, N.C.: University of North Carolina Press, 1967).

Melancton Smith and the Articulation of New York Antifederalism
(1744-1798)

THOMAS SHEVORY
Ithaca College

Born to Samuel and Elizabeth Smith, on May 7, 1744, in Jamaica, New York, Melancton Smith was to become one of the most articulate spokesmen against the Constitution during the period of state ratification. Smith's background was both obscure and modest, but he was well educated at home by his parents. He was what we might today describe as a self-made man. He began working at a young age in a retail store in Poughkeepsie, and developed a reputation as an honest worker who was interested in ideas.[1]

Smith was one of ten delegates from Dutchess County elected to the first provincial congress in 1775. He organized and became captain of the first company of Rangers in Dutchess County; this unit received much favorable recognition for its ability to control Loyalists, of which New York seemed to have more than its fair share. On February 11, 1777, Smith was appointed to a three-person commission for "inquiring into, detecting and defeating all conspiracies . . . against the liberties of America." This was a powerful position which entitled Smith to oversee the administration of oaths and the interrogation and arrest of suspects. During this period, he also served as the sheriff of Dutchess County.[2]

Smith became a friend and political ally of George Clinton during the war and worked within the commissary department of the Continental government during the last years of the Revolution. He acquired considerable property during this period, but maintained a reputation as a man of great integrity. After the war, Washington appointed him to a commission to settle disputes between the army and its contractors. Smith, it is reported, "charged contractors with bad faith and in turn was charged with inducing soldiers to spend pay in his store."[3]

In 1785, he moved to New York City where he became a wealthy businessman and lawyer. He served in the Continental Congress from 1785 to 1788, where his most noteworthy contribution was his service on the committee which developed the final draft of the Northwest Ordinance of 1787. The ordinance was important for three reasons: It gave new states being formed in the territories status equal to that of the original thirteen; it provided that Indian land be bought on fair terms; and it prevented slavery from being established in the new states.[4] Smith's objections to slavery were again made clear during the debates in New York on the new Constitution.

The Poughkeepsie Convention

The signing of the Constitution in Philadelphia on September 17, 1787 was only the first step in the long process of ratification. Final acceptance by the thirteen very independent states was far from assured. When the Continental Congress met on September 28 to consider recommending the document to the states, Smith unsuccessfully objected on the grounds that there was no bill of rights.[5] In 1788 Smith was guaranteed a role in the next stage of the process; he was elected a delegate to the New York ratifying convention, held in Poughkeepsie, to represent Dutchess County as an Antifederalist.[6]

The Antifederalists in New York were followers of Governor George Clinton. Clinton, according to John Fiske, "preferred to remain the most powerful citizen of New York, rather than occupy a subordinate place under a national government in which his own State was not foremost."[7] The Clintonians' principal tactic was to stall a vote on ratification. They hoped that enough states would reject the Constitution so that a vote in New York would be made superfluous.

The New York ratifying convention met from June 17 to July 26. Unfortunately for the Clintonians, New Hampshire became the ninth state to ratify on June 21; and, on July 2, word came that Virginia had approved the new document as well. This did not, however, deter the Antifederalists from their attempts to prevent ratification. Clinton said very little during the Poughkeepsie meeting. According to one source, "he sat quietly in his place and was a force for moderation." He told the Federalists, "I am open to conviction."[8] Forrest McDonald reveals a less laudable picture. According to him, the Clintonians followed the faction's usual practice of "debating endlessly on petty matters," while on important issues "they became silent and voted as a bloc."[9]

In fact, at the convention there were a number of articulate spokesmen against the document. Melancton Smith was certainly the premier Antifederalist advocate. He became involved in a series of exchanges with Alexander Hamilton who, in spite of his disapproval of much of the Constitution during the Philadelphia Convention, became one of its strongest and most outspoken supporters. Hamilton carried many of his arguments from his contributions to *The Federalist* to the convention floor. Thus, the debate between Hamilton and Smith can be seen as a further defense by Hamilton of his arguments in those essays.

Smith *versus* Hamilton

Smith gave five speeches at the Poughkeepsie meeting from June 20 to June 27. He spent much of his time criticizing the method of apportionment in the House of Representatives. He also had objections to the scheme for organizing the Senate. Finally, he objected to the proposal for giving the national government power to tax. Smith's arguments are worth examining in some detail, not only because of their historical value, but because they still have relevance to arguments regarding the democratic character of our national legislative institutions.

The Federalist papers are now justly considered among the finest works of American political thought. The genius of those works is often considered to lie in the ability of their authors to place American constitutional arguments in the broad contexts of Western thought and history. Melancton Smith was not charmed by this style of argumentation, however. He opened his attack upon the Federalist cause by questioning Hamilton's historical and philosophical references. For example, Hamilton referred in writing and speeches to the decline of the Greek city states, which he attributed to their character as confederacies. "It was true," admitted Smith, "that the ancient confederated Republics were all destroyed," but, he continued, "so were those which were not confederated; and all ancient Governments of every form had shared the same fate."[10] Smith also objected to Hamilton's references to Montesquieu. While Montesquieu indeed defended federal systems, he defended confederated ones as well, giving "his opinion, that a confederated Republic has all the internal advantages of a Republic, with the external force of a Monarchical Government."[11]

More was at stake for Smith than particular historical examples or citations. Smith objected to Hamilton's approach to argumentation. One, he implied, could argue continuously about historical antecedents and philosophical references and never reach a conclusion. Or, as Smith put it, "We may wander . . . in the fields of fancy without end, and gather flowers as we go: It may be entertaining—but it is of little service to the discovery of truth."[12] Smith expressed a very American impatience with philosophical disputation. To judge the issues adequately, he asserted, one must attend to an examination of the institutions that the document creates.

The House

Smith's first objection had to do with what he considered as the "injustice" engendered by the three-fifths compromise regarding slaves. Not only was it, he felt, "absurd" to give representation to someone who could never exercise the franchise, but he was alarmed that it gave increased representation, and hence political power, "to those people who were so wicked as to keep slaves."[13] But Smith made these observations while admitting that the compromise was the result of political accommodation, and perhaps even necessary if union with the South was to be had. Still, he clearly did not like it.

Smith's next reservations focused on the size of the proposed House. The wording of Article I was such, argued Smith, that its provisions demanded that representatives be apportioned according to population, that each state be alloted at least one, and that there should never be more than one representative per 30,000 population. This left open the possibility, he argued, that the legislature could reduce its own size, since this was to be a legislative determination, not a constitutional one (except for the first legislature, where actual numbers are specified according to state).[14] Hamilton answered Smith's speech, arguing that a "true and genuine" construction of the Constitution's wording prevented the legislature from arbitrarily lowering the number of representatives.[15] Smith probably had the more accurate reading, although his fears may seem unfounded in retrospect.

From the perspective of political theory, the second part of Smith's argument about size is more interesting. He and Hamilton differed on the relationship between the size of a representative body and its capacity to govern fairly and honestly. Smith took the position that the House, as constituted, with sixty-five members, was not of an adequate size to give representation to the diverse interests within a large country, or, in Smith's words, "it would be incompetent to the great purposes of representation . . . [A] government which is directed by the will of any one or a few, or any number less than is the will of the community, is a government of slaves."[16]

Smith's desire to see the number of representatives increased is an expression of his democratic beliefs. He considered direct democracy as an ideal form, which would be perverted to greater degrees as one collapsed the size of the representative body in proportion to the population. Thus, Smith, like other Antifederalists, considered state governments as more representative and more democratic and feared the powers and potential for corruption of the national legislature, which would have fewer members apportioned to the represented population than the state legislatures, and would therefore be less connected to the people.

Hamilton, in his June 21 speech, expressed little sympathy with this argument. He would not admit that direct democracy was ever an ideal form, stating, "The ancient democracies, in which the people themselves deliberated, never possessed one feature of good government. Their very character was tyranny. [They] presented . . . an ungovernable mob."[17] And whereas Smith argued that full representation was necessary to obtain the "confidence of the people," Hamilton responded that, "The confidence of the people will be easily gained by a good administration."[18] These arguments, which pit democratic rule against stability and the "rationality of administration," are still highly relevant to American political discourse.

In his second speech, which he made on June 21, Smith argued that in larger districts, the wealthy, those whom he referred to disparagingly as the "natural aristocracy," would tend to be elected, while those of the "middling classes" would tend to be excluded. In larger districts, Smith suggested, the middle class would be divided by interests, so that "none but the great" would be chosen, unless the middle classes would be united behind a demagogue, who would be "destitute of principle."[19]

While some, like Hamilton, might have considered selection of the "great and wealthy" a desirable outcome, Smith did not. Those of lesser circumstance, he argued, "are inclined by habit and the company with whom they associate, to set bounds to their passions and appetites." Moreover, they must work at their "respective callings," and hence do not have the luxury of being intemperate. Finally, he said, they know the value of money, since they must work for it, and therefore would not be inclined to increase the burden of taxation on their fellow citizens. The wealthy, on the other hand, "Being in the habit of profuse living . . . will be profuse in the public expense."[20] Hamilton, in response, denied that the wealthy have less virtue than the poor. "Their vices," he said, "are probably more favorable to the prosperity of the state, than those of the indigent and partake less of moral depravity."[21]

A resolution, submitted by Smith, which called for lowering the apportionment ratio to one representative per 20,000 population, was defeated by the convention delegates.

The Senate

On June 24, George Livingston proposed a resolution which provided that senators be able to serve for only one six-year term in a twelve-year period and provided for the possibility of recall by state legislatures. Melancton Smith spoke in favor of this resolution on June 25.

Smith argued that, without some system of mandatory rotation, the Senate would become a "perpetual" body, and that this would be destructive to "established principles of republicanism." Providing for rotation of officers would, on the other hand, "place the senate in the proper medium between a fluctuating, and a perpetual body." Such a perpetual body, Smith argued, would lose its connections to the people. Rotation would require senators to return home where they would enlighten the people and be enlightened by them.

To the argument, frequently made against systems of rotation, that they infringe upon the rights of people to choose their own representatives, Smith responded, "What is government itself, but a restraint upon the natural rights of people? What constitution was ever devised, that did not operate as a restraint on their original liberties?"[22] Smith here expressed the still vital tension in American democratic thinking between the rights of the people to govern themselves, and the constitutional restraints that confine those rights. In doing so, he had shifted his emphasis from the rhetoric of populist democracy to that of natural rights liberalism.

Smith also argued in favor of recall. Interestingly, he never spoke against the system of selecting senators through the state legislatures rather than by direct vote. In fact, he seemed to accept, at this point in the debate, Hamiltonian arguments regarding the inability of the multitude to restrain itself. "I know," Smith stated, "that the impulses of the multitude are inconsistent with systematic government. The people are frequently incompetent to deliberate discussion, and subject to errors and imprudencies."[23] Smith was apparently most interested in voicing his concerns about the continued legitimacy of state governments. Like other Antifederalists, he was concerned that the states' governing authority would be usurped entirely by the new charter. Like other Antifederalists, he had a pronounced tendency to envision states as the shields for liberty and democratic rule. He therefore understood recall as a method of defending the power of state institutions, and, by implication, the rights of the people. Whether or not states are better able to facilitate expressions of democratic rule than national legislative bodies is by no means a settled argument in American political life. But there is little doubt that Smith was correct when he asserted that the institution of a national legislature would tend to diminish the power and prestige of state legislative authorities.

Hamilton argued that recall was unnecessary because the legislature could easily communicate a "spirit of resistance" against corrupt senators which would be a "powerful check to misconduct."[24] To this Smith replied, "This kind of check, I contend, would be a pernicious one; and certainly ought to be prevented. Checks in government ought to act silently, and without public commotion."[25] Ironically, Hamilton, the great Federalist, is here chided by Smith, the populist democrat, for encouraging checks by a form of popular insurrection.

The Power to Tax

The convention took up Article I, section 8 dealing with Congress's powers on June 26. John Williams proposed that Congress be given the power to lay taxes only if requisitions on the states were insufficient. The taxing power was considered as extraordinarily important by friends of the Constitution, especially as they recalled the inadequacies of the requisitioning system to support a regular army during the revolutionary conflict.

Smith argued in defense of the states, asserting that the requisitioning system has "perhaps been too much condemned." If neither the national nor state governments had constitutional restraints on their taxing authority, this would lead to conflicts, a "constant jarring of claims and interests." Ultimately, this would work to the disadvantage of state governments, Smith asserted, and would result in the abolition of state governments entirely.[26] Why the state governments would be held more accountable than the national governments for high taxation is not entirely clear from Smith's speech, nor has the assertion been born out by history. This last speech would have to be considered as his weakest, when evaluated as a prediction of future political development.

Conclusion

It is noteworthy that Melancton Smith, a New York City lawyer and mercantilist, should take up the standard of the Antifederalist. He is a remarkable counterexample to Charles Beard's thesis that those with business interests were among the strongest supporters of the new Constitution, because of its potentially stabilizing effects upon the economy.[27] Smith's modest origins may have encouraged him to identify with the common man more closely than the "natural aristocracy," although it is often true that the self-made man identifies with the class into whose membership he has fought such a hard battle for admittance. Smith's upstate roots may have encouraged him to identify with the Antifederalists. The particulars of Beard's thesis may be wrong, at least in New York, where mercantilists had an economic interest in maintaining their state's power and autonomy under the Articles. Smith's arguments do not seem consistently democratic. He was interested in maintaining state prerogatives. On the other hand, we have no reason to doubt the authenticity of his democratic idealism, especially with regard to his abhorrence of slavery.

In any event, the Antifederalist cause failed in New York. After losing a battle to have the document accepted only with the provision that a bill of rights be added, Smith himself voted in favor of it. "He must have been a man of rare candour," Fiske wrote, "for after weeks of debate he owned himself convinced."[28] McDonald's appraisal, however, is less laudatory. With the possibility of secession a very real threat by the New York City Federalists, the Clintonians realized that they were defeated, McDonald contends. They met in caucus on July 25 to determine who amongst them would vote for ratification, and allow the Constitution to pass by only as narrow a margin as was absolutely necessary. Smith was chosen, along with loyal Clintonian Samuel Jones, because of his residence in a southern county, "and in the event of a rising tide of Federalism in their areas their political careers would be protected by votes for the Constitution."[29]

Smith continued his political attachment to George Clinton as well as his criticisms of the Constitution. He helped to sponsor an unsuccessful movement to call a new constitutional convention in 1789. He was elected to the state legislature in 1791. An early victim of New York's yellow fever epidemic, he died on July 29, 1798.

NOTES:
[1]Dumas Malone, ed., *The Dictionary of American Biography* (New York: Charles Scribner's Sons, 1935), 17: 319. [hereafter, *DAB*.]

[2]*DAB*, 17: 320.

[3]*Ibid.*

[4]See Jay A. Barrett, *Evolution of the Ordinance of 1787* (New York: G.P. Putnam's Sons, 1891; reprinted, New York: Arno Press, 1971), esp. 49–73.

[5]David Ellis, *A History of New York State*, rev. ed. (Ithaca, N.Y.: Cornell University Press, 1967), 124.

[6]*DAB*, 17: 320.

[7]John Fiske, *Essays Historical and Literary* (New York: Macmillan, 1932), 1: 118.

[8]Ellis, 125.

[9]Forrest McDonald, *We the People: The Economic Origins of the Constitution* (Chicago: The University of Chicago Press, 1958), 287.

[10]Herbert J. Storing, ed., *The Complete Anti-Federalist* (Chicago, University of Chicago Press, 1981), 6: 151. [hereafter Storing.]

[12]*Ibid.*

[13]*Ibid.*, 6: 153.

[14]*Ibid.*

[15]Harold C. Syrett, ed., *The Papers of Alexander Hamilton*, 27 vols. (New York, Columbia University Press, 1961-1987), 5: 25. [Hereafter, *Hamilton*.]

[16]Smith, in Storing, 6: 153.

[17]*Hamilton*, 5:39.

[18]*Ibid.*

[19]Smith, in Storing, 6: 158.

[20]*Ibid.*, 6: 159.

[21]*Hamilton*, 5:43.

[22]Smith, in Storing, 6: 165.

[23]*Ibid.*, 6: 166.

[24]*Hamilton*, 5:57.

[25]Smith, in Storing, 6: 167.

[26]*Ibid.*, 6: 170, 171.

[27]Charles A. Beard, *An Economic Interpretation of the Constitution of the United States* (New York: Macmillan Company, 1935).

[28]Fiske, 1: 125.

[29]McDonald, 288.

Robert Yates, Antifederalist

1738–1801

THOMAS E. BURKE
New York State Bicentennial Commission

Robert Yates, a Revolutionary Patriot, jurist, and important Antifederalist critic of the Constitution, was born in 1738 in Schenectady, New York, the son of Joseph and Maria Yates. After receiving a good eduction in New York City, and reading law with William Livingston (later governor of New Jersey), Yates was admitted to the bar on May 9, 1760, at Albany, which remained his residence for the rest of his life. Yates was active in the city as an attorney, surveyor, and political leader. He served for four years (1771–1775) on the board of aldermen. In 1790 he resided in the city's first ward. His household included not only family members, but also two slaves.

In 1766, Yates was present at the first gathering of the Albany Sons of Liberty. During the period of controversy before the Revolution, he was a member of the Albany committee of safety. In 1776 and after, Yates also was a member of the provincial congress and served on the secret committee to obstruct the channel of the Hudson, the committee on arrangements for the Continental regiments, and the important Committee of Thirteen which drafted the first constitution of the state.

Before the new state government was established Yates was appointed, May 8, 1777, a justice of the New York supreme court. During the 1780s, Yates became a recognized leader of the Antifederalists. He was a supporter of Governor George Clinton and, with Clinton, opposed such concessions to the federal Congress as the right to collect impost duties. In 1787, he was appointed with his fellow Antifederalist, John Lansing, Jr., and the Federalist, Alexander Hamilton, to represent New York in the Philadelphia Convention. Yates, with his colleague, Lansing, left the Convention on July 10 on the ground that the Convention, which had been called to revise the Articles of Confederation, was exceeding its powers in attempting to write a new instrument of government. Yates also worried that the consolidation of the states under a national government would impair the sovereignty of New York. After the publication of the federal Constitution, Yates attacked it during the winter in a series of letters signed "Brutus."

More than a decade earlier, during the winter of 1774–1775, Yates had devised his own plan of union, which only recently was discovered among the Yates Papers in the New York State Library, Albany. The unfinished draft ends in the middle of a discussion of qualifications for members of a continental "Council." A large left margin for comments and corrections suggests that it was intended for circulation among Yates's Patriot friends on the Committee of Correspondence. Yates's analysis varies in quality—at times superficial, at others, perceptive.

On the whole, it is a conservative document that occasionally reaches toward the constitutional innovations of the next two decades. Yates was caught up in the current of events and the rapid transition of American constitutional thought. Though he lapsed occasionally into the traditional immutable categories of government—monarchy, aristocracy, and democracy—he also appreciated the "functional" nature of checks and balances and anticipated portions of the debate of 1787. The second major section of his plan dealt with the general subject of imperial reorganization. The subject had long been discussed in New York, and Yates was presumably acquainted with the resulting plans of union. His use of the terms "President," "Council," and "Diet" suggests that he was familiar with Benjamin Franklin's 1754 proposal to the Albany Congress.

However, a plan composed in 1765 by William Smith, Jr., may have had an even greater effect on Yates. Yates had read law under the tutelage of William Livingston in New York City and was familiar with Livingston's acquaintances, including Smith. A requisition system of colonial self-taxation appears in both Smith's 1765 document and Yates's plan nine years later. Also, Smith's proposals for a "Lord Lieutenant," Council, and Assembly more closely resembled Yates's than did Franklin's.

In the midst of the final crisis before the Revolution, Joseph Galloway of Philadelphia raised the subject of union. At the First Continental Congress, Galloway incorporated ideas from the Albany Plan of his old ally, Franklin, into a proposal for reconciliation with Britain. Galloway's ideas may have spurred Yates into writing.

Throughout the draft, and especially in the third section, Yates showed his concern that English common law not be abandoned. Yates demanded that the laws of England be received by his proposed "Diet." His unique contribution was to give a proto-federalist form to the reception of English law by the continental government. Certain legal spheres would be reserved to the separate colonial governments. A number of commercial and intercolonial areas of the law were to be the exclusive preserve of the "Diet"—in effect, enumerated powers. Finally, there were legal actions which might be exercised jointly—that is, concurrently—by the colonial legislatures and the continental government.

Throughout the plan, Yates remained loyal to the empire, and to the moral authority of royal government. He assigned appointive powers to the Crown. It is important to note, however, that Yates's conservatism was not inconsistent with the conservative political stance of other leading New York Patriots. James Duane, John Jay, and Gouverneur Morris were as convinced as Yates that the crisis could be averted by sound, conservative constitutional revision.

Finally, Yates's plan may be viewed as a clue to its author's later Antifederalism. He was a consistent opponent of national consolidation. He opposed the Virginia Plan at the Constitutional Convention of 1787 and worked against ratification of the Constitution in New York. While in Philadelphia, he kept a secret journal of the debates for private circulation for much the same purpose as he probably began the plan of union. His preference for a confederated system can be traced back to his concern for the legal rights of localities, fully documented in his plan of union over a decade earlier.

After the New York ratifying convention's vote to adopt the Constitution on July 26, 1788, the ranks of the former Antifederalist majority began to crumble. In 1789, Yates emerged as the Federalist candidate for governor of New York against the popular Antifederalist incumbent, and his former leader, George Clinton. The Yates forces encompassed both ardent Federalists such as Alexander Hamilton and moderate Antifederalists such as Aaron Burr. Despite Yates's ability to build a coalition under his leadership, Clinton easily defeated him.

Yates continued as a state judge and a member of the state's council of revision. He died quietly in 1801. Twenty years after his death, his Antifederal colleague John Lansing, Jr., now the state's chancellor, saw into print an edition of Yates's notes of debates in the Constitutional Convention of 1787. The *Secret Proceedings . . .* has long been regarded as a valuable corrective to the more detailed and comprehensive notes kept by James Madison, but in the 1980s James H. Hutson of the Library of Congress demonstrated, based on his discovery of two pages of Lansing's verbatim transcript of the lost Yates manuscript, that the published version of Yates's notes was ruthlessly edited by Edmond Genet to turn the *Secret Proceedings* . . . into an anti-Madison tract.

For Further Reading

Yates's plan has been printed in the *William and Mary Quarterly*, 3d ser., 34 (1977): 298–306.

IV. New York's Contributions to American Constitutional Development

Susan B. Anthony

(1820–1906)

M. Jill DuPont

A lifelong commitment to the advancement of women's rights pro-
pelled the career of Susan B. Anthony. Until well into her eighth
decade, this New Yorker adopted, organized, and implemented a
ceaseless national campaign on behalf of woman suffrage. She
and her associates accomplished significant legislative reforms, and
their pioneering work led eventually to the adoption of the Nine-
teenth Amendment.

"**I** love to make history but hate to write it,"[1] Susan Brownell Anthony once proclaimed, yet despite her well-known aversion to the pen, she was the author of many of the most significant reforms achieved by women. Anthony was born on February 15, 1820, in Adams, Massachusetts, the product of a mixed marriage between Baptist Lucy Read and Quaker Daniel Anthony. As a child, Susan possessed both intelligence and ambition, qualities which her father nurtured with private tutoring in addition to village schooling. At seventeen, Anthony attended the Friends Boarding School in Philadelphia; her stay there was shortened due to the Panic of 1837. Forced to auction his cotton mill and homestead, Daniel Anthony purchased a small tract of farmland and settled near Rochester, New York. Susan withdrew from school and took a teaching position in Easton; within two years, she became principal of a nearby boarding school.

In 1846, Anthony became head of the Female Department of the Canajoharie, New York, Academy. While there, she joined the Society of the Daughters of Temperance, thus beginning her public career of reform. At the time, temperance was one of the few acceptable public causes in which women participated, in part because male insobriety threatened the domestic security of women as wives, mothers, and daughters. As a child, Anthony had professed a detestation for both intemperance and slavery, views which were shaped and encouraged by her liberal father. More than any single person in her youth and early adulthood, Daniel Anthony was the pivotal figure in Susan's life. He urged her to be self-sufficient and to employ her energetic intellect in causes which promoted human betterment. When the first Woman's Rights Convention was held in Seneca Falls in 1848, Susan observed the proceedings with detached interest from her post at the Academy. She later discovered that her parents and sister had attended the convention and signed the "Declaration of Sentiments" demanding equal rights for women. When Anthony left school in 1849, disenchanted with teaching, she returned home and "heard nothing but suffrage talk" from her sister, Mary.[2]

Anthony and Stanton

Though Anthony remained ambivalent in her support of woman's suffrage, her return home generated interest in the antislavery crusade. Upstate New York, particularly Rochester, was not only becoming a locus for suffrage sentiment, but already boasted an established antislavery community. Daniel Anthony introduced Susan to abolitionist Frederick Douglass, a meeting which developed into a lifelong—and at times embattled—friendship between the two activists. In 1850 and 1851, the Anthony homestead became a favorite gathering place for men and women immersed in temperance and antislavery work, and it was here that Susan first met William Lloyd Garrison. Anthony attended the Anti-Slavery Anniversary held in Syracuse in 1851, and while there she met Elizabeth Cady Stanton, the preeminent women's rights activist of the time.

Stanton recalled that she liked Anthony "thoroughly from the beginning."[3] More important, it was Stanton who brought Anthony into the women's rights movement with her lucid argument on the centrality of the ballot in the women's fight for independence and first-class citizenship. Anthony had remained uncommitted to women's rights because she was uncertain that suffrage was the key issue for women. Anthony believed that economic independence would create expanded opportunities for the rights of women, fostering a "self-respect which shall scorn to eat the bread of dependence."[4] Stanton convinced Anthony that the ballot would inject the voice of women into governmental and public affairs by rendering them citizens first and women second, paving the way for their advancement in other spheres. Only recently had changes in the property laws of New York entitled married women to hold real estate in their own name. Such legislation would progress piecemeal unless women gained this basic right within a republican government. After attending a Woman's Rights Convention in Syracuse in 1852, Anthony never wavered in her conviction that the right women needed above all others was suffrage.

Stanton and Anthony soon formed an alliance, frequently stormy, that was to last more than fifty years. "We were at once fast friends, in thought and sympathy we were one, and in the division of labor we exactly complemented each other. In writing we did better work together than either could alone," Stanton observed.[5] Stanton articulated philosophical, rhetorical, and theoretical arguments through her talented pen, while Anthony provided the critical thinking, analysis, facts, and statistics which sharpened and refined Stanton's discourse. Their relationship was solidified during the 1850s and 1860s, when they worked to reform legislation regarding divorce, the condition of working women, and suffrage.

Suffragists vs. Abolitionists

In 1852, Anthony served as a delegate to the state Sons of Temperance meeting in Albany. Outraged because she was denied a right to speak because of her sex, Anthony organized a Woman's State Temperance Convention which spawned the Woman's Society at Rochester. This experience demonstrated Anthony's proficient skills as an organizer, encompassing tasks which go largely unrecognized but are indispensable if a movement or organization is to have any success. Her administrative ability—planning and advertising meetings, arranging for halls, and soliciting funds, among other tasks—led to her appointment as the New York agent of the American Anti-Slavery Society in 1856. Reverend Samuel J. May noted that success in New York would depend "more on your personal attendance and direction than upon that of other of our workers."[6] For Anthony, the antislavery cause represented the "brains and conscience" of the reform period, all the more important because it was a movement in which both men and women participated.[7] Moreover, women often likened their own subordinate status to that of blacks, and thus sought to equate the two causes.

The cooperative relationship which existed between reformers working for the cause of blacks and the rights of women was strained, and finally severed, in the years immediately following the abolition of slavery. Advocates for both perceived Reconstruction as the most opportune time for realizing the stated principles of the Declaration of Independence and the Constitution by extending the guarantees of citizenship to those currently without a voice in the political process. It soon became clear to Anthony, Stanton, and others calling for woman suffrage that the energies of Republicans and abolitionists were singularly devoted to securing citizenship and the franchise for blacks. Politicians insisted that only one of the causes, each controversial, could be successfully advanced in Congress at this time rather than both, for "if put on the same level and urged in the same connection neither will be soon accomplished."[8] The antislavery men with whom Anthony had labored so diligently in working for the destruction of slavery, now beseeched her to subsume her goals once again, as this was "the negro's hour."[9]

"I will cut off this right arm of mine before I will work for or demand the ballot for the negro and not the woman," Anthony protested, adding, "The old anti-slavery school says women must stand back and wait until the negroes shall be recognized. But we say, if you will not give the whole loaf of suffrage to the entire people, give it to the most intelligent first."[10] Anthony's comments—and the disparaging, racist rhetoric of other woman leaders—drove a wedge between woman's suffrage leaders and those striving for black enfranchisement. Frederick Douglass—among many—was unsparingly critical of Anthony, noting that "to women the ballot is desirable; to the Negro, it is a matter of life and death."[11] Anthony did not oppose the enfranchisement of blacks, but rather resisted the idea that one cause had to take precedence over the other. Several of Anthony's statements, while undeniably racist in tone, can be more accurately ascribed to her growing frustration rather than prejudice, as she, along with other suffragists, feared their quest for the franchise would be indefinitely postponed, leaving women in their own state of bondage. "Disfranchisement *in a republic* is as great an anomaly, if not cruelty, as slavery itself," Anthony observed with finality.[12]

The Fourteenth Amendment, ratified on July 20, 1868, defined citizenship in such a way as to include blacks and reverse the *Dred Scott* decision of 1857, which declared that Afro-Americans had no claims to citizenship. Woman suffrage leaders objected to Section 2 of the Amendment, which allowed for a reduction of congressional representation for any state abridging the right of *men* to vote. Though Anthony and Stanton later petitioned for the inclusion of "sex" into the proposed Fifteenth Amendment, the version ratified in 1870 asserted that the right to vote could not be denied or abridged only on account of "race, color, or previous condition of servitude."

New Strategies

The setbacks suffered by women in the framing of the Fourteenth and Fifteenth Amendments provided the context for a new direction within the suffrage movement. The two amendments proved to Anthony and other leaders that the Constitution could be made accessible to a previously disfranchised class. Rather than linking their cause to that of blacks, as a result of these amendments, women formed a truly independent and diversified suffrage movement. In 1869, the movement broke into two wings embodying distinct but complementary strategies. Anthony and Stanton formed the National Woman Suffrage Association, which would direct its appeal to Congress for an amendment securing the right to vote against discrimination based on sex. The American Woman Suffrage Association would take its suffrage campaign to the voters of each state and strive to repeat the success of the Wyoming Territory, which approved woman suffrage in that same year, 1869. In addition, in 1868, Anthony had become the publisher and business manager and Stanton the co-editor of *The Revolution*, a feminist paper which served as a vehicle for women to present their claims—primarily suffrage—to the populace, and mobilized the formation of other suffrage papers and organizations throughout the country. This project further alienated abolitionists, who objected to Stanton's and Anthony's enlistment of financial backing from George Francis Train, a despised Democrat who was most visible among a bloc of party members attempting to circumvent black enfranchisement through their endorsement of woman suffrage.

Suffrage leaders also looked more closely at the provisions of the Fourteenth Amendment. Women born or naturalized within the United States were clearly citizens as defined by the first clause of the amendment, and their rights were protected by the second clause which assured that "no state shall make or enforce any law which shall abridge the privileges or immunities of citizens of the United States." Though these "privileges and immunities" were not defined, suffrage leaders believed that the right to vote was a natural right belonging to citizens within a republican government, and thus initiated efforts to test the Constitution through individual attempts at voting.

Anthony became involved in one such test case when she, along with fourteen others, was arrested in Rochester for illegally registering for, and voting in, the November 5, 1872, national election. Anthony and her fellow defendants were examined by officials in the same room in which fugitive slaves were questioned and remanded to their owners in years past. The women were charged with violating Section 19 of the Enforcement Act of the Fourteenth Amendment. They were released on bail until their trial the following spring. Anthony seized this opportunity to speak throughout Monroe County on issues of equal rights, universal suffrage, and constitutional interpretation. She cast her ballot yet again in Rochester's city elections of March 4, 1873, while awaiting trial. Anthony was not accorded the same respectful hearing in Canandaigua's U.S. District Court on June 17 and 18, however. Presiding Judge Ward Hunt, who owed his position to state Republican boss Roscoe Conkling and later served on the U.S. Supreme Court, instructed the jury to find Anthony guilty without deliberation on the trial's second day. Anthony's counsel, former Court of Appeals Judge Henry R. Selden of Rochester, moved for a new trial. The motion was denied. Having witnessed such a blatant violation of her rights, Anthony subsequently used the courtroom as a forum to enumerate the contradictions of constitutional interpretation.

Noting that women were counted in the apportionment of representation and not exempt from taxation as wage earners and property holders, Anthony contended: "Your denial of my citizen's right to vote is the denial of my right of consent as one of the governed, the denial of my right of representation as one of the taxed, the denial of my right to a trial by a jury of my peers as an offender against the law . . ."[13]

Anthony was tried, she observed, by "forms of law all made by men, interpreted by men, administered by men, in favor of men, and against women . . .[14] Not one of her prosecutors, from the "corner grocery politician" who filed the complaint to Judge Hunt, was her peer, for as men possessing the right of suffrage, "each and all are my political sovereigns; and had your honor submitted my case to the jury, as was clearly your duty, even then I should have had just cause of protest, for not one of those men was my peer . . . each . . . was my political superior."[15]

Anthony refused to pay her fine of one hundred dollars, but assumed the legal expenses of, and obtained presidential pardons for, the three election inspectors who had allowed her to register. Hunt did not impose a prison sentence as was his option, for Anthony could have been released on writ of *habeas corpus* and then exercise her right of appeal. Hunt was roundly criticized in the press for his handling—of the trial—though not the verdict. Many editors expressed their concern for the future integrity of jury trials, while simultaneously questioning the leniency of Anthony's penalty. One explanation for Hunt's conduct may be found in the statement of an anonymous juror, who confided at the conclusion of the trial, "The verdict of guilty would not have been mine, could I have spoken, nor should I have been alone. There were others who thought as I did, but we could not speak."[16] In 1875, the Supreme Court held in *Minor v. Happersett* that the Fourteenth Amendment did not confer the right of suffrage upon women, nor did it guard against discrimination based on sex. Following the precedent established in the *Slaughterhouse Cases* of 1873, Chief Justice Morrison R. Waite asserted that the right of franchise was a privilege to be regulated by the individual states, not the national Constitution, effectively ceasing the flurry of test voting.

Anthony further expounded on the rights of women at the Centennial celebration held in Philadelphia in 1876, where, on opposite sides of Independence Hall, two clashing views issued forth on the state of the nation one hundred years after its inception. Anthony was the featured speaker and primary organizer of a large contingent of women gathered in Philadelphia for the purpose of plotting suffrage strategy and exposing the contradictions of the nation's hallowed Declaration of Independence. While affirming that the pivotal right of citizenship, suffrage, was still withheld from women, Anthony also emphasized—in an address bearing Stanton's influential hand—that other rights affecting the status and livelihood of women varied from state to state. In some states, women could possess both property and earnings in her own name; in others, both belonged to her husband. In the case of divorce, some states allowed women to testify in court and retain custody of their children, while other states did not. Finally, the equality of educational and occupational opportunities vastly differed among the various states. A constitutional amendment securing suffrage, Anthony maintained endlessly, in addition to a more liberal reading of the Fourteenth Amendment, would rectify many of these inconsistencies.

The "Anthony" Amendment

In 1878, the Susan B. Anthony Amendment was formally introduced in Congress as the proposed Sixteenth Amendment to the Constitution. Derived almost verbatim from the Fifteenth Amendment, it stated that "The right of citizens of the United States to vote shall not be denied or abridged by the United States or any State on account of sex." A similar amendment had first been introduced in Congress in 1869, with no results; the version submitted in 1878 was the product of a renewed commitment by the NWSA, inspired by the Centennial celebration and Anthony's relentless leadership. The proposed amendment bore her name primarily out of the respect accorded her by the youthful constituency of the NWSA. Anthony, not Stanton, was now considered the driving force behind the suffrage campaign. Stanton, disaffected with the conservatism and narrow vision of suffrage advocates, believed that political disfranchisement was merely a symptom, not the source, of the subjection of women. While Anthony shared the larger feminist concerns of Stanton, she remained convinced that suffrage was the issue which could lead to the resolution of other forms of discrimination. That the amendment of 1878 was not ratified until 1920, as the Nineteenth Amendment, indicates that the issue was equally complex for those devoted to bringing enfranchisement to fruition as well as those women embracing a broader feminist ideology.

Following the Civil War, almost until her death in 1906, Anthony devoted herself solely to the cause of suffrage. Beginning in 1868 and into the 1870s, Anthony attended the Republican and Democratic conventions in an effort to secure support for suffrage through party platforms. She urged each party to uphold its self-proclaimed historical reputation: the Republican party as the party of liberty, while Thomas Jefferson and the Democrats first propounded the theory of "no taxation without representation." With the emergence of the Populist Party in the 1890s, Anthony challenged Populists to adhere to their slogan of "equal rights to all." For the most part, Anthony was given a respectful hearing before the various state and national conventions, while at other times she endured catcalls maligning her appearance. No serious policy was ever adopted as a result of the resolutions she presented, and as long as there was not, Anthony insisted that women withhold their money, allegiance, and energy from political parties.

Anthony also appealed to educational, labor, religious, and philanthropic associations to broaden the movement's base. She wrote countless letters, delivered endless speeches, and organized numerous petition drives. As state organizations were created as offshoots of the NWSA, Anthony was frequently sought out to supervise and participate in the formation of the satellite societies. This was particularly true of the early 1870s, when she and Stanton canvassed several states considering a woman suffrage amendment within their own constitutions. As Anthony grew older, her prominence and esteem grew as well, her reputation alone affording Anthony and the movement a hearing before politicians or conventions. In 1894, at the age of seventy-four, Anthony stumped all sixty counties in New York on the issue of woman suffrage prior to the constitutional convention.

The endless stream of state amendment drives in which Anthony participated produced few victories. In addition to Wyoming, only Utah and Idaho had granted women full suffrage by 1896. Most states and territories gave women a restricted right to vote in school district elections. Anthony, Stanton, and other leaders increasingly looked to the idea of union among suffragists as a solution to the fragmented state of legislation and organizational approaches. Anthony was again the pivotal figure in forming the International Council of Women in 1888, a symbolic union devoted to promoting a sense of sisterhood and developing strategy for the achievement of equal rights for women in virtually all spheres of society in the United States and abroad. Furthermore, in 1890, the NWSA and AWSA united, with Stanton serving as president and Anthony as vice-president. AWSA leaders initially balked at the merger unless Anthony became president, feeling that Stanton was losing interest in the movement and would attract undue criticism because of her radical views of divorce and the Bible. Anthony refused to become embroiled in any political maneuvering, nor did she desire the presidency. Anthony had always willingly deferred to the leadership of Stanton in their organizational pursuits, as she considered Stanton the premier stateswoman and intellectual of the women's rights movement. When Stanton resigned the presidency in 1892, Anthony reluctantly assumed the paramount leadership role of the National American Woman Suffrage Association (NAWSA).

Historian and Publisher

Perhaps the most difficult period of Anthony's life occurred in 1895, when Stanton published Volume 1 of her *Woman's Bible*, a work which reinterpreted and commented upon passages of the Bible which were often used by secular leaders and clergy to sanction the subjection of women. Anthony never shared the stifling views of religion posited by Stanton, in part because of her liberal Quaker upbringing. Moreover, Anthony had frequently expressed her disdain for Stanton's project, and refused to be associated with it. Conservative NAWSA members demanded a political censure of Stanton, and Anthony now found herself in the difficult position of resolving the situation, maintaining her friendship, and retaining her political stature within the organization and movement.

In a statement which also reflected Anthony's dismay at the frequently expedient interpretations of the Constitution, she stated emphatically, "I distrust those people who know so well what God wants them to do, because I notice it always coincides with their own wishes."[17] Anthony further believed that a censure of Stanton would not only disparage the foremost leader of the movement, but set a bad precedent as well in restricting freedom of speech. "When our platform becomes too narrow for people of all creeds and of no creeds, I myself can not stand upon it," she added defiantly.[18] The censure was approved despite Anthony's impassioned objection, and served notice that a new leadership was emerging within the woman suffrage movement.

Anthony resigned the presidency in 1900 at the age of eighty, though her commitment to suffrage remained as fervent as ever. When Stanton's drive for suffrage began to languish among other feminist concerns, it was Anthony who kept this goal in focus for the membership. Her stature had continued to escalate each decade until she was considered the unchallenged leader of the movement in the 1890s. Anthony's resignation in no way signalled her abandonment of the cause to which she had devoted her life.

Anthony stated that she would devote her remaining years to two specific projects: establishing a fund which would be used to finance suffrage work, and finishing the multivolume *History of Woman Suffrage*. The movement had always been hampered by a lack of money, evidenced by the fact that Anthony usually contributed whatever earnings she procured to suffrage work. This shortage of funds affected the ongoing *History of Woman Suffrage*, begun in 1876 and, at the time, in its fourth volume. Anthony, Stanton, and Matilda Joslyn Gage had begun this body of work at Anthony's insistence, for she believed that there must exist, in the words of the participants themselves, an accurate record of the history and ideology of those who forwarded the movement so that it would provide inspiration to suffragists of the future. Anthony had preserved letters, speeches, resolutions, convention accounts, congressional reports, and newspaper clippings which formed the basis of the *History*, and it was Stanton—until her death in 1902—who gave voice to the history. Anthony singlehandedly published Volumes III and IV with her own personal funds, and was initiating work on a fifth volume with Ida Husted Harper when, after a steady decline in health over several years, she died on March 13, 1906.

"First Among the Warriors"

Even well before her death, Chicago *Tribune* editor Joseph Medill noted that Anthony "ranks first among the warriors" in the battle for suffrage, "because she has lived her life in its service and there has been no side issue to it."[19] Anthony rooted almost all of her arguments for woman suffrage in the stated and implicit rights guaranteed by the Constitution. She moved easily between the world of the intellectual and that of the working class, conversant with both the finer points of constitutional interpretation regarding suffrage and the benefits that would accrue to those women seeking to safeguard and improve their person and livelihood. Anthony once stated that the best argument for suffrage was justice, that "the sister should have the same right as her brother, the wife as her husband, the mother as her son . . . I myself could have done more if I had had the tools—the ballot and the opportunities that the ballot gives."[20]

In fact, many of the most significant reforms achieved by women were attained before the franchise was granted in 1920. Ongoing changes in legislation affecting the marital, economic, and educational status of women increased as the decades passed, and the tenacious leadership of Anthony and other women kept the ideas of suffrage constantly before the people until the Nineteenth Amendment was finally ratified. The ballot, itself, did not create the political revolution that was feared by many men: women did not enter politics in any significant numbers, their political voice did not immediately alter the course of social policy, nor were their economic fortunes enhanced overnight. In fact, Anthony may have been more precise in her original assessment that economic concerns were of singular importance in the advancement of women. Yet her most concerted effort to organize working women, through formation in 1868 of the enterprising Workingwoman's Association, proved unsuccessful and may have further solidified Anthony's devotion to securing the franchise. Despite its limitations as a remedy for women's oppression, suffrage was another means by which to achieve the same opportunities as men and reach self-fulfillment.

Anthony's efforts and leadership were instrumental in garnering many of the advances made by women during the nineteenth century. She was not the theorist or writer that Stanton was, but a powerful speaker who was unafraid of the criticism and scorn that she inevitably drew from disapproving men and women. Her executive skills virtually kept the movement running, and her unwavering commitment to suffrage created a steady flow of new—albeit increasingly conservative—leadership into the movement. More than any single person within the suffrage movement, she was acutely aware of the various media through which to direct appeals and exact hearings for the rights of women, including Congress, the courts, local organizations, political parties, newspapers, and the convention platform. Her petition drives became so exhaustive that legislators threatened to withhold this right from women. Anthony's goal in striving for suffrage was to provide women of all aspirations, whether domestic, educational, occupational, or professional, another tool by which to realize their needs and ambitions.

NOTES:

[1] Ida Husted Harper, *The Life and Work of Susan B. Anthony* (1898; rpt., Salem, New Hampshire: Ayer Company, Publishers, Inc., 1983), 2: 913.

[2] Harper, 2: 915.

[3] Harper, 1: 59–60.

[4] Robert Riegel, *American Feminists* (Lawrence: University Press of Kansas, 1963), 77.

[5] Elizabeth Cady Stanton, Susan B. Anthony, and Matilda Joslyn Gage, eds., *History of Woman Suffrage* (1881; rpt., New York: Arno Press, 1969), 1: 459.

[6] Harper, I, 137.

[7] *Ibid.*

[8] Elizabeth Cady Stanton, Susan B. Anthony, and Matilda Joslyn Gage, eds., *History of Woman Suffrage* (1882; rpt., New York: Arno Press, 1969), 2: 317.

[9] Gerritt Smith typified much of this sentiment when he wrote to Anthony, "The removal of the political disabilities of race is my first desire—of sex, my second." Stanton, et. al., 2: 317.

[10] Philip S. Foner, ed., *Frederick Douglass on Women's Rights* (Westport, Connecticut: Greenwood Press, 1976), 33, 87.

[11] Foner, ed., 23.

[12] Mary Jo Buhle and Paul Buhle, *A Concise History of Woman Suffrage: Selections from the Classic Works of Stanton, Anthony, Gage and Harper* (Urbana: University of Illinois Press, 1978), 225.

[13] Buhle and Buhle, 294.

[14] Stanton, Anthony, and Gage, eds., 2: 688.

[15] *Ibid.*

[16] Stanton, Anthony, and Gage, eds., 2: 689.

[17] Buhle and Buhle, 339.

[18] *Ibid.*, 340.

[19] Harper, 2: 549.

[20] Harper, 3: 1162.

For Further Reading

Buhle, Mary Jo, and Paul Buhle. *A Concise History of Woman Suffrage: Selections from the Classic Works of Stanton, Anthony, Gage and Harper.* Urbana: University of Illinois Press, 1978.

Flexner, Eleanor. *Century of Struggle: The Woman's Rights Movement in the United States.* Cambridge, Massachusetts: Harvard University Press, 1959.

Foner, Philip S., ed. *Frederick Douglass on Women's Rights.* Westport, Connecticut: Greenwood Press, 1976.

Harper, Ida Husted. *The Life and Works of Susan B. Anthony.* 3 vols. Reprint ed. Salem, New Hampshire: Ayer Company, Publishers, Inc., 1983.

Lutz, Alma. *Susan B. Anthony: Rebel, Crusader, Humanitarian.* Boston: Beacon Press, 1969.

Riegel, Robert. *American Feminists.* Lawrence: University Press of Kansas, 1963.

Stanton, Elizabeth Cady, Susan B. Anthony, Matilda Joslyn Gage, and Ida Husted Harper. *History of Woman Suffrage.* 6 vols. Reprint ed. New York: Arno Press, 1969.

Truman, Margaret. *Women of Courage.* New York: William Morrow and Company, 1976.

Chester A. Arthur
(1829–1886)

M. Jill DuPont

Though he attained the highest elective office in the nation, few presidents remain as obscure as Chester A. Arthur. He was born in Fairfield, Vermont, in 1829, the son of Baptist preacher William Arthur, an avowed abolitionist rumored to be co-founder of the New York Anti-Slavery Society in 1835, and Malvina Stone, an ancestor of Chief Justice of the United States Harlan Fiske Stone.

From an early age, Arthur received a rigorous education from his father and acquired his abolitionist views. Growing up near Greenwich, New York, he attended the academy in Union Village, and at the age of fifteen matriculated at Union College, pursuing a classical curriculum. Following his graduation in 1848, Arthur began a teaching career and commenced his legal education at the State and National Law School at Ballston Spa. In 1852, he became principal at Cohoes Academy and searched for work in a law office. Arthur joined the firm of abolitionist Erastus D. Culver as a clerk in 1853 and completed his legal training in 1854. He was made a partner in the firm of Culver, Parker, and Arthur following his admission to the bar.

At that time, Culver was representing New York in the *Lemmon* case, the legal culmination of an ongoing battle between the forces of slavery and freedom over the right of slaveowners to travel with their bondsmen in free states. At issue in *Lemmon* was whether slaveowners could bring their slaves into free states without jeopardizing the slaves' status as property. In 1855, Culver was elected city judge of Brooklyn, and Arthur was appointed to the team of lawyers representing the state in subsequent arguments of *Lemmon* before the New York Supreme Court (1857) and the New York Court of Appeals (1860). Though Arthur's precise role remains unclear, several accounts contend that he was sent to persuade members of the state legislature at Albany to pursue the challenge of the case presented by the commonwealth of Virginia.

Arthur was assigned another significant case in 1854, when he represented Elizabeth Jennings, a black public school teacher who had been assaulted on a New York streetcar after refusing to leave a car reserved for whites. Arthur argued successfully that the Third Avenue Railroad Company violated a statute holding common carriers liable for the acts of their agents, and soon thereafter New York railroad companies integrated their cars.

Arthur formed a new legal practice in 1856 with Henry D. Gardiner. The partnership flourished through the Civil War, during which Arthur was appointed quartermaster general and inspector general of the New York state militia by Governor Edwin D. Morgan. Arthur had made the governor's acquaintance in 1854 while serving as a delegate at a convention in Saratoga, a gathering which witnessed the birth of the state Republican Party. In 1863, Arthur returned to his legal practice, where he gained the reputation as an office lawyer reluctant to make court appearances, handling, instead, mostly war claims and negotiations. As his legal career slowed, Arthur turned increasingly to politics, where his prospects fared little better. His fortune changed, however, when he helped elect Roscoe Conkling to the United States Senate in 1867, thus becoming a lieutenant to the dominant figure in New York's Republican political machine. In 1868, Arthur made further inroads into the political scene by becoming chairman of the General Grant Club of New York. His efforts on behalf of Conkling and Ulysses S. Grant led the victorious President Grant to appoint Arthur to the collectorship of the New York Customhouse in 1871.

The New York Customhouse was the cornerstone of the state Republican machine, and also of critical importance to the country in the late nineteenth century. Two-thirds to three-fourths of the nation's customs receipts were collected there. More importantly, the customhouse in New York controlled more government appointments than any other federal office. The collector was thus the primary distributor of lucrative and influential positions in the civil service, and Arthur continually fielded demands for patronage as one of the most vital cogs in Conkling's political machine.

Arthur's tenure as collector coincided with the burgeoning reform movement, which sought to wrest civil service from the control of politicians who frequently sacrificed efficiency and integrity in rewarding their supporters—not necessarily the most qualified applicants—with appointments to public office. Accounts differ as to how conscientiously Arthur applied reform principles in his administration of the customhouse. While he was acknowledged to be an improvement over his predecessor, Thomas Murphy, Arthur's views on the spoils system appeared to mirror those of his political allies and fellow customhouse officials. Grant's hesitant and waning interest in enforcing reform practices only increased the patronage demands received by the New York collector. Frequent investigations most probably kept Arthur somewhat aware of—if not receptive to—reform ideals, and he was reappointed unanimously in 1875 without referral to the Senate, thus becoming the first collector ever appointed to a second term.

The election of Rutherford B. Hayes to the presidency in 1876 brought the New York Customhouse under even greater scrutiny. As historian Ari Hoogenboom has observed, the latter became a "battleground," not so much over the issues of reform and spoils, as the focus of a struggle between two Republican factions. Investigations conducted by a commission chaired by John Jay II revealed that customhouse abuses still prevailed, despite Arthur's insistence that he had been following civil service guidelines in removing solely for cause and promoting for merit. Hayes's campaign to oust Arthur finally succeeded in 1878, accomplishing the purposes of further loosening Conkling's hold on Republican politics in New York and appeasing reformers who sought to bring credibility to public service.

Arthur's removal did not appear to damage his political stature in New York, as he served on the Republican State Committee as its Chairman in 1879 and 1880. He also resumed his law practice at the firm of Arthur, Phelps, Kneval, and Ransom. When James A. Garfield of Ohio, a leader of the reforming "Mugwump" Republicans, won the Republican nomination for president in 1880, Arthur, a prominent member of the antireform "Stalwart" Republicans, was enlisted to round out the ticket as the vice-presidential candidate. Arthur's nomination was primarily strategic: his presence on the ticket could bolster Conkling's weakened and factionalized Stalwarts of New York, while simultaneously garnering the state's critical bloc of electoral votes. Arthur's letter of acceptance indicated he would support efforts to reform the civil service and endeavor to uphold constitutional ideals, particularly those pertaining to the rights of blacks.

Arthur's sincerity was quickly subjected to public examination when President Garfield died from an assassin's bullet six months into his term. Although he had been a Mugwump, Garfield's position on reform had been weak at best, but his death intensified the groundswell for regulations governing the civil service. Arthur's ascension to the presidency raised doubts in the minds of many Americans, as he had little elective leadership experience, dubious political associations, and no real constituency of his own. As the nation's fourth accidental presidency, Arthur's term would resemble those of his predecessors in testing the adequacy and viability of the constitutional system which raised him to office.

In several of his addresses to Congress, Arthur expressed concern over the circumstances which prompted his elevation to the presidency. Garfield had lingered for several weeks after his shooting, too ill to serve as president; Arthur and the nation were adrift without a way to deal with the problem, because the Constitution and federal law were silent on issues of presidential disability. The new president urged Congress to consider with care Article II of the Constitution, requesting more precise guidelines governing presidential succession and the instances in which presidential powers shall devolve upon the vice-president.

As historian and biographer Thomas C. Reeves has noted, one of Arthur's initial tasks as chief executive was the appointment of justices to the United States Supreme Court. His first selection was Horace Gray, a jurist and legal scholar who held a seat on the Massachusetts Supreme Judicial Court. Arthur then drew public criticism for nominating his former political colleague, Roscoe Conkling. The New York senator had no substantial legal training, nor did his record in Congress bespeak achievement. Conkling was confirmed by the Senate, but he rejected the nomination, as he had a similar honor offered by President Grant in 1873. Arthur probably intended the distinction to serve as a personal gesture recognizing Conkling's past assistance; the public perceived his nomination as a sign that Arthur would continue to deal out patronage. Shortly thereafter, Arthur named, and the Senate confirmed, Samuel Blatchford of New York, a reputable judge with ample experience in the federal courts.

For the most part, Arthur's term was marked by his ambivalent relationship with the Forty-Seventh Congress. Congress ignored most of his suggestions, passing a bill on the exclusion of Chinese immigrants over his veto and taking similar action on a "pork barrel" rivers and harbors bill that Arthur believed exceeded the powers of the Constitution. In 1883, when the Supreme Court ruled the 1875 Civil Rights Act unconstitutional, Arthur condemned the decision and declared that he would support any legislation ensuring the equal rights guaranteed by the Constitution—particularly those enumerated in the Fourteenth Amendment. Following the Court's decision, at least five bills were introduced in an attempt to secure rights for blacks, yet Arthur did not act on any of them.

An issue that attracted considerable attention in the late 1870s and 1880s was the status of Native Americans in American society. Affirming the views of other reformers, Arthur hoped for a weakening of tribal affiliations that would lead to the eventual assimilation of Native Americans into society as citizens. As president, he proposed passage of a controversial severalty, law which would allow for twenty to twenty-five years of protection and bring Indian reservations under the umbrella of federal law. Congress defeated several allotment bills during Arthur's term. As Justus D. Doenecke has noted, the suggestions made by Arthur and other reformers were formulated into a national policy in 1887 with the passage of the Dawes Severalty Act. This legislation afforded the heads of families living on reservations the opportunity to acquire land and citizenship, yet also created unforeseen losses for other Native Americans.

Upon becoming president, Arthur had hoped to enact some piece of legislation that would both benefit the people and leave a significant mark on his term. He received some assistance toward achieving this goal following the 1882 congressional elections, a Republican loss, when a previously reluctant Congress rallied around a bill submitted by George Pendleton during its "lame duck" 1882–83 session. The bill, drafted by Dorman B. Eaton and inspired by the executive committee of the New York Civil Service Reform Association, called for the creation of a civil service commission armed with the authority to formulate rules regulating entrance to and promotions within the civil service, monitor the process of reform, and administer exams.

While Arthur initially opposed the use of competitive exams, which he equated with book learning, he later relinquished this position in declaring his support for the Pendleton Act. Once the bill went into effect on July 16, 1883, Arthur set to the task of appointing the three-member Civil Service Commission. Selecting Eaton as chairman, Arthur then chose John M. Gregory—later president of what became the University of Illinois—and Leroy D. Thoman, a young Democratic probate judge from Ohio. Legislators generally acknowledged that in order for the Pendleton Act to be effective, the cause of reform had to have the president's active support. Arthur's appointments appealed to lawmakers and the public alike, for they signalled the President's intention to execute fairly the new law. Doubts remained about Arthur's sincerity, however, for it was common knowledge that he had assisted some friends in New York before the passing of the new law. When he adopted major recommendations made by the commission later in 1883, its members noted, "Our functions cannot be successfully discharged without the constant, firm, and friendly support of the President. That support has never failed." Arthur no longer fulfilled friendly requests for positions in the civil service, and on the whole, administered the Pendleton Act conscientiously. The Republican loss in 1882, the burden of dispensing patronage, and the opportunity to distinguish his presidency all may have influenced Arthur's firm stand in support of reform.

Arthur sought the Republican nomination for president in 1884, but James G. Blaine captured the party's support. That Arthur could not be easily categorized by any single faction contributed to his unsuccessful bid. He was considered too much of a reformer by the Stalwarts who continued to seek patronage, yet not enough of a reformer to those active in the civil service movement. In addition, the balance of power in New York politics had shifted with the demise of Conkling and the congressional loss of 1882—which was attributed primarily to the president and damaged his credibility in his home state. In short, the public still linked Arthur to the old regime despite his sincere effort on behalf of reform, and the manner in which he assumed the presidency prevented him from forming a political base. Arthur's malleability and his association with Conkling had proven an asset in his vice-presidential bid of 1880, but his failure to appeal to any single faction or region during his presidency ended his hopes for reelection in 1884. When he left office, Arthur was approached by New York Republicans about running for the United States Senate, but he refused due to failing health. He died less than two years later in 1886.

In a sense, Arthur's presidency affirmed the fitness of the constitutional provision which brought him to office. While he may be considered only an average president based on the merit of his accomplishments, Arthur was able to dissociate himself from machine politics to the extent that he advanced the cause of reform through the Pendleton Act. He also voiced his opposition to the levying of political assessments, a standard practice during Conkling's reign. Few observers of the period would have believed him able to make such a transition while in office, though he did not entirely abandon his ties to the Stalwarts of New York. In an era in which business leaders often surpassed the prominence of politicians, the Gilded Age provided few distinguished presidents or noteworthy achievements. Though Chester A. Arthur did not necessarily enhance the presidency, neither did he damage its integrity.

For Further Reading

Doenecke, Justus D. *The Presidencies of James A. Garfield and Chester A. Arthur.* Lawrence: University Press of Kansas, 1981.

Hoogenboom, Ari. *Outlawing the Spoils: A History of the Civil Service Reform Movement, 1865–1883.* Urbana: University of Illinois Press, 1961.

Howe, George Frederick. *Chester A. Arthur: A Quarter-Century of Machine Politics.* New York: Dodd, Mead, and Co., 1934.

Levin, Peter R. *Seven By Chance: Accidental Presidents.* New York: Farrar, Straus and Co., 1948.

Murlin, E.L. "The Life of Chester A. Arthur of New York," in E.V. Smalley, ed., *The Republican Manual.* New York: American Book Exchange, 1880.

Reeves, Thomas C. *Gentleman Boss: The Life of Chester Alan Arthur.* New York: Alfred A. Knopf, 1975.

Richardson, James D. *A Compilation of the Messages and Papers of the Presidents 1789–1897,* 20 vols. Washington: Government Printing Office, 1896–1927.

Roger N. Baldwin
(1884–1982)

PAUL L. MURPHY
University of Minnesota

Roger Nash Baldwin was born in Wellesley, Massachusetts on January 21, 1884, the first of six children of Lucy Cushing Nash and Frank Fenno Baldwin. His parents were proper Bostonians. Both sides of the family traced their ancestry to the Mayflower. Frank Baldwin was a prosperous leather merchant who owned several manufacturing companies. All of Roger's forebears were engaged in commerce and industry, although his grandfather gave up his business at the age of forty-two to work in the Boston Young Men's Christian Union, a liberal organization devoted to community service—becoming, to a degree, a role model for the grandson.

Roger Baldwin went to Harvard, where he earned both A.B. and M.A. degrees in 1904 and 1905 respectively. Soon thereafter he took a position as an instructor of sociology at Washington University, St. Louis, a post he held from 1906 to 1909. In 1907 he also became chief probation officer for the St. Louis juvenile court. In the same period he became secretary of the National Probation Association and the St. Louis Civic League. It was during this period that he became actively interested in juvenile justice generally, publishing *Juvenile Courts and Probation* (1912), a handbook of standards and procedures then in practice in various juvenile courts around the country.

Baldwin's vision was becoming increasingly national, however. Stimulated by his friendship with the radical reformer Emma Goldman and her plans for a new society based on social justice and industrial democracy, he moved to New York in 1917, joining the antiwar American Union Against Militarism's (A.U.A.M.) national directing committee. Due to his untiring energy and remarkable organizing skills, Baldwin soon dominated the A.U.A.M. board of directors. Within two months, he had created a Bureau for Conscientious Objectors, and within four, the Civil Liberties Bureau, both within the A.U.A.M. The latter sought legal aid for conscientious objectors. In October 1917, it became an independent organization with Baldwin at its head, and remained so during the war.

Baldwin was drafted himself, but refused to enter the army. He was subsequently jailed. At that time, he resigned the directorship of the Civil Liberties Bureau, turning it over to Albert De Silver, a New York lawyer. After the war and his emergence from prison, Baldwin served briefly as a union organizer during the great steel strike of 1919. But his heart was in civil liberties work, and when, in January 1920, the newly formed American Civil Liberties Union (A.C.L.U.) came into existence formally in New York City, Baldwin took over as director, a position he held until 1950. In that year, he surrendered the day-to-day responsibilities of administering the organization, and became national chairman of the body. In this way he freed himself to engage in a wide variety of civil liberties and human rights activities until his death in 1982 at the age of ninety-eight. Conspicuous was his role in building civil liberties into the postwar Japanese constitution, and his work with the International League of Human Rights following 1946.

From early in his career, Baldwin was conscious of the realities of power relationships in the area of human rights. A philosophical idealist but a tactical realist, his primary concern was with social justice and the achievement of proper social ends. He was convinced that any group that sought to gain full civil liberties within American society had to do so by gaining sufficient power to resist repression. "Those who have economic power," he was fond of proclaiming, "have civil liberties and civil rights," with success clearly tied to the ability to articulate common purposes and to mount successful group action.

Initially, this meant turning principally to labor. "We are not concerned to promote any radical program, or the cause of any class," he stated in 1920. "But the circumstances of industrial conflict today force us chiefly to champion the rights of labor, to meet, organize, strike, and picket, because labor is the class whose rights are most attacked." Labor, then, was to be the beginning, and the A.C.L.U. in its first twenty years scored major breakthroughs; these included repealing state sedition and criminal syndicalism laws, which had been used against labor organizing; fighting the labor injunction through to its successful out-lawing by Congress in the 1932 Norris–LaGuardia Act; and supporting strikes among the unorganized often in remote mining and textile areas, where human rights were being particularly flouted.

But Baldwin's long-range goal was to work for access for a wide range of groups—racial and religious, women as well as men—to the general "blessings of liberty" that the Constitution's preamble had promised. The American Civil Liberties Union under his leadership moved insistently in that direction, defending the Jehovah's Witnesses' religious rights in the 1930s and 1940s; fighting the loyalty hysteria of the late 1940s and 1950s; and working for greater due process guarantees as public demands for equal justice grew in the years following World War II.

But there were more subtle constitutional dimensions to this story. After the alarming repression of the World War I period, particularly in the area of free speech and free press, two schools of the thought had emerged. To one group of legalists, a sensitive and careful new law of civil liberties was required which would provide a body of legal distinctions which courts could apply when Bill of Rights freedoms, particularly First Amendment rights were abused. This group, led particularly by Zechariah Chafee, Jr., of the Harvard Law School but including public lawyers such as Hannis Taylor, Walter Nelles, and Albert De Silver, channeled their energies into refining civil liberties law, and in some cases, creating it.

While not in any way deploring this approach, a second group of legalists had questioned its effectiveness. Baldwin was the strongest voice in this group. He had seen that wartime reliance upon the Constitution and the Bill of Rights had been a conspicuous failure. The courts simply did not protect those rights, for they felt little pressure from any broad constituency to do so and, in fact, felt strong pressures from those in the power establishment not to do so. To Baldwin, if civil libertarian goals were to be achieved—protecting individual rights against the government, extending them by law to groups not having them, and developing new rights not previously protected against governmental infringement—a different type of politics of civil liberties was needed. Here the courts could not be relied upon. Baldwin wrote in 1931 that "the courts do not help much as protectors of rights, for judges write economics as well as law and usually on the side of established property relationships." He was equally jaundiced regarding the majority of the legal community, from the bar associations to the large body of working attorneys in and out of government. Relief from the government's deliberate policy of the criminal prosecution of ideas, expression, and association would have to come through the political process, Baldwin maintained, with the people making the issue of civil liberties a public agenda item, and demanding that they be the arbiters between permissible and punishable behavior. Only if a civil liberties constituency could be developed which would push the issue into the public consciousness and require leaders to take sides on it would the courts ever feel compelled to respond to civil libertarian demands.

Building that constituency became the major goal of the A.C.L.U. in its early years. Under Baldwin's leadership, the body became an agency for attempting to get an ever larger public to see the ominous implications of restrictive laws for themselves and for the nation at large. This meant raising the public's consciousness regarding human rights— dramatizing that what happened to little people, or unpopular people, could happen to anyone. The A.C.L.U.'s hope was that through such efforts, the legal system could be opened gradually to all, thus making vital the concept of the rule of law as a cornerstone of American democracy. This meant working for the sanctity of procedure, without which all contests became subject to the will of the strongest. It embodied the view that commitment to a uniform rule of law and its processes was not only the best, but the only route in deference to the less powerful and to the principles of tolerance, decency, humanity, and right.

It was here that Roger Baldwin came to make his contribution to American constitutionalism. As he wrote late in his career: "If the human race is to survive, we all must come to see that the 'world is my country, and all mankind my countrymen.' Our revolutionary age is moving painfully toward that goal of peace and law with the freedom of peoples from foreign rule, the emancipation of labor, the political equality of women and the rejection of racial white superiority. Our hope must rest on these common goals of most great religions and revolutions."

Aaron Burr

(1756–1836)

RICHARD B. BERNSTEIN
New York State Bicentennial Commission

Aaron Burr's place in American constitutional history differs from that of most of the other famous political figures of his time. Burr did help to shape the American experiment in constitutional government—but not through developing important ideas or articulating well-defined, influential positions on major issues. Rather, his single-minded pursuit of power, and his invention and mastery of what we would recognize as modern political techniques, placed him at the focus of critical junctures in the nation's constitutional development. This biographical essay emphasizes the ways in which his career influenced the history of the United States Constitution.

Early Life

Aaron Burr was born in Newark, New Jersey, on February 6, 1756. His father, Reverend Aaron Burr, was the pastor of the Newark Presbyterian Church and the president of the College of New Jersey (now known as Princeton University). His mother, Esther Edwards Burr, was the daughter of Reverend Jonathan Edwards, the premier theologian of New England Puritanism and one of the greatest figures in American intellectual history.

The sickly child's family disintegrated within two years of his birth. On September 24, 1757, Aaron's overworked father collapsed and died from a fever. Reverend Edwards, named to succeed the senior Burr as president of the College of New Jersey, no sooner arrived in Princeton to assume his duties than he, too, died—on March 22, 1758, from an unsuccessful smallpox inoculation. Sarah Pierpont Edwards and her daughter, Aaron's mother, also died of smallpox. When Esther Edwards Burr died on April 7, 1758, Aaron Burr and his older sister, Sarah, were orphaned.

Sarah and Aaron were brought into the household of their mother's brother, Timothy Edwards, in Elizabethtown, New Jersey. Timothy, like his father and brother-in-law, was a staunch Calvinist who sought to bring up his niece and nephew as obedient, orthodox Presbyterians. Aaron did not adapt well to the discipline and enforced moral behavior of the Edwards household.

Taking refuge in his studies, which were supervised by a series of private tutors, he applied to the College of New Jersey at the age of eleven. Rejected because of his youth, Burr resumed his studies and secured admission to the college as a sophomore two years later. He was a serious and brilliant student; when he was graduated in 1772, he won prizes for Greek, Latin, and reading, and his graduation oration was generally acclaimed. After graduation, Burr sought an appropriate career. Abandoning a short-lived attempt at theological study, Burr turned instead in May 1774 to the study of law with his brother-in-law, Tapping Reeve, a noted attorney in Litchfield, Connecticut.

The American Revolution

In July 1775, two months after the Battles of Lexington and Concord, the nineteen-year-old Burr and his childhood friend Matthias Ogden journeyed to Cambridge, Massachusetts, to enlist with the Continental Army. Captain Burr was assigned to the American military units, commanded by General Benedict Arnold, assigned to invade Canada. Arnold in turn transferred Burr to General Richard Montgomery's command. After Montgomery's capture of Montreal, he led his troops to assist Arnold in besieging Quebec. Although Burr distinguished himself for bravery and gallantry, the attack on Quebec was a fiasco. Montgomery was killed in the first volley; Burr attempted unsuccessfully to drag his body back to the American lines.

When he and the other survivors of the Canadian campaign returned to the United States, Major Burr received an invitation to join the staff of the commander-in-chief of the Continental Army, General George Washington. Burr complained in a letter to John Hancock, president of the Continental Congress and a friend of his late father, that he had no desire to serve with Washington. Nonetheless, he arrived at Washington's headquarters at Richmond Hill in New York City in June of 1776. He lasted only ten days. There is no proof for the many legends about why Burr left Washington's staff, but it is likely that the impatient young officer and the taciturn, slow-thinking general were at odds almost at once. Burr had made a lasting bad impression on Washington and his official ''family.'' Even so, in 1777 Washington approved Burr's promotion to lieutenant colonel. Although this decision made Burr the youngest lieutenant colonel in the Continental Army, he wrote to Washington to inquire why he had not received a higher rank. Given the difficulties in securing promotions, among them the constant bickering between generals in the Continental Army and delegates in the Continental Congress, Burr's protest at this signal advancement must have raised eyebrows at Washington's headquarters.

Burr became a member of General Israel Putnam's staff. He found Putnam, and life at his headquarters, more to his liking. At this time, Burr became involved with Margaret Moncrieffe, a daughter of a British officer stationed on Staten Island. Her unmasking as a British spy damaged Burr's reputation.

In 1779, Washington named Burr to command Malcolm's Regiment, based in New Jersey. This posting and his next (in Westchester County, New York) exposed Burr to the demands of fighting marauding bands of Loyalists, Patriot deserters, escaped slaves, and criminals bent on plundering the hapless farmers of the region. Burr, however, found it wearisome and chafed at being far from the main theatres of war. In the spring of 1779, his weak health compelled Burr to resign his commission.

Burr resumed his legal studies in New York and began to court Theodosia Prevost, the widow of a British officer. At the same time, he began the first of a series of disastrous financial speculations that almost ruined him. In April 1782, Burr passed a special examination and won admission to the New York bar. Three months later, he married Theodosia, and the couple settled in New York City, moving into a house on Wall Street. The Burrs had two daughters, but only the elder, Theodosia (born in 1783), survived beyond infancy.

Soon a successful and prosperous attorney, Burr began to consider a political career. In April 1784 he won election to the New York State Assembly, where he championed the immediate abolition of slavery—a reform not adopted until the early 1800s. He also served as chairman of the assembly's committee charged with revising the state's laws. In a move that would contrast oddly with his later political strategy, he opposed and defeated a bill incorporating the General Society of Mechanics and Tradesmen, fearing that the new society would become the nucleus of a labor aristocracy.

Constitutional Era Politics

Although Burr had won distinction as an attorney and as a rising political figure, he played almost no part in the controversies over the weakness of the Articles of Confederation, the calling of the Federal Convention of 1787, or the debate over the proposed Constitution. Burr's biographers and historians have identified him as a moderate Antifederalist, although it is tempting to conclude that Burr was more interested in building his legal practice and biding his time than in throwing himself into the ratification campaign. His silence during the political battles of 1787–1789 disturbed supporters of the Constitution, however; they began to suspect that his ambition was not leavened by any higher or more serious purpose or interest in the general good.

In 1788, Burr ran again for the state assembly, this time on a ticket clearly identified as Antifederalist, but was defeated. In 1789, Burr injected himself into the strife resulting from the split of the New York Antifederalists after the ratification of the Constitution; in that year's gubernatorial election, he joined with Alexander Hamilton to support Judge Robert Yates, now regarded as a Federalist, in his unsuccessful challenge to the popular incumbent, George Clinton. The victorious Clinton recognized that it might be better to co-opt Burr than to mark him down an enemy; the governor therefore appointed Burr as the state's attorney general.

One of Attorney General Burr's principal responsibilities was to serve as a land commissioner. Traffic in land in the 1780s and 1790s was perhaps the principal form of speculative investment, rivaled only by speculation in federal government securities. Burr dabbled in land investments himself, and narrowly escaped being embroiled in the huge Macomb Land Sale scandal, in which more than three million acres were sold for eight pence each.

Inventing the Republican Party

In January 1791, with the backing of the powerful Livingston family, Burr declared his candidacy for the U.S. Senate against Federalist incumbent Philip Schuyler and defeated him in the Clintonian state legislature.* Schuyler's candidacy was of vital importance to his son-in-law and political ally, Secretary of the Treasury Alexander Hamilton;

---

*At this time, United States senators were chosen by their respective state legislatures. The Seventeenth Amendment (ratified April 8, 1913) provided for the direct election of senators.

Burr's victory over the old general angered Hamilton. In retrospect, we can identify the Burr–Schuyler contest of 1791 as the beginning of the active political hostility between Burr and Hamilton—although there is evidence that this hostility may date to 1789.

Burr's election was a signal victory for the forces coalescing in opposition to Hamilton's fiscal policies and the Washington administration's foreign policy. Senator Burr soon allied himself with Representative James Madison and Secretary of State Thomas Jefferson, and renewed his allegiance to Governor Clinton. Historians agree that political parties had begun to emerge by this period, but Burr played a pivotal role in developing methods of party organization and discipline that eventually made the Jeffersonian Republicans the dominant force in American national politics.

Although it is a truism that political parties are not mentioned in the Constitution, it is equally true that parties have become essential to the conduct of politics and the operation of government under the Constitution. The development of parties may be seen as an informal amendment of the Constitution—or as one of the earliest features of the "unwritten" or customary Constitution. For this reason, the organization of the Jeffersonian Republicans, with its coalition of great and small farmers and urban "mechanics" (workingmen), stands as one of Burr's most important contributions to American constitutional government.

Burr may well have been the first truly professional politician under the Constitution. He displayed a mastery of the skills of political organization and strategy exceeding even those of such master politicians as Madison; in particular, Burr pioneered in developing methods of mobilizing voters at the polls and dramatizing political issues in terms readily comprehensible by voters at all levels of society. His achievements did not win him the admiration of his colleagues or the applause of posterity, however. Rather, in the 1790s Burr began to acquire the reputation of a man whose ambition was selfish only, one who had no interest in the larger issues of politics and government. Burr's defenders protest that he did not permit himself to lose his dispassionate, objective stance and that he thus compares favorably with Federalists such as Hamilton, John Jay, and John Adams or with Republicans such as Jefferson, Madison, and James Monroe. His critics respond that for Burr to show no interest in—let alone commitment to—the great intellectual issues at the heart of American politics in this era confirmed the charges that his ambition was solely for himself.

Burr's senatorial career was competent and respectable, though not distinguished. At one point during the 1792 New York gubernatorial contest, rumors circulated that both the Federalists and the Republicans were considering Burr as a nominee. Due largely to the opposition of Hamilton, the Federalists chose John Jay instead; Governor Clinton's political machine forestalled any challenge to the incumbent's claim to the Republican nomination. Both Burr's personal political appeal and the fluid lines separating the parties help to explain this flurry of interest in Burr as a candidate for governor.

During this period, Burr had leased a large and opulent house in New York City, known as Richmond Hill, which soon became a popular salon for his political allies and legal colleagues. Ironically, this house had been the site of Washington's headquarters during the tense ten-day period in June 1776 when Burr had served on Washington's staff. Burr's frequent journeys to Philadelphia, however, separated him from his wife, who often was too ill to accompany him. On May 18, 1794, Theodosia Prevost Burr died of nephritis, leaving behind her eleven-year-old daughter, Theodosia. Until her tragic death, Theodosia Burr (who married South Carolina planter and politician Joseph Alston in 1801) was her father's favorite confidante and the center of his personal life.

Public and Private Reverses

In 1796, with political lines hardening between Federalists and Republicans, Burr was often mentioned as a potential candidate for president or vice-president on the Republican ticket. He had been a leading opponent of the Jay Treaty with Great Britain, a principal adversary of the Hamiltonian fiscal program, and the favorite politician of the emerging network—which he had helped to create—of Democratic-Republican societies and New York City's Tammany Society. As a result, Burr, together with his ally Governor Clinton, became vitally important to the Republicans; they and their supporters made a national party of what would otherwise have been a sectional (that is, southern) coalition.

The Federalists united behind Vice-President John Adams and Charles C. Pinckney of South Carolina—with a brief show of Federalist interest in placing Burr on the ticket. Although the Republicans had agreed on Jefferson as their presidential nominee and had accepted Burr as his *de facto* running-mate, many Republicans distrusted the New Yorker. As a result, in the electoral tally, he lagged far behind the other three candidates, failing to carry any New England states or even his home state of New York:

John Adams (Federalist) 71
Thomas Jefferson (Republican) 68
Charles C. Pinckney (Federalist) 59
Aaron Burr (Republican) 30

Burr suffered other reverses as a result of the presidential contest of 1796. The Republicans' failures in New York had given the Federalists control of the New York state legislature, which in 1797 rejected Burr's candidacy for a second term in the U.S. Senate and returned Philip Schuyler to the seat that Burr had wrested from him in 1791. Burr's reelection to the state assembly later that year offered small consolation.

Burr returned to his two favorite ways of making money—practicing law and speculating in land. By now he was one of the nation's leading trial lawyers, sharing with Hamilton the domination of the New York legal profession. Burr and Hamilton took part in virtually every major lawsuit in this period—sometimes as colleagues, sometimes as adversaries. Like most successful lawyers in this period, Burr took on students who read law under his direction. These students later recalled not only the legal knowledge he taught them, but also his practical advice, in particular the adages "Law is anything which is boldly asserted and plausibly maintained" and "Written things last." Historians puzzling over the fragmentary and uncommunicative Burr papers have had good reason to grumble at the latter statement.

Burr's ventures in land speculation were much less successful. Moreover, his name was entangled in frequent rumors of a conspiracy to conquer Canada and detach the western lands from the United States to form an independent republic. Whatever plans he had—whether bizarre conspiracies or elaborate schemes for speculation—collapsed in 1797, forcing him to sell the furniture at Richmond Hill to satisfy his many creditors.

The Election of 1800

The conduct of the Adams administration at home and abroad appalled many Americans. Anger at the undeclared naval war with France and the repressive Alien and Sedition Acts of 1798 swelled the ranks of the Republican party, whose organization (devised by Burr) made it all but certain that the party could wrest the presidency from the Federalists.

Once more, the Federalists nominated Adams and Pinckney and the Republicans agreed on Jefferson and Burr. This time, however, Burr's generalship proved decisive. In particular, his shrewd choice of popular presidential electors for the Republican ticket in New York and his mobilization of the members of the Tammany Society made visible the Jefferson–Burr ticket's strength and brought voters to the polls. Burr's brilliant strategy and tactics carried New York for the Republicans. In addition, the fragmentation of the Federalists into Adams men and Hamilton men further weakened the incumbent party, resulting in a landslide victory for the Republican ticket.

The Republican victory of 1800 was tainted, however, by a mischance that few had foreseen. The original version of the electoral college in Article II of the Constitution had provided only that presidential electors would vote for two individuals, without distinguishing between their choice for president and their choice for vice-president. The architects of the electoral college had not foreseen the rise of political parties, nor the idea of a party ticket for president and vice-president. As a result, electors loyally voting for both Jefferson and Burr had created a tie between the two men without intending to do so.

As required by the Constitution, the election was thrown into the U.S. House of Representatives. Aaron Burr's conduct during this period puzzled and vexed both his contemporaries and later historians. His critics charged that he could have resolved the controversy at any time, just by announcing that he was a candidate for vice-president only and that he would ask his supporters to back Jefferson, the intended victor. His defenders reply that he did nothing whatsoever to advance his name for the presidency. (Burr's critics retort that his letter to Albert Gallatin, in which he pledged to accept the presidency only if the interests of the nation and the party demanded it, was hardly a sincere disclaimer of interest in the office.) Burr's defenders also contend that some Federalists sought to complicate the House's resolution of the tie vote, seeking to embarrass the Republicans and, at the same time, hoping that Burr would be more tractable in the presidency than Jefferson.

Despite the interest of some Federalists in manipulating the Jefferson–Burr tie for partisan advantage, Hamilton emerged once again as Burr's foe, pleading with his fellow Federalists not to support Burr because the New Yorker could not be trusted with political power. The extent of Hamilton's influence is unclear, but after more than thirty ballots and with less than two weeks remaining before the inauguration, the House chose Jefferson as the third president of the United States.

The legacy of the Jefferson–Burr tie of 1800 is the Twelfth Amendment, ratified in 1804, which required electors to cast their electoral votes separately for president and vice president. This amendment, which prevented a repetition of the 1800 deadlock, is also important as perhaps the only constitutional provision to recognize (though, of course, not by name) the existence and consequences of political parties in national elections.

Controversial Vice-President

Jefferson was outraged and resentful over Burr's ambivalent conduct in the 1800 election. He and other leaders of the Republican party decided that they could not trust Burr; they therefore froze him out of the Jefferson administration. Not only was Burr excluded from the framing of national policy; even in his home state of New York Republican leaders denied him the opportunity to reward his friends and supporters with federal office—although he did preside over an 1801 convention to consider amendments to New York's Constitution of 1777.

The worst insult to Burr came on February 25, 1804, when the Republican caucus met in Washington, D.C., and nominated Thomas Jefferson for president and George Clinton for vice-president, without even considering Burr's name. Mortified by this treatment and bored with the ceremonial duties of the vice-presidency, Burr began to explore other options—including a defection to the New York Federalists.

Vice-President Burr revealed his unhappiness in the first months of 1804. The Republicans had split between regulars (led by DeWitt Clinton, the nephew of George Clinton) and insurgents. The insurgents nominated Burr for governor; the regulars chose Morgan Lewis, the state supreme court's chief justice, after their first choice, Chancellor John Lansing, Jr., declined to run against Burr. Soon afterward, the Federalists, who chose not to name a candidate from their own ranks, nominated Burr. Aghast, Hamilton yet again declared his opposition to Burr; though some observers scoffed that Hamilton's actions against Burr were rooted in "personal" dislike, Hamilton contributed in some measure to Lewis's defeat of Burr in the April 1804 election.

During the gubernatorial campaign, Burr reportedly had vowed to challenge the first person of consequence to damage his reputation. After the election, Burr learned from a newspaper report that Dr. Charles Cooper had described disparaging comments that Hamilton had made about Burr; among these was a "despicable" (though unspecified) opinion which Hamilton allegedly expressed about Burr. Burr began a correspondence with Hamilton, demanding an explanation. As the exchange of letters continued through the two men's seconds, Burr rejected Hamilton's responses as evasions and pressed him for a full apology for every disparaging comment that Hamilton had made against him. Hamilton refused, and the seconds made arrangements for a duel between the principals.

On the morning of July 11, 1804, Hamilton and Burr met at a dueling ground in Weehawken, New Jersey—just across the river from New York City, where dueling was illegal. Two shots were fired. Burr and his defenders claimed ever afterward that Hamilton had fired first, and at Burr; Hamilton's second and his later defenders retorted that Burr had fired first, that Hamilton had fired involuntarily as Burr's bullet struck him, and that Hamilton was not even aware that he had fired his pistol. The mortally wounded Hamilton was carried back across the river, and died in agony on July 12.

Grand juries in both New York and New Jersey indicted Burr for murder, and the vice-president fled south, where he was welcomed—in a region where dueling was still popular—as a hero who had defended his honor. Federalists and Republicans united to denounce Burr, however, lamenting the loss of Hamilton as a blow to the nation. Both parties were happy to take the opportunity to rid themselves of Burr, whom they regarded as too independent, ambitious, and unprincipled. Meanwhile, every northern state that had not yet outlawed dueling passed statutes doing so, and those where dueling already was illegal stiffened the penalties for the practice.

In his last months in office, Burr made one of his most important contributions to American constitutional law—the only one resulting from deliberate reflection and choice on his part. The Republicans had determined, early in Jefferson's term, to use the mechanism of impeachment to clear the federal bench of Federalist judges. In 1803, they removed senile United States District Judge John Pickering of New Hampshire; in 1804, they impeached Associate Justice Samuel Chase of Maryland. As vice-president, Burr presided over Chase's trial in the Senate. He conducted the trial with dignity and fairness, setting a lasting precedent for future Senate impeachment trials. The Senate acquitted Chase; the enraged president blamed Burr for destroying the Republican purge of the federal courts. Burr's parting speech as vice-president is justly regarded as a model of eloquence and a classic expression of praise for the independence of the Senate:

> [T]his House, I need not remind you, is a sanctuary; a citadel
> of law, of order, and of liberty; and it is here . . . will resistance
> be made to the storms of political frenzy and the silent arts of cor-

ruption; and if the Constitution be destined to perish by the sacrilegious hands of the demagogue or the usurper, which God avert, its expiring agonies will be witnessed on this floor.

Conspiracy, Exile, and Return

In early 1805, Burr left the vice-presidency and national politics. His actions during the next two years are the most mysterious and tantalizing of his career. His enemies charged, and many historians believe, that Burr was bent on a treasonous conspiracy to conquer the western lands and the tottering Spanish empire in Mexico and Central America, in order to create an empire with himself at its head. His defenders suggest either that he only wanted to capture Spain's American possessions, or that he was uncertain of his future but willing to listen to proposals advanced by ambitious and unscrupulous western politicians.

Whatever the case, in 1807 Burr was arrested in what is now Alabama by authority of a presidential proclamation. He was brought to Richmond, Virginia, for trial in the United States circuit court on charges of treason. Representing Burr were former Virginia Governor Edmund Randolph and former Antifederalist Luther Martin; leading the prosecution was United States Attorney George Hay. Presiding over the trial was Chief Justice John Marshall, a bitter opponent of President Jefferson. Jefferson had declared to Congress that Burr's guilt was clear and proven; Marshall was determined that a full and fair trial would resolve the issue.

The Burr treason trial was notable for two significant points of constitutional law. First, a federal court had the authority to issue a subpoena to a sitting president requiring him to produce documents necessary to the conduct of the trial. Burr had asked Marshall to subpoena Jefferson as a witness, which Marshall did, only to work out a compromise with the Jefferson administration to avoid the constitutional crisis that would have resulted had Jefferson refused the subpoena. Second, the trial reaffirmed the narrow definition of treason spelled out in the Constitution. Marshall held that the government had not proved that the former vice president had sought to levy war against the United States or to ally himself with the nation's enemies. The editors of Burr's papers have shown that the principal item of evidence against him, the "cipher letter" which purportedly sketched his plans to sever the western territories from the United States, was actually the handiwork of Senator Jonathan Dayton of New Jersey.

Upon his acquittal, Burr sailed for Europe, where he remained until 1812, traveling from one royal court to another vainly seeking support for vaguely described projects. He returned to New York in June 1812 with fifty dollars in his pocket, and opened a law office in lower Manhattan. Less than a month after his return, his beloved daughter Theodosia Burr Alston, to whom Burr had written a remarkable series of frank letters describing his adventures in Europe, was lost at sea on a voyage to New York. Lost with her were the trunks containing the bulk of her father's papers. Burr stayed in New York until his death in 1836, always short of money yet alarmingly open-handed, supporting himself through his legal practice long after most of his contemporaries had retired. He was regarded then and afterward as a shameless libertine and a figure of almost legendary villainy.

Conclusion

The fame of Aaron Burr is a recurring puzzle for historians of the early national period. Many more Americans are familiar with Burr's name than with James Madison, John Jay, Gouverneur Morris, or all but a few other significant figures in the creation of the United States. The principal source of Burr's fame is his duel with Hamilton in 1804; the tragic, "romantic" fate of Hamilton immortalized his killer as much as himself. Equally influential in the shaping of Burr's posthumous reputation is the classic 1973 historical novel *Burr*, by Gore Vidal (a Burr descendant), which brilliantly reconstructs Burr's world as he might have seen and described it. For these and other reasons, among them his supposed plot to build an empire in the West, Burr is remembered as perhaps the greatest villain in American history. The loss of most of his papers only heightens the degree of mystery, romance, and sinister danger surrounding this enigmatic New Yorker.

Careful examination of the surviving evidence of Burr's life uncovers some answers, but just as many riddles. Rather than an archvillain, he seems brilliant and talented but also directionless and self-destructive. His dispassionate view of American politics and government seems as much the product of indifference to the larger theoretical questions of American public life as of a desire for objectivity.

Burr had no larger goal, no finer motive, than his own advancement and gratification. Nonetheless, he was responsible for major contributions to the development of the American constitutional system, and in many ways represented the future of the nation's politics. Burr, Henry Steele Commager suggested, was the only politician of the early national period who would have done well in modern politics. There is no reason to challenge that statement but good cause to be troubled by it.

---

*I am indebted to Joanne B. Freeman for her insights on the Burr–Hamilton relationship and the theory and practice of dueling in the early national period.

For Further Reading

Kline, Mary-Jo, and Ryan, Joanne, eds. *The Political Correspondence and Public Papers of Aaron Burr*, 2 vols. Princeton: Princeton University Press, 1983.

Lomask, Milton. *Aaron Burr: The Years from Princeton to Vice President, 1756–1805*. New York: Farrar Straus Giroux, 1979.

Lomask, Milton. *Aaron Burr: The Years of Conspiracy and Exile, 1805–1836*. New York: Farrar Straus Giroux, 1982.

Benjamin Nathan Cardozo

(1870–1938)

KERMIT L. HALL

University of Florida

Benjamin Nathan Cardozo (1870–1938) earned a distinguished reputation as a jurist, serving on both the New York Court of Appeals and the United States Supreme Court. His decisions restored judicial restraint and brought about a reevaluation of the role of the courts in the American political system.

Benjamin N. Cardozo was born in New York City on May 24, 1870, to Albert and Rebecca Cardozo, descendants of prominent Sephardic Jews who had arrived in New York City in the eighteenth century. The elder Cardozo was a judge who allegedly did the bidding of Jay Gould in the fight with Cornelius Vanderbilt for control of the Erie Railroad. Albert Cardozo resigned from office in disgrace after a committee of the legislature had recommended his impeachment for corruption.

Benjamin Cardozo received his early education at home. He entered Columbia College at the age of fifteen, finishing at the top of his class. He then attended Columbia Law School, but left after two years, as was then common, to join in practice with his brother. Cardozo never married and lived with his sister, Ellen, until she died in 1929.

Cardozo fashioned an impressive corporate, commercial, and property law practice. So great was the respect accorded his powerful legal intellect that in 1913 the leaders of the New York City bar persuaded the reluctant Cardozo to run for the Supreme Court. Only a month after he began service on this court, the governor elevated him to the New York Court of Appeals.

Cardozo emerged as the most influential judge on what was the nation's most important state appellate tribunal. His success derived from an ability to move the law forward gradually rather than dramatically. To Cardozo, most cases on appeal did not involve much more than applying existing doctrine to a recognizable set of facts. "When Cardozo is through," one legal scholar wrote, "the law is not exactly as it was before; but there has been no sudden shift or revolutionary change."

Cardozo also believed that in a few cases neither precedent nor the facts were clear, and that, as a result, the judge assumed "the function of a lawgiver." "I have grown to see," he wrote, "that the [judicial] process in its highest reaches is not discovery, but creation. . . ." This view of judging was hotly debated in his own time, just as it is today. He was not, however, a simple-minded judicial activist nor a knee-jerk legal realist; instead, he preached the doctrine that judges should defer in many instances to the legislators.

Cardozo was mild-mannered, courtly, and, to some, almost saintly, but such characteristics disguised a less well-known side to his personality. "Very few have ever known," Judge Learned Hand wrote about Cardozo, "what went on behind those blue eyes." The judge's courteous exterior concealed a coldly analytical mind that took "no interest in the identity of the contestants before him." Cardozo compensated for the disgrace of his father with sometimes blind professional detachment, even though he was among his generation's most powerful advocates of the idea that the law had to respond to social change.

Cardozo's scholarly pursuits reflected this concern, and his lectures, books, and articles became classics of modern legal thought. He sought to reconcile the traditional role of the judge in sustaining legal principles with the enormous pressures exerted on the law by industrialization and urbanization. In *The Nature of the Judicial Process* (1921), he argued that for a judge "to determine to be loyal to precedents and to the principles back of precedents, does not carry us far upon the road [to justice]." Rather, Cardozo insisted that an appellate judge always had to fit existing law to changing circumstances. This task was incompatible with the idea that there were fixed, immutable principles of law.

Cardozo's most important state court opinions involved contract and tort law. In *McPherson v. Buick Motor Co.* (1916), for example, the New York court considered whether a seriously injured owner of an automobile with a defective steering wheel could sue the manufacturer, who had built it, rather than the dealer, who had sold it. Traditional doctrine held that there had to be "privity" of contract (that is, a pre-existing direct contractual relationship) between buyer and seller in order to sue. This concept meant that owners of defective automobiles could not get at manufacturers, who sold the cars to dealers rather than directly to the public; they could only sue dealers, who could not satisfy judgements including substantial damages for injuries caused by the defective product. In *McPherson*, however, Cardozo held that they could sue manufacturers, reasoning that "[i]f the nature of a thing is such that it is reasonably certain to place life and limb in peril when negligently made, it is then a thing of danger" and "the manufacturer of this thing of danger is under a duty to make it carefully." Cardozo's opinion in *McPherson* became the starting point for the modern law of products liability.

Cardozo sometimes invoked the law in ways that masked the human consequences of social change. Take, for example, *Palsgraf v. Long Island R.R.* (1928), a classic in American tort law. The cases involved an incident at the Long Island Railroad station in Brooklyn. A railroad guard jostled a passenger, who dropped his package under a moving train. It contained explosive materials, and the resulting detonation of them caused some scales on the train platform to fall on Mrs. Palsgraf. The trial and appeals courts below found in favor of Mrs. Palsgraf. The New York Court of Appeals, however, with Cardozo writing the opinion, overturned the award of damages. Cardozo's writings about the interrelationship of social and legal change would have suggested a finding for the plaintiff. But the coolly analytical Cardozo adopted the position that "the risk reasonably to be perceived defines the duty to be obeyed." He concluded that the railroad could not be held responsible because it could not have reasonably contemplated that the actions of its guard in jostling loose the explosives whose detonation knocked the scales down on Mrs. Palsgraf would have produced Mrs. Palsgraf's injury.

Cardozo also believed that in complex matters judges should defer to legislative authority. In *Kerr S.S. Co. v. Radio Corporation of America* (RCA) (1927), for example, a telegraph company failed to send a coded radiogram and thereby caused great loss to the sender. The question arose whether RCA was responsible for the loss. Cardozo concluded that it was not; to support his position, he invoked the historical rule that a telegraph company was liable only if the general nature of the transaction was revealed to it. He admitted that the rule seemed harsh on senders who of necessity had to keep the text of their messages private. He insisted, however, that such legal innovation "should come through legislation."

Cardozo's influence went beyond his own opinions. As Judge Irving Lehman observed, Cardozo's powerful intellect meant that "his greatest contribution to the development of the common law, is not in his written words—though they will long be read—but in the words spoken in the conference room, heard by few and soon forgotten, yet forgotten only after they had clarified each problem and had served to guide a great court along the road to sound development of the common law.''

When President Herbert Hoover appointed Cardozo to the United States Supreme Court to replace Oliver Wendell Holmes, Jr., in 1932, Cardozo was the most distinguished state judge in America. Even though two other members of the Court were from New York City and another was also a Jew, the support for Cardozo was overwhelming.

On the high bench Cardozo encountered legal tasks of a new order. As a state judge, he had built his reputation dealing with the common law, but on the Supreme Court he had to turn his talents toward constitutional law. His opinions, along with those of the liberal minority of the Supreme Court in the depression ridden 1930s, were important in restoring a sense of judicial restraint and in bringing about a concomitant reevaluation of the Court's role in the American political system.

Because he was the junior justice on the high Court, many important opinions did not go to Cardozo. He did make a real contribution, although rankings by scholars that place him among the Court's ''great'' justices seem unfounded in light of his brief tenure. His lofty judicial reputation rests far more on his brilliant service on the New York Court of Appeals.

Cardozo criticized the restrictive decisions that the Court had made involving state and federal economic regulatory and social welfare legislation. He believed that legislatures had broad power to experiment and that the justices had no business inquiring into the wisdom of their actions. The Court, he said in *Stewart Dry Goods v. Lewis* (1935), should not make itself ''the arbiter between competing economic theories professed by honest men on grounds not wholly frivolous.'' Unlike Louis D. Brandeis, with whom he shared a common view of the judicial role, Cardozo lacked a strongly developed social and economic philosophy that might have guided him toward greater judicial activism.

Perhaps the most difficult issues for Cardozo involved civil liberties, in part because the justice was seldom exposed in his personal life to the kind of conflicts that generated these issues. During his tenure the high Court displayed a growing interest in the relationship between the Bill of Rights and the power of national and state governments to enact laws that impeded individual rights. As an abstract matter, Cardozo believed that no right was absolute and that government, of necessity, had to proscribe certain forms of individual behavior to protect the general welfare. Yet Cardozo was also acutely sensitive to any governmental interference, and he wrote that there could be "no compromise of the freedom to think one's thoughts and speak them."

Cardozo's most famous Supreme Court opinion involved a question of individual rights. In *Palko v. Connecticut* (1937), the justices had to decide whether the limitations of the Bill of Rights could be imposed upon the states through their incorporation in the Fourteenth Amendment. Cardozo wrote for the Court, and his long experience as a state judge with criminal procedure doubtless influenced his opinion. He found that the double jeopardy provision of the Fifth Amendment —the provision at issue in *Palko*—was not binding on the states. Thus, state prosecutors could appeal a jury verdict in a criminal case. But Cardozo added something else to his opinion that proved far more important than the substantive ruling. He concluded that as a general proposition those provisions of the Bill of Rights that were "of the very essence of a scheme of ordered liberty" could be incorporated into the Fourteenth Amendment to limit the powers of the states. Cardozo indicated that the Court would welcome an extension of federal guarantees of freedom of speech, press, and assembly to limit "state action." This formulation is still accepted today, although the Court since *Palko* has included rights that Cardozo would have excluded.

Justice Cardozo died on July 9, 1938, after a long illness. His legacy to American law was to alert judges and lawyers to the modern concept of the function of the courts. With rare insight he discerned the emergent trends in the nation and made both public and private law more responsive to them while maintaining a healthy respect for the principle of judicial restraint.

Columbians as Chief Justices: John Jay, Charles Evans Hughes, and Harlan Fiske Stone *

RICHARD B. MORRIS, PAUL A. FREUND,
and HERBERT WECHSLER

As an appropriate contribution to the federal Constitution's bicentennial, Columbia University devoted its 1987 Gino Speranza Lectures—established at the university by bequest in 1952 to provide lectures on "American traditions and ideals viewed from an historical viewpoint"—to a tribute to the three Columbians who served with distinction in the office of chief justice of the United States. More than a century separated the very first chief justice, John Jay, from Charles Evans Hughes and Harlan Fiske Stone, yet all three shared certain common ground. Although only Jay was a native New Yorker, all three jurists actively practiced law in New York and all three were educated at Columbia—Jay at King's College before clerking for the bar, Hughes and Stone receiving their law degrees from Columbia Law School, the latter serving as its dean over a fourteen-year period.

There are other similarities in the public roles they served. Jay was secretary for foreign affairs and *ad interim* secretary of state, while Hughes was secretary of state in between his years of service as associate justice and then chief justice of the United States Supreme Court. The culmination of Jay's career was his two terms as governor of New York State (1795–1801), while Hughes, who had achieved a nationwide reputation as counsel for the Armstrong Commission, served as the state's governor from 1906 to 1910. For their vision of the Constitution and

*Reprinted, with permission (and corrections), from *New York History* 69 (1988): 133–162.

the contributions they made to its interpretation, we now turn to the scholars who are the acknowledged experts, respectively, on the three chief justices.

It should be added that the forum was chaired by Dean Barbara Aronstein Black of the Columbia Law School, supplemented by valuable commentary by University Professor Emeritus Walter Gellhorn, who, like James Wechsler, had clerked for Stone, and Wilfred Feinberg, Chief Judge of the United States Court of Appeals, Second Circuit, a graduate of Columbia College and, like Black, Gellhorn, Morris, and Wechsler, of the Columbia Law School.

John Jay: First Chief Justice

Richard B. Morris*

John Jay, King's College (now Columbia) '64, was to be the first among equals—serving as chief of a six-man court comprising figures politically congenial—assuming the title of the first chief justice of the supreme court (although the president addressed him as chief justice of the United States). In his 78th *Federalist* letter, Hamilton had gone out of his way to reassure his readers that the judicial branch would always be the "least dangerous to the political rights of the constituents," for unlike the other two branches, "it had no influence over the sword or the purse." However, he was careful not to deny to the federal judiciary the power to invalidate "unconstitutional laws."

In those founding days of our republic, the early academic careers of public officers were usually not held up to the scrutiny of Senate confirmation hearings, the press, and fortunately there was no television, for Jay may have the distinction of being the only chief justice to be suspended from college in his senior year. What happened was preserved in the family tradition, while the official record of the college is conspicuously silent on the affair. It seems that a crowd of students smashed a table in College Hall. That high Tory, Dr. Myles Cooper, King's College's second president, rushed in and proceeded to interrogate the students one by one. None admitted guilt or knowing the culprit. When Jay's turn came, he denied doing it but admitted knowing who did. He refused, however, to inform against a fellow student. Hailed before a faculty committee, Jay looked up his copy of the college statutes and could find no obligation of one student to inform on another. On the other hand, the statutes did enjoin obedience and proper deportment.

The long and the short of it was that Jay was suspended, but an indulgent faculty permitted him to return to college in time for commencement, and his name appears first on the list of graduates, which included only one other at that time. Jay had already shown himself to be a principled and unbending young man.

*The late Richard B. Morris, editor of *The Papers of John Jay,* was Gouverneur Morris Professor of History Emeritus at Columbia University.

No one really knew the exact role the Supreme Court would play when the six judges took their oaths and received their commissions. The Judiciary Act of 1789 had burdened the Supreme Court justices with the arduous duties of circuit riding, which they early decried, even being prepared to cut their salaries if that burden could be removed—a notion, by the way, seemingly inhibited by Article III, section 1, which states that the judges' compensation "shall not be diminished during their continuance in Office."

In any case, among the Founding Fathers who shaped the destiny of the new nation, John Jay has not received adequate recognition for his seminal contributions as statesman and Constitutional expositor. Circumstances have conspired to keep Jay out of the spotlight which has played on the central figures in the great Constitutional drama: He did not attend the Constitutional Convention. Unlike other major figures of the time, save Franklin and Hamilton, he never became president (although he did obtain a number of electoral votes for that office). Yet no one who did not serve in the presidency had the opportunity to distinguish himself in as many different high state and federal offices as Jay. Save for perhaps John Quincy Adams, no one else can claim to have been principal in the negotiation of two major treaties of the United States with foreign nations.

Constitutional historians have not dealt charitably with Jay. His term on the Supreme Court has, as I propose to show, been dismissed as a period of marking time. To take two most recent examples: A recent volume on the early history of the court is subtitled "Antecedents and Beginnings" and devotes a mere three out of seventeen chapters to the high court, 1790–1801, and two chapters to the circuit court, while the succeeding volume dealing with the Marshall court, 1810–1815, bears a subtitle "Foundations of Judicial Power: John Marshall." This ignores the fact that the foundations of national power were laid in the pre-Marshall court and were built upon and invested with prestige and boldness of purpose in contrast to the relatively prudent and even nonpolitical course that Marshall steered through stormy waters.

The fact is that of all the high Federalists, save perhaps Hamilton, John Jay, a central figure in Confederation years by reason of his post as secretary for foreign affairs, held the most advanced views of centralization, of the subordination of the states to the federal government, and of the separation of powers. He had collaborated with Alexander Hamilton and James Madison in writing *The Federalist*, along with a powerful polemic, *An Address to the People of the State of New York*, published in the spring of 1788, with its trenchant and irrefutable exposé of the weaknesses of the Confederation. In correspondence with Thomas Jefferson and George Washington, Jay had previously advocated the separation of powers and checks and balances, and he had persuaded the Confederation Congress to adopt the resolution holding treaties to be part of the supreme law of the land—an injunction to the states later embodied in the supremacy clause of the Constitution.

If Jay's Court rendered relatively few decisions (although the chief justice himself handled some 400 cases on circuit), the justices of the Supreme Court riding circuit took advantage of their confrontation with the local populace to include in their charges to grand juries expositions of the Constitution and the national political scene. Far from feeling that such comments were improper, they deemed it incumbent upon the court to instruct the public in the essence of the brand new Constitutional system in whose construction they themselves had labored so strenuously. In the early days, Jay's charges, when delivered in the northern circuit, were courteously received; but it took courage to tell an audience of French sympathizers (when the French Revolution and the wider European involvement had divided the American people) that they should be neutral in their conduct or to tell the host of southern debtors that they were honorbound under the treaty with Great Britain of 1783 to pay their prewar debts due British creditors. Taking into consideration the prevailing ignorance about the Constitution and the widespread opposition on the part of segments of the American people to its ratification, the Jay Court felt they were dutybound to use the grand jury charges as a vehicle to educate and enlighten the nation. In the post-Jay years, Associate Justice Samuel Chase's grand jury charges assumed the character of violent diatribes, and almost brought about his impeachment.

In considering Jay's impact on our Constitutional history, I should like to concentrate on the chief justice's view of the separation of powers, of the subordination of the states, and the supremacy of treaties.

The issue of separation of powers arose early. In November 1790 Alexander Hamilton, secretary of the treasury, submitted to Jay the question as to whether all branches of the government should intervene and assert their opposition to the principle of states' rights recently enunciated by the Virginia legislature. That body, under prodding from Patrick Henry, had condemned Hamilton's proposal for the assumption of the debts as unconstitutional. Hamilton sounded distraught. "This is the first symptom of a spirit which must either be killed or will kill the Constitution of the United States." Hamilton's feverish comment was no more out of character than Jay's cool response. He considered it inadvisable. "Every indecent interference of state assemblies will diminish their influence. The national government has only to do what is right, and, if possible, be silent.''

When in July of 1793 Secretary of State Thomas Jefferson passed on to Jay a request of President Washington for "the opinions of the judges of the Supreme Court" on various aspects of the executive regulations adopted under the Proclamation of Neutrality, Jay awaited the assembling of the full Court before replying. When he answered in August at some length, he pointed out that "the lines of separation drawn by the Constitution" provided checks upon each branch of the government by the other. Hence, since they were judges of a court of last resort, they felt it improper to decide extrajudicially on such matters, "especially as the power given by the Constitution to the President of calling on the heads of department for opinions, seems to have been *purposely* as well as expressly united in the executive department." Jay's memorable argument was unanswerable, and ended the notion of extrajudicial opinions. But I should add that the doctrine of separation of powers did not deter Jay privately from giving solicited advice to President Washington regarding both domestic and foreign matters, including matters of war and peace. He even wrote a draft of the famous Neutrality Proclamation.

Of Jay's major decisions, his first was his vote in *Chisholm v. Georgia* to uphold the suability of states in federal tribunals. *Chisholm v. Georgia* was grounded in a suit brought by the executors of a citizen of South Carolina, who under contract had supplied the State of Georgia with cloth and clothing during the war. When the case first arose in the Georgia Circuit Court, Governor Edward Telfair was served, and entered a plea denying the jurisdiction of the court on the ground that Georgia was a free and sovereign state. After preliminary hearings in Georgia, the case was put on the Supreme Court calendar for August 1792. When the case came up for argument, Georgia again refused to appear, its distinguished counsel, Alexander J. Dallas and Jared Ingersoll, denied the court's jurisdiction, entering a formal remonstrance which Attorney General Edmund Randolph sought to refute. Randolph argued that the Constitutional provision giving the Supreme Court jurisdiction in cases in which a state was a party covered the cases in which the state was the defendant as well as the plaintiff and cited the Judiciary Act of 1789, which empowered the court to issue all writs necessary for the exercise of its jurisdiction.

Before a large audience the court rendered its decision in February 1793, the majority upholding its jurisdiction over the case, Iredell alone dissenting. Long recognized as a stalwart adherent of popular sovereignty, James Wilson was equally stalwart in his support of national sovereignty. Wilson's views on the suability of states by private citizens of other states should hardly have come as a surprise, since he had stated these views both at the Pennsylvania ratifying convention and in his law lectures at the College of Philadelphia.

But it is the chief justice's notion of sovereignty and his exposition thereof in this case which should concern us today. Jay contended that the sovereignty of the country as a whole passed from the *Crown* of Great Britain to the *people* of the colonies under the Declaration of Independence, and that "the people in their collective and national capacity, established the present Constitution." "The sovereignty of the nation is in the people of the nation," so ran his exposition, "and the sovereignty of each state in the people of each state." Thus the chief justice anticipated by twenty-six years John Marshall's classic finding in *McCulloch v. Maryland* that "the government of the Union then is emphatically and truly a government of the people."

As for the dissenter, James Iredell of North Carolina, the intensity of states' rights feelings and the hostility of the exercise of federal jurisdiction could not be lost upon him. Adopting a narrow construction of the Judiciary Act, which implied that *Congress possessed the power to confer* such jurisdiction but had *actually not done so*, Iredell's dissent was founded on his conception of the *reserved powers of the states*. Clearly Iredell's opinion could find support in Hamilton's cautionary note about the judiciary in *The Federalist*, and in the arguments at the Virginia ratifying convention by James Madison and John Marshall.

And clearly the other states thought so, for *Chisholm v. Georgia* burst like a bomb upon an unsuspecting nation, and the majority decision was repudiated by the Eleventh Amendment, adopted in 1798.

What is notable and lasting about the majority opinion in *Chisholm v. Georgia*, so quickly overruled by Constitutional amendment, is that it raised the crucial question of the base upon which the powers of the federal government rested. Did these powers emanate from the states or from the people as a whole? Jay and Wilson had declared the people to be the source of authority. In the years to come, when the states' rights doctrine threatened the cause of national unity, Jay's position in *Chisholm* was continually called to mind and reaffirmed. On the Supreme Court bench John Marshall asserted the people to be the source of authority in decisions such as *McCulloch v. Maryland*; Daniel Webster proclaimed it from the floor of the Senate; and Chief Justice Salmon P. Chase reaffirmed the doctrine in the years following the Civil War.

The conclusion of that terrible conflict would finally vindicate Jay's concept, set forth seventy years before, of one nation and one people, consisting of "free and equal citizens," with "equal justice for all."

If there was one question upon which the leading framers of the Constitution were united it was on the *obligation of contracts*, and there was widespread opposition to the issuance of paper money by the states and to a variety of moratory legislation on behalf of debtors. Shays's Rebellion, it must be remembered, had only just wound its way down within weeks of the Constitutional Convention. Jay's attitude did not remain in doubt. Sitting on circuit for the District of Rhode Island (long a hotbed of pro-debtor agitation), the chief justice handed down a ruling in an unreported case which the court files still preserve. This was the lawsuit of *Alexander Champion and Thomas Dickason v. Silas Case.* The suit turned on an act of the Rhode Island General Assembly, passed in February 1791, allowing debtors a three-year extension to settle accounts with their creditors and for an exemption for all arrests and attachments for such term. The court invalidated the statute on the ground that it conflicted with the obligation of contract clause of the Constitution, and the legislature of Rhode Island concurred meekly in the decision.

On the other hand, the storm over the collection of debts due by Virginia debtors to British creditors made before the war proved more than a tempest in a teapot. The issue involved the provisions of the treaty of peace with Great Britain, which provided creditors shall meet with no lawful impediment to the recovery of the full value in sterling money of all bona fide debts heretofore contracted. For Jay, as secretary for foreign affairs during the Confederation years, the failure of certain state courts to enforce this treaty pledge provided some justification for England's unreadiness to fulfill her part of the treaty—that is, to withdraw from the frontier. Also he had made no secret of his views.

The argument over British debts reached a climax in the notable case of *Ware v. Hylton.* Not by coincidence had Jay, in a charge to the grand jury in May of 1793, declared that "debts fairly contracted should be honestly paid." Immediately after this bold charge came the hearing of *Ware v. Hylton.* In this case in the Virginia circuit court Jay's was the minority opinion, the majority holding that the payment under Virginia law to the state loan office covered that portion of the debt represented by the face amount of the certificate, but even the majority refused to accept the defendant's plea that the Treaty of 1783 was not controlling. When the case reached the Supreme Court, Jay had already resigned as chief justice to accept the elected post of governor of New York, but the Court unanimously upheld his earlier dissenting view.

Justice Chase held that the British treaty must prevail over state laws, for under the Constitution a treaty supercedes all state laws which derogate from its provisions.

In the year 1794, however, this and other controversial issues had clouded relations between Great Britain and the United States. To settle outstanding grievances President Washington dispatched John Jay to the Court of Saint James's on a controversial diplomatic mission. This was a regrettable precedent, for Jay did not resign from the Court until his return from England, and a justice of the Supreme Court can hardly serve on a controversial diplomatic mission without bringing the Court into politics or raising the implication that somehow such presidential nominations for extrajudicial duties constitute a reward for conduct on the bench. Jay's acceptance seems inconsistent with his strict views on the separation of powers, but, as he explained it to his wife, the pressing public considerations impelled him "to put duty above ease and domestic concerns"—in fact, this meant the longest separation from his beloved wife Sally in their very happy and close-knit marriage.

Jay, as a diplomat in England, had been criticized for settling for relatively minor gains—although the withdrawal of the British Army from the frontier posts hardly falls in that category; but the terms of the treaty divided the nation and spurred an opposition party, which the framers of the Constitution had never contemplated.

Although Jay did not sit in the great Carriage Tax Case, in which the Court rendered its decision interpreting the meaning of the words "direct tax" as used in the Constitution and upholding the validity of the act of Congress, he did as early as 1790, in a unanimous memorandum to President Washington, suggest that one section of the Judiciary Act requiring Supreme Court justices to sit in circuit was unconstitutional, both as regards the distinction the Constitution makes between judges of the Supreme Court and inferior courts and legislation which, by providing the same salary for two jobs, in effect reduced the compensation of the Supreme Court judges. Furthermore, the act required the high Court to rule on errors of its own members sitting in circuit. Attorney General Randolph was sympathetic, and passed the memorandum on to Congress—which did nothing. In a second protest in 1792, the Court merely stressed hardship and not unconstitutionality. But except for a brief respite at the end of Adams's term, the Supreme Court judges, whether Constitutionally or not, were required to engage in the arduous duties of circuit riding until late in the nineteenth century.

Before leaving Jay's role on the bench, reference should be made to his landmark decision in *Glass v. Betsy.* Speaking for the court and reversing the decision of the District Court of Maryland, Jay asserted the full power of the United States District Court, under its admiralty jurisdiction, to determine the legality of prize ships brought into ports of the United States by any foreign nation, in this instance French privateers, and denied the right of any foreign nation, in the absence of treaty stipulation, to establish a court for the exercise of such jurisdiction within the territory of the United States. Charles Warren has observed that "no decision of the court ever did more to vindicate our international rights, to establish respect among other nations for the sovereignty of the country."

In retrospect, Jay's contribution to the Supreme Court in its formative years takes on significant dimensions despite the paucity of business that came before the tribunal in its early days. He and his associates brought the federal court system in close contact with the people of the states by their arduous circuit riding and relatively crowded dockets.

Although he had been New York State's first chief justice, Jay had not practiced law for many years and his decisions do not bear the stamp of a technician in the law. Instead, he is remembered as a creative statesman and an activist chief justice whose concepts of the broad purposes and powers of the new nation under the Constitution were to be upheld and spelled out with boldness and vigor by John Marshall. In bringing the states into submission to the federal government, in securing from both the states and the people reluctant recognition of the supremacy of treaties, and in laying the foundation for the later exercise by the Supreme Court of the power to rule on the Constitutionality of acts of Congress, Jay gave bold direction to the new Constitutional regime. His tireless efforts both before and during his tenure as chief justice to endow the national government with energy, capacity, and scope and to assert the authority of the people over that of the states attest to his vision, courage, and tenacity. It remained for others to spell out the safeguards for individual liberties and the limitation on national power which are so essential to the maintenance of a democratic society in a federal republic. As a humanitarian and civil libertarian (a leading opponent of slavery), John Jay, the patrician, could take pardonable pride in the result.

Jay has been painted by historians and a recent columnist as starchily aristocratic, a supernationalist who first coined the term "Americanize." I think he deserves a better epitaph, and I can think of no better one than his own words in a letter to Benjamin Rush, penned a few years before he ascended the high Court: "I wish to see all unjust and all unnecessary discriminations abolished, and that the time may soon come when all our inhabitants of every colour and denomination shall be free and equal partners of our political liberty."

Chief Justice
Charles Evans Hughes

PAUL A. FREUND*

To the dwindling band of us who witnessed Charles Evans Hughes at the center of the Bench, his commanding, magisterial presence seemed preordained by nature. It comes as a surprise, then, to learn that early in his tenure as associate justice (1910–1916) he was on the verge of a breakdown, unsure of his capability, thinking of resignation, agitated, a deeply troubled figure whom Chief Justice White, in a late night walk with him, tried to calm and to reassure. The conventional explanation is that he took his seat without a break and a rest from the crowded final period of his governorship of New York, and that he found early on that he required an annual vacation: he was one of those, like Brandeis, who could do a year's work in eleven months but not in twelve. Hughes himself recognized his need early in life. It was in 1894, as he recorded in his *Autobiographical Notes*, that he "discovered" Switzerland.

This explanation, in Hughes's case, implies more than a sensitive nervous system; it signifies a temperament of great intensity, utter immersion in the work at hand, the severest demands on his own powers. As chief justice he and his wife declined all evening social invitations except for Saturdays. Their Saturday evenings were booked a year in advance. Efficiency was his watchword. In middle life he gave up smoking; this, he said characteristically, increased his efficiency twenty-five percent.

He arrived regularly at his office at 8:30, after a brisk walk. He managed with just one law clerk, who was a fixture for a number of years. He never missed a day of the Court's sessions, except for a period of illness in 1939 lasting several weeks. The circumstances are revealing. The justices were assembled at a celebration of the sesquicentennial of Congress. Hughes was scheduled as a major speaker. He approached the rostrum with faltering steps, and spoke under an obvious strain, without notes. At the end of the ceremony he motioned to his

---

*Paul A. Freund is Carl M. Loeb University Professor Emeritus at Harvard University.

colleagues, "Come on, Brethren, we have work to do." It was a Saturday, conference day. Justice Roberts urged the Chief to postpone the conference, to no avail. That evening the Hugheses were hosts on their weekly allowable social event. That night Hughes collapsed; a physician was called, and diagnosed a bleeding ulcer.

On the Bench his concentration was total. He transfixed counsel with a steady gaze, betraying a readiness to intervene by a flickering of the eyelids. His questions were designed to bring a case into focus. He would say, "Doesn't your case come to this?" Or "Isn't this your real point?"—followed usually by counsel's answer, "Your Honor, you have stated it better than I could." And, he could rescue counsel floundering under a battering from elsewhere on the Bench.

It would be a mistake to picture Hughes as a cold and calculating machine. When he resigned as associate justice to run for the presidency in 1916, Holmes wrote of him in a letter to the eminent legal scholar Sir Frederick Pollock: "I shall miss him consumedly, for he is not only a good fellow, experienced and wise, but funny, and with doubts that open vistas through the wall of a nonconformist conscience." This warmer side of his nature showed itself in his role as chief justice.

To those who knew him as chief justice at close range, only his neatly trimmed white whiskers were frosty. I have pertinent testimony from two men who were members of the Senate when Hughes was nominated in 1930 and who voted against his confirmation—C.C. Dill of Washington, known in the West as the father of Grand Coulee Dam, and Hugo L. Black. Some years ago in Spokane I spoke with Senator Dill, who at ninety had total recall. He had voted against Hughes, he said, because Hughes as counsel for private power interests during his interregnum (1916-1930) had advocated private operation of Muscle Shoals and had argued that a licensee of the Federal Radio Commission to operate a radio station enjoyed a vested right, not to be displaced save for fraud or the like. The latter issue reached the Supreme Court in 1933, and Dill, having heard reports that the decision was about to be announced, was in the courtroom, deeply apprehensive. To his happy surprise, Hughes delivered a ringing opinion upholding the Commission's authority to conduct a renewal hearing on a competitive basis. At the adjournment, Dill betook himself to the Chief's chambers, was ushered in, and said, "Chief Justice, I am here to eat crow." Hughes threw back his head and laughed. "Don't you know, Dill, that as a lawyer you do your best for your client, and as a judge you decide in the public interest?" After that, Dill recalled, whenever he presented a constituent for admission to the Supreme Court bar, Hughes would say to the applicant, "You are fortunate to have Senator Dill as your sponsor."

The second witness to Hughes's mellower nature was closer to the daily life of the Court. I spoke with Justice Black near the close of his tenure. He recalled that early in his service certain columnists (Hughes liked to call them daily calumnists) wrote that Black was writing dissenting opinions too indiscriminately. The Chief came to him and said, "I hope you are not going to be influenced by what you may have read about your dissenting opinions. Dissents have been the lifeblood of this Court."

Thirty years later, Black was still moved by the episode. It was all the more impressive because Hughes was known to be generally averse to dissents in practice, however much he had lauded them philosophically as appeals to the "brooding spirit of the law."

Perhaps the most exacting duty of a chief justice is the task of presiding at conference. When I asked Black about Hughes in this role he said simply, "We haven't had anyone like him since." This from one who served under three successors. Justice Brandeis, who retired while Hughes was Chief, was more descriptive. He said, with admiration, "Sometimes our conferences lasted six hours and Hughes would do almost all the talking." Still, Justice Frankfurter asserted, discussion was actually freer under Hughes's strict enforcement of orderly progression among the Brethren than in the more at-large speaking tolerated under his successors. It evidently took some courage and preparation to contest Hughes's statement and analysis of a case, delivered from scanty notes which he consulted sparingly.

As chief justice, Hughes proved to have more effective political sense than he showed as a candidate for president. A supreme test came with President Roosevelt's Court plan early in 1937. Hughes was asked to testify before the Senate Judiciary Committee, and although inclined at first to do so, was dissuaded by the advice of Justice Brandeis that he should not appear. On the Saturday before the opposition witnesses were to be called, Senator Wheeler went to see Brandeis in the hope of getting a statement. Brandeis said that any statement should come from the chief justice, and when Wheeler protested that he did not know Hughes, Brandeis replied that Hughes knew Wheeler and what he was trying to accomplish. Thereupon Wheeler phoned Hughes, was welcomed at the Chief's house, and arranged that a letter be drafted by Hughes for presentation on Monday. Over the weekend Hughes composed the letter, refuting the administration's claim that the Court needed additional members to cope with its docket, and submitting that more justices would be counterproductive: more to hear, to confer, to consult, to write, to agree. Probably the most telling part of the letter was the statement that it was joined by Justices Brandeis and Van Devanter, and that although there was not time to consult others, Hughes was confident it had the support of all the members of the Court. Hughes explained the episode at the next conference of the Court, and no complaint was voiced. Nevertheless, in other quarters Justice Stone objected, not without reason, to the gratuitous assertion about those who had not been consulted, and to an oblique advisory opinion in the letter to the effect that for an enlarged Court to sit in panels might violate the constitutional mandate of "one Supreme Court."

When Senator Wheeler picked up the letter late on Sunday, Hughes remarked, pointing to the concurrence of Brandeis and Van Devanter, "They are the Court." They were, of course, the respected senior members of the liberal and conservative blocs on the Court.

Hughes may have been thinking of the occasion in 1935 when he testified in opposition to Senator Black's bill to expedite appeals in certain federal constitutional cases; on that appearance he was flanked by the same colleagues, Brandeis and Van Devanter. The fraternal relationship of Hughes and Brandeis merits some brief attention. When the colleagues of Justice Holmes concluded sadly that the time for his retirement had come, Hughes approached Brandeis to deliver the message to the old warrior. Brandeis countered that the message had best come from the Chief, who acquiesced and carried out the mission. As Holmes's law clerk recounts the experience, Hughes left the Holmes house with tears in his eyes, and on the way out met Brandeis coming in, surely not by accident. At the close of several terms Brandeis indicated to Hughes that he was ready to retire, but was persuaded by the Chief to continue, until in the spring of 1939 Brandeis made the final decision; turning to the clerk of the Court at the close of a session, he said "I'll not be in tomorrow."

A Chief's relations with his colleagues are most subject to strain in the assignment of opinion-writing. If presiding at conference is the most exacting function, assignment is the most delicate. When Hughes was in the majority on a divided Court, he sought to entrust the opinion to a moderate member. In cases of extraordinary moment, such as the Gold Clause cases and the Labor Relations Act decisions, he understandably acted as spokesman. In some instances there were considerations of individual appropriateness. Several cases involving enlarged review of the fairness of criminal trials of Negroes were assigned to Justice Black. The Social Security cases were assigned to Justice Cardozo, even though he was in a minority on the threshold question of standing to sue. The first and ill-fated flag salute case was assigned to Justice Frankfurter, because of his moving statement at conference on the role of the public schools in fostering a spirit of national unity amid diversity—this despite the advice of Frankfurter and Roberts that the opinion should be taken by Hughes himself. (It would have helped Frankfurter's place in history if their advice had been accepted.)

The assignment process was not without criticism. Justice Stone let it be known that in his view Hughes was self-centered in this regard, keeping too many of the major cases for himself, and also choosing to author decisions for a "liberal" majority while designating others to write for a conservative majority. When the criticism came to Hughes's attention after his retirement, he sought to deflect it by stating that he had wanted to assign the Gold Cases to Stone, but that Stone in conference took a position different from that of either bloc of justices. (Justice Stone did indeed write a separate concurring opinion, which, in my estimation, was the only completely honest opinion intellectually in the whole lot.)

At oral agreement, Hughes brought a case into focus and often rescued a counsel from an onslaught from the Bench. One or two examples will suffice. In the Ashwander case, preferred stockholders of Alabama Power Company sued to enjoin the company from carrying out a contract with the Tennessee Valley Authority for the sale of properties at Muscle Shoals, on the ground that TVA was unconstitutional. Counsel for the plaintiffs began by luridly describing the plans and programs of TVA for the entire Tennessee River and its tributaries. Hughes grew impatient. "Would you mind telling us at once what this suit is, who brought it, and against whom?" Counsel was "just coming to that," but had to be pressured again to state the issue before the Court. It was, he said, "the validity of the program of the Tennessee Valley Authority." To which Hughes countered, "It is the validity of a contract, is it not?" With that the focus was set, the bounds were drawn, and TVA escaped the first barrage against it.

In the Gold Cases, turning on devaluation of the dollar, Solicitor General Stanley Reed was the unhappy target of a bombardment from Justice Pierce Butler, who wanted to know whether the government could call a dime a dollar, could make 15 grains of gold the equivalent of 25 grains, could indeed make one grain of gold satisfy a promise to pay the 25 grains. Reed was reduced to saying, "I presume it could." At this point Hughes intervened. "Well, the Government could provide for paper money, could it not . . ." "And is it the effect of the *Legal Tender* decisions that although money may have been borrowed on a gold basis, the Government may provide for repayment on a paper basis?" Reed was too battle-weary or too painfully honest to appreciate the neatness of Hughes's question. He responded, "Do you mean by 'borrowed on a gold basis' that that was written into the obligation?'' The rescue operation was thus almost aborted. Hughes tried again. ''No, I am not speaking of the gold clause; but I am speaking of the borrowing of money which, at the time it was borrowed, was worth a certain amount of gold, and I am asking if the *Legal Tender* decisions did not have the effect of deciding that the Government could thereafter constitutionally provide for the discharge of that debt in paper money.'' The words ''on a gold basis'' were the one perfectly designed bridge to throw up between the precedents of 1870 and the case at bar; the one formula whose careful ambiguity was capable of tempering the shock of repudiation with the shock of recognition.

We are now led to the final aspect of our subject, the substantive positions of Chief Justice Hughes.

Justice Brandeis used to say that the way to deal with the irresistible (like the ''curse of Bigness'') was to resist it. I hardly think that Hughes would have made that response. More like Margaret Fuller, he would accept the universe, at least where the issue was one of centralizing power and not of fundamental human rights. A forecast of his views on national power over the economy was provided during his earlier service on the Court, in what was perhaps his proudest opinion, the *Shreveport* case. The Interstate Commerce Commission, to equalize railroad freight rates between equidistant points, had ruled that a carrier must either lower its interstate charges or raise its intrastate rates—despite a provision in the Interstate Commerce Act prohibiting the Commission from regulating intrastate rates. The Commission, Hughes reasoned, was not violating its charter; it was regulating not intrastate rates ''as such,'' but the ''relationship'' between the two sets of rates. The opinion is doubly revealing—not only for Hughes's sympathetic acceptance of national power, but for his ability to surmount subtly an inconvenient clause or an embarrassing precedent. After all, in similar vein he sustained a law that forbade employers from discharging an employee for refusing to promise not to join a union (the *Coppage* case), while not overruling a prior decision (the *Adair* case) that had overturned a statute outlawing the firing of employees who joined a union. Yellow-dog contracts, it seems, came in different shades, making it possible to discern more clearly the legitimate claims of organized labor.

It should not have been too surprising that in the New Deal period, even putting aside the danger of President Roosevelt's Court Reorganization Plan, Hughes was able to support a state minimum wage law without overruling the *Adkins* precedent, on the ground that the new law took account of the needs of the employer as well as of the employees. Or that, after joining a majority striking down the wage and hour provisions of the Guffey Coal Act, he could deliver a ringing opinion upholding the collective-bargaining provisions of the Labor Relations Act. Or that, while chastising the government for abrogating gold clauses in its outstanding bonds, sounding like Secretary of State Hughes lecturing Latin American states on the immorality of default, he could nevertheless give victory to the Treasury, exonerating it of any obligation to pay a premium on the bonds, since the bondholders could not prove any "damages"—as if a creditor holding a monetary obligation for an arithmetically determined sum must show "damages" in order to recover. In what was surely the nadir of constitutional law, when a majority ruled invalid under the commerce clause a federal railway pension plan because philanthropy toward ex-employees was unrelated to efficiency of railway operations, Hughes put aside his allergy to 5–4 decisions and wrote an uncharacteristically stinging dissent. If his position on key issues had carried the day in the Court, the Court plan may well have been averted.

True, he joined in overturning the Recovery Act and the Agricultural Adjustment Act, but the former was sinking under the weight of failing enforcement and was due to expire by its own terms in a few weeks, while in the latter case Hughes had tried to base the decision on the curable ground of excessive deligation of power, but was forestalled at conference by Justice Stone, who argued cogently that the principle of Congressional ratification of executive action would be compromised by the Chief's suggestion. At all events, Hughes did insist on an espousal in Roberts's opinion of the broad view of the spending power, which proved valuable in the subsequent Social Security cases, however paradoxically it was treated in the AAA case itself.

The juridical universe that he accepted, adroitly at times, was not *toto caelo* at odds with that of Franklin Roosevelt. Relations between the two men, both schooled in the political life of Albany, never became embittered. When the Chief administered the presidential oath to FDR for the third time, in 1941, he was tempted to say, he reminisced, "Franklin, don't you think this is getting a trifle monotonous?"

The drama of the Court crisis, which turned mainly on national power over the economy, has obscured the seminal contribution of the Hughes Court in the area of civil liberties and civil rights. The change in 1930 from Taft and Sanford to Hughes and Roberts was one of the identifiable watersheds in the Court's history. A remarkable series of decisions, generally authored by Hughes himself, established new benchmarks in freedom of the press, of speech, and of assembly. Local dictators like Mayor Frank Hague and Governor Huey Long received their come-uppance. Governor Sterling of Texas was held subject to the injunctive power of a federal district court. The reach of habeas corpus was extended. Racial segregation in higher education was struck down. These decisions were the doctrinal wellsprings for the post-World War II surge in the Court's guardianship of procedure, participation, and personhood. As the struggles over national power fade into the inevitabilities of battles long ago, these other advances will stand out as the most memorable legacy of the Court under Hughes.

Harlan Fiske Stone

HERBERT WECHSLER*

Of all the "Columbian" Chief Justices whose careers we celebrate today, Harlan Fiske Stone was surely most "Columbian" of all. He was an alumnus of the Law School in the class of 1898; that was, however, but the start of his relation to the school. He served as a lecturer in law from 1899 to 1903, adjunct professor from 1903 to 1905, and professor and dean of the faculty from 1910 to 1923, when he resigned to devote himself to full-time practice. Thus he gave some nineteen years to teaching at Columbia, endearing himself to the students of that time to a spectacular degree. The ranks of those students have, of course, grown thinner with the passing of years, but they are still more than "a happy few"; and all seem eager to discourse at length about the imprint of Stone's classes.

Stone's contribution to the Law School was, however, not confined to personal achievement in the classroom. During his thirteen years as dean, his targets went beyond establishing a firm tradition of great teaching and attention to the growth of students' minds. What he developed was a complex of ideas concerning what law is and is not, how it could be thought about most usefully, and what it could be made to be. He had a vision of a school that conceived of law as "neither formal logic nor the embodiment of inexorable scientific law" but rather as "a human institution, created by human agents to serve human ends." He sought to recruit a faculty who, seeing law for what it is, would by their teaching, scholarship, and public service facilitate its prudent adaptation as conditions changed or time threw up new problems and new social needs. I do not mean, of course, to represent him as a great reformer; he was not. His concern, which he believed should also be the school's concern, was, in his modest terms, for "law improvement," the enduring task of nurturing the systematic and objective reassessment and refreshment of existing legal institutions. He thought that the then leaders of the bar had failed in the performance of that vital function, as undoubtedly they lamentably had; and he trusted to the schools

*Herbert Wechsler is Harlan Fiske Stone Professor Emeritus of Constitutional Law and special lecturer at Columbia University Law School.

to fashion future leaders who would understand and would discharge the duties of a great profession. It is not too much to say that the Law School's character in modern times derives, and hopefully will long continue to derive, from Stone's conceptions of law teaching and of law, developed and articulated here well over half a century ago.

Stone's decision in 1923 to devote his energies to full-time practice, a decision motivated in some part at least by his distaste for Nicholas Murray Butler, was promptly frustrated by President Calvin Coolidge in 1924. Congressional investigation of the work of the Department of Justice under Harry M. Daugherty, President Warren G. Harding's appointee as attorney general, had uncovered a malodorous condition that could be remedied only by his replacement. Coolidge called on Stone, whom he had known at Amherst, to take on the rescue operation, a summons Stone did not believe he could refuse. His appointment, warmly acclaimed in Congress and the press, was followed promptly by the reconstruction that was urgently required. In a bare nine months as the Attorney General, Stone won widespread recognition for the integrity, courage, candor and skill that he displayed in rehabilitating the department. It was not surprising, therefore, that when Associate Justice Joseph McKenna retired after long service on the Supreme Court, Coolidge nominated Stone as his successor. The nomination was widely applauded in the Congress and the press, notwithstanding a flurry of opposition led by Senator George Norris of Nebraska, who sought to picture Stone as a representative of Wall Street. When the votes on confirmation were counted in the Senate, only six were cast in opposition. One of these, that of Senator Norris himself, was recanted sixteen years later when Stone was unanimously confirmed as chief justice. "In the years that have passed," the senator said, "I became convinced, and am now convinced, that in my opposition to the confirmation of his nomination I was entirely in error. . . . It is a great satisfaction to me to rectify, in a very small degree, perhaps, the wrong I did him years ago." The statement tells us something nice about George Norris. It tells us even more about the magnitude of Stone's achievement as an associate justice in the years from 1925 to 1941.

When Stone came to the Court, the dominant problem of American public affairs was that of marshaling the capacities of government to promote individual and social welfare by ordering the economic forces that industrial enterprise had unloosed. Efforts to fashion constructive legislative intervention had encountered conceptions antipathetic to government that had prevailed for a long time. Such conceptions might be defeated at the ballot box; it was more difficult to overcome them on judicial review by the Supreme Court. Restrictive applications of the due process and equal protection clauses of the Fourteenth Amendment weighed heavily upon the power of the states to formulate measures, with further restrictions derived from the negative implications of the commerce clause if the activity was interstate. At the same time, the power expressly conferred on Congress "to regulate commerce . . . among the several states" was interpreted so narrowly that it precluded national action of fundamental economic reach. However the issue might be posed in concrete cases, the portent was that governmental action must confine itself to very modest limits if the judicial test were to be survived.

In the overthrow of this entrenched position Justice Stone played a heroic part. The pioneering work had, to be sure, been done for years by Justice Holmes and Justice Brandeis. That Stone would largely share and strongly fortify their dissenting views was not apparent at the start of his judicial career, but before long became quite clear. By 1929, Chief Justice William Howard Taft was voicing his chagrin that, as he put it, Stone "has ranged himself with Brandeis and with Holmes in a good many of our constitutional differences." Justice Benjamin N. Cardozo replaced Justice Oliver Wendell Holmes, Jr., in 1932 and cast his lot with the dissenters, but that, of course, produced no change in the numerical division of the Court. By 1937, however, in the shadow of the Roosevelt Court Reorganization Plan, Chief Justice Charles Evans Hughes and Justice Owen J. Roberts joined Brandeis, Stone, and Cardozo in determining the course of the decisions. As the Old Guard justices departed in the four succeeding years, to be replaced by Roosevelt supporters, the "historic shift of emphasis in constitutional interpretation," as Stone modestly described what had occurred, transformed the jurisprudence of the Court relating to the issues that had been in controversy for so long.

These issues, it is useful to recall, varied significantly during Stone's long tenure. For roughly the first decade, they primarily involved the validity of state attempts to cope with economic problems by regulation and taxation. Thereafter, the issues involved primarily the validity of national attempts to come to grips with problems thought by both the president and Congress to defy an insular solution, the host of measures that derived from the New Deal. Throughout, but especially in the last years, there also were more poignant issues to be faced: the claims of individuals that fundamental areas of personal freedom and autonomy (civil liberty, if you will, and civil rights) were protected against governmental infringement by the Bill of Rights and Civil War Amendments.

Whatever the issue, Stone's approach to its resolution was animated by the insight that the words of the Constitution were not to be read "as we read legislative codes which are subject to continuous revision with the changing course of events, but as the revelation of the great purposes which were intended to be achieved by the Constitution as a continuing instrument of government."

Stone's work in dealing with these issues is embodied in more than 200 opinions for the Court or in dissent that cannot possibly be summarized in a brief paper. It may, however, be instructive to provide some illustrations of the contribution that he made.

1. *State Regulation.* When Stone was appointed to the Court, the majority held fast to the dogma that governmental regulation of prices or of wages was invalid, an impairment of the liberty of contract deemed to be protected by the Fourteenth Amendment. In 1927 and 1928, Stone dissented vigorously on the issue of price, perceiving "no controlling difference between reasonable regulation of price . . . and other forms of appropriate regulation . . . ," a position that prevailed in 1934 when minimum prices fixed under the New York fluid milk law were sustained. With price regulation out of the shadow, the question of wage remained. That issue came to the Court in 1936, to be turned aside on highly technical grounds that Stone considered insufficient. His dissent protested, "It is not for the courts to resolve doubts whether the remedy by wage regulation is as efficacious as many believe, or is better than some other or is better even than the blind operation of uncontrolled economic forces. The legislature must be free to choose unless government is to be rendered impotent." A year later, the battle was over when the Washington minimum wage law was sustained.

From that time forth there was no doubt that whatever lines might ultimately be drawn, the states had regained the power to govern, save as their power might be limited or preempted by the national authority in areas in which it is supreme.

2. *The Powers of Congress.* Prior to the explosive issues engendered by the Roosevelt program, the scope of the great vehicles of national power embodied in the Constitution had not during Stone's service been the subject of important consideration. When the first test of the New Deal came in an attack on the Petroleum Code, the Code was held invalid on the ground of excessive delegation, Justice Stone joining in the judgment. The Gold Clause cases followed with a narrow escape for the government in the case of the government bond, Justice Stone concurring only in result. Promptly thereafter, the Railroad Retirement Act, mandating that the interstate roads establish pensions for their super-

annuated employees, was held invalid—not only on due process grounds that could be remedied but also on the fatal ground that it was not a regulation of "commerce," with Brandeis, Stone, and Cardozo joining in Hughes's powerful dissent. Three weeks later the N.I.R.A. was struck down, the Court unanimous that the delegation was too wide and that the labor provisions of the Live Poultry Code dealt with a local matter beyond reach of Congress.

The Tennessee Valley Authority Act was, to be sure, sustained at the next term, Chief Justice Hughes writing the opinion, but the Agricultural Adjustment Act fell with a declaration that Congress could not use the national spending power to induce farmers to reduce their crops, agricultural production being the exclusive concern of the states. The Bituminous Coal Conservation Act was next to go on the ground that mining coal also was "production" and not commerce, notwithstanding the dependence of much of the country on its availability and use; labor conditions in the mines were also the exclusive concern of the state. Read together, the decisions seemed to doom the Social Security Act, and it was difficult to see how the National Labor Relations (Wagner) Act could succeed under the standards by which the Coal Act had failed. Hughes and Cardozo each filed dissents in the Coal Case in which Brandeis and Stone concurred. The dissent in the Agricultural Adjustment case was written by Justice Stone, with only Brandeis and Cardozo in support.

Justice Stone's dissent in the case of the A.A.A. marks in many ways the high point of the struggle. Because Congress, it was assumed, could not compel a farmer to reduce his crops, it could not (by a magnificent *non sequitur*) "indirectly accomplish those ends by taxing and spending to purchase compliance." So Justice Roberts had reasoned for the Court. The position was ridiculed by Justice Stone:

> The government may give seeds to farmers but may not condition the gift upon being planted in places where they are most needed or even planted at all. The government may give money to the unemployed but may not ask that those who get it shall give labor in return, or even use it to support their families . . . All that, because it is purchased regulation infringing state powers, must be left for the states, who are unable or unwilling to supply the necessary relief.

Even more significant, however, than Justice Stone's position on the merits was his reminder that the only check upon the Court is "our own sense of self-restraint," that "the conscience and patriotism of the Congress and the Executive" are also "a restraint on the abuse of power," and that "interpretation of our great charter of government" leads to destruction when it "proceeds on any assumption that the responsibility for the preservation of our institutions is the exclusive concern of any one of the three branches of government."

This was more than an answer on the specific issues in the case. It was a frontal challenge to the majority of the Court. In the struggle that followed in the Congress and the country, it was the battle cry of the attack.

The story moves quickly thereafter. Early in February 1937, the president proposed his Court reorganization plan in a message to Congress; it would have authorized the president to appoint, with the consent of the Senate, an additional justice of the Supreme Court for each justice over seventy years of age who did not retire on full salary, save that the number of justices could not at any time exceed fifteen. At the height of the great debate upon the plan, the Court sustained the collective bargaining provisions of the Railway Labor Act in an opinion by Justice Stone. Two weeks later the National Labor Relations Act survived the judicial test, Chief Justice Hughes writing the opinion for five members of the Court. The judgments sustaining the Social Security Act followed, Cardozo writing in support of the federal statute and Stone in support of the enactment of a state.

Decisions of the next few years made clear how far the terms of settlement of the great crisis finally accorded to the national authority the powers that a modern nation needs. One of the most important of these judgments was Stone's opinion in the Darby Lumber case in 1941, sustaining the Fair Labor Standards Act of 1938. Federal authority, he held, may deal directly with the conditions of production for interstate commerce. The old Child Labor Act decision of 1918, *Hammer v. Dagenhart*, in which Justice Holmes filed his great dissent, was with much satisfaction overruled. The opinion finally rejected the idea that radiations from the Tenth Amendment limited the scope of national authority. The amendment reserved what was not delegated but did not "circumscribe the delegations.

In a very different field from commerce, Stone affirmed in *United States v. Classic* the power of Congress to penalize abuses in the conduct of primaries to select candidates for federal office, specifically, the denial of the right of a qualified elector to vote. The decision laid the predicate for the later ruling forbidding the longstanding exclusion of Negroes from Democratic primaries in the South, a crucial step in the modern enfranchisement of blacks and the political rejuvenation of a vital portion of the country.

It would distort Justice Stone's participation in the reformulation of constitutional doctrine to epitomize his contribution in terms of the vindication of government alone. For it is the paradox of the period that new areas of constitutional protection were emerging even as the power to govern was being sustained. Thus the First Amendment freedoms of religion, speech, and press were held, with Stone's support, to be protected against action of the state by the due process clause of the Fourteenth Amendment and were accorded a progressively expansive meaning. Stone wrote little in this field, but what he wrote was of immense importance, culminating in his lone dissent in the compulsory flag salute case of 1940, which was adopted by the Court in 1943. The Constitution, he admonished, "expresses more than the conviction of the people that democratic processes must be preserved at all costs. It is also an expression of faith and a command that freedom of mind and spirit must be preserved, which government must obey, if it is to adhere to that justice and moderation without which no free government can exist." That moving statement made forty-seven years ago epitomizes the main thrust of constitutional development and exegesis in our time.

Any appraisal of the influence that courts or judges of the past have exerted on the future is a problematic venture. I make bold nonetheless to say that the fact that the power to govern is unchallenged now in areas where government is sorely needed, that our federalism is more viable than it once was, that civil rights and civil liberty are more secure, may be attributed in part to the persuasiveness of Stone's opinions in his twenty-one years of service on the Supreme Court.

The Electoral College in the Early Republic, 1787-1804: The New York Experience

TADAHISA KURODA
Skidmore College

Writing under the pseudonym "Publius," Alexander Hamilton wrote in *The Federalist No. 68*, "The mode of appointment of the Chief Magistrate of the United States is almost the only part of the system, of any consequence, which has escaped without severe censure or which has received the slightest mark of approbation from its opponents." But that provision of Article II of the Constitution left open questions for political leaders in the nation and states to resolve, and hence led to controversy. The electoral college as we know it today was as much the creation of those who implemented the Constitution in New York and elsewhere as it was of the framers of the Constitution in the Philadelphia Convention.

With potential regional voting blocs in both New England and the South, the middle states, particularly Pennsylvania and New York, could sway the outcome of presidential contests. Those individuals who could affect New York's vote, therefore, had great influence: George Clinton in 1789, 1792, and again in 1804, Aaron Burr in 1796 and 1800, and Alexander Hamilton throughout this period. No state in the early republic played a more important role in working out the meaning of the electoral college than New York, and there is no more interesting example of the role of politics in interpreting the Constitution than in New York's experience with presidential electors.

George Clinton, a revolutionary soldier-patriot, committed republican, and first governor under the constitution of 1777, was the dominant political figure of the period in New York. Reelected in 1780, 1783, and again in 1786 when he ran unopposed, Clinton depended on the support of farmers from semi-subsistence areas of central and northern New York. His republicanism emphasized the state as the basic unit, direct rather than virtual representation, and the yeoman farmer as the backbone of the citizenry. He and his followers generally preferred direct democratic government, based on the numerical majority, but would compromise and accept more sophisticated and complex structures where necessary. They were on the whole satisfied with the political situation as shaped by the New York constitution and the Articles of Confederation, which granted substantial autonomy to the state.[1]

Clinton recognized that his opponents, the advocates of the Constitution, drew strength from New York City and Albany, particularly from their professional and mercantile classes, and from the commercial farmers of the lower Hudson. Known as the Federalists, they favored a more complex republic of checks and balances, but they would make accommodations to numerical majorities when necessary. Their nationalism and support for a stronger central government derived at least in part from their desire to place political power where they could have access.[2]

Clinton and the Antifederalists contributed relatively little to the making of the Constitution in the Philadelphia Convention. Moreover, they could not prevent its adoption—even in their own state, where they held a clear majority in the ratifying convention meeting at Poughkeepsie in June and July of 1788. In the ensuing weeks and months they tried to unite behind a common plea for amendments to make sure that the Constitution would be safe for their constituents.

1789

In September of 1788, the Confederation Congress announced that on the first Wednesday in January, 1789, the states that had ratified the Constitution should appoint presidential electors; on the first Wednesday in February the electors should assemble in their respective states and vote for president. On the first Wednesday in March, the new government would begin functioning at "the present Seat of Congress." This decision, the result of a stalemate between factions contending for the other sites, gave New York City the much sought after honor and advantage of hosting the new government.[3]

Each state had to adopt procedures in compliance with the Constitution for the election of United States representatives, senators, and presidential electors. Accordingly, Governor Clinton called for a special session of the state legislature to meet in Albany in December, less than one month before electors were to be appointed. Senate clerk Abraham Bancker noted that the Federalists had a majority in the state senate, and the Antifederalists a majority in the assembly: "consequently we must expect many of our acts to be negatived by each other in the course of Sessions, which, by the bye, is likely to be a very long one."[4]

The Federalists were determined to protect their interests in the upcoming presidential and congressional elections and to deny the Clintonian organization any advantage. They wanted George Washington for president with a trustworthy partner, like John Adams, for vice-president, and sought to make certain that no Antifederalist, especially Clinton, embarrassed Washington or the new government with a successful challenge for either position. They also sought clear majority control of the United States Senate and House, which would examine all proposals for amendments to the Constitution. Having barely won the ratification battle in Poughkeepsie, they were not about to lower their guard and be surprised by the Clintonians. On the other hand, the Clintonians determined to flex their political muscle, win support in Virginia and the other states, and press for a bill of rights.[5]

The larger Antifederalist assembly favored choosing electors by the joint ballot of the legislature, while the smaller Federalist senate preferred a concurrent vote which would effectively give each house four electors to appoint. Clinton threw his sympathies on the side of the assemblymen, elected in counties by freeholders, rather than on that of the senators, chosen in four large districts by those meeting a substantial property-holding requirement. The two houses tried to break the deadlock with joint conferences on January 5 and February 3, to no avail.

Thus February came and went, and New York's legislature failed to agree on a mode for choosing electors, and New York, therefore, cast no votes for president. Federalist Jeremiah Mason celebrated the occasion by writing to a New York friend, "Your neglecting to choose electors will make the election of a federal President more certain. As some of your electors would probably have been Antifederal."[6] Mason understood that the Constitution's directive that each elector cast two votes for president left uncertain which candidate ultimately would have the greatest number of votes. Antifederalist electors could have held the balance of strength between George Washington and John Adams, and tipped the scales in favor of the latter. Because George Clinton maintained a close friendship with George Washington throughout these trying times and because many Antifederalists held the former commander of the Continental army in high regard, there was in actuality less likelihood of such plotting over the presidency than Federalist partisans imagined.

The presence of New York electors might have denied the Federalists the vice-presidency, however, for in their desire to guarantee Washington's election and to defuse any Antifederalist challenge to him, they had arranged for some of the electors to throw their second votes to a person other than Adams. Antifederalist Melancton Smith believed, ". . . it is very probable our State and Virginia would agree in the person for vice President—and by their union might very probably determine the choice. I think it would be the means of promoting amendments, if a vice president was chosen who is heartily engaged in the business."[7] Even a strong third-place finish would have given notice that Antifederalism remained a force to contend with. But the Antifederalists in New York pursued a course of action which foreclosed these prospects. Washington and Adams were duly elected, though Adams received one vote less than a bare majority of the votes cast.

1792

By 1792, New York and the nation experienced significant changes which affected the political climate for the second presidential election. For example, the state no longer focused on disputes about ratification of the Constitution but faced new issues like public land policy and banking. Meanwhile, the Washington administration had begun to make a record, especially on matters of patronage and fiscal policy, which drove the Livingston family out of the Federalist camp and into Clinton's. Second, responding to state constitutional requirements for reapportionment, the legislature created new counties in 1791 (Saratoga, Otsego, Herkimer, and Tioga), which large Federalist landowners, such as William Cooper, came to dominate. Finally, Congress required all states to appoint electors within thirty-four days of the first Wednesday in December, when they were to cast their votes for president.[8] New York state legislators moved promptly to set up procedures for choosing electors. They concluded that thirty-four days provided too short a time to conduct popular elections in a state so large as New York, and decided to make the appointments themselves. It is not at all evident, however, that elections could not have been concluded within the time prescribed, for Massachusetts, Pennsylvania, and Virginia, states as large as New York, as well as New Hampshire, Maryland, and Kentucky, opted for popular participation. Probably, the legislators responded to other factors. First, since New York held state elections in April, popular elections for electors in the fall imposed additional costs and inconvenience. Second, debate over how to conduct such elections, whether by districts, at large, or some other means, could lead to delay, and the legislators did not want to repeat the 1789 embarrassment of failing to cast votes for want of electors. Third, the assemblymen and the senators believed that they could represent their constituents faithfully, and were entitled to appoint electors under the provisions of the Constitution. Legislatures in Connecticut, Rhode Island, Vermont, New Jersey, Delaware, North and South Carolina, and Georgia did likewise.[9]

The legislature could either appoint persons for this office without passing any law; adopt a resolution; or pass a law. In selecting the last option, the New York legislature brought into the process the governor and the council of revision, which could negative any legislative act.

In April of 1792 the legislature enacted a law stipulating that the assembly and senate convene on the first Tuesday in November and by joint ballot choose electors in the ratio of 4:3:3:3 for the southern, middle, western, and eastern districts. This ratio assumed that New York would have thirteen electors or some multiple of thirteen at a time when Congress was considering reapportionment of the House in accord with the 1790 federal census. The governor and council of revision approved.[10]

In the fall, however, the newly elected pro-Clintonian legislature had to revisit the presidential electors' law. By then Congress had assigned ten representatives to New York and hence allowed it twelve electors. On November 6, the legislature repealed that portion of the April law which set the 4–3–3–3 ratio, and the measure hurried through both houses by November 8.[11]

This attempt to allocate proportions of electors to four state senate districts failed, and it had important implications for the future of the electoral college. Reapportionment after each decennial census meant that the state could expect to have a different number of representatives and thus of presidential electors every decade. Then the legislature would have to draw up new congressional districts, and that occasion could be expected to prompt highly partisan debate and argument. The difficulties of drawing acceptable district lines for representatives would be compounded if New York decided to have district elections for presidential electors. Not only would these have to be redrawn every decade, but the lines could not be identical with congressional districts because the number of electors assigned to a state always exceeded the number of representatives by two. For New York, the convenient choices were narrowing to at-large legislative appointment or at-large election of electors, and there were as yet few advocates for the latter.[12]

On November 19, 1792, the legislators promptly moved to appoint electors. They did not cast votes for persons who would exercise independent judgment but for those who could be depended on to vote the way they were supposed to vote. Almost all of the successful candidates for electors had been loyal Clintonians for many years, while the unsuccessful ones had in numerous instances acted in support of John Jay's formidable challenge to Clinton in the controversial gubernatorial race in the spring.[13]

The electors met as directed at the Poughkeepsie courthouse on December 5, 1792, and they cast twelve votes for George Washington and twelve votes for George Clinton. They made a sparse record of their actions, and reported very correctly to the president of the United States Senate that they had voted by ballot for two persons, one of whom was properly from a state other than New York. In the nation at large, George Washington received 132 electoral votes, a unanimous vote of the electors; John Adams won seventy-seven, George Clinton fifty, and others, five. The Clintonian electors in New York and elsewhere used their votes in such a way that they were in fact casting one vote for president and one vote for vice president even though their formal report to the president of the Senate made no such distinction.[14]

1796

From 1792 on, the Federalists relentlessly attacked Governor Clinton with charges of land scandals, partisan patronage policies, and election fraud. They also stood by the policies of the Washington administration, including neutrality, the recall of the controversial French diplomat Edmond "Citizen" Genet (who renounced his French citizenship and married George Clinton's daughter), and the Jay Treaty with Great Britain. In the spring of 1795 they ended Clinton's string of six consecutive terms and elected the absent Chief Justice Jay governor for the first of two terms with a Federalist legislature behind him. Despite these reverses, the Republicans began to make inroads into Federalist strongholds in the new upstate counties and among the working classes in New York City. These gains would loom large later in the decade.[15]

A Federalist legislature adopted a law for presidential electors on March 26, 1796, which followed the principal features of the 1792 act. Later in the spring, voters, not knowing for sure who would be candidates in the upcoming presidential contest, elected a Federalist legislative majority to choose electors in the fall.[16]

What made this presidential contest novel was the absence of Washington from the lists. His farewell address appeared in newspapers across the country in September of 1796. Meanwhile, informal caucuses in the Congress had fastened upon John Adams of Massachusetts and Thomas Pinckney of South Carolina for the Federalists and Thomas Jefferson of Virginia and Aaron Burr of New York for the Republicans as presidential candidates.[17]

Determined to prevent Jefferson's elevation to the presidency, Alexander Hamilton encouraged New Englanders and Southern Federalists to support Adams and Pinckney equally, and hoped southern Republicans might vote for Jefferson and Pinckney. Such a strategy could have made Pinckney president and Adams vice president. New Englanders, suspecting Hamilton's motives and fearing the outcome, gave Adams solid support but intended to throw away some potential votes for Pinckney. Northern Republicans supported Jefferson and Burr, but southerners, particularly Virginians, backed Jefferson solidly and planned to scatter their second votes.[18]

On the first Wednesday in December, the twelve Federalist electors of New York gathered in the town of Hudson, where they cast twelve votes for John Adams and twelve votes for Thomas Pinckney. They were then "attended by several gentlemen from this city and Claverack, partook of an elegant entertainment, prepared for the occasion by Mr. Gordon; and drank several patriotic toasts."[19]

When the votes from all the states became known, the nation learned that Federalist John Adams had been chosen president and Republican Thomas Jefferson, vice president.

1800

The deepening political divisions between Federalists and Republicans, particularly after the XYZ Affair, the undeclared war against France, and the Alien and Sedition Acts, promoted a wave of proposed constitutional amendments from Federalists in Massachusetts, Connecticut, and Maryland to ensure that only native born Americans could serve in the executive and legislative branches of the national government. The presidential election of 1796, which had produced a Federalist president and a Republican vice-president, also prompted concern, even alarm, among Federalists who now sought a reform that would provide "That the electors of the President and Vice–President of the United

States, shall designate upon their ballots the name of the person they elect to either of the above offices."[20]

Republicans in New York countered with democratic initiatives, one of which provided for popular election of presidential electors on a district basis. In 1799 and 1800 John Swartwout of New York City, a close ally of Aaron Burr; Jedidiah Peck, one of the new upstate Republicans from Otsego; and Moses Philips of Orange attacked the practice of legislative appointment of electors used in 1792 and 1796. They pointed out that a majority of one in the legislature gave the state's entire electoral vote to one party. District elections, they calculated, would result in proportional distribution of electors among the candidates of the two parties, and hence provide a much fairer measure of popular sentiment.[21]

Federalists blundered badly in the way they defended legislative appointment of electors. John V. Henry of Albany declared that ". . . whenever the people choose electors, . . . it is not done with that purity which it might be done by their representatives," because they are not as well informed as the legislators who "have more expanded minds." Josiah Masters of Rensselaer dug a deeper hole still by claiming, "The people are not so capable of choosing as the legislature. What do they know about the general government, or about foreign affairs. Nothing." Henry and Masters assumed an elitist, anti-democratic posture, and linked that with the Federalist Party in New York.[22]

The Federalist majority defeated the reform proposed by the Republicans, and confidently asserted the rights of the legislature through joint ballot to appoint electors; they believed they would thereby secure for the Federalist presidential candidates the entire vote of New York as Clintonians in 1792 and Federalists in 1796 had done. But they courted political dangers in putting themselves against a rising tide of popular sentiment and aligning themselves in the public mind with intolerance and aristocracy. The Federalists in New York gave the Republicans ample ammunition to reverse their recent defeats in the assembly.

In a brilliant strategic move, Aaron Burr organized the 1800 Republican campaign for the legislative elections in New York City. He secured the agreement of some of the best known members of the party, including George Clinton, Horatio Gates, Brockholst Livingston, and Jacob Broome, to run for the assembly. He and his allies prepared lists of prospective voters and turned them out on election day, and pulled off a shocking Republican victory in the city. This triumph pointed toward a decisive Republican majority in any joint session of the legislature that would meet in the fall to appoint electors. The legislative elections in the spring had become clearly linked to the presidential election.[23]

Disappointed, frustrated, and driven by his passion to defeat the Republican presidential candidates, Alexander Hamilton pleaded with Governor and fellow Federalist John Jay to have the current Federalist legislature provide for district election of electors so that the newly elected Republican legislature could not name the entire slate in the fall. The temperate and responsible Jay rejected the idea which, if attempted, might have provoked a furious popular outcry against the Federalists and undermined the people's faith in the electoral process.[24]

Republicans reported rumors that Federalists would try to frustrate the wishes of the people by absenting themselves to prevent a senate quorum and thereby block the appointment of electors. Another rumor suggested that Governor Jay would not call a special session of the legislature to appoint electors. These fears were put to rest when on December 6th the assembly and the senate named twelve electors.[25]

The New York electors met at the house of Stephen Holmes in Hudson and by ballot cast twelve votes for Thomas Jefferson and twelve votes for Aaron Burr. These votes were pivotal in giving the Republicans a national victory. But, in their desire to avoid the division which led Federalist electors in 1796 to get Adams the top office while losing the second, Republican electors throughout the United States cast their votes equally for Jefferson and Burr. As a consequence, Republicans discovered to their chagrin that the lame duck, Federalist-controlled House of Representatives, elected in 1798, would determine whether Jefferson or Burr would become president. The House after lengthy deliberations chose Jefferson, but Republicans felt great anxiety about the process.

Having won decisively in 1800 in New York and the nation, Republicans sought to leverage their popular support into control of both the presidency and the vice-presidency without relying on the House to break tie votes. They also wanted to avoid giving the minority Federalist electors the opportunity of casting a few votes for one or the other of the Republican candidates and thereby selecting the more acceptable person for president. They therefore adopted the previous Federalist idea of a "designation" amendment to require each presidential elector to cast one vote for president and one for vice-president.

In the late 1790s when they were a minority, New York's Republicans sought district election of presidential electors, and ostensibly they favored this change after 1800. In 1802 a largely Republican state assembly and Federalist senate urged Congress to consider a national constitutional amendment that would require both district election and designation. But acting more and more as members of the majority party in the state and the nation, Republicans emphasized the second aim.[26]

In February of 1802, Benjamin Walker of New York presented to the House of Representatives a resolution from New York proposing a designation amendment, and in April and again in October, DeWitt Clinton introduced motions in the U.S. Senate for a similar reform. The Congress discussed these and like-minded proposals through 1802 and 1803 before submitting a final version to the states in early 1804. Interestingly, some Federalists, speaking now for the minority, asked in vain for an amendment to require popular election of electors in districts.[27] Designation would assure Republicans control of both presidential and vice-presidential offices, but also had the effect of diminishing the stature of the latter. No more would vice-presidents be presidential candidates who finished second, but figures who added political strength to the head of the ticket.

In 1804 New York's Republicans secured state ratification of the Twelfth Amendment, and made no further concerted effort to install district elections for electors. Having a sure command of the majority in the legislature and popular support that would maintain control for the future, the Republicans saw legislative appointment as just fine with them.

Conclusions

The New York experience with presidential electors in the early republic showed that not only did the Constitution's provisions for the electoral college influence the conduct of politics in the state, but those politics in turn shaped the meaning of that Constitution. First, the political debate between Republican and Federalist political leaders in the period from 1788 to 1804 made clear that electors were not to exercise independent judgment in casting their votes, but to vote in accordance with the wishes and interests of the party responsible for getting them appointed. Second, having weighed the merits of popular election or legislative appointment, New York opted for the latter. Reasons of convenience, constitutionality, political utility, and the likelihood that the state's entire electoral vote would go to the victorious party informed that choice. Third, Republicans, who had challenged some of these points by recommending district election of electors when they were a minority, shifted position once they became a majority, and accepted them after 1800 when they focused on designation as their principal aim. A later generation tried a short-lived experiment in 1825 with popular election by district, but turned in 1829 to a general ticket which, like legislative appointment, maintained the prospect of a winner-take-all result. With minor changes here and there, that system has come down to our own day, sustained by the mutual interests of the two major parties in the state.

NOTES:

[1]Stephen L. Schechter, "Clintonism and the New Federalism in New York State," in this volume.

[2]Jackson T. Main, *Political Parties Before the Constitution* (Chapel Hill, 1973), ch. 3.

[3]Merrill Jensen and Robert A. Becker, eds., *The Documentary History of the First Federal Elections* (Madison, 1976) 1: 132-133.

[4]Abraham B. Bancker to Evert Bancker, Albany, December 20, 1788, in Bancker Family Papers, New-York Historical Society (NYHS).

[5]Tadahisa Kuroda, "New York and the First Presidential Elections," *New York History* (July 1988), 19-51.

[6]Jeremiah Mason to John Woodworth, New Haven, January 26, 1789, in Gorden Den Boer, Lucy Trumbull Brown, and Charles D. Hagermann, eds., *The Documentary History of the First Federal Elections* (Madison, 1986), 3: 35.

[7]Melancton Smith to John Smith, New York, January 10, 1789, John Smith Papers, NYHS.

[8]Alfred F. Young, *Democratic Republicans of New York* (Chapel Hill, 1967), Part III; *Laws of the State of New York (1789-1796)* [Albany, 1887], 15th session, ch. 72, preamble.

[9]Neal Pearce, *The People's President* (New York, 1968), ch. 3 and Appendix B; Richard P. McCormick, *The Presidential Game* (New York, 1982), ch. 3.

[10]April 12, 1792, *Journal of the Senate of the State of New York*, 15th session; *Laws of the State*, III, ch. 72, 15th session.

[11]November 19, 1792, *Journal of the Assembly of the State of New York*, 16th session; *Laws of the State*, III, ch. 1, 16th session.

[12]Massachusetts resorted to an unusual formula to avoid the creation of separate districts for representatives and for electors. It allowed voters in each district to cast ballots for a representative and an elector. The General Court appointed two additional electors.

[13]Compare information in lists such as Stephen L. Schechter, "A Biographical Gazetteer of New York Federalists and Antifederalists," in Stephen L. Schechter, ed., *The Reluctant Pillar* (Troy, 1985), 157-206, with information about pro-Clinton and pro-Jay committees given in [New York] *Daily Advertiser* and the *Poughkeepsie Journal* throughout the spring and summer of 1792.

[14]See the manuscript report from New York's electors in the National Archives.

[15]Young, *The Democratic Republicans of New York*, Parts IV-V.

[16]*Laws of the State*, ch. 32, 19th session.

[17]Noble S. Cunningham, *The Jeffersonian Republicans in Opposition* (Chapel Hill, 1957), ch. 5.

[18]Alexander Hamilton to . . ., New York, November 8, 1796, and Theodore Sedgwick to Alexander Hamilton, Stockbridge, November 19, 1796, in Harold C. Syrett, ed., *The Papers of Alexander Hamilton* (New York, 1974), 20: 376-377, 402-407.

[19]*The Argus, or Greenleaf's New Daily Advertiser,* December 17, 1796.

[20]January 18, 1799, *Journal of the Assembly,* 22nd session.

[21][New York] *Republican Watch Tower,* April 9, 1800.

[22]*Ibid.*

[23]Cunningham, *op. cit.,* chs. 8-9.

[24]Alexander Hamilton to John Jay, New York, May 7, 1800, in Syrett, ed., *The Papers of Alexander Hamilton* (New York, 1976), 24: 464-467. The editor in note 4 on 467 points out that the Governor wrote at the bottom of the letter: "Proposing a measure for party purposes wh. I think it wd. not become me to adopt."

[25][New York] *Republican Watch Tower,* October 18, 1800 and October 25, 1800.

[26]February 16, 1801, *Journal of the Assembly,* 24th session; January 30, 1802, *Journal of the Assembly,* 25th session; January 26 and 29, 1802, *Journal of the Senate,* 25th session.

[27]February 15, 1802 in the House, and April 12 and October 21, 1803 in the Senate, *The Annals of Congress.*

David Dudley Field

(1805–1894)

WILLIAM P. LAPIANA
New York Law School

An important and influential member of the New York bar, David Dudley Field took a leading role in the public life of New York and of the nation following the Civil War. He was the author of procedural court reforms mandated by the New York State Constitution of 1846.

David Dudley Field was born on February 13, 1805, the son of a clergyman. By the time of his death in 1894, he was one of the most successful, yet most notorious, members of the American legal profession. Though born in Connecticut, he was also most definitely a New Yorker. He played an important part in the transformation of the New York legal system brought about by the Constitution of 1846. He was a dominant presence at the New York City bar from the 1860s through the 1880s. With his partners, Thomas G. Shearman and John W. Sterling (who went on to found the firm that still bears their names), he participated in the litigation surrounding the battles for control of the Erie Railroad and other ventures of Jay Gould and his associates. He was an important figure in the defense of the notorious Tammany leader William Marcy "Boss" Tweed. On a higher stage, he took a leading role in several important United States Supreme Court cases growing out of the conduct of the Civil War and Reconstruction. In short, Field was seldom absent from the public life of New York and of the nation in the period following the Civil War.

Although he was the eldest son of a successful clergyman, Field, like his younger brother, Stephen, and his nephew, David Brewer, both of whom became justices of the Supreme Court, sought his fortune in the law. It was not a surprising choice for an ambitious young man growing up as part of the first generation to take American independence for granted. The rapid growth of the young nation provided a wide arena for the fulfillment of personal dreams of material success. The United States was no longer overwhelmingly agrarian. With the increasing importance of commerce seems to have come an increasing secularization of society which reduced the prestige, both social and economic, of the clergy. For those of a literary bent, who were more at home with words than the skills of entrepreneurship and who, in an earlier day, would have seriously considered the ministry as an outlet for their talents, the law exerted a strong attraction. Not only was legal business more plentiful than ever as the economy became more dependent on trade and manufacturing, but the legal profession had assumed a peculiar importance in American life.

National Politics

Alexis de Tocqueville, the young French magistrate whose journey to the United States in the 1830s inspired him to write *Democracy in America*, described the American legal profession as an aristocracy of intellect. The young Frenchman was accurately reporting the American legal profession's self-image, or at least that held by those self-consciously learned and professional lawyers with whom he came into contact. For these men, the job of lawyering had to be connected intimately with the proper functioning of the American polity. Not only were the most important questions of the day ultimately fought out in the courts and subject always to the ultimate test of constitutionality, a test applied by courts, but the very substance of American life ultimately was defined by the principles of the common law.

Those rights of Englishmen for which the Revolution had been fought were only imperfectly specified in the various constitutional provisions, both state and federal, which named them. Their fullest vigor could be found only in their application in the daily work of the courts of justice. It was the job of lawyers and judges to understand the principles of the common law through the study and use of legal science. Legal science, in turn, was the application to legal questions of the techniques of investigation which were valid for all sciences, be they natural sciences like chemistry or moral sciences like law. In the English-speaking world of the early nineteenth century, scientific method was inductive; that is, it involved the careful observation of facts—which, in law, were the decided cases—and the drawing from those facts of the priciples which lay behind them. Those principles formed a coherent moral system; they had to, for in the end they were the product of the mind of God.

Field accepted part of this vision of the lawyer's role. Throughout his life he concerned himself with national politics and played an important role in several of the great cases which came before the United States Supreme Court after the Civil War. In each of these cases, Field argued positions which limited the power of the federal government. He feared a "consolidated" government with all power centralized in Washington, a fear made plausible, first, by the invigoration of federal power in response to the numerous tasks involved in fighting the Civil War, and, second, by the attempts of Congress to control the reconstruction of the defeated South. In Field's view, the preservation of the "rule of law," threatened by the expedient ignoring of principle in the face of wartime needs, required the preservation of the states as the most important governmental entities in the nation.

His positions in the five cases he argued before the Supreme Court, always as part of a team of lawyers, therefore either denigrated federal power directly or attacked the authority of the state governments imposed by congressional Reconstruction and supported by the military power of the federal government. These cases were: *Ex parte Milligan*, 71 U.S. 2 (1866); *Georgia v. Grant*, 73 U.S. 241 (1868); *Ex parte McCardle*, 74 U.S. 506 (1868); *Cummings v. Missouri*, 71 U.S. 277 (1866); and *United States v. Cruikshank*, 92 U.S. 542 (1876).

Milligan grew out of President Abraham Lincoln's suspension of the writ of habeas corpus, as ratified by Congress in 1863. In seeking to overturn a death sentence imposed by a court martial upon Confederate sympathizer Lambdin P. Milligan, Field successfully argued that citizens in the Union states could not be prosecuted by military tribunals when civilian courts were still in operation. Field also argued that military government was inconsistent with the Constitution even in the former Confederate states, a position he took in *McCardle* and *Grant*. The Court was unable to decide either *McCardle* or *Grant* on the merits, because Congress hastily enacted a statute stripping the Court of jurisdiction to decide cases challenging the statutes comprising the congressional Reconstruction program.

In *Cruikshank*, Field challenged the constitutionality of the Enforcement Act of 1870, which was designed to provide a federal forum for the prosecution of those who deprived citizens of their civil rights. Field argued vigorously for the position that the rights guaranteed by the Reconstruction Amendments (XIII, XIV, and XV) could not be directly enforced by the federal government. At most, he declared, the federal courts could only nullify discriminatory state action. While the justices did not accept Field's reasoning and did not invalidate the law, they did construe it so narrowly as to make it all but useless.

Cummings, the fourth case Field argued before the Court, best illustrates many of the key principles of Field's constitutional thought. At issue in *Cummings* was a test oath prescribed by the Missouri constitution of 1865. Public officials, voters, jurors, lawyers, teachers, and clergymen were all required to swear to their past and future loyalty to the United States and the state of Missouri. The purpose of the oath was to exclude Confederate sympathizers from public life. Cummings, a Roman Catholic priest, refused to take the oath. In his argument before the Supreme Court, Field emphasized the oath's similarity to an *ex post facto* law. In effect, Missouri was punishing Cummings by forbidding him to carry on his profession because he might have given comfort to those engaged in the rebellion, an offense which would include the most basic acts of charity offered to the dying, acts which most certainly were not illegal at the time they were committed. The crucial part of Field's argument was the categorization of Cummings's disqualification as a punishment. If the oath were merely a qualification for taking up an office, its prescription would be well within the power of the state. Field argued, however, that among the inalienable rights of the American people was the right to follow one's calling. It is clearly a punishment to be deprived of such an unalienable right. In an opinion written by Justice Stephen Field, a divided Supreme Court not only approved this reasoning but did so in words paraphrased from David Field's argument.

David Field's position in *Cummings* was consistent with his opposition to federal authority and his resulting preference for the states. By restraining Missouri, he was helping to assure the dominance of state government, the important level of government in the American system, by white males—many of whom, indeed, had sympathized with the rebellion. He was no believer in African–American suffrage or, for that matter, in the propriety of extending the vote to recent immigrants. His argument had another side as well. By providing a rationale for finding rights outside the constitutional text embodied in the vague language of "inalienable rights," he helped his brother, Stephen, create the doctrine of substantive due process that so dominated constitutional jurisprudence in the late nineteenth-and-early twentieth centuries.

Judicial Reform

While David Dudley Field took seriously the lawyer's role as guardian of the temple of the Constitution, he had little sympathy with law as morality or with legal science as the discovery of the moral order of the universe. On the contrary, as a law reformer as a practitioner, his stated goals were simply to make the legal system more efficient, and to improve its ability to decide the cases that came before it. The courts' job was to keep the wheels of commerce turning and to serve litigants by providing a forum where a hearing could be obtained, a suitable remedy decreed, and the remedy easily and efficiently enforced. There was little room in the legal world of David Dudley Field for elaborate consideration of the moral worth of clients and their causes. In a way, he never understood, let alone accepted, the virulent criticism levelled at him for representing Jay Gould and William Marcy Tweed. Field was his client's servant. He was also, at least in his eyes, the servant of the people of the State of New York, and he was determined to give them the legal system they needed.

It was in this earlier phase of his career that Field made his most lasting contributions. His constitutional jurisprudence, if not obsolete, at least has long been a minority position, but that is not the case with his views on the way courts should be run. Today, even most lawyers do not generally realize that the various systems of procedural rules governing all litigation in the Anglo–American world trace their descent to a greater or lesser degree to the code of civil procedure that David Dudley Field wrote for the state of New York in the late 1840s. Fewer still know that the creation of that code was mandated by a provision of the New York Constitution of 1846 that Field helped to create through his advocacy. As different as the antebellum world is from our own, it still rules our legal life through the influence of a single statute of the state of New York which, in turn, was very much the product of a single individual.

Field himself was not elected to the Constitutional Convention of 1846, but the judiciary article of the document which the convention produced and which the people approved reflected his thought. He was appointed to the post-convention committee that created the reformed procedural code which the new constitution required.

Field's legal system had no room for separate courts of law and of equity. He believed that the remedies of the legal system should be available in one place. Any other system led only to the duplication of effort and needless expense. Moreover, both legal and equitable remedies should be available in one suit. If the controversy required a jury to resolve questions of fact, one would be impanelled. Issues properly equitable would be reserved for the judge. Additionally, the broadest possible rules of joinder were to be used in order to encourage the settling in one suit of all controversies arising from a single situation. Finally, the forms of action at the common law were to be abolished root and branch. No longer were real situations to be masked behind the stereotyped language of the common-law writs. No longer would the legal system tolerate the interminable exchange of complex documents designed to reach an "issue" on which trial could be held. An aggrieved party filed a complaint stating the facts on which relief should be granted. The defendant replied in an answer; the plaintiff could reply to that; and the pleadings were over.

While the substance of this system of procedure was rapidly enacted into law, many judges and not a few lawyers opposed its effective operation. In many cases in the Field Code's first years, judges again and again stated that while the new code abolished the forms of action as collections of words, it did not abolish trover, replevin, trespass *de bonis asportatis*, and all the rest as concepts. Somehow, these judges maintained, they were inseparable from the law itself and existed in a realm which mere legislative power could not reach. Eventually, however, the new ways became established, and the procedural face of the common law was forever changed.

Changing procedure also helps to change substance. The forms of action which Field worked so hard to abolish had provided the framework for organizing the multitude of cases which make up the common law. Their eventual dissolution led to a new era of theorizing and conceptualizing, especially in legal education. The "case method" of instruction, still the basis of American legal education today, was created by Christopher Columbus Langdell who, before he became dean of Harvard Law School, practiced law for more than ten years in the new world which Field's code created in New York. The code required that the plaintiff's first pleading, the complaint, contain facts on which recovery could be based. Understanding whether or not a client had a claim, therefore, depended on what fact patterns led to recovery. That investigation led to a careful consideration of precedent, a case method of practicing law. In turn, the resulting profusion of fact patterns led to attempts to create theories which would bind the facts into a coherent whole. A new academic enterprise was born.

There were other factors in the rise of modern legal education, but there was none more important than the change in ways of thinking about law that the Field Code helped to create. Both modern legal practice and modern legal thought find at least some of their roots in the work of David Dudley Field, not as an advocate before the Supreme Court, but as a reformer of procedure and as a student of the practice of law.

For Further Reading

Field, David Dudley. *Speeches, Arguments, and Miscellaneous Papers of David Dudley Field*, edited in 3 volumes by A.P. Sprague. New York: D. Appleton and Company, 1884–1890.

Reppy, Alison, ed. *David Dudley Field: Centenary Essays Celebrating One Hundred Years of Legal Reform.* New York: New York University School of Law, 1949.

Van Ee, Daun. *David Dudley Field and the Reconstruction of the Law.* New York: Garland Publishing Co., 1986 [originally unpub. Ph.D. dissertation, Johns Hopkins University, 1974].

William Dameron Guthrie: The Case of the New York Conservative and the Birth of Fundamental Family Liberties*

BARBARA BENNETT WOODHOUSE
University of Pennsylvannia School of Law

Four decades separate the United States Supreme Court's decision in *Meyer v. Nebraska* in 1923 from the line of cases beginning in 1965 with *Griswold v. Connecticut* and leading to *Roe v. Wade* in 1973. These modern cases secured the individual's rights to decide when and whether to bear children and to have custody and control of those children. In the wake of these cases, vast areas of law relating to families and children that formerly were regulated freely by the states are now subject to constitutional scrutiny. The Supreme Court has struck down state laws that regulated contraception and abortion, penalized unwed parents and illegitimate children, and placed restrictions on marriage and divorce. These opinions cited *Meyer* as a foundation case for the proposition that the freedom to marry, conceive, and raise children is a fundamental right implicit in our concept of ordered liberty and protected by the Constitution.

The *Meyer* decision is commonly perceived as a liberal landmark. Yet study of its history and social context discloses strange anomalies. *Meyer* was the product of a pitched battle between radical reformers and conservatives, in which the combatants were arrayed in alliances that might surprise and puzzle modern observers. Few have noticed that the conservatives claimed *Meyer* as a decisive victory. Also forgotten is the key role played by a prominent New Yorker at the birth of the constitutional doctrine of family liberties.

Guthrie and the Movement for Americanization

In the winter of 1922, New Yorker William Dameron Guthrie barricaded himself in his law library. Guthrie, a medium sized, meticulously attired gentlemen of sixty-two, formal in speech and manner, seemed an unlikely model for the role of gladiator. Yet he knew that a critical struggle lay ahead. At stake, Guthrie believed, were the very soul of the family, the survival of the parochial school, and even the future of the nation. Guthrie, a wealthy Catholic lawyer and influential constitutional theorist, had been enlisted for the coming confrontation by the Rt. Revs. Alexander Christie and Edward Joseph Hanna, the Catholic archbishops of Oregon City and San Francisco. His orders: Stop the Oregon School Law—a law that would abolish private and parochial schooling in the State of Oregon and violate the God-given right of parents to control the education and upbringing of their own children.[1] Surrounded by casebooks and constitutional treatises, including his own volumes on *Magna Carta* and *The Fourteenth Amendment* and his briefs to the Supreme Court in *Champion v. Ames* (1903) and *McCray v. United States* (1904) (respectively the famed *Lottery* and *Oleomargarine* cases), Guthrie plotted his defensive strategy.

Guthrie was no newcomer to the battle to protect the autonomy of the family from government encroachments. A staunch believer in delimiting the power of government over men's lives, it was Guthrie who had devised the constitutional arguments that ultimately persuaded the Supreme Court to declare Congress powerless to effect local labor and health reforms through its commerce and taxing powers. Eighteen years before, Guthrie had fought the oleomargarine tax, arguing eloquently in the Supreme Court. He had lost that battle, but, in the past four years, he had seen his vision vindicated of a Court that would stand as a bulwark against excessive government regulation. In 1918, the high Court had invalidated the Owen–Keating child labor law in *Hammer v. Dagenhart* and in 1922 the Child Labor Tax in *Bailey v. Drexel*, each time declaring that Congress had overstepped its authority and intruded on areas of domestic concern reserved by the Constitution to the states. Who could doubt Guthrie's contribution to these conservative victories? Chief Justice William H. Taft's opinion in *Drexel* handed down

May 15, 1922, virtually adopted Guthrie's losing brief in the *Oleomargarine Case*, page for page and paragraph for paragraph.[2]

But Guthrie believed that there was more at stake in attempts to regulate the wages and working hours of children than the mere division of power between state and federal governments. He shared with many fellow conservatives the belief that these so-called "child protective" laws were the first step toward nationalizing the children of America and undermining their parents' supremacy as governors of hearth and home. In Guthrie's view, social legislation that displaced the parents' authority over their children's study, work, and upbringing violated rights—guaranteed by the Fifth, Fourteenth, and First Amendments—to liberty of contract and to personal and religious freedom.

Clearly, the Oregon School Law could and must be challenged as unconstitutional. But the Oregon law would not go into effect until 1926. Now, in November 1922, a far more immediate threat loomed in the shape of *Meyer v. Nebraska*, a case that was to be argued before the Supreme Court in February 1923.

The Nebraska law at issue in *Meyer* required that all elementary school classes, whether public, parochial or private, be taught in English. This law seemingly had little impact on private schooling in the City of New York, where English was the standard language of instruction, but Guthrie recognized the danger. In ruling on the Nebraska language law, the Supreme Court might employ language that would sanction the states' authority, in the name of the public good, to control not only *what* private schools might teach but *whether* they might teach. A broadly written ruling would be a step along the road to abolition of the parochial school.

Both the Nebraska law and the Oregon law were products of complex forces converging at a particular moment in the nation's history. The Great War with Germany was over, and the nation seemed poised at the edge of a new era. Yet anti-German sentiment lingered, adding urgency to the credo of the Americanization movement: in order for the foreign-born citizen to participate fully in American life, he or she must be assimilated into the melting pot of American culture. In the years since the war, lawmakers in many states had passed laws requiring that all subjects in the elementary grades be taught in English. One such law passed the legislature of Nebraska in 1919. It prohibited teaching in foreign languages in the primary grades of all schools, public or private.

The Nebraska language law was not an isolated phenomenon. In the same year, sixteen states enacted similar laws, and by 1921 some thirty-one states had laws on their books making English the sole language of instruction in public or in all schools.³ In part, these language laws can be traced to wartime anti-German prejudice. They had deeper roots, however, in the longstanding tension between rural nativist groups in the midwest and the large German, Polish, and Scandinavian communities in those states. These immigrant groups formed self-sufficient enclaves with clubs, parochial schools and churches, and banks and insurance companies where all business was conducted in the language of the home country. To their neighbors, coming from a tradition which mixed populism and progressivism with a distrust for anything foreign, this failure of the immigrant community to assimilate seemed at once a threat to the "American" way of life and a golden opportunity for benevolent reform. Responding to this public ambivalence, school boards vacillated between pluralist policies, such as offering classes in foreign language and culture to attract immigrant students, and restrictive rules that sought to force assimilation by suppressing foreign language study.

In St. Louis, Missouri, for example, in the year 1860 the school population stood at approximately 15,000 students. To the consternation of local educators, nearly one-third of these schoolchildren attended private schools where German was the language of instruction. In order to entice these children to the melting pot of the public school system, the St. Louis School board in 1864 rescinded its longstanding "English only" policy and initiated a German-language curriculum. By 1887, opponents of German-language schooling had gained ascendancy and succeeded in abolishing the program. A similar shift from English-only rules to foreign language curriculums and back again occurred in such cities as Chicago and San Francisco. In the 1890s Minnesota struck a compromise—all schools must be taught in English, but teachers were permitted to use the pupil's native language as an aid in teaching English. Thus, the theme of assimilation through the mandatory teaching of English was not simply a by-product of wartime panic, but also an outgrowth of preexisting political, social, and cultural tensions.⁴

In retrospect, it is tempting to think of "Americanization" as a code word for discrimination and the bigoted reaction to exaggerated wartime propaganda. In the early 1920s, however, it was viewed by the public and by prominent educators as a serious answer to a serious problem. "Americanization of the immigrant" became the catch phrase to identify a group of policies aimed at assimilating the immigrant into American life. Fluency in English was widely regarded as a key tool in this reform movement.

In April 1918, United States Secretary of the Interior Franklin K. Lane called a conference on Americanization in Washington, D.C., that was attended by governors, social workers, industrialists, and educators from eighteen states. The comprehensive plan of education and cooperation with immigrant groups adopted by convention included a recommendation that "in all schools in which the elementary subjects are taught they shall be taught in the English language only." In the same year, at the Fifty-sixth Annual Meeting of the National Education Association, a number of speakers urged the importance of English as a medium of Americanization. By the 1919 annual meeting held in Milwaukee, the association had formally adopted a recommendation in favor of laws mandating English as the language of instruction in all schools and for compulsory classes in Americanization for any persons unable to read and write English at the sixth-grade level.

The popular press lent enthusiastic support. *Outlook* magazine's April 24, 1918, issue carried an article entitled "A Pioneer Movement for Americanization," praising the vision of the originator of the English-language laws. The article began with a quote—"To speak German is to remain German." But its discussion focused on the social and economic problems of immigrant children raised in ignorance of the English language. *The Literary Digest*, while celebrating cultural diversity, treated Americanization as a serious endeavor. Throughout 1918 and 1919, it ran a series of features entitled "Education in Americanism" on the different immigrant groups and their cultural heritages. The emphasis was pluralist; however, the theme of fluency in English reappears repeatedly in discussions of each group's ability to contribute to American life. *The Literary Digest* of March 30, 1918, printed a survey of the use of German in public schools. The article pointed out that German was used as the exclusive language of instruction in certain Nebraska Lutheran schools. The *Digest* noted that this interfered with the pupils' acquiring fluency in English and cited with apparent approval a string of newspaper editorials criticizing the practice.

In this mixed climate of prejudice and genuine concern, and with both outgoing and incoming governors supporting it, the Nebraska legislature in 1919 passed the Siman Act, named for its sponsor, Senator Harry Siman, forbidding the teaching of foreign languages below the eighth grade. The law was narrowly construed in *Lutheran Synod v. McKelvie* as banning only the teaching of foreign languages insofar as they replaced the required school curriculum. The Missouri Synod of the Lutheran Church, however, hoped to see the law struck down entirely as a violation of First Amendment religious freedoms.[5]

From the beginning, the test case mounted by the Missouri Synod had the ring of a religious liberty case. There was little indication that *Meyer v. Nebraska* would become a seminal case on parental rights.

The protagonist, Robert T. Meyer, was a quiet, mild mannered and God-fearing man in his forties, the father of five. He taught in the little white clapboard schoolhouse of the Evangelical Lutheran Church that stood at the crossroads in Zion Corners, Hamilton County, Nebraska. One summer day in 1920, he was observed by county officials instructing a ten-year-old child in the story of Die Himmelsleiter (Jacob's Ladder) from a German Bible text. The lesson took place during a newly instituted "recess" which school officials admitted had previously been devoted to formal studies. Meyer was convicted of violating the Siman law and fined $25, but he refused to pay and challenged the constitutionality of the law. His case was argued on religious freedom grounds to the Nebraska Supreme Court on January 2, 1922. The Nebraska high court upheld the law, in an opinion that broadened the Siman Act's prohibition to cover all times when pupils were assembled in school for the purposes of instruction. Justice Charles B. Letton, the author of the earlier opinion in *McKelvie*, dissented vehemently. He pointed not to religious freedom but to the fundamental "God-given and constitutional right of a parent to have some voice in the bringing up and education of his child." Encouraged by this dissent, the synod appealed to the United States Supreme Court, this time relying primarily on the Fourteenth Amendment property rights of schools to operate business enterprises and of teachers to earn their living without government interference.

Meanwhile, the far more radical reform movement to abolish private schools had been gathering force in the middle and western states.[6] The same legislature that adopted the Siman Act had come within one vote of adopting a revolutionary proposal—a law compelling all pupils to attend public schools. Similar measures were proposed but defeated in Michigan, Washington, Ohio, and California. Then in 1922, in Oregon, a popular initiative mandating public schooling for all children under sixteen years of age was proposed and carried by a vote of 115,506 to 103,685. The Oregon initiative was sponsored by the American Legion, the Federated Patriotic Societies, and the Scottish Rite Masons, but was also heavily backed by the Ku Klux Klan. The guiding sentiment behind this law was a combination of anti-Catholic and anti-foreign prejudice and a conviction that private and parochial schools were breeding grounds of Bolshevism.[7]

The propaganda circulated in favor of the initiative added a new theme to the assimilationist rhetoric of the language laws. The public schools were to be the enforced melting pot where foreigner and native, rich and poor, would be mixed together, producing the "true American." According to the law's defenders, "children must not under any pretext, be it based upon money, creed or social status be divided into antagonistic groups."[8] This rhetoric of social levelling echoes the Populist movement of the 1890s and the Jacksonian ideal of democracy. Whatever their origin, these ideas must have been profoundly disturbing to observers from the eastern establishment, where the freedom to educate one's children according to one's position in society was a cornerstone of class distinction.

In contrast to public reaction to the language laws, reaction to the idea of compulsory public education was highly unfavorable. In its January 6, 1923, issue, *The Literary Digest* came out against the Oregon Law. With the exception of the Scottish Rite paper, *The New Age*, newspapers throughout the country opposed it. Some, like the Houston Chronicle, labelled it "Prussian to the Core"; others described it as an infrinqement on religious or intellectual freedom; still others, like *Catholic World*, condemned it as an intolerable interference with parental authority.[9]

The Guthrie *Amicus* Brief as Prelude

William Dameron Guthrie was an excellent choice to lead the battle against the Oregon law. He was a staunch Catholic whose ancestors had come to the New World from Ireland in 1718. As a boy, Guthrie had lived in France, and he spoke fluent French. For awhile he attended New York City public schools, but was forced to leave school at the age of sixteen to support his mother and sisters. Young Guthrie was hired by the law firm of Blatchford, Seward, Griswold & Da Costa as a stenographer. By the time he turned twenty, he had determined to become a lawyer. He enrolled at Columbia University, attending both senior and junior law classes simultaneously, and working as a court reporter to pay his fees. He never completed a Columbia degree, however, for he passed the New York bar exam in 1880, shortly after his twenty-first birthday, and promptly rejoined the Blatchford firm as a practicing lawyer.[10]

Success came quickly. Within four years he was a partner at the firm. Still in his mid-thirties, he had attained the pinnacle of advocacy, as one of the lead counsel who persuaded the justices of the United States Supreme Court to declare taxes on corporate income unconstitutional. The marathon argument and reargument of *Pollock v. Farmers' Loan and Trust Co.* consumed eight days of the Court's calendar in March and May of 1895 and resulted in an opinion drastically restricting the federal powers of taxation.

Pollock was the first in a string of masterful arguments. By the time of the Nebraska and Oregon cases, Guthrie had amassed a comfortable fortune defending the property rights of powerful corporations and businessmen. Elected president of both the New York City and New York State bar associations, he had become a man of power and influence. A member of the Union, Metropolitan, Union League, Century, Downtown, Catholic, and New York Yacht clubs, he was married but childless.

Guthrie was also one of the foremost scholars of the constitutional theory of substantive due process—holding that the Fourteenth Amendment meant that government could not intrude on certain fundamental personal liberties. As Ruggles Professor of Constitutional Law at Columbia University from 1913 to 1922, he was well known for his works construing Magna Carta and the Fourteenth Amendment's due process clause as embodying guarantees against government interference in a man's freedom to employ his property as he wished. Guthrie's reverence for individual rights and liberties often translated into protection of vested property interests, even where they clashed with laws designed to protect children. He was a gifted legal theorist whose briefs had been highly influential. Historian Benjamin Twiss credits Guthrie with laying the groundwork in his briefs in the *Lottery* and *Oleomargarine* cases for the argument that ultimately won *Hammer v. Dagenhart* and the *Child Labor Tax* case, establishing that Congress lacked constitutional authority to regulate the ages, hours, or wages of child workers. It was not that Guthrie lacked sympathy for what Justice Oliver Wendell Holmes, Jr., in his *Dagenhart* dissent, had called the "ruined lives" of these young sweatshop and factory workers. Guthrie had supported early initiatives by local government to combat the worst excesses of child labor. But Guthrie believed fiercely in the sanctity of the patriarchal family. He opposed federal child labor laws as well as other education and maternity bills as unwarranted government interference in the private sphere of family life.

Guthrie's deep conservatism won him few friends among Columbia's liberal faculty. Writing in *The New Republic* on December 29, 1917, Charles A. Beard complained that Guthrie owed his professorship to his reactionary views and his powerful contacts on the board of trustees and that his appointment to the Ruggles chair had been a "backstairs" strategy by the university's conservative administration to thwart a leading liberal candidate. Even those who respected Guthrie's intellect charged him with a certain rigidity of mind. His writings and speeches indeed reveal a man of strong convictions who believed that the Constitution and religion stand as twin bulwarks against assaults on traditional values. Among the values he sought to defend were the absolute inviolability of individual liberty and property interests, religious but not racial tolerance, the sanctity of parental authority, and old-fashioned individualism.[11]

When the Oregon School Law was passed on November 7, 1922, Guthrie mobilized for immediate action. By its terms, the Oregon statute would not take effect until 1926. Yet Guthrie was faced with an acute emergency—the pending Supreme Court consideration of *Meyer v. Nebraska* which, it was feared, would implicate issues critical to the Oregon case. On February 20, 1923, he filed an *amicus* or "friend of the court" brief, co-authored by Bernard Hershkopf. The sole objective of the *amicus* brief was to alert the Court to the controversy over abolition of private schools and to forestall the Court from deciding *Meyer* in language that might adversely affect the challenge to the Oregon school law.

Unheralded and apparently unnoticed by subsequent historians, the Guthrie brief was a stunning success. First, it provided Justice James C. McReynolds, author of the *Meyer* opinion, with his keystone argument—the discussion of education of the child under Plato's *Republic* as antithetical to American tradition. Second, it brought the nascent issue of abolition of private education into the foreground of the justices' thinking. As Chief Justice William Howard Taft later remarked to Guthrie, the opinion in the Nebraska case ultimately controlled the decision of the Oregon cases. The language of *Meyer* was so comprehensive and far reaching that it applied alike to the German-language laws and the Oregon School Law.[12]

The Guthrie brief was explicitly addressed not to the language laws, on which it pointedly expressed no opinion, but to the issues raised by the Oregon School Law's state monopoly of education. The brief touched lightly on religious and intellectual liberty and on the property rights of teachers. However, the first theme mentioned, and the one most thoroughly developed, was Guthrie's theory that the state's usurpation of parental authority was fundamentally un-American:

> The most casual perusal of the Oregon act will at once disclose that it is, indeed, an extraordinary and revolutionary piece of legislation. It adopts the favorite device of Communistic Russia—the destruction of parental authority, the standardization of education despite the diversity of character, aptitude, inclination and physical capacity of children, and the monopolization by the state of the training and teaching of the young. The love and interest of the parent for *his* child, such a statute condemns as evil;

the instinctive preferences and desires of the child itself, such a law represses as if mere manifestations of an incorrigible or baneful disposition.

Anything more un-American and more in conflict with the fundamental principles of our institutions, it would be difficult to imagine. It had always been supposed that "the law does not interfere with the freedom of private instruction." The notion of Plato that in a Utopia the state would be the sole repository of parental authority and duty and the children surrendered to it for upbringing and education was long ago repudiated as impossible and impracticable in a workaday world where men and women lived, loved, had children and sought advancement in the struggle of life.

The Guthrie brief closed with a paragraph discussing the historical relationships between suppression of literature and suppression of religious liberty and urging the Court to reserve decision on the issue of state monopoly of education until the Oregon School Law came before it.

As a mere "friend of the Court" and not a party, Guthrie did not take part in the oral argument. But his strategy clearly influenced Arthur Mullen, who argued the case for schoolmaster Meyer. Chief Justice Taft and Justice McReynolds were by far Mullen's most active questioners. Like Guthrie, Mullen drew the coming threat to private education into the foreground. "Now, language prohibition," he told the justices, "arose in our legislature under these circumstances: It came immediately after the War, in the legislature of 1919. Early in that session a bill was introduced, and passed through the house, and was beaten by a vote of only one majority in the senate, that forbade absolutely the maintenance of primary private schools in that State. . . . *That is the atmosphere under which the act was passed.*"

Mullen had come to the lectern assuming that McReynolds, a fundamentalist from the Bible Belt, would vote against religious toleration and in favor of Americanism. Yet Justice McReynolds immediately targeted the issue of the abolition of private schools. Prompted by McReynolds's questioning, Mullen devoted the most extensive, uninterrupted portion of his presentation to the Court to this point. Throughout his oral argument, Mullen skillfully blended conservative themes such as parental authority, property rights, and the fear of Communism with progressive or libertarian themes such as religious liberty, intellectual freedom, and the values of ethnic pluralism. One theme, however, prevailed. No less brilliant a legal stategist than Clarence Darrow, evaluating the oral argument in *Meyer*, maintained that it was the specter of abolition of private education that won over Justice McReynolds and carried the day.[13]

March, April, and May passed and the Court had not yet rendered a decision. Then on June 4, 1923, Justice McReynolds took the bench and read aloud his opinion for the Court striking down the Nebraska law.

The *Meyer* Opinion

The opinion in *Meyer* is viewed today as the foundation on which the Court has built modern constitutional doctrines protecting personal liberty and family privacy. Yet the task of writing the opinion had been assigned to the archconservative Justice McReynolds. It is one of the greatest anomalies of Supreme Court history that the single enduring opinion by the reactionary McReynolds should be this liberal keystone. But William Guthrie, by alerting McReynolds to the looming Oregon School Law's attack on the privileges and class divisions nurtured by private education, had tapped in McReynolds a well of deeply felt societal values.

Substantive due process analysis is notoriously dependent upon a judge's personal moral vision of human liberty. This may account for the peculiar lack of legal argument in *Meyer*. The Guthrie brief was only eight pages long; the text of McReynolds's opinion in *Meyer* occupies less than eight pages of the United States Reports. Guthrie cites little case law and McReynolds virtually none. Both of these authors seem to violate the rule laid down by Justice Oliver Wendell Holmes, Jr., that "law does not exist without some definite authority."[14] Apparently, Guthrie's vision and that of the equally conservative Justice McReynolds meshed in some important way. But McReynolds put his own authoritarian and patrician stamp on the analysis. Coming from McReynolds, it is hardly surprising that among the fundamental constitutional liberties first identified in *Meyer* were the parental "right of control" of the child and the duty to provide the child "with an education suitable to his station in life."

McReynolds and Guthrie seemingly had little in common. Born in 1862, McReynolds was the oldest son of a doctor. Descended from Scots–Irish stock who had arrived in America in 1740, he was educated in private preparatory schools and went on to Vanderbilt College and the University of Virginia School of Law. According to historian Alexander Bickel, McReynolds certainly belonged to the professional upper class, if not the southern landed gentry. William E. Leuchtenburg paints a vivid picture of the man: "Slender, erect, slightly over six feet tall, he had piercing steel-blue eyes and carried himself like a Roman senator."

His politics were true to his patrician roots. In 1896, violently opposed to the Populist ideals of William Jennings Bryan, he had run for Congress as a "Gold Democrat" and lost. Appointed to the Court by President Woodrow Wilson (who had previously named him Attorney General) because of his reputation as a trust buster, on all other issues he demonstrated an unflagging and radical conservatism. One of the "Four Horsemen" whose bitter resistance to Franklin D. Roosevelt's New Deal legislation precipitated the famous "Court-packing" scheme, he registered 310 dissents in his twenty-six years on the bench—apparently a Supreme Court record.[15]

By all accounts, McReynolds was the most bigoted and illiberal man ever to have sat on the Supreme Court. Contemporaries described him as "petty," "overbearing," "rude," and "savage." He openly despised Jews, women lawyers, the *nouveau riche*, blacks, and legislators. His anti-Semitism was legendary. He treated his Jewish colleagues Louis D. Brandeis, Benjamin N. Cardozo, and Felix Frankfurter, with disdain, remarking that " for four thousand years the Lord tried to make something out of Hebrews, then gave it up as impossible and turned them out to prey on mankind generally—like fleas on the dog." McReynolds would not attend social functions at which the Jewish justices would be present, as he objected to dining "with the Orient."

There was, however, a hidden sentimental side to his nature, seldom revealed in public life. He was fond of children and adopted thirty-three British refugee children during World War II. He left a part of his estate to a seminary for young ladies. The eligible McReynolds remained a bachelor. While at college, he had formed an intense romantic attachment for Willella Pearson, the daughter of a Presbyterian minister; but she died at the age of twenty-four. Almost sixty years later, when McReynolds was eighty, he placed a plaque in her village church with a tribute composed by him. After his death it was learned that he had never married because he had resolved to remain true to her memory.

As a jurist, Justice McReynolds is far more famous for his personal idiosyncrasies and blistering dissents than for the opinions he wrote. Perhaps because of his cantankerous personality, he was usually assigned to draft opinions on minor questions in such fields as admiralty law. Whatever induced Chief Justice Taft to assign McReynolds the *Meyer* opinion, it was clearly not McReynolds's libertarian views or his sympathy for the downtrodden German–American. He publicly castigated those "malevolents from Germany, a country then engaged in hunnish warfare and notoriously encouraged by many of its natives who, unhappily, had obtained citizenship here." He exonerated the public official in *Berger v. United States* who had made anti-German remarks as showing only a proper "detestation for all persons of German extraction who were at that time wickedly abusing privileges granted by our indulgent laws."

Not surprisingly, McReynolds's opinion gave short shrift to the issues of ethnic bias and religious bigotry and even appeared to excuse the anti-German impetus for the Nebraska law as "easy to appreciate" and stemming from "unfortunate experiences during the late war and aversion to every characteristic of truculent adversaries. . . ." The Court had read and heard powerful religious and intellectual liberty arguments, yet McReynolds stressed the statute's interference with teachers' property rights and, above all, the rights of parents to control the activities of their children. After repeating the Nebraska court's findings on the necessity for restricting German language instruction, he identified the problem as whether the statute unreasonably infringed on liberty guaranteed by the Fourteenth Amendment.

Just what liberties should be included under the list of those guaranteed by the Constitution had been the subject of some debate. McReynolds added to the list of "liberties" enumerated in earlier cases such as the dissent in the *Slaughterhouse Cases* (1873) and the opinion in *Allgeyer v. Louisiana* (1897) the right "to acquire useful knowledge, to marry, establish a home and bring up children." He went on to note that "corresponding to the right of control, it is the natural duty of the parent to give his children education suitable to their station in life."

The dramatic centerpiece of the opinion, however, is its discussion of child-rearing policies in the Ideal Commonwealth of Plato and under the Spartan system—a discussion which seems far more appropriate to the issue of compulsory public education than to the Nebraska Language Law. Both Plato's Commonwealth and Sparta are alike in taking the child from its parents and placing its education exclusively in the hands of the state. According to McReynolds, "[a]lthough such measures have been deliberately approved by men of great genius, their ideas touching the relation between individual and State were wholly different from those upon which our institutions rest."

Curiously, although the opinion appeared to owe a great deal to Guthrie's *amicus* brief, McReynolds barely mentioned the religious liberty and intellectual freedom arguments developed there and at oral argument. The rights of children also receive cursory attention. Overall, McReynolds's opinion may be seen as raising, in a more sophisticated form, the question asked by the Oregon School Law opposition pamphlets: "Who Owns Your Child?" According to McReynolds, the parents' dominion over the child is a vested, fundamental right protected from state infringement by the Fourteenth Amendment. In McReynolds's view, "the parents' power to control the education of their own," like liberty of contract and private ownership of property, is not merely a feature of social organization which may be tampered with in the name of reform. It is a liberty enshrined in the Constitution.

Justice Oliver Wendell Holmes, Jr., joined by Justice George Sutherland, dissented from the *Meyer* majority opinion, in its companion case, *Bartels v. Iowa* (1923). Holmes framed the issue as whether the Nebraska law posed an unreasonable restriction on the Fourteenth Amendment liberties not of the parent but of teacher or scholar. Although he clearly found the language laws personally distasteful, Holmes wrote:

> It is with hesitation and unwillingness that I differ from my brethren with regard to a law like this. . . . [I]f there are sections in the state where a child would hear only Polish or French or German spoken at home I am not prepared to say that it is unreasonable to provide that in his early years he shall hear and speak only English at school. I think I appreciate the objection to the law but it appears to me to present a question upon which men reasonably differ and therefore I am unwilling to say that the Constitution of the United States prevents the experiment being tried.

Holmes, in dissenting, remained true to the views expressed in his *Lochner* and *Dagenhart* dissents, and in countless other cases in which the Court had invalidated legislative reforms. Holmes believed that the Constitution was not intended to enact the status quo into law, to stifle reform or to prefer any one social or economic system. In Holmes's view, the Framers of the Constitution had entrusted these policy choices to the people's elected representatives, and judges must be loath to second-guess the legislature unless its acts were plainly arbitrary or violated clear and explicit constitutional prohibitions.[26]

Scholarly commentary on *Meyer* was divided. Its critics followed Holmes in questioning the appropriateness of the Court's substituting its judgement in educational matters for the judgment of local officials, educators, and the electorate. They arged that the critical importance of education to the welfare of the state traditionally had been held to justify wide latitude under the police power first in compelling parents to forego their children's labor in the farm or factory and later in setting uniform curricular requirements conducive to good citizenship.[17] Nonetheless, Guthrie had succeeded in his project—he had laid a solid foundation for his triumph two years later in the Oregon School Law case, *Pierce v. Society of Sisters*.

The Oregon School Law in Court

In the Oregon School Law case, parental rights as a bulwark against the threat to private education were debated openly by both sides. In addition to the powerful precedential effect of *Meyer*, the Society of Sisters now asserted a higher authority: "patriarchal government was established by the Most High . . . [and] rests on foundations far more sacred than the institutions of man."[18]

William Guthrie was again in the front lines of the battle in *Pierce*. He headed one of two teams of lawyers writing for the Catholic parochial school challenging the law, but now he held the high ground. He had the advantage of being able to point to his own analogy to Plato which Justice McReynolds had adopted from Guthrie's brief in *Meyer* and made the law of the land. The discussions of parental authority, religious freedom, and traditions of individualism in *Pierce* were heated. Each side accused the other of playing into the hands of Bolshevists, syndicalists, and Communists. However, the battle had already been won in the sweeping language of *Meyer v. Nebraska*. Justice McReynolds, this time writing for a unanimous Court, repeated his reasoning in *Meyer*, and further expanded upon it.

> The fundamental theory of liberty on which all governments in this Union repose excludes any general power of the State to standardize its children by forcing them to accept instruction from public teachers only. The child is not the mere creature of the State; those who nurture him and direct his destiny have the right, coupled with the high duty, to recognize and prepare him for additional obligations.

The rhetoric that sounded feverish and exaggerated in the context of English curriculum laws now seemed an apt description of the perils of a state monopoly of education. It is not surprising that there were no dissents. Exclusive state control of all organs of education and the closing of all religious schools posed a grave threat to the existence of an independent, informed electorate and implicated the constitutionally explicit rights of free speech and free exercise of religion. It was also a frontal assault on a certain way of life. As the brief for the Society of Sisters pointed out:

> If the state can thus destroy the primary school, it can destroy the secondary school, the college and the university. Harvard, Yale,

Columbia, Princeton . . . [a]ll could be swept away, and with them
would depart an influence and an inspiration that this country can
ill afford to lose.

Whether the justices were influenced by a belief in the First Amendment values of independent education or by a belief in the conservative
mission of their class, they could hardly fail to disapprove a social experiment which would threaten the survival of both.

The liberty announced in *Meyer* to control one's children has remained something of a conundrum. As the defenders of the Oregon
law remarked, "[I]t is a strange perversion of the meaning of the word
'liberty' to apply it to a right to control the conduct of others."[19] Yet
the Court asserted the existence of such a constitutional liberty without
citing a single precedential authority.

In fact, the issue had been addressed earlier, in a 1904 case not
discussed by either Guthrie or McReynolds. In *Wadleigh v. Newhall*,
a father seeking to regain custody of his children argued that his Fourteenth Amendment rights had been violated by state action. The United
States Circuit Court for the Northern District of California rejected the
father's claim that parental custody rights were encompassed in the liberty protected by the due process clause.[20] This ruling was compatible
with evolving legal scholarship. Nineteenth-century legal scholars, mirroring the young Republic's reverence for the freedom of each individual,
had begun to depict parental rights not as absolute but as corollary to
specific parental duties. Parental control of the child was viewed not
as a liberty of the parent but as a necessary restraint on the child's liberty.
The parents' right to a child's earnings and services created not a right
but rather a duty to train and educate the child.[21] Now, as if someone
had gotten hold of the wrong end of the telescope, the viewpoint shifted
to parental control of children as a fundamental liberty personal to the
parent.

Guthrie Battles the Child Labor Amendment

The battleground also shifted. Having won the war to protect
parents' rights to choose their children's education, Guthrie turned his
attention to the ongoing struggle to secure parents' rights to the labor
of their children. With Guthrie's help, the movement to enact federal
laws regulating child labor had been defeated when the Supreme Court,
with McReynolds and the other "Four Horsemen" in the lead, ruled
in *Hammer v. Dagenhart* (1918) and in 1922 in *Bailey v. Drexel Furniture Co.* (*Child Labor Tax Case*) that Congress lacked the power to

regulate these areas of domestic concern. However, the opponents of child labor attempted an end run around the intransigent justices. They drafted an amendment to the United States Constitution that would authorize Congress to regulate the employment of children under the age of eighteen years.

The movement to regulate child labor, like the Americanization movement, had a complex history. Since colonial times, children had worked on family farms and as apprentices. But the Industrial Revolution, with urban factories and textile mills and company-owned farms ushering in a new mechanized age, changed the face of child labor immeasurably. In 1910, one out of every six children between the ages of ten and fifteen was a wage-earner. The comforting picture of children learning a skill or tending farm animals at their parents' side gave way to the economic reality of sixty-hour weeks in the perpetual gloom of the factory, mill, or coal mine or in the blazing sun of huge, company-owned sugar beet farms.[22]

Reform-minded Progressives, joined by trade unionists and religious leaders, established the National Child Labor Committee in 1904 and in the next two decades made enormous strides toward raising the ages and reducing the hours of child workers. Still, their goal of enacting uniform protective laws in every state remained elusive. Powerful interests opposed the reform movement. In the South, low wages were deemed essential to the revitalization of the textile industry, while in the conservative business community of the North, there was widespread distrust of any federal economic regulation, including the child labor laws and the proposed amendment. Echoing Guthrie's arguments in the *Meyer* and *Pierce* cases, ideological opponents of the amendment predicted that it would undermine parental authority, with the downfall of the Republic and revolution sure to follow.

A fact often forgotten in modern discussions of child labor is that attempts to regulate it threatened both the economy and the politics of the patriarchal family. Debates on child labor often analogized parents' interests in their children to property rights in chattels and livestock. Some argued that even horses were protected from their owners' abuse by law, while others equated the furor over child labor with the furor over slavery. In a letter to Congress, former United States Senator Charles Spalding Thomas of Colorado suggested that the evil of child labor, like the evil of slavery, was exaggerated since "men in general do not treat their property" with brutality.[23] The notion that children are a form of parental property formed a recurrent theme. The Child Labor Amendment was condemned as a sinister plot to deprive parents of their property and nationalize the economic value of the country's children. According to Senator Eugene Ransdell of Louisiana,

> Parents will remain in the background after being permitted to bring children into the world and nurture them in their toddling infancy. Just as soon as the children are large enough to be of some assistance to their real parents they must be delivered to their statutory father in Washington.[24]

Among the most avid opponents of the Child Labor Amendment were many influential Catholic organizations, churchmen, and laymen. They viewed the amendment with alarm as transferring to the state powers that ought to belong to parents. The American Bar Association also adopted a resolution opposing it.[25]

In the last year of his life, Guthrie led the successful opposition in New York State to the Child Labor Amendment. By 1934, New York had become the crucial state in the ratification process. Guthrie spoke not only for the Catholic community but also as leader of the American Bar Association committee opposing the amendment. He spoke to women's clubs, appeared at legislative hearings, delivered radio addresses, and and wrote an influential "Argument in opposition to ratification" presented to the Legislature of the State of New York in 1934 when it considered and ultimately defeated the amendment. In this brief, he painted a picture of moral decay, with idle children devoid of individualist values failing to milk the cows or gas up the family Ford or help their widowed mothers with the dishes. Parents who had been deprived of their children's services would be forced to turn to the taxpayer for support. Guthrie's argument concludes with extensive quotations from the Supreme Court opinions in *Meyer* and *Pierce*. As he had sown the language creating a parental right of control, so he reaped the benefits of a new constitutional doctrine in his fight against the Child Labor Amendment.

On February 25, 1934, Guthrie addressed the citizens of New York on WOR radio.[26] He condemned the Child Labor Amendment as a

> menace to the family, to the home, and to our local self-government. . . . Under its language Congress could regulate the help children might give their parents in the home and on the farm, and . . . control the education of children under the guise of limiting or regulating their mental labor.

The amendment was defeated. Again, on January 23, 1935, Guthrie debated against New York City Mayor Fiorello LaGuardia before a crowd that overflowed the Senate Chamber in Albany. He charged that the amendment would bring the federal government into the sacred precincts of the home and reach the farm boy picking blueberries on the mountain, the schoolboy delivering newspapers, and the boy earning money to pay his way through college. A second time the amendment was defeated.[27]

On the morning of December 8, 1935, Guthrie's friend and neighbor John W. Davis, the 1924 Democratic presidential candidate, went to call on Guthrie at "Meudon," his Long Island estate. Davis was announced. As he ascended the stairs to the second-floor study, he heard Guthrie fall to the floor. Davis reached his friend's side as Guthrie lost consciousness, stricken by a sudden heart attack. He died later that day. Guthrie was seventy-six years of age. In a eulogy before the Association of the Bar of the City of New York, Davis evoked the lawyer and the man:

> Short is the lawyer's life and shorter still his fame. Soon or late oblivion awaits us all. As those who stand in its shadow, we owe it to ourselves and to posterity to make lasting record of worthy men that they may live on without visible symbol, woven into the stuff of other men's lives. None better deserves such honor at our hands than William D. Guthrie. Let us write him down a learned and able lawyer, a wise and prudent counsellor, a patriotic and loyal citizen, a gentleman unafraid.[28]

Today, Davis's words seem clairvoyant. Although Guthrie's name has been all but forgotten, his words and ideas truly are woven into the stuff of constitutional law.

The Ironic Fate of Guthrie's Contribution

What William Dameron Guthrie's amazement would be, however, could he see the pattern that has emerged from the thread of *Meyer* as it has figured in the "new" substantive due process. Guthrie died believing that he had won a decisive victory in the battle to stem federal powers and to protect the traditional family. Yet today Guthrie's landmark cases supply the constitutional rationale for doctrines that are viewed by modern conservatives and states' rights advocates as undermining local political prerogatives and drastically eroding the traditional family.

This transmutation of *Meyer* was partly a product of drastic shifts in political and judicial power in the turbulent depression era. The conservative victory over the expansion of federal powers was especially short-lived. At the time of Guthrie's death, the nation faced a deepening economic crisis. Yet Justices James C. McReynolds, George Sutherland, Willis Van Devanter, and Pierce Butler, joined by Justice Owen Roberts, continued to invoke the Constitution to block Franklin D. Roosevelt's New Deal programs at every turn. Personal liberties and liberties of contract guaranteed by the due process clause, coupled with a narrow view of the commerce clause, left small constitutional margin for government to intervene in the economy. In its 1936 term, the Supreme Court overturned one after another of FDR's legislative projects, turning the tide of opinion against the "Nine Old Men" and their conservative vision of the Constitution. Then on February 5, 1937, Roosevelt sent to Congress the notorious "Court-packing plan" that would have allowed him to add as many as six new justices to the Court.[29] Less than two months later, the Court handed down its opinion in *West Coast Hotel Co. v. Parrish*, validating a minimum wage law and essentially repudiating Guthrie's absolute view of due process as forbidding substantive economic regulation. "Liberty under the Constitution is necessarily subject to due process restraints," the Court announced, "and regulation which is reasonable in relation to its subject and is adopted in the interests of the community is due process." By 1938, it was widely believed that the Court's decisions in *Whitfield v. Ohio* (1936) and *Kentucky Whip and Collar Co. v. Illinois Central Railroad Co.* (1937) had opened the way to federal regulation of child labor.[30] Opponents of child labor turned their energies to drafting new federal legislation and the Child Labor Amendment became obsolete.

But what of the notion that the Constitution prohibits state intervention in non-economic aspects of family life? Curiously, although the economic branch of substantive due process perished in the New Deal, the substantive due process doctrines of liberty in family matters announced in *Meyer* and *Pierce* survived unscathed.[31] Half a century later, they formed a part of the doctrinal foundation, in cases like *Griswold v. Connecticut, Roe v. Wade,* and *Stanley v. Illinois*, of an expansive liberty in all matters touching on the decision to procreate and on parent/child relationships. It is an enduring irony that these cases, presently condemned by many who view themselves as champions of traditional family values, should owe their existence to the archconservative Justice McReynolds and to the prominent New York Catholic lawyer and scholar whose most cherished goal was to protect and preserve the patriarchal family from the threat posed by centralized federal power. The Constitution has been called a "living" document. And constitutional rights—once brought to life—begin a history of their own, outlasting the personal moral visions of their creators and critics alike.

NOTES

*Thanks to Jennifer Giblin and Randi Stock for their invaluable research assistance.

¹William D. Guthrie, "The Oregon Compulsory Public School Law," *Columbia Magazine* (June 1924).

²Benjamin R. Twiss, *Lawyers and the Constitution: How Laissez Faire Came to the Supreme Court* (Princeton, N.J.: Princeton University Press, 1942), Ch. 10; Stephen B. Wood, *Constitutional Politics in the Progressive Era: Child Labor and the Law* (Chicago: University of Chicago Press, 1968), 148, 155–159, 280–281.

³On the English-only movement, see Robert N. Manley, "Language, Loyalty, and Liberty: The Nebraska Council of Defense and the Lutheran Church, 1917–1918," *Concordia Hist. Inst. Q.* 37 (1964): 1; Kenneth B. O'Brien, Jr., "Education, Americanization, and the Supreme Court: The 1920s", *American Quarterly* 13 (1961): 161; William G. Ross, "*Meyer v. Nebraska:* A Judicial Janus," *Cinn. L. Rev.* 57 (1988): 125; I.N. Edwards, "Legal Status of Foreign Languages in the Schools," *The Elementary School Journal* 29 (Dec. 1923): 270–273.

⁴Paul E. Peterson, *The Politics of School Reform: 1870–1945* (Chicago: University of Chicago Press, 1985), 52 ff.; Selwyn K. Troen, *The Public and the Schools, Shaping the St. Louis System, 1838–1920* (Columbia, Mo.: University of Missouri Press, 1975), 53–57; Wayne E. Fuller, *The Old Country School: The Story of Rural Education in the Middle West* (Chicago: University of Chicago Press, 1982), 199.

⁵For *Meyer's* procedural history and legal strategy, see Arthur F. Mullen, *Western Democrat* (New York: Wilfred Funk, Inc.: 1940); Ross, "Judicial Janus."

⁶On the movement to abolish private schools, see David Tyack, Thomas James, and Aaron Benavot, *Law and the Shaping of Public Education, 1785–1954* (Madison: University of Wisconsin Press, 1987), 177; Lloyd P. Jorgenson, "The Oregon School Law of 1922: Passage and Sequel," *Catholic Hist. Rev.* 54 (1968–1969): 455; Timothy M. Pies, "The Parochial School Campaigns in Michigan," *Catholic Hist. Rev.* 72 (April 1986).

⁷The nativist movement is chronicled by John Hingham in *Strangers in the Land: Patterns of American Nativism, 1860–1925* (New York: Atheneum Press, 1965), and Robert Murray, *Red Scare: A Study in National Hysteria, 1919–1920* (New York: McGraw-Hill, 1955).

⁸The quote is from the ballot argument, reprinted in the Supreme Court Record, *Pierce v. Society of Sisters,* Appellee Society of Sisters Brief (Kavanaugh), Appendix B, 97.

⁹Jorgenson, "Oregon School Law," collects quotations from numerous contemporary magazines, newspapers, and periodicals.

[10]My account of Guthrie's life and work draws upon a variety of sources, including Joseph S. Auerbach, *The Bar of Other Days* (New York: Harper Bros., 1940), Ch. 25; Twiss, *Lawyers and the Constitution*, Ch. 10; Julius Goebel, Jr., ed., *A History of the School of Law of Columbia University* (New York: Columbia University Press, 1955), 208-211; Guthrie's obituary, "W.D. Guthrie Dies Suddenly at 76," *New York Times* (Dec. 9, 1935) 21:1; and Matthew Dolan's profile in the *Dictionary of American Biography,* Supp. 1 (New York: Charles Scribner's Sons, 1944), 367-368.

[11]Guthrie's most representative writings are gathered in William D. Guthrie, *Lectures on the Fourteenth Amendment* (New York: Johnson Reprint Corp., 1970 ed.) and *Magna Carta and Other Addresses* (Freeport, N.Y.: Books for Libraries Press, 1969 ed.).

[12]Guthrie, "The Oregon Compulsory Public School Law," *Columbia Magazine* (June 1924).

[13]13. Mullen, *Western Democrat*, 225.

[14]The famous quotation is from Justice Oliver Wendell Holmes, Jr.'s dissent in *Black and White Taxicab & Transfer Co. v. Brown & Yellow Taxicab & Transfer Co.*, 226 U.S. 518, 533 (1928).

[15]This sketch of Justice McReynolds draws heavily upon Alexander M. Bickel's memorable portrait in Alexander M. Bickel and Benno C. Schmidt, Jr., *The Oliver Wendell Holmes Devise History of the Supreme Court of the United States, Vol. IX: The Judiciary and Responsible Government, 1910-1921* (New York: Macmillan, 1984), 341-357. Other sources include William Leuchtenburg's sketch in *The Dictionary of American Biography*, Supp. 4 (1946-1950), 536, and Roger Jacobs, ed., *Memorials of the Justices of the Supreme Court of the United States*, (Littleton, Colo.: Fred B. Rothman & Co., 1981), 373 ff.

[16]Max Lerner, ed., *The Mind and Faith of Justice Holmes, His Speeches, Essays, Letters and Judicial Opinions* (New Brunswick, N.J.: Transaction Publishers, 1989), 317-321.

[17]O'Brien, "Education, Americanization, and the Supreme Court," 165 & n. 21 and 166 & n. 22, citing comments of Ellwood Cubberly, Dean of Stanford University School of Education, and I.N. Edwards, Professor of Education at the University of Chicago.

[18]Record, *Pierce v. Society of Sisters*, Appellee Society of Sisters Brief, 41.

[19]Record, *Pierce v. Society of Sisters*, Supplement to Brief of Appellant, Governor of State of Oregon, 8.

[20]The *Wadleigh* opinion is reported at 136 Fed. 941 (1905).

[21]Michael Grossberg, *Governing the Hearth: Law and the Family in Nineteenth Century America* (Chapel Hill, N.C.: University of North Carolina Press, 1985), 281-285; Steven Mintz & Susan Kellogg, *Domestic Revolutions: A Social History of American Family Life* (New York: Free Press, 1988), 54-55, 128-129.

[22]On children's work in early America, see John Demos, *A Little Commonwealth* (New York: Oxford University Press, 1972), and Edmund S. Morgan, *The Puritan Family* (New York: Harper & Row, 1966). For child labor in the nineteenth and early twentieth centuries, see Stephen B. Wood, *Constitutional Politics in the Progressive Era: Child Labor and the Law* (Chicago: University of Chicago Press, 1968), 1-22; Viviana A. Zelizer, *Pricing the Priceless Child: The Changing Social Value of Children* (New York: Basic Books, 1985), 56 ff.

[23]65 *Congressional Record* 10077 (1924).

[24]*Ibid.* at 10097.

[25]On Catholic opposition to the amendment, see Vincent A. McQuade, *The American Catholic Attitude on Child Labor Since 1891* (Washington, D.C.: Catholic University Press, 1938); Greene, "The Catholic Committee for Ratification of the Child Labor Amendment, 1935-1937: Origin and Limits," *Catholic Historical Review* (April 1988), 248-250, 258. For Guthrie's role in the Bar's and church's opposition, see William D. Guthrie,

Argument in Opposition to Child Labor Amendment (New York: New York Bar Association, 1934); "LaGuardia Urges, Guthrie Assails Child Labor Ban," *New York Times* (Jan. 24, 1935) 1:5.

[26]Guthrie's radio address is reprinted in *American Bar Association Journal* 20 (1934): 404–406.

[27]"LaGuardia Urges, Guthrie Assails Child Labor Ban," *New York Times* (Jan. 24, 1935) 1:4.

[28]Quoted by Auerbach, *The Bar of Other Days*, 282–283. See also "Guthrie Dies Suddenly at 76," *New York Times* (Dec. 9, 1935) 21:1.

[29]An excellent synopsis of the Court-packing plan and its aftermath may be found in Henry J. Abraham, *Justices and Presidents: A Political History of Appointments to the Supreme Court*, 2nd ed. (New York: Oxford University Press, 1985), 206–210.

[30]"Information as to Referendum on Child Labor," *American Bar Association Journal* 23 (1937): 819, 823–824.

[31]Laurence H. Tribe, *American Constitutional Law*, 2nd ed. (Mineola, New York: Foundation Press, 1988), 1318.

Learned Hand*

(1872–1961)

GERALD GUNTHER
Stanford Law School

Learned Hand is widely viewed, with Oliver Wendell Holmes, Louis D. Brandeis, and Benjamin N. Cardozo, as among the leading American judges of the twentieth century. His influence on constitutional law stems more from his extrajudicial advocacy of judicial restraint and his modest, yet creative, performance on lower federal courts in fifty-two years of judging than from the relatively few constitutional rulings among his nearly 3,000 decisions.

Christened Billings Learned Hand, the son and grandson of upstate New York lawyers and judges, Hand dropped the Billings after graduation from Harvard Law School in 1896. Hand surrendered to family pressures in turning to law rather than pursuing his interest in philosophy engendered by his Harvard College teachers, including William James, Josiah Royce, and George Santayana. In six years of practice in Albany and seven in New York City, he performed competently but considered himself inadequate. But the young lawyer's associations with New York City intellectuals and reformers prompted President William Howard Taft to name the thirty-seven-year-old Hand to the federal trial bench in 1909. President Calvin Coolidge elevated him to the Court of Appeals for the Second Circuit in 1924, where Hand served for the rest of his life.

*Reprinted from the *Encyclopedia of the American Constitution*, edited by Leonard W. Levy, Kenneth Karst, and Dennis J. Mahoney. ©1986 by Macmillan Publishing Company, a Division of Macmillan, Inc. All rights reserved.

Hand's persistent belief in judicial restraint antedated his appointment to the bench. He had been strongly influenced by James Bradley Thayer at Harvard Law School. His major publication before the judgeship was an article attacking *Lochner v. New York* (1905). His deepseated skepticism and allergy to absolutes, as well as his devotion to democratic policymaking and his unwillingness to be ruled by a bevy of Platonic Guardians, made him disdainful of judges ready to pour subjective philosophies into vague constitutional phrases. He was unwilling to suppress his hostility to judicial activism, developed in the era of the "Nine Old Men" and its use of substantive due process to strike down economic regulation, in the post-1937 years, when the philosophy of Harlan Fiske Stone's footnote to *United States v. Carolene Products Company* (1937), with its preference for personal rather than economic rights, gained ascendancy.

In his early years as a federal judge, Hand participated widely in extrajudicial activities. He was a member of the group that founded *The New Republic* magazine, and he helped draft Theodore Roosevelt's Bull Moose platform in 1912. Indeed, he was so devoted to the Progressive cause that he permitted his name to be entered as that party's candidate for the New York Court of Appeals in 1913.

After World War I, Hand decided that his position precluded extrajudicial involvements in controversial issues. But he had frequent occasion to continue airing his views of the judicial role in papers and addresses, many of which are collected in *The Spirit of Liberty* (1952). Hand's Holmes Lectures, delivered at Harvard three years before his death and published under the title *The Bill of Rights*, were an extreme restatement of Hand's hostility to the *Lochner* interventionist philosophy. The lectures even questioned the judicial enforceability of vague Bill of Rights provisions.

Hand's judicial reputation rests mainly on his craftsmanlike performance in operating creatively within the confines set by the political branches. His strength is best revealed in the way he handled many small cases in private law and statutory interpretation. He probed deeply to discover underlying questions, rejecting glib formulations and striving for orderly sense amidst the chaos of received legal wisdoms. Although constitutional issues seldom came before his court, he touched upon a wide range of them, from favoring strong enforcement of Fourth Amendment guarantees in *United States v. Rabinowitz* (1949) to offering innovative views on defining obscenity in *United States v. Kennerly* (1913).

Hand's most important judicial contributions dealt with political speech under the First Amendment. His most enduring impact stems from his controversial decision in *Masses Publishing Co. v. Patten* (1917). The ruling, overturned on appeal, protected the mailing of antiwar materials in the midst of national hostility to dissent. Hand's approach shielded all speech falling short of incitement to unlawful conduct. Two years later, the Supreme Court, in its first confrontation with the problem, refused to go so far as Hand had. Instead, *Schenck v. United States* (1919) launched the clear and present danger test, under which the protection of speech turned on guesses about its probable impact. In a rare disagreement with his one judicial idol, Oliver Wendell Holmes, Hand criticized Holmes's approach, in *Abrams v. United States* (1919) as well as *Schenck*, as an inadequate bulwark against majoritarian passions. With the Supreme Court adhering to Holmes's standard for decades, Hand assumed that his *Masses* approach had failed. But in 1969, Hand's incitement test, combined with the best elements of Holmes's approach, became the modern standard for First Amendment protection, in *Brandenburg v. Ohio* (1969).

Hand is equally well known for recasting and, many believe, diluting the clear and present danger test by affirming convictions of the Communist leaders in *United States v. Dennis* (1950). This ruling reflected not only Hand's mounting skepticism about judicial protection of fundamental rights but also his consistent obedience to Supreme Court pronouncements. In affirming the *Dennis* convictions, Chief Justice Fred M. Vinson's plurality opinion adopted Hand's reformulation as the proper criterion. Hand, however, remained convinced even in the 1950s that his *Masses* approach offered better protection to dissenters.

The distinctive traits of Hand's model of judging—open-mindedness, impartiality, skepticism, restless probing—came naturally to him. Those traits were ingredients of his personality by the time Hand became a judge. Philosopher and humanist as well as judge, Hand remained intellectually engaged, ever ready to reexamine his own assumptions.

Hand's unmatched capacity to behave according to the model of the modest judge was not wholly a conscious deduction from the theory of judicial restraint instilled by Thayer and confirmed by Hand's early experiences. It was at least as much a product of Hand's temper and personality. The doubting, open-minded human being could not help but act that way as a judge. Hand's major legacy, to constitutional law as well as to all other areas of the law, lies in his demonstration that detached and openminded judging is within human reach.

For Further Reading

Hand, Learned. *The Spirit of Liberty: Papers and Addresses*, ed. Irving Dilliard. New York: Knopf, 1952.

_____ *The Bill of Rights*. Cambridge, Mass.: Harvard University Press, 1958.

Shanks, Hershel, ed. *The Art and Craft of Judging: The Decisions of Judge Learned Hand*. New York: Macmillan, 1968.

John Marshall Harlan
(1899–1971)

MICHAL R. BELKNAP

California Western School of Law, San Diego

Justice John Marshall Harlan was a persistent champion of judicial restraint and federalism during a sixteen-year career on the Supreme Court that began in 1955 and ended shortly before his death on December 29, 1971. He was the second man bearing that name to occupy a seat on the nation's highest bench. The first was his grandfather, who served from 1877 to 1911. Like the first Justice John Marshall Harlan, who is best remembered today for his lonely protests against racially insensitive rulings negating the Fourteenth Amendment's promise of equal rights for blacks, his namesake often swam against the prevailing judicial tide of his day. His repeated pleas for judicial restraint and federalism made the second Justice Harlan the great dissenter of the Warren Court.

This constant critic of reform by judicial decision came originally from Chicago, where he was born in 1899. After attending elementary and secondary schools in the United States and Canada, Harlan enrolled at Princeton University, from which he graduated in 1920. He then attended Balliol College, Oxford, as a Rhodes Scholar, staying on to study law and eventually earning both a B.A. and an M.A. degree. Upon his return to America, Harlan, as befit the grandson of a Supreme Court justice and the son of an attorney, began preparing for a legal career. He became an apprentice with the Wall Street law firm of Root, Clark, Buckner, and Howland, meanwhile continuing his formal education as a part-time student at the New York Law School. In 1924 he received an LL.B. from that institution.

Harlan's association with Root, Clark continued for more than three decades. During his years with the firm he represented boxer Gene Tunney and participated in highly publicized cases involving Bertrand Russell and the estate of multimillionaire spinster Ella Wendell. He also argued several appeals before the United States Supreme Court.

Several periods of public service interrupted Harlan's lengthy tenure with Root, Clark. From 1925 to 1927 he served as an assistant United States attorney for the Southern District of New York. In that capacity he participated in the prosecution of former Attorney General Harry Daugherty for official misconduct. In 1928 Harlan took leave from Root, Clark to serve as a special New York state prosecutor in an investigation of municipal graft in Queens. During World War II, he served in the Army Air Force, rising to the rank of colonel and winning several decorations for his work in operational analysis and postwar planning. In 1951 he became general counsel to the New York State Crime Commission.

Harlan finally left Root, Clark for good in early 1954 to take a seat on the United States Court of Appeals for the Second Circuit. He had served for less than a year on that prestigious tribunal when, on November 8, 1954, President Dwight D. Eisenhower elevated him to the Supreme Court. Southerners, who were angered by the Court's 1954 *Brown v. Board of Education* decision striking down school segregation and who feared this new Justice Harlan might share his grandfather's hostility to racial discrimination, managed to delay his confirmation for several months, but on March 28, 1955, he was finally able to take his seat. He served until September 1971, when terminal cancer forced him to resign from the Court.

During his time on the Court, Justice Harlan was one of its hardest-working members. He wrote 168 opinions for the Court, 296 dissents, and 149 concurrences. During the ten-year period that began with the 1958 term, he wrote more opinions per term than any other justice. His writing style was sometimes dull and pedantic, but his opinions were always scholarly and carefully crafted. He earned a well deserved reputation as a "lawyer's judge."

Harlan also became known as an advocate of judicial restraint on a Court noted for its liberal activism. Under the leadership of Chief Justice Earl Warren, the Supreme Court broadly interpreted such constitutional guarantees as the due process and equal protection clauses of the Fourteenth Amendment to combat social and political injustice and promote egalitarianism. As far as Harlan was concerned, his colleagues had a "mistaken view" of both the Constitution and their own function:

> This view in a nutshell is that every major social ill in this country can find its cure in some constitutional "principle," and that this court should "take the lead" in promoting reform when other branches fail to act. The Constitution is not a panacea for every blot upon the public welfare, nor should this court, ordained as a judicial body, be thought of as a general haven for reform movements.[1]

During his early years on the Supreme Court, Harlan aligned himself with Justice Felix Frankfurter, the leading proponent of the idea that the judiciary should leave policy-making to the elected branches of the government. After Frankfurter's retirement in 1962, he carried on alone their crusade for judicial restraint.

Marching to a different drummer from that guiding most of his colleagues, Harlan dissented from many of the most important decisions of the Warren Court. He protested its revolutionary one-man-one-vote rulings, which required that seats in state legislatures[2] and the U.S. House of Representatives[3] be apportioned on the basis of population. He refused to join in decisions declaring the poll tax unconstitutional[4] and turning a Reconstruction civil rights statute into an open housing law.[5] Two of the Warren Court's most significant and controversial criminal justice decisions, *Miranda v. Arizona*[6] and *Mapp v. Ohio*,[7] elicited dissents from Harlan.

His persistent criticism of rulings widely applauded by liberals tended to create the impression that Harlan's jurisprudence was a product of political conservativism. However, at times he could adopt positions that were surprisingly liberal. At the height of the McCarthy era, Harlan warned his fellow Americans that the greatest danger confronting the nation was "that we shall fall prey to the idea that in order to preserve our free society, some of the liberties of the individual must be curtailed, at least temporarily. . . ."[8] In 1957 he acted on this conviction, writing an opinion for the Court overturning the convictions of fourteen California Communist leaders for violation of a sedition statute known as the Smith Act.[9] This decision forced the government to abandon a legal attack on the Communist Party that it had been waging for nearly a decade with that law as its weapon. During the Vietnam War, while such conservatives as President Richard Nixon and California Governor Ronald Reagan were condemning the tactics of youthful protesters, Harlan extended constitutional protection to their activities. He spoke for the Court in cases in which it overturned a conviction for casting contempt on the American flag[10] and held for his fellow Justices that the First Amendment precluded California from punishing for disturbing the peace a young man who had appeared in a county courthouse wearing a jacket with the words "FUCK THE DRAFT" emblazoned across the back.[11] Harlan even supported the controversial *Griswold v. Connecticut* decision, which announced the existence of a right of marital privacy protected by the due process clause of the Fourteenth Amendment.[12]

Such a right was, he insisted, "implicit in the concept of ordered liberty." It was, therefore, protected against state interference by the Fourteenth Amendment. Harlan disagreed with his usually liberal colleague and close friend, Justice Hugo Black, who argued that all of the provisions of the Bill of Rights had been incorporated into the due process clause. Indeed, he opposed even the selective incorporation by which the Warren Court applied most, but not all, of those guarantees to the states through the Fourteenth Amendment. As far as Harlan was concerned, all that the due process clause demanded of the states in their dealings with individuals was that they accord them "fundamental fairness."

Harlan expected more from federal authorities. When a case involved the application of some provision of the Bill of Rights to the national government, he was likely to take a quite advanced position, joining forces with the most liberal and libertarian of his colleagues. For, although reluctant to see the Supreme Court impose national standards on the states, he was a supporter of civil liberties.

Nor was Harlan hostile to most of the reforms that his colleagues sought to advance with their decisions. Generally, his differences with the Warren Court's majority concerned means, not ends. Harlan disagreed with the Court's activist members not about what reforms would be good for American society, but about how those reforms should be achieved. For example, he shared his colleagues' belief that the poll tax ought to be eliminated. "But," as Harlan saw it, "the fact that the *coup de grace* has been administered by this Court instead of being left to the affected states or to the federal political process should be a matter of continuing concern to all interested in maintaining the proper role of this tribunal under our scheme of government."[13] As far as Harlan was concerned, reform should come through legislative action. He also worried that his colleagues were pursuing it in ways that would undermine American federalism.

As Professor Henry J. Bourguignon has pointed out, Harlan "placed [the] principle of federalism at the peak of his hierarchy of constitutional values."[14] He believed that state legislatures should be left free to experiment and to find their own solutions to the problems that confronted their constituents. He dreaded the displacement of local practices by national standards, imposed from above by the Supreme Court in Washington. That is why Harlan dissented from *Mapp*, which required the states to exclude illegally seized evidence from their criminal trials, and from *Miranda*, which forced them to give detailed warnings to suspects before interrogating them. While it was in criminal justice cases that he most often stressed the importance of federalism, that principle was, as Judge J. Harvie Wilkinson has observed, "the transcendent theme of his legal career" and "the cornerstone of his judicial perspective."[15]

The only value that could rival federalism for pre-eminence within Harlan's scheme of values was judicial restraint. The foundation blocks on which his jurisprudence rested were respect for the states and deference to the political branches. To Harlan, preserving these principles seemed more important than curing the ills of society or improving the performance of government. He assigned higher values to judicial restraint and federalism than to the reforms for the attainment of which his colleagues seemed willing to sacrifice these precepts. This outlook placed him at odds with a majority of the Warren Court. It determined that, like his grandfather before him, the second Justice John Marshall Harlan would be remembered primarily as a dissenter.

NOTES:

[1] *Reynolds v. Sims*, 377 U.S. 533, 634 (1969) (dissenting opinion).
[2] *Ibid*.
[3] *Wesberry v. Sanders*, 376, U.S. 1, 20 (1964) (dissenting opinion).
[4] *Harper v. Virginia Board of Elections*, 383 U.S. 663, 680 (1966) (dissenting opinion).
[5] *Jones v. Alfred H. Mayer Co.*, 392 U.S. 409, 449 (1969) (dissenting opinion).
[6] 384 U.S. 436, 504 (1966) (dissenting opinions).
[7] 367 U.S. 643, 672 (1961) (dissenting opinions).
[8] David L. Shapiro, ed., *The Evolution of a Judicial Philosophy: Selected Opinions and Papers of Justice John N. Harlan* (Cambridge, Mass.: Harvard University Press, 1969), 288.

[9]*Yates v. United States*, 354 U.S. 298 (1957).

[10]*Street v. New York*, 394 U.S. 576 (1969).

[11]*Cohen v. California*, 403 U.S. 15 (1971).

[12]381 U.S. 479, 499 (1965) (concurring opinion). See also *Poe v. Ullman*, 367 U.S. 497, 539–555 (1961) (dissenting opinion).

[13]*Harper v. Virginia Board of Elections*, 383 U.S. at 680–681 (1966) (dissenting opinion).

[14]"The Second Mr. Justice Harlan: His Principles of Judicial Decision Making," *Supreme Court Review* 1979 (1979): 252.

[15]"Justice John M. Harlan and the Values of Federalism," *Virginia Law Review* 57 (1971): 1186.

Robert H. Jackson: Independent Advocate

(1892–1954)

DENNIS J. HUTCHINSON

University of Chicago

Robert Houghwout (pronounced HOW-it) Jackson was a highly successful upstate lawyer who took a six-month leave from his practice in 1934 to head the Bureau of Revenue in Washington, D.C. He never returned, and successively ran the tax and antitrust divisions of the Department of Justice before becoming solicitor general, attorney general, and associate justice of the Supreme Court of the United States (1941–1954)—the eleventh New Yorker to sit on the Court. Jackson is now best remembered as the chief prosecutor at the Nuremberg War Crimes Trials (1945–1946), but his work both in the Department of Justice and on the Court helped to change the terms of American constitutional discourse.

Early Life

Jackson was born on February 13, 1892, at Spring Creek, Pennsylvania, to a farming family that could trace its English ancestry to a forebear who was a barrister of the Middle Temple and to colonial immigrants. Young Jackson was the product of a demanding rural upbringing and little formal education. The family moved when Jackson was five to Frewsburg, New York, and Jackson attended first Frewsburg and then Jamestown high schools, where he was class orator. He did not attend college, but at the age of eighteen—against his father's advice—apprenticed himself to a local lawyer with whom he read law before completing a two-year law course in twelve months at Albany Law School. In whatever spare time he had, he listened to oral arguments before the New York Court of Appeals. In later life, Jackson would credit his taste for literature and his capacity to turn a phrase to his English teacher at Jamestown, Mary Willard: "To those who feel the poverty of a life of sales talk by day and small talk by night, she threw open the treasure houses of accumulated scholarship of ages and bid us enrich ourselves there, limited in what we carry away only by the effort we give to the taking."[1]

Jackson returned to Jamestown in 1913 to begin practice with his cousin, and during the next twenty years built an extraordinarily successful practice in the small town (pop. 31,000 at his admission to the bar). His annual income often exceeded $30,000 even during the Depression. Despite entreaties to devote his time exclusively to one client or another, Jackson remained fiercely independent and maintained a general practice. He was an active Democrat in an overwhelmingly Republican area, and held no public office (other than a short stint as acting corporation counsel of Jamestown). He later recalled knowing of only one Democratic officeholder during the two decades he lived in Jamestown.

Public Service Career

Jackson worked for Franklin D. Roosevelt's gubernatorial campaign but turned down Roosevelt's proposal to appoint him to the Public Service Commission. Jackson enjoyed a thriving practice, prominence in his community, a small yacht, and a stable of horses. Perhaps more than anything else, he enjoyed his independence—a self-styled autonomy that he saw as almost inherited by blood from his headstrong ancestors.

When Roosevelt was elected president in 1932, Jackson—in the words of his keenest observer—"didn't take kindly to the importunities to leave this all for Washington. His was not the crusading public spirit. But he finally succumbed to a short tour of duty as general counselor to the Bureau of Internal Revenue. Washington, D.C., was very far, indeed, from Jamestown, N.Y. Jackson was invited to Washington not to be given a job but to do a job. There were hundreds of lawyers with better political credentials than his clamoring for assignments. But the New Deal needed experienced professional talent."[2]

Jackson's most publicized work at the Bureau, which lasted four times as long as expected, was the prosecution of Andrew W. Mellon— former ambassador to the Court of St. James's and former secretary of the treasury—for tax evasion, which resulted in a $750,000 judgment for the government. From Treasury, Jackson became assistant attorney general in charge first of the tax division (1936) and then the antitrust division (1937). He became solicitor general in 1938, attorney general in 1940, and Associate Justice of the United States Supreme Court in 1941. During the 1936 presidential campaign, Jackson crisscrossed the country making speeches for Roosevelt, with whom he developed a close relationship. Jackson was now not only one of the New Deal's most prominent lawyers, but also a presidential intimate in a world where that status was highly coveted. As his political star rose, Jackson was identified as one of the most liberal members of the administration and even was touted by some for vice-president. His only flirtation with elective office—for governor of New York in 1938—died aborning when Governor Herbert Lehman consented to renomination.

Although Jackson enjoyed the star status that FDR's second administration brought him, his deepest enjoyment came as solicitor general. It was the perfect wedding of his independence and his forensic brilliance. Justice Louis D. Brandeis is said to have remarked—in what later could be seen as both a right-handed and left-handed compliment—that Jackson should have been made solicitor general for life.[3] He was not a keen administrator, although he relished the eventual cabinet position.

Both as solicitor general and as attorney general, Jackson began to develop a constitutional view that later received its fullest voice in the opinions he wrote during his thirteen years on the Supreme Court. His advice to Roosevelt in 1940 on the provision of weapons to England[4] was informed by a conscientious yet practical feel for separation of powers, and his book *The Struggle for Judicial Supremacy* (1941), published shortly before his appointment to the Court, was a sustained critique—thinly disguised as a narrative with commentary—of what he saw as the pre-1937 Supreme Court's arrogation of political power under the name of constitutional interpretation.

Jurist

Once on the Court, Jackson—like many other Roosevelt appointees—wrote opinions that consolidated the constitutional vision of the New Deal, which had finally triumphed in 1937 when the Court retreated from its path of constitutional obstructionism in the face of the so-called "Court-Packing Plan" (a post-election scheme which Jackson was often erroneously credited with engineering)[5] He wrote for a Court that took Congress's power over interstate commerce to—and perhaps, he privately thought, past[6]—the limit,[7] and provided the most coherent image to date of the interstate "free market" contemplated by the commerce clause,[8] a view often blurred by earlier judicial deference to local power.

Yet the Roosevelt Court quickly exhausted the New Deal agenda, and the constitutional fields of fire shifted from familiar questions of federalism and national power to more urgent issues of civil liberty as the country plunged into World War II. Jackson produced his most stirring opinion in his second term, *West Virginia Board of Education* v. *Barnette*,[9] in which the Court held unconstitutional a state statute requiring public school students to pledge allegiance daily to the flag. Two young Jehovah's Witnesses claimed the statute violated the injunction in Exodus against embracing graven images. Jackson declared for the Court: "The very purpose of the Bill of Rights was to withdraw certain subjects from the vicissitudes of political controversy, to place them beyond the reach of majorities and officials and to establish them as legal principles to be applied by the courts. One's right to life, liberty, and property, to free speech, a free press, freedom of worship and assembly, and other fundamental rights may not be submitted to vote; they depend on the outcome of no elections."[10] He concluded, in his most-quoted testament: "If there is any fixed star in our constitutional constellation, it is that no official, high or petty, can prescribe what shall be orthodox in politics, nationalism, religion, or other matters of opinion or force citizens to confess by word or act their faith therein."[11]

Jackson also wrote forcefully, if not as memorably, in dissent against the Court's later decision that the government's war-time relocation from the West Coast of Japanese—citizen and alien alike—was not a violation of the due process clause of the Fifth Amendment.[12]

Postwar Experience

As the war in Europe wound down, Jackson accepted another presidential assignment that he again expected would be of brief duration: chief prosecutor at the International Military Tribunal in Nuremberg. Jackson helped to forge the agreement among the Allies establishing the terms of the trials and then undertook what turned out to be the year-long task of overseeing the assembly of documentary evidence to be presented and of conducting the critical stages of the trials. Jackson was widely criticized at home, both for being away from the Court for an entire term and for conducting what one member of the Court privately called a "high-grade lynching party."[13] Despite daily frustrations over logistics and what he viewed as unfair criticism of some of his questioning, Jackson later claimed to be more proud of what was accomplished at Nuremberg than of any other achievement in his career. Jackson returned to the Court in 1946, after a temperamental outburst from Nuremberg over the ethical standards of Justice Hugo L. Black (who, Jackson believed, had blocked his elevation to the chief justiceship when Harlan F. Stone died in April 1946).

The postwar Court faced dockets crowded with issues involving freedom of speech and racial discrimination. Jackson joined decisions invalidating racially restrictive covenants and segregated public education at the graduate level, but he recoiled at what he saw as increasing judicial opportunism—a penchant to turn slogans and results into constitutional doctrine. He rebelled at expansions of the freedom of speech clause[14] and the due process clause[15] in cases where he saw complexity while majorities saw imperatives. His opinions had a tendency to be biting, but as the chief justiceship of Fred Vinson wore on, Jackson's words became caustic. He began to rehearse his longstanding anxiety over judicial arrogation of power in lengthy opinions and, more memorably, in frequently quoted barbs: "We are not final because we are infallible, but we are infallible only because we are final."[16] And: "There is a danger that, if the Court does not temper its doctrinaire logic with a little practical wisdom, it will convert the constitutional Bill of Rights into a suicide pact."[17] One of his most discerning students, Paul A. Freund, captured the power of Jackson's pen: "He had style to delight, grace and power of expression to captivate. If his style was like pearls, they were occasionally—as was said of the style of a Scottish judge, surely a forebear—pearls dissolved in vinegar."[18]

Jackson's Legacies

Freund's observation, made at a memorial service after Jackson's death in 1954, is obviously accurate but can be overread. Over time, Jackson has become something of a judicial Cheshire Cat, whose opinions fade until only the style is left. And it is true that he does not compare well to his successor, John Marshall Harlan, for relentless logic or precision. Although too many Jackson opinions contain startling logical gaps or muddling of issues, he was more than a stylist who papered over underdeveloped arguments or impatience with vivid turns of phrase.

Part of the reason that the substance of his work seems less accessible today is that his most important contributions were made in fields that now seem commonplace or arcane. His writings on the commerce clause are fundamental, and his opinions on the full faith and credit clause—what he called "the lawyer's clause of the Constitution"[19]—are singularly valuable. His concurring opinion in the Steel Seizure Case[20] is still the analytical touchstone for questions of executive power.

"Like the proverbial rules of law," Freund wrote, "Justice Jackson's thoughts can be put into a nutshell but surely one cannot keep them there."[21] Jackson—ever the maverick—resists neat categorization even at this remove. During an era in which the Court became polarized, with outside champions for each view, Jackson remained his own man. He resisted what he saw as social engineering in the form of adjudication, but he joined the decisions dismantling the formal structure of Jim Crow; he wrote eloquently of freedom of conscience, but he refused to turn the First Amendment into a talisman for immunity from reasoned governmental activity; he was criticized for being indifferent to censure of dissidents,[22] but he wrote—in wartime—a careful opinion stripping the government's power to bring easy prosecutions for treason.[23] Jackson's enduring sin in a simplified world was to see, with lawyer's eyes, the problems and complexities of his task. His judicial philosophy, shaped as it was by acute sensitivity to the limits of the law and role of courts, was working itself out even at his sudden death.

Freund's remarks at the memorial service touch on the sources of that evolving view:[24]

> If he wrote for the lawyers he knew and yet reached an immeasurable audience, is it too much to suggest that his basic ideas had their origins in the community he knew as a lawyer and yet that they derived from sources far more general and remote? The sense of cohesion, the response to the pull of the widening community, the appreciation of mobility of men and resources,—were not these naturally cultivated in one who had been brought up in Warren County, Pennsylvania to live in upstate New York and who came to represent commercial interests operating in the vicinity of state boundaries? The fierce attachment to the cause of spiritual integrity, the right to choose one's fellowship or if need be to walk alone, to enjoy the now exuberant companionship of like minds and now the privacy of the spirit curtained against intrusion from whatever source without,—were not these too part of a Jamestown inheritance? Tradition spoke through Justice Jackson with his own strong and distinctive accent, but recognizable still as the authentic American voice.

Despite twenty years in Washington, D.C., Jackson never lost his affection for Jamestown. His suburban Virginia estate, Hickory Hill, recalled, with its stables and isolation, his upstate origins. In a spiritual sense, then, perhaps Jackson never really left. His influence on modern constitutional thought, on both the molecular and molar levels, is more enduring than his personal reputation, which may in time be rehabilitated, as we see him in better perspective and therefore may—as Auden wrote of Paul Claudel—forgive him for writing well.

NOTES:

[1]Quoted in Eugene C. Gerhart, *America's Advocate* (Indianapolis: Bobbs–Merrill, 1958), 33.

[2]Philip B. Kurland, "Robert H. Jackson," in Leon Friedman & Fred L. Israel, *The Justices of the United States Supreme Court, 1789-1978: Their Lives and Major Opinions* (New York: Chelsea House, 1980), 4:2546.

[3]See *id.* at 4:2559.

[4]See Gerhart, ch. 13; Jackson, "A Presidential Legal Opinion," *Harvard Law Review* 66 (1953): 1353.

[5]William E. Leuchtenburg, "The Origins of Franklin D. Roosevelt's 'Court Packing' Plan," *1966 Supreme Court Review* 347.

[6]A.T. Mason, *Harlan Fiske Stone: Pillar of the Law* (New York: Viking Press, 1956), 594-95.

[7]*Wickard v. Filburn*, 317 U.S. 111 (1942).

[8]*H.P. Hood & Sons v. Du Mond*, 336 U.S. 525 (1949).

[9]*West Virginia Board of Education v. Barnette*, 319 U.S. 624 (1943).

[10]319 U.S. at 638.

[11]319 U.S. at 642.

[12]*Korematsu v. United States*, 323 U.S. 214, 242 (1944).

[13] *Per* Stone, C.J., quoted in Mason, *Stone*, 716.

[14]See *Terminiello v. Chicago*, 337 U.S. 1, 13 (1949).

[15]*American Communications Association v. Douds*, 339 U.S. 382, 422 (1950).

[16]*Brown v. Allen*, 344 U.S. 532, 540 (1953).

[17]*Terminiello v. Chicago*, 337 U.S. at 37.

[18]*Proceedings of the Bar and Officers of the Supreme Court of the United States, April 4, 1955: In Memory of Robert Houghwout Jackson* (Washington: 1955), 52.

[19]Jackson, *Full Faith and Credit: The Lawyer's Clause of the Constitution* (New York: Columbia University Press, 1945).

[20]*Youngstown Sheet & Tube Co. v. Sawyer*, 343 U.S. 579, 634 (1952).

[21]*Proceedings,* at 46.

[22]*Douds; Dennis v. United States*, 341 U.S. 494, 561 (1951). See generally Louis L. Jaffe, "Mr. Justice Jackson," *Harvard Law Review* 68 (1955):940.

[23]*Cramer v. United States*, 325 U.S. 1 (1945).

[24]*Proceedings*, 52-53.

James Kent:
American Conservative
(1763–1847)

JAMES P. FOLTS
New York State Archives & Records Administration

James Kent was born in what is now Putnam County in 1763. His father was Moses Kent, a lawyer who was the son of Rev. Elisha Kent, a Presbyterian minister. James Kent's mother was Hannah Rogers, daughter of a Connecticut physician. Like his father and grandfather Kent, James Kent attended and graduated from Yale College. There he studied mathematics, grammar, logic, philosophy, history, English literature, and the Greek and Latin classics. One summer, a teenaged James Kent was initiated into the mysteries of the common law through a reading of Sir William Blackstone's *Commentaries on the Laws of England*. Kent decided to follow a legal career. Since colleges did not yet offer law degrees, James Kent read law while serving a clerkship in the office of Egbert Benson, a Poughkeepsie attorney who was currently attorney general of the new state of New York. Kent was admitted to the bar in 1785. Around this time he fell in love with Elizabeth Bailey, the daughter of John Bailey, in whose house Kent boarded. James Kent and Elizabeth Bailey were married and lived together happily for sixty-two years, until his death in 1847.

For a while James Kent was content in the law practice he set up in Poughkeepsie. The leisurely practice of a country lawyer did not make Kent rich, but it did give him time to read systematically the English law reports and the Latin classics. The learning he acquired benefitted him for the rest of his career. Kent soon became interested in politics. He became friends with Alexander Hamilton, and like Hamilton, strongly supported ratification of the federal Constitution in 1788. (Kent

attended the daily sessions of the ratification convention in Poughkeepsie.) Kent was elected to the New York Assembly on the Federalist slate
in 1790 and again in 1792. In the gubernatorial election of 1792, Kent,
a good Federalist, attacked the Antifederalist election officials who, it
was widely believed, had rejected an election canvass from Otsego which
would have made Federalist John Jay governor. While this affair helped
gain Kent a Federalist nomination for the U.S. House of Representatives in 1793, it also persuaded the Antifederalist majority in his district to vote for his opponent Theodorus Bailey—Kent's brother-in-law.

Professional Career

Weary of politics and hoping to further his legal career, Kent now
removed himself and his family to New York City. At first, clients did
not beat a track to his door. With the help of Federalist friends, Kent
obtained an appointment as the first lecturer in law at Columbia College. Kent held the appointment from late 1793 through 1798, when he
resigned. His courses were not very well attended after the first year,
and the student fees were correspondingly small. Kent was learned in
the law but not a great lecturer. Furthermore, he was interested in larger
questions of jurisprudence, not in training would-be attorneys in the
daily routine of their profession. Kent's theme in his course was the
distinctiveness of American law. He thought American law took the best
from English law but avoided its aristocratic and antiquated features.
This theme would later appear in Kent's *Commentaries on American
Law,* the great work of his retirement years.

Besides lecturing on the law, Kent continued his practice with increasing success. He followed politics closely, and publicly defended
Chief Justice John Jay's 1794 treaty with England. This treaty resulted
in the king's troops evacuating several Great Lakes forts; it also guaranteed debts owing from citizens of the United States to British subjects, or vice versa, even during wartime. (The latter provision was very
unpopular.) When John Jay was elected governor in 1795, he apppointed
James Kent recorder (city judge) of New York City and County and
also gave him a lucrative post as master in chancery (an officer who
took depositions for Court of Chancery cases). An even higher honor
came in 1798, when Kent was appointed a justice of the Supreme Court
of Judicature, the highest court in the state.

Supreme Court justices presided over trials, both civil and criminal,
in circuit courts held in every county of the state. The justices also decided questions of law raised during pleading or trial, or brought to

them by writs of error or certiorari from the lower courts. With his appointment to the Supreme Court, James Kent and his family moved from New York City to Albany, the state capital since 1797. There, Kent was more centrally located to make the long, arduous journeys required of a circuit judge. In visiting the new western counties to hold court, Justice Kent was impressed by the orderly behavior of the Federalist Yankees of Ontario County, and dismayed by the boisterous behavior of the Jeffersonian Republican inhabitants of Tioga and Delaware counties. However, Kent's most productive work as a supreme court justice was done in his capacity of appellate judge. Kent later remarked that when he first became a supreme court judge, "we had no law of our own, and nobody knew what it was." In fact, for many decades New York had had a sophisticated court system and legal procedure, adopted from English models. What Kent probably meant was that New York judges did not ordinarily draft written opinions but rather delivered their decisions orally from the bench. This practice made it difficult to learn what precedential cases existed.

Justice Kent initiated the practice of issuing regular written judicial opinions. In 1806, soon after being appointed chief justice of the state supreme court, Kent appointed his friend William Johnson as the official case reporter for the New York courts. Johnson's reports of New York court decisions were soon accepted throughout the nation as definitive statements of legal doctrine. Many of the opinions in these reports had been written, often anonymously, by the chief justice, who in learning and industry overshadowed his colleagues on the bench.

Chancellor Kent

In 1814, after serving on the supreme court for sixteen years, ten years as chief justice, James Kent was appointed chancellor, to preside over New York's Court of Chancery. This court, a court of equity, operated differently from the supreme court, a court of common law. The supreme court's procedures and remedies were rigidly defined by centuries of precedents, carried over to New York from the English common law courts. A litigant in a court of law could recover only money damages or possession of real or personal property. Juries were powerless to dispense other remedies that might be consistent with justice. Because of the deficiencies of the common law, equitable remedies had been developed in the court of the royal chancellor, who acted as the "King's conscience." The English court of chancery eventually came to have a well defined jurisdiction and procedure. Chancery handled cases of mortgage foreclosures; cases involving trusts, especially trusts set up for women, children, and incompetents; partnership and certain corporation cases; and special orders such as subpoena, injunction, and specific performance. The New York court of chancery handled all this business, as well as divorce cases, which in England lay within the jurisdiction of the church courts. Kent's decisions and opinions as chancellor continued to be reported by his colleague, William Johnson. Far more than any chancellor before him, Kent shaped equity law in New York, and his decisions and opinions were frequently cited by judges in other states. In equity, as in law, Kent usually followed the pertinent decisions of English judges, but he was also occasionally influenced by the continental civil law and by the utilitarian legal philosophers. Many of his most important cases reflected American circumstances, particularly in the area of economic development.

Delegate to the New York State Constitutional Convention, 1821

James Kent's service as chancellor was terminated by the provision of New York's constitution that judges must retire at age sixty. But Kent's judicial retirement in 1823 also coincided with political and constitutional changes. The constitutional convention of 1821 replaced New York's original 1777 constitution with a new instrument which made state government more democratic and strengthened the separation of powers among the three branches of government. Kent was elected a delegate to the 1821 convention. He was one of a minority of conservative, often former Federalist, delegates who were on the losing side of almost every crucial vote. Still, Kent's presence and participation helped assure that the conservative positions were defended with intelligence and dignity.

Kent was not a naysayer to every proposal for change. One of the main issues at the 1821 convention was the appointing power, and even Kent conceded that reform here was needed. Since 1777, the council of appointment, a board of four senators picked annually by the assembly, had possessed the power, jointly with the governor, to appoint major state officers as well as a multitude of local officers, including county clerks, sheriffs, justices of the peace, and commissioned militia officers. Whenever political control of the assembly changed hands, the new council of appointment usually replaced literally thousands of local office holders with persons loyal to the prevailing political faction. The result was constant political intrigue and numerous incompetent appointees. Everyone, except for a few top politicians, was tired of the system.

The 1821 convention voted unanimously to abolish the council of appointment. Under the new constitution, which went into effect in 1822, the secretary of state, comptroller, treasurer, attorney general, and surveyor general were nominated by the legislature. The governor appointed all judges, with consent of the senate. Justices of the peace were to be nominated jointly by the county board of supervisors and the county judges. If they disagreed on the nominees, the governor was to pick justices of the peace from the lists prepared by the judges and supervisors. (In 1826, this cumbersome system was abolished, and justices of the peace were henceforth elected by the voters in each town and city ward.) Under the 1822 constitution, the governor appointed the adjutant general and the major generals of the state militia, but all other militia officers were to be chosen by their men. Higher ranking officers were still commissioned by the governor. County clerks and sheriffs were now elected, rather than appointed, as before.

Constitutional Reform

A second body established by the 1777 constitution and abolished by the 1821 convention was the council of revision. This council consisted of the governor, the chancellor, and the justices of the supreme court. It was empowered to review all bills passed by the legislature. If it appeared "improper" to the council that a bill should become law, the council had ten days to return it to the legislature, along with its objections in writing. If the legislature passed the bill again by a two-thirds majority in both houses, the bill became law despite the council's objections. Four of the judges on the council of revision were delegates to the 1821 convention. They defended the council's role in reviewing legislation, but did not fight very hard to keep it from being abolished. They pointed out that the council of revision had in fact rejected only about 2 percent of all bills passed by the legislature, usually because the judges believed the bills to be unconstitutional. James Kent denied that he ever allowed political considerations to influence his votes in the council of revision. However, Democrats considered at least a few of the council's vetoes to be politically motivated. The convention in general wanted to get the nonelected judges out of the business of reviewing and vetoing legislative bills. By a unanimous vote, the convention gave to the governor the power to veto bills within ten days of receipt, and to the legislature the power to override the governor's veto by a vote of two-thirds of the members present in each house. The appellate courts continued to possess the power to rule on the constitutionality of a statute, if it pertained to a case before them.

The convention battle lines between conservatives (usually Clinton Democrats and old Federalists) and liberals (mostly Van Buren Democrats) were clearly drawn in the debates and votes on how long the governor should serve in office. Liberals thought a powerful governor should be held strictly and frequently accountable to the voters. Therefore they supported a one-year term of office. Conservatives wanted the governor to have a three-year term, so that he would be somewhat removed from party politics and have time to learn his job. After much debate, the convention, by a bare majority, approved a two-year term.

The most hotly debated issue at the 1821 convention was suffrage, particularly the right to vote for state senators. The 1777 constitution had sharply limited the right to vote for members of the assembly and senate and for governor. Voters in assembly elections had to own land worth $50 exclusive of any liens thereon, or rent property worth $5 and pay taxes on it. Voters for senator and governor had to own land worth $250 exclusive of all liens. The convention voted by a large majority to abolish the property qualification for voters and to allow any adult white male who paid taxes, worked on the roads, or served in the militia to vote in both local and state elections. Conservative delegates tried to restore the $250 property qualification for voters for senators. James Kent argued eloquently, though in vain, against the "extreme democratic principle" of universal manhood suffrage. He believed that "democracy" in ancient Rome and revolutionary France had "been productive of corruption, injustice, violence and tyranny." A portion of political power ought to remain with the agricultural freeholders on whose labors, Kent believed, the state's prosperity depended. Such men were the "safest guardians of property and laws." The growing numbers of poor people in the cities, led by demagogues, would covet the property of the rich and try to seize it. Kent believed that "society is an association for the protection of property as well as of life, and the individual who contributes only one cent to the common stock, ought not to have the same power and influence in directing the property concerns of the [social] partnership as he who contributes his thousands." Universal male suffrage would expose the rights and property of a minority (in this case, native born farmers) to the whims of the majority (poor, landless immigrants in the cities). Only a "stable senate" elected by men of property would protect property, liberty, and justice.

Other convention delegates forcefully argued that no special qualifications should be necessary to vote for senators. They pointed out that thousands of citizens had signed petitions calling for extension of the suffrage. Many propertyless men had fought to protect the state during the recent war with Britain. Few other states now required voters to own property. The senate and assembly would be in constant conflict if they were elected by different classes of voters. Factory owners and poor laborers surely had the same interest in protecting property rights as farmers did. The balance of power between the two houses of the legislature and the three branches of government was a better guarantee of liberty than a senate chosen by a restricted electorate. After three days of intense debate, the arguments for a practically universal adult white male suffrage prevailed. The suffrage clause was again approved, by a vote of 100 to 19, and the proposed amendment requiring a voter to possess $250 worth of real property to vote in senate elections was rejected.

The political rights of one group excluded from voting—blacks— were vigorously debated. The 1777 constitution had not required any special qualifications for free blacks to vote, for at that time almost all blacks in New York were slaves. The legislature abolished the slave trade within the state by an act of 1785, gave freedom to children of slaves by an act of 1799, and provided for total abolition of slavery in ten years by an act of 1817. The constitutional convention of 1821 debated whether blacks should have the same right to vote as whites. Almost all the delegates believed that blacks were not ready for the responsibility of voting. Conservatives like James Kent, as well as some Democrats like Martin Van Buren, argued that blacks should nevertheless enjoy the same political rights as whites. However, the majority of the convention delegates voted (72–31) to impose on blacks a $250 property qualification for the right to vote. (New York's restriction on blacks' right to vote remained in place until the fifteenth amendment to the U.S. Constitution was ratified in 1870.)

James Kent and other conservative delegates voted against the property qualification for black voters. Democratic observers at the convention thought it was "curious" how former Federalists, like Kent, and supporters of DeWitt Clinton voted to include blacks in the electorate on the same terms as whites. It was probably no coincidence that most black voters had voted for Federalist candidates. However much the convention delegates might have denied it, they considered politics as well as principles when deciding how to vote.

Party politics were at no time more in evidence than when the convention debated how to reform the judiciary. The convention's Democratic majority wanted to remove the five incumbent supreme court justices. Chief Justice Ambrose Spencer and at least two other justices had taken an active part in politics, in opposition to the "Bucktails," the dominant Democratic faction led by Martin Van Buren. The Bucktails now controlled the legislature and showed what they thought of the judges by voting in 1820, and again in 1821 and 1823, to reduce the judges' salaries. The convention neatly solved the vexing problem of the judges by voting, by a large majority, to abolish the present supreme court and establish a new one. Hence the incumbent judges were automatically retired. The convention held James Kent in grudging respect and allowed him to stay in office as chancellor until his sixtieth birthday in 1823, the constitutional age limit.

More important for the good administration of justice, the convention reduced the number of supreme court justices from five to three and created eight new judicial circuits, each presided over by a judge having both law and equity jurisdiction. The chancellor continued to preside over the court of chancery in Albany. The new judgeships were not only political plums; they were also badly needed to handle the growing caseload of the superior courts. The reorganization of the judiciary by the 1821 constitutional convention set the stage for later judicial reforms. The partial combination of law and equity jurisdiction was completed when the 1847 constitutional convention abolished the court of chancery and merged it into the supreme court. The circuit courts set up by the 1822 constitution were in some respects the predecessor of the modern appellate division of the supreme court, established in 1896.

Key Decisions

If James Kent seemed to be out of step with the advances of political democracy in the constitutional convention of 1821, his court decisions and opinions reveal that he was a man of his time in one important respect: he strongly sympathized with the development of a modern commercial economy. Kent was well read in the English economists Adam Smith, Thomas Malthus, and David Ricardo, as well as American writers on economics such as Alexander Hamilton and John McVickar, Kent's own law student. Kent was interested in how wealth was produced and distributed and came to admire modern technology. Though Kent at first thought Robert Fulton's steamboat a "useless piece of machinery," he soon took a ride on the *Clermont* and wrote to his wife that he was "delighted with the paddling!" Kent visited a new textile factory in New England and marvelled at the complex spinning machines.

In his judicial opinions, Kent advocated and assisted the development of free enterprise in New York. He approved of New York's general incorporation act of 1811, which allowed business corporations to be formed more easily, without getting a special law passed each time. Kent advocated free trade and therefore opposed any legal limitations on the activities of out-of-state corporations. He accepted the legal doctrine of *caveat emptor* ("buyer beware"), as long as there was no deceit or contract warranty. He supported the chartering of banks and the expansion of credit. Kent helped develop the first legal rules for bank checks, a new form of money, and he narrowed the legal use of sealed contracts, which could not be assigned freely like promissory notes. Kent believed that government regulation and promotion of the economy was a good thing, within limits. Thus his decisions on the bench favored "natural monopolies" granted for a limited period of time—patents, copyrights, and transportation franchises like Fulton and Livingston's steamboat monopoly (later overturned by the United States Supreme Court in the case of *Gibbons v. Ogden*). Kent was also an enthusiastic supporter of the Erie Canal. He upheld the legality of a statute providing for compensation to landholders when the state took their property under eminent domain for canal construction.

James Kent cannot be termed a libertarian in his economic views and court decisions. He believed that judges were responsible for upholding a moral order in society, and he was ready to protect the rights of those who were threatened by impersonal forces of money and economy. Hence he upheld the government's right to regulate both public health and food prices in time of necessity. Contrary to many economists of his day, Kent supported New York's usury law, which limited interest to 7 percent. Bankruptcy laws displeased him, because he thought debtors were legally and morally responsible for paying their creditors. Kent held that corporation shareholders should be personally liable for corporation debts, because this would discourage overly-risky corporate ventures. (Kent's view on shareholder liability did not prevail, and the limited liability of corporations became accepted legal doctrine.) Kent thought that government as well as individuals and corporations should be fiscally prudent. He abhorred a large, permanent public debt, believing that it led inevitably to heavy taxes, speculation, inflation, and stagnation. Finally, Kent believed that judges should protect the unfortunate. As chancellor, he several times upheld the rights of widows and orphans whose property had been mismanaged by trustees. In one of his most important decisions, Kent extended the jurisdiction of the court of chancery to include protection of the property of the mentally retarded.

The "American Blackstone"

After Kent's retirement from the court of chancery, July 31, 1823, he and his wife moved back to New York City, where their grown children lived. Kent set up a law practice advising other lawyers and soon accepted a part-time post as professor of law at Columbia College, the post he had held back in the 1790s. Kent liked teaching a little better the second time around. He taught law for two years, but his students were not very numerous. He disliked preparing and giving lectures and was glad to give it up. However, Kent's law lectures were the basis for his great work, the *Commentaries on American Law,* which occupied his long years of retirement and earned him the honorable nickname of the "American Blackstone."

Kent's work in fact did not imitate Blackstone's *Commentaries on the Laws of England* very closely. Blackstone's work was divided into two sections, one on "rights," the other on "wrongs." The rights of legal persons were discussed under categories such as the King, Parliament, master and servant, husband and wife, parent and child. The rights of property involved the nature, sources, and alienation of title to real and moveable property. "Private wrongs" involved a discussion of the courts of common law and equity and their actions, procedure, and remedies. Blackstone's *Commentaries* concluded with a discussion of "public wrongs"—crimes and the criminal courts. Kent's *Commentaries* were a distinctively American product. The work was focused on the American constitutional system. The longest part of the *Commentaries* dealt with the Constitution and the complementary powers of the federal and state governments (especially the organization and jurisdiction of the courts). Blackstone's *Commentaries* dealt only peripherally with constitutional law. Kent, unlike Blackstone, recognized and discussed the multiple legal systems that influenced American law—not only the English common law but also Roman civil law (in its ancient, medieval, and modern incarnations) and the modern law of nations, first expounded by Hugo Grotius in the seventeenth century.

Kent's *Commentaries* most closely resembled Blackstone's when he discussed the legal relationships between persons and the various kinds of real and personal property. But Kent again departed from Blackstone's model by greatly condensing the sections on civil actions and procedure and omitting crimes and criminal courts altogether. On the other hand, unlike Blackstone, Kent discussed at great length various types of commercial contracts and negotiable instruments such as bills of exchange, partnerships, maritime law, and insurance. Blackstone's *Commentaries* looked backward through the centuries and systematized a legal system which in all essentials was medieval. James Kent admired, even revered, the achievement of the English common law. But his *Commentaries on American Law* looked forward as well as backward, and described a legal and constitutional system suited, as he believed, to the needs of a young, expanding republic.

FOR FURTHER READING

John T. Horton, *James Kent: A Study in Conservatism, 1763–1847* (New York, 1939) is a readable biography. Shorter accounts of Kent's life and work are in the *Dictionary of American Biography*, 10: 344–47, and Kent's own "Autobiographical Sketch," *Albany Law Journal* 6 (1872): 41–45. Kent's son, William Kent, compiled *Memoirs and Letters of James Kent* (Boston, 1898). Detailed studies of Kent's judicial opinions are Joseph Dorfman, "Chancellor Kent and the Developing American Economy," *Columbia Law Review* 61 (1961): 1290–1317; Thomas P. Campbell, Jr., "Chancellor Kent, Chief Justice Marshall and the Steamboat Cases," *Syracuse Law Review* 25 (1974): 497–534; and two articles by Donald M. Roper, "James Kent and the Emergence of New York's Libel Law," *American Journal of Legal History* 17 (1973): 223–31, and "The New York Supreme Court And Economic Development, 1798–1823," *Working Papers from the Regional Economic History Research Center, Eleutherian Mills–Hagley Foundation,* vol. 3, no. 3 (1980): 58–89. Also by Roper is "The Elite of the New York Bar as Seen from the Bench: James Kent's Necrologies," *The New-York Historical Society Quarterly* 56 (1972): 199–237. The best published accounts of New York's 1821 constitutional convention are Charles V. Lincoln, *The Constitutional History of New York* (Rochester: 1906), 1: 613–756, and Jabez D. Hammond, *The History of Political Parties in the State of New-York* (Albany: 1842), 2: 1–85. A sample of Kent's writing is his "Lecture, Introductory to a Course of Law Lectures [1824]," in *The Legal Mind in America from Independence to the Civil War,* ed. Perry Miller (Garden City: 1962), 92–105.

Samuel Nelson

(1792–1873)

JENNI PARRISH
University of Pittsburgh Law School

Many New Yorkers have had distinguished careers with both state and federal courts. One nineteenth-century jurist, Samuel Nelson of Washington County, served as Chief Judge of the New York State Supreme Court, and from 1845 to 1872 as Associate Justice of the United States Supreme Court. During his twenty-seven year term, Mr. Justice Nelson wrote opinions on several significant constitutional matters, including the Dred Scott case.

Samuel Nelson was born on November 10, 1792, in the town of Hebron in Washington County, New York. Of Scotch–Irish ancestry, he spent his boyhood on the family farm, but did so well in the local school that it was decided he should pursue the ministry. After three years of academy education, he entered Middlebury College in Vermont at the age of fifteen, supported by funds raised by his father through the sale of a Negro girl. After graduation in 1813, he abandoned the idea of the ministry and decided to pursue the law as a career. In Salem, New York, he apprenticed in the law office of Judges Savage and Woods. Two years later he moved to Madison County with Judge Woods, was admitted to the bar in 1817, and married the judge's daughter, Pamela.

Shortly thereafter, he set up an independent and successful practice in Cortland, New York. He was postmaster of the town from 1820 to 1823. In 1821, he represented Cortland County at the state constitutional convention. While he did not play a major role, he spoke out against frequent elections, stating that "unless they could be conducted with more temperance and sobriety than they had been heretofore, . . . even once in three years was often enough for this community to be agitated and convulsed, and all the social enjoyments which make life desirable, interrupted by the violence of the election." Regarding the expansion of the franchise, Nelson followed the lead of Governor Martin Van Buren who urged expanding the right to vote. However, Nelson was not prepared, as was a small contingent of the delegates, to adopt full manhood suffrage.

From 1823 to 1831, Nelson served on the New York State Supreme Court's Sixth Circuit. Under the state constitution, which Nelson helped to write, the Sixth Circuit covered nine counties and had original jurisdiction over all suits in equity brought in that circuit.

In 1825, Nelson, now widowed, moved to Cooperstown where he married Catherine Ann Russell, with whom he would have two daughters and a son.

In 1831, he was appointed an associate judge on the New York State Supreme Court, advancing to the position of chief judge in 1837. He replaced John Savage, who had taught him law in Salem more than twenty years before. Nelson was evaluated by a contemporary as follows: "Nature intended him for a judge. All of his leading mental characteristics were of the judicial type. . . . His fund of 'common sense' was inexhaustible. . . . His opinions are pervaded by a humane and liberal spirit. . . . [They] were read and admired for their terseness, directness, lucidity and practical comprehension of the cases under consideration, by the members of the bench and bar throughout the country. . . ."

A sampler of the many issues Judge Nelson considered during his tenure on the state bench would include the following: In *People v. Morris*, 13 Wend. 325 (N.Y. Sup. Ct. 1835), a grocer was indicted under a state statute for selling liquor without a tavern keeper's license. The grocer insisted that under his village's act of incorporation, which predated the state statute, he had been granted such license and the statute was inoperative in his case. Furthermore, he argued that two-thirds of the legislature had to assent to such alteration of a public corporation. Nelson disagreed and affirmed the judgment below, holding that a mere majority of the legislature could pass laws affecting public corporations (the two-thirds rule applied only to private corporations). Besides this clarification, Nelson also stated: "It is an unsound and even absurd proposition, that political power, conferred by the Legislature, can become a vested right as against the government. . . ." The case decided that state statutes applied to the entire state and that no municipality was exempt unless clearly and specifically exempted by the legislature.

In *Morris*, Nelson had stated that a two-thirds vote of the legislature was required to create or alter the charters of private corporations. This decision was to be used as a check on the power of banks and other private corporations. By the time of *Thomas v. Dakin*, 22 Wend. 9 (N.Y. Sup. Ct. 1839), Nelson's fears of banking institutions proved well founded. "Free" banks, not incorporated by the legislature, had been established; the defendant in this case refused to acknowledge indebtedness to one of these free banks, claiming it was an illegally created corporation. Judge Nelson affirmed the lower court's decision for the plaintiff bank, upheld the legality of free banks as corporations, and discussed the differences between public and private corporations at length. While Nelson's views were clear, such problems with New York banks would not finally be resolved until 1846 with the creation of a new state constitution.

In *Taylor v. Porter*, 4 Hill 140 (N.Y. Sup. Ct. 1843), Nelson dissented from the majority view that a state statute authorizing the laying out of private roads was unconstitutional and void. He insisted: "The construction of roads and bridges . . . [is] indispensable to the prosperity of a country. . . . Private roads . . . are often as necessary . . . as those of a public nature."

In *The Mayor of the City of New York v. Nichols*, 4 Hill 209 (N.Y. Sup. Ct. 1843), Nelson found that a city ordinance requiring inspection of pressed hay contravened a state ordinance which did not require such inspection, and therefore declared the city ordinance void. This holding was consistent with Nelson's general willingness to uphold the power of the state legislature whenever possible.

Nelson considered very different kinds of issues in the divorce case of *Burr v. Burr*, 7 Hill 207 (N.Y. Sup. Ct. 1843), where the wife who had been subjected to "a course of systematic cruelty and oppression" at the hands of her millionaire husband was awarded alimony of $10,000 per year. Nelson upheld the award after giving a discourse on matrimony and marital property rights in mid-nineteenth century New York.

In December 1843, Justice Smith Thompson of New York died, leaving a vacancy on the United States Supreme Court. Over the next eighteen months, President Tyler considered numerous replacements, including Martin Van Buren (to eliminate his leading competitor for the Democratic presidential nomination); John C. Spencer, a New York Whig who had held several posts in the President's cabinet; John Sergeant and Horace Binney, both Philadelphia lawyers; William L. Marcy of New York; Senator Silas Wright of New York; and New York's Chancellor Reuben H. Walworth, before finally offering the position to Samuel Nelson. Nelson accepted the position and was sworn in on March 5, 1845. His twenty-seven years on the nation's highest Court spanned a time of great change in this country.

Nelson kept a very low profile on the Court until the *Dred Scott* decision (*Scott v. Sandford*, 60 U.S. [19 How.] 393 [1857]), probably the most important and controversial decision handed down during Nelson's tenure. Nelson was originally chosen to write the majority opinion in this case, which focused on the status of a slave who had lived for a time in Illinois, a free jurisdiction. Nelson's opinion held that the laws of Missouri, a slave jurisdiction, determined Scott's status after he returned there from Illinois. Under those state laws, he was still a slave. Feeling that this narrowly framed proslavery opinion did not go far enough, and fearing the strength of his colleagues' antislavery dissents, Chief Justice Roger B. Taney of Maryland undertook to write the majority opinion himself. Taney's opinion decided not only the issues Nelson had dealt with but went on to conclude that the Missouri Compromise was invalid and that a Negro could never be a citizen of the United States. The judicial restraint exercised by Justice Nelson in this highly emotional case was not to prevail.

Nelson was neither happy nor enthusiastic about the outbreak of the Civil War. While he remained loyal to the Union, he tended to be regarded suspiciously within the Lincoln administration as one sympathetic to the Copperheads, and thus disloyal to the United States.

A number of wartime issues were raised by cases coming before the Supreme Court in the 1860s. As might be expected, Nelson considered each issue thoughtfully and reached conclusions which were not necessarily popular in the United States. *The Prize Cases*, 67 U.S. (2 Black) 635 (1863), held that Lincoln's blockade of the southern states was lawful even before Congress officially declared war: "A Civil war is never solemnly declared; it becomes such by its accidents—the number, power and organization of the persons who originate and carry it on." Nelson dissented from this view, stating that a state of war did not exist until Congress acted on July 13, 1861; therefore, he argued, the president's actions were outlawed.

Justice Nelson also participated in two other well known Civil War cases. In *Ex Parte Vallandigham*, 68 U.S. (1 Wall.) 243 (1863), he concurred with the majority in confirming that the decision of a military commission which imprisoned an Ohio citizen because of public utterances disloyal to the Union during wartime was not reviewable by the Court. However, in *Ex Parte Milligan*, 71 U.S. (4 Wall.) 2 (1866), Nelson agreed with the majority that a military commission did not have jurisdiction to try a citizen of Indiana who was not in the military, concluding that the defendant deserved a jury trial in either federal or state court.

While he was not generally active in politics after becoming a judge, there was one unsuccessful attempt to elect Nelson to the United States Senate from New York in 1845. In 1864, Governor Horatio Seymour of New York pressed the Democratic Party to nominate Nelson for president, but was not successful. In 1871, Justice Nelson was appointed by President Ulysses S. Grant to serve on a joint high commission to resolve disputes of maritime and international law between Great Britain and the United States. His tenure on this commission was brief. Failing health forced his retirement from the Court and active public life in November 1872. He returned to Cooperstown, where he died on December 13, 1873.

In conclusion, it can be said of Justice Samuel Nelson that he was a thorough, fair-minded, and precise judicial craftsman during fifty of the most tumultuous years in this nation's history. He served with merit on both the state and federal bench.

Rufus Wheeler Peckham, Jr.

(1837–1909)

SCOTT HORTON, ESQ.
Patterson, Belknap, Webb & Tyler
New York, New York

*We know Justice Rufus Wheeler Peckham, Jr. principally through
the devastating critique of his great antagonist, Oliver Wendell
Holmes, Jr. Peckham, the great advocate of* laissez faire *economics, wrote the United States Supreme Court's opinion in* Lochner
v. New York, *198 U.S. 45 (1905), the lodestar of a judicial doctrine
known to later generations as substantive due process. Peckham's
contribution to the development of this doctrine has a significant
place in American constitutional history*

Rufus Wheeler Peckham, Jr.,
was born in 1838 into a well-known family of upstate lawyers and politicians. His father, Rufus Wheeler Peckham, Sr., was a Democratic member of the United States House of Representatives and a judge of the
New York Supreme Court and Court of Appeals; his brother, Wheeler
H. Peckham, became one of the leading corporate lawyers of his day,
a president of the state bar, and himself an unsuccessful nominee for
the United States Supreme Court.

The Peckhams devoted a considerable part of their professional
energy to battling with Tammany Hall for control of the state Democratic Party machinery; they also committed themselves to representing
major corporate interests, particularly railroads. George F. Baker, Jim
Fisk, Jay Gould, James J. Hill, J. Pierpont Morgan, William Rockefeller,
James Speyer, and Cornelius Vanderbilt were among the many tycoons
of industry who figured among Rufus Peckham's clients and confidants.
These preoccupations no doubt strongly influenced Peckham's judicial
philosophy, which was fiercely partisan and political in approach. Contemporary observers and later scholars concurred that Peckham con-

tinued to serve the interests of his chosen constituency with great effect after his lawyering career ended and his tenure on the bench began.

State Judicial Service: Substantive Due Process Presaged

In 1883, following a failed effort to win election to the New York Court of Appeals, Peckham launched his judicial career on the New York Supreme Court in Albany County. Within three years, however, Peckham, with strong backing from his political mentor Grover Cleveland, succeeded in gaining election to the Court of Appeals, the state's highest court, where he served for a decade.

Peckham's dissenting opinion in *People v. Budd*, 117 N.Y. 1 (1889), is particularly noteworthy as an indicator of the course of his later judicial philosophy. At issue in *Budd* was the constitutionality of a New York statute which fixed maximum charges for grain elevators. The Court of Appeals sustained the statute, but Peckham dissented vigorously. Peckham criticized his colleagues for political partisanship, writing that "all men, however great and however honest, are almost necessarily affected by the general belief of their times." Yet Peckham, no less than his colleagues, was driven by a political credo. He maintained that allowing the government to intervene in the economy would "wholly ignore the later and as I firmly believe the more correct ideas which an increase of civilization and a fuller knowledge of the fundamental laws of political economy, and a truer conception of the proper functions of government have given us at the present day." Because, in Peckham's view, the transparent motivation for such legislation as the measure challenged in *Budd* was the government's preference for one "class" (impoverished farmers) against another (the "capitalist" grain factors), it would commence "a new competition for the possession of the government so that legislative aid may be given to the class in possession thereof in its contests with rival classes or interests in all sections and corners of the industrial world." The Constitution, Peckham insisted, provided a firm bulwark against state intervention in favor of the underprivileged: "Such species of legislation . . . is so plain an effort to interfere with what seems to me the most sacred rights of property and the individual's liberty of contract that no special intendment in its favor should be indulged in." Peckham rejected all such reforms as infected with an ideology abhorrent to the American ideal: "The legislation under consideration is not only vicious in its nature, communistic in its tendency and in my belief wholly ineffective to permanently obtain the results aimed at, but illegal."

Peckham's dissent in *Budd* outlined the underpinnings of a doctrine that later scholars have called "substantive due process." Professor Laurence H. Tribe has aptly defined substantive due process:

> To say that governmental action violates "substantive due process" is to say that the action, while adhering to the forms of law, unjustifiably abridges the Constitution's fundamental constraints upon the content of what government may do to people in the name of "law." . . . It thus restricts government power, requiring coercive acts of the state to have public as opposed to merely private ends, defining certain means that government may not employ absent the most compelling necessity, and identifying certain aspects of behavior which it may not regulate without a clear showing that no less intrusive means could achieve government's legitimate public aims.[1]

In the years following the Civil War, the Supreme Court and many lower state and federal courts applied this general pattern of reasoning to protect economic liberties from state government regulation. Peckham was an enthusiastic adherent of this point of view.

Judge Peckham Becomes Mr. Justice Peckham

In 1895, the death of Justice Howell E. Jackson created a vacancy on the United States Supreme Court. President Grover Cleveland quickly nominated his Albany protege Rufus Peckham to succeed Jackson, and the Senate acted equally promptly in confirming the nomination. Peckham's first years on the Court were unremarkable. Although he dissented in two controversial cases, *Holden v. Hardy* (1898) and *Jacobson v. Massachusetts* (1905), he did not prepare written dissents, following the custom of his time. Both cases rejected Fourteenth Amendment challenges to state statutes exercising the states' police powers: *Holden* sustained a Utah statute limiting the working hours of men employed in certain extractive (e.g., mining) industries to no more than eight hours per day, except in certain emergencies. *Jacobson* upheld a Massachusetts statute providing for compulsory vaccination.

Lochner v. New York and Substantive Due Process

In his ninth year on the Court, Peckham wrote the majority opinion in *Lochner v. New York*, 198 U.S. 45 (1905). He seized the opportunity presented by the *Lochner* opinion to convert his New York Court of Appeals dissent in *Budd* into federal constitutional precedent and to articulate the rationale of his dissents in *Holden* and *Jacobson*.

New York had enacted a statute limiting the number of hours an employee could work in a bakery to no more than sixty in any week. Lochner, the owner of a bakery in Utica, was convicted of violating this statute. He appealed his conviction to the United States Supreme Court, arguing that the statute was not a reasonable exercise of the state's police power and therefore was an infringement of his constitutional freedom of contract. The justices accepted Lochner's argument by a vote of 5-to-4. Peckham's majority opinion in *Lochner* is a classic statement of economic substantive due process.

Peckham declared that the right of employee and employer to contract freely for the performance of labor lies at the heart of the Fourteenth Amendment. While the state may interfere with this relationship, he continued, its right of intervention is narrowly circumscribed. When the freedom of contract collides with limitations imposed under color of the state's police power, the Court must inquire: "Is this a fair, reasonable, and appropriate exercise of the police power of the state, or is it an unreasonable, unnecessary, and arbitrary interference of the right of the individual to his personal liberty, or to enter into those contracts in relation to labor which may seem to him appropriate or necessary for the support of himself and his family?" In Peckham's view, the process of answering this inquiry should not include any special presumptions in favor of the legislator. Indeed, Peckham held for the Court, the burden was on the proponent of the legislation to establish that the statute at issue has a legitimate and proper purpose. Note that Peckham's reasoning, both in his *Budd* dissent and in *Lochner*, requires the judge to conduct an independent evaluation of both the validity of the public interest to be protected and the appropriateness of the statutory means the state uses to protect that interest. Despite Peckham's denials, the effect of *Lochner* was to elevate the Supreme Court to the status of a superlegislature reconsidering the wisdom of legislatures.

Peckham and his colleagues maintained that the Thirteenth, Fourteenth, and Fifteenth Amendments had one essential purpose: to further economic rights such as freedom of contract. Thus, in the Court's hands, these constitutional provisions had the effect of frustrating the efforts of Progressives and other reformers to enact and enforce legislation protecting consumers, promoting health, and improving safety in the workplace. In addition to their invocations of constitutional principle, Peckham and his allies believed that the doctrine of substantive due process was a valuable protection of the industrial sector, the new mainspring of the American economy, against the regulatory barrage of the Progressive movement.

By contrast with his devotion to economic substantive due process, which sanctioned activist courts in striking down social legislation, Peckham was appalled by the idea, later validated by the Supreme Court, that the Fourteenth Amendment might provide a means to apply guarantees of the federal Bill of Rights to limit the powers of state and local government. For example, in *Maxwell v. Dow*, 176 U.S. 581 (1900), he concluded that the states were free to establish criminal procedures clearly infringing provisions of the Bill of Rights.

The Decline—and Resurgence?—of Substantive Due Process

Justice Oliver Wendell Holmes, Jr., already highly regarded by Progressives and leading legal scholars, dissented from *Lochner*, maintaining that the legislature had the right to enact such legislation as the maximum-hour law challenged in *Lochner* and dismissing the doctrine of substantive due process as a cloak for judicial imposition of a particular set of economic beliefs under the cover of constitutional law. "The Fourteenth Amendment," he insisted, "does not enact Mr. Herbert Spencer's *Social Statics*"—a popular and widely read exposition of *laissez faire* doctrines. Nonetheless, Peckham's views held sway (with minor fluctuations) on the Supreme Court for several decades—that is, through the first years of the New Deal.

Even Peckham himself may have had doubts about the wisdom of *Lochner*. It is, at first glance, difficult to explain his conclusion to vote to uphold, in *Muller v. Oregon*, 208 U.S. 412 (1908), a statute proscribing the employment of women in certain trades for periods longer than ten hours per day. Peckham concluded that the statute was a valid exercise of the state's police power, despite a challenge on freedom-of-contract grounds virtually indistinguishable from the arguments he accepted in *Lochner*. Peckham's position in *Muller v. Oregon* probably can be traced to his paternalistic attitudes toward women, rather than his reconsideration of *Lochner*.

The *Lochner* doctrine did not fall from favor until a new majority emerged on the Supreme Court during the administration of President Franklin D. Roosevelt. In the 1950s, it seemed that substantive due process was dead and unmourned; Peckham's opinion in *Lochner* was generally reviled as a case study of precisely what the Supreme Court should not do. In the late 1960s and 1970s, however, a new variant of substantive due process emerged. Proposed by Tribe and other constitutional scholars, this new version of substantive due process is designed to protect non-economic fundamental rights, such as the right of sexual privacy and the right of choice with respect to pregnancy and abortion.[2] Opponents of the new substantive due process charge that it is *Lochner*-ism, seeking to taint it by association with the discredited handiwork of Rufus Peckham, Jr. The debate continues, ensuring that the influence of Justice Peckham will continue to brood over American constitutional law for the foreseeable future.

NOTES

[1]Laurence H. Tribe, "Substantive Due Process of Law," in Leonard W. Levy, Kenneth Karst, and Dennis Mahoney, eds., *The Encyclopedia of the American Constitution*, 4 vols. (New York: Free Press/Macmillan, 1986), 3: 1796–1803 (quote at 1796).

[2]See generally Tribe, "Substantive Due Process of Law;" Laurence H. Tribe, *Constitutional Choices* (Cambridge, Mass.: Harvard University Press, 1985); Laurence H. Tribe, *American Constitutional Law*, 2d ed. (Mineola, N.Y.: Foundation Press, 1988), 1302–1435.

Franklin D. Roosevelt*
(1882–1945)

ARTHUR M. SCHLESINGER, JR.
Graduate School of the City University of New York

Franklin Delano Roosevelt, four-time President of the United States, received his formal instruction in the constitutional system at Harvard College (1900–1904) and Columbia Law School (1904–1907). The mood of the Progressive period, however, was more potent than academic doctrine in shaping his understanding of the constitutional process.

His kinsman Theodore Roosevelt, for whom he cast his first presidential vote in 1904, saw the Constitution "not as a straitjacket . . . but as an instrument designed for the life and healthy growth of the Nation." T.R. further saw the courts as "agents of reaction" and the President as the "steward of the people." If necessary, the President must be prepared to act as the savior of the Constitution against the courts, a role in which T.R. cast himself when he proposed the recall of judicial decisions in 1912. Service under Woodrow Wilson confirmed the young Franklin Roosevelt's belief in a spacious reading of executive authority, and experience as assistant secretary of the navy in wartime Washington showed him how emergency expanded presidential initiative.

After the Wilson administration, Roosevelt's return to legal practice was interrupted when he was crippled in 1921 by poliomyelitis. Elected governor of New York in 1928, he soon confronted the consequences of the Wall Street crash of 1929. He foresaw no constitutional objections to his state programs of unemployment relief, public power

*Reprinted from the *Encyclopaedia of the American Constitution*, edited by Leonard W. Levy, Kenneth Karst, and Dennis J. Mahoney, ©1986 by Macmillan Publishing Company, a Division of Macmillan, Inc. All rights reserved.

development, and land planning. "The United States Constitution," he said in a 1930 speech, "has proved itself the most marvelously elastic compilation of rules of government ever written." Though Roosevelt's purpose in that speech was to vindicate states' rights, he proved marvelously elastic himself when elected president in 1932. Favoring the concentration of power at whatever level of government he happened to be serving, he became thereafter a resolute champion of federal authority.

"Our Constitution," he said in his first inaugural address, "is so simple and practical that it is possible always to meet extraordinary needs by changes in emphasis and arrangement without loss of essential form." He hoped, he continued, to preserve the normal balance between executive and legislative authority. However, if the national emergency remained critical, "I shall ask the Congress for the one remaining instrument to meet the crisis—broad Executive power to wage a war against the emergency." He thus combined optimism about the essential elasticity of the Constitution with an understanding that extraordinary executive initiative must rest, not on inherent presidential power, but on the delegation to the President of powers possessed by Congress. To this he added a certain pessimism about the federal courts, assuming, as he had said during the 1932 campaign, that the Republican party had been in "complete control of all branches of the Federal Government . . . the Supreme Court as well."

For this last reason he was in no hurry to send New Deal legislation through the gantlet of the Supreme Court. The first major test came in February 1935 over the constitutionality of the congressional joint resolution of June 1933 abrogating the so-called gold clause in public and private contracts. If the Court invalidated the resolution, the result would increase the country's total debt by nearly $70 billion. Roosevelt prepared a radio speech attacking an adverse decision and planned to invoke emergency powers to mitigate the effects. But while the Court, in *Perry v. United States* (1935), held the repudiation of the gold clause unconstitutional with regard to government bonds (though not to private obligations), it also held that, because the plaintiff had suffered no losses, he was not entitled to compensation. The administration's monetary policy remained precariously intact.

But three months later in a 5–4 decision the Court nullified the Railroad Retirement Act as an invalid use of the commerce power. Then on May 27, in *Schechter Poultry Corp. v. United States* it struck down the National Industrial Recovery Act on two grounds: that the act involved excessive delegation of power by Congress, and that it exceeded the reach of congressional power under the commerce clause. The vote against the National Recovery Administration was unanimous, as were two other decisions the same day—"Black Monday" in the eyes of New Dealers—one holding the Frazier–Lemke Farm Bankruptcy Act unconstitutional, the other denying the President the power to remove a member of a regulatory commission without congressional consent. If the Court was warning Roosevelt not to go to extremes, Roosevelt responded by warning the Court not to go to extremes either. Calling the *Schechter* decision "more important probably than any decision since [*Dred Scott v. Sanford* (1857)]," he said that it carried the Constitution back to "the horse-and-buggy definition of interstate commerce."

Undeterred, the Court majority prosecuted its attack. In January 1936 six Justices in *United States v. Butler* pronounced agriculture a "local" subject, beyond Congress's power, and set aside the Agricultural Adjustment Act. Justice Harlan F. Stone protested a "tortured construction of the Constitution" in an eloquent dissent. The Court majority, however, proceeded to strike down the Guffey Bituminous Coal Conservation Act, the Municipal Bankruptcy Act, and, finally, in *Morehead v. New York ex. rel. Tipaldo* (1936), a New York minimum wage law. The Court, Roosevelt now said, had thereby created a " 'no man's-land' where no Government—State or Federal—can function." Between 1789 and 1865 the Court had declared only two acts of Congress unconstitutional; now, between 1934 and 1936, it invalidated thirteen. Doctrines propounded by the Court majority held out small hope for the Social Security Act, the Wagner National Labor Relations Act, and other New Deal laws awaiting the judicial test. Roosevelt concluded that "[John] Marshall's conception of our Constitution as a flexible instrument—adequate for all times, and, therefore, able to adjust itself as the new needs of new generations arose—had been repudiated."

By 1936 apprehension was spreading about the destruction of the New Deal by the unelected "Nine Old Men." Congress and the law schools were astir with proposals to rein in the Court. Roosevelt outlined three possibilities to his cabinet: limiting the power of the Court to invalidate congressional legislation; making an explicit grant to Congress of powers now in dispute; or ("a distasteful idea") packing the Court by appointing new judges. The first two courses required constitutional amendments. Roosevelt soon decided that an amendment would be difficult to frame, even more difficult to ratify, and in any event subject to judicial interpretation. The problem lay not in the Constitution but in the Court. In early 1936 he instructed Attorney General Homer Cummings to prepare in utmost secrecy a plan, short of amendment, that would overcome the Court's resistance.

Roosevelt did not make the Court an issue in the 1936 campaign. But his smashing victory in November convinced him that the moment had arrived. Cummings proposed legislation providing for the appointment of new Justices when sitting Justices failed to retire at the age of seventy. Roosevelt sprang the plan in a message to Congress on February 5, 1937. Claiming overcrowded dockets and overworked and overage judges, Roosevelt requested legislation that would enable him to appoint as many as six new Justices.

Postelection euphoria had evidently marred Roosevelt's usually astute political judgment. Wider consultation might at least have persuaded him to make his case as an honest confrontation of power. The pretense that he was seeking merely to ease the burdens of the Court relied on arguments that Chief Justice Charles Evans Hughes soon demonstrated in a letter to the Senate Judiciary Committee. By the time Roosevelt began to present the true issue—''We must take action to save the Constitution from the Court and the Court from itself''—his initial trickiness had lost the court plan valuable momentum.

The Chief Justice had further resources. On March 29, in *West Coast Hotel v. Parrish*, a 5–4 Court upheld a Washington minimum wage law, thereby in effect overruling the *Tipaldo* decision taken the preceding term. The "switch in time" that "saved nine" was provided by Justice Owen J. Roberts; because *Parrish* had been argued in December, Roberts's second thoughts, if affected by external circumstances, responded to the election, not to the Court plan. In March, the Court also upheld a slightly modified version of the Farm Bankruptcy Act rejected two years earlier. In April, in *National Labor Relations Board v. Jones & Laughlin Steel Corporation*, the Court approved the National Labor Relations Act in a 5–4 decision in which, as Roberts later conceded, both he and Hughes reversed the position they had taken in condemning the Guffey Act the year before. In May the Court upheld the Social Security Act.

In two months, the Court, under the pressure of the election and the Roosevelt plan, wrought a constitutional revolution, recognizing in both federal and state governments powers it had solemnly denied them in the two previous years as contrary to the Constitution. It greatly enlarged the federal commerce power and the taxing and spending power, gave new force to the general welfare clause, altered the application of the due process clause to the states, and abandoned the doctrine of excessive delegation as a means of invalidating federal legislation.

The Court's revisionism, by lessening the felt need for reform, strengthened opposition, already vehement, to the President's plan for the Court. Democrats joined Republicans in denouncing "court-packing." In May the decision of Justice Willis Van Devanter to resign, opening the way for Roosevelt's first Supreme Court appointment, further weakened pressure for the plan. In the interests of Senate passage, Roosevelt promised the vacancy to the majority leader Senator Joseph T. Robinson. As Robinson was both old and conservative, he was an anomalous reform choice. By summer Roosevelt was belatedly ready to entertain compromise. But Robinson's death in July brought the bitter struggle to an end.

The insouciance with which Roosevelt presented the Court plan exacted heavy costs in the future of his domestic program, the unity of his party, the confidence of the electorate, and his own self-confidence. Still, the plan attained its objective. As Robert H. Jackson summed it up, "The President's enemies defeated the court reform bill —the President achieved court reform." The plan forced the Court to abandon rigid and restrictive constitutional views; at the same time, the plan's rejection eliminated Court packing as a precedent for the future. History may well conclude both that Roosevelt was right to propose the plan and that the opposition was right to beat it.

In the next half dozen years Roosevelt made the Court his own, appointing Hugo L. Black (1937), Stanley F. Reed (1938), Felix Frankfurter (1939), William O. Douglas (1939), Frank Murphy (1940), James F. Byrnes (1941), Robert H. Jackson (1941), and Wiley B. Rutledge (1943) as Associate Justices and Harlan F. Stone as Chief Justice (1941). In time the Roosevelt Court itself split between the apostles of judicial restraint, who had objected to the methods of the "Nine Old Men," and the activists, who had objected only to their results. But the new Court was united in affirming the reach of the national government's constitutional power to meet the social and economic problems created by the Great Depression.

With the status of New Deal legislation thus assured, Roosevelt's next tangle with constitutional issues took place in foreign affairs. The Court in *United States v. Curtiss-Wright Export Corporation* (1936) had unanimously endorsed the propositions that "the powers of external sovereignty did not depend upon the affirmative grants of the Constitution" and that the President had in foreign affairs "a degree of discretion and freedom from statutory restriction which would not be admissible were domestic affairs alone involved." But Congress still had statutory control over vital areas of foreign policy. Neutrality, for example, had been a congressional prerogative since 1794. While Roosevelt requested discretionary neutrality legislation, he saw no practical choice but to accept mandatory laws passed by a stubbornly isolationist Congress. These laws placed the administration in a foreign policy straitjacket from which it sought to wriggle free to the very eve of Pearl Harbor.

Congress, too, retained the constitutional power to declare war. As Roosevelt reminded the French prime minister during the fall of France in 1940, assurance of aid did not imply military commitments; "only the Congress can make such commitments." And legislative power extended to a variety of defense questions. When Winston S. Churchill asked for the loan of old American destroyers, Roosevelt initially responded that "a step of that kind could not be taken except with the specific authorization of the Congress." Later Roosevelt was persuaded that he could make the transfer through executive action. Attorney General Robert H. Jackson's official opinion to this effect rested not on claims of inherent power as President of commander-in-chief but on the construction of laws passed by Congress. Critics found the argument strained, but public opinion supported the action.

The decisive step marking the end of American neutrality was the Lend–Lease Act, passed after full and vigorous debate in March 1941. Once Congress had authorized the lending and leasing of goods to keep Britain in the war, did this authority not imply an effort to make sure that the goods arrived? So Roosevelt evidently assumed, trusting that a murky proclamation of "unlimited national emergency" in May 1941 and the impact of Nazi aggression on public opinion would justify his policy. When Grenville Clark urged a joint resolution by which Congress would explicitly approve measures necessary to assure the delivery of supplies, Roosevelt replied in July that the time was not "quite right." The renewal of the draft the next month by a single-vote majority in the House of Representatives showed the fragility of congressional support. By autumn the navy, on presidential orders and without congressional authorization (until Neutrality Act revision in November), was fighting an undeclared war against Germany to protect convoys in the North Atlantic.

Roosevelt's actions in the latter part of 1941, like Abraham Lincoln's after the fall of Fort Sumter, were arguably unconstitutional, though not without historical precedent. He did not seek to justify the commitment of American forces to combat by pleas of inherent power as President or as Commander-in-Chief, and thereby proposed no constitutional novelties. If pressed, he perhaps would have associated himself with John Locke, Thomas Jefferson, and Abraham Lincoln in asserting not continuing presidential power but emergency prerogative to be exercised only when the life of the nation was at stake.

Entry into war, as always, increased unilateral presidential authority. When under the New Deal Roosevelt had acted most of the time on the basis of specific statutes, as a war President he acted very often on the basis of general powers claimed as "Commander-in-Chief in wartime" and on emergency powers activated by proclamation and conferred on an all-purpose agency, the Office of Emergency Management. Of the agencies established in 1940–1943 to control the war economy, only one, the Office of Price Administration, rested on a specific statute.

This statute ironically provoked Roosevelt's most notorious assertion of unilateral authority. The Price Control Act contained a farm parity provision deemed threatening to the anti-inflation program. Roosevelt told Congress in September 1942 that, if it did not repeal the provision within three weeks, he would refuse to execute it. "The President has the powers, under the Constitution and under Congressional Acts," he declared, "to take measures necessary to avert a disaster which would interfere with the winning of the war." He added, "When the war is won, the powers under which I act automatically revert to the people—to whom they belong."

The international threat, as always, increased pressure of civil liberties. In 1940, while protesting his sympathy with Oliver Wendell Holmes's condemnation of wiretapping in *Olmstead v. United States* (1928), Roosevelt granted his attorney general qualified permission to wiretap "persons suspected of subversive activities against the United States." Given the conviction Roosevelt shared with most Americans that a Nazi victory in Europe would have endangered the United States, he would have been delinquent in his duty had he not taken precautionary measures. Though we know now that the internal menace was exaggerated, no one could be sure of that at the time.

Roosevelt, however, extended his concern to include Americans honestly opposed to intervention, directing the Federal Bureau of Investigation to investigate isolationists and their organizations. There was so little government follow-up of Roosevelt's prodding, however, that the prods were evidently taken by his subordinates as expressions of passing irritation rather than constant purpose. In 1941 Roosevelt appointed Francis Biddle, a distinguished civil libertarian, as attorney general and kept him on the job throughout the war despite Biddle's repeated resistance to presidential requests that threatened the Bill of Rights.

Roosevelt's preoccupation with pro-Nazi agitation increased after Pearl Harbor. "He was not much interested in the theory of sedition," Biddle later recalled, "or in the constitutional right to criticize the government in wartime. He wanted this anti-war talk stopped." In time, his prods forced a reluctant Biddle to approve the indictment of twenty-six pro-Fascist Americans under a dubious application of the law of criminal conspiracy. A chaotic trial ended with the death of the judge, and the case was dropped.

Biddle also resisted the most shameful abuse of power within the United States during the war—the relocation of Americans of Japanese descent. Here Roosevelt responded both to local pressure, including that of Attorney General Earl Warren of California, and to the War Department, where such respected lawyers as Henry L. Stimson and John J. McCloy demanded action. Congress ratified Roosevelt's executive order before it was put into effect, so the relocation did not represent a unilateral exercise of presidential power. The Supreme Court upheld the program in the Japanese American Cases (1943–1944).

Still, despite Roosevelt's moments of impatience and exasperation, his administration's civil liberties record during World War II was conspicuously better than that of the Lincoln administration during the Civil War or of the Wilson administration during World War I. In 1944 the American Civil Liberties Union saluted "the extraordinary and unexpected record . . . in freedom of debate and dissent on all public issues and in the comparatively slight resort to war-time measures of control or repression of opinion."

Roosevelt's presidency vindicated his conviction that social reform and military victory could be achieved without breaching the Constitution. A believer in a strong presidency, he was himself a strong president within, on the whole, constitutional bounds. His deviations from strict constitutional propriety were mostly under impressions, sometimes mistaken, of clear and present international danger. Those of his successors who claimed inherent presidential war powers went further than he ever did.

Roosevelt was a political leader, not a constitutional lawyer, and he correctly saw that in its major phase constitutional law is often a question of political and economic philosophy. No doubt his understanding of the practical necessity of consent was more important than technical appreciation of constitutional limitations in keeping his actions within the frame of the basic charter. But his presidency justified his inaugural assertion that the Constitution could meet extraordinary needs by changes in emphasis and arrangement without loss of essential form. His legacy was a revivified faith in the adequacy of the Constitution as a progressive document, equal to domestic and foreign emergency and "capable of meeting evolution and change."

For Further Reading

Alsop, Joseph, and Catledge, Turner. *The 168 Days*. Garden City, N.Y.: Doubleday, 1938.

Biddle, Francis. *In Brief Authority*. Garden City, N.Y.: Doubleday, 1962.

Freedman, Max, ed. *Roosevelt and Frankfurter: Their Correspondence, 1928–1945*. Boston: Little, Brown, 1967.

Jackson, Robert H. *The Struggle for Judicial Supremacy: A Study of a Crisis in American Power Politics*. New York: Knopf, 1941.

Mason, A.T. *Harlan Fiske Stone: Pillar of the Law*. New York: Viking, 1956.

Schlesinger, Jr., Arthur M. *The Age of Roosevelt*, vols. I–III. Boston: Houghton Mifflin, 1957–1960.

The Sesquicentennial of the Constitution: Franklin D. Roosevelt and His Monument in Poughkeepsie

WILLIAM B. RHOADS
State University College at New Paltz

In 1937–38, New Yorkers, afflicted with an economic depression at home and fearful of belligerent dictatorships abroad, celebrated the sesquicentennial of the adoption and ratification of the United States Constitution. On one level, the celebrations provided light patriotic entertainment: for example, the WPA Federal Theatre Project marked the opening of Constitution Week in 1937 with a Torch of Liberty pageant at the foot of the Statue of Liberty, followed by the release of thick smoke from the statue's torch, accompanied with music provided by the Fire Department Band. Yet the events also encouraged many Americans to reaffirm their faith in the eternal validity of the Constitution, attacked as it was by extremists of the Left and Right. Education was a vital part of the work of the U.S. Constitution Sesquicentennial Commission directed by Representative Sol Bloom (Democrat–New York): the young were to be made aware of their constitutional heritage through school essay and oratorical contests; the population as a whole was to be bombarded with speeches, facsimiles of the Constitution, and commemorative postage stamps.[1] Art, too, was called upon to instruct. Portraits of the signers of the Constitution were exhibited at the Corcoran Gallery in Washington, and Howard Chandler Christy was commissioned to make a "correct" view of the signing of the Constitution as the official sesquicentennial poster.[2]

New York State's ratification of the Constitution in Poughkeepsie on July 26, 1788 was commemorated around the state. The main celebration took place, appropriately, in Poughkeepsie. President Franklin D. Roosevelt pressured Assemblyman Irwin Steingut, chairman of the Constitution Sesquicentennial Commission of the State of New York, to focus the celebration on Poughkeepsie, arguing that "if there had been no Poughkeepsie, there would have been no Union of the United States of America!" Roosevelt made his personal interest in the event clear by telling Steingut that his "great-great-grandfather [Isaac Roosevelt] was one of the leading proponents of the ratification," and "I . . . want my great-great-grandfather honored." On July 26, 1938, FDR himself was to be aboard the *U.S.S. Houston*, vacationing in the Galapagos Archipelago, but that day he sat in his cabin and wrote out his greetings, which were at once transmitted by radio to his Dutchess County and Poughkeepsie neighbors.[3]

A second Poughkeepsie celebration was planned for September 17, 1938, with the expectation that FDR would speak at the site of the new post office. In August, he wrote privately to his friend, Poughkeepsie's leading historian, Helen Wilkinson Reynolds, that "the Poughkeepsie committee on the celebration is merely having some kind of parade and the whole party looks as if it would be more like an Elks' Convention." Presidential displeasure resulted in FDR's remaining in Washington and transmitting his address by radio.[4]

Commemoration

Probably of more lasting impact than any of the speeches heard in Poughkeepsie in 1938 has been Gerald Foster's mural, "The Ratification Convention, 1788,"* ordered by President Roosevelt in 1937, installed in the Poughkeepsie Post Office in 1938, and in 1988 the official poster of the New York State Commission on the Bicentennial of the U.S. Constitution. This mural was part of a vast New Deal program to bring art to the American people by incorporating murals depicting American history, life, and landscape in some 1,100 post offices across the country between 1934 and 1943. Even though Roosevelt had, as the artist George Biddle said, "no artistic sense . . . [he] could not tell a good sculpture or a good picture from a bad one," he was a firm supporter of Edward Bruce's Section of Painting and Sculpture in the Treasury Department, which was responsible for post office construction and decoration. Roosevelt recognized that the Section, under Bruce, shared his concern that post office murals factually render historical or contemporary scenes. FDR's Dutchess County friend, the artist Olin

---

*For a detail of this mural, see p. 190 in this volume.

Dows, knew from personal experience that "his approach [to art] was historical . . . on the record . . . [artists] might create." For Archibald MacLeish, Librarian of Congress under Roosevelt, the president was "a political leader whose intellectual preoccupation was history."[5] Consequently, FDR understood the role that art based on historical themes could play in influencing the mind of the public.

Roosevelt was particularly devoted to the history of Dutchess County, his birthplace and the home of some of his colonial ancestors. This devotion found expression in his encouragement of Helen Reynolds to write *Dutch Houses in the Hudson Valley before 1776* (1929), and his supervision of the design and construction of Val-Kill cottage (1924–25) at Hyde Park for Eleanor Roosevelt. The cottage, at Roosevelt's insistence, was closely modeled after the Dutch colonial fieldstone houses of the county.[6]

Presidential Directives

When president, FDR took pleasure in exercising similar control over selected federal building projects. On August 3, 1936, he gave instructions that the post office projected for Poughkeepsie should follow the lines of the long-demolished Dutchess County Courthouse of 1809 and should be built of irregular fieldstone. The 1809 courthouse stood on the site of its predecessor, completed shortly before it was occupied by the 1788 ratification convention. Roosevelt was aware of the significance of the 1780s courthouse as the location of what was generally considered "the most important and dramatic event" to occur in Dutchess County, and he undoubtedly would have preferred to reconstruct it, but little information survived about its appearance. Moreover, Helen Reynolds believed some of its walls survived in the 1809 structure, whose form was well known through photographs.[7]

Two weeks after FDR specified the architectural source, Elinor Morgenthau, wife of Treasury Secretary Henry Morgenthau, alerted Edward Bruce that the president was "keen to have murals in the Poughkeepsie Post Office." Bruce and the Section treated this as a mandate to produce "an unusually fine job"—one which would ultimately result in five murals costing three times the $4,200 customarily allocated to comparable post offices.[8]

By January 1937, the Director of Procurement reported "that the President is interested in having historical subjects treated." On March 2, Roosevelt met with the Section and handed over a list of topics for the murals, including the "Signing of Ratification of the U.S. Constitution 1788." Subsequently, the president decided that, instead of the signing, an earlier and more dramatic moment should be represented. This was the point when the Federalists (including Isaac Roosevelt) and some of the Antifederalists arrived at a crucial compromise in which the Antifederalists whose votes were needed for ratification were assured that a bill of rights soon would be added to the Constitution. Three Dutchess County Antifederalists, led by Melancton Smith, were critical to the success of this compromise, a fact not lost to FDR who, in his speech at the laying of the post office cornerstone, proudly noted that "it took leadership on the part of the Dutchess County delegates to suggest a compromise."[9]

The Interpretation

The Section selected Gerald Foster, a Princeton graduate who had studied at the Art Students' League and in Paris and Rome, to carry out the three murals on seventeenth- and eighteenth-century Poughkeepsie. Foster's painting style, compared by critic Edward Alden Jewell to the "preternatural clarity" of Luigi Lucioni and Charles Sheeler, was well suited to the role of historical muralist. His successful recreation of the story of Molly Pitcher at the Battle of Monmouth in a mural (1935–36) for the Freehold (New Jersey) Post Office encouraged the Section to assign him the three Poughkeepsie panels. According to the Section, Foster was "an ardent student of the Revolutionary War period," and so took great care to insure the historical accuracy of his details, which the Section, and especially FDR, viewed as essential for mural art.[10]

Eric Kebbon, architect of the Poughkeepsie Post Office, spoke to the artist "enthusiastically" about Barry Faulkner's two murals (1936) in the National Archives Building in Washington, which portrayed the most significant men associated with the signing of the Declaration of Independence and adoption of the Constitution.[11] Faulkner's figures, garbed in period costume, were placed outdoors in a grandiose setting of monumental classical architecture akin to that of the National Archives Building, but far removed from the modest Georgian of their actual meeting place, Independence Hall.

Foster rejected the pomposity of Faulkner's murals in favor of the more literal approach of his Molly Pitcher panel. He would paint the ratification following the tradition established by John Trumbull in his canvases of the Declaration of Independence (1787–1824), where the participants were shown in the meeting room with all faces more or less visible and details of the room's architecture and furnishing clearly represented.[12] Foster may also have been influenced by *The Signing of* *the Constitution* (1856) by Junius Brutus Stearns, a painting selected by FDR as the basis for the 1937 three-cent stamp commemorating the sesquicentennial.[13] The stamp's designer added a Roman fasces* and a torch to the border to signify power and enlightenment. Some Americans were dismayed to find the Fascist symbol on their postage stamps. They had nothing to fear in regard to Foster's mural, however, for he excluded all trappings of dictatorship. Where Lee Lawrie's sculpture, *Drafting the Constitution*, presented a table with massive legs in the form of fasces, Foster pictured only the simple furniture of eighteenth-century Dutchess County.[14]

Foster was told by the Section that the president wanted him to consult Helen Reynolds, whom FDR considered the ranking expert on Dutchess County history. Roosevelt would ultimately judge Foster's work from the standpoint of historical accuracy, and he rightly believed that Reynolds would direct the artist to appropriate historical sources and make certain they were followed in the murals.

Foster spent much time doing research in Poughkeepsie. In July, Reynolds reported to the president that the artist was "going very carefully into local details. I have enjoyed collaborating with him and found him thorough in his investigations and sympathetic with the subject matter." The artist "found about a dozen portraits of delegates to the convention," including Gilbert Stuart's of Isaac Roosevelt, which he studied at the Roosevelt home in Hyde Park.[15]

Collaboration

Reynolds, author of two volumes on the early architecture of the area, worked closely with Foster in determining the architectural details of the court room. Since no record remained of the room's original appearance, details were copied from other eighteenth-century Dutchess County interiors. The windows and their paneled jambs were modeled after the John Brinckerhoff house (1738) in the town of Fishkill, a house visited by Washington during the Revolution. The wall paneling on the right side of the mural was inspired by woodwork in the General Jacobus Swartwout house (c. 1760) in the town of Wappinger. Swartwout was an Antifederalist delegate to the convention. The benches follow the spartan form of the seating preserved in the Nine Partners Friends' Meetinghouse (1780) in South Millbrook. The Windsor chair of the presiding officer was justified as a type advertised in local newspapers in

---

*The Latin word *fasces* refers to a bundle of rods with an ax with projecting blade at its center, borne before ancient Roman magistrates as a badge of authority.

the 1780s, while the mahogany drop-leaf table was an heirloom preserved by generations of Van Kleecks—their ancestor had entertained some of the delegates perhaps at this very table, thought Helen Reynolds. The framed map hanging on the rear wall copied a map in the Adriance Memorial Library which showed Poughkeepsie in 1790, and so, as Reynolds told readers of the *Star-Enterprise*, it gave "an accurate idea of the tiny hamlet where the convention held its sessions."[16]

Foster did not attempt the portrayal of all sixty-five delegates. No authentic portraits could be found of many, and by reducing the number pictured to twenty-three, he could avoid the crowded and stilted poses Trumbull had been forced to adopt. In addition to the likeness of Isaac Roosevelt, Foster later identified those of Melancton Smith, George Clinton, Alexander Hamilton, and John Jay as "authentic."[17] Others were improvised, although Reynolds was under the impression "that of the number possible to show in the mural, the faces of nearly all are actual likenesses." John Poehler, Foster's assistant, painted him as Cornelius Schoonmaker, while Foster painted Poehler as Richard Morris.[18] Perhaps Foster recalled that Raphael and Michelangelo had included portraits of themselves in their Vatican frescoes.

The attention of most of the convention is focused on the Federalist and Antifederalist leaders, Alexander Hamilton and Governor George Clinton, who shake hands as they have been brought together by a key Antifederalist, Dutchess County's Melancton Smith, who places his hand encouragingly on Clinton's shoulder. Only Cornelius Schoonmaker (with Gerald Foster's face) turns his Antifederalist visage entirely away from the central drama. On this warm day (a window is open), the delegates stand and sit informally but with coats and neckcloths firmly in place. Facial expressions reflect the gravity of the deliberations; only Dirck Wyncoop, an Antifederalist, applauds. No one notices the mouse witnessing the event from a hole in the baseboard directly below the clasped hands of Clinton and Hamilton.[19] Foster's break with decorum was mild in contrast to Diego Rivera's surreptitious inclusion of Lenin's head in a Rockefeller Center mural (1933) or Rockwell Kent's equally notorious insertion of a cryptic revolutionary message in a mural (1937) in the Post Office Department Building in Washington.[20]

Foster's mural emphasizes the cordial resolution of conflict and the quiet triumph of the Federalists who dominate the panel.[21] Thirteen Federalists are shown with only ten Antifederalists, even though the Antifederalists had won more than two-thirds of the convention seats. Antifederalist leader Clinton is seen from behind, while the three most prominent figures in the center of the panel are Federalists: Hamilton, Jay, and Roosevelt. The prominence given Isaac Roosevelt appears unwarranted by historical accounts of the convention[22] and was probably a consequence of Foster's desire to please his great-great-grandson. In fact, Foster's design appealed to Franklin Roosevelt, and by November 29, 1937, it had his enthusiastic approval.[23]

A Monument to FDR

FDR's keen interest in the ratification mural was partly a reflection of his general concern for American, New York, and Dutchess County history, especially as it related to his ancestors, but the very bitter debate over his own presidential role as upholder of the Constitution must have made him all the more eager to have the mural put before the public. In the 1936 presidential campaign, Roosevelt's Republican enemies described him and his New Deal policies as forces destructive of constitutional government. Alf Landon charged that "it is the essence of the New Deal that the Constitution must go in order to give men in Washington the power to make America over, to destroy the American way of life and establish a foreign way of life in its place." Former New York Governor Nathan L. Miller insisted, according to the *New York Times*, that FDR meant "to overthrow the Constitution and establish a new form of government alien to the American system, in defiance of his oath to defend the Constitution."[24]

Roosevelt's self-defense culminated the evening before election day in an extemporaneous speech given from the balcony of a Poughkeepsie hotel, the Nelson House, to a crowd of more than 5,000 gathered in a drizzly Market Street. He assured them that he, like most American voters, sought "progress" while "retain[ing] our American form of government." As evidence of his commitment to constitutional rule, he gave the assembly a short history lesson:

> About a block from where I stand . . . there was a little old stone building and in the year 1788 there was held there the constitutional convention of the State of New York.
> My great, great-grandfather was a member of the convention. The question was, should New York ratify the Federal constitution . . . in the absence of a Bill of Rights . . . ?
> . . . finally, the delegates . . . up there in the little old stone building, ratified it only on this condition. 'In full faith and confidence that a Bill of Rights would be added to the Constitution . . . .' And largely because of the insistence of the State of New York . . . almost immediately the new government submitted to the

States the first ten amendments of the United States Constitution.
And so you will see that not only in my own person but also
by inheritance I know something not only about the Constitution
. . . but also about the Bill of Rights.

How many of his antagonists could claim to have an understanding of
the Constitution from the very blood in their veins?[25]

Franklin Roosevelt believed in a usable past. Some parts of the
ratification story were not usable—for example, the fact that Isaac
Roosevelt was a New York City Federalist, a conservative who saw no
real need for a Bill of Rights.[26] Much more usable were the facts that
his ancestor had voted for ratification and that Dutchess County men
had been instrumental in working out the final compromise.[27] Here were
models for his own actions as a statesman named Roosevelt from Dutchess County.

FDR was all too aware that his New Deal programs were imper-
manent. As he told Edward Bruce, "there 'ain't no sich thing' as a
masterpiece of permanence in the art of living or the art of government."
But, "when a great picture has been painted and touched up a little
here and there, it becomes at last a permanent contribution to civilization for all time."[28] The post office, sturdily built of local stone and
modeled after a venerable courthouse, provided what the president expected would be an enduring shelter for a mural, reminding present and
future generations of the contributions Dutchess County and Isaac
Roosevelt had made to the creation of the country.

Secretary Morgenthau, speaking at the post office cornerstone
ceremony, publicized FDR's personal selection of the mural subjects,
and the president never tired of telling audiences of his kinship with
Isaac the ratifier, so that the mural was clearly meant to certify forever
Franklin Roosevelt's deep-rooted allegiance to the American Constitution. The building, with its murals, was indeed, as Morgenthau proclaimed, "a monument to him."[29]

NOTES:

[1] *New York Times*, September 13, 1937 and June 4, 1937; " 'We the People'—and
the Constitution," *Recreation* 30 (March 1937): 587–89. See generally Michael Kammen,
A Machine That Would Go of Itself: The Constitution in American Culture (New York,
1986), 282–312.

[2] *New York Times*, September 13, 1936 and February 14, 1936. While the poses
of the signers were to be "correct," the poster included an allegorical, winged woman:
New York Times, September 13, 1936. Later, in 1939, the House of Representatives com-

missioned Christy to do a large painting of the signing; the resulting canvas was widely scorned. *New York Times*, June 24, 1939; Jane Watson, "Christy and the Capitol," *Magazine of Art* 33 (July 1940): 431-32.

[3] Franklin D. Roosevelt (FDR) to Irwin Steingut, May 19, 1938, in Kevin J. Gallagher, "The President as Local Historian: The Letters of F.D.R. to Helen Wilkinson Reynolds," *New York History* 64 (April 1983): 159; FDR to Steingut, May 26, 1938, President's Personal File (PPF) 1230, Franklin D. Roosevelt Library, Hyde Park, N.Y. (FDRL); Secretary Early to Comdt. 12th N.D., July 26, 1938, PPF 1230, FDRL. The only public gathering in Poughkeepsie on July 26, 1938, to commemorate the sesquicentennial was held by the Communist Party in the Moose Hall; FDR's greetings seem not to have been transmitted there. *Poughkeepsie Eagle-News*, July 26 and 27, 1938.

[4] FDR to Helen Reynolds, August 23, 1938, in Gallagher, "President as Local Historian," 160; *New York Times*, August 30, 1938 and September 17, 1938.

[5] Marlene Park and Gerald E. Markowitz, *Democratic Vistas: Post Offices and Public Art in the New Deal* (Philadelphia, 1984), xvii; George Biddle indirectly quoted by Rexford G. Tugwell, *The Democratic Roosevelt* (Garden City, 1957), 294-95; Willium B. Rhoads, "The Artistic Patronage of Franklin D. Roosevelt: Art as Historical Record," *Prologue* 15 (Spring 1983): 12-21; Olin Dows Papers, FDRL; Archibald MacLeish, "He Cherished American Culture," *New Republic* 114 (April 15, 1946): 540.

[6] William B. Rhoads, "Franklin D. Roosevelt and Dutch Colonial Architecture," *New York History* 59 (October 1978): 430-38.

[7] Notes on conference of August 3, 1936, in C.J. Peoples to Henry Morgenthau, July 8, 1937, National Archives; Federal Writers' Project, *Dutchess County* (Philadelphia, 1937), 14; Helen W. Reynolds, "The Court House of Dutchess County," *Dutchess County Historical Society Year Book* (1938): 79-80.

[8] Elinor Morgenthau to Edward Bruce, August 18, 1936, Edward Rowan to Inslee Hopper, August 28, 1936; Rowan to Mrs. Morgenthau, September 1, 1936; Rowan to Supervising Architect, December 10, 1937, Record Group (RG) 121, National Archives.

[9] Peoples to McReynolds, January 29, 1937; Hopper to Mrs. Morgenthau, March 5, 1937, RG 121; Helen W. Reynolds, "The Constitutional Convention of 1788 as Shown in a Mural for the New Post Office," *Poughkeepsie Star-Enterprise*, July 7, 1938; *New York Times*, October 14, 1937. For an account of the reaching of the compromise, see Linda Grant De Pauw, *The Eleventh Pillar: New York State and the Federal Constitution* (Ithaca, 1966), 241-54.

[10] *New York Times*, March 15, 1938 and May 6, 1932; Hopper to Foster, March 20, 1937, RG 121; Forbes Watson, "The Return to the Facts," *Magazine of Art* 29 (March 1936): 150-53; Park and Markowitz, *Democratic Vistas*, 76. Foster's other two Poughkeepsie murals were a view of the center of Poughkeepsie, including the courthouse, about 1750, and a view of Indians and settlers about 1690. The Section may also have chosen Foster because of his ability to render boats, one of FDR's great interests. See *New York Times*, April 29, 1934. The Poughkeepsie murals of boats on the Hudson were not, however, executed by Foster.

[11] Foster to Hopper, July 25, 1937, RG 121; *New York Times*, November 15, 1936.

[12] Thomas Jefferson, principal author of the Declaration, advised Trumbull in the creation of his painting. See Irma B. Jaffe, *Trumbull: The Declaration of Independence* (New York, 1976), 64-65. It is not known whether Roosevelt, who greatly admired Jefferson, knew of this joint effort.

[13] *Art Digest* 12 (December 15, 1937), 14. FDR also chose the reddish purple color of the stamp: Acting Third Assistant Postmaster General to FDR, September 2, 1937, Official File (OF) 19, FDRL.

[14] *New York Times*, August 29, 1937 and September 12, 1937.

[15] Hopper to Foster, March 20, 1937, RG 121; Reynolds to FDR, July 24, 1937, PPF 234, FDRL. After Foster completed his three Poughkeepsie murals, Reynolds recommended to the President that he be allowed to carry out the last two murals in the

post office, but two other artists were chosen by competition. Reynolds to FDR, April 8, 1939, OF 400, FDRL.

[16]Helen Wilkinson Reynolds, *Dutch Houses in the Hudson Valley Before 1776* (New York, 1929), 334, 384; Helen Wilkinson Reynolds, *Dutchess County Doorways* (New York, 1931), 225-27, plates 52, 105-06; Reynolds, "Constitutional Convention."

[17]Foster to author, July 25, 1979. The 23 figures are identified in the *Poughkeepsie Eagle-News*, September 17, 1938, superseding the identification attached to Bruce to FDR, November 19, 1937, OF 400, FDRL. From the left, Smith is 7th, Clinton 8th, Hamilton 9th, Jay 11th, and Roosevelt 13th. At least one other portrait, Robert R. Livingston's (6th from left), seems authentic. See Ruth Piwonka, *A Portrait of Livingston Manor 1686-1850* (n.p., 1986), 57.

[18]Reynolds, "Constitutional Convention;" Foster to author, August 7, 1979. Schoonmaker is second from left, Morris the last seated figure on the right.

[19]Foster to author, November 21, 1980, explained that "John Poehler . . . put it [the mouse] in when he was rendering the furniture pieces and principally the base boards. It was just a gag and we figured it would delight any school children touring the post office. . . . Maybe a little naturalism is in the best tradition. You remember, of course, the dog defecating in one of Rembrandt's paintings." The most famous mouse of the 1930s was Mickey Mouse (created 1928), but the mouse in an eighteenth-century setting anticipates Amos, Benjamin Franklin's companion in Robert Larson's *Ben and Me* (Boston, 1939).

[20]Karal Ann Marling, *Wall-to-Wall America: A Cultural History of Post Office Murals in the Great Depression* (Minneapolis, 1982), 31, 141-42.

[21]The Section described the action in the mural as "Governor Clinton congratulating Alexander Hamilton on his victory." See "Description of Poughkeepsie Murals" in Bruce to FDR, November 19, 1937, OF 400, FDRL. The mood of the painting seems to coincide with that found by Richard B. Morris, "John Jay and the Adoption of the Federal Constitution in New York," *New York History* 68 (April 1982): 162, who observes that "the cause of the Constitution owed most to the fact that men of good will remained conciliatory and flexible. . . ."

[22]De Pauw, *Eleventh Pillar.*

[23]Bruce to Reynolds, November 29, 1937, RG 121. The Section had some suggestions for improvements to the ratification design: Rowan to Foster, March 1, 1938, RG 121, questioned Hamilton's small size and urged that he be given a more masculine stance. In February 1938, Bruce introduced Foster to FDR at the White House: Foster to Rowan, February 17, 1938, RG 121. In October, Bruce invited FDR to inspect the murals installed in the post office, but FDR declined and probably never saw the finished murals: Bruce to FDR, October 11, 1938 and FDR to Steve, October 17, 1938, OF 400, FDRL.

[24]*New York Times*, October 27, 1936 and February 14, 1936; and also H.L. Mencken, "A Constitution for the New Deal," 1937 article from *American Mercury* and *Reader's Digest*, reprinted in Kammen, *Machine*, 407-409, and the discussion in *ibid.*, 269-273.

[25]*New York Times*, November 3, 1936; Ted Morgan, *FDR: A Biography* (New York, 1985), 27, suggests FDR "understood by birthright what the framers were seeking."

[26]During the Revolution, Isaac retreated from New York to his wife's family estate in Dutchess County. On Isaac, see Kenneth S. Davis, *FDR: The Beckoning of Destiny* (New York, 1972), 18-20.

[27]FDR, radio address on Constitution Day, September 17, 1938, *The Public Papers and Addresses of Franklin D. Roosevelt, 1938* (New York, 1941), 525-28.

[28]FDR to Bruce, October 2, 1941, *F.D.R., His Personal Letters*, 4 vols. (New York, 1947-1950), 4: 221.

[29]Address of Henry Morgenthau, Jr., at the laying of the cornerstone of the Poughkeepsie Post Office, October 13, 1937, Morgenthau Diary, vol. 92, 60-61, FDRL.

Elihu Root

(1845–1937)

TIMOTHY J. HOULIHAN

Elihu Root was characterized by Chief Justice Charles Evans Hughes as "most astute among lawyers, most shrewd among diplomats, most wise among statesmen."[1] Root's career as a corporate attorney made him rich; his political career, as a cabinet member in two Republican administrations and as a United States Senator, won him fame; and his efforts on behalf of the Carnegie Endowment for International Peace won him the Nobel Prize. When he died at the age of ninety-two, Root left a complex legacy of conservatism and reform dominated by his achievements in the fields of world peace and international cooperation.

Born in Clinton, N.Y., on February 15, 1845, Elihu was the third son of Oren and Nancy Buttrick Root. His father was a professor of mathematics at Hamilton College, from which Elihu graduated in 1864. After one year of teaching at Rome, N.Y., he began his study of law at New York University, and continued to support himself through teaching in private academies. He completed his studies in 1867, and was admitted to the New York bar in the same year.

For the next few years, Root practiced corporation and real estate law with his partner, John H. Strahan. Together they built a reputation for ability, accumulated corporate clients, and climbed New York's social and economic ladders. Root first came into the public eye as the junior assistant to the army of lawyers who defended Boss William M. Tweed and William H. Ingersoll in 1873 against charges of graft and public corruption. In later life his opponents, especially William Randolph

Hearst, often brought up Root's connection with the Tweed case in attempts to discredit him and his policies. Even at the time, his family questioned the wisdom of the Tweed connection. The young Elihu, however, found it hard to imagine that he would ever be singled out for his very minor role in the case.[2]

In 1878, Root married Clara Wales, the daughter of a prominent New York City Republican. Together they had three children: Elihu, Jr., Edward, and Clara. Throughout his long career, Root's family remained the focus of his private life and the object of much affection.

By the 1890s Root was one of the most sought-after attorneys in the country. Between 1890 and 1898, Root defended the government of the United States, the Comptroller of the State of New York, the City of New York, The New York Times Publishing Company, The New York Press Company, at least six railroads, Theodore Roosevelt, August Belmont, and Frederick Vanderbilt. He was counsel for many of the nation's largest trusts, including the sugar trust, the lead trust, the whiskey trust, and Standard Oil Company.[3] Root's ability to grasp quickly the intricate details of difficult cases, his flawless logic, and his talent for convincing juries made him a valuable attorney and advisor for both corporations and individuals.

Early in his career, Root identified himself with the Republican party in New York. He joined the Union League Club and other prominent Republican societies. While he ran for public office only once (an unsuccessful race for Judge of the Court of Common Pleas in 1879), he held a long string of appointed positions. In 1883, President Chester A. Arthur installed him as United States Attorney for the Southern District of New York. He also represented the Twenty-first Assembly District on the Republican County Committee for several terms, and was chairman of the County Committee in 1886. As a leader of the reform element of the party, he was active in the Committee of Thirty, which rebelled against the Republican county machine.

Root was a delegate-at-large to the New York State Constitutional Convention of 1894. As chairman of the judiciary committee, he strove to simplify the administration of justice and to safeguard the interests of the small litigant. He also spoke out at the convention against women's suffrage and state aid to sectarian educational institutions, and in favor of legislative control over campaign spending. Root combined a strong sense of social conservatism with an equally strong desire for decent government.[4] In 1898, he was a delegate to the Republican State Convention at Saratoga, where, in an address before the convention, he established the legal eligibility of Theodore Roosevelt for the governorship. His friendship and support of Roosevelt served both men well, and lasted until Roosevelt's break with the Republicans in 1912.

In 1899, Root sacrificed his lucrative private career and accepted an appointment as Secretary of War from President William McKinley. McKinley was in search of a lawyer to reorganize the chaotic War Department and to direct the government of the recently acquired islands of the Philippines, Cuba, and Puerto Rico. Root proved himself capable to the task. He created the new War College, instituted the General Staff, reorganized the administrative system of the department, and applied civil service rules to the promotion of officers. He pushed an army reorganization bill through Congress, and pressed for the enlargement of West Point.

As the architect of United States colonial policy, Root demonstrated both his great ability to organize and direct a complex operation and his political and social conservatism. In Puerto Rico, Root moved quickly to establish a relief fund for the victims of a tropical hurricane. He then lobbied the president to abolish all customs tariffs between the United States and Puerto Rico in order to insure the economic viability of the island. Root's political system for Puerto Rico included a governor and a legislative council appointed by the president. Native membership in the council was permitted, but they would be in a minority. There was to be no elective assembly. Root justified his system on the grounds that the high level of illiteracy in Puerto Rico limited the practicality of democratic government. While McKinley defended Root's plan, Congress insisted on more home rule for the island, including an elective lower house for the assembly. The House of Representatives also insisted on a minimal tariff on imports. The Foraker Act, signed by McKinley on April 12, 1900, incorporated congressional demands.[5]

Cuba presented a more complex problem for Root and for the United States. The Teller Amendment to the war resolution specifically disclaimed any attempt by the United States to annex the island, but Root, and many others, insisted that strategic and economic concerns made Cuba too vital for the immediate withdrawal of troops. Root's plan for the island was incorporated into the Platt Amendment to the Army Appropriation Act of March 2, 1901. This amendment assured the United States of the opportunity to buy or lease naval sites in Cuba, and prohibited the Cubans from permitting foreign colonization on their soil. Thus the withdrawal of American troops on May 20, 1902, did not signal an end to American interest in Cuban affairs. Rather, through the Platt Amendment, that interest was enshrined in the Cuban Constitution.

In the Philippines, Root made use of his remarkable capacities for organization and logistics. Confronted with an armed insurrection, Root proceeded to build an enormous army, unleash his commanders in the field, and crush the opposition to American occupation. The atrocities committed by both American and Philippine troops unleased a groundswell of anti-imperialist sentiment in the United States. Root and McKinley, however, continued to defend the necessity of military rule throughout the insurrection. With the coming of peace, Root directed McKinley's Philippine Commission, headed by William Howard Taft, to organize a civil government for the island and, on September 1, 1900, to take over the legislative functions of the military regime. In the Philippines, as in Puerto Rico and in Cuba, Root distrusted the combination of a democratic political system with a largely uneducated population. In his own words: "I do not believe any people, three-fourths of whom are contented to remain unable to read and write, can for any very long period maintain a free government."[6] He defended the right of all people in United States territory to the protections of the Constitution, but he believed those rights could best be preserved through rule by the educated elite.

Root served as secretary of war from August 1, 1899, to February 1, 1904, under McKinley and then Theodore Roosevelt. Root briefly returned to his legal career, but Roosevelt persuaded him to accept the position of secretary of state, a post he held from July 1, 1905, until January 7, 1909.

As secretary of state he reorganized the consular service, bringing to that service the same principles of order and administration he brought to the War Department. Root also initiated the first "good neighbor" policy with Latin America. His goodwill tour of Mexico and South America in 1906 strengthened the commercial and political bonds between the region and the United States. The tour, and his service as honorary president of the Pan-American Congress, led directly to the Central American Peace Conference which established a Court of Arbitration for international disputes in Latin America.[7]

In the Far East, Root successfully lessened Japanese-American tensions with his negotiation of a gentlemen's agreement over immigration, an artibration treaty, and the Root-Takahira Agreement of 1908. In the first of these, the Japanese pledged to restrict voluntarily the entry of Japanese laborers in the United States. The arbitration pact brought several areas of dispute under diplomatic consideration and reduced suspicion between the two nations. In the 1908 agreement, the two parties agreed to perpetuate John Hay's "Open Door" policy in

China. Though Root has been severely criticized for his conciliatory attitude toward the Japanese, his policies were consistent with his life-long reliance on negotiation and arbitration in his efforts to preserve peace.[8]

In March 1909, Root was chosen by the New York Legislature to serve as United States senator. The next six years were both frustrating and triumphant for the aging politician. He was angered by the growing power of Progressives in his beloved Republican party. He distrusted the climate of social and political experimentation of the second decade of the twentieth century, and frequently argued with the Republican leadership. He split with President William Howard Taft over interpretation of the Hay–Paunceforte agreement. He felt American vessels should pay the same tolls for use of the Panama Canal that other nations paid.[9] Root also split with his longtime friend, former President Roosevelt, when Roosevelt left the Republicans to form his own Progressive Party.

Root's triumphs came as counsel for the United States in the North Atlantic Fisheries Arbitration in 1910, during which he settled long-standing disputes with Britain over boundaries and fishing rights. He became a member of the Permanent Court of Arbitration at The Hague, and, in 1910, Root was offered the presidency of the Carnegie Endowment for International Peace. For his efforts in the pacification of Cuba and the Philippines, his part in the negotiations between the United States and Japan, his stance on the Panama Canal tolls, and his work on behalf of the Carnegie Endowment, Root was awarded the Nobel Prize for Peace in 1912. Negotiation and arbitration had their rewards, both for the nations involved and for Root.

After his retirement from the Senate, Root served as president of the New York State Constitutional Convention of 1915. He dominated the drafting of the new constitution, and championed the reorganization and improvement of the executive and the judiciary. In contrast to his position in Cuba and the Philippines, in New York Root opposed a literacy test for voters. In November, however, Root had to face the rejection of his constitution by the public.[10]

Though a loyal Republican throughout his life, Root rallied support for the Wilson Administration during the war effort. As a result, Wilson appointed him Ambassador Extraordinary as head of a mission to Russia in 1917. Root's failure realistically to assess the situation, affected no doubt by the constant reassurances of the new Russian government, led Wilson to condemn the mission as a fiasco. For the rest of the war, and the rest of the Democrat's administration, Root held no official position in the government. Root's split with Wilson was aggravated after the war by the issue of the League of Nations. While Root supported the notion of international cooperation, he rejected the Covenant as brought back from Paris by Wilson. As was the case with Henry Cabot Lodge, Root's essential disagreement was with Article X of the Covenant, which obligated members of the League to preserve the territorial integrity and political independence of all states which were also members. Root believed that the United States in particular had not only a right but an obligation to interfere in the affairs of all nations in the western hemisphere, and possibly beyond. Though he is sometimes accused of writing the anti-League plank of the Republican platform in 1920, Root's stance was simply one of reservation. He supported the candidacy of Warren G. Harding precisely because of the Ohio Republican's support for an "association of nations." Root drafted his own world association plan in which the permanent World Court at The Hague would be combined with certain parts of the League proposal. The so-called "Root Protocol," defeated in the Senate, would have allowed the United States to join the World Court without official ratification of the League. With his usual sense of caution and conservativism, Root continued to champion the cause of arbitration and negotiation.[12]

As an elder statesman, Root continued to be an advocate of the peaceful settlement of international and domestic disputes. In 1921, he was a delegate to the Washington Conference for the Limitation of Armaments, at which a number of nations agreed to prohibit the use of poison gas and chemical weapons as well as the use of submarines against merchant shipping.[13] In domestic affairs, Root settled a jurisdictional dispute between the plasterers' and bricklayers' unions in New York City. He also defended an organization of brewers in their attack on the Volstead Act which, it appears, Root considered unconstitutional and an infringement on individual rights.[14]

On Sunday, February 7, 1937, Root died in his home in New York City, surrounded by his family. Elihu Root described himself as "a lawyer first and all the time," and he brought to every position he held his tremendous capacity to organize and rationalize complex situations.[15] For many, Root was the epitome of conservatism, and his opinions on social and political issues were shaped by his cautious sense of the role of government and his paternalistic sense of the mission of the United States. But when Root died, the world lost one of the most persuasive and effective advocates of international cooperation and world peace.

NOTES:

[1]Quoted in *New York Times*, February 7, 1937, 38.
[2]Phillip C. Jessup, *Elihu Root* (New York, 1938), 1: 83.
[3]*Ibid.*, 183–184.
[4]*Ibid.*, 173–182.
[5]Richard W. Leopold, *Elihu Root and the Conservative Tradition* (Boston, 1954), 25–38; Jessup, *op. cit.*, ch. 11–19.
[6]Jessup, 1: 305.
[7]Leopold, *op. cit.*, ch. 3.
[8]*Ibid.*, 59–62; Jessup, 2: 3–65.
[9]Jessup, 2: 266–268.
[10]*Ibid.*, ch. 40.
[11]*Ibid.*, 367.
[12]Leopold, 130–150; Jessup, ch. 45.
[13]Leopold, 158–161.
[14]*New York Times*, February 7, 1937, 38.
[15]Jessup, 1: 114.

Elizabeth Cady Stanton
(1815 –1902)

M. JILL DuPONT

Unlike many historical figures, Elizabeth Cady Stanton cannot be measured in terms of specific events or monumental tracts. Rather, it is the collective whole of her thoughts, writings, and actions which defines her legacy as the intellectual pioneer of the women's rights movement. Stanton's public struggle was also a private one, as she grappled with traditional and nontraditional conceptions of womanhood in the nineteenth century. As biographer Lois Banner has observed, Stanton's ideology was "intertwined" with her autobiography: "Her life was her primary source for her ideas, which in turn influenced her behavior."[1]

Elizabeth Cady was born in Johnstown, New York, in 1815. Throughout her childhood, Elizabeth strived to emulate and win the approval of her father. Daniel Cady served in the New York State Legislature from 1808 until 1814, when he was elected to Congress. His bid for reelection in 1816 failed, as did the campaigns of most Federalists. After a stint as a circuit court judge, Cady served as an associate justice of the New York Supreme Court from 1847 until 1855. A respected and successful lawyer, Cady attracted some of the finest male minds to clerk and study under his tutelage. Elizabeth spent much of her youth ensconced in her father's office, absorbing his discussions with clients or perusing the volumes lining his bookshelves. She was particularly affected by the plight of a mother who wished to divorce her intemperate husband, but who was told by Cady that existing laws could not prevent the loss of her children, possessions, or earnings. Elizabeth, distraught, decided to cut out the discriminatory statutes from her father's law books with a knife, but was restrained by Cady before she could do so. Daniel Cady admired his daughter's intelligence and passion, but was secretly disappointed that she had not been born a boy. A young man of her abilities entertained limitless opportunities, while women remained restricted by their gender.

Elizabeth did not work as eagerly to impress her mother. Though defined by her daughter as "queenly,"[2] Margaret Livingston Cady exhibited many of the same qualities that Elizabeth later manifested. As with most nineteenth-century women, Margaret Cady's primary duties were confined to the domestic sphere. She did not urge Elizabeth to pursue any calling other than that of wife and mother, yet Margaret displayed an independent will which her daughter inherited. She voiced her displeasure with Daniel Cady's opposition to abolition and women's rights, and when Elizabeth later gravitated toward reform activities, her mother was quietly proud.

Elizabeth attended and excelled at coeducational Johnstown Academy until the age of fifteen. Upon her graduation in 1830, she matriculated at Emma Willard's Troy academy, which offered the most rigorous and comprehensive education for women at the time. (Colleges did not yet admit women, a fact which prevented Elizabeth from attending Union College, her university of choice.) Her experiences at these two institutions contributed to Cady's lifelong advocacy of coeducation.

Cady did not have any career prospects or ambitions upon graduating from Troy in 1833. She began spending time at her cousin Gerrit Smith's farmstead in Peterboro, where she found herself attracted to the social reformers who gathered there. Smith's home also served as a station on the Underground Railroad, and Cady was thus exposed to the plight of slaves and abolitionists working for their freedom. In 1839, Cady met Henry Stanton, an executive with the American Anti-Slavery Society. They were married in 1840 as part of a trip to the World Anti-Slavery Convention in London. Cady kept her own name and adopted her husband's, reasoning that she was exercising an option similar to that of slaves who chose new names upon gaining freedom.

While attending the convention, Cady Stanton was incensed by the treatment of female delegates, who were not allowed to participate in the proceedings nor granted seats on the convention floor. Her focus abruptly shifted from slavery to the bondage of women. Cady Stanton had the good fortune to meet Lucretia Mott, a prominent abolitionist preacher who was the leading woman delegate. The two became inseparable companions, with Mott acting as mentor to the younger Cady Stanton, who sought her advice on social and theological issues. The two resolved to hold a convention to discuss women's rights upon their return to the states.

The first eight years of Cady Stanton's life, however, were consumed by domesticity. In 1842, Henry established a law practice in Boston, the intellectual center of reform activity. Motherhood—what she termed "the most important of all professions"³—afforded Cady Stanton an opportunity to formulate her own philosophy of child rearing. She shunned many of the traditional approaches to raising children and followed her instincts instead, manifesting two central tenets of her awakening feminism: self-reliance and woman's independence. These two qualities would later form the heart of Cady Stanton's reform ideology. By 1846, "The novelty of housekeeping had passed away, and much that was once attractive in domestic life was irksome."⁴ The Stantons moved to Seneca Falls in 1847, an isolated town which accentuated Cady Stanton's restlessness. Saddled with three young boys and envious of her husband's freedom to do as he pleased, she renewed her commitment to a women's rights convention.

A week before their proposed convention in Seneca Falls in 1848, Lucretia Mott, Cady Stanton, and several other women met to prepare a document that would articulate the legal, political, social, educational, and economic grievances of women. Cady Stanton suggested that they use the Declaration of Independence as their model, a move which connected their cause to the American symbol of liberty and rooted Stanton's own political philosophy in the theory of natural rights.⁵ Of the eighteen grievances they compiled, none was as controversial as Stanton's demand for suffrage, a resolution which was narrowly approved at the convention's sessions on July 19th and 20th. Suffrage was hotly debated again at the Rochester convention which followed on the heels of Seneca Falls, but by the Worcester gathering of 1851, suffrage served as the instrumental component of any platform on women's rights, and bonded together women who differed on other aspects of feminism.

Cady Stanton wrote much of the Declaration of Sentiments of 1848, drawing on her knowledge of women's legal disabilities, personal experience, and Lucretia Mott's economic concerns. The 1848 convention established Stanton as a leading feminist, spawned the women's rights movement around her demand for the ballot, and allowed Stanton to merge some of her personal grievances into a public cause. Many accounts credited Mott with inspiring the inaugural women's rights convention, but in a letter to Stanton in 1854, she said "Remember the first convention originated with thee . . . I have never liked the undeserved praise . . . of being the moving spirit of that occasion, when to thyself belongs the honor."[6]

The Women's Movement

Throughout the 1850s, Cady Stanton explored and nourished her maturing feminism through articles published in *The Lily, Una,* and the *New York Tribune.* Both *The Lily* and *Una* were journals published by and devoted to the education and elevation of women. Cady Stanton contributed essays encompassing diverse aspects of feminism, including motherhood, employment, coeducation, married women's rights, divorce, and suffrage. Her intellectual inspiration came from a variety of sources: earlier feminist tracts penned by Margaret Fuller and Mary Wollstonecraft, the essays of Ralph Waldo Emerson, and later, John Stuart Mill's *On The Subjection of Women.* Each work dealt with themes Cady Stanton would enunciate throughout her career, namely, self-reliance, the oppression of women, individual relationships between men and women, and the cultural—rather than innate—differences between the sexes.

Yet Cady Stanton was not yet ready to relinquish the satisfaction and self-confidence she derived from motherhood. She bore four more children in the next decade (the last in 1859), thus dividing her time and energy between the public and private spheres. Her link to the women's rights movement during the 1850s was Susan B. Anthony, whom Cady Stanton had met at an Anti-Slavery convention in 1851. Their friendship was a "blend of opposites."[7] Anthony lacked the intellectual capabilities of Cady Stanton, yet possessed the organizational skills and attention to detail that Stanton abhorred. Stanton's ideas were formulated into a plan of action and carried out by Anthony, whose drive and persistence were limitless. "I forged the thunderbolts, and she fired them," Stanton recalled fondly.[8]

In 1848, Stanton had initiated a movement centering on her stunning resoluion for suffrage. By 1853, she confided to Anthony, "I feel this whole question of women's rights turns on the point of the marriage relation, and sooner or later it will be the question for discussion."[9] As the decade progressed, marriage became the focal issue for Stanton. She delivered stirring orations before the state legislature in Albany urging the passage of a comprehensive bill ensuring property rights to married women, culminating in the Married Women's Property Act of 1860. Her address before the legislature in 1854 was compelling, for she argued that

The wife who inherits no property holds about the same legal position that does the slave of the Southern plantation. She can own nothing, sell nothing. She has no right even to the wages she earns; her person, her time, her services are the property of another. . . .[10]

Stanton contended that "men and women are alike"—a position denied by woman's standing before the law—and thus asked for "no better laws than those you have made for yourself."[11] At the Tenth National Woman's Rights Convention of 1860, she reiterated this theme:

There is one kind of marriage that has not been tried, and that is, a contract made by equal parties to live an equal life, with equal restraints and privileges on either side. Thus far, we have had the man marriage and nothing more. From the beginning, man has had the sole and whole regulation of the matter. He has spoken in Scripture, he has spoken in law . . . as a judge and legislator, he still holds the entire control.[12]

Though most women agreed with Stanton's assessment of the marital relation, they did not readily embrace her proposed solution: liberalized divorce. Stanton held that marriage should not be regulated by either civil or canon law, but regarded as a simple contract to be dissolved for reasons privy to the husband and wife alone. If legislative involvement was necessary, Stanton believed laws should make divorce easier to obtain and marriage more difficult to undertake.[13] At the heart of Stanton's campaign for married women's property rights and divorce— along with economic opportunity, political equality, and coeducation— was her crusade to instill a sense of independence among women and to realize this sentiment in the law and public opinion. She believed that women should marry out of choice, not necessity. Simply put, Stanton held that individual happiness promoted a better community. A bad marriage perpetuated detrimental effects upon society, for "A child conceived in the midst of hate, sin, and discord, nurtured in abuse and injustice, cannot do much to bless the world or himself."[14]

Crusader

Stanton strayed even further from the mainstream of the women's rights movement following the Civil War. Reasoning that the law prevented women from voting but not seeking office, Stanton campaigned for a seat in the House of Representatives in 1866, thus becoming the first woman to run for Congress. Her bid was primarily symbolic, as she did not invest herself in the campaign and received only twenty-four of twenty thousand votes. Meanwhile, the battle for black and woman suffrage was growing increasingly bitter. While Stanton coolly observed that "Every argument for the negro is an argument for women and no logician can escape it," she advised women that "it becomes a serious question whether we had better stand aside and see Sambo walk into the kingdom first."[15] When black suffrage appeared a certainty, Stanton noted that "In securing suffrage but to another shade of manhood, while we disfranchise fifteen million tax-payers, we come not one line nearer the republican idea."[16]

Suffrage had always been just one element of Stanton's comprehensive feminism. She believed it futile to concentrate on only one aspect of woman's degradation, when discrimination existed in almost every sphere of society. While the defeat of woman suffrage during Reconstruction provided the impetus for the formal organization of a woman suffrage movement, Stanton turned her attention to problems neither men nor women wished to confront: rape, prostitution, and infanticide. She addressed many of these issues in the pages of *The Revolution*, a journal begun in 1868 with Susan B. Anthony and financed by Democrat George Francis Train. Stanton displayed more of an urban emphasis with her focus on the sexual exploitation of women, in addition to her campaign for the eight-hour workday, the conditions of working women, and wage discrimination. She also discussed her opinions on birth control, marital discontent, and divorce.

Stanton's views received a practical test in 1868 when Hester Vaughan, an immigrant servant, was raped by her employer, became pregnant and gave birth, and was subsequently found guilty of infanticide and sentenced for murder. Stanton argued that the man involved was as guilty as Vaughan, and insisted that equal moral standards be applied to both men and women. Moreover, Stanton pointed out that jury service was still restricted to men, a fact which may have contributed to the court's verdict. Stanton found this case symptomatic of the unpublicized abuses also endured by married women who had no legal recourse to the sexual exploitation they suffered at the hands of husbands:

> Marriage today is in no way viewed as an equal partnership, intended for the equal advantage and happiness of both parties. Nearly every man feels that his wife is his property, whose first duty, under all circumstances, is to gratify his passions, without the least

reference to her own health and happiness, or the welfare of their offspring, and so enfeebled is woman's judgment and moral sense from long abuse, that she believes so too, and quotes from the Bible to prove her own degradation.[17]

Stanton pleaded with legislators to regard marriage as a civil contract like any other, "subject to the laws of all other contracts, carefully made, the parties of age, and all agreements faithfully observed."[18] Divorce at the will of the parties, Stanton maintained, "is not only a right, but (that) it is a sin against nature, the family, the state for a man or woman to live together in the marriage relation in continual antagonism, indifference, disgust."[19]

Stanton's radical foresight distanced her from the conservative forces of the woman suffrage movement. That two branches of the movement were created in 1869 was as much a factor of personality conflicts as strategical philosophy. The American Woman Suffrage Association (AWSA) refused to have their quest for suffrage clouded by the controversial issues raised by Stanton, who, despite serving as president for many years, was frequently disdained and ignored within the ranks of the National Woman Suffrage Association (NWSA) as well. Although Stanton had initiated the drive for political equality in 1848, Anthony embraced the crusade and achieved a revered stature of almost religious proportions within the suffrage movement. Stanton never fully devoted herself to the NWSA and appeared satisfied with writing the organization's official documents, including the centennial declaration of 1876 —a piece heralded for its facile enumeration of the constitutional and social disabilities faced by women, but which was not considered as revolutionary as her 1848 address.

Despite the existing tension between Stanton's radicalism and the movement's single-issue conservatism, Stanton was reelected to the presidency in 1878. Yet, as she indicated to Anthony in a letter in 1876, Stanton's discontent was deepening:

> As I sum up the indignities toward women, as illustrated by recent judicial decisions—denied the right to vote, denied the right to practice [law] in the Supreme Court, denied jury trial—I feel the degradation of sex more bitterly than I did on that July 19, 1848.[20]

Stanton shifted her assault on discrimination to organized religion, which she felt sanctioned and encouraged the subjection of women. Beginning in 1878, she appealed to the NWSA to adopt resolutions condemning the Bible and church oppression of women, but her actions only widened the rift existing between herself and the organization. The NWSA wanted no part of any controversial ideology which would detract from their goal of suffrage or alienate potential supporters. In addition, the suffrage movement found itself influenced by a growing Christian constituency. Stanton's resolutions were consistently defeated, and once again she found herself in the minority.

Feminism and Ideology

In the 1880s, Stanton collaborated with Anthony and Matilda Joslyn Gage on the first three volumes of the *History of Woman Suffrage*. Stanton ended her affiliation with the project in 1886, in a sense terminating her association with the suffrage movement as well. Though she was elected president of the newly formed NAWSA (through a merger of the AWSA and NWSA) in 1890, Stanton's election was unpopular and engineered only through Anthony's influence and insistence. Stanton resigned in 1892, confiding to Gage that she was "sick of the song of suffrage."[21] In 1888, Stanton had written,

> The National has been growing political and conservative for some time. Lucy [Stone] and Susan [Anthony] alike see suffrage only. They do not see woman's religious and social bondage, neither do the young women in either organization.[22]

Stanton investigated this religious bondage more fully in Parts I (1895) and II (1898) of *The Woman's Bible*, an undertaking conceived in the early 1880s and brought to fruition with an editorial staff composed of more than twenty women. The polemical work commented upon Bible passages which portrayed women as strong and independent, as well as those which seemed to degrade and encourage subjection of their gender. In her introduction to the first volume, Stanton observed:

> When, in the early part of the Nineteenth Century, women began to protest against their civil and political degradation, they were referred to the Bible for an answer. When they protested against their unequal position in the church, they were referred to the Bible for an answer.[23]

Stanton insisted that organized religion ingrained a sense of inferiority among women which prohibited their self-emancipation. Stanton's belief was reinforced from her earliest lecture tours, when she was confronted by audiences of women who listened eagerly to her sentiments on marriage, divorce, and birth control, then cited passages from the Bible which prevented them from subscribing to Stanton's views. *The Woman's Bible* was regarded seriously by neither the general public nor religious orders, and was formally repudiated at the NAWSA convention of 1896.

In her final years, Stanton assumed rather conservative stances on issues peripheral to feminism. She favored American expansionism on the grounds of America's innate superiority, supported government policy detrimental to Native American autonomy, and campaigned for educated suffrage—particularly as it applied to immigrants. One of Stanton's foremost passions, reading, became an impossibility as her eyesight failed in her last few years. When Susan B. Anthony heard of Stanton's death on October 26, 1902, she reflected on her personal loss:

> Well, it is an awful hush—it seems impossible—that the voice is hushed that I longed to hear for fifty years—longed to get her opinion of things—before I knew exactly where I stood.[24]

The majority of Stanton's contemporaries were not ready for her multifaceted feminism. The constant ideological sparring which occurred between Stanton and narrowly focused suffragists usually ended short of the free discussion Stanton longed for. Only through discussion of their differences, Stanton contended, could the contours of feminism be defined, results attained, and ambitions uplifted. Though her views on divorce, birth control, and religion in particular were perceived as radical at the time, they became integral components of the twentieth-century women's rights movement—just as her proposal for suffrage evolved from a bold request to the basis of the nineteenth-century movement.

Though Stanton's feminism assumed a variety of forms throughout her lifetime, her message remained virtually unchanged: the opportunity for women to achieve self-reliance, independence, and happiness. In her address before the Seneca Falls Convention of 1848, Stanton declared that

> Men's intellectual superiority cannot be a question until woman has had a fair trial. When we shall have had our freedom to find

out our own sphere, when we shall have had our colleges, our professions, our trades, for a century, a comparison then may be justly instituted.[25]

It was Stanton's hope that women would marry out of choice, not necessity. She spoke harshly of marriage because she felt few couples achieved the ideal of a complete spiritual and intellectual union based on equality. To reach this goal, Stanton not only argued for legislative reform increasing the marital and career options for women, but frequently chided and mocked those women who proclaimed themselves satisfied with their lot in life. "No matter how much women prefer to lean," Stanton observed,

> to be protected and supported, nor how much men desire to have them do so, they must make the voyage of life alone and for safety in an emergency they must know something of the laws of navigation.[26]

Stanton articulated this theme until the year she died. In what she considered her finest address, "Solitude of Self," Stanton asked for "the complete development of every individual, first, for his own benefit and happiness;" for "whatever the theories may be of woman's dependence on man, in the supreme moments of her life, he cannot bear her burdens."[27]

NOTES:

[1]Lois Banner, *Elizabeth Cady Stanton: A Radical for Women's Rights* (Boston: Little, Brown and Co., 1980), 71.

[2]Elisabeth Griffith, *In Her Own Right: The Life of Elizabeth Cady Stanton* (New York: Oxford University Press, 1984), 10.

[3]Margaret Forster, "Elizabeth Cady Stanton, 1815–1902," in her *Significant Sisters* (New York: Oxford University Press, 1984), 216.

[4]*Ibid.*, 218.

[5]Banner, 41; Griffith, 54.

[6]Alma Lutz, *Created Equal: A Biography of Elizabeth Cady Stanton* (New York: John Day Co., 1940), 54.

[7]Banner, 59.

[8]*Ibid.*

[9]Ellen Carol DuBois, ed., *Elizabeth Cady Stanton, Susan B. Anthony: Correspondence, Writing, Speeches* (New York: Shocken Books, 1981), 55.

[10]"Address to the Legislature of New York on Women's Rights," February 14, 1854. Reprinted in DuBois, ed., 48.

[11]DuBois, ed., 19.

[12]From "Debates on Marriage and Divorce," in Mary Jo Buhle and Paul Buhle, *A Concise History of Woman Suffrage* (Urbana: University of Illinois Press, 1978), 176.

[13]Griffith, 103.

[14]Letter to Anthony, March 1, 1853. Reprinted in DuBois, ed., 55.

[15]From "Gerrit Smith on Petitions." Reprinted in DuBois, ed., 122; Buhle and Buhle, 219.

[16]From National Women's Rights Convention of 1866. Reprinted in Buhle and Buhle, 223.

[17]Lutz, 164.

[18]From "Home Life." Reprinted in DuBois, ed., 134.

[19]From "Speech to the McFarland–Richardson Protest Meeting." Reprinted in DuBois, ed., 129.

[20]Lutz, 239.

[21]Banner, 160.

[22]*Ibid.*, 154.

[23]Elizabeth Cady Stanton, *The Woman's Bible*, vol. 1 (1895; reprint. New York: Arno Press, 1972), 9.

[24]Griffith, 218.

[25]From "Address Delivered at Seneca Falls," July 19, 1848. Reprinted in DuBois, ed., 29.

[26]Forster, 206.

[27]From "Solitude of Self." Reprinted in DuBois, ed., 248, 251.

For Further Reading

Banner, Lois. *Elizabeth Cady Stanton: A Radical for Women's Rights* (Boston: Little, Brown and Co., 1980).

Buhle, Mary Jo, and Buhle, Paul. *A Concise History of Woman Suffrage: Selections from the Classic Works of Stanton, Anthony, Gage and Harper* (Urbana: University of Illinois Press, 1978).

DuBois, Ellen Carol, ed. *Elizabeth Cady Stanton, Susan B. Anthony: Correspondence, Writings, Speeches* (New York: Shocken Books, 1981).

Forster, Margaret. "Elizabeth Cady Stanton, 1815–1902." In her *Significant Sisters* (New York: Oxford University Press, 1984).

Griffith, Elisabeth. *In Her Own Right: The Life of Elizabeth Cady Stanton* (New York: Oxford University Press, 1984).

Lutz, Alma. *Created Equal: A Biography of Elizabeth Cady Stanton* (New York: John Day Co., 1940).

Stanton, Elizabeth Cady. *The Woman's Bible*, Vol. 1. Reprint ed. (New York: Arno Press, 1972).

Alvan Stewart
(1790–1849)

WILLIAM M. WIECEK
Syracuse University

Born in 1790 at South Granville, New York (near the Vermont border), Alvan Stewart studied law in the offices of Chancellor Reuben Walworth and then established his legal practice in Cherry Valley, in central New York. In 1832, he removed his practice to Utica, which remained his home for the rest of his life. He began his career as a reformer by joining the teetotalling wing of the temperance movement, and he retained an interest in that cause throughout his long and turbulent career. Like many other abolitionists of his time, he originally favored colonizing the freed slaves, either in Africa or elsewhere outside the continental United States, on the grounds that blacks were a source of corruption and strife in white society. But, like all other *immediatist* abolitionists (that is, men and women who favored the immediate abolition of slavery), Stewart withdrew his support from the colonization movement at some time in the early 1830s. He was a founder and the first president of the New-York State Anti-Slavery Society (NYSA-SS) (1835). Stewart steadfastly worked for the cause of immediate abolition until his death, which occurred in New York City in 1849.

Setting Abolitionist Principles and Tactics

Stewart joined with the other founders and leaders of the revitalized national antislavery movement in supporting the principles set forth in the "Declaration of Sentiments" adopted by the American Anti-Slavery Society (AA-SS) at its founding in 1833. These included:

1) Slavery was a moral evil, violating the laws of God and the principles of natural justice.

2) Slavery was inconsistent with the principles of republican government and the ideals of the Declaration of Independence.

3) Slavery was to be abolished immediately, and without compensation to the masters; both gradualism and colonization were wrong.

4) Blacks must "share an equality with whites, of civil and religious privileges."

5) Slavery was primarily the constitutional responsibility of the states, not the federal government.

6) The movement, however, would work for certain specified political objectives at the federal level, including the abolition of the slave trade and of slavery in the District of Columbia.

Changing Political and Constitutional Course

Throughout the 1830s, however, the movement's repeated frustrations and defeats led Stewart to reconsider the utility of these principles. These setbacks included violent attacks on abolitionists by an anti-abolitionist mob in Utica in October 1835; the stinging 1836 denunciation of abolitionists by New York's Democratic Governor William Marcy; the movement's failure to secure repeal of either the 1821 New York Constitution's $250 suffrage qualification for blacks or the 1817 New York statute permitting slaveholders visiting the state to keep their slaves with them as slaves for up to nine months.

Rethinking his commitment to the principles of the abolitionist movement led Stewart to change his mind about two key aspects of the prevailing abolitionist orthodoxy—the abolitionists' lack of interest in general electoral politics and their constitutional position that slavery was a matter only for the states and that the federal government had no authority over slavery.

Politics: Although abstaining from electoral politics, abolitionists never had refrained entirely from political action. Throughout the 1830s, they repeatedly petitioned Congress for antislavery objectives, such as repeal of the 1793 Fugitive Slave Act, and had continued the long tradition of lobbying state legislatures for such reforms as the enactment of laws protecting free blacks from kidnapping. Despite their pursuit of these antislavery reforms through the political process, abolitionists had not explored the usefulness of more conventional political activity— that is, running avowed abolitionist candidates for office.

Stewart and other upstate New York abolitionists, including Myron Holley and Gerrit Smith, decided that their abstention from electoral politics was self-defeating. Abolitionists, they agreed, would be more likely to achieve their objectives by running their own candidates for office where both Democrats and Whigs were hostile to them, and perhaps even by fielding entire antislavery tickets. As his contribution to this change of strategy, Stewart won over the membership of the NYSA-SS. Antislavery conventions in Warsaw and Albany, New York (1839–40) created the Liberty Party, nominating the converted slaveholder James G. Birney as its presidential candidate.

The abolitionist movement did not endorse this change of strategy unanimously. William Lloyd Garrison, based in Boston, and his followers denounced such overt political action as sinful; they condemned Birney, Stewart, and other politically active abolitionists for betraying the original principles of the AA–SS. In turn, the political abolitionists dismissed the Garrisonians' ever more radical theological doctrines as moral solipsism that would not free any slaves. A schism in the abolitionist movement began to form in 1839.

Constitutional Doctrine: The dispute over political tactics mirrored a dispute over constitutional doctrine in the ranks of the abolitionists. Mulling over the possibilities of political action under the United States Constitution, Stewart found himself increasingly attracted to an idea that had not won many converts or systematic exposition: that slavery was inherently unconstitutional as a violation of the Declaration of Independence and the United States Constitution. This idea led Stewart, in turn, to repudiate the fundamental belief, shared by abolitionists and nonabolitionists alike, that the federal government had no power to abolish slavery. In September 1837, Stewart declared before the NYSA-SS that the due process clause of the Fifth Amendment to the United States Constitution empowered the federal government to abolish slavery everywhere.

The Garrisonians, who regarded the entire Constitution as "a covenant with death and a compromise with hell" because of what they saw as its avowedly proslavery doctrines, found Stewart's new constitutional argument against slavery just as indefensible as was his enthusiasm for conventional political activity. After 1840, the constitutional and political schism in abolitionist ranks became permanent, destroying the consensus that had assembled under the 1833 AA–SS principles and producing at least two main factions, moderate abolitionists and Garrisonians, in opposition to the third, the political abolitionists.

Moderate abolitionists rejected Stewart's argument for congressional power to abolish slavery in the states, believing instead that the federal government could only confine it to the states where it existed and otherwise must abstain from supporting it. After the political crises caused by the Mexican War (1846–48) and the 1848 Wilmot Proviso (which would have banned the extension of slavery into any territory acquired as a result of that war), the moderate abolitionists carried their constitutional beliefs into the Free Soil Party (1848) and eventually into the Republican Party, becoming the mainstream of the fragmented abolitionist movement.

Garrisonians, for their part, condemned all forms of political action, denounced radicals like Stewart, and proclaimed that the United States Constitution was a proslavery compact to be spurned by all righteous people.

Stewart as Antislavery Litigator

Meanwhile, Stewart continued to propagate his belief that slavery was unconstitutional. Though his regular Utica law practice suffered, he litigated—albeit without success—to have his views accepted as law. His major opportunity came not in his home state but in New Jersey, which in its 1844 Constitution had declared that "all men are by nature free and independent." In two 1845 cases, *State v. Post* and *State v. Van Beuren*, Stewart appeared as counsel, arguing that this new constitutional provision of its own force abolished the vestiges of slavery that had remained in New Jersey after its 1804 and 1820 *post-nati* gradual emancipation statutes. The New Jersey Supreme Court of Judicature rejected this argument by a 3-to-1 vote, holding that the new constitution did not disrupt existing social arrangements.

Stewart's Fifth Amendment due process argument had a fatal flaw. In *Barron v. Baltimore* (1833), Chief Justice John Marshall held for the United States Supreme Court that the federal Bill of Rights (including, of course, the Fifth Amendment) was not a restraint on the states. (Stewart might have argued from analogy to comparable law-of-the-land or due-process clauses in the state constitutions, but he never made such an argument.) Perhaps for that reason, or perhaps because his lawyer's instincts led him to seek other bases for argument, he sometimes relied on other parts of the federal Constitution, and on the Declaration of Independence, as textual foundations for his antislavery arguments. He cited the various clauses of the Preamble, the commerce clause (for federal power to prohibit the international and interstate slave trade), Congress's regulatory power over the District of Columbia, the First Amendment (for protection of abolitionists' rights of speech, press, and petition), and the clause in Article IV providing that the United States shall guarantee to every state a republican form of government. He also invoked any state constitutional provision that came to hand, as he had in his New Jersey arguments.

Conclusion

Stewart enjoyed a reputation in the antislavery movement as a forceful, humorous speaker and as a courageous organizer. He was not, however, an original or deep thinker. His surviving arguments, speeches, and essays are rhetorical rather than reflective, emotive rather than thoughtful. As suggested by the flaw in his due-process argument exposed by *Barron*, his legal reasoning was shallow and opportunistic. Other abolitionists, such as William Goodell, were more thorough; other abolitionist lawyers, such as Salmon P. Chase and Samuel Sewall, were more effective litigators; still others, such as James Alvord, were more successful lobbyists. Yet for all the rhetorical superficiality of his argument, Stewart deserves the credit for originating and promoting one of the most influential ideas of late nineteenth-century law: that the due process clauses convey a substantive right to liberty and property which a claimant can demand that courts protect. This idea, known as *substantive due process*, served other ends than the freedom of black Americans fifty years after Stewart's death, but it remains, despite its weaknesses, one of the most original and influential concepts in abolition's armory of legal weapons.

Suffragists Protest the Constitution *

September 17, 1887

SALLY ROESCH WAGNER

When the centennial of the Constitution reached its crescendo on September 17, 1887, with the Grand Federal Procession down the historic streets of Philadelphia, thousands of demonstrators were on hand protesting their perceived exclusion from the American Dream. "U.S. CONSTITUTION, EVEN THE SCORE. MEN: 200, WOMEN 0," one popular button read. While the parade replicated the original procession which celebrated the ratification of the Constitution, the protesters were also repeating a history of their own.

Suffragists 100 years ago confronted the president with a written protest when the nation's leaders met in Philadelphia to celebrate the Constitution's centennial. "We cannot allow the occasion to pass without reminding you that one-half the people who obey the laws of the United States are unjustly denied all place or part in the body politic," these early feminists proclaimed. "In the midst of the pomps and glories of this celebration, women are only on-lookers, voiceless and unrepresented."

When the nation celebrated the hundredth anniversary of the signing of the Constitution on September 17, 1887, women had neither the right to vote nor equal protection under the law. To suffragists, the centennial represented "a century of injustice." They wrote: "This denial of our chartered rights, this injustice of which we complain, is inflicted

*Adapted from Sally Roesch Wagner, *A Time of Protest: Suffragists Challenge the Republic, 1870–1877* (Sacramento, 1987).

in defiance of the provisions of the Constitution you profess to honor. When we examine that instrument, we find it is declared in the Preamble that it was: 'Ordained and established by "The People of the United States." ' One-half of the people of the United States are women, yet they are allowed no voice, direct or indirect, in framing this Constitution, or executing its provisions. We protest, therefore, that the words of the Preamble have been falsified for a hundred years."

The 1887 protest was not the suffragists' first. In fact, it was part of an organized campaign of demonstrations that had begun with the government's celebration of the Boston Tea Party in 1873. Charging that "Taxation without Representation is Tyranny," the New York Woman Suffrage Association followed in the footsteps of the patriots of 1773 by forming an antitax league and refusing to support the government until they were given equal representation.

Unable to vote legally, suffragists by the hundreds around the country committed civil disobedience—by voting. But it was the best-known suffragist in America, Susan B. Anthony of Rochester, who was arrested for committing the "horrendous crime" of voting. Viewing her arrest as politically motivated, Anthony and her co-worker, Matilda Joslyn Gage of Fayetteville, New York, made a total of thirty-seven speeches to potential jurors in Ontario County in the twenty-two days before the trial began. Gage ended her impassioned appeal by saying: "To you, men of Ontario County, has come an important hour. . . . To you, freedom has come looking for fuller acknowledgment, for a wider area in which to work and grow. Your decision will not be for Susan B. Anthony alone; it will be for yourselves and for your children's children to the latest generations. . . ." Unfortunately, the jurors were barred from acting. Judge Hunt, without consulting the jury, found Susan B. Anthony guilty of voting, and fined her $100. She refused to pay, declaring that "Resistance to tyranny is obedience to God."

Three years later, these two New York women risked arrest at the major centennial celebration in Philadelphia by making an illegal presentation of a Declaration of Rights of Women, dedicating their action to "the daughters of 1976, so they might know that their mothers of 1876 had impeached the government for its treatment of women."

Declaring that the existing political parties had "raised no great moral or political issue" but rather "presented to people the same old platitudes," the suffragists formed an Equal Rights Party and ran Belva Lockwood, a well known woman lawyer, for president in 1884. Matilda Joslyn Gage joined Moses Richardson of Lockport, New York, as elector-at-large on the ticket. Their party platform called for "equal and exact justice" for all citizens, regardless of "color, sex or nationality," as well as an international peace pact (because "war is a relic of barbarism belonging to the past") and an end to monopolies ("the tendency of which is to make the rich richer, and the poor poorer"). Lockwood and her running-mate, Marietta Stow, made a respectable showing; they received 4,149 popular votes and the entire electoral vote of Indiana.

When the Statue of Liberty was unveiled in 1886, women's rights advocates called it "the greatest hypocricy of the 19th century" to depict liberty as a woman "while not one single woman throughout the length and breadth of the Land is as yet in possession of political Liberty." During the dedication ceremony, the New York City Woman Suffrage Association circled Bedloe's Island, registering their protest in a rented steamer decorated with highly visible suffrage banners. The radical suffragists staged their final protest during the 1887 ceremonies which brought to a conclusion the series of celebrations in commemoration of the birth of the nation.

"The matter of finding a fitting occasion on which to present the protest to the President was one which caused us considerable anxiety," said Lillie Devereux Blake, President of the New York Woman Suffrage Association, who was chosen to make the presentation on behalf of the suffragists. After much debate, they chose the public reception President Cleveland was holding on Saturday morning as the most fitting occasion. A double row of policemen guarded the small room in which the president was to receive guests, and Blake, initially denied admittance, quickly talked her way in. "Precisely at nine o'clock, the cheering outside announced the coming of the Chief Magistrate," Blake reported. "A moment later, he entered the room and was presented to the city officials. Then there was a pause, and this was my opportunity. I at once advanced, holding a copy of the protest with the autograph signatures." President Cleveland shook Blake's hand with a promise that he would give the document his careful consideration. Despite his assurance and those of later presidents, it would be another thirty-three years before the Constitution gave women the right to vote.

Women Lawyers
of New York State

KAREN BERGER MORELLO, ESQ.

Soon after Sandra Day O'Connor was nominated to the United States Supreme Court in September 1981, she appeared at confirmation hearings held by the Senate Judiciary Committee. Senator Robert Dole of Kansas, noting the age of the Supreme Court and the significance of her appointment, welcomed O'Connor by saying, "Better one hundred ninety years late than never—you are among friends."[1] While obviously intending to put O'Connor at ease, Dole's remarks pointed out the uneasy fact that for most of our history women have been excluded from participation in the legal system and from attaining positions of importance within the legal profession.

Justice O'Connor is destined to have a place in history, but the names of few—if any—of the women lawyers who came before her are widely known. Although women practiced law in America since colonial times, little more than a hundred years ago the United States Supreme Court ruled that a female's "natural and proper timidity and delicacy" made her unfit for many occupations, most particularly the law.[2] The giants of the legal profession—men such as Harlan Fiske Stone, Roscoe Pound, and Clarence Darrow—consistently opposed the entry of women into the law and sought to keep them on the fringes of the profession. The reasons for such extraordinary resistance to women lawyers can never be fully explained, but it is likely that it has to do with the law's close relationship to power in our society. When Barbara J. Harris studied nineteenth-century professional women, comparing the difficulties women faced in entering the legal and medical professions, she found that women faced greatest opposition from the bar. Harris and others who have examined the role of women in the legal system note that while entry into the medical profession might be justified as a natural extension of women's nurturing role, the law clearly was an all-male domain, closest to the center of power, that was not to be invaded or changed by females.[3]

In the fight to keep women out of that domain, bar associations claimed that women lacked the strength to handle heavy caseloads, and newspapers charged that attractive women would unfairly sway juries. Law business was conveniently discussed in men-only private clubs; bar groups restricted their memberships for such "practical" reasons as not having adequate bathroom facilities; law schools operated on a quota system if they admitted women at all; and interviewers for law firms routinely told female applicants, "We're not hiring any women this year." Even when the clients and cases were rewarding, women faced so much opposition to their participation in the law that for many it proved to be a difficult and lonely profession.

This was especially true for New York's women. Although Anna Meyanders successfully argued her own case in a colonial court and Elizabeth Holt published the 1784 Sessions Law of the State of New York, not until 1886 did women officially begin practicing law in the state. One consequence of the New York bar's resistance was that a good many talented women left the state to pursue legal careers.

Lemma Barkaloo, America's first female law student, was a Brooklyn girl who in 1868 hoped to attend Columbia Law School. Her application and those of two other female students were quickly rejected. Columbia Trustee George Templeton Strong recorded in his diary:[4]

> Application from three infatuated young women to the [Columbia] Law School. No woman shall degrade herself by practicing law in New York especially if I can save her. . . . "Women's Rights Women" are uncommonly loud and offensive of late. I loathe the lot.

Barkaloo was forced to travel to St. Louis, Missouri, to obtain a legal education. She did exceptionally well at the Washington University Law School and in 1870 became Missouri's first woman lawyer. Remarkably, when Barkaloo died several years later of typhoid fever, the *United States Biographical Dictionary* insisted that the real cause of her death was "over-mental exertion."[5]

America's first black woman lawyer, Charlotte E. Ray, moved to Washington, D.C., to study law. At Howard Law School, Ray stunned officials with her sharp intellect. One trustee noted with amazement in Howard's 1870 Annual Report that "there was a colored woman who read us a thesis on corporations, not copied from the books but from her brain, a clear incisive analysis of one of the most delicate legal questions."[6] Ray also was the first woman lawyer in Washington, D.C. She later returned to New York City.

Brooklyn Heights native Lavinia Goodell was a successful editor in New York City. Realizing that she would be unable to study or practice law in New York, she moved to the Midwest. In 1874, she became Wisconsin's first woman lawyer, and she and attorney Angie King formed the nation's first female law partnership.

Also during this period, Belva Lockwood, from Lockport, New York, traveled to the District of Columbia to study and practice law. Lockwood was outraged when a federal judge refused to allow her to argue a case before him. He insisted that she hire a male replacement. Lockwood said that she realized that "it was a crime to be a woman but it was too late to put in a denial so I pled guilty."[7] Her substitute, she recalled, "said very badly in three days what I could have said well in one hour."[8] Lockwood went on to become the first woman lawyer to argue a case before the United States Supreme Court. Not only did she maintain a lucrative law practice—in 1884 she ran for president of the United States on the Equal Rights ticket, well before women had the constitutional right to vote.

America's first woman judge, Esther Morris, was born and raised in Spencer, New York. After the Civil War, she moved to frontier Wyoming. She held court in a log cabin in South Pass City and insisted that all rifles and pistols be left outside the front door. When a number of men, most notably her husband John, insisted that a woman should not hold judicial office, Morris ignored her critics and held her husband in contempt of court.

Finally, in 1886, New York seemed ready for change. Albany teacher and suffragist Kate Stoneman took the New York State bar examination and passed it with distinction. She expected her application for admission to the bar to be a simple formality. But a three-judge panel of the state supreme court refused her application, insisting that the clear intent of the state legislature was to "bar female citizens from this office."[9] The justices expressed their own private view that there was no call for women lawyers in New York and doubted that there ever would be. Stoneman disagreed. She campaigned successfully for a change in New York's gender-restrictive admissions statute and devoted the rest of her life to working on issues of importance to women.

New York's leading legal newspaper, the *Daily Register* (in its present incarnation, the *New York Law Journal*), opposed the Stoneman campaign for admission of women to the New York State bar. It responded to her efforts by printing an editorial called "New Anticipations" claiming that women would treat the law as they treat fashion: one year contracts would be drawn short, the next year women lawyers would want them drafted stylishly long.[10] Fortunately, neither the *Daily Register* nor its views on women survived.

In 1890, New York University Law School hired Dr. Emily Kempin, a distinguished legal scholar from Switzerland, to teach a course in Roman law. Kempin was the first woman law professor in the United States. Concerned that American women did not have sufficient understanding of their rights under the law, Kempin started the Woman's Law Classes at NYU; these classes trained nearly every woman who became an attorney in New York State around the turn of the century.

In the early 1900s, only small numbers of women were practicing law in New York State, but they were working actively to increase the legal rights of women and to obtain a constitutional amendment for women's suffrage. A Women Lawyer's Club formed in New York City and active in both New York and New Jersey began publishing a national newsletter in 1911. The organization grew to become the National Association of Women Lawyers, which continues to represent women attorneys today.

Crystal Eastman, co-founder of the American Civil Liberties Union, was appointed in June of 1909 to the New York State Employers' Liability Commission. During the next two years, she drafted New York's Workmen's Compensation Law. Also in this period, Jessie Ashley, a radical feminist, defended Elizabeth Gurley Flynn of the International Workers of the World (I.W.W.) against a 1913 federal prosecution for subversive activities and campaigned unsuccessfully for election to the New York State Court of Appeals.

In the years preceding and following the First World War, women lawyers continued to campaign vigorously for suffrage and for the right of women to sit on juries. They participated in demonstrations, marched down New York City's Fifth Avenue, and chained themselves to the gates of the White House in Washington, D.C.

As the campaign for women's rights intensified, women also scored impressive gains in the federal and state legal systems. Rose Rothenberg became New York State's first female prosecutor, and in 1918 Clarice Baright became the first woman to try a case before a U.S. Army general court-martial when she defended a client at Camp Upton on Long Island. (It was not until 1973, however, that Beatrice Burstein became the first woman elected to the New York State Supreme Court from the Tenth Judicial District.)

In 1919, Jean H. Norris, New York's first woman judge, was appointed to the New York City Magistrate's Court. Norris was a brilliant tax lawyer who had important ties to the politically powerful Tammany Hall. Regrettably, less than ten years later, after an investigation by Judge Samuel Seabury, the Appellate Division of the state supreme court removed Magistrate Norris from the bench for misconduct.

The 1920s saw the appointment of the first woman to the federal judiciary when, in 1928, President Calvin Coolidge named Genevieve Rose Cline to the United States Customs Court in New York City. In 1924, in another milestone, Catherine Noyes Lee became the first female associate hired by a major Wall Street law firm. It was also during this decade that Columbia Law School finally opened its doors to women students. Early women graduates recalled their male classmates making a sport out of stamping their feet in unison whenever a woman was called on in class.

During the Depression years, women lawyers formed a number of women's bar associations in New York to counter the resistance that women faced from their county bar associations. Bessie Geffner, who helped found the Queens County Women's Bar Association in 1931, recalled, "The excuses always were the same. No bathroom facilities, women wouldn't like the rough language, the men wouldn't be comfortable, but that's exactly what they were—excuses. They simply didn't want to acknowledge the existence of women lawyers."[11] Not until the early 1960s were women permitted to join the "regular" Queens County Bar Association.

In the mid-1930s, Eunice Hunton Carter became the first black woman prosecutor in New York State. She then joined Thomas E. Dewey's "crimebusting" special prosecutor's office, and is credited with initiating the investigation that led to the conviction of mob leader Charles "Lucky" Luciano.

In the 1940s and 1950s, a few Wall Street law firms hired their first female associates and in 1944 Soia Mentschikoff became the first female partner of a major law firm.

Cecelia Goetz, now a United States bankruptcy judge in New York, gave the opening argument for the prosecution in the Krupp trial at Nuremberg, Germany, following the close of the Second World War, but in order to be a prosecutor at Nuremberg she had to obtain a "waiver of disability" under U.S. Army law. Her "disability" was that she was a woman.

The 1960s were an important time of transition. Early in the decade, women were being rejected from jobs in both the public and private sectors because of their admitted plans to marry. Geraldine Ferraro, who later became a member of the United States House of Representatives and was the 1984 Democratic candidate for vice-president, recalls having lost an offer from the Manhattan district attorney's office: "They said I would get pregnant right away and it would be a waste of their training." [12] Up until 1967, some New York law schools continued "Ladies' Day," the once-per-semester ritual made famous at the Harvard Law School in which women students were called on to recite for the entertainment, not education, of the professor and the male students.

The activism of the late 1960s led many women to challenge existing attitudes and practices. Law clinics at Columbia and New York University made headlines by filing actions against major law firms that discriminated in the hiring and promotion of attorneys and against male-only scholarship programs and clubs. Karen DeCrow and Faith Seidenberg, two lawyers from Syracuse, New York, successfully challenged in federal court the all-male drinking policy at New York City's famed McSorley's Old Ale House.

By the 1970s, enrollment of women in law schools in New York and throughout the United States increased to such an extent that approximately one-third to one-half of all students were female. Ruth Kessler Toch became New York's solicitor general. In 1979, Amalya Kearse became the first black woman member of the United States Court of Appeals for the Second Circuit. Bella Abzug, the outspoken activist United States Representative, helped to found the National Women's Political Caucus, and Representative Elizabeth Holtzman was recognized for her work on the House Judiciary Committee's deliberations on the impeachment of President Richard M. Nixon.

The achievements of women lawyers continued into the 1980s with the appointments of Sandra Day O'Connor to the United States Supreme Court in 1981, Judith S. Kaye to the New York State Court of Appeals in 1983, and Barbara Aronstein Black as the first woman dean of Columbia Law School in 1986.

In recent years, women have become increasingly vocal about their achievements as well as their ambitions, and this, coupled with the extraordinary rise in the number of women joining the bar, promises to bring about dramatic changes in coming decades. In the last fifteen years, the number of women practicing law throughout the United States has increased tenfold—from 12,000 to 120,000. The American Bar Association estimates that, if this trend continues, by the end of this century half of the attorneys in the United States will be women.

The courage and persistence shown by New York's early women lawyers have made it possible for today's women to use their full capacities in the law and to make real choices about their lives and their careers. In the late 1700s, William Sampson, a prominent New York lawyer, criticized attempts by colonial attorneys to imitate the style and thinking of British barristers: "Must we tread always in their steps, go where they go, do what they do, and say what they say?"[13] Sampson urged his fellow lawyers to create instead a distinctly American legal system, one that would be responsive to the needs of a new nation. Over two centuries later, women lawyers are adopting similar views, insisting that their contributions to the law be not as associate males but as independent actors who by their very presence are changing the nature of the legal profession and our system of laws as well.

NOTES:

[1]*New York Times*, September 10, 1981, II, 14, col. 1.

[2]*Bradwell v. Illinois*, 16 Wall. 130 (1872).

[3]See generally Barbara J. Harris, *Beyond Her Sphere: Women in the Professions in America* (Westport, Conn.: Greenwood Press, 1978).

[4]Allan Nevins and Milton Halsey Thomas, eds., *The Diary of George Templeton Strong* (New York: Macmillan, 1952), 4: 256.

[5]Quoted in Karen Berger Morello, *The Invisible Bar* (New York: Random House, 1986), 46.

[6]General O.O. Howard, Third Annual Report, Howard University, Washington, D.C., July, 1870, quoted in Morello, *Invisible Bar*, 146.

[7]Morello, *Invisible Bar*, 31–32.

[8]*Ibid.*, 33.

[9]*In re Stoneman*, 53 Am. Rep. 323 (N.Y. Sup. Ct., 1886).

[10]*Daily Register*, January 22, 1886.

[11]Author's interview with Bessie Geffner, January 16, 1982.

[12]Author's interview with Geraldine Ferraro, December 12, 1983, quoted in Morello, *Invisible Bar*, 185.

[13]Quoted in Morello, *Invisible Bar*, xv.